✓ B&T
2v. $30.00

Modern America

Number 4

THE NEW DEAL

Volume Two

The New Deal

The State and Local Levels

Edited by

John Braeman
Robert H. Bremner
David Brody

OHIO STATE UNIVERSITY PRESS : COLUMBUS

Library of Congress Cataloguing of Publication Data

Braeman, John.
  The New Deal.

  Modern America; 4)
  CONTENTS: v. 1. The national level—v. 2. The state and local levels.
  Includes index.
  1. United States—Politics and government—1933–1945. 2. Unites States—Social
conditions—1933–1945. I. Bremner, Robert Hamlett, 1917–   joint author. II. Brody,
David, joint author. III. Title. IV. Series.   1-28-76
E806.B72   320.9'73'0917   74–20843
ISBN 0–8142–0200–4 (v. 1)   0–8142–0201–2 (v. 2)

Contents

Introduction

Students of the New Deal have traditionally tended to focus their attention upon events in Washington—Roosevelt and his advisers, the myriad of new federal agencies spawned during the 1930s, and the Congress. But in recent years, a growing number of scholars, recognizing the degree of decentralization of political power and governmental administration found in the United States, have begun to investigate another dimension of the New Deal: its impact upon the states and localities. The landmark work in directing historians' interest to this aspect of the New Deal was James T. Patterson's *The New Deal and the States: Federalism in Transition* (1969). And though no writer has yet followed Patterson in making a full-scale study of federal-city relations during those years, urban historians have shown increasing awareness of the New Deal's impact and role at the municipal level.

Yet paradoxically the result of this new interest has been further to downgrade the significance of the New Deal as an instrument of fundamental changes in American life and society. To quote Patterson, "The New Deal, far from being a dictatorial blueprint, was more like an overused piece of carbon paper whose imprint on the states was often faint and indistinct."[1] A recent student of American urban development has similarly concluded that "the federal response to depression in the cities was conservative. The New Deal's urban policy neither envisaged nor produced a radical transformation of metropolitan form and structure."[2] The purpose of the papers in this volume is to test these generalizations through in-depth studies of the impact of the New Deal upon different states and cities.

Three of the papers deal with highly industrialized and urbanized states. Harold Gorvine, formerly of Oakland University, seeks to explain why the popularity of, and support for, the New Deal in Massachusetts so swiftly receded. He puts the blame upon Democratic factionalism, a backlash against increased state government spending from businessmen and local taxpayers' associations, and the growing conviction among Bay Staters that the national administration's policies favored the South and West at their expense. "All in all," he concludes, "given the makeup of the Massachusetts political scene from 1932 to 1938, a New Deal administration on Beacon Hill, cooperating fully with Washington, was never a real possibility." Richard C. Keller, of Millersville State College, traces the rise, achievements, and downfall of Pennsylvania's "Little New Deal." Under Governor George H. Earle III, the Democrats pushed through "the most sweeping reform program in Pennsylvania's history . . . to improve the social and economic conditions of the people of the state." And though the Republicans regained power in the 1938 elections and retained a firm grip upon the state until the 1950s, the GOP could not—and did not—"turn back the legislative clock very far." In contrast, David J. Maurer, of Eastern Illinois University, shows the inadequacies of Ohio's relief efforts even at the height of the New Deal nationally. The continuing strength of traditional attitudes regarding self-help, private initiative, and local responsibility, uninspired and even reactionary gubernatorial leadership, the hostility of businessmen to higher taxes, the lack of political muscle by those needing relief, and rural domination of the legislature "defeated legislation designed to provide funds and progress in welfare administration in the state."

Three papers deal with Southern states. Virginia was probably more hostile to the New Deal than any other state. Robert F. Hunter, of Virginia Military Institute, ascribes this hostility to the fact that "the New Deal had little to offer that would meet Virginia's social and economic needs." At the same time, "What the New Deal even vaguely and inferentially promised to do for the Negro in Virginia was regarded by many Virginians as a threat to the established social order. . . ." John Robert Moore, of the University of Southwestern Louisiana, shows how the development in Louisiana of "a strong federal-state partnership" in responding to the depression was blocked by the power and ambitions of Huey Long, how Long's political heirs made their peace with the Roosevelt administration, and how the resulting flood of federal money, jobs, and building projects into Louisiana not only solidified the power base of Long's successors but brought far-reaching benefits to the state's "masses." Yet while New Deal funds and programs carried forward the "revolution" begun in Louisiana by Huey Long, Keith L. Bryant, Jr., of the University of Wisconsin —Milwaukee, concludes that the impact of the New Deal upon Oklahoma was, "at best, only marginally evolutionary." "Even federal programs to alleviate economic distress in Oklahoma proved to be of minimal value to most residents," and the New Deal wrought in the Sooner State "few long-lasting socioeconomic changes" and "only the most modest political changes."

Four papers deal with the Rocky Mountain states. Whereas F. Alan Coombs, of the University of Utah, finds the effect of the New Deal upon Wyoming politics to have been "minimal," Michael P. Malone, of Montana State University, credits the New Deal with having had "a major impact upon Montana's political order" by promoting "a powerful liberal coalition of farmers and workers that shook the state's political structure and endured until after World War II." But even Malone concedes that "the New Deal's over-all effect" was "less than 'revolutionary.' . . . The New Deal altered but did not permanently reshift the main currents of Montana's political history." Taking a broader-gauged approach, James F. Wickens, of Chabot College, shows how Colorado, in desperate need of federal assistance, welcomed those New Deal programs that "served Colorado's parochial ends." But this acceptance of much of the New Deal did not transform the political culture of the state. Colorado, Wickens concludes, "came through the 'Roosevelt Revolution' with much of its states' rights philosophy intact" and with its traditional attitudes born of the frontier experience still powerful. On the other hand, William Pickens, presently a graduate student at the University of California—Davis, ascribes to the New Deal a much more far-reaching influence upon New Mexico. The 1930s made New Mexico into a Democratic stronghold, brought a more positive attitude on the part of state government toward its social responsibilities, and produced expansion and increased professionalization of state activities.

Robert E. Burton, of California Polytechnic State University, surveys the impact of the New Deal upon a Pacific Coast state, Oregon. He concludes that the changes which took place during the 1930s in "Oregon's socioeconomic and political patterns" fell "far short of revolution." Oregon's economy remained dependent upon the products of forest and field. And though the state did assume greater responsibility for relief and welfare, Republican domination "was only temporarily broken" thanks to conservative control of the Democratic party and the Republicans' willingness to accommodate to the New Deal.

The final two papers deal with the impact of the New Deal upon cities. Bruce M. Stave, of the University of Connecticut, appraises the mixed results of the New Deal in Pittsburgh. On the one hand, the New Deal transformed Pittsburgh from a Republican bastion into a Democratic stronghold and provided the sinews by which Democratic leader David E. Lawrence built a powerful local machine. On the other, although federal monies made a major contribution toward dealing with the city's massive unemployment and housing problems, the New Deal failed to solve Pittsburgh's more basic problems of economic stagnation and physical decay. Lyle W. Dorsett, of the University of Denver, shows how Kansas City, unlike Pittsburgh, had taken effective steps before the New Deal to meet the depression crisis through a large-scale public works program instituted by Democratic boss Tom Pendergast. The Kansas City works program "became the inspiration and model for part of the New Deal." And federal assistance under the New Deal "beautified and modernized Kansas City" while solidifying the Pendergast machine's power not merely locally but statewide.

Given these differing effects of, and responses to, the New Deal from state to state and from locality to locality, what conclusions can be drawn about its impact? Perhaps the most striking is the necessity of making a distinction between the short- and the long-run influence of the New Deal. By 1933, state and local governments had irrefutably demonstrated their incapacity to deal with the crisis. The growing centralization of economic life—and the resulting nationwide scope of the depression—largely precluded successful state and local efforts to promote recovery. The complexity and interdependence of the American economy limited the possibilities for meaningful reform at the state and local levels even if the will had existed. And a host of additional factors—dwindling tax revenues, constitutional or statutory limitations upon indebtedness, rural overrepresentation in state legislatures, outmoded administrative structures, weak and mediocre political leadership, and the continuing strength of traditional beliefs about limited government, budget-balancing, local responsibility, and individual self-reliance—prevented effective state and local action to relieve the millions in distress.

After 1933, the federal government moved in to fill the gap. The New Deal was largely successful in providing immediate relief, reforming the worst abuses of the existing system, and promoting at least partial recovery. But the same factors that had blocked effective state and local response to the depression crisis continued to hamper the development of a working federal-state-local partnership in implementing the New Deal measures. For the most part, conflict more than cooperation marked the relationship between the federal government, on the one side, and state and local governments, on the other, during the 1930s. The requirement of state or local matching funds for such New Deal programs as the Federal Emergency Relief Administration and the Public Works Administration, Washington's demands for centralization and professionalization of welfare administration, and the efforts by state and local politicians to exploit the federal largess for their own political advantage led to continuing friction. Although the carrot of federal grants and the stick of the federal payroll tax forced the states into participating in the programs established by the 1935 Social Security Act, state cooperation was often reluctantly given and benefits tended to be kept at the lowest possible levels. State and local governments proved even more niggardly in their treatment after 1935 of those requiring assistance who were not covered by the Social Security Act programs or given jobs by the Works Progress Administration.

A major factor in the limited long-run impact of the New Deal was the limited durability of the political realignment wrought by the New Deal at the state and local levels. The popularity of the New Deal during Roosevelt's first term swept Democrats into office nearly everywhere throughout the country. The new voting alignments proved most lasting in the larger urban centers. But over-all the Democratic tide receded more swiftly—and more strongly—at the state and local levels than at the presidential level. There were many reasons for this decline in Democratic strength at the state and local levels. The success of the New Deal in providing immediate relief and stimulating partial recovery undercut grass-roots pressure for further reform. At the same time, the New Deal's failure to bring full recovery—made painfully manifest by the recession of 1937–38—disillusioned many former supporters. Different states and localities benefitted—at least in their own perceptions—unequally from the New Deal programs. Local issues and personalities remained powerful forces in shaping voting behavior. Fewer low-income voters turned out in off-year elections than in presidential years. Influential local vested interests resisted higher taxes, and the rise of a militant labor movement frightened middle-class voters. The more astute Republicans neutralized the Roosevelt appeal by accepting the basic tenets of the New Deal. And traditional attitudes about the role of government, states' rights, free enterprise, pay-as-you-go, and individual self-reliance continued to exert strong appeal.

But a large part of the explanation for the rapid waning of Democratic support lies in the unattractiveness of state and local Democratic parties. Too often the men swept into office on Roosevelt's coat-tails were, to borrow James L. Sundquist's categories, "patronage oriented" rather than "issue oriented." Many were conservatives hostile to the New Deal and its works and thus unable to retain the backing of large numbers of voters attracted to the programs of the national administration. And the Democratic successes after long years in the political wilderness stimulated or exacerbated a destructive factionalism within the party—a factionalism at times growing out of ideological differences, but more frequently reflecting simply a clash of personalities or a struggle for power. As a result, the return of Republican dominance in many states would not be challenged until the post–World War II years when a new generation of "programmatic liberals"—men and women inspired by the New Deal experience—succeeded in winning control of, and revitalizing, their local Democratic parties.[3]

JOHN BRAEMAN
ROBERT H. BREMNER
DAVID BRODY

1. James T. Patterson, *The New Deal and the States: Federalism in Transition* (Princeton, 1969), p. 126.

2. Zane L. Miller, *The Urbanization of Modern America: A Brief History* (New York, 1973), pp. 168–69.

3. For a perceptive discussion of the political realignment produced by the New Deal, see James L. Sundquist, *Dynamics of the Party System: Alignment and Realignment of Political Parties in the United States* (Washington, D.C., 1973), pp. 183–244.

THE NEW DEAL

Harold Gorvine

The New Deal in Massachusetts

ALTHOUGH THE NEW DEAL HAD SIGNIFICANT EFFECTS ON BOTH
party politics and state and local government in Massachusetts, its impact
was limited by local and regional factors with which Washington found it
difficult to contend. One set of problems related to continuing factionalism
within the Massachusetts Democratic party and the weakness of the
Democratic state organization. The second involved a struggle between
national and state authorities over allocation of relief funds and control of
the relief program. A third centered on a clash between the special sectional interests of New England and national policy. The result of the
interplay of all these factors was that after reaching a high point of
influence in Massachusetts in 1934, the New Deal sank to a nadir in 1938.

During the 1920s, the Republicans had controlled the politics of the
state. Although Massachusetts had once taken the lead in welfare legislation, its legislature passed no major reform bills between 1920 and 1928. In
1929, the General Court (as the legislature had been known since colonial
times) rejected an old age pension plan, a bill outlawing yellow dog
contracts, and a measure regulating public utilities. Furthermore, urban-
rural splits and ethnic divisions between old-stock Americans, on the one
hand, and Irish and new immigrants on the other hand, led to a concentration on cultural issues such as prohibition and state regulation of parochial
schools rather than on economic reform.[1]

By 1928, however, an emerging Democratic coalition had begun to
wrest political power from the Republicans in Massachusetts. The new
alignment consisted mainly of Irish and new immigrant voters. Minor
elements were a few Yankee Democrats, labor leaders, advanced liberals,

and discontented old-stock Republicans. By 1932, three years of the depression had put the state GOP on the defensive; indeed, it seemed to be in danger of becoming the minority party. Its membership consisted chiefly of old-stock citizens of the towns and suburbs and of the upper economic groups, both of whom viewed the Republican party "as the sole safeguard of the country's economy, or of its cultural traits and standards."[2]

The New Deal and the personal popularity of President Roosevelt gave added momentum to this process of political change. Voters shifted party allegiance; the state government embarked on new programs of relief, spending, and public welfare; and the relationships between Washington, Beacon Hill, and the municipalities grew increasingly tangled. Both Democrats and Republicans underwent internal conflicts over control of state party organizations and policy. The results of these struggles affected not only the political futures of the parties themselves but also the course of state government and the nature of its relationship to New Deal agencies in Washington. This article will focus mainly on the period from 1932 to 1936, with some attention to the two following years.

The Democratic factionalism was a carry-over from the years preceding the New Deal. In one sense, the Democratic party was two parties—one centered in Boston and its immediate vicinity, and the second, in western Massachusetts. The largest block of Irish and new immigrant voters came from the Boston area, but the party also needed votes from other large urban centers to win statewide elections.[3]

In 1930, the Democrats won both the governorship and the second United States Senate seat. The Democratic gubernatorial and senatorial nominess, Joseph B. Ely and Marcus Coolidge, were Yankee Democrats from western Massachusetts. In his quest for the nomination, Ely had contended with the Irish Catholic mayor of Boston, James Michael Curley, who was supporting another candidate in the expectation that he, Curley, would succeed to the governorship in 1932. In this clash, Senator David I. Walsh, an Irish Catholic from western Massachusetts, had sided with Ely.[4]

The contest for power between the Curley and Walsh-Ely factions was more than a matter of personalities. It was also part of the continuing struggle between the Boston and western Massachusetts Democrats for control of the party. The Bostonians had been slowly winning this battle over the years. Thus, between 1900 and 1911, only 25 percent of the Democratic nominess for statewide office had come from Boston and vicinity. After the introduction of the primary election in 1911, that percentage climbed to 46.4 in 1912–20, 44.1 in 1922–30, 65.6 in 1932–40, and 82.9 in 1942–52.[5]

Professor V. O. Key, Jr., has pointed out that despite this change "the division of the Democratic vote between Boston and vicinity and the rest of the state remained fairly constant." Thus, between 1900 and 1952 the Boston area supplied "about one-half of the statewide Democratic primary votes against around one-third of the statewide general election vote for Democratic candidates." When Democratic victories in statewide elections became a real possibility, the Democratic state committee and state conventions found it increasingly difficult to get organization candidates approved in the primaries. That is, Boston Democratic politicians like Curley could thwart the party machinery by using their influence with their local followings to win nominations in the primaries.[6]

In the process, the Democratic state organization was weakened at times to the point of ineffectiveness. Moreover, Key points out,

> the gradual increase in the proportions of Democratic nominations captured by Bostonians did not reflect by any means solely the fortunes and exertions of prominent factional leaders. It came more and more to result from the unguided and unbossed actions of primary voters in supporting names familiar to them, usually those of local notables.[7]

The continuing factionalism and the inability of any one faction to retain effective control of the party made it very difficult for national Democratic leaders to deal with the Massachusetts political scene. For example, the feud between the Walsh-Ely and Curley groups continued in 1932 when Ely, Walsh, and most Massachusetts Democrats endorsed Al Smith for the Democratic presidential nomination. Mayor Curley, on the other hand, supported Roosevelt, probably because he hoped to use him to further his own plans to become governor.[8]

Curley's management of the campaign was a disaster for the Roosevelt forces. Roosevelt's aide, Louis Howe, later explained that the mayor had not made "the slightest attempt . . . to get out the rural vote." Instead, he had "insisted on making it a city fight throughout the state with all the organization and voting officials under the control of Walsh and Ely." Howe also complained that Curley had not kept his promise "to have the campaign run by a committee of six mayors with himself only responsible for Boston"; consequently, "at least four [of] the mayors" had backed away from Roosevelt. The campaign ended with Massachusetts sending a slate of Smith delegates to the Democratic National Convention.[9] After

Roosevelt's nomination in Chicago, Senators Walsh and Coolidge came out for FDR, while Ely seemed to sulk. Both Ely and Roosevelt carried the state.[10]

After Roosevelt's victory in November, Mayor Curley expected that he would receive a choice federal position. The new president, who probably had not forgotten the recent fiasco in Massachusetts, refused to appoint Curley either as secretary of the navy or as ambassador to Italy. Looking back in 1959, James Roosevelt wrote that his father

> no more would have considered naming the flamboyant Boston political brawler to head his beloved Navy Department than he would have appointed the Grand Wizard of the Ku Klux Klan as Ambassador to the Vatican.[11]

When the president finally offered the mayor the ambassadorship to Poland, Curley angrily turned down the job.[12] He then began to consider running for governor in 1934. He also tried to persuade Postmaster General James A. Farley to channel federal appointments in Massachusetts through him.[13]

For several months, the president proceeded quite cautiously in filling federal posts in Massachusetts. However, with but a few exceptions, the administration distributed patronage without consulting Walsh, Ely, or Curley. For example, by the end of September 1933 Washington had given five major jobs to two Smith men, two FRBC (For Roosevelt before Chicago) people, and one individual who had been neutral in the Roosevelt-Smith struggle of 1932. The Smith men were state Democratic chairman Joseph A. Maynard, collector of the Port of Boston, and Mary H. Ward, immigration commissioner. The two FRBC appointees were Francis J. W. Ford, United States attorney, and Somerville Mayor John J. Murphy, United States marshal. Collector of Internal Revenue Joseph Carney had been neutral in 1932.[14]

Except for the selection of Murphy, Washington had ignored Curley. Senator Walsh also had not endorsed any of the five in advance, except for Maynard. Federal authorities similarly had failed to consult Ely.[15]

Apparently Washington was trying to build a Roosevelt group that would be independent of both the Walsh-Ely and Curley factions—a kind of third force in Massachusetts Democratic politics. Direction for this drive came from James Roosevelt, who was living in the Boston area.[16] Postmaster General James A. Farley was never in complete sympathy with the "freeze-out" of Senator Walsh, and consequently, during the early months of 1934, he was working to bring about a truce with the senior senator over the Massachusetts situation.[17]

Despite such attempts to maintain a facade of public unity, an intense struggle for power was taking place. Early in 1934, state Representative Michael J. Ward of Roxbury organized the Boston Democratic Club, made up exclusively of Boston Democratic legislators and city councilors. In March, the club elected James Roosevelt as its president. The members then accepted his suggestion that they unite for the election of delegates to the coming state Democratic preprimary convention in June, without pledging themselves at this time to any candidate or slate of candidates. When some of the members suggested that State Chairman Maynard might try to put through a slate of delegates in Boston, Roosevelt replied, "We'll have to go out and lick them. I'll stand by you fellows."[18]

The intraparty feud also spilled over into the activities of federal relief agencies in Massachusetts. In March 1934, all three members of the state's Civil Works Administration board resigned in protest over a drastic reduction in the Massachusetts job quota. Washington then named Joseph Carney to head the Federal Emergency Relief Administration (FERA), which was replacing the CWA. (In 1933, local newsmen had attributed Carney's nomination as collector of internal revenue to the influence of James Roosevelt.)[19]

The 1934 appointment of Carney to head the FERA thus exacerbated the divisions within the Democratic party. Prior to assuming his new post, Carney had been sounding out prospective delegates to the coming Democratic preprimary convention and had been advising them to stand together. Therefore, when he began to replace FERA staff, many local Democrats felt that he was trying to rid the agency of all non-Roosevelt men; but at this point they realized that appeals to Washington would be futile.[20]

In one sense, the battle reduced itself to a struggle between federal and state officeholders. The Smith backers of 1932 were the state officeholders who had been appointed by Ely, whereas the FDR supporters of 1932 were now either federal officeholders or "me too" men willing to back the president in the hope of gaining some political office.[21]

By August 1934, the Roosevelt administration had practically dismantled the Ely political machine. This, of course, had been a gradual process, and the governor inadvertently had aided the administration by announcing as early as January that he would not run again. Ely had been proud of three of his appointments—Professor Frank B. Sayre as commissioner of correction; Edwin S. Smith as commissioner of labor and industry; and Judge

John J. Burns to the Superior Court. By August, all three had "deserted" to the New Deal. Smith, for example, was now a member of the National Labor Board. Federal authorities had also succeeded in obtaining Maynard's resignation from the Democratic state chairmanship in accord with a ruling that a man could not hold an appointive and party post simultaneously.[22]

Why the administration chose to ignore Curley, Walsh, and Ely is something of a puzzle. In the case of Curley, it was probably due to his mismanagement of Roosevelt's preconvention campaign in Massachusetts in 1932, and his attempt to use the campaign purely for his own political profit.

When the *Boston Transcript*, on 30 July 1933, first published the story of the patronage row, it reported that the administration felt that Walsh and Ely had not cooperated with Washington. This charge was not true; on the contrary, both men had supported the New Deal during the Hundred Days. The governor did not make his first attack on the NRA until 21 September 1933.[23] It is probable, then, that the main reason for the freeze-out of Walsh and Ely was their opposition to Roosevelt's nomination—the so-called FRBC test.

After September 1933, Ely became increasingly anti–New Deal. The patronage quarrel with the president was one factor in the break. Furthermore, Ely was a conservative Democrat who was afraid of an overcentralization of power in Washington. Writing in 1944, he explained that though he had supported the 1932 national Democratic platform, by late summer of 1934 he had concluded that the New Deal was aiming at "control of the intricacies of business and agriculture." Because he could not support such policies, he had decided to retire from political office so that he could be free to express his opinions.[24]

Senator Walsh, on the other hand, pursued an independent course of his own. Walsh, who was the first Irish Catholic governor of Massachusetts (1916–19), was elected to the United States Senate in 1918. He was defeated for reelection in 1924 but in 1926 was returned to the Senate, where he remained until 1947. His supporters included a variety of conflicting groups—Irish and Yankee Democrats, new immigrant and Negro voters, independents, Republicans, New Dealers, anti–New Dealers, labor, and conservative Massachusetts businessmen and industrialists (for whom he had become the spokesman after the death of Senator Henry Cabot Lodge).[25]

The special interests of Massachusetts, particularly the depressed condition of the state's textile industry, helped to shape his stands in Congress. Thus, he demanded the erection of tariff walls against Japanese textile imports, the elimination of North-South wage differentials in the NRA's textile code, and repeal of the AAA's cotton-processing tax, which was paid by the millowners. In his view, all of the processing taxes placed "an unfair burden on the consumers of the industrial areas of the East."[26]

Walsh also was wary of Washington's possible acquisition of too much power at the expense of the states, although he recognized the need for federal intervention in key areas of the national economy. For example, he came to oppose the whole idea of an AAA. Thus, when the Roosevelt administration was pushing for a second AAA measure to replace the one declared unconstitutional by the Supreme Court, Walsh denounced it as "a measure of dubious constitutionality, of indefinite grant of bureaucratic power and control over agriculture and of incredible financial burden."[27]

His stand on the NRA was the clearest example of the senator's ambivalence about the proper role of the federal government in American economic life. In December 1934, he seemed to be leaning in the direction of giving more power to the National Recovery Administration. One of its shortcomings, he explained, was that the minimum wage provision was "not a law but merely an agreement among businessmen." Moreover, Congress had given the administration the "power to issue licenses to businesses," but this was never done. "I wonder if it shouldn't have been in force to strengthen the whole ERA [sic] structure." He added that when the NRA came up for renewal in July, "the big businessman should not be lost sight of." Workers had "a right to get enough to live according to decent standards." But, he emphasized, it was not the small businessman who had "suffered most under NRA. The real sufferer is the big producer who is tied down by labor demands." In March, he came out for extension of the NRA, "along the lines proposed by the President, with certain modifications and limitations."[28]

The federal government's relief policies also troubled Walsh. In September 1935, he stated that although the federal government ought to provide "any money necessary to relieve suffering and distress caused by the depression," it should allocate "the funds to the several states and give them the responsibility of distributing [them]." He did "not believe in the work-relief program as such" because when Washington entered "the domain of substituting a job for the obligation of relieving . . . distress, this is no place to stop unless you provide a job for all of the 10,000,000 unemployed." He also expressed concern over the piling-up of the national debt.[29]

In Walsh's view, the Social Security Act was the best bill passed in 1935, although he believed that more of the policy-making details should have been left to the states. He hoped that the administration had left reform behind and henceforth would concentrate on recovery. In July, Walsh had voted against the Public Utilities Holding Company Act, a reform measure.[30]

In 1935, Walsh also opposed the administration's tax program, which he described as a reform measure that had been presented as a revenue bill. Although he conceded that there was an inequitable distribution of wealth in the United States, he argued that the best remedy was "to equalize opportunity and to insure a fair distribution of the rewards of labor and capital. But this proposal for the redistribution of wealth would result only in a redistribution of poverty. It would mean state socialism and all that implies."[31]

The following year, he came out against the president's request for a tax on individual corporate surpluses, for he feared that "because of its large per capita savings, New England will be called upon to carry a large part of the new tax load." He predicted that the proposed graduated tax on undistributed corporate savings would "stunt the growth of small corporations and foreclose their opportunity to become big."[32]

Walsh's stands in Congress also grew out of the conflicting demands of his constituency. Thus, his stands on federal-state relations, relief, spending, taxation, and the Public Utilities Holding Company Act pleased his conservative Republican and business backers, whereas his opposition to the AAA found favor in both business and labor circles in Massachusetts.

His fight for the Wagner National Labor Relations Act and the Walsh-Healy Act of 1936, which set minimum labor standards for businesses and states that received contracts from the federal government, also kept him in labor's good graces.[33] His shifting position on the NRA was the clearest illustration of his efforts to straddle the conflicting interests of business and labor groups within his constituency.

Senator Walsh, then, was in some respects an old-style progressive, who was finding it rather difficult to adjust to New Deal liberalism and to the Roosevelt administration's handling of patronage in Massachusetts. However, he did not follow the example of the more conservative Ely, who, along with Al Smith, bolted the president in 1936. Instead, he allowed himself to be named to the Massachusetts slate of Roosevelt delegates to the Democratic National Convention.[34]

Relations between Washington and the other leading Democrat in the state, James Michael Curley, also continued to be strained. In 1934, Curley had won the gubernatorial nomination and election after a bitter intraparty battle. During his two years as governor, the Roosevelt administration favored neither his faction nor that of Walsh. Although Walsh managed to place some people in minor jobs, most of the major appointments were made without his approval. The administration similarly ignored Curley for the most part in distributing important federal appointments.[35]

For example, in June 1935, the president named Judge William M. Welch of Northampton, a Walsh man, as collector of internal revenue for the state. However, two months later Roosevelt nominated former Gardner Mayor George C. Sweeney to a federal judgeship in Boston—a move interpreted by the *Springfield Republican* as a " 'slap' at Walsh . . . Curley and other old-time Democratic leaders," and a victory for former Collector of Revenue Carney. Sweeney had been one of the few Massachusetts mayors to come out for Roosevelt before Chicago. Walsh then tried to have a Bay State Democrat named to the spot Sweeney was vacating, that of assistant United States attorney general, but Attorney General Homer Cummings informed him that the job would go to one of the lawyers in the Justice Department.[36]

The clearest illustration of the Roosevelt administration's attitude toward Curley came in 1935 when the term of Boston Postmaster William E. Hurley, a career man and a Republican, expired. Curley quickly threw his support behind Peter F. Tague, who was a friend of both the governor and the president. Walsh, on the other hand, had come out for Hurley's retention on the grounds that the Boston postmastership should be freed from patronage politics. The matter dragged on from February to October when Farley named Tague acting postmaster. Curley's friends were jubilant; but Washington officials emphasized that President Roosevelt's personal acquaintance with Tague was the deciding factor.[37]

The most detailed account of the episode was written by John Bantry, a news analyst for the Democratic *Boston Post*. He explained that as soon as Farley had taken over the Post Office Department, "a flood of promotions and supervisor jobs, dictated in Washington, [had] descended on Postmaster Hurley." Only the intervention of Senator Walsh had halted this raid. Under the Farley regime, continued Bantry, every promotion in the Boston post office had been a political one.

Once the new Boston post office was ready for occupancy, Washington instructed Hurley that James Roosevelt would fill all the positions in the building "from head janitor to scrub-woman." This provoked loud protest from local congressmen, resulting in "a further order . . . to give the Boston Congressmen some of the places, but not to give Senator Walsh a thing." The original request for the Tague appointment, explained Bantry, came not from Curley but from Tague himself. "Later the whole situation became twisted into a test of Governor Curley's prestige."[38]

The president, concluded Bantry, had fully intended to put an end to politics in the Post Office Department, "but the exigencies of . . . Farley's political strategy . . . prevailed." The latter believed that FRBC men deserved rewards and that Republicans must be removed.[39]

As during Ely's second term, the federal officeholders at the time of Curley's governorship continued to constitute a third Democratic faction, separate from the Curley and Walsh groups and even hostile to them. Indeed, many old-line Democratic politicians felt that too many Republicans had received New Deal positions and that the federal officeholders were indifferent to the Democratic party's political welfare in the state. Furthermore, the governor complained publicly about the appointment of out-of-state men to key posts in Massachusetts.[40]

Washington, in turn, was rather wary about interfering in the Massachusetts situation. One federal department head told a new Bay State appointee, "Be very careful now and don't get into any political jam or take sides in this Massachusetts political row. The safest course is not to give Walsh or Curley anything."[41]

The federal officeholders, however, lacked a leader. James Roosevelt had moved to Washington early in 1935; and though he still intervened occasionally on the Massachusetts political scene, he was now somewhat removed from the struggle for power there. The result was that the Roosevelt administration lacked a well-placed, loyal, and powerful spokesman in Massachusetts.[42]

Clearly, then, the Roosevelt administration had not been able to use its patronage powers effectively to build a loyal New Deal wing of the Democratic party in Massachusetts. Instead, Washington had antagonized both the Curley and the Walsh-Ely Democrats. This combination of local factionalism and growing antagonism between the state and national Democratic parties created many difficulties when Washington and Beacon Hill tried to cope with the problems of government spending for relief.

During 1931, Governor Ely abandoned pay-as-you-go ideas for public works schemes; but in 1932, he retreated from this policy. Mayor Curley, on the other hand, pressed for public works at federal expense. During these two years, the Massachusetts Republicans continued to advocate "economy and sound administration" and to condemn any trend towards "radicalism."[43]

The Republicans still controlled the state legislature, although the Democrats had increased their seats in the Senate from ten to fourteen out of a total of forty. At the opening session of the 1933 General Court, GOP legislative leaders, Senate President Erland F. Fish and Speaker of the House Leverett Saltonstall, both called for economy. Saltonstall, however, conceded that the cities and towns needed aid.[44]

Governor Ely, in his inaugural speech, also stressed the necessity for strict economy. The governor continued the pressure for retrenchment in his budget message of late January. The total expenditures requested amounted to $56,990,305, which was about 6 percent below the 1932 figure and 12 percent below that of 1931. He admitted that the municipalities would find scant relief in his budget. He also proposed a pay cut for all state employees and the withholding of appropriations from various state departments and two state teachers' colleges.[45]

Reaction to the governor's proposals was immediate. Letters poured in from schoolteachers' federations, public employee associations, and representatives of every group whom the proposed economies would affect. The legislators themselves, Republicans as well as Democrats, reacted to these pressures by showing increasing signs of rebellion against their parties' leadership.[46] The anti-economizers were not a tightly knit unit; rather, many separate groups fought for their own special interests. For example, the projected elimination of the state teachers' colleges at North Adams and Hyannis met the stubborn resistance of almost all the senators from western Massachusetts. Each of the state departments marked for extinction also found its special pleaders. Thus, representatives of social welfare organizations, labor, and foreign-born groups protested against the governor's proposal to abolish the Division of Immigration and Americanization.[47]

The opponents of salary cuts were equally determined. One unidentified, excitable legislator exlaimed that he would have to be etherized before he would vote for them. Representative C. F. Nelson Pratt, a liberal Republican, told the Joint Ways and Means Committee, "The way to prosperity is to end wage slashing, and our vote in the House will tell its story to private industry. Not one dime will be cut."[48]

Also aligned on the side of the anti-economizers was the Equal Tax League led by Frank Goodwin, an independent Republican. The avowed purpose of the league was to make "the wealthy tax dodgers pay; to prevent wage and salary cuts; to prevent the curtailment of necessary governmental services, and thereby to maintain the present standard of living." Many city employees in Boston refused to join because they did not view the stated purposes of the league as the real ones. Rather, they believed that Mayor Curley was secretly backing the league in order to advance his own political interests.[49]

The economizers, reflecting the viewpoints of homeowners, local taxpayers' associations, and big banking and business interests, were also divided. For example, the National Economy League concentrated its attention on the problem of veterans' compensation and the reduction of the costs of national government, whereas most local taxpayers' associations concerned themselves almost wholly with economy in local, county, and state governments. The Home Owners' Protective Association, organized originally in Springfield and copied elsewhere, stressed not only thrift and the easing of the burden on real estate but also demanded reduction in the interest rate on mortgages and a change in the tax system to reduce the burden of property taxes.[50]

The question of new taxes also caused controversy. The local taxpayers' associations and big banking and business interests coupled their demands for government economy with "an equally urgent declaration against the imposition of new taxes." Both Governor Ely and Speaker Saltonstall emphasized the need for new taxes after expenses had been curtailed, in order to balance the budget without placing an unbearable load on real estate. Despite a 45 percent shrinkage in the state's revenue and the possibility of the commonwealth's doubling its tax on realty, reluctance to face up to the problem of tapping new sources of tax revenue persisted.[51]

Despite fierce opposition, the economy drive did make some slow progress early in the session. Late in March, for example, the House voted to cut the salaries of state employees by 10 to 15 percent, a reduction that was to end in December 1934. The vote was 174 to 56—131 Republicans and 43 Democrats for, and 47 Democrats and 9 Republicans against.

Speaker Saltonstall was better able to maintain control of the Republicans than was Ely of the Democrats. The 47 Democrats who voted no explained to the governor that they came from districts where citizens opposed income reductions of any kind. In the Senate, only 5 Democrats voted no, and 26 Republicans and 9 Democrats voted in the affirmative.[52]

In late April, the Massachusetts battle over government spending and taxation took a new turn when Congress passed the La Follette-Costigan bill, which established the Federal Emergency Relief Administration and allocated $500 million for distribution to the states. Of this sum, $250 million was for grants-in-aid, to which the recipient states had to contribute three dollars for each dollar of federal money. The FERA could give the remaining $250 million to states that were encountering emergencies. The unemployed were to receive these funds as a dole.[53]

The prospect of acquiring a share of these funds, and the mounting financial plight of the cities and towns, reversed the course of the economy drive in Massachusetts. Lieutenant Governor Gaspar G. Bacon, a Republican, denounced the La Follette-Costigan bill as "pernicious," but recommended that Massachusetts take advantage of it. Governor Ely, similarly opposed to the bill on principle, argued that if the commonwealth did not take her share, some other state would.[54]

The economy drive broke down conclusively on 5 June, when the House of Representatives rejected the Ways and Means Committee's $30,000,000 tax revenue bill, including a proposal for a retail sales tax. This bill had been based on Ely's recommendations. Lined up behind the sales tax were local government interests generally, who wanted both to continue adequate public services and to ease the burden on real estate. Opponents of the proposal included organized labor, merchants, retailers, local chambers of commerce, and business organizations. Moreover, Democratic members of the House from poor urban districts realized that the measure was unpopular with many of their constituents.[55]

In place of the Ways and Means bill, the House considered the Halliwell bill, which provided that the state would borrow $30,000,000 by issuing bonds, the money to go to the cities and towns as loans. The basis for distribution was to be the increase in 1932 local expenditures for public welfare and other doles over what was spent in 1929. Municipalities had to use all money thus obtained either for welfare or reduction of their tax rates. Massachusetts would then be in a position to begin receiving FERA funds.[56]

After a flurry of legislative maneuvers, the House and Senate passed the bill with an avalanche of votes, by 190 to 1 in the lower chamber and 26 to 2 in the upper house. The governor signed the bill into law on 1 July. Included in the final version of the bill was a three-year 6 percent tax on most intangibles (stock dividends of Massachusetts corporations, previously tax-free). The purpose of this provision was to furnish revenue to finance repayment of the bond issue.[57]

Two other acts involved the commonwealth in increased indebtedness. The tax title bill, passed early in the legislative session, authorized the state to borrow not more than $10 million, which it in turn would lend to the cities and towns. (The state was to repay this money not later than 30 November 1939.) Second, under the National Industrial Recovery Act the Public Works Administration could offer a state a direct subsidy of 30 percent of the cost of labor and materials and allow the state to borrow the remaining 70 percent from federal monies. In order to qualify Massachusetts for PWA funds, the legislature authorized the commonwealth to raise $22,000,000 by obtaining a $4,000,000 grant and an $18,000,000 loan from the federal government. On the last day of the legislative session, the House passed the measure 192 to 1, and in the Senate 21 Republicans and 8 Democrats voted yes and 1 Republican voted no (the remaining ten senators were absent or did not vote). Ely quickly signed the bill into law.[58]

The following year Governor Ely once again made economy the major theme of his annual address to the General Court. However, as Ely himself had admitted late in November of 1933, "How can you economize when every agency of the federal government seems devoted to the spending of money?" Moreover, the operation of the New Deal, especially the National Recovery Administration, had raised commodity prices, thus making the costs of government on all levels higher. Finally, the direct debt of Massachusetts had increased by $57,000,000 as a result of the tax title act, the Halliwell Bill, and state construction under the PWA.[59]

Ely undermined his own position by advocating the restoration of one-third of the salary cuts of state employees. Once again the Democrats in the House rebelled against the governor's leadership. A coalition of 37 Republicans and 79 Democrats voted for full restoration, and 96 Republicans and only 5 Democrats voted no. The governor, however, stood firm for his original proposal, which eventually passed both houses. However, when Ely and Frederick Mansfield, the new mayor of Boston, tried to get the legislators to approve cuts in the wages of employees of the city of Boston, the House turned them down. Forty-four Republicans joined 65 Democrats in rejecting the measure, and 68 Republicans and 10 Democrats voted for it. The Senate concurred with the House's action without debate. The General Court also restored several state government divisions it had abolished in 1933.[60]

Clearly, the Republican leadership, too, was finding it difficult to hold its members in line on issues involving government spending.

Once more the governor tried to persuade the legislature to pass a sales tax, with the proviso that the prime necessities of life would be exempt. The same groups that had defeated the proposal in 1933 opposed it again. The upshot was that at the end of May the House referred the matter to the next annual session. The General Court also turned down proposals for a graduated income tax, an increase in the gasoline levy, and other taxation measures.[61]

Since Ely had decided not to run for a third term, Curley moved to win his party's gubernatorial nomination. The Democratic preprimary convention, however, nominated a protégé of Ely, Charles Cole, rather than Curley. The former Boston mayor, however, conducted a vigorous primary campaign, during which he pictured himself as the victim of bossism at the state convention. Both candidates tried to tie themselves to President Roosevelt and the New Deal; the president, however, refused to be drawn into the battle. Curley defeated Cole by 280,405 to 129,025—a margin of 151,380 votes. Most observers agreed that Curley's espousal of the president's policies was the dominant factor in his upset win, since some of Cole's chief supporters, such as Governor Ely, were critics of the New Deal. Significant, too, was the fact that this was the first time in the history of the state that Democratic primary voters outnumbered Republicans.[62]

Curley's Republican opponent for the governorship was Lieutenant Governor Gaspar G. Bacon. But Bacon never had a real chance for victory. Late in August he made a strong anti–New Deal speech. However, he soon retreated from this position and spent the rest of the campaign trying to dissociate national issues from the Massachusetts election. At the close of the campaign, he desperately assured voters that a vote for him would not be an act of disloyalty to the president; the issue, Bacon insisted, was "honesty vs. Curleyism."[63]

Tactics posed no problem for Curley, who continued to bind himself securely to his "Work and Wages" slogan, to the president, and to the New Deal.[64] Although President Roosevelt refused to participate personally in the Massachusetts contest, James Roosevelt and Farley now endorsed Curley, in contrast to their proclaimed neutrality during the Curley-Cole primary battle.[65]

On election day, Curley polled 736,463 votes; Bacon, 627,413; and

Frank Goodwin, a third candidate (independent), 94,141. Curley's margin of victory was 109,050. Senator Walsh swamped his Republican opponent by a vote of 852,776 to 536,692. In the congressional races, the Democrats unseated two incumbent Republicans. The Democrats won all the other statewide offices, except for that of secretary of state. The GOP managed to retain control of both houses of the legislature, but the Democrats scored five upset wins in the Senate and twenty-two in the House. The new lineup in the latter stood at 125 Republicans and 115 Democrats; in the Senate, 21 Republicans, 19 Democrats. The Republicans also lost several county offices.[66]

The Democrats were now in an even stronger position in Massachusetts than after the 1932 election. All newspapers agreed that the president and the New Deal were the main factors in the returns. The New Deal even showed surprising strength in rock-ribbed Republican towns and won in "every city save those which [had] been overwhelmingly Republican in the past."[67]

The new governor interpreted his election victory as signifying that the voters and legislators were prepared to back more spending by the state, local, and federal governments in order to cope with the continuing economic and financial crisis in Massachusetts. In his inaugural address on 3 January 1935, Curley proposed increased cooperation with the federal government and the adoption of a "Work and Wages" program to replace the public welfare allotments. He explained that he had asked the commonwealth and its municipalities to draft a public works program, "anticipating their requirements based upon a fifty percent contribution by the Federal Government." (Curley had no reason to expect that Washington would actually make such a large contribution.) The governor's budget message of 24 January called for total expenditures of $61,149,530 and a 10 percent surtax on income, corporation, and inheritance taxes for two years.[68]

The first really controversial "Work and Wages" bill was Curley's proposal to reduce the hours of employees of state institutions to 48 per week. (Ely had vetoed a similar bill in 1934.) The governor's skillful lobbying and the basic appeal of the bill carried it to victory over the objections of its opponents, who claimed that it was too costly and that it was a way for Curley to find jobs for "his kind of deserving Democrats." The key to victory was Republican votes. In the House, 99 Democrats and 24 Republicans voted for the measure, and 74 Republicans and only 3 Democrats voted against it. In the Senate, the vote was along party lines, except for Senate President James Moran, a Republican, who voted for the bill, and another Republican allowed himself to be paired with an absent Democrat.[69]

The next struggle over state spending came over Curley's proposed $35,000,000 bond issue to establish state work relief projects that would be separate from the federal program. The bonds were to be paid for over a fifteen-year period, out of the existing state gasoline tax. Opponents of the bill, such as the Associated Industries of Massachusetts and the Boston Chamber of Commerce, predicted that the bond issue would "accelerate the process of removal [of existing industries] and . . . discourage the entrance into the Commonwealth of new [ones]." Among other groups fighting the bill were spokesmen for real estate owners, automobile interests, apartment owners, and the Massachusetts Federation of Taxpayers' Associations.[70]

The governor, however, prevailed by accepting the House Ways and Means Committee's modifications of his proposal: two separate bond issues totaling $20,800,000, to be amortized out of the gasoline tax. Despite the efforts of the House GOP leadership, many Republican legislators deserted to the governor. On 1 August 1935, the House voted for a $13,000,000 bond issue for construction. The vote was 157 to 78. Forty-three Republicans voted with Curley, while only 2 Democrats voted no. (The affirmative vote was only one more than the two-thirds required to enact a borrowing bill.) In the Senate, 11 Republicans joined 18 Democrats to put the measure across.[71]

Although Speaker Saltonstall mustered enough Republican votes to prevent passage of a second bond issue, GOP ranks had broken on spending bills. On the whole, the governor displayed an impressive degree of control over the 1935 legislative session, the longest to that date. The General Court approved expenditures of $75,500,000, including the $13,000,000 bond issue and a state budget of about $62,500,000. Only the 1931 legislature had spent more—$79,600,000. A balanced budget—on paper, at any rate—was achieved by setting the state tax (levied by the state on the cities and towns) at $10,000,000, transferring $9,500,000 from the highway fund to the general fund, and passing a one-year 10 percent surtax on incomes. Several proposals for new taxation, including a sales tax and a constitutional amendment to permit graduated state income taxes, were stymied.[72]

Curley kept up the pressure for increased government spending in his budget message of January 1936. This time he asked for $69,162,710.69

to finance ordinary governmental activities and a bond issue of $9,196,140 for building construction. He also called for increased taxes on liquor, slot machines, dog racing, and tobacco, as well as a one-year extension of the 10 percent surtax on incomes. These measures, he estimated, would reduce the state tax from $10,000,000 to $3,000,000. No mention was made of a sales tax.[73]

Opponents of Curley's spending and taxation proposals, including the Massachusetts Federation of Taxpayers' Associations and Republican legislative leaders, began a five-month struggle to cut expenditures. The governor's foes accused state department heads of lavish and wasteful spending.[74] For a short time, it looked as though the economizers might be victorious when a number of Democrats (who were dissatisfied with the governor's monopoly of patronage) and Curley Republicans voted for spending cuts. Curley, however, used his control over the distribution of state jobs to bring the dissidents back into line. In the final Senate vote, 8 Republicans joined 18 Democrats to give the restored Curley budget an easy 26 to 11 (the latter all Republicans) victory. On the final roll call in the House, 4 Republicans abstained while 9 voted with the Democrats.[75]

The final state budget for 1936, including the unspent portion of the $13,000,000 bond issue and funds for flood relief, totaled $72,500,000, though Curley's proposal for a new bond issue to finance the construction of additional state buildings did not pass. The commonwealth, however, had not succeeded in coming up with adequate sources of new tax revenues. The General Court had approved continuation of the 10 percent income surtax, a 40 cent tax on each gallon of alcohol used for commercial purposes, and continuation of an increase in the state gasoline tax, but it had rejected a graduated income tax, a new tax on intangibles, and a retail sales tax, among others.[76]

Governor Curley's success in getting spending bills through the nominally Republican legislature was due in large part to his ability to carry enough Republican votes when he needed them. For example, Republican state representative Christian Herter charged that a legislator who voted against the governor's "Work and Wages" program found that "the unemployed of his district had no chance of getting a state job." Whether or not this allegation is completely true, it is certain that Curley did reward the "renegade" Republican lawmakers with "pick-and-shovel" patronage. Furthermore, forty- and fifty-year-old legislators, who had no prospect of going any higher in politics, were "constantly scheming to get a good appointive job." Consequently, the governor did "not need to offer jobs for votes. He [was] bombarded with offers of votes for jobs."[77]

Another factor in Curley's success was the weakened condition of the Republican party after its electoral defeats of 1932 and 1934. As the *Worcester Telegram* put in in August 1935,

> What the Massachusetts Republicans need is a party. There are the Republicans who vote with the Democrats at the nod of the Democratic Governor; there are those who are for liberal expenditures; there are those who are for paying as the state goes; there are the young Republicans . . . ; there are the embattled women who are militant and the most convincing; there is the patient and cautious State Committee which hopes for the best; *but there is still no rallying around anyone or anything.*[78] [Italics mine.]

Furthermore, the Massachusetts Republicans found it difficult to come up with positive alternatives to Curley's spending proposals. From 1932 to 1934, Governor Ely had cast himself as an economizer; as a result, the demands for government spending had focused equally on the governor's office and the state legislature. When Governor Curley and most of the Democratic legislators aggressively pressed for government spending, those Republican lawmakers who championed economy found themselves on the defensive.

During his two-year term, Curley, who had won the endorsement of the AFL State Federation of Labor in his 1934 campaign, worked hard to get the General Court to liberalize the commonwealth's labor laws. The results were impressive: an anti-injunction measure patterned after the federal Norris-LaGuardia Act; unemployment insurance legislation; revisions in the state's workmen's compensation act; clarification of the state's minimum wage law; a bill providing for the payment of the prevailing rate of wages on state public works; and expansion of the 48-hour work week for women to include additional classes of workers.[79]

Despite his many legislative successes during his two years in the State House from 1935 to 1937, Governor Curley probably did more than any other single Democrat to damage his party's political prospects. Once in the governor's chair, he moved to purge Ely's appointees instead of trying to heal the party's differences.[80] Curley also found himself in trouble in other Democratic quarters because the depression had created a tremendous pressure on legislators from their constituents for jobs. Although this situation was not his fault, he handled it maladroitly. As the *Springfield*

Republican put it on 10 May 1936, "The Curley administration has been more of a personal administration than a party administration. Many Democratic leaders have had no contact with it."[81]

Even more pointed were criticisms from Democrats like Abner S. McLaud of Greenfield in western Massachusetts. Writing to Farley in the midst of the 1936 campaign, he argued that though Curley had done many commendable things, he had been "in some instances tactless and ruthless." In particular, McLaud charged, the governor had used his "Work and Wages" program "in an endeavor to build up a personal organization." He also claimed that Curley's appointment of unfit men to various departments had caused demoralization in the state service.[82]

Other critics of the governor were far less balanced in their views. For example, in 1936 three magazine articles appeared, each savagely attacking Curley's integrity, motivation, and competence. In February, Ray Kierman charged that during his first year in office Curley had set up a dictatorship similar to that of Huey Long in Louisiana. Two months later, Louis M. Lyons described the governor's appointees, mostly Irish, as "the smallest and cheapest political heelers that ever shined their trousers in the seats of public office in Massachusetts."[83]

In September, Joseph F. Dineen, who thirteen years later wrote a sympathetic biography of Curley, described him as "The Kingfish of Massachusetts." Said Dineen,

> Eighteen thousand state employees dare not speak out against the governor. . . . Camp followers are in charge of police departments, the state's educational system, civil service, public works, and all available judicial and administrative positions. The right to pardon criminals has been invested in Curley's controlled council and is exercised freely. With quick coups and an iron hand, he has usurped the power of all public officials and centered it in himself.[84]

As Duane Lockard has pointed out, Curley never exercised anything approaching the power that Huey Long wielded in Louisiana. However, the charges and scandals ruined Curley's chances to win another statewide election, even though he was nominated twice more by the Democrats.[85] In the process, moreover, he further weakened and divided the Democratic party in Massachusetts.

Furthermore, relations between federal and state relief agencies were continuously complicated by the divisions within the state Democratic party. For example, friction developed over the procedures of the Public

Works Administration. In 1933, Massachusetts established an Emergency Finance Board to assist its municipalities. After Congress passed the NIRA, with its provisions for public works, the General Court conferred on this board the duty of approving projects in order to prevent the cities and towns from burdening themselves too heavily with debt. However, PWA authorities appointed a federal board for Massachusetts, with former Republican Governor Alvan Fuller, a longtime critic of Ely, as chairman. Secretary Ickes, who was in charge of the PWA, refused to have anything to do with state agencies in allocating the funds at his disposal.[86]

This provoked an immediate protest from Ely, who early in August 1933 telephoned Ickes and asked him to promise that he would give no public works money to any Massachusetts municipality without the prior approval of the state's Emergency Finance Board. Ickes replied that if the administration adopted such a policy with respect to Massachusetts, this would embarrass it in other states. An angry exchange followed, and the secretary finally hung up.[87]

Ely continued to press his viewpoint on Ickes, though without apparent success. The issue was resolved, at least on the surface, when Fuller declared at his board's first formal meeting that he intended to cooperate to the fullest extent with the state's Emergency Finance Board.[88]

Further delays ensued in getting PWA projects started in Massachusetts because of disagreements between Governor Ely, Republican legislators, and PWA authorities in Washington over financial arrangements. Finally, in late February 1934, Secretary Ickes' office announced an agreement by which Massachusetts, waiving the privilege of federal loans, would take 30 percent grants from PWA and finance the rest by selling her bonds on the open market.[89]

When Curley became governor, he bombarded Washington with requests for outright federal grants. At one point, he submitted a figure of $600,000,000. The administration, of course, was not prepared to accede to the governor's extravagant request. In mid-April 1935, President Roosevelt announced that most of the public works money from the $4,800,000,000 congressional appropriation would be available in the form of loans to states, cities, and towns.[90]

Curley's next move was to name former state senator James P. Brennan of Cambridge, a Democrat, as Massachusetts' special envoy to Washington. His job was to speed up the flow of federal funds into the state. Ickes and WPA chief Harry Hopkins ignored Brennan throughout the month of May. Matters were complicated further by lack of cooperation between

Walsh and Curley, who had still not settled their differences. Moreover, the state's Democratic congressmen, as well as Senators Coolidge and Walsh, resented Brennan's mission because it seemed to suggest that they were not doing their best for their constituents. The congressmen were also angry at Curley, Walsh, and Coolidge for not having consulted them on patronage. By September, the congressmen therefore had decided to strike out on their own in political matters.[91] All these political crosscurrents helped snarl the flow of federal relief money into Massachusetts.

Curley in particular was determined to direct federal relief expenditures in the state. Harry Hopkins, however, was equally persistent in his efforts to keep federal relief as free as possible of political pressures. Thus, when Carney resigned as state FERA chief, Walsh and Curley each sought to name his successor. The administration, however, ignored both men and selected Arthur G. Rotch, a Republican. Rotch made one stipulation to his accepting the appointment—that he be free to overlook political patronage considerations. This was granted. When the transition was made from the FERA to the WPA, Rotch stayed on.[92]

Governor Curley had been in office hardly a month when rumors began to circulate that he was trying to have Rotch removed. Democrats from all over the state took part in a well-orchestrated series of attacks on Rotch. One of the major complaints was his alleged allocations of more aid to Republicans than to Democrats. State Auditor Thomas H. Buckley accused him of discriminating against Democrats in selecting his supervisors. Other officials blamed WPA delays and snags on Rotch's alleged incompetence. Rotch, for his part, told Curley that his office would have to approve all of the governor's WPA proposals before they could be sent to Washington.[93]

The moving force behind the anti-Rotch campaign seems to have been Governor Curley, who continued to blame federal authorities for the slowdown in the state's "Work and Wages" program. Rotch, in turn, had the support of Senator Walsh and the Massachusetts Federation of Taxpayers' Associations. However, in the face of so much opposition, the administration was finally forced to replace Rotch. The Democratic politicians in Massachusetts were, as always, divided over the choice of a successor. The administration consulted none of them, and Hopkins replaced Rotch with an out-of-state Democrat, Paul Edwards, who was serving as assistant regional WPA administrator for New York and New England. The Edwards appointment provoked still another round of protest from Bay State Democrats.[94]

Once on the job, Edwards apparently did manage to mollify some of his critics, but many local Democrats continued to grumble. For example, Mayor Lawrence E. Crowley of Brockton, writing to Farley in September 1936, reported that the Irish Democrats had been angry at Rotch for placing "administration of the E.R.A. in the towns in the hands of the Republican selectmen." However, there was still "a great deal of dissatisfaction" in Brockton even after Edwards had made some changes. Joseph Carney further pointed out to Farley that many Irish Democrats viewed Edwards as "a Jewish gentleman of New York City . . . [who had] put a great many of his own people in peak places" in the WPA.[95]

The difficulties faced by both Rotch and Edwards were partly due to the circumstances of municipal politics. As Congressman Richard M. Russell of Cambridge explained it to Farley, Edwards had been consulting local authorities when he named relief supervisors. This of necessity resulted in "a tremendous preponderance of Republicans" because though only 6 of the 39 cities had GOP administrations, 301 of the 316 towns were governed by Republicans. (Russell discounted the official nonpartisan character of many local elections.)[96]

The distribution of relief funds in Massachusetts was further complicated by the fact that the state maintained an outmoded organizational framework that had not been changed significantly since 1919. Each municipality, no matter how small, had a separate board of public welfare, generally staffed by part-time officials. The state supervised neither the local public welfare agencies nor the general relief program. The municipalities were completely responsible for financing relief, with the exception of a few special categories of assistance for which the state appropriated small sums. (This is why, in June 1935, a spokesman for Harry Hopkins could charge, with only slight exaggeration, that the commonwealth had not spent any money for direct relief.)[97]

According to a study made by William Haber and Herman M. Somers, the FERA exercised "considerable influence, if not control, over the administration of public relief" in many states. However, in Massachusetts the FERA functioned as "an independent agency responsible directly to the national officials," and had less influence than it did elsewhere over state and local relief agencies.[98]

In 1934 the FERA in Massachusetts began to set up work relief projects in many municipalities. The division of responsibility between federal authorities (work relief), municipal public welfare boards (direct relief), and private agencies created all kinds of anomalies. For example, late in

November 1934, FERA field agent Robert Washburn reported to Harry Hopkins that people on public welfare in Boston "could count on medical attention, necessary glasses, dentures, and the rest, from the city," but those working on FERA projects were ineligible for public welfare and had to apply to private charities if they could not afford such necessities. The private charities, Washburn continued, were doing whatever they could but were asking, " 'How long are we going to furnish necessary medical aid free to Federal relief cases?' "[99]

Washburn also noted that the division between public welfare and the FERA was responsible for the FERA's establishing projects "in the various towns on the basis of . . . relief need and not on the basis of how rapidly worthwhile work projects can be developed." The FERA had further ruled that it would give work only to breadwinners with two or more dependents. Only in the city of Worcester did Washburn find the budget that public welfare set for its individual clients the same as that established by the FERA.[100]

Both Washburn and another FERA investigator, Martha Gellhorn, reported a general feeling that, at the local level where job distribution was decided, the FERA was even more susceptible to political influence than was public welfare. According to Mrs. Gellhorn, individuals who applied for FERA work relief had to wait from three weeks to three months to get it, and there were "always four times as many applicants as jobs." Nevertheless, Washburn also found a general acceptance by businessmen and the public of "the necessity of relief" and the need for federal aid to the localities, although some businessmen were critical of "extravagance and waste" in the programs. However, Washburn warned,

> The whole set-up, especially the confusion resulting from the separation of PW and ERA work relief, has left a dangerous bewilderment in the minds of public and relief clients, who continue unanimously to acquiesce in . . . [rather] than support—the program, partly because they have faith it won't have to last much longer and partly because of emotional sympathy with the New Deal.[101]

The most persistent complaint of many New Englanders, Democrats and Republicans both, from 1933 on, was that their part of the country was not receiving its fair share of federal money.[102] Just what constituted a fair share varied with one's point of view. Local interests wanted as much as they could get, and it was therefore good tactics continually to cry for more and more. Bay Staters often drew comparisons with other states, especially those of the South and West. The situation, however, differed from state to state. For example, as bad as economic conditions were in New England, they were much worse in the South.

In his recent book *The New Deal and The States*, James T. Patterson has argued that the New Deal grants-in-aid policy did not favor the poorer states over wealthier states like Massachusetts. That is, the poorer states received the least per capita aid. Patterson concludes,

> Federal grant policy was more concerned with securing state participation than with discovering the extent of need. Indeed, Roosevelt made little effort to equalize wealth by state or region, or even to establish a minimum state payment for various kind of welfare. Far from being deliberately discrimina-tory, New Deal aid policy perpetuated the existing imbalance between rich and poor states in America.[103]

Despite all of the delays, Massachusetts did receive federal money for relief. For example, in December 1934, the FERA reported that 690,000 people—sixteen percent of the population of the state—were receiving public funds for relief. For all of 1934, a total of $72,960,000 had been spent; of this, $40,191,000 had come from federal funds. By June 1935, the number on relief had increased to 722,000 or roughly twenty percent of the population. Total expenditures for 1935 climbed to $105,575,000, with the federal share increasing to $67,160,000. These figures include expenses beyond what finally went to recipients of relief.[104]

When the transition was made in 1935 from the FERA to the Works Progress Administration, delays in Washington led to delays in Mas-sachusetts. After the president signed a $4.8 billion Emergency Relief Appropriations Act in April, FERA head Harry Hopkins and Interior Secretary Harold Ickes began a year-long struggle for control of the new program. Roosevelt named Hopkins to direct the WPA, and Ickes con-tinued as head of the Public Works Administration. The WPA stressed light public works, which could be begun quickly, and the PWA em-phasized heavy and durable projects, which required a longer period of time to plan and to implement.[105]

Thus, a good deal of the delay in getting federal projects under way in the state was due to factors over which Curley had no control. For example, the administration's refusal "to approve extensive projects where the cost of materials [ran] high" blocked a large part of his program. Another handicap was the one-year time limit on the completion of all projects. This involved the president's preference at that time for the speedier WPA approach over the slower PWA.[106]

The Ickes-Hopkins feud further slowed things down. On 11 September 1935, for instance, Hopkins was continuing to throw out "permanent construction projects calling for a high average cost per man year," thus imperiling the PWA programs of both the state and its municipalities. It was not only Curley's plans that were shunted aside. The application of Boston's Mayor Frederick Mansfield for a new city hall received similar treatment. As late as July of the following year, Roosevelt's preference for small projects and the WPA approach was deferring presidential approval of $20,000,000 worth of PWA projects, including a proposed $5,000,000 addition to the Suffolk County Courthouse.[107]

Moreover, for part of Rotch's tenure the process of filling the WPA quotas of Massachusetts lagged behind most other states; but by November 1935 the relief pace in Washington and in Massachusetts was quickening. Nevertheless, local politicians continued to complain that under Rotch's management the WPA was "unnecessarily slow" in meeting its quotas.[108] It is not possible to say how much the delays were due to Rotch's management, how much to the situation in Washington, and how much to Curley's attempts to control the distribution of federal relief funds in Massachusetts. All played a part.

In a 343-page report, filed with Washington in September 1935, Rotch estimated that during the last fiscal year the FERA had spent $70,000,000 to employ an average of 115,000 persons on 8,400 projects. Since 1 April 1934, the agency had disbursed $84,925,000. At its peak, it had had 134,000 men working. In all, 28,399 projects had been filed, of which 6,923 had been completed or nearly so by 1 July.[109]

In late September, the WPA inaugurated 20 to 30 projects in the state. On the twenty-seventh, the president approved $13,181,189 for 166 PWA enterprises. The PWA grants were only 45 percent of the amount required; the local units had to supply the rest. The WPA, on the other hand, paid about 90 percent of the cost of the projects to its employees, and the cities and towns contributed the remaining ten for materials and equipment. By 1 December, 100,000 were working for the WPA throughout the commonwealth, thus absorbing the bulk of FERA personnel. By 5 March 1936, the WPA was employing its full quota of 120,094.[110] On 23 April 1936, Paul Edwards issued a report, putting the number working on WPA undertakings at 120,212, of whom 118,729 had come from relief rolls.[111]

By June, WPA personnel were down to 103,000, in accord with a nationwide policy of gradual reduction up to 1 July. However, when taken in conjunction with those on other federal projects and federal road work, the statewide figure added up to 112,000. In fact, many towns were falling below their quotas as private industry absorbed some of the unemployed. In the city of Boston, however, Edwards found one out of every four on relief. The improvement elsewhere in the state enabled the WPA chief to modify his program in order to ease Boston's burden. In December 1936 the total number of persons receiving public relief funds in Massachusetts stood at 210,000.[112]

At the beginning of the fiscal year, 1 July 1936, the Works Progress Administration reduced its employees in Massachusetts from 93,860 to 89,350. The federal government made available $350,000,000 for the continuation of WPA activities throughout the nation. Of this sum, New England received $25,333,500, and Massachusetts, $16,428,125—according to the *Boston Herald*, "the sixth largest share of the total disbursement made from the $1,425,000,000 appropriated under the 1936 emergency relief act for expenditure on projects already approved by the W.P.A." [113]

Meanwhile, PWA funds began to arrive, although at a slower rate than WPA money. On 30 May 1936, grant payments for thirteen different projects were announced. A month later Secretary of the Treasury Henry Morgenthau, Jr., approved $4,000,000 in building projects for Massachusetts, including a new marine hospital and thirteen post offices. On 30 July 1936, Senator Walsh announced that for the fiscal year terminating on 30 June, $159,186,026 had been allotted to Massachusetts for all agencies operating under the works program. Of this sum, $58,831,934 had gone to the WPA.[114]

Allocation of funds was only one of the problems arising from the federal relief program. Another was the question of WPA wages. President Roosevelt wanted a "security wage," which would be more than the relief dole but not great enough to discourage people from seeking private jobs. The AFL, fearful that this might drive down private pay rates, argued for a wage level commensurate with the prevailing local standard. The wage row continued to smoulder throughout the summer months of 1935. AFL President William Green, labor spokesmen in Massachusetts, Governor Curley, and two federal works administrators for Massachusetts protested against the security wage. The result was a compromise. In September, Hopkins gave the state administrators the discretionary power to decide hours of work for each semimonthly pay period, but the WPA would keep its old monthly maximum in wages. In some cases, such arrangement made the security wage equal to the prevailing union wage—if the hours were reduced sufficiently. Thus, the WPA could accede to labor's hourly wage demands without exceeding the monthly security level. In June 1936, Hopkins made this informal arrangement official.[115]

The Roosevelt administration's determination to use the work relief program as a means of clearing the welfare rolls also caused friction with labor during 1935 and 1936. The requirement stipulated that 90 percent of the total employed must come from the welfare rolls. The Building Trades Council complained that the rules were forcing their union workers to go on relief. Despite threatened strikes and a request from Governor Curley that the WPA raise from 10 to 25 percent the number of its employees chosen from outside the public welfare lists, Hopkins did not give in.[116]

In New England, the growing discontent with the New Deal extended beyond relief to other matters. Once again, many Bay Staters, Democrats as well as Republicans, became increasingly convinced that Washington was favoring the South and the West at the expense of their section.

The source of the discontent was the steady decline of the Massachusetts textile and shoe industries, a decline that reached back to the 1920s and earlier. The crux of the difficulty lay in the migration of cotton textiles to the South Atlantic states and of the boot and shoe industry to the Midwest. Various reasons were assigned for the primacy of other sections over New England: "closer proximity to raw materials or to a large market for the finished product," discriminatory freight rates, cheaper fuel, cheaper power or water supply, lower taxes, lower wages, and "greater freedom from trade union activity." During the 1920s, many Bay Staters labeled the state's progressive labor laws a handicap. Others pointed out that New England industrialists had tied their property up in inherited trusts. The sons then became "coupon clippers," and the actual operation of the textile industry fell into the hands of absentee managers "with little industrial interest or know-how."[117]

The depression made matters even worse. Massachusetts cotton textile manufacturers welcomed the NRA in 1933; and even in mid-1934, when other businessmen were beginning to express some doubt, the textile magnates were still firmly behind the measure. The reason for their strong support was that although the cotton textile code permitted the mills of the South to pay a lower minimum wage than those of the North, it did at least establish a floor below which the southern mills could not go. The suspension in 1933 of the six o'clock law (a Massachusetts statute that forbade the employment of women and children in textile plants after 6 P. M.) also helped to correct the sectional imbalance somewhat. However, the existence of any wage differential at all between North and South was a bone of contention between northern mill men and the NRA textile code authority.[118]

Early in 1935, New England mill owners, labor leaders, state legislators, governors, and citizens in affected communities launched an organized campaign aimed at getting the Roosevelt administration to abolish the cotton processing tax, a levy laid by the Agricultural Adjustment Administration on textile manufacturers so that the federal government could make benefit payments to cotton farmers. The mill owners, already financially hard-pressed, passed the cost of the tax on to their customers; and this, they felt, was keeping down the volume of their sales. On this issue, the southern mill owners agreed with their northern counterparts, as they did on the need to block Japanese textile imports. The southerners, of course, disagreed with the northern demand for abolition of the one dollar per week minimum wage differential, which favored the South. The New England mill owners found other allies in the South—in the cotton exporters, who feared that they were losing ground in foreign markets. On the other side of the issue, firm supporters of the AAA's cotton policy were the Roosevelt administration and the landowning cotton planters.[119]

Not all textile owners blamed the cotton processing tax for their problems. For example, J. Foster Smith, agent for the Pequot Mills of Salem, Massachusetts, pointed to overproduction as the chief difficulty. He contended that the solution lay in "greater cooperation between the manufacturers," who should "join to regulate supply and demand."[120]

In reply to the continuing complaints, the National Industrial Recovery Board of the NRA authorized depressed divisions of the cotton textile industry to reduce operations 25 percent below the existing code standards. This was to be achieved by allowing cuts in labor time from the 40-hour-weekly code maximum to as low as 30. The board also gave permission for a 25 percent decrease in machines. The NIRB hoped that these moves would spread available business throughout the industry and thus halt the "wholesale shutdowns" of the previous several weeks. The board viewed these changes as temporary. These moves, in turn, provoked protests from spokesmen for the United Textile Workers Union.[121]

Bipartisan opposition among Massachusetts politicians to the processing tax continued to mount. The president, however, refused to yield. Back in New England, a group of manufacturers was laying plans to test the constitutionality of the processing taxes in court. Roosevelt moved to divert the storm by appointing a cabinet committee to probe the textile situation, but protests continued to flow into Washington from Massachusetts.[122]

The conflict over policy was a basic one. As the liberal *Nation* put it:

> The textile problem cannot be safely treated in isolation. In fact, the issue as it presents itself is essentially a *sectional conflict* [italics mine]. On the one side is a decadent New England industry dependent on the tariff for its existence and desiring above all else an abundant supply of cheap cotton. On the other is the cotton growing industry, which, because of its dependence on foreign markets, must have either a reduction of tariff or an indefinite continuation of the present reduction-subsidy policy. Reconciliation of this conflict is impossible.[123]

The Supreme Court decision striking down the NRA as unconstitutional created a state of near panic in the textile industry. Efforts by the cotton mill men to maintain code standards voluntarily broke down by January 1936. Furthermore, the mills received little comfort from the Roosevelt administration. In August 1935, the president's cabinet committee recommended continuation of the processing tax and steps to control Japanese textile imports, but preferably by means of a voluntary agreement with Japan. The committee dodged the thorny question of wage differentials by calling for further study. The only aid that northern textile mill owners received from Washington during the rest of 1935 was in the form of government orders for cotton cloth.[124]

The lawsuit instituted against the AAA by William M. Butler and James A. McDonough of the Hoosiac Mills of New Bedford ended with the Supreme Court's declaring the AAA unconstitutional in January 1936.[125] However, the underlying problems of the industry remained unsolved.

The boot and shoe industry also continued to decline. Early in 1935, both owners and workers in desperation demanded that the NRA revise the shoe code. The resultant hearings revealed sharp differences. The manufacturers contended that they moved factories away from unionized centers not to obtain lower wages but to escape labor troubles. The union spokesmen demanded reorganization of the code authority; establishment of fixed minimum wages for skilled, semiskilled, and unskilled workers; and elimination of the existing sectional and population wage differentials, which, by allowing management to pay lower wages in smaller towns, had helped country districts attract shoe plants out of Massachusetts. The code authority refused to reconsider the code, and there the whole matter stood until the Supreme Court voided the NRA.[126]

All of this sectional unrest among New Englanders, and Bay Staters in particular, raised questions about the future political prospects of the New Deal in the Northeast. As early as October 1934, news analyst John Bantry reported that the rank-and-file Democratic politicians of Massachusetts, especially the Irish leaders, distrusted President Roosevelt's "brain trust" and were "cool to the N.R.A., the agricultural programme, the trend toward inflation and the large expenditures." In February 1936, Bantry observed that Democratic politicians in Boston still were suspicious of New Deal policies and were convinced that the president had not "played his political cards well" in Massachusetts.[127]

Governor Curley took an equivocal stance. That is, though he criticized New Deal policies that were out of favor in New England, he was careful to maintain a public position of personal loyalty to the president. Early in February 1936, he announced that he would campaign for a slate of Democratic National Convention delegates pledged to FDR.[128]

Several of the letters from Massachusetts Democrats to Farley in August and September of 1936 expressed doubts about election prospects. James Roosevelt, writing from Boston on 17 September, summarized these concerns. He feared that if the election were held on that day, Massachusetts would not go for Roosevelt. "A considerable number of Independent voters" had not yet made up their minds. The state Democratic ticket, he felt, was "not as good as the Republican ticket" and was made up of individuals "not willing to cooperate" with the national ticket. Another problem was "the influence of Father Coughlin." Thomas O'Brien of Boston, the Union party's candidate for vice-president, was also running for the office of United States senator from Massachusetts; and Coughlin's influence in Massachusetts was "probably stronger than in any other state." The Union party's candidates, James Roosevelt concluded, would "pull more [votes] from Democrats than [they would from] Republicans."[129]

Many local Democrats, such as Abner McLaud, Joseph A. Maynard, collector of the Port of Boston, and Mayor Lawrence Crowley of Brockton, recognized that Curley, who hoped to be elected to the Senate on the president's coattails, was the weakest link in the Democratic campaign. John Donahue, a representative from Haverhill to the state House of Representatives, even went so far as to suggest that the directors of the Democratic national campaign in Massachusetts try to dissociate it from the record of the Curley administration.[130]

In October, the president's campaign in Massachusetts picked up momentum, partly in response to a vigorous speaking tour by James Roosevelt on his father's behalf.[131] On election day, President Roosevelt carried Massachusetts by a margin of 174,103 votes over Republican Alfred Landon. The totals were 942,716 to 767,613. Thus, Roosevelt more than doubled the 63,000-vote plurality by which he had taken the state in 1932. The Union party ticket of William Lemke and Thomas O'Brien polled 118,639 ballots. Curley lost the Senate seat to Republican state Representative Henry Cabot Lodge, Jr. The final returns gave the governor 739,751 votes; Lodge, 875,160; and O'Brien, 134,245.[132]

Many factors were responsible for Curley's loss: his excesses as governor; his barely disguised feud with the president; the O'Brien candidacy, which drew votes from Curley in cities like Boston and Somerville (where Father Coughlin had been gaining support among the Irish); and Lodge's drawing power in the cities because of his liberal record on labor legislation. Furthermore, the president had not endorsed Curley during his campaign tour of Massachusetts.[133]

Curley's loss was not the only sign of Democratic weakness in Massachusetts. In late August, Congressman Arthur D. Healy complained to Farley that there seemed to be "a lack of cooperation and coordination among the candidates for statewide offices. We congressional candidates," he continued, "are left entirely on our own and must rely upon ourselves entirely for re-election." A month later, another Democrat, Michael T. Golden of Woburn, reported to Farley that gubernatorial candidate Charles F. Hurley was "playing a lone hand and [was] doing nothing to advance the President's position."[134]

The upshot was that Hurley was elected, but by a bare 38,177-vote margin. The Republicans gained two congressional seats, two statewide offices, control of both houses of the legislature and the governor's executive council, and "nearly a full complement of county officers." Leverett Saltonstall lost the lieutenant governorship to his Democratic opponent by a bare 9,197 votes.[135] Clearly, then, even the appeal of Roosevelt and the New Deal at the height of the president's popularity in 1936 could not stem the erosion of Democratic power in Massachusetts.

Governor Hurley's actions accelerated the process. During his two-year term, Hurley was hostile to the Roosevelt administration, protesting strongly against its attempt to gain passage of the child labor amendment. He had his troubles within the state, too. By July 1938, he and the Republican-controlled legislature were deadlocked over the latter's refusal to enact his proposed expenditures for a large work relief program. (By the end of August, however, the legislature had appropriated $77,000,000, the second-largest sum to be appropriated by a General Court in Massachusetts until then. Thus, despite the persisting political wrangles, state government spending continued to increase.) Furthermore, Hurley had not repaired the damage to state service that Curley's appointments had caused.[136]

In an attempt to win a second term, Hurley publicly embraced the New Deal in July 1938. However, he was challenged in the Democratic primary by Curley, who charged that the governor had "betrayed" President Roosevelt. Curley also contended that he had put more men to work on the state payroll during his own administration than had Hurley, and he promised to cut the minimum age for old-age assistance from 65 to 60. Curley won the September primary and asserted that he was running "only . . . to prevent the election of a reactionary Republican." His GOP opponent, Leverett Saltonstall, stated that he stood for "an honest State budget, ever recognizing the fact that until such time as private business is ready to take care of the unemployed it is the duty of the government to provide jobs for those who want to work but are unable to get work." He also promised to "fight for a tariff policy that will protect Massachusetts labor, Massachusetts industry and the American standard of living."[137]

On election day, Saltonstall defeated Curley by a decisive margin of over 100,000 votes. Curley failed to carry the normal Democratic vote in any part of the state, showing weakness in both the industrial areas and the towns. Even Democrats in Boston, as well as other sections, refused to vote for him. For example, his running mate for lieutenant governor ran ahead of him in the city of Boston. The Democratic revolt against Curley carried some of the GOP candidates for statewide office to victory as well, and the Republicans kept control of the executive council and both branches of the legislature, and retained their ten congressional seats. After the election, Democratic Congressman William Granfield estimated that "thousands of Democrats refused to vote for the head of the ticket, and many of them supported the Republican ticket from top to bottom."[138]

The *New York Times* pointed out that there had been "not so much an increase in the Republican vote as . . . a definite reduction in the Democratic vote. . . . The Republicans drew out their normal Presidential election year vote while the Democrats had only their normal off-year vote."[139]

This was Curley's third successive defeat, for in 1937 Republican

Henry Parkman and Democrat Maurice Tobin had formed an alliance that foiled Curley's bid for the Boston mayoralty. Tobin was elected mayor and Parkman corporation counsel. In 1938, many Boston and suburban Irish deserted Curley again and voted Republican, even though organized labor had endorsed his candidacy.[140]

One *New York Times* account asserted that "national issues [had] played no part in the campaign." Joseph Dineen, writing in the *Nation* in August 1939, argued that though the New Deal was "still popular, . . . Roosevelt and the Democratic Party [had] slipped, substantially in the towns and less noticeably in the cities." He attributed this to "rifts within the party."[141]

Some of Farley's Democratic correspondents from Massachusetts, however, pointed to other factors in the situation. They viewed the WPA as "a political liability." WPA workers wanted more money, which they were promised by the Republicans. Those who had not been able to get on the WPA also voted Republican, and there was growing public resentment over "W.P.A. gangs soldiering at their work." Furthermore, small businessmen had been "infected with the idea that the [Roosevelt] administration [was] anti-business." Congressman Joseph Casey argued that "men who were formerly New-Dealers [sic] . . . are opposed to our spending program because of its resultant high taxes." Besides, one correspondent from the western part of the state reported "a definite swing to the right in Mass[achusetts], as the result of dissatisfaction with [the] present Administration's left wing attitude, [the attempted] purge [of anti–New Deal congressmen and senators], etc."[142]

The local intraparty strife involved more than the Curley-Hurley split. Senator Walsh and former Governor Ely took no part in the campaign. Furthermore, the whole statewide ticket came from metropolitan Boston; outstate Democrats were not included at all.[143]

As Professor Key has pointed out, Walsh, with his combination of Democratic, independent, and "on occasion, Yankee Republican support," could win elections to the United States Senate, but he could not hold a large enough following among Democrats to control his own party in the state. Curley, on the other hand, "built a political career on his uncompromising championship of the Boston Irish." However, he was victorious in only one statewide race, "that for governor in 1934, a year when probably Democratic popular strength in the nation generally reached its peak." Although he could win statewide nominations, his rough political style alienated independents, Republicans, and enough Democrats to deprive him of victory in the general election.[144]

The Republicans, moreover, according to Farley's Democratic correspondents, conducted a well-organized, well-financed campaign. By contrast, these same Democrats complained about lack of funds for western Massachusetts and rural districts. Congressman Casey reported that the Republicans

> ran a magnificent campaign in that they ignored the Yankee Republicans upon the theory that they had no place else to go . . . and they played for racial groups, particularly the French, Polish and Italians. They promised them everything. They would put their leaders on the payroll. They even paid off church mortgages in order to encourage good will with the pastors.[145]

The Republicans thus were able to capitalize on the resentment felt by the new immigrants and their children against the Irish for their failure to share patronage and political power equitably.[146]

Perhaps most important, the Massachusetts GOP had been moving in a more liberal direction on questions of economic policy. For example, since 1933 enough Republicans in the lower house had joined Democrats in voting for various pieces of labor legislation to put the measures across. (However, Senate Republicans in many cases had resisted prolabor bills more stubbornly than their GOP colleagues in the House and had thus managed to defeat some bills; and even in the House a hard core of conservative Republicans had opposed such proposals.)[147] When Saltonstall became governor, liberals and conservatives in his party struggled to influence his stands on labor legislation.[148]

The 1938 election marked the beginning of a GOP resurgence in Massachusetts. Between 1938 and 1952, the Republicans captured the governorship four times, and Bay State voters often split their tickets.[149]

By August 1939, the depression was diminishing in Massachusetts as her industries began to feel the effects of war orders.[150] In the six preceding years, the state had faced hard questions involving government spending, relief activities, taxation, business recovery, and labor matters. If the answers of Massachusetts politicians were less than forthright, this was partly due to the ambiguities of national policy and politics.

Furthermore, both Democrats and Republicans in the Bay State felt that they had to defend the special interests of Massachusetts and New England, no matter what. The situation was made worse by the struggle over allocation and control of relief funds, the persistent factionalism within the Massachusetts Democratic party, and the continuing feuds between the Roosevelt administration and various state Democratic factions. All in all, given the makeup of the Massachusetts political scene from 1932 to 1938, a New Deal administration on Beacon Hill, cooperating fully with Washington, was never a real possibility.

1. J. Joseph Huthmacher, *Massachusetts People and Politics, 1919–1933* (Cambridge, Mass., 1959), pp. 59–71; James T. Patterson, *The New Deal and the States: Federalism in Transition* (Princeton, N.J., 1969), pp. 17, 22–23.

2. Huthmacher, *Massachusetts People and Politics*, pp. 260–62.

3. Duane Lockard, *New England State Politics* (Princeton, N.J., 1959), pp. 125–27.

4. Huthmacher, *Massachusetts People and Politics*, pp. 200–202; *Who's Who in Massachusetts*, 2 vols. (Boston, 1942), 2:223; Dorothy G. Wayman, *David I. Walsh: Citizen-Patriot* (Milwaukee, 1952), p. 60.

5. Lockard, *New England State Politics* p. 126; V. O. Key, Jr., *American State Politics: An Introduction* (New York, 1956), p. 155.

6. Key, *American State Politics*, p. 158.

7. Ibid., p. 160.

8. Huthmacher, *Massachusetts People and Politics*, pp. 232–56; James MacGregor Burns, *Roosevelt: The Lion and the Fox* (New York, 1956), pp. 131–32.

9. Burns, *Roosevelt*, pp. 131–32.

10. Huthmacher, *Massachusetts People and Politics*, pp. 232–56.

11. Sidney Shalett and James Roosevelt, *Affectionately F.D.R.* (New York, 1959), p. 184.

12. James Michael Curley, *I'd Do It Again* (Englewood Cliffs, N.J., 1957), pp. 246–52; Joseph F. Dineen, *The Purple Shamrock* (New York, 1949), pp. 200, 204–10.

13. Untitled newspaper clipping, 1 May 1933, and *Boston Globe*, 5 May 1933 (clippings), David I. Walsh Scrapbooks (Holy Cross College Library).

14. *Boston Herald*, 24 September 1933; *Boston Transcript*, 24 September 1933.

15. *Boston Herald*, 24 September, 1 October 1933.

16. *Boston Transcript*, 30 July 1933, 9 March 1934; *Boston Post*, 9 March 1934 (clipping), Walsh Scrapbooks.

17. *Boston Post*, 10 April 1934 (clipping), Walsh Scrapbooks.

18. *Boston Transcript*, 9 March 1934; *Boston Post*, 9 March 1934 (clipping), Walsh Scrapbooks.

19. *Boston Transcript*, 30 July 1933; *Springfield* (Mass.) *Republican*, 21 March 1934.

20. *Boston Post*, 9 March 1934 (clipping), Walsh Scrapbooks; *Springfield Republican*, 1 April 1934.

21. *Springfield Republican* 1 April 1934.

22. *Boston Herald*, 5 August 1934.

23. *Boston Globe*, 2 July 1933 (clipping), Walsh Scrapbooks; *Boston Transcript*, 30 July 1933; Joseph B. Ely, *Addresses and Messages to the General Court* (Boston, 1934), pp. 418–22.

24. Joseph B. Ely, *The American Dream* (Boston, 1941), pp. 89, 125.

25. Huthmacher, *Massachusetts People and Politics*, pp. 172–213; Lockard, *New England State Politics*, pp. 127–28; *Boston Post*, 11 March 1934; *Haverhill* (Mass.) *Gazette*, March 1936 [sic] (clippings), Walsh Scrapbooks.

26. *Boston Transcript*, 8 March 1935; *Boston Post*, 17 March 1935; *Providence Journal*, 2 April 1935 (clippings), Walsh Scrapbooks.

27. *New York Herald Tribune* 9 February 1936; *Boston Transcript*, 2 May 1936; *Southbridge* (Mass.) *Evening News,* 26 June 1936 (clippings), Walsh Scrapbooks.

28. *Berkshire* (Pittsfield, Mass.) *Eagle,* 5 December 1934; *Boston Transcript,*23 March 1935 (clippings), Walsh Scrapbooks.

29. *Minneapolis Star*, 17 September 1935; *Minneapolis Journal*, 17 September 1935; *Minneapolis Tribune,* 18 September 1935 (clippings), Walsh Scrapbooks.

30. *Censor*, July 1935; *Minneapolis Journal*, 17 September 1935 (clippings), Walsh Scrapbooks.

31. *Boston Herald*, 26 July 1935 (clipping), Walsh Scrapbooks.

32. *Boston Transcript*, 24 April 1936; untitled newspaper clipping, 20 June 1936 (clippings), Walsh Scrapbooks.

33. *Boston Transcript*, 16 March, 30 April 1935; *Boston Post*, 22 July 1935; untitled newspaper clippings, 25 July 1935, 10 February, 30 June 1936 (clippings), Walsh Scrapbooks.

34. *New York Times*, 25 February, 1 March 1936.

35. *Worcester* (Mass.) *Gazette*, 11 September 1935; *Boston Post*, 27 October 1935 (clippings), James Michael Curley Scrapbooks (Holy Cross College Library).

36. *Boston Post*, 11 June 1935; untitled newspaper clipping, 27 August 1935 (clippings), Walsh Scrapbooks; *Springfield Republican*, 21 August 1935 (clipping), Curley Scrapbooks.

37. *Boston Herald,* 9 January, 5 October 1935; *Boston Transcript*, 24 January 1935 (clipping), Curley Scrapbooks; *New York Times*, 3 February 1935.

38. *Boston Post*, 27 October 1935 (clipping), Curley Scrapbooks.

39. Ibid.

40. *Lowell* (Mass.) *Leader*, 12 June 1935 (clipping), Curley Scrapbooks; *Boston Herald*, 21 June 1935, 2 June 1936.

41. *Boston Post*, 22 September 1935 (clipping), Curley Scrapbooks.

42. *Springfield Republican*, 5 May 1935 (clipping), Curley Scrapbooks; *Boston Herald*, 24 November 1935.

43. Huthmacher, *Massachusetts People and Politics*, pp. 219–28.

44. Ibid., pp. 247–56; *Journal of the House of Representatives of the Commonwealth of Massachusetts: 1933* (Boston, 1933), pp. 14–16; *The Commonwealth of Massachusetts: The Journal of the Senate for the Year 1933* (Boston, 1933), pp. 4–5.

45. Ely, *Addresses and Messages*, pp. 33–48, 152–58; *Boston Herald*, 25 January 1933.

46. *Boston Transcript*, 27, 31 January 1933; *Springfield Republican*, 27, 29 January 1933.

47. *Springfield Republican*, 27 January, 10, 19 February 1933; *Boston Transcript*, 9 February 1933.

48. *Springfield Republican*, 16 February 1933.

49. *Boston Herald*, 3 December 1932; *Springfield Republican*, 20 February 1933.

50. *Springfield Republican*, 21 February 1933.

51. Ibid., 16 February 1933.

52. Ibid., 5, 29, 30 March 1933; *Massachusetts House Journal: 1933*, pp. 362–64, 380–84, 572–74; *Massachusetts Senate Journal: 1933,* pp. 314–16, 448.

53. Patterson, *New Deal and the States*, p. 50.

54. Gaspar G. Bacon, *Individual Rights and the Public Welfare* (Boston, 1935), pp. 152–54; Ely, *Addresses and Messages*, p. 403; *Boston Herald,* 7 May 1933.

55. Ely, *Addresses and Messages*, pp. 171–76; *Boston Transcript*, 20 April 1933, 31 May 1934; *Springfield Republican*, 25, 26 April, 14, 17, 28 May 1933, 5, 6, 26 January, 6 May, 29 June 1934.

56. *Springfield Republican*, 4, 6 June 1933.

57. Ibid.; *Boston Transcript*, 1 July 1933; *Massachusetts House Journal: 1933*, pp. 1179–81; *Massachusetts Senate Journal: 1933*, p. 921.

58. *Boston Transcript,* ca. March 1933 (clipping), Walsh Scrapbooks; ibid., 21 June 1933; *Springfield Republican,* 13 July 1933; *Boston Herald,* 24 July 1933; *Massachusetts House Journal: 1933,* pp. 1328–30; *Massachusetts Senate Journal: 1933,* pp. 1024–25.

59. Ely, *Addresses and Messages,* p. 56; *Boston Herald,* 21 November, 31 December 1933; *Springfield Republican,* 10 January 1934.

60. Ely, *Addresses and Messages,* pp. 50, 250–51; *Massachusetts House Journal: 1934* (Boston, 1934), pp. 355–57, 1219–20; *Massachusetts Senate Journal: 1934* (Boston, 1934), pp. 961–62; *Boston Transcript,* 26, 27, 30 April 1934; *Springfield Republican,* 29 June 1934.

61. Ely, *Addresses and Messages,* p. 56; *Springfield Republican,* 5, 6, 26 January, 6 May, 29 June 1934; *Boston Transcript,* 31 May 1934.

62. *Boston Herald,* 15, 21, 22 June 1934; *New York Times,* 19 September 1934; *Boston Globe,* 2, 22 September 1934; *Boston Post,* 22 September 1934; *Springfield Republican,* 30 September 1934; Commonwealth of Massachusetts, *Public Document No. 43: Election Statistics, 1934* (Boston, 1934), p. 86.

63. Bacon, *Individual Rights and the Public Welfare,* pp. 253–56; *Springfield Republican,* 30 September 1934; *Fitchburg* (Mass.) *Sentinel,* 31 October 1934; *Worcester Sunday Telegram,* 4 November 1934; *Boston Herald,* 4, 5 November 1934. In September, Bacon offered a ten-point program. Some of his proposals, such as "necessary relief for the unemployed," unemployment insurance, and "necessary public works to provide jobs," indicate the extent to which the New Deal set the tone of the state campaign. The only hints of criticism of the New Deal made by Bacon were the planks calling for "honest spending of the people's money" and "removal of restrictions on business so men and women can be taken off relief rolls and placed on payrolls" (*Boston Herald,* 25 September 1934).

64. *Boston Herald,* 27, 30 September 1934; Curley, *I'd Do It Again,* p. 263; Dineen, *Purple Shamrock,* p. 217.

65. *Boston Herald,* 14, 15 June, 22 September, 21 October 1934; *Boston Post,* 16 June 1934; *Springfield Republican,* 21, 28 October 1934; *East Boston Free Press,* 27 October 1934 (clipping), Walsh Scrapbooks; Shalett and J. Roosevelt, *Affectionately F.D.R.,* pp. 217–18; Arthur M. Schlesinger, Jr., *The Coming of the New Deal* (Boston 1958), p. 506.

66. *Public Document No. 43: 1934,* p. 240–45, 278–79, 281–84; *Boston Herald,* 7, 8 November 1934.

67. *Boston Herald,* 7 November 1934; *Boston Post,* 7 November 1934; *Worcester Telegram,* 8 November 1934.

68. James Michael Curley, *Addresses and Messages to the General Court, Proclamations, Official Addresses, Correspondence and Statements of His Excellency Governor James M. Curley, 1935–1936* (n.p., 1936), pp. 7–41; *Boston Herald,* 24 January 1935; *Springfield Republican,* 24 January 1935 (clipping), Curley Scrapbooks.

69. *Boston Transcript,* 29 June 1934; *Boston Globe,* 5 June 1935 (clipping), Curley Scrapbooks; *Boston Herald,* 6, 25 June, 4, 25 July 1935; *Springfield Union,* 26 June 1935 (clipping), Curley Scrapbooks; *Christian Science Monitor,* 27 June 1935 (clipping), ibid.; *Massachusetts House Journal: 1935* (Boston, 1935), pp. 1427–29. Moran was in the political debt of the Democrats because Curley and the Democrats in the state Senate had supported him for the presidency of the body over the incumbent Erland Fish. Moran rewarded the Democrats by giving them 14 of the 34 Senate chairmanships (see Curley, *I'd Do It Again,* p. 264; *Boston Herald,* 1, 2, 8, 11, 18 January 1935).

70. *Boston Transcript,* 28 June 1935; *North Adams Transcript,* 28 June 1935; *Leominster Enterprise,* 29 June 1935; *Springfield Republican,* 30 June, 3 July 1935; *Boston Post,* 12 July 1935 (clippings), Curley Scrapbooks; *Boston Herald,* 28, 29, 30 June 1935.

71. *Boston Herald,* 20 July, 2, 3 August 1935; (Boston) *Daily Record,* 7 August 1935 (clipping), Curley Scrapbooks; *Massachusetts House Journal: 1935,* pp. 1576–78; *Massachusetts Senate Journal: 1935* (Boston, 1935), pp. 1217–18.

72. *Christian Science Monitor,* 15 August 1935 (clipping), Curley Scrapbooks.

73. Curley, *Messages,* pp. 147–53; *Boston Herald,* 22 January 1936.

74. *Boston Herald,* 24 January, 4, 8, 12, 14, 15, 16 February 1936.

75. *Boston Herald*, 16, 17, 18, 22, 24, 26 April, 7, 8, 14 May 1936; *Christian Science Monitor*, 17, 18 April, 15 May 1936; *Springfield Republican*, 26 April 1936; *Boston Advertiser*, 3 May 1936 (clipping), Curley Scrapbooks; *Boston Transcript*, 15 May 1936.

76. *Christian Science Monitor*, 3 July 1936 (clipping), Curley Scrapbooks.

77. *Worcester Post*, 1 October 1935; *Boston Post*, 24 May 1936 (clippings), Curley Scrapbooks.

78. *Worcester Telegram*, 4 August 1935 (clipping), Curley Scrapbooks.

79. *Boston Globe*, 8 August 1935, 7 June 1936; *Christian Science Monitor*, 15 August 1935, 3 July 1936 (clippings), Curley Scrapbooks; *Proceedings of the Fiftieth Annual Convention: Massachusetts State Federation of Labor* (Boston, 1935), pp. 42, 51.

80. *Boston Post*, 21 February 1935 (clipping), Curley Scrapbooks; *Boston Herald*, 21 February, 28 November 1935; *Boston Globe*, 14 March 1936 (clipping), Curley Scrapbooks.

81. *Springfield Republican*, 10 May 1936 (clipping), Curley Scrapbooks.

82. Abner S. McLaud to James A. Farley, 8 September 1936, OF 300, Democratic National Committee, James A. Farley Correspondence on Political Trends, Massachusetts, 1936, Box 81, Roosevelt Papers (Franklin D. Roosevelt Library) (hereafter cited as OF 300, Box 81, Roosevelt Papers).

83. Ray Kierman, "Jim Curley, Boss of Massachusetts," *American Mercury* 37 (1936): 137–51; Louis M. Lyons, "Jim Curley and His Gang," *Nation* 142 (1936): 540–42.

84. Joseph F. Dineen, "The Kingfish of Massachusetts," *Harper's Monthly Magazine* 173 (1936): 343–57.

85. Lockard, *New England State Politics*, p. 129.

86. *New York Times*, 13 August 1933.

87. Harold L. Ickes, *The Secret Diary of Harold L. Ickes*, 3 vols. (New York, 1953–54), 1:73–74. When Ickes had lunch at the White House on 13 August 1933, "the President said that the best story that had come out of Washington since March 4, was the conversation I had over the telephone with . . . Ely. . . . He said it was grand" (*Diary*, 1:80).

88. Ely, *Addresses and Messages*, pp. 415–18; *New York Times*, 13 August 1933.

89. *Boston Transcript*, 24 February 1934.

90. *Quincy* (Mass.) *Patriot-Ledger*, 7 February 1935 (clipping), Curley Scrapbooks; *Boston Herald*, 13, 14 April 1935; *Boston Post*, 20 April 1935 (clipping), Curley Scrapbooks.

91. *Worcester Telegram*, 8 May 1935; *Boston Traveler*, 21 May 1935; *Boston Transcript*, 13 September 1935 (clippings), Curley Scrapbooks; *Boston Post*, 24 May 1935 (clipping), Walsh Scrapbooks.

92. *Lynn* (Mass.) *Telegram News*, 15 September 1935; *San Francisco Chronicle*, 26 November 1935 (clippings), Curley Scrapbooks; *Boston Herald*, 26 November 1935.

93. *Boston Post*, 2 February 1935; *Boston Traveler*, 23 August 1935; *Wakefield Item*, 12 September 1935; *Gloucester Times*, 29 November 1935; *Quincy Patriot Ledger*, 30 November 1935; *New Bedford Standard-Times*, 3 December, 1935; *Boston Traveler*, 5 December 1935; *Springfield News*, 13 December 1935 (clippings), Curley Scrapbooks; *Boston Herald*, 21 June 1935.

94. *Worcester Telegram*, 1 December 1935; *Fitchburg Sentinel*, 13 December 1935; *Boston American*, 1 February 1936; *Boston Advertiser*, 2 February 1936 (clippings), Curley Scrapbooks; *Boston Herald*, 25, 26 January, 1 February 1936.

95. Joseph P. Carney to Farley, 5 August 1936; Lawrence E. Crowley to Farley, 29 September 1936, OF 300, Box 81, Roosevelt Papers.

96. Richard M. Russell to Farley, 11 August 1936, ibid.

97. William Haber and Herman M. Somers, "The Administration of Public Assistance in Massachusetts," *Social Service Review* 12 (1938): 398, 409–10; *Boston Herald*, 25 June 1935. Massachusetts had enacted an old age assistance bill in 1931, four years before the passage of the federal Social Security Act. Together the state and federal governments paid about five-sixths of the costs of old age assistance in Massachusetts, but they found it difficult to supervise the programs because they had to deal with so many local boards (Haber and Somers, "The Administration of Public Assistance in Massachusetts," pp. 397–98, 409–10).

98. Haber and Somers, "The Administration of Public Assistance in Massachusetts," p. 398.

99. Robert Washburn to Harry Hopkins, 10 November 1934, FERA-WPA Narrative Field Reports, "Federal Emergency Relief Administration Survey of Conditions November, 1934 to January, 1935," box 59, Hopkins Papers (Franklin D. Roosevelt Library).

100. Washburn to Hopkins, 3, 10 November 1934, ibid.

101. Washburn to Hopkins, 3 November, 7 December 1934; Martha Gellhorn to Hopkins, undated (probably late November 1934), ibid. Martha Gellhorn's over-all view of the relief picture was much more pessimistic than Washburn's. The latter, despite "the critical tone of much" that he had written, was surprised that "under the circumstances the relief job that is being done is an [sic] efficient as it is" (Gellhorn to Hopkins, undated [probably late November 1934]; Washburn to Hopkins, 7 December 1934, ibid.).

102. For example, Massachusetts Tax Commissioner Henry Long contended that in the long run Massachusetts and other eastern states would have to pay a large part of the taxes engendered by the New Deal spending programs, "although perhaps in the next generation" (*Boston Post*, 10 February 1935 [clipping], Curley Scrapbooks).

103. Patterson, *The New Deal and the States*, p. 200.

104. *Statistical Abstract of the United States: 1935* (Washington, 1935), p. 327; *Statistical Abstract of the United States: 1936* (Washington, 1936), p. 335. The *Statistical Abstract* for 1936 states that the money spent "includes in addition to relief extended to cases under the general relief program (direct and work relief) obligations incurred for special programs, for administration, and, since April 1934, for purchase of materials, supplies and equipment, rental of equipment, earnings of nonrelief persons employed, and other expenses incident to Emergency Work Relief Program" (p. 335).

105. Arthur M. Schlesinger, Jr., *The Politics of Upheaval* (Boston, 1960), pp. 270, 343–51.

106. *Ibid.*, p. 344; *Boston Post*, 19 June 1935 (clipping), Curley Scrapbooks.

107. *Boston Herald*, 11 September 1935, 12 July 1936; *Springfield Republican*, 15 September 1935 (clipping), Curley Scrapbooks.

108. *San Francisco Chronicle*, 26 November 1935; *Christian Science Monitor*, 1 February 1936 (clippings), Curley Scrapbooks.

109. *Boston Herald*, 6 September 1935.

110. *Christian Science Monitor*, 21 September 1935, 5 March 1936; *Boston Globe,* 28, 29 September 1935 (clippings), Curley Scrapbooks; *Boston Herald*, 1 December 1935.

111. *Boston Post*, 24 April 1936 (clipping), Curley Scrapbooks.

112. *Berkshire Eagle*, 1 May 1936 (clipping), Curley Scrapbooks; *Boston Herald*, 4 June 1936; *Statistical Abstract of the United States: 1937* (Washington, 1937), p. 335.

113. *Boston Herald*, 30 June, 1 July 1936.

114. *Boston Herald*, 30 May, 25 June 1936; *Boston Post*, 30 July 1936 (clipping), Curley Scrapbooks.

115. Schlesinger, *Politics of Upheaval*, pp. 268–69; *Boston Herald*, 22 May, 26 June, 28 July, 1, 7, 9, 10 August, 20, 21 September 1935, 24 June 1936.

116. *Boston Herald*, 28, 29 July, 15 August 1935, 11, 19 January, 13 March, 24 June 1936.

117. Huthmacher, *Massachusetts People and Politics*, pp. 126–31; Commonwealth of Massachusetts, *Final Report of the Special Commission on Stabilization of Employment* (Boston, 1933), p. 78.

118. *Massachusetts Senate Journal: 1933*, p. 978; *Massachusetts House Journal: 1933*, pp. 1271–73; *Boston Transcript*, 6 July 1933, 30 June 1934; *Boston Herald*, 17 July 1933.

119. *New Bedford Standard-Times*, 16 February 1935 (clipping), Curley Scrapbooks; *New York Times*, 3 March 1935; "Cotton Goods: Houses and Roads Fail to Stem a Slump," *News-Week*, 30 March 1935, pp. 33–34; *Boston Herald*, 1 April 1935; "The AAA and the Textile Crises," *Nation* 140 (1935): 496; "Revolt in the Cotton South," *Literary Digest*, 4 May 1935, p. 31.

120. *Boston Post*, 10 April 1935 (clipping), Curley Scrapbooks; *Boston Herald*, 12 April 1935.

121. "King Cotton's Headache," *Business Week*, 30 March 1935, p. 11; *Boston Herald*, 27 March, 2 April 1935.

122. *Boston Transcript*, 10 April 1935 (clipping), Curley Scrapbooks; *Boston Herald*, 11, 14, 20, 22 April 1935; "Cotton Manufacturers Make Last Ditch Fight against Tax," *News-Week*, 20 April 1935, p. 27; *New York Times*, 22 April 1935.

123. "The AAA and the Textile Crises," p. 496.

124. *Boston Herald*, 30 May, 22, 29 August, 23 November 1935; *Christian Science Monitor*, 30 January 1936 (clipping), Curley Scrapbooks.

125. *Boston Herald*, 7 January 1936; *Christian Science Monitor,* 30 January 1936 (clipping), Curley Scrapbooks.

126. *Boston Herald*, 16, 30 January, 23 March 1935; *New York Times*, 18 February 1935. Early in May, a committee appointed by Governor Curley submitted its report, which also concluded that the NRA wage differentials were detrimental to the Massachusetts shoe industry. A second source of unrest was labor troubles. Third, the report criticized the leasing system of the United Shoe Machinery Corporation as "adaptable to facile movements by the manufacturers, putting the shoe industry on roller skates." Fourth, the committee found that cities and towns in other states—Rhode Island and Maine, for instance—were deliberately campaigning to draw the shoe industry away from Massachusetts. *New York Times*, 18 February 1935; *Lynn Daily Evening Item*, 3 May 1935 (clipping), Curley Scrapbooks.

127. *Boston Post*, 7 October 1934, 2 February 1936.

128. *New York Times*, 7 February 1936.

129. James Roosevelt to Farley, 17 September 1936, OF 300, box 81, Roosevelt Papers.

130. McLaud to Farley, 8 September 1936; John Donahue to Farley, 10 September 1936; Lawrence E. Crowley to Farley, 29 September 1936, ibid., Joseph A. Maynard to Farley, 28 October 1936, Democratic National Campaign Committee, Presidential Election Forecasts, October 1936, Massachusetts, box 11, Democratic National Committee, Records 1928–48 (Franklin D. Roosevelt Library) (hereafter cited as Box 11, Democratic National Committee Records).

131. McLaud to Farley, 7 October 1936, OF 300, box 81, Roosevelt Papers; Maynard to Farley, 28 October 1936, box 11, Democratic National Committee Records.

132. Commonwealth of Massachusetts, *Public Document No. 43: Election Statistics, 1936* (Boston, 1937), pp. 343, 389; *Boston Transcript*, 4 November 1936.

133. Dineen, *Purple Shamrock*, pp. 245–47; *Public Document No. 43: 1936*, pp. 379–89; *Boston Transcript*, 4, 5 November 1936; *Christian Science Monitor*, 4 November 1936.

134. Arthur D. Healy to Farley, 24 August 1936; Michael T. Golden to Farley, 29 September 1936, OF 300, box 81, Roosevelt Papers.

135. *New York Times*, 5 November 1936.

136. Ibid., 7 July, 25 August 1938; Joseph F. Dineen, "The New Yankee G.O.P." *Nation* 148 (1939): 169–70.

137. *New York Times*, 7, 9 July, 21, 22, 25 September 1938.

138. Ibid., 9 November 1938; William J. Granfield to Farley, 3 January 1939, OF 300, James A. Farley Correspondence, "Election Forecasts and Results, 1938," Massachusetts, box 87, Roosevelt Papers (Franklin D. Roosevelt Library) (hereafter cited as OF 300, box 87, Roosevelt Papers).

139. *New York Times*, 9 November 1938.

140. Dineen, "The New Yankee G.O.P.," pp. 169–70.

141. *New York Times*, 20 November 1938; Dineen, "The New Yankee G.O.P.," p. 169.

142. Owen Johnson to Farley, 21 November 1938; J. M. Deely to Farley, 5 December 1938; Joseph Casey to Farley, 16 December 1938; Justin L. McCarthy to Farley, 22 December 1938, OF 300, box 87, Roosevelt Papers.

143. Casey to Farley, 16 December 1938; Granfield to Farley, 3 January 1939, ibid.

144. Key, *American State Politics*, pp. 158–60.

44 THE NEW DEAL

145. Deely to Farley, 5 December 1938; Casey to Farley, 16 December 1938; McCarthy to Farley, 22 December 1938, OF 300, box 87, Roosevelt Papers.

146. Huthmacher, *Massachusetts People and Politics*, pp. 262–65.

147. For example, in 1936 the legislature considered the "baby" Wagner Act, which would have established a state labor relations board to guarantee labor the right to collective bargaining in intrastate commerce. The bill went down to defeat in the Senate on a 19 to 18 roll call. The split was strictly along party lines, the Republicans voting against the legislation and the Democrats for it.

Another proposal, the so-called anti-spy bill, called for "legal curbs on the activities of private police and detectives in labor disputes." This measure passed the House by a vote of 104 to 81—84 Democrats and 20 Republicans for; 79 Republicans, 1 Democrat, and 1 undetermined against. In the Senate, however, 20 Republicans voted no and 17 Democrats yes. *Christian Science Monitor*, 10, 13, 17 June, 3 July 1936 (clippings), Curley Scrapbooks; *Boston Herald*, 17 June 1936; *Massachusetts House Journal: 1936* (Boston, 1936), pp. 1087, 1383–85; *Massachusetts Senate Journal: 1936* (Boston, 1936), pp. 1082–83.

148. Dineen, "The New Yankee G.O.P.," p. 170.

149. Huthmacher, *Massachusetts People and Politics*, pp. 262–65.

150. Dineen, "The New Yankee G.O.P.," pp. 170–71.

Richard C. Keller

Pennsylvania's Little New Deal

AS THE FOURTH DECADE OF THE TWENTIETH CENTURY OPENED, Pennsylvania remained the keystone in the arch of victory so often achieved by the Republican party. Since 1860 the commonwealth had turned against the presidential candidate of the GOP only once, giving its electoral vote to that irregular Republican, Theodore Roosevelt, in 1912. A single Democrat had been chosen as Pennsylvania's governor in all the years since the Civil War, and the second of his two terms had ended during the 1890s.

The one-party character of Pennsylvania politics had resulted from the success of the political machine built by Simon Cameron, Matthew Quay, and Boies Penrose. Backed by business and industrial interests, these politicos had made the state a stronghold of economic conservatism. As a result, conditions of economic feudalism still existed in the Keystone State. Private industrial police kept the workers docile both on and off company property; women worked up to 54, and fourteen-year-old children up to 51, hours per week for incredibly low pay; union labor received few rights and little protection from legislatures submissive to the industrial interests.[1]

On the last day of 1921, however, the Cameron-Quay-Penrose dynasty ended abruptly with the death of Senator Penrose, for he had prepared no successor to carry on his work. The factionalism so often found in a one-party region now rose to the surface, and three centers of power emerged in Pennsylvania. The strongest of these centered in Philadelphia, where the Vare brothers had built a Republican stronghold. William S. Vare inherited the organization after the death of his brothers and proceeded to ally himself with bankers, railroads, and coal companies in the eastern part of the state.[2]

In the western part of the state, the city of Pittsburgh came under the rather loose control of the Mellon interests during the 1920s. The Mellon family had taken no active part in Pennsylvania politics until Andrew, the financier, received the appointment as President Harding's secretary of the treasury. When the state's two United States senators died within a year, the fight over the spoils caused some lesser political leaders to look to the west for the means of achieving harmony. Although the newly appointed secretary lacked the temperament to throw himself into the fray, his nephew William Larimer Mellon was eager to do so. This businessman-turned-politician proceeded to weld the warring GOP politicos of Pittsburgh into a temporarily united machine, and saw his choice elected mayor of the city.

Outside the two largest cities of the commonwealth, the strongest figure in the Republican party was Joseph R. Grundy, in the words of Penrose, "the best money collector and the worst politician since Julius Caesar."[3] His position as head of the Pennsylvania Manufacturers' Association made him the spokesman for small business in the Keystone State and enhanced his influence in the smaller cities and towns, as well as with the leaders of the "courthouse gangs" in the rural counties.

By 1926, Mellon had allied himself with Grundy, who was looking for a lever to use against Vare, and Mellon himself was chosen Republican state chairman.[4] The alliance remained uncertain, however, for Grundy could not even wholly dominate politics in eastern Pennsylvania, since the Vare machine stood squarely in his path. As a result, both Mellon and Vare would occasionally seek to unite their forces for immediate advantage, leaving Grundy isolated since he could not think of aiding Vare. To Grundy, who held old-fashioned ideas concerning morality, Vare and his organization were unutterably corrupt; and he would not deal with them.

The fratricidal nature of Republican politics after the death of Penrose prepared the way for the party's decline, for the ensuing political infighting allowed progressive ideas, which had earlier left Pennsylvania relatively unaffected, to gain a foothold. Gifford Pinchot—conservationist, progressive, associate of the late Theodore Roosevelt—set out to capture the GOP gubernatorial nomination in 1922. Though born in Connecticut, Pinchot considered Milford, Pennsylvania, his home and returned to that base after his years of service as head of the Bureau of Forestry.

Pinchot had thrown his hat into the ring earlier when he opposed Penrose for the U.S. Senate seat in 1914, but lost; eight years later, a new situation made him a formidable opponent for the candidate offered by Vare. Popular distaste for the machine rule that held the cities in subjection combined with the prohibition issue to bring about a split in the Republican party between the rural and urban areas. Moreover, for the first time women were going to help choose gubernatorial candidates, and Pinchot was both anti-machine and a militant dry, attitudes thought to be popular with rural and female voters.[5]

Even with such advantages, however, Pinchot would probably have been defeated if it had not been for the assistance given him by Joseph R. Grundy. Unwilling to support the candidate selected by Vare, Grundy chose to aid Pinchot rather than see the Philadelphia boss take over the state patronage. The manufacturers' spokesman believed Pinchot would run the state economically and keep taxes down, which was more important than his progressive attitudes. So, with Grundy turning a deaf ear, Pinchot toured the state denouncing not only boss rule but also the corrupt alliance between business and politics, while proclaiming loudly the rights of organized labor. In the primary, Pinchot won a narrow 9,000-vote victory, then easily brushed aside the weak opposition of the Democratic candidate in November to become a governor of a type Pennsylvania had not seen for generations.[6]

Pinchot's first term as governor was not overly progressive, however, since control of the General Assembly remained in the hands of the factions opposed to him. Nor did Grundy carry his backing of the new governor to the point of supporting his legislative program.[7] The four years were notable chiefly for the political infighting that occurred among the various GOP groups.

The most devastating of these conflicts saw Vare and Pinchot fight incumbent United States Senator George Wharton Pepper for the nomination for his position. Constitutionally ineligible to succeed himself as governor, Pinchot fought hard to go to the Senate but ran a bad third in the primary. Pepper came to the Philadelphia city line leading Vare by 140,000 votes, but the machine counted him out. Vare carried but two of Pennsylvania's sixty-seven counties and yet won by over 80,000 votes.[8] Corruption had run rampant, and after Vare's victory in November, Pinchot issued a "certificate of doubt," declaring that Vare's election had been "partly bought and partly stolen." Finally, after three years of investigation and delay, the United States Senate rejected Vare; and Governor John Fisher, a product of the Mellon-Grundy alliance, appointed Joseph R. Grundy to fill the vacancy.[9] This held the promise of even more bitter political battles as the gubernatorial election year of 1930 opened.

Victory in the primary of 1930 was vital to both factions, and each chose a champion to carry its banner. Vare selected Francis Shunk Brown, former attorney general of the state, and his choice to retire Grundy from the Senate was President Hoover's secretary of labor, James J. Davis. The Mellon-Grundy forces picked Grundy's York County lieutenant Samuel S. Lewis to run for governor, and Grundy had little trouble gaining support in his effort to hold the Senate seat.[10] But the arrangement did not hold up. As a newspaper columnist had predicted earlier, "The leaders find it impossible to dismiss the threat personified by the . . . tall thin figure of Gifford Pinchot. . . . If Pinchot runs, he may be depended on to raise blazes all over the Commonwealth."[11]

Pinchot did indeed announce his candidacy for a second term and frightened Mellon into abandoning Lewis, for the Pittsburgh leader hated the former governor for his attempts to embarrass the secretary of the treasury on the prohibition issue and was unwilling to risk a Pinchot victory because of a split in Republican ranks. Lewis, reluctant from the start, withdrew from the race, and this event served to revivify one of the strangest alliances in politics, that of Pinchot and Grundy. Only a few weeks earlier, Pinchot had described Grundy as the greatest enemy of organized labor on this continent. Despite this, Grundy linked his name with Pinchot's on sample ballots in some counties, for he knew that, though the former governor would do him no favors, neither would he fire state officeholders in order to build a personal machine. Pinchot remained the silent partner, not uttering a word on behalf of Grundy, though he did not endorse the latter's opponent.[12]

If the contest for the gubernatorial nomination had been confined to Pinchot and Brown, the latter would almost certainly have won. But in 1930, the specter of prohibition haunted aspirants for public office. Pinchot had the reputation of being a confirmed dry; and Brown, though he was backed by the wet Vare organization, publicly straddled the issue. Accordingly, a third candidate who stood uncompromisingly for repeal remained in the race and drew 281,000 votes, most of which would otherwise have gone to Brown. Pinchot thus won a 20,000 vote victory.

The Philadelphia machine drew small solace from the fact that Davis defeated Grundy in the Senate race.[13]

Bitter at seeing Pinchot and Grundy once more block his ambition to control the state government, Vare tried a desperate gamble to recoup his political fortunes. Though the Democratic gubernatorial candidate, West Chester laywer John M. Hemphill, had drawn only 121,000 primary votes against the combined total of over 1,500,000 for the three major Republican aspirants, the Philadelphia organization determined to back him. They hoped to utilize regular Republican hatred of the insurgent GOP nominee along with the rising tide of anti-prohibition sentiment to swing enough support behind Hemphill to enable him to defeat Pinchot and give them a share of the state patronage.

To accomplish this, a Liberal party was formed, and petitioned for a place on the ballot. Backed by Vare and the adherents of the "wet" primary candidate, this party was merely a device by which loyal members of the GOP could vote against Pinchot without seeming to support someone under the Democratic label. Though ostensibly a national movement, the Liberal party had on its Pennsylvania ticket only one name, that of Hemphill.[14]

This maneuver set the stage for serious defections from the Republican ranks. Pennsylvania Railroad chief W. W. Atterbury resigned as national committeeman in order to support Hemphill, and soon virtually the entire Philadelphia machine openly joined him. Early in October, about a score of financial and industrial leaders in the Pittsburgh area signed a statement supporting the Democratic standard-bearer, an indication of the Mellon influence. Not all the straying came from Republican ranks, however; an estimated 200,000 Democrats bolted to Pinchot on election day because of the prohibition issue.[15] One observer summarized the confused turn of events by saying, "The campaign will go down in history as one in which the most stalwart regulars of the Republican Party preached irregularity, and irregulars of the most pronounced type took for their slogan the doctrine of regularity."[16]

But Pinchot had put together a coalition that gave him victory. The rural areas, the mining regions, and an Allegheny County Republican organization that defied the Mellons combined to give the former governor a margin of 80,000 votes. Surprisingly, the smaller cities and towns, normally a tower of strength for Pinchot, swung toward the Democrats. Whether the depression or prohibition had more effect in causing that result is difficult to say. In 1932, however, most of those same places landed in the Hoover column.[17]

To the casual observer, the election of Pinchot obscured the shattered state of Republican politics in Pennsylvania. Not only was there no statewide organization to call the tune, but the centers of power that did exist often clashed violently. Although Grundy and his small-town allies could often work harmoniously with the Mellons, the influence wielded by the latter was in decline. A power struggle was taking place within the Pittsburgh GOP, and this resulted in a weakening of its effectiveness in party circles. The Vare organization, still powerful, remained isolated in its Philadelphia bastion. Yet even here the seeds of disaster had been sown. By supporting the Democratic candidate against Pinchot, Vare had demonstrated to his followers that voting the other party's ticket could sometimes be justified. In a few years, the Negro and the nationality groups would use this newly found independence against the Vare machine.

The impact of the depression added a new note to the factionalism of Pennsylvania politics. Pinchot had promised to further the interests of labor and other previously neglected groups, and he entered the executive mansion in 1931 determined to take action. This would split the party still more. With the second Pinchot administration likely to provide a bitter struggle between Republican liberals and conservatives, and with Pennsylvania entering the depths of the depression under Republican executives in state and nation, the GOP's hold on the Keystone State was in jeopardy.

Events during Pinchot's second term bore out this gloomy foreboding. During the 1930 campaign, the governor had asked a prophetic question: "Is it not time for a new deal? Is it not time to have the affairs of the Republican party . . . administered by public servants who are not willing to serve solely their own selfish interests?" In keeping with this theme, Pinchot had called for up-to-date labor legislation, old age pensions, clean elections, equalization of taxation, and effective regulation of utilities.[18] These proposals might have suffered the same fate as they had during his first term of office, but different social forces operating in the new decade insured that such ideas could not be ignored. Pinchot had the opportunity to preside over the shift in the Keystone State from the routine affairs of the 1920s to the explosive issues of the depression. In doing this, he anticipated some of the activities soon to take place in Washington and helped lay the foundations for the Little New Deal in Pennsylvania.

Although Pinchot could count on a tenuous majority for his proposals in the House, his enemies dominated the Republican caucus in the State Senate by two votes.[19] Thus, fight as he did for utilities reform, abolition of the coal and iron police, improvement in the conditions of work for women and children, and softening of the harsh labor injunction, the governor managed to force only watered-down versions of several items through the General Assembly. By 1933, however, the odds against the passage of such legislation changed somewhat. The severity of the depression plus the upsurge of the Democratic party in 1932, particularly in the large urban areas of the state, brought repercussions. In both Philadelphia and Pittsburgh, the Republican organizations suddenly decided to support social legislation so as to retain their hold on those cities. The representatives from those areas combined with the Pinchot Republicans and most of the Democrats in the House, where the minority party had nearly tripled its membership over the previous session, to push the governor's program through.[20]

But the Senate remained the citadel of the status quo. Joseph Grundy's Pennsylvania Manufacturers' Association exerted disproportionate influence in the senatorial districts, dominated as they were by the smaller cities and boroughs of the commonwealth. Under the direction of these forces, the Senate became the burying ground for most of the measures for social reform, for Grundy had come out in open opposition to Pinchot because of his relief and labor proposals.[21]

Even with such opposition, Gifford Pinchot's second term as governor contributed more to advance the cause of social reform in Pennsylvania than had been accomplished in decades, if not generations. The first old-age pensions in the state; improvement in the child labor law, plus ratification of the national constitutional amendment; abolition of the yellow-dog contract; a more advantageous workmen's compensation law; and a bill weakening the labor injunction, all ran the gantlet of the two houses of the General Assembly. In addition, the governor was permitted to establish commissions that investigated sweatshops and public utility regulation, focusing the merciless spotlight of publicity on both.[22]

Despite the importance of such measures, demands for relief for the victims of unemployment dominated most of Pinchot's term, for the depression had a staggering effect upon the economy of Pennsylvania. Although business of all kinds had suffered heavily, industry in particular had been dealt a crippling blow. The value of all products turned out by industrial plants in the Keystone State fell from $8,162,000,000 in 1929 to $3,118,000,000 in 1932. Wages and salaries dropped almost as drastically, from $2,237,000,000 in 1929 to $1,032,000,000 in 1932.[23] Unemployment quickly became a major problem. By April 1931, Philadelphia had 25.6 percent totally unemployed and 13.8 percent more working only part time. Using a novel method of poll-taking, that of having teachers ask school children about their parents, Governor Pinchot estimated that 900,000 people, or 26.2 percent of the working force of the state, were out of work in September 1931. By the next year, the Department of Welfare estimated that a third of the people of the state were entirely without income from wage earners.[24]

In the face of this disaster, the relief agencies of Pennsylvania completely broke down. An antiquated system of County Poor Boards represented the state's approach to the problem; 425 boards under the control of 920 directors handled all public relief in the state. Although in operation continuously only from 1882, these boards were a heritage from Elizabethan days. The Poor Boards had the power to tax, and they were now expected to meet the challenge of the depression. But even by raising taxes fifty percent in four years, the Poor Boards by 1932 were making a per capita grant to the needy only twenty percent as large as ten years before. Nor could private charity take up the slack. Karl de Schweinitz, secretary of the Philadelphia Committee for Unemployment Relief, reported that private funds had given out and noted that the hospitals had definite cases of starvation. Contributions to charitable groups in Pittsburgh in 1931 totalled $2,000,000 to care for the families of 150,000 unemployed. During the same year, however, Richard B. Mellon announced a gift of $4,000,000 to build the East Liberty Presbyterian Church, which he hoped "would do its part to reassure those who fear that the country is doomed to become engulfed in materialism."[25]

Governor Pinchot wanted to act vigorously to meet the emergency, but the cost of his proposals shocked the rural legislators who had previously been his chief support in the General Assembly. Calling a special session in 1931 to deal with relief, Pinchot declared:

> The Declaration of Independence tells us that the right to life, liberty, and the pursuit of happiness is inalienable. But in an emergency like this that right means nothing to millions of men and women unless it carries with it not only the right to live but also the right to work. For the right to work is included in the right to live.[26]

Although in calling the session the governor had asked for $35,000,000 in tax money for relief purposes, he found himself stymied by the state's constitution. The attorney general advised Pinchot that the basic law forbade any state appropriation to any person or community for charitable purposes; so the chief executive then asked the legislature to allow the borrowing of money by issuing Prosperity Bonds.[27]

Still at odds with the governor, members of the GOP in the State Senate agreed with President Hoover that unemployment was temporary and local in character; they saw no need for Pinchot's program. After a prolonged hassle, the legislature scrapped both the governor's proposals and the attorney general's view of the state constitution by passing an appropriation of $10,000,000 for relief, but providing no means of raising the money to pay for it. One critic noted that both Hoover and Pinchot had asked their legislative bodies not to appropriate money without making revenue available, but the Pennsylvania Assembly had applauded Hoover and condemned Pinchot. The final act in this farce occurred when the Pennsylvania Supreme Court upheld the appropriation as constitutional, but ordered $10,000,000 taken from funds for state institutions so as to keep the state within its debt limit.[28]

Long an advocate of "taking the farmers out of the mud," the governor established the goal of putting macadam on the farm-to-market roads of the state. Using unemployment as a rationale, he anticipated the Civilian Conservation Corps by setting up labor camps for young men hired by the state to work on the roads. Critics charged that Pinchot was trying to "pave his way to the Senate" and that money used in this more expensive work-relief could have been spent on food for the hungry. Pinchot himself admitted that road-building would not solve the problem and that direct relief was less costly; he now became an enthusiast for federal aid to the needy and made strenuous efforts to induce Washington to act.[29]

Faced with a growing revolt in the legislature against increased relief expenditures, Pinchot asked the Reconstruction Finance Corporation to lend Pennsylvania some of the recently appropriated relief funds. The RFC did so, but insisted that the state raise enough money to pay its reasonable share and establish an agency at the state level to supervise relief spending. This last demand led to the creation of the State Emergency Relief Board, which supervised the work of the County Poor Boards, but the commonwealth's share of relief money slipped steadily until it reached the nadir of five-tenths of one percent of the total late in 1934.[30]

For the remainder of the Pinchot administration, a three-way struggle ensued. The governor pressed the General Assembly for adequate relief money, but the realities of Pennsylvania politics prevented any real cooperation. Fearful that Pinchot's popularity might fan his already strong political ambitions if he were permitted to carry out the kind of relief program he wanted, Republican leaders staked their hopes on national aid or the belief that the depression would disappear naturally. Though the setting up of the SERB constituted the brightest spot in Pennsylvania's relief picture, the legislature continued to transfer money from other funds for relief purposes and left to the next General Assembly the responsibility for enacting the tax measures necessary to keep federal money flowing into Pennsylvania. Business and industry, so influential among legislators, shied away from large-scale state aid because of the probability that it would have to be financed by taxes on their holdings and profits. So long as these same forces controlled the state government, Pennsylvania's needy would fare badly. While the national administration of Franklin Roosevelt was willing to help, Pennsylvanians looked to a shift in the political complexion of their state to end the deadlock.

In January 1935, Governor Pinchot made his farewell address to the General Assembly and monotonously ticked off the list of his proposals for social legislation that they had spurned. He then declared with an air of self-justification:

> It is well within the truth to say that if the General Assembly had enacted these measures as they were laid before it, or a majority of them, the next Governor of Pennsylvania would have been a Republican and not a Democrat.[31]

Pinchot was able to change his party with dereliction of duty because the Democratic party had suddenly been transformed from a perennial also-ran into a winner. For decades, Democratic gubernatorial candidates had been losing by hundreds of thousands of votes; in 1926, Eugene C. Bonniwell failed to carry a single county. As late as 1930, the Democrats could not win even with substantial Republican support.

As yet no section of the commonwealth could be called normally Democratic. The ten most Democratic counties of the 1920s and early 1930s included a smattering of coal-mining areas—though not the most important ones—with agricultural counties making up the remainder. Even these counties did not always return a Democratic majority. Until 1934, not one important industrial county appeared among the Democratic top ten. The labor force in the state, largely unorganized except for the miners, apparently saw no reason to support the Democratic party. The Negro and nationality groups formed the backbone of the Vare machine in Philadelphia and of such Republican organizations as John Fine's in the coal-mining county of Luzerne. Where the Democrats did well in elections, they very likely did so on the basis of local issues or of unusually attractive candidates in the region. The party could not depend upon solid support in any section of the state or from any important group.[32]

As will any perpetual minority in politics, the Democratic party in some areas had begun to function as an adjunct of the GOP. One political columnist reported, "In Pennsylvania the Democratic organization is hardly more than the morganatic wife of the Republican."[33] As a concomitant to their minority role, the Democrats had the problem of developing the leadership necessary to lift their followers out of the doldrums and to win new adherents. Occasionally, Democratic leaders had to defy elements within their own party in order to fight the Republicans for political supremacy. In Philadelphia, John O'Donnell held sway over the Democratic party, but he would not fight Vare for control of the city and survived on the patronage crumbs thrown his way by the Vare machine. By this arrangement, Vare registered enough of his men as Democrats to help swing the primary vote to the O'Donnell faction, but the latter did not work hard to bring out the Democratic vote in the general election. O'Donnell reputedly admitted to J. David Stern, the *Philadelphia Record* editor: "Vare's my best friend and patron. He gave me my job and has been supporting the Democratic party for years. Bill Vare, himself, pays the rent of our headquarters."[34]

Nothing better demonstrated the value placed by the Democrats on nominations by their party than the events that took place early in the year 1930. Both candidates selected to run for the top state offices turned down the assignments, the choice for governor withdrawing in order to seek the position of Grand Exalted Ruler of the Elks![35] Rank-and-file Democrats might be pardoned for wondering when a leader who could unify and rebuild the party would appear.

Actually, such a person had been on the scene for some time; he needed only the right conditions in which his talents could operate. After the election of Woodrow Wilson in 1912, Joseph F. Guffey, A. Mitchell Palmer, and Vance McCormick won control of Pennsylvania's Democracy. Guffey's power was primarily in the western part of the state, where his Pittsburgh organization struggled through a series of losing elections for many years. In 1931, however, in a bold move Guffey abandoned his previous support of Al Smith and announced that most of Pennsylvania's delegation to the Democratic National Convention the next year would back Franklin D. Roosevelt for the nomination. At the convention, Guffey watched proudly as his state cast more votes for Roosevelt than did any other delegation. After the election, even though Hoover carried the Keystone State, no doubt remained as to who dominated the Democratic party in Pennsylvania. When James A. Farley gave him control of federal patronage in the state, Guffey proceeded to build a powerful organization. One of the most important cogs in his machine was David L. Lawrence, who had become Allegheny County Democratic chairman in 1920 and moved into the position of state chairman in 1934.[36]

Philadelphia presented a problem, however. The Democratic National Committee had tried to deflate O'Donnell's power in 1928 by placing party affairs in the hands of a special campaign committee; but after O'Donnell backed Roosevelt in 1932, the party had to stick with him for a time. J. David Stern, editor of the pro-Democratic *Philadelphia Record*, provided the impetus for the removal of O'Donnell. Stern went to John B. Kelly, a former bricklayer who had become a wealthy contractor, and persuaded him to try to oust O'Donnell. Kelly formed a team with another Philadelphia contractor, Matthew H. McCloskey, Jr., and with the support of the state organization they entered a slate of candidates against O'Donnell's in the 1933 primary. Vare faced a challenge on his own ticket that year and could not permit so many of his people to register as Democrats to help his ally; so the Kelly slate won a smashing victory. O'Donnell retained his position as city chairman until the next year, but his reign was clearly ended.[37]

There is no question, however, that the most important reason for the revival of the Democratic party in Pennsylvania was the New Deal in Washington. Because of its activities, new leaders came into the party and important voting groups swung to its banner. As early as 1932, Robert L. Vann, editor of a Negro newspaper in Pittsburgh, offered Joseph Guffey his loyalty and promised to help move others of his race to the Democrats. Vann advised Negroes to turn Lincoln's picture to the wall, since that debt had been paid in full. Though Vann had some effect in Pittsburgh in 1932, the real switch of this group came only after the New Deal had swung into operation. The change was felt in Pittsburgh before Philadelphia, for many Negroes were employed in heavy industry in the former city and had been hurt by the depression more severely. By 1934, the Negro areas of Philadelphia had begun to shift to the Democrats; and in 1936, the slide became an avalanche. The upper- and middle-class Negroes moved quickly into the Democratic column, but those in the depressed river wards followed more slowly. Vare had stronger control in the latter areas, which may account for this phenomenon.[38]

As Samuel Lubell has pointed out, the so-called hyphen groups, the nationality blocs, began to desert to the Democratic party as early as 1928, when Al Smith's candidacy produced an upsurge in Democratic strength in the largest cities. The activities of Catholic Democrats such as Lawrence in Pittsburgh and Kelly in Philadelphia gave impetus to the change, but again the work of the New Deal in lending assistance to those affected by the depression turned the tide into a flood. The Italian sections of Philadelphia shifted from 22.6 percent Democratic in 1932 to 52.2 percent favoring the party in 1934. Among Italians, as with Negroes, the districts highest in economic status went Democratic more quickly than those with more poverty.[39]

One more link completed the chain that led to Democratic victory. Leaders of organized labor, accustomed to Republican domination of Pennsylvania politics, had not given support to the Democratic cause. Only the GOP had been in a position to advance the objectives of labor through legislation; consequently, the Republican candidates had generally gained the endorsement of labor groups. As late as 1930, when the Democrats had a fighting chance of victory because of important Republican support for their gubernatorial candidate, labor's headquarters still remained silent.

Then came the depression under a Republican administration, and this drove labor closer to the Democratic camp. The activities of the New Deal reflected a profound change in the national government's attitude toward the worker, and in 1933 the legislative program announced by the minority Democrats in the Pennsylvania Assembly contained many proposals favorable to labor. As a result, union leaders in the commonwealth began to abandon the Republican party. Such men as John L. Lewis of the United Mine Workers and John Phillips, president of the Pennsylvania Federation of Labor, started to cooperate with the Democratic organization. Perhaps the master stroke of the Democrats was the slating of Thomas Kennedy, secretary-treasurer of the UMW, for lieutenant governor in 1934. These events marked, as Joe Guffey said, the beginning of the alliance between labor and the Democratic party in the Keystone State.[40] Before the mid-1930s then, the Pennsylvania Democracy had broader support, better organization, and top-level leadership, and could look to an early realization of its ambition to control the state government.

By 1934, the American people were in the midst of a period of experimentation and change destined to be the most far-reaching in their history. Franklin D. Roosevelt had begun his New Deal; and, whether one loved or hated him, none could deny that he had stirred the country out of the lethargy brought on by the depression. Enough had been accomplished in a year to cause Pennsylvania Democrats to look forward to the gubernatorial election with some optimism. The AAA had attacked the farm problem, and the farmers' income was rising; the banking crisis had been met, and most banks were sound again; the National Industrial Recovery Act had granted the laborer the right to organize and to bargain collectively, and union strength was increasing. Of greatest urgency, the FERA had placed the distribution of relief on a more stable and adequate basis, thereby removing some of the sense of desperation from the unemployed. In little over a year, the FERA poured almost $95,000,000 into direct relief activities for Pennsylvanians, and the Civil Works Administration about $45,000,000 more in work relief.[41] The New Deal offered the Democratic party in Pennsylvania these broad coat-tails for use in its campaign.

Hopeful that the popularity of the New Deal would sweep them into control of the state government, Democratic leaders met several months before the primary to draw up a slate to achieve that purpose. Joe Guffey persuaded the State Committee to tap George H. Earle III as its candidate for governor. A novice in politics, Earle's background read like a review of American history. Descended from a Mayflower voyager, George Earle also numbered among his ancestors an anti-slavery Quaker named Thomas Earle, who had been the Liberty party's candidate for vice-president in 1840. "Mad" Anthony Wayne and Lucretia Mott appeared in the Earle genealogy, and the candidate's father had headed a reform slate in the city of Philadelphia in 1911.

Though a lifelong Republican, Earle's social consciousness led him to question the wisdom of Hoover's policies toward the national crisis. By contributing a large sum to the Democrats in 1932, Earle attracted the attention of Guffey, who got him a diplomatic post.[42] Hoping to win independent support for the 1934 campaign, Guffey thought that Earle would be preferable as a gubernatorial candidate to anyone from among the old-line Democrats. Guffey himself received the nomination for the United

States Senate seat held by David A. Reed. After brushing aside weak opposition in the primary, Earle and Guffey looked to the fall campaign and the battle against William A. Schnader, attorney general of the commonwealth, and Reed, who had beaten Pinchot for the Senate nomination.

As expected, the New Deal held the spotlight of attention during the campaign. Speaker after speaker announced that the only issue the voters needed to consider was that of the New Deal versus the Old Deal, Main Street versus Wall Street, the Roosevelt program versus a return to Hooverism. Democratic State Chairman David Lawrence accused the Republicans of a "tory plot to break the back of the New Deal" and said that the GOP in Pennsylvania was "shooting over the heads of the local opposition in order to destroy the Roosevelt administration." If their tactics succeeded in Pennsylvania, Republicans would have a firm base from which to upset the New Deal in 1936. Lawrence summed up the attitude of his party by stating that all other issues were "bunk."[43]

Senator Reed concurred in this judgment. Still clinging to a laissez faire philosophy, he denounced the "futile and fantastic experiments" of the New Deal and warned that "America is being fed poison from which it will take decades to recover." Ultra-conservative Reed had not even been satisfied with the policies of Herbert Hoover. During those years, the senator had lamented, "I do not often envy other countries their governments, but I say that if this country ever needed a Mussolini, it needs one now." Schnader followed the same general line, demanding that the national government allow the state to work out its own problems and warning against the "national goosestep."[44]

A massive shift in voter registration toward the Democrats, plus the defection of some top-level GOP leaders, foreshadowed the election result. Not only did the Republican registration lead fall by over 800,000, but GOP figures such as Charles Margiotti, a power in western Pennsylvania, and Richard Beamish, Pinchot's secretary of the commonwealth, came over to the Democrats. In addition, Negro Republican leaders in thirty-four Philadelphia wards pledged their support to the entire Democratic slate; and Negro business and professional people organized a committee of one hundred to work for the Democratic ticket, the first time such a group had ever done so. Election day saw George Earle win the governor's chair for the Democrats for the first time since the 1890s, and Joe Guffey become the party's first popularly elected senator in the history of the state. In addition, the Democrats won control of the lower house of the legislature for the first time since 1877.[45]

Joyful Democrats hoped they had put an end to the Republican dynasty in Pennsylvania. With their party in power in both nation and state, they saw a rare opportunity to put together an organization, based solidly on patronage and service, that could go on winning elections for many years. Pittsburgh had come into the Democratic camp and would stay there. Though Philadelphia would remain Republican in local elections throughout the Roosevelt era, William S. Vare had died in 1934 and the GOP machine was badly weakened. More startling, many of the smaller cities and towns of the commonwealth went Democratic in 1934, indicating that the depression had worked its political magic on the middle class. When added to the newly won votes of labor, the nationalities, and the Negroes, this seemed a portent of massive Democratic power.

Though decades of domination by ruthless political machines and industrial overlords had laid the groundwork and the depression had provided immediate motivation, this overwhelming political change needed one man to act as catalyst: Roosevelt. Any candidate who could claim political alliance with the president held a decided advantage in the election of 1934. Perhaps the Negroes provided the best example, for among them the image of FDR was particularly strong. One Negro who had voted Republican all his life admitted: "I didn't pay no attention to the party. I saw Roosevelt's picture and I know what he done for me when I was hungry. Anybody that has that picture beside him can get my vote." A black Republican ward leader in Philadelphia lamented, "I can beat the Democrats, but that d---- Roosevelt has taken Lincoln's place." George Earle showed that he understood the source of his victory by stating: "I literally rode into office on the coat-tails of President Roosevelt, and I have no hesitation in saying so."[46] The party now looked to the next legislative session to begin building the record that would enable them to make this dream of continued power a reality.

In his inaugural address, George Earle promised the people of the commonwealth: "We are going, along with the rest of the nation to a new ground. Politically and economically a change is necessary." To effect change, the incoming administration took the New Deal as a model and tried to reproduce its image in Harrisburg. Used at first as an epithet by unfriendly newspapermen, the term "Little New Deal" caught on as a description of the Earle administration and was accepted by friend and foe alike. The Pennsylvania Democrats took advantage of the fact that the national New Deal had been in operation for two years and had provided something in the nature of a program for the Pennsylvanians to adopt. For the next few years news stories publicized the Little Wagner Act, the Little NRA, the Little Brain Trust, and Little Fireside Chats as the Democrats of the Keystone State tried to build a following among the disgruntled and the dispossessed.[47]

The needy presented the most immediate problem. Though unemployment figures had been falling steadily since March 1933, some 836,000 persons, representing 22.5 percent of the total laboring force of the state, remained out of work. Appropriated relief funds expired the day before Earle assumed office, and the national government took over the entire financial burden for three months, pouring $68,000,000 into the state; but Harry Hopkins warned that Pennsylvania must provide $5,000,000 a month for relief after 15 April. In line with this, the governor asked the General Assembly to appropriate $120,000,000 to the needy from his proposed $203,000,000 in new and increased taxes for the biennium.[48]

Earle's program, with minor modifications, easily passed the House, but the Senate presented an entirely different picture. The nineteen Democrats there represented a huge increase over the seven they had been able to muster for the previous session, but they still faced a phalanx of thirty-one Republicans. And the Senate soon riddled the work of the House. Burying the governor's program in committee, the GOP leaders in the upper chamber advanced their own relief and taxation proposals, cutting those of Earle by more than half. When the governor refused to accept this, Senate majority leaders demanded a meeting with Hopkins, whom they hoped to convince of the soundness of their position. Earle arranged the interview and accompanied them to Washington, but he had already taken action to assure a desirable result. In a call to Hopkins, Earle had urged the relief administrator to hold firm and make the Pennsylvania legislature provide the necessary money. "Even the Republican Press had gone over to us. I think we will have to stand on this. I think if we give them an inch now we will never get it." Hopkins did not budge from his earlier position, advising the Republican senators to get together with Governor Earle on a tax program.[49]

At this point, Republican ranks split asunder. The governor's "Little Fireside Chats" had had their effect; a GOP senator lamented that each address was followed by hundreds of letters and phone calls urging support for Earle's proposals. Eight Republican senators now pledged to back the governor's plans for relief and taxation, so long as he made his demands for only one year. Most of the bolters represented the mining and industrial areas where strong sentiment for adequate relief appropriations had developed, and they believed their leaders had misread the public pulse. This break in the ranks brought the Senate leaders to heel. They met with the governor and in a short time hammered out an acceptable program. Earle won but a limited victory; a special legislative session in the 1936 election year was assured.[50]

In addition to requesting relief appropriations, Governor Earle had asked the General Assembly for legislation to allow the commonwealth to participate in federal relief and public works programs. Huge congressional appropriations had been made, and the state stood to gain by about $250,000,000 if it passed the necessary authorizations. But here the Senate balked. Of nearly a score of bills for this purpose passed in the House, only three received final approval in the upper chamber. Though a bill to set up a system of unemployment insurance by tying it to the Social Security bill then moving through Congress passed the House by a vote of 189-2, the Senate ignored it. The Republican majority in the latter house demonstrated its attitude toward federal-state cooperation to meet the problems of the depression by passing, over Democratic protests, a bill to tax the obligations of the Home Owners' Loan Corporation and other nongovernmental agencies established by Congress.[51]

Attempts to bring about social and economic reform followed the same pattern in the 1935 legislative session. The Little New Deal set out to redeem the party's pledges and, underlining the demands of its newfound labor ally, free the Pennsylvania worker from industrial serfdom. Consequently, the governor requested legislation to eliminate child labor, reduce the working hours of women and grant them minimum wages, abolish industrial police and company-paid deputy sheriffs, regulate industrial homework, set up an NRA for the state, and improve workmen's compensation. Earle reminded the lawmakers that both the Democratic and Republican platforms had contained many of these items.[52]

Democrats in the House responded by approving virtually intact all but one of the administration measures. The lone exception was Pennsylvania's version of the NRA, which lost because of the Supreme Court's decision declaring the national law unconstitutional. Upon reaching the Senate, these bills were handed to a committee whose chief function was to give them decent burial. The few reform measures that did emerge from committee greatly altered the Democratic proposals, and the conference committee applied the coup de grace by failing to agree. Only two labor measures successfully passed the gantlet of the Senate: a more stringent child labor law, and a bill outlawing the hated coal and iron police. Passing the latter bill amounted to kicking a dead horse, for Governor Pinchot had refused to commission such officers, and Earle had continued the precedent. The only other important reform measure to pass the 1935 General Assembly was an equal rights bill, to prevent racial discrimination in public accommodations. It received bipartisan support, for the Republicans were anxious to win back Negroes to their former loyalty.[53]

As the session closed, Democrats looked upon the results with mixed emotions. Their tax and relief programs had been generally approved, but only for one year. The drive for liberal labor legislation had resulted in almost complete failure, and only a few other reforms were adopted. Democratic leaders realized that if the Little New Deal were to become a reality it would have to come quickly, for periods of active reform are usually short. If the Pennsylvania Democrats could not capitalize on the spirit of the times and soon gain effective control of the government at Harrisburg, their opportunity might well be gone.

To the governor and his party, 1936 looked like the year of decision. They needed to hold their control in the State House of Representatives while winning seven additional seats in the Senate. The party carrying the state's popular vote by any reasonable majority could be pretty well assured of taking more than half the House seats, but malapportionment of senatorial districts, plus the constitutional provision that only half of the fifty senators shall be elected every two years, made that contest more difficult. Pennsylvania Democrats knew that their only chance of success was to grasp President Roosevelt's coattails firmly, make him the main issue, and work for a big electoral margin. If control of the State Senate could not be achieved, the nation might have a New Deal, but Pennsylvania would not.

With Pennsylvania suddenly transformed into a two-party state, Democrats pursued their goal vigorously. Governor Earle declared, "The real issue is Roosevelt," and toured the commonwealth denouncing his opponents. He pointed to the Republican Senate's obstruction of relief money for the needy, noted the loss to the Pennsylvania taxpayer caused by the failure to enact an unemployment compensation law, and denounced the Republican do-nothing philosophy of government. Earle condemned the GOP for nominating among their candidates for the State Senate two convicted criminals, a third candidate who had been tried twice for election fraud, and another who had been disbarred. "Take a good look at the men who are leading the Republican Party in Pennsylvania today," the governor urged the people of the state, "and then decide whether you want to support them."[54]

During the election campaign, a relief crisis required the attention of a special session of the General Assembly and gave Democrats the opportunity to point to Republican obstruction in providing adequate help for the needy. Although the establishment of the Works Progress Administration had aided Pennsylvania through the transfer of 263,637 needy cases to WPA jobs, the state's relief situation had not really improved. When the authorities in Washington set up the work relief program, the problem of direct relief had been turned back to the states. Pennsylvania then had to care for the 192,261 cases remaining on its rolls in March 1936. This cost the commonwealth approximately $8,000,000 a month, a higher sum than it was forced to provide under the previous arrangement with Hopkins. Angrily, Earle assailed the Republican Senate for making relief funds available for only one year; with a two year appropriation, he might have been able to secure from Hopkins the $5,000,000 monthly limit on the state's contribution for both years.[55]

Faced with this situation, the governor asked the special session to appropriate $70,991,000 for relief, hoping that the sum would last until next year's legislature could act. Again the GOP-dominated Senate balked, offering only half as much. In addition, they authorized a probe of WPA operations in the state, hoping to uncover some good campaign material. When a federal court order stopped the investigation and Governor Earle refused to accept their drastic cut in relief funds, the Republican senators sat on their hands amid the mounting furor. A jobless army descended on Harrisburg and lobbied furiously for relief money while the governor toured the state making "Little Fireside Chats" in the home districts of the GOP senators. The combined pressure brought about a compromise reluctantly accepted by both sides—$45,000,000 for relief to cover an indefinite period. Earle had persuaded Hopkins to hold open the WPA rolls to 15 June, despite the January deadline; this removed 30,000 more employables from the state's relief list and made the compromise palatable. But the Democrats had gained additional campaign ammunition.[56]

All signs indicated a Democratic victory. The party's registration figures rose markedly while the number of Republicans on the rolls remained static. As in 1934, there were important Republican defections to Democratic ranks, and organized labor lined up solidly behind Roosevelt. The *Journal* of the United Mine Workers stated: "The issue of 'Stand by Roosevelt' will overshadow everything else." The Pennsylvania Federation of Labor, the railroad brotherhoods, the Amalgamated Clothing Workers, Labor's Nonpartisan League all backed FDR and the Democrats. Worried Republican leaders in Philadelphia, hoping to save the state candidates, distributed sample ballots marked straight Republican and for Roosevelt, showing the voters how to split the ticket.[57]

The election result exceeded the Democrats' wildest expectations. Not only did FDR sweep the state by over 660,000 votes, but the Little New Deal tightened its hold on the State House by capturing 154 of 208 seats and won control of the Senate for the first time since 1871 by taking 18 of the 25 contests. They would have a two-thirds margin in the upper chamber, with 34 seats. Roosevelt carried Pittsburgh by 190,000 votes and Philadelphia by 210,000, along with winning 41 of the state's 67 counties.[58]

Election statistics dramatized the extent of the political revolution wrought by the New Deal in the Keystone State. The urban and mining counties went overwhelmingly Democratic, holding the GOP to victory in a handful of forest and farming areas. In both Pittsburgh and Philadelphia, the Democracy carried every ward with a Negro majority, with margins of increase greater than in other wards. In Philadelphia, nearly all the wards with mostly foreign-born residents gave FDR a higher percentage of the vote than did the city as a whole; this did not happen in a single ward with a majority of native-born Americans.[59]

As the first payment on the campaign promises, Earle took advantage of the fact that legislative terms begin on 1 December following the election and called the General Assembly into special session on that day. He made only one request of the legislature: enact an unemployment compensation law before the 31 December deadline for compliance with the Social Security Act. With Democrats now controlling both houses, the legislators shouted the proposals through in the record time of five days.[60] The Little New Deal was in full swing.

After the bitter political struggles of the past few years, the harmony of the 1937 legislative session seemed almost anticlimactic. While New Dealers struggled in Washington with Roosevelt's judicial reorganization plan, New Dealers in Pennsylvania made up for lost time by whooping through the legislation that would complete the Little New Deal. Governor Earle led the way by exhorting the General Assembly:

We have before us a tremendous responsibility and an unprecedented opportunity. Liberal forces control both Executive and Legislative branches of our State Government for the first time in 91 years. It is now our duty to translate that liberalism into positive effective action.[61]

The legislature responded with the most sweeping reform program in Pennsylvania's history as the Democrats used their power to improve the social and economic conditions of the people of the state. No one doubted that organized labor stood to gain heavily from the legislation passed by the Little New Deal. Not only had labor leaders supported the Democrats in their bid for power, but a top official of the United Mine Workers, Thomas Kennedy, occupied the lieutenant governor's chair. Within a few months, these notable labor laws had been enacted: the regulation of industrial homework; the abolition of privately paid deputy sheriffs; a strengthened anti-injunction law, the first occupational disease act in the state's history, plus a vastly improved workmen's compensation act; the Little Wagner Act; a minimum-wage, maximum-hour law for women—one was passed to cover men, too, but the courts voided it.[62]

Other reforms were not neglected. Among the more important achievements was the replacement of the antiquated County Poor Boards with a permanent Department of Public Assistance, thereby placing the administration of relief on a much more stable basis. Now, instead of a patchwork system in which each of sixty-seven counties set up a Poor Board in a variety of ways and established tax rates of many different figures, taxes would be imposed by the commonwealth at a uniform rate and administered by a state agency in a more equitable manner. The Public Service Commission, subject of a scathing denunciation by Gifford Pinchot during his tenure of office for failing to protect the consumers, was "ripped" out and a new Public Utilities Commission installed in its place. In addition, farmers received the benefits of a Little AAA, primarily a soil conservation program, and a milk control law to benefit the producers rather than the middlemen. The state's first teacher tenure law protected this group against politically minded school boards, and a Bureau of Civil Liberties was set up to handle complaints along those lines. Nearly all the aforementioned items were enacted over the intense opposition of the Republican minority.[63]

With their successes in welding together a coalition of minority groups into an electoral majority and in enacting a model of the New Deal reform program in Pennsylvania, it is surprising that the tenure in office of the

Democratic party was not longer. But success had caught up with the Democrats, and the 1938 election dealt them a resounding defeat.

Among the reasons for this blow was the fact that the party's nominations had become highly desirable, and many aspiring leaders discovered their latent talents. A bitter primary fight developed, with Senator Guffey and State Chairman David Lawrence leading opposing factions in battling for the gubernatorial nomination for their candidates. This contest turned into a battle for control of the state organization.[64]

In 1934, at a time when the Democrats were struggling out of oblivion, the party could still offer one of its highest nominations to an amateur in politics. Now, after four years of power, the professionals scrambled for position. Apparently David Lawrence could easily have gained the nomination for governor; but he was a Catholic, and a private poll indicated the religious issue would damage his candidacy. Thus, he stepped aside in the interests of victory.[65] Guffey and Lawrence together had enough strength to name any candidate they wanted, but these two leaders were fighting each other for control of state patronage. Guffey felt confident that he could win with Lieutenant Governor Thomas Kennedy as his standard-bearer, for this would assure the support of John L. Lewis and his CIO. The anti-Guffey forces chose a little-known western Pennsylvania Democrat, Charles Alvin Jones, a man unacceptable to the senator.

New Deal leaders in Washington tried to prevent a party-rending fight in the Keystone State by calling a conference of the top Pennsylvania Democrats and reputedly getting them to agree to the nomination of William C. Bullitt, ambassador to France, for governor. But this arrangement, if it existed, fell apart within twenty-four hours, and the struggle resumed.[66] Governor Earle, caught in the middle while running for a United States Senate nomination, almost became a pawn in the contest. Hoping to open up a place for Kennedy on a united ticket, Guffey sought a position for Earle in the Roosevelt cabinet. There had been too much speculation in the news media, however, about Earle as a possible presidential candidate in 1940, and James A. Farley may have torpedoed this idea.[67]

Splits of all kinds plagued the Democratic party during the primary campaign. The governor, following a conference with Roosevelt, announced his support for Jones and stated that FDR had severed relations with John L. Lewis, though the White House did not confirm this assertion. Not only did Senator Guffey continue to support Kennedy, but he encouraged Philadelphia Mayor S. Davis Wilson to run against Earle. The American Federation of Labor denounced Kennedy as a CIO candidate and refused to support him until the CIO unions returned to the fold.[68]

Nothing better demonstrated that this was a fight not for principle but for control of the party than the fact that all concerned agreed that what Pennsylvania needed was more of the New Deal. This placed the Roosevelt administration in a dilemma, for unlike some primaries they were intervening in elsewhere in the country, all the major candidates in Pennsylvania were liberal Democrats. Since a Guffey lieutenant ran the WPA in the Keystone State, Earle telegraphed Hopkins that it was being used to fight the Democratic organization. When President Roosevelt announced that the WPA must not be used for political purposes, the Kennedy forces were hurt, for now there was nothing to offset the use of state employees by the Earle-Lawrence faction. Then, on the day before the primary, Democratic National Chairman James A. Farley issued a statement calling for the nomination of Earle and Kennedy. His plea failed. Earle won an easy victory, but Kennedy narrowly lost to Jones.[69]

Farley loyally announced that Pennsylvania Democrats had been absolutely within their rights in disregarding part of his suggestion and called for united support for the nominees.[70] With the Republicans having rejected Gifford Pinchot's candidacy and nominated Arthur H. James, a Superior Court judge who bitterly denounced the New Deal, the stage seemed to be set for a classic contest over the Roosevelt-Earle policies. The Democrats seemed reasonably united again and might have had an even chance to win the election, but a new complication had arisen.

A lesser candidate for the Democratic gubernatorial nomination, Attorney General Charles Margiotti, saw that his campaign was getting nowhere and made sensational charges against officials of the Earle administration. He accused them of selling legislation and receiving kickbacks from contractors on state projects. The resultant furor damaged Democratic election prospects badly. The governor quite naturally fired Margiotti as attorney general, then tried to prevent the Republican district attorney of the capital city area from launching a grand jury probe that was admittedly a "fishing expedition."[71] Failing to stop the investigation by judicial processes, Earle called a special session of the General Assembly and asked the legislators to take the play away from the grand jury and conduct the probe themselves. The Assembly rushed the bills through, but they were declared unconstitutional, and the grand jury proceeded.[72] Though no convictions resulted from the Margiotti charges, the Democrats faced the general election under a cloud.

Organized labor continued its political duality into the fall campaign. Lieutenant Governor Thomas Kennedy appealed to the half million who had voted for him to work for a Democratic victory in November, and the Pennsylvania CIO responded by pledging its support for the slate, as Kennedy wished. But the American Federation of Labor refused to join the coalition, for William Green, AFL president, urged the election of Senator Davis over Earle. Then, just before the election, the director of organization for the AFL, Louis G. Hines, asked Pennsylvania workers to vote the Republican ticket to prevent "Communist-controlled CIO leadership in Pennsylvania." The State Federation of Labor also backed the GOP candidates and called Arthur James, who had worked as a breaker-boy in the coal fields, a "true son of the mining region."[73]

Adding to Democratic woes, relations between Washington and Harrisburg became more confused as the year wore on. In August, the press revealed that all Democratic governmental employees in the state and all WPA workers had received a letter over the signature of Senator Guffey from the Democratic State Committee requesting funds for the campaign. Guffey and Lawrence promptly denied that the letter had been authorized.[74] A short time later, Democratic Senator Morris Sheppard of Texas, chairman of the committee charged with investigating compliance with the federal election laws, asserted that the charges were true, that all letters sent out with Guffey's letterhead violated the law. Acting WPA administrator Aubrey Williams vigorously denied this allegation, despite a report from one of his field investigators who charged that one district manager sent cards to his supervisors telling them to "be present for roll call" at a Democratic club meeting and to bring their workers along. At that time they would be instructed on campaign plans and how to solicit votes.[75]

This new falling-out among Democrats may have occurred because of the recently formed alliance between the Republicans and the southern Democrats in Congress. Guffey had been the most unyielding advocate of Roosevelt's court reorganization plan, and many southern Democrats were unlikely to desire Earle as another Guffey-style liberal in the Senate. In any case, the charges about political use of the WPA refused to blow over, and just before the election the president publicly deplored coercion of such federal workers and declared that it must be stopped.[76]

The campaign itself reflected the standard pro–New Deal, anti–New Deal split. Democrats wrapped the mantle of Roosevelt about themselves and declared, "We must preserve the progress we have made toward the new Democracy—the Democracy of liberalism and equal opportunity for all." Republican candidates were equated with Hoover and reaction and accused of wanting to destroy the Little New Deal. For his part, Judge James accused the Democrats of a "hymn of hate" against business and denounced them for accepting Communist support.[77] Unfortunately, too many extraneous issues prevented the people of the Keystone State from making a decision based largely on the value of the New Deal, both state and national.

Gradually, defections from Democratic ranks began to foreshadow the outcome. Labor was already split, with an important faction working for Republican success. Suddenly, Robert L. Vann, the Pittsburgh publisher who had started the swing of Negroes to the Democrats in 1932, declared that he and other Negro leaders would support James. Vann added that he had confidential information from Senator Guffey to prove that Negroes were not being treated fairly by the Earle forces. Soon thereafter some followers of Lieutenant Governor Kennedy began to switch their organizations to the support of James. This happened in Luzerne and Schuylkill counties, important mining areas, and in Allegheny county, site of the Democratic stronghold of Pittsburgh. James S. Doyle, vice-chairman for the Kennedy campaign, announced, "Our people would rather give James everything than allow Davey Lawrence to get another ounce of power." President Roosevelt delivered what may have been the final blow by deciding against a trip to Pennsylvania to aid the party; then, in a radio address near election day, ignoring Democratic candidates in Pennsylvania while specifically endorsing them elsewhere.[78]

On November 8, the expected disaster took place. Judge James defeated Charles Alvin Jones in the gubernatorial race by almost 290,000 votes, and Earle lost his bid for the Senate by 400,000. An analysis of the vote indicates that the Democrats were defeated by a moderate drop-off in their majorities in the industrial regions and a severe loss in the rural areas. Defections by the Negro leaders apparently had little effect, for the geographic areas dominated by that race gave the party higher majorities than ever before. In the mining areas as well, the Democracy increased its margin. But in the industrial towns and cities, the loss of AFL support hurt badly. The worst losses of all occurred in the areas where the GOP had traditionally done well until the impact of the depression had caused many votes to shift to the Democrats. Now, after the battle over the Supreme Court, with charges of political use of the WPA, under the cloud of the

Margiotti accusations, and with the middle class somewhat better off economically, the small towns and farming regions returned to the Republican fold. In addition to these liabilities, the Democrats bucked a nation-wide trend to the GOP.[79]

The election results also put an end to the mild Earle-for-President boom that had been going on since the 1936 convention. The Pennsylvania governor had captivated many Democrats at that time, and some delegates had termed Earle FDR's "political crown prince." He was promised support for 1940, and the *New York Daily News* commented: "Watch this boy Earle." Interest in the governor's candidacy continued after the convention; a year later, Governor Ayres of Montana remarked that he considered Earle the most available candidate the party had. Earle apparently did little to encourage this attention, for he announced that Roosevelt was his choice for 1940. But the resounding defeat the governor suffered at the hands of Senator Davis snuffed out whatever chance he might have had for the Democratic nomination.[80]

The smashing of George H. Earle's political career was not the only result of this election. In January 1939, a governor sympathetic to business interests would take office, and at least one branch of the legislature would be controlled by his party. Perhaps the Democrats could prevent the mutilation of many of their achievements, but new legislation of a liberal nature was unlikely. The Little New Deal had ended.

For the most part, the administration of Arthur James did not turn back the legislative clock very far. Perhaps the GOP had intended to make a sharp break, but political and economic realities decreed otherwise. The system of relief established by the Democrats remained virtually intact under Republican rule, and the new administration furnished adequate money for the needy. Economics dictated the first action, politics the second. The cost of abandoning the centralized relief system would have been too much of a burden on the taxpayers of the commonwealth, and GOP did not wish to go into the next election campaign facing the charge of being too stingy to those on relief. Although some changes took place in the administration of aid—notably the insistence on work from the able-bodied—few, if any, abuses were reported. And despite his remarks during the campaign, the governor expressed his willingness to accept PWA, WPA, and other aid from Washington. All he asked was that control of WPA be given to the state, which did not happen.[81]

Having made the decisions about rleief, James found that the desired tax reductions had become impossible of achievement. Since it was politically undesirable to try to shift the burden of taxation away from the higher income groups, James had no better solution to offer than the reenactment of all emergency tax measures of the Little New Deal. One writer observed that the governor had now walked the main plank he had offered as a candidate. The reason for this, political columnist John M. Cummings noted, was that "Governor James, since January, had been fortified with fiscal information not available to Candidate James." The Republican legislature regretfully but dutifully enacted the measures.[82]

The laborer suffered more than any other group at the hands of the James administration. The GOP-dominated Assembly weakened the Little Wagner Act, emasculated the Workmen's Compensation Act, and reduced the effectiveness of several other labor laws. But much of the forward-looking labor legislation of the Little New Deal remained; and it seemed likely these gains would endure. The greatest change in the commonwealth in the New Deal years had been one of attitude; there now existed among the people an awareness of the conditions under which the working man should labor and the realization that the power of government could be used to impose these conditions.[83]

Perhaps the chief difference between the Earle and the James administrations lay in their objectives. The Little New Deal had pressed for sweeping reform; the Republicans chipped away at the gains won by various interests in Pennsylvania society and barred further advances along similar lines. Even had the Democrats won the 1938 election, however, a continuation of large-scale progressive legislation would have been improbable. The national New Deal had ended, and the effects of this would likely have influenced the government at Harrisburg. Moreover, the antiquated Pennsylvania Constitution still blocked some changes desired by the Democrats; until revision of that document occurred, the completion of reform could not be effected.

As Pennsylvania returned to its traditional Republican pattern, it became clear that the Little New Deal had been an aberration caused largely by the shifting tides of national policies. Despite the success of the Earle administration during the middle 1930s, at no time did Democratic voter registration come within half a million of the Republican. In 1934 and 1936, Keystone State voters had given the Democrats temporary majorities because of the popularity of the administration in Washington. With the waning of the New Deal, the GOP in Pennsylvania reasserted itself with victories at the polls, except when FDR was on the ballot. Only in the 1950s, after the capture of Philadelphia city hall by Joseph S. Clark, did the

Democrats gain enough strength to turn Pennsylvania into a two-party state. Beginning in 1954, Democrats won three of the next five gubernatorial elections, three of four presidential contests, and in 1970 captured legislative control of the State Senate for the first time since 1936. It was the Little New Deal, hanging grimly to Roosevelt's coattails, that had brought the Democrats out of the doldrums, though only subsequent events turned them into perennial contenders in the elections of the state.

1. Frank Butler and Robert Taylor, "Coal and Iron Justice," *Nation* 129 (1929): 404–5; Gifford Pinchot, *Final Message to the General Assembly of the Commonwealth of Pennsylvania by Gifford Pinchot, Governor* (n.p., n.d.), p. 27.

2. Louis F. Budenz, "Vare's Last Triumph?", *Nation* 129 (1929): 349–50; "Who Won in Pennsylvania?", *New Republic*, 4 June 1930, pp. 59–60.

3. Walter Davenport, "Double-Cross Marks the Spot," *Collier's,* 25 October 1930, p. 12.

4. Harvey O'Connor, *Mellon's Millions: The Biography of a Fortune* (New York, 1933), pp. 259–60.

5. "Progressivism in Pennsylvania," *New Republic*, 31 May 1922, p. 5.

6. Speech material about Joseph R. Grundy, Box 2106, Gifford Pinchot Papers (Library of Congress); Commonwealth of Pennsylvania, *Smull's Legislative Hand Book and Manual of the State of Pennsylvania, 1921–22* (Harrisburg, 1922), p. 765.

7. Abraham Epstein, "After Four Lean Years," *New Republic*, 1 June 1927, pp. 39–40.

8. Clinton Rogers Woodruff, "Pennsylvania's Primary," *National Municipal Review* 15 (1936): 388–90; Fullerton Waldo, "The Outcome of the Republican Primaries in Pennsylania," *Outlook* 143 (1926): 173–74.

9. Morton Keller, *In Defense of Yesterday* (New York, 1958), pp. 193–95; Maynard C. Krueger, "Election Frauds in Philadelphia," *National Municipal Review* 18 (1929): 295–97.

10. Richard J. Beamish, "Pennsylvania's Battle Royal," *Nation* 130 (1930): 564; *Pittsburgh Post-Gazette*, 12, 13 March 1930; *Philadelphia Record*, 4 January 1930.

11. Bernard Haggarty in the *Philadelphia Public Ledger*, 9 January 1930.

12. Gifford Pinchot to *Wilkes-Barre Telegram*, 19 December 1929. Box 1940, Pinchot Papers; "Who Won in Pennsylvania?", pp. 59–60; *Philadelphia Public Ledger*, 4 April 1930; *Philadelphia Inquirer*, 13 April 1930.

13. Commonwealth of Pennsylvania, *The Pennsylvania Manual, 1931* (Harrisburg, 1931), pp. 596–97.

14. Samuel Harden Church, *The Liberal Party in America* (New York, 1931), p. 31; *Philadelphia Inquirer*, 22 September 1930.

15. *Philadelphia Public Ledger*, 10, 11 October 1930; *Philadelphia Inquirer*, 11 October, 9 November 1930.

16. *Philadelphia Public Ledger*, 12 October 1930.

17. *The Pennsylvania Manual, 1931*, pp. 502–3; *The Pennsylvania Manual*, 1933, pp. 431–574.

18. *Philadelphia Inquirer*, 29 October, 26 March 1930.

19. *Harrisburg Telegraph*, 1 January 1931.

20. *Philadelphia Record*, 6 January 1931; *Harrisburg Telegraph* 8 December 1933.

21. *Harrisburg Telegraph*, 14 November 1933.

22. Pinchot, *Final Message*, pp. 5, 27, 33–34.

23. Commonwealth of Pennsylvania, *Industrial Statistics for Pennsylvania, 1916 to 1956* (Harrisburg, 1959), pp. 2–5.

24. "Unemployment in Philadelphia, April 1931," *Monthly Labor Review* 21 (1930): 36; Commonwealth of Pennsylvania, Executive Minutes, 1 January 1931 to 31 December 1935, p. 97 (unpublished, Public Records Office, Harrisburg, Pa.); U.S. Congress, Subcommittee of Committee on Manufacturers, United States Senate, *Federal Cooperation in Unemployment Relief*, 72d Cong., 1st Sess. (1932), pp. 11–12.

25. Commonwealth of Pennsylvania, *Poor Relief Administration in Pennsylvania* (Harrisburg, 1934), pp. 41–42, 50, 79, 83; Broadus Mitchell, *Depression Decade* (New York, 1947), p. 105; Commonwealth of Pennsylvania, *Unemployment Relief in Pennsylvania* (Harrisburg, 1933), p. 66; Dwight Macdonald, "Pittsburgh: What a City Shouldn't Be," *Forum* 50 (1938): 56.

26. *Harrisburg Evening News*, 28 October 1931.

27. *Legislative Journal of the Commonwealth of Pennsylvania, 1931* (State Library, Harrisburg), p. 45; "Message to the Special Session . . . ," Executive Minutes, 1 January 1931 to 31 December 1935, p. 98.

28. *Washington Observer*, 18 December 1931; interview with William A. Schnader, 16 December 1958; Commonwealth *v.* Liveright, 208 *Pennsylvania State Reports* 35 (1932).

29. *Philadelphia Inquirer*, 26 March 1930, "Emergency Labor Camps in Pennsylvania," *Monthly Labor Review* 34 (1932): 1289–91; Isidor Feinstein, "A Gentleman in Politics," *American Mercury* 28 (1933): 84; *Harrisburg Evening News*, 28 June 1932.

30. *Harrisburg Telegraph*, 20 August 1932; *Monthly Report of the Federal Emergency Relief Administration, October 1 through October 31, 1934*, OF 444, Box 3, Roosevelt Papers (Franklin D. Roosevelt Library).

31. Pinchot, *Final Message*, pp. 5–6.

32. Harold F. Alderfer and Fannette H. Luhrs, *Gubernatorial Elections in Pennsylvania, 1922–42* (State College, Pa., 1946), pp. 11, 13, 15, 24; James Erroll Miller, "The Negro in Pennsylvania Politics with Special Reference to Philadelphia since 1932" (Ph.D. diss., University of Pennsylvania, 1945), pp. 11, 121–23; interview with John S. Fine.

33. Davenport, "Double-Cross Marks the Spot," p. 32.

34. Austin F. MacDonald, "The Democratic Party in Philadelphia," *National Municipal Review* 14 (1935): 297; "The Reminiscences of J. David Stern," Oral History Research Office, Columbia University, pp. 45, 51.

35. *Philadelphia Record*, 21 March 1930.

36. Joseph F. Guffey, *Seventy Years on the Red-Fire Wagon* (n.p., 1952), p. 75; Frank Hawkins, "Lawrence of Pittsburgh: Boss of the Mellon Patch," *Harper's*, August 1956, pp. 56–59.

37. "The Reminiscences of J. David Stern," pp. 51–52; *Philadelphia Record*, 20, 27 September, 1933, 8 July 1934.

38. *Pittsburgh Courier*, 17 September 1932; Miller, "The Negro in Pennsylvania Politics, "pp. 190, 229–30.

39. Samuel Lubell, *The Future of American Politics* (New York, 1952), pp. 34–41; Hugo V. Maiale, *The Italian Vote in Philadelphia between 1928 and 1946* (Philadelphia, 1950), pp. 53, 156.

40. Guffey, *Seventy Years*, pp. 130–31.

41. *Unemployment Relief in Pennsylvania* (Harrisburg, Pa., 1935), pp. 34, 44.

42. Personal Files A to G, 1935–39, George H. Earle III Papers (in private possession, Bryn Mawr, Pa.); "The Labor Governors," *Fortune*, June 1937, p. 143; "Labor Governor," *Time*, 4 July 1937, p. 12.

43. *Philadelphia Record*, 29 September, 3, 19 October 1934; *Pittsburgh Post-Gazette*, 9, 27 October 1934.

44. *Pittsburgh Post-Gazette*, 9 April 1934; U.S. Congress, Senate, *Congressional Record*, 72d Cong., 1st Sess. (1932), 75, pt. 9: 9644; *Philadelphia Inquirer*, 5, 16 August 1934.

45. Commonwealth of Pennsylvania, *The Pennsylvania Manual, 1935–36*, pp. 420–21, 422; *Pittsburgh Post-Gazette*, 6 October 1934; *Philadelphia Record*, 5, 6 November 1934; *Greensburg Daily Tribune*, 8 November 1934.

46. Miller, "The Negro Vote in Pennsylvania Politics," pp. 228, 190; "Address . . . at Meeting of Columbia Chamber of Commerce, Columbia, South Carolina," Speech and News File 80, Earle Papers.

47. "Inaugural Address of George H. Earle, Governor of Pennsylvania, January 15, 1935," Executive Minutes, 1 January 1931 to 31 December 1935, p. 431, Public Records Office, Harrisburg, Pa.; Don Wharton, "Cheerleader," *Today*, 1 August 1936, pp. 8–9.

48. "Employment in Pennsylvania, December, 1934," *Monthly Labor Review* 40 (1935): 876; News Release, Governor's Office, 25 March 1935, Speech and News File 68; "Message to the General Assembly. February 12, 1935," Speech and News File 67, Earle Papers.

49. "Mr. Hopkins Telephone Conversation with Governor Earle and Mr. Kalodner," 18 April 1935, State Files 248, 1933–36, Pennsylvania 400, Federal Emergency Relief Administration Records, Record Group 69 (National Archives); *Harrisburg Telegraph*, 1 May 1935.

50. *York Gazette and Daily*, 10 May 1935; *Philadelphia Record*, 2 May 1935; Iris Richey, ed., *The Pennsylvania Manual, 1957–58* (Harrisburg, n.d.), pp. 977–82; *Lancaster Intelligencer Journal*, 9 May 1935, 5 June 1935.

51. "To the Honorable, the Senate . . . ," 19 June 1935, Speech and News File 70, Earle Papers; *Philadelphia Record*, 6, 23 June 1935; *Harrisburg Telegraph*, 26 February 1935.

52. "To the Honorable, the General Assembly . . . ," 28 January 1935, Speech and News File 67, Earle Papers.

53. Interview with Herbert F. Cohen, 8 July 1956; "Terror in Pennsylvania," *New Republic*, 21 August 1935, p. 35; *Harrisburg Telegraph*, 4 June 1935.

54. "Address of George H. Earle, . . . , September 8, 1936," Speech and News File 78; "Address of George H. Earle, . . . , September 24, 1936," Speech and News File 79, Earle Papers.

55. Fred Fuller Shedd, "Pennsylvania Studies Its Relief Rolls," *Review of Reviews* 93 (1936): 32; "Address of George H. Earle, . . . , April 14, 1936," Speech and News File 75; Earle to Charles A. Waters, 11 May 1936, Speech and News File 76, Earle Papers.

56. "Message to the Special Session . . . , May 4, 1936," Speech and News File 76, Earle Papers; *Harrisburg Telegraph*, 7 July 1936; United States *v*. Owlett, U.S. District Court, Middle District, Penna., 7 July 1936, 15 F. Supp. 736, Pa. 610, Special Litigation Folders P-Z, FERA Records; *Philadelphia Record*, 15 July 1936; news information, 30 July 1936. Speech and News File 78, Earle Papers.

57. C. H. Westbrook, ed., *The Pennsylvania Manual, 1937* (Harrisburg, 1938), pp. 166, 183; *Philadelphia Record*, 18 October, 16 September 1936; *United Mine Workers Journal*, 15 May, 1 October 1936; Jesse Laventhol, "Pennsylvania Hits the Roosevelt Trail," *Nation* 143 (1936): 515.

58. *The Pennsylvania Manual, 1937*, pp. 176, 185, 212; *Harrisburg Evening News*, 4 November 1936.

59. *The Pennsylvania Manual, 1937*, pp. 185, 240, 251, 270, 289, 315–16; Miller, "The Negro Vote in Pennsylvania Politics," pp. 240–42; U.S. Bureau of the Census, *Fifteenth Census of the United States: 1930. Population*, 3:750.

60. *Legislative Journal of the Commonwealth of Pennsylvania, Second Extraordinary Session, 1936* (Harrisburg, 1936), p. 101; *Harrisburg Telegraph*, 1 December 1936.

61. "Message to the General Assembly by George H. Earle, January 5, 1937," Executive Minutes, January 3, 1936 to December 31, 1943, p. 89.

62. Wayland F. Dunaway, *A History of Pennsylvania* (New York, 1948), pp. 501–5; Holgate Bros. Company *v*. Bashore, 331 *Pennsylvania State Reports* 225 (1938).

63. Dunaway, *A History of Pennsylvania*, pp. 501–5; Bruce Bliven, Jr., "Pennsylvania Under Earle," *New Republic*, 18 August 1937, p. 39.

64. Interview with Roy Furman, 15 January 1959.

65. Guffey, *Seventy Years*, pp. 103–4; *Pittsburgh Sun-Telegraph*, 27 February 1938.

66. Guffey, *Seventy Years*, pp. 106–7; interview with David L. Lawrence, 20 May 1959.

67. *Philadelphia Inquirer*, 23 January 1938; 9 February 1938. Twenty years later, Farley denied any knowledge of this matter (James A. Farley to the author, 10 December 1958).

68. *Lancaster Intelligencer Journal,* 18 March 1938; Guffey, *Seventy Years*, p. 109; *Pittsburgh Post-Gazette*, 8 April 1938.

69. Earle to Harry L. Hopkins, undated telegram, Personal File H to Z, 1935–39, Earle Papers; *Philadelphia Inquirer*, 22 March 1938; *Philadelphia Record*, 17 May 1938; Commonwealth of Pennsylvania, *The Pennsylvania Manual, 1939*, pp. 147–48.

70. Press release by James A. Farley, Bureau of Publications, Democratic National Committee, OF 300, Pennsylvania, Roosevelt Papers (Franklin D. Roosevelt Library).

71. *Philadelphia Inquirer*, 26 April 1938; "Address of Charles J. Margiotti . . . , April 28, 1938," Campaign Literature during Governor's Senatorial Campaign, Box 104, Earle Papers; *Philadelphia Record*, 9 May 1938; *Pittsburgh Post-Gazette*, 19 May 1938.

72. "Addresses before the Special Session . . . , July 25, 1938," Box 104, Earle Papers; Dauphin County Grand Jury Investigation Proceedings (No. 2), 332 *Pennsylvania State Reports* 342 (1938–39).

73. *Lancaster Intelligencer Journal*, 21 September 1938; *Philadelphia Inquirer*, 12 October, 10 September 1938; *Philadelphia Record*, 17 August 1938; *Washington Observer*, 5 November 1938.

74. *Lancaster Intelligencer Journal*, 10 August 1938; *Philadelphia Record*, 17 August 1938; Senator Sheppard—Questionnaire re: expenses as candidate for United States Senate, Personal File H to Z, Earle Papers.

75. *Philadelphia Inquirer*, 11 October 1938; *Harrisburg Patriot*, 26 October 1938; Banks Hudson to Harry B. Wirin, Pennsylvania 610, Special Folders re: Political Coercion, Box 2380, Works Progress Administration Records, Record Group 69 (National Archives).

76. *Philadelphia Inquirer*, 5 November 1938.

77. "Statement of Governor George H. Earle," undated, Correspondence, Box 104, Earle Papers; *Lancaster Intelligencer Journal*, 6 November 1938; *Harrisburg Patriot*, 2 September 1938; *Philadelphia Record*, 26 October 1938.

78. *Pittsburgh Post-Gazette*, 19, 24 October 1938; *Philadelphia Record*, 23 October 1938; *Philadelphia Inquirer*, 29 September 1938; *York Gazette and Daily*, 5 November 1938.

79. *The Pennsylvania Manual, 1939*, pp. 153–56, 174–325; Miller, "The Negro Vote in Pennsylvania Politics," pp. 250–54; *Washington Observer*, 9, 10 November 1938.

80. *Philadelphia Evening Public Ledger*, 24 June 1936; *Pittsburgh Sunday Sun-Telegraph*, 28 June 1936; undated clipping, Scrapbook for 1936, Earle Papers; Lewis H. Marks to Joseph Tinney, 7 September 1937, Correspondence, Box 104, Earle Papers; *Harrsiburg Telegraph*, 23 June 1937.

81. "Inaugural Address of Arthur H. James, Governor of Pennsylvania, January 17, 1939," Executive Minutes, 3 January 1936 to 31 December 1943, pp. 255–56, Public Records Office, Harrisburg, Pa.

82. Burtt Evans and Samuel Botsford, "Pennsylvania after the New Deal," *New Republic* 6 May 1940, p. 599; *Philadelphia Inquirer,* 31 May 1939; *Lancaster Intelligencer Journal,* 2 May 1939.

83. *Harrisburg Telegraph*, 6 June 1939; *Legislative Journal of the Commonwealth of Pennsylvania, 1939*, 4:4633, 4057; 5:5060–62.

David J. Maurer

Relief Problems and Politics in Ohio

IN JANUARY 1933, OHIO, LIKE THE REST OF THE STATES IN THE union, trembled on the edge of disaster. In some counties of the state, more than 70 percent of the population depended upon relief for survival. Heavily industrialized counties like Cuyahoga, Summit, Stark, Lucas, and Mahoning were particularly hard hit. Toledo for some time fed its hungry adults for six cents a day.[1] In early March, demonstrations and riots occurred in Cleveland, Canton, and Mansfield in front of city halls and relief offices and in city council chambers. The demonstrators demanded decent relief allowances for food and rent.[2] In the rural and mining counties, where relief organizations never had existed or had collapsed under the pressure of the relief load, the situation was even more critical. J. R. Stockham, a social worker, reported:

> In 1933, a group of miners, men who had been miners in the marginal mines of Athens County, marched into Glouster, Ohio which was the trade center of the surrounding area. Each man was armed with a gunny sack; each man was uttering demands for food—food for his family, food for himself. . . . This march was a spontaneous local move. There were no outside agitators. The group was composed of Americans of English and Welsh descent, grandsons and great grandsons of the miners who came at the opening of the Hocking Valley field in the fifties and sixties.[3]

In Akron, Sheriff Ray Potts ordered his deputies to use force in order to evict unemployed persons who could not pay their rent.[4] Physicians in Akron examined 22,026 school children and found that approximately 10 percent suffered from malnutrition.[5]

Such conditions did not develop overnight. Like many other states between 1929 and 1933, Ohio groped with the problem of providing relief for an increasing number of citizens. The financial crash in October 1929 was a shocking and even ruinous event to many Ohioans, but the slowing down of the economy and subsequent layoffs caused the most widespread distress. The percentage of the total work force that was unemployed rose from 13.3 percent in 1930 to 37.3 percent in 1932. The average number of unemployed was 307,000 in 1930; 576,000 in 1931; and 869,000 in 1932.[6] After exhausting credit at grocery stores and depleting the financial reserves of friends and relatives, the majority of the unemployed turned to public and private relief agencies when they could not find jobs and had exhausted their savings. Between 1929 and 1931, private charities markedly increased their assistance to the unemployed. A comparison of the first three months of 1929 with the same period in 1931 reveals that voluntary expenditures for relief in certain Ohio cities rose 240 percent.[7] In some communities, private charity, ad hoc citizens' committees, and local government cooperated in establishing bread and soup lines, garden projects, and milk distribution centers. In spite of such efforts, only a fraction of those needing help were aided by private efforts. By 1932, private unemployment relief funds represented only a small percentage of total expenditures for relief.[8]

Although private charity's efforts were helpful, the growing number of unemployed had to depend on relief provided by local government. Ohio's relief policies, typical of those of the eastern and midwestern states, dated with only slight modification from the nearly nineteenth century. Under these laws, the township trustees furnished outdoor relief to needy residents and the county provided aid to transients and the disabled. In 1913, a state department of welfare was established to oversee the dispensation of relief, but it could only suggest policies and practices.[9] Between 1930 and 1933, the state's efforts to relieve the plight of its citizens were sporadic and unimaginative. Consequently, the burden of relief for the unemployed rested largely on the shoulders of municipal, township, and county governments.

Ohio cities diverted an increasing amount of money from general revenue, generated by real estate taxes, to relief purposes. Ohio's major urban areas spent local public funds for public relief totaling $619,000 in 1929; $2,120,000 in 1930; $6,027,000 in 1931; and $14,254,000 in 1932.[10] Several cities developed work relief projects, mostly of the pick and shovel variety in the city parks or on the streets, but most communities spent the lion's share of relief expenditures on direct relief because it was cheaper.[11] In Ohio's rural and mining counties, township and county officials struggled to maintain, as tax receipts dwindled drastically, even the appearance of relief.[12]

As early as 1931, in spite of the efforts of private charity and increased expenditures by local government, it was apparent to some observers that depression problems went beyond the capacity of local government. During the gubernatorial campaign the previous fall, incumbent Republican Governor Myers Y. Cooper campaigned on his efforts to relieve unemployment. He had created a special committee to speed up public works projects in the state. His opponent, George White of Marietta, and other Democrats exploited the "hard times" issue.[13] White won and the Republicans' lopsided control of the previous General Assembly was reduced to a small majority. Although this new General Assembly was described as liberal and progressive and Governor White had benefited from the depression-created dissatisfaction, both legislature and governor preferred to rely on local action. The legislature passed measures permitting cities and townships to sell bonds for relief purposes. A bill introduced by Republican State Senator Robert A. Taft of Cincinnati to consolidate welfare activities in a single department in each of Ohio's counties died in committee. An unemployment insurance proposal, called the Ohio Plan, was also killed by the legislature.[14] This response is not surprising when it is recalled that an overwhelming majority of average Americans and their political leaders believed that the economic downturn was only temporary and that any tampering with the system such as centralization of relief or unemployment insurance was likely to delay recovery.[15]

By the end of 1931, it was plain that as the need for relief continued to grow, efforts made during the year were inadequate. S. P. Bush, Ohio's representative to the President's (Hoover) Organization on Unemployment Relief (POUR), which sought to coordinate information on relief activities, reported:

> Based on reports from all subdivisions of the state there is an existing deficiency as of this day, in relief funds of $2,750,000, and estimates based on reports from all subdivisions indicate a deficiency of $16,000,000 in relief funds needed for the period of 1932.[16]

Newspapers throughout Ohio told of the consequences of the lack of relief funds: evictions, demonstrations, scavenging in garbage cans, and soup kitchens.

Distressed by the suffering of the jobless and the failure of local communities to raise necessary funds, Governor White called three special sessions of the General Assembly in 1932. Because of the severity of the depression and the fact that 1932 was an election year, the first breaches in the wall of tradition were made at these sessions. For example, very little opposition arose over legislation creating a State Relief Commission (SRC). For the first time, the state acknowledged that the local communities could not solve the relief problem by themselves. The SRC was to cooperate with national, state, and local unemployment relief commissions. It coordinated the distribution of Red Cross flour, blankets, and garments. On 7 March and 5 July 1932, President Hoover transferred federal surplus wheat and cotton to the Red Cross, which prepared the raw commodities and distributed them to the states for families on relief. When the Reconstruction Finance Corporation (RFC) was authorized by Congress in the Emergency Relief and Construction Act of 1932 to lend money to the states for relief purposes, the SRC processed the applications of local subdivisions. Prior to June 1933, Ohio received $18,937,305 from the RFC.[17]

The state was fortunate that the SRC had been established and could serve as the agent for RFC funds because the legislature was unwilling to provide a significant amount of state funds for relief purposes. The General Assembly merely increased the power of local governments to raise funds and diverted a couple of million dollars from other tax sources for relief. Faced with the possibility of a budget deficit, the legislators and the governor believed that it was politically impossible to provide substantial aid for relief activities; in order to balance the budget, the governor approved legislation reducing salaries of state employees.

One of the considerations behind the concern for a balanced budget in the minds of the legislators and governor was the hope that the voters, in an election year, would be impressed with the politicians' fiscal orthodoxy. In 1932, the conventional wisdom, expressed in campaign speeches, stressed the belief that balanced budgets would restore confidence and a healthy economy. This tactic did not hurt the Democrats in Ohio, although the party probably benefited more from the belief that the Republicans had done little to combat the ravages of the depression and the Democrats might institute needed changes. George White won easily over his Republican opponent, David Ingalls, a wealthy Clevelander, and the Democrats gained control of the lower house of the General Assembly.[18] Both candidates were generally kown as successful and somewhat conservative businessmen, but White's victory can be attributed to the feeling that Democrats were committed to providing relief.

The meaning of the election returns was not lost on White. In January 1933, the governor called for state support of relief; he estimated that $35,000,000 would be needed to provide food, clothing, fuel, and shelter for the unemployed in 1933. Three months later, in April, he observed that this estimate was too low and that the state would need an additional $13,000,000 to provide even minimum protection for the unemployed. White believed the state should now shoulder at least one-quarter of the relief burden. He asked the General Assembly to enact a series of nuisance taxes and transfer highway construction funds in order to raise $12,000,000 for a relief fund. The legislature responded with legislation raising $2,000,000, remitting taxes to landlords housing relief clients, and exhorting Ohio's citizens to purchase American-made and American-raised products.[19] In short, the Ohio General Assembly continued to rely upon local government to cope with the relief problem and probably hoped the local authorities could be aided by the incoming Roosevelt administration.[20]

In March 1933, the federal government began to establish programs designed to assist state and local governments in coping with the impact of the depression. Only a few disgruntled persons objected. Senator Simeon D. Fess of Ohio, an archconservative Republican and spokesman of prohibitionist sentiment in the state, said, "I can hardly find parliamentary language to describe the statement that the states and cities cannot take care of conditions in which they find themselves but must come to the Federal Government for aid." His colleague in the House of Representatives, Republican John B. Hollister, successor to Nicholas Longworth's Cincinnati seat, asked "Is there anything left of our Federal system?"[21] Another point of view was expressed by a Dayton man who wrote Democratic Congressman (and later governor) Martin L. Davey: "I honestly believe that Franklin D. Roosevelt was the answer that an All Wise, Just God sent, to the prayers of millions of discouraged Americans of all classes who got down on their knees and prayed for assistance."[22]

Ohio's share of federal funds in 1933 totaled $27,893,871.89. The increased participation of the federal government in relief expenditures in Ohio came at a crucial moment. In June 1933, the state contributions to the cost of relief reached its lowest point, $161,948.61, and the federal government increased its share by $600,000. In May 1933, Harry Hopkins, Roosevelt's relief administrator, designated the State Relief Commission as the administrative agent for Ohio. In June, the commission's executive director, Ellis O. Braught, added an auditor, a nutrition specialist, and a statistician to his small staff. The succeeding months, preceding the opening in November 1933 of the Civil Works Administration program, saw further staff additions to conform to the new federal programs. These included a distributor of surplus commodities, a director of transient activities, and an agent in charge of the first CCC enrollment, and office personnel were augmented accordingly.[23]

The State Relief Commission urged creation of local groups in the counties to administer the relief program under state direction. A brief look at the county machinery prior to the CWA reveals county relief organizations in only thirty of the eighty-eight counties. In these thirty counties, the SRC established contacts with a country relief director who was paid from county funds. His nominal position was assistant clerk to the Board of County Commissioners; and he managed on a countywide basis that part of the relief program being financed with federal, state, or local funds earmarked for relief. In large counties, the director headed a fairly complex staff of relief workers, all paid from county funds and working exclusively for the county relief administration. In the fifty-eight remaining counties, county commissioners, city officials, and township trustees administered all relief funds, both general and emergency, in accordance with traditional public relief practice. In many cases, however, they acted with the advice of voluntary boards, known as county relief committees.

Beginning in August 1933, each county was required to set up a relief administration under the State Relief Commission and State Civil Works Administration. The staff in each county unit included a director, a casework supervisor, a team of investigators, and clerical workers. In these fifty-eight counties, the state paid the salaries of the director rather than the county. All but one county accepted the conditions outlined by the SRC by 1 December 1933.

In conclusion, it should be noted that the central authority and assistance outlined here were part of the emergency laws and depression situation. The Ohio poor law with its twin principles—residence as eligibility for relief and local responsibility—remained on the books. The hope that Ohio would return to the previous system of local control by some 4,000 township trustees, 110 city safety and service directors, and 88 boards of county commissioners continued to survive. This desire for local relief autonomy managed to subvert to a certain extent some of the programs engaged in by the FERA and the State Relief Commission.[24]

Between May 1933 and December 1935, the Federal Emergency Relief Administration, operating through the State Relief Commission, provided the major defense against the miseries of the Great Depression. Most of Ohio's relief population depended on direct relief—about 1,000,000 persons a month between July 1933 and October 1935. They received orders from their local county relief organizations providing food, clothing, rent, and other necessities. In most cases, support was at or below the subsistence level. Some young men and veterans took advantage of the work and training program of the Civilian Conservation Corp (23,530 in November 1935). Although hampered by local politics and pressures, the FERA made great progress toward two of its primary objectives: adequate relief and useful work projects for employable persons. These goals were attained because of the establishment of special forms of assistance for the various groups in need. Thus, the FERA in Ohio developed a transient relief program, an emergency education plan, a college student aid scheme, the Ohio Rural Rehabilitation Corporation (ORRC), and a self-help cooperative program, the Ohio Relief Production Units, Incorporated (ORPU). The programs of the Federal Surplus Relief Corporation and the Civil Works Administration in Ohio were undertaken by Ohio's FERA administrators.[25]

The Work Project Development Committee, created in March 1933 by the State Relief Commission, had drawn up plans for numerous small projects around the state for parks, roads, and minor improvements in public buildings. The largest expense in the plans was labor costs. During the summer of 1933, the FERA provided funds and administration of work relief on SRC projects. Both the SRC and the FERA viewed direct cash or in-kind relief as merely emergency measures. Also, leaf-raking and other "made work" schemes were kept to a minimum by undertaking projects deemed worthwhile by local governments.

Work relief was greatly expanded when President Roosevelt signed an Executive Order (6420-B) on 9 November 1933 announcing the creation of the Civil Works Administration. From 24 November 1933 to 31 March 1934, the CWA in Ohio put a weekly average of 205,000 men to work at a payroll cost of $45,000,000. Altogther Ohio received CWA funds totaling $57,985,555.[26] A smaller number of white collar and women workers handled clerical and skilled jobs under the CWA's auxiliary, the Civil Works Service (CWS). A chief engineer was placed in charge of each of the state's twenty-nine engineering districts. He guided the district projects and was responsible for its operation.

Workers in the Ohio CWA, particularly the skilled ones, did not always receive the wages suggested by the administration in Washington. Thirty-seven and a half percent of the unskilled workers in Ohio failed to get the recommended 50 cents per hour, and skilled workers received only 75 cents per hour instead of the indicated $1.20 per hour. Architects were paid an hourly rate of 75 cents to $1.08. Ohio's relief population increased so fantastically that more and more workers were incorporated into CWA projects. Unfortunately, the funds available from Washington did not increase.[27]

Political difficulties complicated work for the CWA in Ohio. Charges of political partisanship in hiring practices were raised in Springfield, Cleveland, Dayton, and Toledo. Investigation proved the charges were groundless, but the allegations always received more newspaper coverage than reports of the investigations that exonerated local CWA officials. The most serious political interruption of the CWA program occurred in Youngstown. A number of newspaper stories telling of favoritism toward Democrats reached Harry L. Hopkins in Washington. Calling on Frank D. Henderson, adjutant general of the Ohio National Guard and chairman of the SRC, to make a complete investigation of the CWA organization in Mahoning County, Hopkins vowed that funds would not be issued to Youngstown unless political interference ceased. Several weeks later Henderson reported to Hopkins.

> Mahoning County has presented a problem due to the political complications involving both of the major parties. Both the Democratic and Republican Parties have attempted to use the relief administration politically in the past, which, together with inefficient handling and irregularities, led to the action . . . of placing a SRC employee from outside of Mahoning County in charge of the Relief and CWA administration in the county. . . . Youngstown has a great many political factions all of whom want to run the show. All groups oppose the new appointee, Ray Noble, the best proof that it [his administration] is impartial.[28]

In Ohio, the CWA program involved approximately 6,000 work projects, and nearly half of these were completed before the termination of the program on 31 March 1934. The remaining 3,000 projects were either continued as a part of the FERA works program, or discontinued without loss or other inconvenience to the public. Typical CWA projects included a new library at Yellow Springs in Greene County, a new city hall in Marysville, and swimming pools in Orrville and Alliance. Because of the

CWA, Ohio boasted thousands of miles of newly paved or graded and ditched streets and roads, hundreds of new public park facilities, and a host of other welcome public improvements that would have been impossible without federal funds. The most important gain was putting men to work.

In the spring of 1934, when the CWA was dismantled, the FERA works program took over the task of providing jobs through work relief. From July 1934, when the FERA began to operate effectively, to June 1935, when it was liquidated prior to the establishment of the WPA, a monthly average in Ohio of 1,119,508 men and women received relief. A number of these, approximately 65,000, felt fortunate to be engaged on work relief projects. The greater cost of work relief, as compared to direct relief, limited the amount of projects and the number of employables on relief that could be funded.[29]

The FERA work program primarily benefited relief clients in urban areas. In order to cope with rural destitution, the SRC set up, with FERA funds, the Ohio Rural Rehabilitation Corporation (ORRC). A statewide survey of rural families on relief conducted in the spring of 1934 revealed that of the approximately 66,000 families, only 16,000 lived on, or operated, farms. The other 50,000 were nonfarming families, living in rural areas near factories in which they had formerly been employed. Before the organization and incorporation of the ORRC, the SRC formed a Family Recovery Division that provided individual farmers with funds for seeds, equipment, and necessary repairs on dwellings that could be made habitable by relief clients for relief clients. Between May and July 1934, the Family Recovery Division helped support an average of 13,300 families a month. In August, the ORRC aided 5,530 participants. The number supported continued to edge downward in succeeding months. The ORRC's purpose was not wholesale relief but a plan that looked toward the eventual return to self-support of those destitute families on rural relief demonstrating possibilities for rehabilitation. The officers of the Corporation, Executive Director Frank D. Henderson, the former chairman of the SRC, and trustees C. C. Stillman, J. R. Allgyer, and L. L. Schoenmann, counseled a careful selection of cases to insure complete rehabilitation. The figures above indicate that many thousands in the previous program were not good risks and returned, wholly dependent, to the general relief rolls.[30]

By the end of 1934, of farming relief families selected 1,546 had enjoyed such benefits from the Rural Rehabilitation Corporation's program that they were again self-supporting. The outstanding feature of the program was the extension of loans in the form of feed, fertilizer, seed, equipment, livestock, or other capital goods. All loans were made against notes payable to the corporation. Repayment could be in cash, produce, or labor on local work projects, which meant rural community efforts such as canning, sewing, rug-making, or repair of usable buildings in the area. In 1935, the functions of the ORRC were absorbed by the Resettlement Administration, and contractual obligations were liquidated as soon as possible.

In the minds of the participants, the program was a success. One of the farmers who wrote to Henderson said:

> Now I am farmer, on my way to security and independence. . . . I produced this season 308 shocks of corn, and 100 shocks of fodder, and raised to maturity 85 of the 100 baby chicks which were supplied to me. I have obtained 17 head of cattle. . . . a pump . . . a milk house and 300 rods of fence. The acreage that I have planted for 1935, or have ready for planting, will yield at an average rate of production and average prices, $1245.00. . . . We are on the way up again.[31]

As a scheme of rehabilitation, however, the ORRC did not even attempt to solve problems of over 90 percent of the rural destitute. Between September 1934 and June 1935, the maximum monthly number of families receiving aid was 4,976, and the usual monthly figure was 2,800. The highest monthly expenditure totaled $291,509.13, but the average hovered around $128,000.00.[32] Although the overwhelming number of the rural poverty-stricken were given general relief and many benefited from several of the other FERA programs, the back-to-the-farm scheme was an illusion for most.

Experimentation remained the order of the day in 1934. In June, the SRC organized the Ohio Surplus Relief Corporation (later and more familiarly known as the Ohio Relief Production Units, Inc.) to try the idea of leasing idle industrial plants throughout the state and putting relief clients to work producing items of clothing, furniture, bedding, and the like, which were needed badly by the other relief clients of the state. The formation of this corporation paralleled the popularity of the "production for use" idea in other parts of the country.

Workers were paid in cash at NRA code rates in amounts up to their former relief budget and in labor credits that could be exchanged for products manufactured at other ORPU factories. Unfortunately, the labor credit system was not effective. The twelve factories put in operation by the

ORPU produced garments, stoves, chinaware, furniture, and blankets. The worker quickly acquired these items and then began to accumulate unwanted labor credits. Since his cash income was restricted to food, rent, fuel, and utilities, the ORPU employee wanted an increase in cash wages so he could pay off debts, receive medical care, and do other things not called for in the relief budget. Within three months after the first plant went into operation, the policy of paying employees partly in cash and partly in labor credits was discontinued. In place of this unworkable plan, the cash payments increased to a more liberal figure, and at the same time the number of hours worked by each employee was reduced. Several shifts of workers kept the plants in operation 40 hours per week, but the individual worker put in only 24 to 30 hours per week.

Even though the corporation provided employment for approximately one thousand workers a month beginning 2 July 1934 to May 1935 and received praise from factory owners (anxious to see their plants busy and at least rent-producing) and the accolades of the towns where ORPU plants were located, the ORPU disbanded. Only a crude distribution system could be devised by ORPU because it did not sell to the public. A small group of salesmen energetically attempted to sell to local relief administrations, but this market was limited; and the buyers were under pressure to restrict their purchases to local business and manufacturing concerns. The lack of a market seriously undermined the ORPU's effort to be self-sustaining. The corporation did not lose a great deal of money, but returns never exceeded costs.[33]

To Ohio's host of unemployed, the ORPU scheme was of little benefit; but for those who shared in the venture, the ORPU provided almost a year of steady employment at decent wages. The limited experiment in state capitalism failed as an answer to the relief crisis because of the variety of objections to its functions. Labor unions protested that the ORPU might interfere with union organization and take jobs away from unionized workers in private industry. Local private concerns feared they would lose the business of their local relief units if the latter bought from ORPU plants. Moreover, since the scheme was competitive with private industry, there was general disapproval even though some businessmen approved. Noncompetitive schemes were a great deal more popular.

Other programs developed in Ohio included relief for transients, educational projects, and aid for college students. The establishment of the transient program sprang from the recognition that wandering, homeless persons constituted a special relief problem. Most of the transients were native-born, and the majority were residents of the state in which they were traveling. A study in Columbus found that in almost every case the transient was earnestly seeking work.[34]

Prior to the establishment of the Transient Division, the transient was often treated in some areas of Ohio like an outlaw and was ejected from the town as quickly as possible. In the larger cities, some private groups attempted to aid the transient, but the shelter offered was very poor at best. Medical care, rehabilitation, and recreation were nonexistent. In Columbus, some of the facilities were little better than pest holes, particularly the shelters for Negroes.[35] Early in August 1933, a state plan for aid to transients with cost estimates was prepared and submitted to Washington. On 17 August, the federal director of transient activities advised that Ohio's plan and application had been the first received from any state, and he earmarked $50,000 in FERA funds for the Ohio transient program during the month of September.

Thanks to an early start in the program, Ohio was able to secure some outstanding supervisors and social workers for its bureaus. Central shelters were quickly established in Cleveland, Cincinnati, Toledo, Columbus, Akron, Dayton, Canton, and Portsmouth to provide immediate necessities and to separate the transient family from wandering men and boys. Families were kept in the community in an effort to keep the children in school and the head of the household close to possible employment in an urban work relief project. Ohio established ten camps for individual men and boys. The camps provided medical, recreational, educational, and work facilities. The work projects were construction-type, and between February 1934 when the first camp opened and March 1936 when the last closed, the men of the Ohio Transient Division worked 2,866,645 man hours on useful labor programs. Between July 1934 and November 1935, the division supervised the care, on the average, of 11,376 individuals a month at a cost of approximately $179,000 per month. The program spent $4,033,435.94 in Ohio from September 1934 to April 1936.[36]

Two other specific programs of the FERA in Ohio revolved around education. The emergency education program of the FERA was designed to meet the needs of teachers who were unemployed and destitute. The program not only gave work to teachers (a monthly average of 1,600 Ohio teachers received employment between December 1933 and November 1935)[37] but aided communities generally by providing adult education, literacy classes, vocational training and rehabilitation, and nursery schools. Without displacing any regularly employed teachers, the emergency education activities of the FERA filled a real need.

Among the black population of Ohio, there were disproportionately large numbers of well-qualified teachers on relief. The Ohio Emergency Schools Administration made certain that Negro teachers were hired in proportion to their numbers. This action stands out as one of the successes of the program. The pay to the teachers ranged from 80 cents per hour in the rural counties to $1.00 per hour in the cities, for a maximum of fifteen hours per week. The first concern of the program was to combat illiteracy, but the scope of the program was quickly broadened into areas helpful to the morale and possible economic well-being of the state's citizens. Twelve thousand Ohioans enrolled in literacy classes, and approximately eighteen thousand took vocational training classes. Other classes also enrolled thousands in adult education and nursery schools.

College men and women were aided by the College Student Aid Program. In 1934-35, a monthly average of 5,100 Ohio students participated in the program.[38] Students in fifty-nine Ohio colleges and universities worked at approximately ten thousand jobs, half of them on campus and the other half with off-campus agencies. Many students worked in college offices at tasks that had gone undone because of a lack of funds. Professors once again had laboratory assistants and grading assistants. Off-campus jobs included work at relief agencies, clerical work in records offices and outdoor work.

How successful was the FERA in providing relief for Ohio citizens and in providing a basis for efficient programs in the future? In the beginning, there was a great deal of confusion in investigative policies, accounting, office location, and official status, as well as continual worry over sources of funds.[39] Rural counties lacked knowledge of how to handle the overwhelming relief problem. A case study of rural Belmont County pointed out that the relief organization failed to improve the lot of 10 percent of the population even after a year of operation. Local politicians and self-interested individuals often opposed a humane but costly solution.[40] In Fairfield County (44,010 population), relief families without any means of providing shelter for themselves were forced to live in horse stalls at the county fairgrounds in 1934. The Fairfield County Relief Commission could pry only a pittance for relief from the county commissioners, who were split politically. Since the expenditure of federal and state funds depended on local participation, little could be done to correct a deplorable situation. Five dollars was the average monthly relief payment. The county averaged 3,000 relief cases a month and spent only $15,000 per month.[41] But despite these shortcomings, the federal government developed a relief operation that put thousands to work on relief projects and aided hundreds of thousands through direct relief between 1933 and 1935.

For the most part between 1933 and 1935, Ohio's political leaders preferred to allow the burden of relief to rest upon the federal government. The Ohio General Assembly was called into special session in the spring of 1934, and Governor White urged the legislature to consider state financing of relief and total centralization of relief administration in Ohio. The legislators refused to go beyond previous commitments to the SRC and legislation allowing local governments to issue bonds for relief purposes. In spite of the criticism of many of the state's major newspapers and citizen's groups for this stand, the legislators feared voter retaliation that might come from unbalanced budgets and changes in the state's permanent relief policy.

The conservative attitude of the politicians was briefly challenged in 1933 by the rise of the pension issue. By the initiative process, a pension plan to aid impoverished persons at age 65 who had resided in the state for fifteen years was approved by the voters. The plan called for a maximum monthly grant of $25.00. Although it was estimated that there would be over 400,000 eligible recipients according to the 1930 census, only 36,543 were receiving benefits by the end of 1934 and the average montly grant was $6.54.[42] Governor White urged that a state income tax be approved to finance the old age pension plan, to retire local governments' poor relief bonds, for increased aid to school districts and municipalities, and for increased funding of relief operations in the state. A combination of rural legislators and Chambers of Commerce killed the income tax proposal and substituted a sales tax bill, which White approved of at the last minute (December 1934). The governor hoped that the measure could raise a part of the $24,000,000 that the FERA administrator, Harry Hopkins, said Ohio should be contributing in 1935 toward its share of the relief burden in the state.

Thus, Ohio depended to a great extent on the federal government for funds in order to keep from sliding back to the pre-1933 relief situation when local authorities had reached their financial limits and the General Assembly refused to vote additional funds. Governor White stood almost alone in the state government after 1933 in recognizing that the depression was not a temporary aberration and that the dispensation of relief could no longer be handled by methods suitable to an agrarian society. His fellow citizens preferred to believe that the problem would soon disappear or that the federal government would solve their problem at little cost to them. This attitude would cause grave political problems in Ohio in 1935 and in succeeding years. It would also cause significant federal intervention in Ohio's relief problems.

In 1934, Governor White decided to run for the Senate but lost in the primary to Vic Donahey, who went on to crush incumbent Republican Senator Fess in the general election. Martin L. Davey, a Democrat, won the governorship by 65,406 votes in a hotly contested election with his Republican opponent Clarence J. Brown.

Martin L. Davey grew up in Kent, Ohio and, after briefly attending Oberlin College, entered his father's business, The Davey Tree Expert Company. Davey was successful in building a national reputation for the company in the 1920s. A recognized leader in the community, he was elected mayor of Kent and represented his district in Congress for several terms. He lost the race for governor in 1928 against Myers Y. Cooper, but in 1930 he was back in Congress. Govencr Davey, throughout his political career, made use of the radio. Up until 1934, his weekly radio program "Trees" interested thousands of potential voters in his subject and the man. After his election he used a statewide hook-up for "fireside chats."[43]

During his gubernatorial campaign, Davey announced his intention to return the administration of relief to local officials. He argued that the state could not afford to maintain a system that encouraged graft and chiseling. The *Cleveland Plain Dealer* was shocked by Davey's attitude. Davey's policy would give "the relief set-up to the politicians" when "relief should be divorced from politics."[44] Davey refused to backtrack. On the eve of his election, he reiterated his position that relief should be handled locally in the smaller cities. He contended that township trustees, who knew the problems of their communities best, should administer relief.[45] His stand reinforced and strengthened the attitude the legislature had assumed in 1933 and 1934.

Outgoing Governor White possibly feared what Davey and the 91st General Assembly would do to Ohio's relief program. On the very day Davey was inaugurated, Governor White sent a last message urging the legislators to raise taxes for relief.[46] On 22 January 1934, eight days later, Governor Davey presented his State of the State message. He stated that he did not know what the state's share of the relief burden would be. He insisted that he would not approve any new taxes for any cause but that the state would answer the "urgent human appeal" for relief if the federal government could not provide work for the unemployed.[47]

The General Assembly complied with Governor Davey's request and did not raise taxes. Amended Senate Bill No. 114 and House Bill No. 501 provided the machinery whereby counties could raise money for relief purposes through the issuance of bonds. Otherwise, the legislature did not see fit to meet the unemployment relief problem in Ohio. The state of Ohio's expenditures for general and special relief programs in 1935 totaled $8,414,075.[48]

In February, Davey charged that the federal administration of relief in Ohio was "cruel, inhuman and wasteful." He might have added that the state's local relief administrators refused to yield to his demands for political patronage. Charles C. Stillman, FERA administrator in Ohio, was dismissed by Davey because he opposed the governor's requests for administrative posts for Democrats loyal to Davey in the relief apparatus. Harry Hopkins launched an immediate investigation and found evidence that Davey and his subordinates had used pressure in seeking relief posts for their followers and that they had tried to pressure firms doing business with the Ohio Relief Administration to contribute funds to make up Davey's campaign deficit and his inaugural expenses. As a result of the investigation, President Roosevelt, in a letter to FERA Administrator Hopkins stated:

> I have examined the evidence concerning corrupt political interference with relief in the State of Ohio. Such interference cannot be tolerated for a moment. I wish you to pursue these investigations diligently and let the chips fall where they may. This Administration will not permit the relief population of Ohio to become the innocent victims of either corruption or political chicanery.[49]

When Hopkins repeated this charge and specifically mentioned Davey, the governor called the FERA Administrator a liar and actually filed a libel charge. The charge issued against Hopkins was withdrawn shortly, but the governor redoubled his attack on the centralized relief system. As a result of the investigation, on 1 March 1935 the federal government took over the administration of relief in Ohio. Stillman was returned to his position as relief administrator, and the FERA worked with local governments to handle the dispensation of relief until the FERA was phased out in favor of a new approach begun in late 1935.

On 8 April 1935, President Roosevelt approved the Emergency Relief Appropriation Act of 1935 (WPA). This law represented a new direction in relief in the United States. The Works Progress Administration was to provide a federal work relief program for unemployed employables throughout the country. Relief of unemployables was to be handed back to the states. And the Social Security Act of 1935 signed by the president in August provided, among other things, grants to the states for aid to the unemployables (dependent children, the handicapped, and indigent aged). The passage of these two measures established the principle that government was responsible for the well-being of its citizens in an industrial and urban society.

Ohio did not become an enthusiastic partner in this new approach. Politicians in both parties sought political advantage in the operation of the WPA and in the categorical aid programs of the Social Security Act. The state shirked its financial responsibility for relief of those not enrolled in various federal programs. It also dragged its feet in establishing an effective permanent statewide relief organization even after it became evident that the local communities lacked the financial resources for providing relief. Between 1935 and 1940, the state of Ohio depended on the WPA to provide relief for the bulk of the unemployed, and on the local communities for aid to the remainder of those persons not covered by the categorical aid provided by the Social Security Act.

WPA activities in Ohio included road-building and construction (schools, sewer systems, parks, public buildings, and so on). High school and college youth were given jobs by the WPA-created National Youth Administration (NYA) in order to keep them in school and off the glutted labor market. A whole series of programs were instituted to provide worthwhile tasks for white collar and professional groups: music, art, writers and theater projects, educational and public health programs, and research and statistical surveys.

In Ohio, as in most states, the WPA program built on FERA personnel. C. C. Stillman, director of the FERA in Ohio, was named administrator of the WPA in Ohio and held both jobs from 1 July 1935 to 31 October 1935, when he resigned as WPA administrator to resume his duties as director of the School of Social Administration at Ohio State University. Harry Hopkins named Dr. Carl Watson of Findlay, Ohio, to Stillman's position. Watson, long associated with welfare work, proved an excellent administrator.

WPA projects put 29,925 persons to work by September 1935. By 28 March 1936, over 186,000 persons found jobs with the WPA.[50] By September 1936, the WPA had completed or was working on 9,436 projects in Ohio at a cost of $313,901,543.56.[51] Regulations required that at least 95 percent of the people employed on projects be selected from those certified by local relief agencies as receiving, or being in need of, relief. In the main, the WPA in Ohio was successful in finding qualified persons from its certified clients; and in November 1938, only 2.4 percent of the total people employed on projects were noncertified. The average monthly number of workers employed by the WPA in Ohio, 1936 to 1939, were: 1936, 158,544; 1937, 104,077; 1938, 231,234; and 1939, 187,045.[52]

C. C. Stillman, although not officially connected with the WPA in 1939, remained close to the organization. On 22 February 1939, in a radio broadcast, Stillman summed up the accomplishments of the WPA to that date: he noted that in addition to the millions of hours of useful labor by the unemployed, the state benefited from the construction or improvement of thousands of public buildings, bridges, roads, recreational facilities, hot lunches in the schools, concerts, health clinics, and thousands of other projects.[53]

To many in the state, the greatest achievement was the fact that the WPA in Ohio took thousands of men and women off the relief rolls and put them to work on worthwhile projects. At its peak in 1938, the WPA employed 279,067 men and women on its projects at a statewide average wage of $58.21 a month. General relief provided only a maximum of $26.65 a month.[54]

An indication of Ohio's dependence on the WPA to provide relief for its citizens is found in Donald Howard's comparative study of WPA activities. Howard points out that Ohio exceeded the national WPA employment average by 30 percent or more in 1938 and 1939. In those years, Ohio had more men and women working on WPA projects than any other state save one.[55]

Many of the complaints about the WPA involved politics. Democrats claimed too many Republicans held jobs, and Republicans asserted that the Democratic administration employed only party members. Typical of the complaints heard by the Ohio WPA was the allegation by J. Fuller Trump of Springfield, Ohio. Trump, in the insurance business and treasurer of the Clark County Democratic executive committee, charged that the WPA organization was run entirely for the benefit of Republicans and was corrupt. An investigation by the district director resulted in the exposure of Trump as a political malcontent who sought revenge because of failure to get a part in a WPA Theater Project play.[56]

Charges of a more serious nature resulted from an investigation of Black Legion activities in Allen County.[57] The Black Legion, a paramilitary, crypto-fascist group was active in Ohio, Michigan, and Indiana during the mid-1930s. The Legion members believed that their 100 percent Americanism could be forced on their fellow citizens by flogging and murder. Beginning in May 1936, their activities were exposed in a series of sensational indictments for murder in Detroit, and the organization was quickly disbanded. In June 1935, State Representative H. T. Phillips, a Republican from Athens County, stated that special investigators for his legislative committee estimated that 82 percent of the Allen County Relief Administration were members of the Black Legion. Their numbers and positions allegedly enabled them to control the relief or discriminate in favor of their organization. Dr. Carl Watson, WPA administrator in Ohio, in his report to Washington stated:

> Fred Roose, WPA Director in District 13 which includes Allen and eleven other northwestern Ohio Counties says he is positive no present or former Black Legion member occupied any position under WPA that would permit him to influence labor policies or exercise discrimination.[58]

Additional problems in providing relief were created by Governor Davey. C. C. Stillman in a memo to George Babcock, WPA regional director, noted: "It is the opinion of many close observers . . . that the Governor of Ohio [Davey] is not interested in suggesting or encouraging any suitable program to meet the needs of Ohio people on relief."[59] Yet despite Davey's opposition to federal relief policies, he sought political advantage from them as long as they existed. In 1936 and again in 1938, charges were made that Governor Davey attempted to use the WPA for his own political purposes. Both times, WPA officials at the state and federal level objected strenuously to state and national party officials. In 1938, Davey's supporters not only pressured WPA workers for funds and votes but used some workers for campaign work while they were on project time. Several workers and foremen were dismissed for this partisan activity.

Charges of WPA political activity did not end with Governor Davey. John W. Bricker, a Republican, elected governor in 1938, echoed charges heard throughout the nation that Washington juggled WPA employment quotas for partisan advantage. Colonel F. C. Harrington, national WPA Works Projects Commissioner, replied that federal and state WPA officials had diligently rooted out evidence of political activity. He alleged that an increase in Ohio's WPA rolls was largely a result of the Bricker administration's failure to provide relief for thousands of Ohioans.[60]

Ohio had to provide relief for "unemployables" and "unemployed employables (not eligible for WPA projects)" turned back to the state after the WPA was established. Only a little over 100,000 were recipients of categorical aid from the state and Social Security Act grants to the states. Several hundred thousand persons not aided otherwise had to depend on the resources of their local governments and the meager contributions of the state. In 1936, Ohio spent considerably less than Illinois, which aided approximately the same number of those on relief. Illinois paid out $43,138,734 in relief funds; Ohio expended only $25,196,559. Pennsylvania, whose relief rolls were one and a half times greater than Ohio's, disbursed three times as much for relief.[61] In 1936, the General Assembly's appropriation for relief provided nine dollars per family in rural sections; ten dollars per month in semiurban counties, and twelve dollars in counties with large cities.[62] The following year, the state provided even less aid for relief.[63] During 1938 and 1939, the state of Ohio assumed only 16 percent of the cost of public aid borne by the federal, state, and local governments.[64]

In March 1937, a relief crisis broke out when Ohio's large cities announced that local funds were exhausted. Governor Davey, asserting no state money was available, urged the legislature to draw up a city enabling act to permit the municipalities to provide the revenues for half the cost of relief in their own communities.[65] The legislature did not see fit to take action on the governor's suggestion or anyone else's, and so additional suffering had to be borne by those already vulnerable.

During Governor Bricker's first term stopgap legislation (diversion of revenue from highway funds and nuisance taxes) continued to be the order of the day. Both the governor and the General Assembly urged local governments to assume the relief burden. Inadequate standards of relief began to deteriorate further. The number of general relief cases (families and individuals) rose from 86,737 in 1938 to 94,161 in 1939. On the other hand, Ohio's general relief expenditures decreased by nearly $2,000,000.[66] More than ever before, in the depression years, the relief burden fell on the local communities and the WPA.

Investigations into the relief situation in Toledo and Cleveland produced reports of desperate conditions. A study of 155 individuals and childless couples in Cleveland who, between 23 November and 7 December 1939, had been denied relief from the Emergency Division of Charities and Relief, revealed that as a result of this action 138 persons suffered from inadequate diets. They subsisted on such foods as

1) stale bread, tea, and beans; 2) fried mush; 3) apples, cereals and butter; 4) stale bread and occasional meals; 5) commodities and occasional food from relatives, neighbors or landlord; 6) apples, corn meal and sandwiches; 7) oatmeal; 8) apples, beans and squash.

One "frail looking man of 60" who lived alone "in rooms without heat except as he . . . [found] wood in the neighborhood" was reported to have "lived on apples and food which his landlord . . . on W. P. A. could give him, what he could salvage from garbage cans, and what he could beg from the market. He had no electricity and no coal oil for his lamp."[67]

A study conducted under the auspices of the Toledo Council of Social Agencies covering a 10 percent sample of 3,253 "employable" cases cut from relief rolls in September 1939 presented similar evidence of unmet needs. Findings indicated that early in November 1939 more than 67.4 percent of those included in the survey were "in varying degrees of actual need," many "living under unbelievable conditions." Investigators revealed that scavenging for food was common. Cases in "actual want" were reported as suffering from "lack of food and clothing and from illness resulting from insufficient fuel and/or food." More than a third of the families with children of school age stated that their youngsters had been absent from school during October 1939 because they lacked necessary food and clothing. Among 259 cases of the 325 studied for which data was available, nine families were found to have been evicted between the time relief was cut off and the time the study was made. Evictions were in process in eight more cases and had been threatened in another thirty-one.[68]

In December 1939, Mayor Harold H. Burton of Cleveland, a Republican, announced that the failure of the state government to provide funds forced the city to cut relief orders. Those lucky enough to remain on relief received 16 cents a day per person for food. The mayor blamed Governor Bricker for the suffering of the unemployed in Cleveland and elsewhere in the state. His eye on the Republican presidential nomination, Bricker engaged during November and December in a bitter debate with New Deal leaders over relief. He charged that the desperate relief situation in several Ohio cities had been created by the Roosevelt administration to embarrass him into calling the General Assembly and asking for an increase in taxes. Roosevelt responded that the state of Ohio provided average relief benefits of $16.65 per individual while the neighboring state of Pennsylvania expended $27.00. Governor Bricker also wanted to evade increasing old-age assistance payments from $30 to $40. Federal action required an increase in state contributions; and if the General Assembly met, it would have to raise revenue for this purpose, and this meant new taxes or an unbalanced budget. Mayor Burton claimed that the governor's scheme to enhance his political prestige by balancing the budget, creating a general fund surplus, and by refusing to contract a state debt for relief caused misery throughout the state.[69]

Other commentators, not politically involved, agreed with the mayor and added that the governor was successful because of an alliance with the rural majority in the Ohio General Assembly. The rural lawmakers had no desire to change the extent of the relief appropriations. Their counties benefited from the geographic distribution of relief, and the needs of those counties were met. For instance, rural Monroe County received $44.43 per case per month (1939) but spent only $21.17; it pocketed $23.26. Cuyahoga County received the largest state relief appropriation of all the Ohio counties, but divided among its numerous unemployed it amounted to only $5.99 per case per month. This meant that the county had to raise the difference between what it received from the state and what it spent per case.[70]

In 1940, the employment rate began to rise, and the worst features of Ohio's relief structure were somewhat obscured. Better economic conditions allowed the governor and the General Assembly to meet the state's minimum relief needs and thereby balance the budget without serious political repercussion. The great unemployment and relief problems were solved by conditions over which the state did not have control.

The resistance of Ohio to the idea that relief for the unemployed and unemployables was beyond the capacity of poor laws developed in the previous century kept the state from creating a workable federal-state partnership. The federal government went more than half way in creating programs and in funding them. Of the three Ohio governors between 1931 and 1940, only George White showed an awareness of the dimensions of the relief problem in modern society. By the end of his second term, he was calling for state control, professional leadership, and increased funding of relief. He proposed that the state assume the greater part of financing relief programs by raising revenue through an income tax. Together, he believed, the federal and state governments could remove the burden of relief from the shoulders of local government and provide an efficient, nonpartisan solution to a basic problem in modern America.

His successors, Davey and Bricker, all too often allowed political ambition to determine their course of action. The conventional wisdom dictated holding on to the familiar when change was occurring so rapidly. Those needing relief lacked political muscle, and since they were in a minority and federal programs provided help to blunt the worst of conditions, some politicians ignored their responsibility to all of their constituents. Neither Democrat Martin Davey nor Republican John Bricker wanted the onus of raising taxes. On several occasions, organized groups threatened a taxpayer revolt. Chambers of Commerce in the state believed that industry and commerce would be driven from Ohio if taxes were increased. Another reason for the resistance to increased taxes was the urban-rural split in the General Assembly. Rural legislators, Republican and Democrat, viewed the welfare problem as an urban one. A coalition of rural legislators and business community representatives defeated legislation designed to provide funds and progress in welfare administration in the state. As a consequence, Ohio's dependence on the federal government for welfare, already apparent prior to 1940, continued to increase.

1. Mauritz A. Hallgren, "Bankers and Bread Lines in Toledo," *Nation* 134 (1932): 397.

2. At this time, food allowances were so inadequate and the need for rent relief so pressing that very few persons considered the necessity of medical care and clothing (*Cleveland Plain Dealer*, 5 March 1933).

3. J. R. Stockham, "An Analysis of the Organizational Structure, Aims, and Tactics of the Workers' Alliance of America in Franklin County and Cuyahoga County, Ohio and in Hennepin County, Minnesota" (MASA thesis, Ohio State University, 1938), p. 1.

4. *Akron Beacon Journal*, 26 February 1933.

5. Leo Gallin, "The Plane of Living of Families on Public Relief in Akron, Ohio" (MASA thesis, Ohio State University, 1935), p. 34.

6. Committee on Economic Security, *Social Security in America*, published for the Social Security Board (Washington, 1937), Table 5, foldout between pp. 58–59.

7. Bureau of the Census, *Relief Expenditures by Governmental and Private Organizations, 1929 and 1931* (Washington, 1932), p. 9.

8. Cincinnati's experience was typical. The Community Chest used 60 percent of its budget for relief of the unemployed in 1931. In 1932, overwhelmed with those requesting aid, the need to support its traditional concerns, and with revenue declining, it cut unemployment relief to 12.4 percent of its

budget. Community Chest of Cincinnati and Hamilton County, *Twenty-Five Years, 1915–1940* (Cincinnati, 1940), p. 15.

9. American Public Welfare Association, *Poor Relief Laws: A Digest of Existing State Legislation* (Chicago, 1934), pp. 18–19. Aileen E. Kennedy, *The Ohio Poor Law and Its Administration* (Chicago, 1934), pp. 105–12.

10. The major urban areas were, in alphabetical order: Akron, Canton, Cincinnati, Cleveland, Columbus, Dayton, Springfield, Toledo, and Youngstown (Enid Baird, *Public and Private Aid in 116 Urban Areas, 1929–38* [Washington, 1942], pp. 87–95).

11. See Joanna C. Colcord et al., *Emergency Work Relief* (New York, 1932), pp. 27–30, 254–55.

12. *Cleveland Plain Dealer*, 6 February 1931.

13. *New York Times*, 17 October 1930; Eugene Roseboom and Francis Weisenburger, *A History of Ohio* (Columbus, 1953), p. 516.

14. The Ohio Plan for unemployment insurance was a pioneer effort. It called for a statewide pooled fund with employee and employer participation under public control. See Paul H. Douglas, *Social Security in the United States* (New York, 1939), p. 14. The Ohio Plan contrasted sharply with the American Plan; this proposal called for employer contribution and employer control.

15. For a full discussion of this point see Herbert Gaylord Warren, *Herbert Hoover and the Great Depression* (New York, 1959); Albert U. Romasco, *The Poverty of Abundance: Hoover, the Nation, the Depression* (New York, 1965); J. Joseph Huthmacher, *Senator Robert F. Wagner and the Rise of Urban Liberalism* (New York, 1968), chaps. 6–8.

16. Gifford Files, Group No. 73 (Series No. 50), State Representative Reports, President's Organization on Unemployment Relief Records, (National Archives). The creation of POUR, *in a limited way*, illustrated that the relief problem was beyond the scope of individual communities (William F. McDonald, *Federal Relief Administration and the Arts* [Columbus, Ohio, 1969], p. 15).

17. Gertrude Springer, "The New Deal and the Old Dole," *Survey Graphic* 22 (1933): 351.

18. White defeated Ingalls by over 200,000 votes. The state senate was divided between both parties. Franklin Roosevelt and Democratic congressional candidates did very well. Republicans were surprised by the magnitude of the Democratic party victory in Ohio.

19. *Laws of Ohio* (Columbus, 1933–34), 155, pt. 1: 50, 51, 61, 62, 194, 195, 672.

20. The *Cleveland Plain Dealer*, 8 June 1933, blasted the legislature for its evasion of duty, especially since the leadership in both political parties had announced that they would act after the federal government outlined its program.

21. Quoted in Arthur M. Schlesinger, Jr., *The Coming of the New Deal* (Boston, 1959), p. 264.

22. John P. Ries to Martin L. Davey, 18 September 1934, Davey Papers, Box 1 (Ohio State Museum).

23. State Relief Commission, *Manual* (n.p., 1933), pp. 303–12.

24. Dayton H. Frost, *Emergency Relief in Ohio* (Columbus, 1942), pp. 40–45.

25. The Federal Surplus Relief Corporation spent over $5,000,000 in Ohio prior to 1936 in distributing surplus commodities and for feeding drought-stricken cattle in Delaware, Ohio. The fattened cattle were slaughtered, and the meat was distributed through relief channels.

26. Frost, *Emergency Relief in Ohio*, p. 48; Mary V. Daugherty, ed., *The State Relief Commission and Its Activities* (Columbus, 1935), p. 35.

27. Administrative Reports, 6 December 1933, Box 25; 1 March 1934, Box 35, Civil Works Administration Records (National Archives), hereafter cited as CWA Records.

28. F. D. Henderson to Bruce McClure, 12 December 1933, Administrative Reports, Box 35, CWA Records.

29. This was a decline from the 200,000 monthly average employed by the CWA. For work relief figures for 1934–35, see T. E. Whiting, ed., *Final Statistical Report of the FERA* (Washington, 1942), p. 245. See also Searle F. Charles, *Minister of Relief: Harry Hopkins and the Depression* (Syracuse, N.Y., 1963), pp. 61–65; McDonald, *Federal Relief Administration and the Arts*, p. 67. The average monthly earnings of a CWA worker nationwide was $60.00, and under the Emergency Works Program of the FERA, it was $28.00.

30. Whiting, *Final Statistical Report of the FERA,* pp. 233–34.

31. Quoted in Frost, *Emergency Relief in Ohio*, pp. 137–39.

32. Whiting, *Final Statistical Report of the FERA*, pp. 233–34.

33. Frost, *Emergency Relief in Ohio*, Appendix H, p. 405.

34. R. L. Konigsberg, "Social Factors in the Transiency of Boys" (MASA thesis, Ohio State University, 1935).

35. J. D. Rinehart, "A Study of the Transient Problem in Columbus and Franklin County" (MASA thesis, Ohio State University, 1938).

36. Frost, *Emergency Relief in Ohio*, Appendix F, pp. 171, 394–95.

37. Whiting, *Final Statistical Report of the FERA*, pp. 228–30.

38. Ibid., pp. 231–32.

39. Cuyahoga County Relief Commission (CCRC), "Minutes," 17 July 1933, Files of the Cuyahoga County Welfare Department, Cleveland, Ohio.

40. D. L. Gates, "A Survey and Analysis of the Content of the Relief Families of Belmont County, Ohio" (MASA thesis, Ohio State University, 1934).

41. Relief payments in Pickaway County were as low as $2.00 a month per person (P. O. Josephson, "A Study of the Influence of the FERA and the SRC upon the Administration of Relief in Eight Selected Counties" [MASA thesis, Ohio State University, 1936], pp. 58–60, 89).

42. Roseboom and Weisenburger, *History of Ohio*, p. 521; Florence E. Parker, "Experience under State Old Age Pension Acts in 1934," *Monthly Labor Review* 41 (1935): 303–12. Although this plan was funded by the state, the counties bore the burden of relief for dependent children and the handicapped (approximately 30,600 recipients in November 1934).

43. Ralph J. Donaldson, "Martin L. Davey," in Ohio State Archaeological and Historical Society, ed., *The Governors of Ohio* (Columbus, 1954).

44. *Cleveland Plain Dealer*, 10 October 1934.

45. Davey to Chester P. Brown, 1 November 1934, Box 1, Governor Davey Papers.

46. Ohio Senate *Journal*, vol. 116, 91st Session (Columbus, 1934), pp. 25–26.

47. Ibid., pp. 51–52.

48. Whiting, *Final Statistical Report of the FERA*, p. 316.

49. *FERA Monthly Report*, March 1935, p. 18.

50. *Report of the President of the U.S. to the Congress of the Operations under the ERA Acts of 1935 and 1936* (Washington, 1937), p. 49.

51. Ibid., pp. 65, 161.

52. Donald S. Howard, *The WPA and Federal Relief Policy* (New York, 1943), p. 538.

53. Radio Address, WOSU, 22 February 1939, C. C. Stillman Papers, on file in the Director's Office, School of Social Administration, Ohio State University.

54. Ohio Department of Public Welfare, *Public Aid in Ohio, 1938–1941* (Columbus, 1942), p. 9 and table 3.

55. Howard, *The WPA and Federal Relief Policy*, pp. 537–42.

56. Letters on the Trump Affair, "State" Series, Ohio, Box 610, Works Progress Administration, Record Group 69 (National Archives), hereafter cited as WPA Records.

57. "The most generally accepted account is that the Black Legion originated in Ohio in 1931 when several hundred men who had violated the rules of the Ku Klux Klan dyed their robes black and formed a separate organization" (Morris Janowitz, "Black Legion on the March," in Daniel Aaron, ed. *America in Crisis* [New York, 1952], p. 305).

58. Carl Watson to Col. L. Westbrook, WPA Assistant Administrator, 28 May 1936, "State" Series, Ohio, Box 610, WPA Records. WPA files indicate that all charges of political activity, no matter how absurd, were thoroughly investigated.

59. C. C. Stillman to George Babcock, 24 October 1935, "State" Series, Ohio, Box 610, WPA Records.

60. Ibid.; *New York Times*, 29 November 1939.

61. Whiting, *Final Statistical Report of the FERA*, pp. 305, 316, 318.

62. Ohio Senate *Journal*, vol. 116, pt. 27, 91st Session (Columbus, 1937), p. 509.

63. Whiting, *Final Statistical Report of the FERA*, pp. 316, 397.

64. Ohio Department of Public Welfare, *Public Aid in Ohio, 1938–1941*, table 2.

65. Ohio Senate *Journal*, vol. 117, 92d Session (Columbus, 1938), pp. 342–43.

66. Ohio Department of Public Welfare, *Public Aid in Ohio, 1938–1941*, table A, p. 6, and table 16.

67. American Association of Social Workers, Cleveland Chapter, *The Humane Side of a Relief Crisis* (Cleveland, 1939), pp. 20–25.

68. Toledo Council of Social Agencies, *The Toledo Relief Survey* (Toledo, 1939), pp. 2, 18–19.

69. *Cleveland Plain Dealer*, 8 December 1939. For all the charges and countercharges, see the *New York Times*, 23 November-22 December 1939.

70. Clayton Fritchey, "Relief in Ohio," *American Mercury*, May 1940, pp. 74–81.

Robert F. Hunter

Virginia and the New Deal

PROBABLY NO STATE IN THE UNION RECEIVED THE NEW DEAL WITH less hospitality than the Old Dominion. The reaction was not totally negative, for many Virginians demonstrated enthusiasm for Roosevelt, listened to his "fireside chats," and responded to his personal appeal by voting for him in substantial majorities. Yet the New Deal had little to offer that would meet Virginia's social and economic needs, as they were conceived by Virginia voters and their political leaders. In the New Deal programs for money, banking, agriculture, industrial recovery, relief, public works, and social security, they found little that roused their enthusiasm and much that provoked hostility. Moreover, some even perceived underlying it all a threat to the traditional social order.

The Democratic party dominated Virginia politics, but Virginia was not a democratic community in the 1930s, if indeed it ever had been since the seventeenth century.[1] V. O. Key in his classic *Southern Politics in State and Nation* (1949) called Virginia a "political museum piece" in the style of eighteenth-century England, an apt comparison, for it was generally agreed that Harry Flood Byrd had the Old Dominion in his pocket.

Byrd had been the dominant personality in Virginia politics for a decade when Franklin D. Roosevelt was elected president in 1932. Byrd emerged in 1922 as the new leader of the political organization developed during the progressive era by Senator Thomas S. Martin.[2] Three years of uncertainty followed Martin's death in 1919. Then young (35) State Senator Harry F. Byrd, lineal descendant of the renowned William Byrd of Westover, son and nephew of leaders in Virginia politics, and a successful newspaper publisher and apple grower, wisely allied with Senator Claude Swanson against Governor Westmoreland Davis. In the 1922 contest between Davis and Swanson for the latter's seat in the United States Senate, Byrd as the new chairman of the Democratic State Central Committee engineered an overwhelming victory for Swanson. Byrd easily won the governorship as the recognized leader of the Democratic party in Virginia in 1925.

Byrd was a very popular governor, and for good reasons. His social credentials were impeccable, his business acumen impressive, and his political sway with the legislature was so thorough that he was in a position to formulate and execute his own program. He was no "do-nothing" governor, but prompted a flurry of activity as a "business progressive" leader.[3] He employed a professional research agency from New York to study Virginia's government, and on the basis of its report reorganized the state government along lines conducive to greater efficiency. In addition, Byrd recommended a long list of constitutional amendments to the legislature, most of which were adopted. Notable was the short ballot, which meant a reduction in the number of elective officials with a consequent saving in campaign expenditures and an increase in the governor's power of appointment. Economy in government was Byrd's major concern as governor, and one of his amendments virtually forbade the commonwealth to borrow money. Without a vote of the people, the state government could issue short-term notes only to meet casual deficits in revenue, to redeem a previous liability of the state, to suppress insurrection, repel invasion, or defend the state in time of war. This rule, the basis of Virginia's highly touted "pay-as-you-go" policy, was occasioned by an unsuccessful campaign during the 1920s to put over a bonded indebtedness program to build highways. Byrd fought the spenders to a standstill, then fixed the constitution to cripple the chances of a successful new movement for borrowing money on the state's credit for any kind of public service program —roads, schools, or anything else—for years to come.

Byrd also persuaded the legislature to reduce taxes on property and investments, which enhanced his popularity among the small number of Virginians who were active voters, most of whom were property-owners and investors. This arrangement prompted critics of the Byrd regime in and out of Virginia to brand it a Tory government, of, by, and for the property-owners. An unknown wag once said that Virginia's government was "of the Byrds, by the Byrds, and for the Byrds." This was a half-truth at best, for there existed no insurmountable obstacles between the white voter and the ballot box, or even between the black voter and the ballot box to the same degree as in other southern states. So long as Virginia voters were convinced that the "organization" provided honest and economical government, few felt any compulsion to vote. Many allowed their poll taxes to lapse, thereby disfranchising themselves, quite agreeably to the Byrd organization since it reduced the cost of rounding up the faithful few who could be depended upon to vote right. This was by definition a politics of apathy.

The nomination of New York's Alfred E. Smith for the presidency in 1928 threw Virginia Democratic leaders into consternation. The event occurred in the middle of Byrd's term as governor and coincided with the reelection bid of Carter Glass for his second full term in the United States Senate. Democratic organization leaders swallowed hard and supported Smith, but the voters did not follow their lead, with the result that Virginia cast its electoral votes for Hoover in 1928. In later years, after World War II, Byrd would approve tacitly the support of Republican presidential candidates by Virginia Democratic voters, a policy labeled "golden silence." But the time was not yet ripe for that, nor would it become so during the New Deal years. The "Hoovercrat" party in Virginia proved to be short-lived. In the gubernatorial election of 1929, Republican hopes in the candidacy of William Moseley Brown were dashed when the electorate overwhelmingly endorsed the organization-approved candidate, John Garland Pollard. A student of this election says it not only signified Virginia's return to the Solid South, but also gave a resounding stamp of approval to Byrd's program.[4] The Virginia electorate echoed that approval repeatedly during the New Deal years in their voting behavior.

As the Democratic National Convention of 1932 approached, a Roosevelt-Smith deadlock followed by a compromise candidate loomed as a possibility. Byrd went to a Chicago preconvention meeting of party leaders determined to support Jouett Shouse for the presidency, but found little support for Shouse. So he reluctantly agreed to back Roosevelt "when the time should come." But on the third ballot at the convention, which nearly brought disaster to Roosevelt, Byrd disappointed Roosevelt by failing to deliver Virginia's twenty-four favorite-son votes. Byrd, writes Frank Freidel, "seemed more interested in a deadlock."[5] Although not enthusiastic for Roosevelt, Glass did finally make a single campaign speech one week before election day assailing Hoover for spending too much money. "At the expense of the taxpayers," Glass declared, "President Hoover has converted the Treasury at Washington into a national pawnshop and infected the central government with the fatal germ of financial socialism."[6] Nearly 300,000 Virginians voted for Roosevelt, about a 2½-to-1 victory over Hoover, the greatest number of votes cast in the history of Virginia elections to that time in spite of the relatively small turnout. Glass was disturbed at the size of Roosevelt's nationwide victory and called it "too great for comfort." It portended, he said, "much trouble for those of us at Washington who want to see sane things done and insane things prevented."[7] And when Glass was offered the post of secretary of the treasury, he declined when Roosevelt refused to rule out inflation of the currency.[8] Thus, Glass and Byrd were anti–New Dealers even before the New Deal began, Byrd because of his own ambition for the White House, Glass because of his fear of inflation.

Rumors of a cabinet appointment for Byrd circulated in spite of his obvious anti–New Deal stance, but by Christmas he had decided against accepting one if offered.[9] Roosevelt appointed Swanson to be secretary of the navy, thereby creating a vacant Senate seat to which Governor Pollard quickly appointed Byrd.[10] He ran successfully against Republican Henry Wise for Swanson's unexpired term in November 1933, and in 1934 was elected for the first of six times to a full term in the Senate.

Byrd repeatedly denied that he intervened in the electoral process in Virginia state politics from his senatorial post, but the evidence that he possessed and used influence is too convincing to be disbelieved. Nearly every Virginia Democrat who ran for the office of governor, congressman, or member of the state legislature did so only after clearance by the organization. The name of the Byrd-approved candidate quickly passed down to the courthouse "rings" that comprised the local element in the structure, and the regular registered Democratic voters, some of whom had their poll taxes paid for them by the organization, predictably endorsed him. Some exceptions to this occurred, but the organization was flexible enough to give ground on occasion.

Two gubernatorial elections were held in Virginia during the New Deal, in 1933 and 1937. George C. Peery of Tazewell had Byrd's support in the first of these. Peery was regarded as no more a reformer than Pollard, if as much; and a Norfolk lawyer, Vivian L. Page, challenged him in the primary with a call for Virginians to "rise up and force from the administration extension of the Roosevelt 'new deal' to this State." Two more Democratic aspirants announced for the post, Page withdrew, and Peery received nearly two-thirds of the primary votes. Byrd faced a greater challenge in the gubernatorial contest of 1937, and was forced to give ground. James H. Price, lieutenant governor under both Governors Pollard and Peery, announced in July 1935, without benefit of Byrd's prior approval, that he intended to run for governor in 1937. Byrd made no public statement about Price's candidacy for eighteen months, until the end of 1936. Two days before Christmas, the organization's opposition to the popular Price collapsed suddenly and completely as the members of the "high command" in Richmond, including Byrd's right-hand man, State Comptroller E. R. Combs, announced their support of Price. All Byrd would say was, "I have no desire whatsoever to exert a personal influence over political affairs in Virginia except to lend my support as a citizen to a more efficient and progressive government in the State, and to this end I will always cooperate."[11] It was no secret that Byrd would have preferred another candidate, but none could be found to challenge Price. Byrd settled instead for making a shambles of Price's governorship by means of an intransigent legislature.[12]

Virginia's delegation to the House of Representatives during the New Deal years was remarkably stable. The nine members who were there during the Hundred Days were still there at the beginning of Roosevelt's third term, with the exception of Andrew Jackson Montague, who died in 1937.[13] Divergence among them did not appear during the Hundred Days, when none of them voted against anything, but such harmony could not last. Glass and Byrd were followed by Congressmen Colgate Darden, Willis Robertson, and Howard Smith in a march to the right. Darden later became governor, and then president of the University of Virginia. Robertson's leadership in money and banking legislation was widely recognized before he replaced Glass in the Senate in 1946. Judge Smith acquired a reputation as a formidable enemy of organized labor, and in 1938 easily brushed off a challenge for his seat from young William E. Dodd, Jr., who was sponsored by both the administration and John L. Lewis. John Flannagan of Bristol and Clifton Woodrum of Roanoke were the most consistent supporters of the president. Flannagan stood alone after 1937, however, and managed it mainly because his home base, the "Fighting Ninth" District in the far southwest corner of the state where Byrd's power was minimal, was a traditional stronghold of Republicans and anti-machine Democrats. The Norfolk area (Second Congressional District) was another spot where the organization had political problems, not so much because Republicans abounded there as because it was urban. Byrd disparaged it as "the most ardent New Deal district in the State," and a self-styled New Dealer, *Portsmouth Star* publisher and editor Norman R. Hamilton, a bitter foe of the Byrd organization, defeated incumbent Colgate Darden for his House seat in 1936. During his term in Congress,

however, Hamilton voted to return to committee four out of five administration bills, so the administration understandably gave him no help in
1938. James Farley, in relaying information to Roosevelt about the
Darden-Hamilton contest, called Darden "a straight-shooter and . . . a
man out in the open in his opposition."[14] The New Deal opponents were
without question the strongest figures in the Virginia delegation to the
House of Representatives during the New Deal years.

Byrd was elected to the Senate for a six-year term in 1934, so his seat
was not involved in the elections of 1936 or 1938. Glass had been elected in
1922 and 1928, and was up for his third term in 1936. He received the
endorsement of the *Richmond Times-Dispatch* in August 1935, "irrespective of whether he has opposition, and no matter who his opponent is, if
any." Randolph Leigh of Fairfax was romantically inclined enough to
challenge the entrenched senator in the Democratic primary. His quixotic
campaign lasted five months, and was totally extinguished months before
the primary. "We have not always agreed with the senior Senator, but we
accept unreservedly the universal verdict that he is able, fearless, and
sincere," wrote *Times-Dispatch* editor Virginius Dabney, a liberal who
was frequently in sharp disagreement with the policies of the Byrd organization. "The fate of Mr. Leigh is likely to be the fate of any man who enters
the lists against him."[15] In November, 234,980 Virginians voted for
Roosevelt over Landon, and 244,518 voted for Glass over his unknown
Republican challenger. Glass received nearly 10,000 more votes than the
president in Virginia without exerting himself to make a single campaign
speech. Byrd even improved on that record in 1940 when he received over
38,000 more votes than Roosevelt in Virginia. Byrd, unchallenged by a
Republican candidate, received 274,260 votes, and 235,961 Virginians
voted for Roosevelt over Willkie. The Byrd organization was never more
firmly entrenched than it was in 1940. Instead of being forced to the wall by
the New Deal, it had recaptured a temporarily lost political stronghold in
the Second Congressional District and had brushed off self-styled New
Dealers as challengers.

The New Deal economic programs could hardly have been expected to
generate enthusiasm in such a political environment. However, it was not
merely the political strength of anti–New Deal forces that acted as a
damper. The programs themselves were with few exceptions substantially
ill-suited to Virginia's social and economic needs, not only as such needs
were conceived by the political leaders, but even as they actually existed.

The depression did not affect Virginia so adversely as other states for a number of reasons. Virginia was underdeveloped industrially and so lacked the masses of industrial unemployed. An accurate figure for Virginia's unemployed in 1933 is difficult to obtain, but a reasonable estimate places it between 75,000 and 100,000, or between three and four percent of the state's population of two-and-a-half million. Moreover, her leading industry was cigarette manufacturing, which had a reputation for being "depression proof." Consumption figures showed that cigarette smokers consumed tobacco as much during depression as during prosperity; presumably smokers consumed tobacco as a luxury when employed and as consolation when unemployed, at about the same rate. Other industries important in Virginia such as chemicals and rayon were not as seriously affected by the drop in demand and production as the average American industry. In agriculture, Virginia was less committed to commercial crops dependent upon distant markets, but devoted more of her cultivated acres to diversified farming for subsistence or local markets. Therefore, Virginia farmers, though not wealthy, suffered less from the depression than cotton or wheat growers.[16]

In no areas of New Deal activity did Virginia cooperate less with the federal government than in relief to the unemployed and the construction of public works under both PWA and WPA. The formula for dollar-matching in the FERA program was not based exclusively upon population but included other factors such as per capita wealth, income, and tax-paying ability. Relief Administrator Harry Hopkins was given discretion in working out a formula (and making exceptions to it) for the distribution of funds. When he announced in July that the states would be required to match federal relief funds "in whole or in part," Governor Pollard admitted he had been avoiding the issue by reminding inquirers that the Virginia General Assembly was not scheduled to meet in 1933. But when assemblymen themselves called for a special session in August, the governor said, with one eye on the clause in the Virginia Constitution that forbade borrowing for such purposes, "If the question is put up to us, we shall have to meet it, and the only way to do it is by raising taxes." Pollard then appealed to Byrd, who attempted to persuade the FERA that the $3 million Virginia was spending annually on roads constituted direct unemployment relief. When in March 1934 Hopkins made it clear that he wanted Virginia to put up $2 million in order to qualify for $4 million in federal relief funds, Governor Peery followed the lead of his predecessor and sat on his hands.[17]

In the fall of 1934, Virginius Dabney of the *Times-Dispatch* was becoming embarrassed by the state government's attitude toward relief. A survey of Virginia and her neighboring states revealed that the unemployment and relief conditions shown in tables 1 and 2 existed on October first:

TABLE 1

UNEMPLOYMENT

State	Population	Unemployed	Percentage of Population
Virginia	2,435,000	84,863	3.4
North Carolina	3,244,000	83,363	2.5
West Virginia	1,761,000	95,213	5.4
Maryland	1,653,000	84,502	5.1

TABLE 2

RELIEF

State	Active Relief Caseload	Number of People	Percentage of Population
Virginia	36,418	156,597	6.4
North Carolina	77,105	331 551	12.2
West Virginia	82,619	355,262	20.2
Maryland	41,387	177,964	10.7

Virginia had a smaller relief load in proportion to population than any of her neighbors, but eligibility requirements were between two and six times as stringent. The average of relief given throughout the state in September (1934) was $9.50 per case, or $2.20 per relief individual. The average for the nation was over $20 per case, and for North Carolina it was $9.48, for West Virginia $14.42, and for Maryland $30.24. Therefore, Virginia's standard of relief was about the same as North Carolina's, but 35 percent below that of West Virginia and over 70 percent below that of Maryland. It was harder for a needy family to get on relief in Virginia, and when accepted, it received less help.[18]

When Glass, Byrd, and Peery fended off complaints from Washington by contending that Virginia paid heavy federal taxes—a specious argument since Virginia ranked high only because cigarette manufacturers purchased tax stamps to affix to cigarette packages—and that the state was spending $3 million a year on highways and calling it work relief, Hopkins became increasingly angry. But the anticipated "crackdown" by Hopkins on Virginia never came, even though the state government never produced the matching funds. Although he withheld funds from certain other states for such cause, Hopkins was aware of the power of Byrd and Glass in the Senate and respected it.[19]

Widespread comment about the allegedly demoralizing effects of relief payments prompted the *Times-Dispatch* to send a staff writer, Cabell Phillips, on a tour of selected counties. In Virginia's Northern Neck (near Washington, between the Potomac and the Rappahannock), Phillips found the most resentment against the FERA. Within a stone's throw of the capital, "the economic and social dominance of a feudal aristocracy" was preserved as nowhere else in Virginia. The large landowners resented this threat to the dependence of their workers on themselves. Across Chesapeake Bay in Accomac County (the Eastern Shore), he found virtually no dissension; fruit and vegetable growers and fishermen, all hit by low prices, were grateful for FERA help. At South Boston, in the heart of the tobacco region, the director of the emergency crop loan office told Phillips there was some superficial opposition to the FERA on the ground that it had made labor scarce, but the majority of the families he knew were "eager to get off the rolls and back on their feet as quickly as possible." Concluding his survey, Phillips believed the effects of relief were in fact demoralizing, but there was no evidence that relief had affected the available supply of farm labor. "There is probably no agency of the New Deal more completely victimized by misunderstanding and prejudice than the FERA," he concluded. "It is the vociferous minority, plus a few Bourbons of the 'let them eat cake' school of social thought, who have made relief a whipping boy for the shortcomings of markets, crops, the weather or their own initiative."[20] FERA assistance in Virginia was welcomed only by those who received the checks. Their numbers were kept few and their checks small insofar as the state's policy-makers had power to control them.

A portion of the National Industrial Recovery Act, passed in June 1933, established a $3.3 billion fund out of which the president was authorized to make loans to states, cities, and counties for the construction of public works. Borrowers were required to repay only 70 percent of the amount; the other 30 percent was a grant. Both Glass and Byrd held Harold Ickes of the PWA in as high esteem as they did anyone in Roosevelt's administration—higher than most. Governor Pollard appointed a three-man State Advisory Board for Public Works in August 1933. Highway construction was a type of public work that Byrd could hardly oppose, and a $16 million loan from the PWA fund for that purpose in Virginia was anticipated. Ironically, Byrd's own handiwork as governor proved an obstacle: the Virginia Constitution forbade the state's borrowing money for such purpose, and the president, aware of this, indicated he would withhold approval. The Virginia legislature promptly enacted a new "bond code" permitting the cities and counties to qualify for PWA loans and grants; but this did little good in the case of highway building, for the Byrd reforms had included also the transfer of all authority of public roads in Virginia to the state government. All of the PWA money expended in Virginia with few exceptions was for public buildings.

With $16 million for highways out of reach, Byrd shifted to a plan for building a scenic highway along the crest of the Blue Ridge Mountains in Virginia and the Great Smoky Mountains in North Carolina. When it was first proposed in September 1933, the *Times-Dispatch* editor credited Governor Pollard with the idea, although Byrd, Robert L. Doughton of North Carolina, and Roosevelt himself would have taken exception to such claim. In any event, it was Byrd who headed a committee of Virginians who successfully sought federal support for the project.

The Virginia PWA Advisory Board completed its work and relinquished office in March 1934, leaving its executive officer and state engineer, Colonel James A. Anderson, to supervise the execution of projects under way. Greeted at first by Virginians as a gigantic pork barrel that would bestow upon favored constituencies "white elephants in granite and steel commemorating the short-sighted benevolence of some pandering congressman," PWA had to be "sold" to Virginians by the board. The board performed its public relations task well, and Colonel Anderson did his more complex job even better. A characteristic type in the administration of the Virginia government, Anderson graduated from the Virginia Military Institute in 1913, emerged from the war a lieutenant colonel at 26, and joined the VMI faculty. In 1933, he became consulting engineer for the State Advisory Board for Public Works, did the board's supervisory work himself, and became acting director, then director, of the PWA program in Virginia. In three years, he handled $23 million in federal funds and supervised 157 projects scattered over the state. Not one to project himself into the limelight, Anderson ran his office with quiet efficiency, where many noted the absence of confusion in spite of the rush of business. Not a great deal of public service was rendered, but that which was provided was administered with efficiency and integrity. The Byrd organization insisted upon this.[21]

By the fall of 1933, it was evident that PWA was moving too slowly to provide work relief for needy unemployed and that the FERA was unable to cope with the problem because of its size. Three million families in the nation receiving less than twenty dollars a month presented a staggering challenge. Hopkins persuaded Roosevelt to detach $400 million from PWA funds and allow him to set up an emergency work relief program to be called the Civil Works Administration. Its twenty weeks of tenure were stormy, no less in Virginia than elsewhere. Virginia received immediately over $500,000 for 188 projects, and before CWA closed shop in Virginia at the end of March 1934 nearly $12 million had been spent. The state administrator of both the CWA and the FERA, William A. Smith, distinguished himself by working often eighteen hours a day with "if anything, too much conscientious devotion to duty, [and] moreover, a rare quality of sympathy and understanding for the people he tried to help."[22] The conscience of William Smith, however, did not permeate the CWA throughout Virginia, for it was reported that in various counties the "courthouse gangs" were "handling CWA money like so much plunder." The nation was rocked by a widespread CWA scandal in January 1934, and Virginia's part in it was not entirely innocent. The CWA, virtually thrown together overnight, had no chance to protect itself against predators; and no one can claim that the species was extinct in Virginia, regardless of the Byrd organization's deserved reputation for honesty in handling public funds.[23]

The transition was begun early in 1935 from the direct relief program of the FERA to the work relief program of the WPA. When the new $4.88 billion work relief bill was proposed in Congress in January, it encountered trouble in the Senate, Glass leading an uprising against the bill in the Appropriations Committee that he chaired. Three Virginia members of the House of Representatives also rebelled against the work relief bill; Darden, Robertson, and Smith objected to giving the president a free hand with so much money.[24] Byrd led a floor fight against the entire works measure as soon as it left committee; he proposed an amendment to cut $3 billion out of the $4.88 billion appropriation, insisting that "great public works and social service should await recovery." Besides, said Byrd, the PWA still had over $1.5 billion unspent after two years—why add another $4 billion now? In fact, much of the $1.5 billion that had been spent by the PWA had not gone for relief. "We find honeycombed through the Secretary's report such allocations as $13 million to the NRA, $700,000 to the FPC, and $500,000 to the general accounting office," he protested. "I do not see that these funds were used for relief work."[25] But his amendment was lost, and the entire $4.88 billion was appropriated.

The FERA came to an end in Virginia as it did in other states in November 1935, while the transition to the WPA was in progress. In sixteen states, the number of WPA workers in proportion to population exceeded the national average in each year between 1936 and 1939, inclusive, three of them southern border states (West Virginia, Kentucky, and Oklahoma). On the other hand, in seventeen states the proportion never reached the national average in any one of the four years, including Virginia. The Old Dominion had a WPA enrollment of 58 percent of the national average in 1936, dropped to 45 percent in 1938, and climbed back to 50 percent in 1939. When WPA workers across the nation averaged $45.92 per month in 1936, Virginians on the WPA received $25.40. By 1940, Virginians had been raised to $39.12, but the national average meanwhile had gone up to $50.81.[26] In terms of expenditures of the WPA by states, Virginia ranked at the very bottom. The average per capita expenditure for the nation for WPA purposes during the four years (1936–39) was $12.29—for Virginia, $4.46. No other state was so low on this scale.[27]

The program of relief payments to the unemployed from either the federal or the state treasury was unpopular in Virginia. Foot-dragging in Richmond was obvious in implementing state participation in the FERA program, and the transition from the FERA to the WPA did not alter the picture greatly. Since more WPA money was spent in Pennsylvania than in the entire South, southern politicians opposed the federal relief programs for reasons similar to the antebellum issue over internal improvements. It was not that the southern states eschewed the federal benefits so much as that they resented paying federal taxes only to see the lion's share of benefits paid to states outside the South. Relief was an urban problem, and Virgina was still a rural state. Add to that the conditioned reflex of Virginia's political leaders against federal expenditures for public services as a matter of principle, and Virginia's low regard for the WPA was hardly surprising.

The program for industrial recovery found even less acceptance in Virginia than the New Deal relief programs. Virginia's largest industry was tobacco manufacturing, with cotton textile production a poor second. More than that, textiles and other Virginia industries such as coal, foodstuffs, pulp and paper, chemicals, and rayon saw depression demand drop less than in most industries. There did not arise from Virginia any demand for such meddling in the affairs of business and industry as was represented by the National Recovery Administration.

The basic goals of the NRA seemed to be to help industrial leaders rationalize their production systems to control output and raise prices, and then through Section 7(a) to encourage unions to organize and engage in collective bargaining. Cigarette manufacturers had no need of such aid, for they had adequate control of output and prices by means of their well-organized oligopoly. Therefore, they resented the implications of Section 7(a) all the more and fought off the imposition of any "code of fair competition" for over eighteen months, at which time the NRA was nearing the end of its days.[28]

Cotton textile production in Virginia ranked sixth in the South, even though Virginia boasted the largest number of spindles under one roof at Dan River Mills in Danville. President Robert R. West of that company played an important role in the drafting of NRA Code Number One, the Cotton Textile Code,[29] but still had doubts about the program's prospects for success. When a fellow manufacturer suggested refusing to pay the processing tax and another urged closing mills in protest, he upbraided them, saying, "For us to visit upon our people the affliction of loss of employment, purely out of spite toward an inept Government, is entirely out of reason."[30] The program was not a success in textiles partly because many mill executives were not interested in a static share of the market, and partly because nearly all of them resented Section 7(a).

The most persistent complaint was that the NRA discriminated against small business. "Thousands of the very concerns which are publicly exhibiting the blue eagle are privately cursing the symbol as a black buzzard," Carter Glass wrote Walter Lippmann.[31] NRA chief Hugh Johnson admitted to Glass that it was a problem, but the trouble as he saw it was that small business offended even more than big business in exploiting labor.[32] Clothing manufacture, for example, essentially an adjunct of the cotton textile industry in the South, was a source of complaints that the smallest firms could not, and many of the larger firms would not, abide by the NRA codes.[33] The impact of the NRA upon the food products industry provoked a chorus of complaints about the wage and hour rules. Prices for bakery goods, remarked a small Richmond baker, "naturally are set by the larger factors in the industry and the smaller must conform." They had to pay higher wages for shorter hours, plus "more than double the former price for flour," and then accept for nearly half their output the prices prevailing before any of these changes.[34] In August 1934, members of the Baltimore Canned Food Exchange, which operated canneries, declared it impossible to pay the wage scale of the canning industry code because competitors in Virginia were paying less than code wages. An NRA official, asking Carter Glass about a report that he had encouraged canners to ignore NRA rules, had the temerity to threaten curtailment of FERA purchases of canned tomatoes in Virginia, and received a scorching reply. Glass had indeed received complaints from canners in the initial stages of the NRA to the effect that the requirements threatened them with bankruptcy. When he had taken up the question with Hugh Johnson, Glass had received what seemed to him the "brutal answer" that marginal firms unable to pay code wages for code hours would have to go out of business. "The NRA has impaired scores of the smaller industries of the country, especially in the South, and is proceeding to destroy others," Glass charged. "If you or any of the other bureaucrats connected with the system have any pride in the accomplishment, you are welcome to it."[35]

Local NRA compliance boards in Virginia had their problems. "There is a sincere desire on the part of the best element in this vicinity to make the [President's Reemployment] Agreement workable," reported a Norfolk compliance board official in November 1933, "but there is, I feel a lack of appreciation of what the President's Agreement could do with the cooperation of all concerned."[36] In Richmond, the Standard Drug Company deliberately sold merchandise at below-code prices beginning in the fall of 1934, and formally entered a demurrer against an injunction on the ground that both the NRA act and the code were unconstitutional. The company carefully avoided selling in interstate commerce in order to avoid a federal injunction, and competitors who tried to obey the code soon gave up the effort. A Washington NRA official declared in disgust in February 1935 that there was no hope for favorable action in the Virginia state courts whether or not the NRA was renewed for another two years. He added, "It is a question of either testing out the meaning of the phrase 'in or affecting interstate commerce' now, or else sitting by and watching the breakdown of this Code spread over the entire country."[37] The test came in May with the Schechter decision, which the NRA failed by a unanimous verdict of the Supreme Court. Meanwhile, the breakdown of the NRA codes was well advanced in Virginia months before that time. In fact, no important Virginia industry gave them the support necessary to make them fulfill their purpose.

Only gradually did it appear that in areas other than money, banking, securities, and perhaps electric power did the New Deal propose to reform existing institutions with permanent alterations. In agriculture, the purposes of the New Deal government were not altogether clear at the outset, certainly not to Senator Byrd. He voted for the AAA when it was passed in May 1933, in the reasonable belief that its purpose was to provide relief to the farmer and nothing more. Senator Glass, on the other hand, voted against it and every other farm bill considered during the New Deal. Most of the House delegation became steadily more skeptical of the farm program. Burch showed interest in the tobacco program, and Bland exerted himself for Eastern Shore potato growers; but only Flannagan was a consistent supporter of the AAA. The New Deal farm program was received in Virginia with a minimum of enthusiasm mainly because it had little to offer Virginia farmers, with the exception of tobacco growers. The family farm predominated in Virginia agriculture, with comparatively little commitment to either cotton or tobacco.

The most important trend in early twentieth-century southern farming was the increase in number and decrease in average size of farms, which accompanied an increasing commitment of land use to cotton and tobacco and increasing yields per acre in both crops. Virginia farmers did not expand their production of either cotton or tobacco commensurately, even though Virginia farms decreased in size and expanded in number. Virginia cotton, grown only in a few Southside counties, averaged less than 60,000 bales a year before the New Deal and dropped to 37,000 bales by 1933, a fraction of one percent of the nation's crop. The high cotton prices of the 1920s deteriorated until by 1932 five-cent cotton returned less than the cost of production. Cotton production in the United States was shifting westward until by mid-century well over half of the nation's crop was grown west of the Mississippi River. Cotton growers in Virginia, marginal in both the geographic and the economic sense, were in economic straits from which the AAA program proved powerless to retrieve them, for whatever price improvement the AAA effected was offset by their increasing costs.

Virginia was the leading tobacco-growing state from early times into the early twentieth century, when it lost ground to other states. North Carolina in the 1930s grew forty percent of the nation's tobacco, Kentucky about twenty percent, and Virginia ranked third with about ten percent. During the New Deal, tobacco acreage came under strict controls while tobacco growers increased average yields per acre phenomenally.

As soon as the New Deal leaders thought the banking crisis was in hand in March 1933, Roosevelt asked Congress for a program of farm relief, granting powers to Secretary of Agriculture Henry A. Wallace to lease lands to remove them from production of cotton, wheat, corn, hogs, cattle, sheep, rice, tobacco, and dairy products. Virginia cotton growers were slow to sign contracts with the AAA in 1933, but more entered the program in 1934 and 1935. Participation of Virginia cotton growers rose from 36 to 69 percent in 1934, and to 93 percent in 1935. The reason for it is not hard to find: the Bankhead Cotton Control Act of 1934 introduced compulsory in the place of voluntary controls, utilizing the tax-exemption certificate or warrant as the control device for enforcing crop quota agreements. When the cotton crop was being harvested and ginned in the late summer of 1934, it appeared that the Bankhead Act had been a success, although it was difficult to separate its effects from those of the severe drought and the boll weevil. In Virginia, where the drought and the boll weevil had little effect, cotton growers exceeded their allotments, resulting in a Virginia market for unneeded tax-exemption certificates, worth between $15 and $20 a bale, in the hands of southwestern cotton farmers who fell below their quotas. The Bankhead Cotton Control Act had played an unexpected role as crop insurance, with Virginia growers helping to pay the premiums.[38] But Virginia enemies of the AAA cotton program found it unassailable in light of strong support for it in the Gulf Coast cotton states.

Tobacco was declared a basic crop in the AAA of 1933, but more effort was expended in working out a satisfactory parity base than in developing an acreage-reduction program. The period between August 1919 and July 1929 was agreed upon as a parity base, during which prices averaged about twenty cents per pound.[39] When the markets opened in late August 1933, opening floor prices averaged between ten and twelve cents, and tobacco growers in neighboring North Carolina loudly demanded a tobacco "holiday": that is to say, a government order to close the tobacco auction markets until the tobacco manufacturing companies could be persuaded to offer better prices.[40] To clear the confusion, the AAA decided to deal directly with the companies and in October worked out an agreement. The buyers agreed to pay an average minimum price of 17 cents per pound for all flue-cured tobacco—which comprised roughly half the total crop —purchased between 25 September 1933 and 31 March 1934 for use in the

United States, an estimated 250 million pounds (the amount unsold on 25 September). If any buyer averaged under 17 cents, he agreed to pay the difference to the secretary of agriculture, who would distribute it to growers. In addition, if any buyer failed to purchase his "normal quantity," he agreed to pay the secretary 17 cents for each pound short. Meanwhile, a hurried campaign was conducted to sign up growers to agreements to limit acreage and production. The arrangement worked a minor miracle for tobacco growers. As in neighboring tobacco states, Virginia growers' 1933 income was more than triple their 1932 income—up from $2.6 million to $9.1 million.[41] The joy of the tobacco growers was not shared by tobacco manufacturers, who depended heavily on foreign markets. William T. Reed, president of Larus and Brother Company of Richmond and close personal friend of Senator Byrd, complained that his company's export business, which netted $100,000 annually, had been hurt already by the reciprocal trade agreements program. "With the added expenses that are now being put on us," he concluded, "there is nothing left for us to do but go outside."[42] Reed was planning to establish new factories in Newfoundland and Australia.

The details of the tobacco program for 1934 were publicized in December 1933. Since the object was to reduce the total flue-cured crop from over 700 million pounds to about 500 million pounds, growers were expected to cut acreage about thirty percent. The farmer could choose as his base acreage either his average for 1931-33 or 85 percent of the average for any two of the three years. For each acre removed from tobacco the government would pay a rental of $17.50. The farmer would receive in addition, at harvest time, upon evidence that he had complied with the acreage reduction program, a parity payment amounting to 12½ percent of the net sales prices of his 1934 tobacco, provided average market prices did not exceed 21 cents.

Supporters of the farm program feared that not enough growers would participate in the programs in both the cotton and the tobacco areas in the spring of 1934 to make them effective. Accordingly, Congress passed the Bankhead Cotton Control Act in April and the similar Kerr-Smith Tobacco Control Act in June. The tobacco act provided for the reinforcement of existing acreage control contracts by the issuance of tax-free warrants to cover marketing allotments. Tobacco marketed without a warrant would be assessed an amount equal to as much as one-half the market price at the discretion of the secretary of agriculture. "I do not think this legislation will be very bad," Byrd assured his friend Reed. "I went over the Kerr bill before it was passed and added a number of amendments."[43] Unlike the Bankhead Cotton Act, warrants were not transferable from one grower to another, which made tobacco control even more rigid than cotton control and precluded any crop insurance function, but it effectively discouraged overplanting by signers of contracts.[44] With Virginia tobacco growers as with those in other states, the larger producers reaped most of the federal benefits, and the small producers had difficulty even retaining their diminutive allotments.[45] Therefore, the principal support for the AAA in Virginia came from the large tobacco growers.

Henry Wallace proposed amendments to the AAA in May 1934 that irritated Senator Byrd, who had voted against the NIRA because it gave Hugh Johnson the power to license businesses. Now Wallace wanted the AAA changed so that farmers who violated AAA regulations could be denied licenses for shipment. "I regard this authority as un-American and better suited for the Soviet government of Russia," Byrd exclaimed,[46] and his radio address against the Wallace amendments received nationwide attention. The episode was repeated in the spring of 1935, and Wallace took Byrd's attack seriously enough to appear in Richmond to defend his plans. Flanked by Norman Hamilton and John Flannagan, he spoke to 1,500 Virginia farmers and argued that the licensing provision should be called a "code of fair play." Without mentioning Byrd by name, he ridiculed the charge that individual farmers would be licensed, and insisted that the AAA sought to give farmers "a device for group action comparable to those long used by industry and labor."[47]

Roosevelt hosted a farmers' rally at the White House two weeks later, on 15 May. First, the farmers heard Wallace adjure them not to be misled by " 'bloody shirts,' Wall Street 'Jeffersonians' and other deceptions practiced for generations." Then they heard the president condemn the enemies of the farm program as "liars." Roosevelt said he was talking as "farmer to farmer," and had no use for "pussy foot words." The suggestion for this farmers' rally had come from Texas; but of the throng of 5,000, fully 1,500 were North Carolina farmers, while Virginia farmers were conspicuously absent.[48]

The first AAA was on the verge of extinction by the Supreme Court as the year 1935 drew to a close, after nearly three years of turbulent effort to wrestle with the farm problem. Voices of criticism and widespread apathy had greeted such efforts in Virginia even among tobacco growers, and the statistical record bears this out. As of 31 December 1935, the AAA had spent $1.2 billion in the nation; Virginia, with a population of about two percent of the nation's and still predominantly an agricultural state, had received $7.9 million, or seven-tenths of one percent.[49]

Congress passed the Soil Conservation and Domestic Allotment Act in February 1936, with a declared purpose "to promote the conservation and profitable use of agricultural land resources by temporary Federal aid to farmers," but there was little doubt that its stated purpose was not the primary one.[50] Instead, the sponsors of the new law were interested mainly in reducing the production of the major cash crops and transferring income to farmers, without the processing tax and without disobeying the Supreme Court's verdict in *United States* v. *Butler*. Congress and the Department of Agriculture developed throughout 1937 the structure of a new farm bill that became law early in 1938. The bill passed the House during the special session on 11 December 1937, but in the Senate, Byrd estimated the cost at $1.5 billion annually and declared it entirely at cross-purposes with all previous farm legislation. Earlier legislation had as its stated purpose the relief of the farmer, he insisted, whereas this new farm bill apparently proposed to guarantee "parity prices" from henceforth forevermore to the producers of five major crops. Senate Agriculture Committee Chairman "Cotton Ed" Smith himself, Byrd noted, said that there was no way of estimating "within $200,000,000 or $300,000,000" how much it would cost every year.[51] Byrd supported the farm bill in the final Senate vote in February 1938, but Senator Glass remained irreconcilable. "Congress seems completely willing to take any poison labelled 'Farm Remedy,' " fumed Glass.[52] Except for parity payments and the purchase of surplus commodities, Byrd believed that the programs of the agriculture department and its agencies were "perhaps the most beneficial expenditures that are being made by the Federal Government." The main problem, as he saw it, was that Roosevelt had "created a spending consciousness on the part of Congress and time and time again has urged that only by excessive spending can the country be restored to prosperity."[53] This was Glass's theme in reverse; Glass usually insisted that it was not the president who was to blame for excessive spending, but Congress.

The basic objective of the New Deal farm program was to reduce the output and restore the domestic price for the producers of commercial crops. The domestic allotment plan was better designed for western wheat farmers and growers of corn and hogs whose market was more exclusively domestic, than for tobacco and cotton growers whose market was largely foreign, or at least had been a few years earlier. It was not designed at all for a farm problem of the nature of that in Virginia, where the principal problem lay in the smallness of the farms. Virginia's 170,000 to 200,000 farms during the 1930s averaged 94 acres each. In 1959, after Virginia farmers had taken over a million acres (out of about 17 million) out of cultivation in 15 years and reduced the farm labor force by 30 percent, Virginia still had a small-farm problem. Nearly two-thirds of her farms had gross annual sales of $2,500 or less, too little to permit the farmer to modernize or expand. Only the top 20 percent of Virginia farms had annual sales of $5,000 or more. The New Deal and its AAA programs had done little or nothing to assist the small farmer to become more self-sufficient, and nowhere was this better exemplified than in Virginia.

The Social Security Act was another New Deal reform program that was ill-received and only partially accepted in Virginia. When Senator Robert Wagner introduced the Social Security bill in the Senate early in 1935, Byrd spent a week adding figures, then stood vigorously opposed to the proposed law. He estimated it would cost an average state such as Virginia about $21 million per year to care for old-age dependents, which would force the state to increase the tax burden by 130 percent. Byrd's estimate of the cost was based upon the assumption that about half of all persons 65 or over would be eligible to receive benefits, or about 77,500 Virginians. His $21 million per year would pay each about $22.50 per month, but the United States Labor Department officials had a radically different set of figures. They estimated that 7,000 Virginians would be eligible and would receive about $15 per month, making a total annual cost (for Virginia) of $1,260,000. The *Times-Dispatch* editor believed the Labor Department figures were more realistic, and added, "The most disturbing aspect of Senator Byrd's statement is to be found in the fact that nowhere in it does he indicate that he regards social security legislation as either necessary or desirable." India and China, he noted, were the only other major nations that lacked social security laws.[54]

This was Byrd's second major revolt against the administration, and, coming just before the revolt of Darden, Robertson, and Smith against the work relief bill, may have prompted it. Governor Peery quickly rose to stand to the right of Senator Byrd. He declared that Virginia, regardless of any action Congress might take, would not set up an old-age pension system of any kind,[55] and during the New Deal it did not. Peery would not commit himself concerning Virginia's participation in the old-age assistance plan for the needy aged—as distinct from the Old Age and Survivors' Insurance program (OASI)—but instead assigned the director of the State Bureau of Legislative Research, William R. Shands, and State Tax Commissioner C. H. Morrisett to make a study of the question and report to him. The state lacked the information requested; Virginia had 127,000 persons over 65, of whom 72,000 were over 70, but no one could say how many of these were needy. Not even the federal Social Security Board could be helpful, lacking reliable data with which either to confirm or refute the wide-ranging and contradictory estimates of cost of either the pension plan or the plan to assist the needy aged.[56]

The unemployment insurance provisions of the Social Security Act imposed a one percent payroll tax on employers, with 90 percent of the proceeds returnable to the state if it had an acceptable unemployment insurance program of its own. State Senator Aubrey Weaver added an amendment to the unemployment insurance bill, then in committee in the Virginia legislature, to the effect that the act should go into force "if and when" the United States Supreme Court should declare constitutional the unemployment insurance sections of the Social Security Act. State Senator John S. Battle offered a different amendment providing that Virginia should participate in the social security program fully; then if the Supreme Court should declare the federal law invalid, the state law should likewise become invalid and the money returned to contributors. In the Virginia General Assembly of 1936, however, the Senate killed the old-age assistance bill and the House killed the unemployment insurance bill. All that was salvaged was a commission to study the problem and report to the next session in 1938.[57]

The Virginia Manufacturers' Association, which had lobbied for the Weaver amendment, had won the first round in the General Assembly, but at great risk. The VMA was ready to gamble that the Supreme Court would declare the federal act unconstitutional; but if it was wrong and the Supreme Court upheld the law, Virginia industries stood to lose about $2.5 million in payroll taxes without a cent coming back. Even worse, Virginia industries would be out nearly $7.5 million if the Court's decision was delayed two years, since the rate for the second year was two percent as against one percent the first year.

The Virginia Consumers' League, a branch of the National Consumers' League, a liberal pressure group particularly interested in labor legislation, was established in September 1936, and immediately went to work lobbying for the unemployment insurance bill. Its leaders stressed that during the 1936 session of the Virginia General Assembly, one of the most reactionary on record, not one social security or labor bill of importance was passed, and the trash cans were stuffed with defeated bills for unemployment insurance, old-age pensions, old-age assistance, an eight-hour bill for women, a stricter mine safety law, an improved workmen's compensation law, and a minimum wage law for women and minors. The VCL urged the adjourned legislators to demand a special session, under the rule in the Virginia Constitution that if two-thirds of each house called for it, the governor was required to call it.[58] When this movement was gathering momentum in November, Peery pointed out that, since 32 states besides Virginia had not passed an unemployment insurance law, Congress would probably extend the time in which the states could come under the provisions of the law. Such lame excuses did not neutralize the pressure for a special session; in December two-thirds of the members of both legislative houses signed the petition requesting it. In language that clearly conveyed his unhappiness over having to take such a step, Peery yielded and called for the special session. After all the bickering in getting it called, the session was humdrum, for within three days the resurrected unemployment insurance bill was passed with a single dissenting vote in each house. The presumption is very strong that the leaders of the VMA, witnessing the great victory of the New Deal in the November election, decided they had made a mistake in lobbying against unemployment insurance.[59]

The Supreme Court upheld the unemployment insurance, old-age assistance, and old-age pension provisions of the Social Security Act in May 1937. Six months later Carter Glass, hostile as ever, called the act "a Frankenstein and very vicious evidence of the government's purpose to thrust itself into matters which are not properly of government concern."[60] At this time when Virginia voters elected James H. Price governor, Virginia was the only state in the union that had not enacted into law a federal-state old-age assistance program. The Virginia Old-Age Assistance Commission reported to Governor Peery in December 1937 that the average monthly subsistence need for eligible white Virginians over 65 was $11.58; for Negroes, $9.05. It estimated that the total cost of old-age assistance in Virginia would be $5 million the first year, increasing to $6.6 million per year in ten years. The commission recommended that cities and counties share in the expense of financing old-age assistance, and that local boards determine the eligibility of applicants subject to review by a state board.[61]

In his inaugural address in January 1938, Governor Price said that he "warmly favored" the cooperation of Virginia in the Social Security program. However, he believed that the maximum payment for old-age assistance should be fixed at $15 or $20 per month rather than the federal maximum of $30. "It should be made perfectly clear that Old Age Assistance, as the term implies, is intended to be . . . based upon the actual needs of the individual case and is not to be regarded as a pension," said Price.[62] Immediately, identical bills were introduced in the Assembly and passed within a month, which brought Virginia into line with the other 47 states, all of which now had unemployment compensation and old-age assistance programs.

Although no state action was required for its implementation, the Old Age and Survivors' Insurance program remained distasteful to Byrd and the "organization" until the Truman years. In 1952, after a new federal law of 1950 extended OASI coverage to such previously uncovered categories as farmers, the self-employed, domestic servants, and teachers, Virginia integrated the OASI program with a retirement program for state employees. This signaled a belated capitulation by the Byrdmen.

Meanwhile, the Assembly appropriated $3.3 million for the biennium beginning 1 July 1938 for old-age assistance, relief for the needy blind, and for about 3,000 of an estimated 10,000 eligible dependent children. Both bills were amended to accord with Price's suggestion to cut the maximum monthly allowance for the needy aged from $30 to $20. The state appropriation comprised 62.5 percent of Virginia's share and the localities put up the other 37.5 percent, the federal government matching the combined funds. Out of an eventually estimated 39,000 needy aged in Virginia, this program reached about 18,000. Virginia's lateness in adopting the old-age assistance program "makes it all the more essential that the system she is now to set up should be adequate," commented the *Times-Dispatch*. "Is this the best the Legislature can do for the needy aged of the Old Dominion?"[63]

It was not the best Virginia could do. Economist Clarence Heer, discussing the financing of the program in the South in January 1938, noted that the tax programs of southern states tended to be heavily regressive, with emphasis on general and specific sales taxes. "Because of the low average level of income in the South," he observed, "the Southern states in particular have not been able to raise much revenue from the so-called ability taxes."[64] Therefore, the social security program imposed a heavy financial burden on all the southern states, but not as heavy on Virginia as upon most of the others. Average taxable wages per employee for eleven southern states were $572 ($675 for whites, $289 for Negroes). For Virginia, the figure was $657 ($765 for whites, $335 for Negroes.[65] Moreover, Virginia did not then have a general sales tax. All things considered, Virginia exhibited an unbecoming lack of concern for the problems of her underprivileged citizens in comparison with other southern states. Apathy on the part of the electorate may have played a role in this, but it is difficult to avoid tracing responsibility directly to Byrd, leader of the " 'let them eat cake' school of social thought."

An easily identified group of underprivileged Virginians were the Negroes, who numbered about 650,000 of the state's population of 2.5 million, or 26 percent. The New Deal did not accomplish very much for the Negro in the nation, but it is becoming clearer after thirty years, as Frank Freidel and others have pointed out, that race relations played a more vital role during the New Deal years than contemporaries appeared to think.[66] What the New Deal even vaguely and inferentially promised to do for the Negro in Virginia was regarded by many Virginians as a threat to the established social order, which they resented and resisted. There were exceptions to this, as some reflective citizens had second thoughts about the Negro in Virginia society. In retrospect, it appears to have been a transitional period in race relations whether all accepted the idea of change or not.

Virginia had a good record in comparison with most southern states in the matter of disparity between expenditures per pupil for white and Negro students in public schools. In the 1930s, Virginia spent a little over 50 percent more per white pupil, whereas South Carolina, Alabama, Louisiana, and Georgia each spent about 400 percent as much for each white pupil, and Mississippi about 600 percent. Nevertheless, the education of whites and Negroes during the New Deal years in Virginia was entirely separate and entirely unequal from the first grade through graduate school. At the graduate level, there was not a single state-supported institution where a Negro could pursue graduate or professional work as late as 1937 in Virginia.[67]

When the National Association for the Advancement of Colored People (NAACP) was attempting to get Negro students into graduate schools in Virginia and elsewhere in 1936, Virginia Negroes had their own state-supported four-year college at Petersburg, Virginia State College for Negroes, which offered no graduate or professional training of any kind. Four peripheral southern states—West Virginia, Missouri, Maryland, and Oklahoma—had adopted a diversionary tactic by offering state assistance to qualified Negro graduate schools outside the state; and in 1936, the Stephens-Dovell Act established such a program in Virginia. PWA and WPA grants to the Virginia State College for Negroes doubled the value of its physical plant (to about $2 million) between 1933 and 1937, but there were still no plans for graduate or professional training. When the NAACP pressed harder for the admission of Negroes to the University of Virginia, the State Board of Education authorized the Negro institution at Petersburg to offer graduate courses beginning in the summer of 1937.[68]

The all-Negro Virginia Teachers' Association advanced the cause of racial equality when it won its case in a federal circuit court in Norfolk in 1940 for equal pay for public school teachers with equal qualifications and experience. Salary differentials, said the court, were "as clear a discrimination on the grounds of color as could well be imagined." School boards in 45 of Virginia's 100 counties and eight of her cities agreed to equalize salaries rather than go to court within three years.[69]

Negroes in Virginia during the New Deal were the victims of indifference in the field of general employment. The NRA was of no particular benefit to them and even appeared to be a new handicap, since with higher pay and shorter hours under the codes, white unemployed were willing to displace Negroes in such jobs as waiters, messengers, janitors, truck drivers, and elevator operators. Patterns of anti-Negro discrimination were probably no different in Virginia from those in the rest of the South in such activities as the FERA and the CCC. Although the FERA forbade it, the rules were applied differently to Negroes. The need of a Negro for relief was more rigorously questioned, he received a lower weekly stipend, he was dropped from the rolls upon employment for even a few days at a pittance of wages, and for work relief purposes he was usually classified as unskilled regardless of his training. FERA officials opposed local prejudice on the subject in vain.[70] It was much the same in the Civilian Conservation Corps, in which the Negro never received his fair share. Robert Fechner, the director, was a Tennesseean with the usual intransigent view of the Negro that refused to countenance integrated CCC camps or even the location of all-Negro camps near conservative white communities. Roosevelt appointed Fechner and acquiesced in his reflecting the prevailing white opinion.[71]

The Social Security Board was equally of little help to the Negro. When plans were announced in 1937 for the expansion of the Virginia Employment Service with the aid of federal funds under the Social Security program, the executive secretary of the Richmond Urban League had hopes of getting a number of Negro appointees placed in some of the 33 new Virginia offices around the state. The Virginia program director abruptly informed him that no Negroes would be used, and when he appealed to the Social Security Board in Washington, he received a vague, noncommital answer.[72]

To some Negroes, it was apparent that they would have to assume the initiative for their own advancement. A group of 400 Negro women factory workers at Richmond's I. N. Vaughan Company, where they were paid three dollars a week (five cents an hour for a sixty-hour week) as tobacco stemmers in a rehandling plant, walked out on 6 May 1937, without any prompting by outside agitators. They appealed to the Richmond agent of the ultraconservative Tobacco Workers' International Union (AFL), who rejected their cause as "hopeless," but the Southern Negro Youth Congress helped them organize an independent union and present their demands to the company. Within two days they had secured better wages, a forty-hour week, and recognition of their union. Immediately, 400 more stemmers at the nearby Carrington-Michaux plant duplicated their performance, and within a year three more Richmond stemmeries had their workers organized and in possession of contracts with management. The CIO wasted no time in taking over these new unions, but when it attempted to organize tobacco workers in other branches of the industry, the CIO ran into an awakened TWIU, now belatedly interested in organizing Negro tobacco workers in Virginia. Wherever Negroes were organized, they were segregated into separate unions, which limited interracial cooperation to the leaders. However, by 1940 joint committees were meeting monthly in Richmond to discuss problems common to both Negro and white tobacco workers, in clear defiance of the TWIU leadership.[73]

Disfranchisement of the Negro after Reconstruction developed in an uneven pattern within the South. Probably at no time and certainly not in every place were Negroes totally excluded from the ballot box. In the widespread effort to exclude them following the Mississippi Constitution of 1890, the South Carolina Constitution of 1895, and the abortive Populist effort to unite the races politically, Negroes were barred from voting generally by legal means of residence, literacy, and tax requirements, laced with extralegal intimidation and fraud. Virginia was no exception to the rule.

When segregation practices became increasingly onerous following World War I, Richmond Negroes organized a "lily-black" Republican party in 1921, with a slate of Negro leaders for governor, lieutenant governor, United States senator, and superintendent of public instruction. They attracted so few votes that it was clear the Negro could make his vote more effective in the regular Democratic primaries, if he could vote in them.[74] The Norfolk *Journal and Guide*, one of the leading Negro newspapers in the South, deserted the party of Lincoln for the party of Al Smith in 1928, and in 1930 Negroes switched to the Democratic party in a nationwide trend. Voting registrars blocked Negro voters in Virginia in the 1930s, but few other white persons were involved in such activity. Charles S. Johnson, in gathering material for *Into the Main Stream*, found that Virginia Negroes voted in both local elections and statewide primaries in small numbers.[75] But then white persons in Virginia voted in small numbers. Actually, the Negro had little interest in Democratic primaries until shortly before the New Deal. A majority of Negro voters in the nation supported Hoover, but those who did not probably voted more against Hoover than for Roosevelt, since there was little in Roosevelt's record as governor of New York and nothing in the Democratic national platform that indicated concern for Negro problems.

About 30,000 Virginia Negroes were registered voters in the 1930s out of a total adult Negro population of about 360,000, or one out of twelve. As more Negro voters switched to the Democratic party, some politicians made an effort to win even this handful of votes, sometimes with rueful results as Norman Hamilton discovered in his congressional campaign against Colgate Darden in 1938. Hamilton set up a campaign headquarters in the heart of Portsmouth's Negro district, staffed by Negroes. The Darden forces could not resist the temptation to hang the label "nigger lover" on Hamilton, which he declared cost him the election, but there is no evidence that Darden personally approved of the tactic.

Registrars blocked would-be Negro voters as a general rule during the 1930s. One type of block was the so-called understanding and educational requirement, which actually consisted of unfair questions. For example, a Negro would be asked to name the counties in a congressional or judicial district or to quote specified sections of the state constitution, questions that would have stumped even the registrars. When professors at Hampton Institute were turned away the system had exceeded reasonable limits, declared the Virginia State Supreme Court of Appeals in the 1931 case of *Davis* v. *Allen*. Even so, the practice continued into the 1940s until hounded into obscurity by the Virginia NAACP. A second type of block was the blank application form, upon which a Negro registrant would be expected to enter the correct information without guidance, a transparent device that made a Negro's chances for getting his name on the list virtually nil, unless the registrar chose to include him. Some were included. A recent student of the Negro in Virginia politics finds that the Byrd organization disapproved of the actual intimidation of Negroes, and "even appeared to frown upon the use of the blank form." Even so, its use continued into the 1930s and even later in some areas. The number of Negro voters increased more rapidly after 1940 in Virginia with the Virginia Voters' League, organized in 1941 by history professor Luther P. Jackson of the Virginia State College for Negroes, laboring to overcome the political apathy that was as natural to Virginia Negroes as to Virginia whites.[76]

The Old Dominion did not impose upon Negroes the device common in states of the deep South: the white primary. The United States Supreme Court in *Nixon* v. *Herndon* (1929) declared the Texas white primary law contrary to the Fourteenth Amendment. Texans subsequently arranged for payment of the expenses of primaries by the party organization itself, thus divorcing the state government from direct involvement. The Supreme Court in *Grovey* v. *Townsend* (1935) confirmed the legality of the Texas ploy. Meanwhile, Judge C. Vernon Spratley of the Circuit Court of Elizabeth City County had declared in 1933 that Virginia Negroes could not be excluded from the primaries solely because of their race. "Judge Spratley's decision has been accepted in Virginia, and Negroes are allowed to take part in the Democratic primaries when their qualifications are adequate," Virginius Dabney asserted following the *Grovey* v. *Townsend* decision. "That is at it should be." The editor supposed that some southern states would be encouraged by the latest ruling to reorganize their primaries and pay expenses from Democratic party funds, but he did not expect Virginia would do so, because with the expense of a statewide primary then ranging from $25,000 to $30,000, it cost more money that it was worth. As he predicted, the Virginia Democratic leaders decided to permit Negro members of the party to participate and allow the general taxpayers to continue paying the cost. After all, the risk involved was extremely slight; apathy alone was sufficient to preclude any mass movement to the polls of either Negroes or whites in Virginia.[77]

Some thoughtful and informed southerners during the New Deal had second thoughts concerning the Negro and white supremacy. Douglas Southall Freeman, Richmond newspaper editor and biographer of Robert E. Lee, for one, told Harry Byrd that he had come to know Walter White of the National Association for the Advancement of Colored People, and he was much impressed by White's ability, integrity, and character. In fact, said Freeman, his contacts with White and other NAACP officials had made him realize "how much of the prejudice existing in the South against this organization is without foundation."[78] When William Watts Ball, editor of the *Charleston* (S.C.) *News and Courier*, expressed fear for the future of white supremacy when "a Franklin Roosevelt party, of Southern sympathies" no longer occupied the White House, Virginius Dabney sharply countered, "It is high time that Southerners stopped losing sleep over 'white supremacy.' It was a live issue during reconstruction days, but today it is almost as dead as Bildad the Shuhite."[79] It was neither that remote nor that dead, but what seemed to be happening along the color line in Virginia if not in the nation in the 1930s was a complex pattern of breakthroughs and reinforcements, resulting in a ragged racial barrier by the close of the decade. Negro leaders of that era were still willing to exhibit the patience of Job in waiting for the reinforced areas of segregation and discrimination to be broken through.

The New Deal deserved credit for some of the breakthroughs in spite of Roosevelt's reluctance to tackle the race issue. When individuals or agencies of the administration took the initiative in a situation involving race, Roosevelt watched and waited without intervening. In the Division of Subsistence Homesteads, for example, the 31 projects under construction in 1935 included not a single one for Negroes, whereas on the basis of population alone three of them should have been, and on the basis of need, more than that. Therefore, the DSH announced that no new homesteads would be started until Negroes shared in the program, a commitment that led to the building of Aberdeen Gardens at Newport News, Virginia. Negro skilled and unskilled labor was used as fully as possible in the construction of 205 low-cost houses (about $3,000 each), which were sold to Negroes carefully selected for their ability to keep up payments on a forty-year mortgage at three percent interest.[80]

It seems clear that the Negro's place in Virginia society was beginning to change for the better during the New Deal years, whether as a result of the New Deal, the paternalistic concern of white Virginians, or his own efforts. To this extent, the stage was being set for the accelerated changes and intensified resistance of the postwar years.

It also seems clear that the political, economic, and social condition of Virginia during the 1930s was not conducive to a cordial and receptive attitude toward the New Deal. Spending borrowed money on public service programs of dubious relevance to the needs of the Old Dominion held little charm for an electorate that had found the champion of its basic convictions in Harry F. Byrd. The Byrd organization, inclined against the

New Deal by temperament, conviction, and interest, was strong in Virginia politics in 1932 and had grown steadily stronger by 1940. New Dealers, both genuine and self-styled, flailed feebly at the organization in 1936 and 1938, and the voters rejected them.

More than the political strength of the New Deal opposition was involved. The economic goals of the New Deal programs were substantially out of harmony with Virginia's needs. The industrial depression was not as severe in Virginia as in many other states because the few industries Virginia had developed were not afflicted by as great a drop in demand as the average American industry. The NRA with its rationalization of output and price control was not needed, particularly in Virginia's leading industry, and its Section 7(a) with its encouragement to labor unions was hotly resented. There was less need for relief to the unemployed, though probably more need than the Byrd organization seemed willing to recognize. Virginia nearly refused to cooperate with the FERA altogether, and was at the bottom of recipients of WPA aid. Not only were the political leaders opposed to federal spending for such purposes, but Virginia in the 1930s was still predominantly a rural state and relief was essentially an urban problem. But not even the agricultural program of the New Deal was designed to suit Virginia's needs. Virginia was mainly a community of small family farms producing a diversified output for subsistence or local markets, whereas the AAA's domestic allotment plan was designed primarily to aid the big western wheat, corn, and hog growers. Southern cotton and tobacco growers were of secondary concern, for little or no effort was made to recapture their once-important export markets, and the family farm was left to shift for itself. Virginia's political leaders were dismayed when it became clear that the farm program was one of reform and not merely relief.

Social security was a New Deal reform program that seemed more out of harmony with Virginia's needs in the eyes of its leaders than was actually the case, and possibly for that reason, more concessions were made to New Deal policy in this area than in other economic programs. Even so, the portions of the program accepted were held to a minimum. Probably Virginia's greatest social and economic need in the 1930s was for an improved system of public education, and New Deal efforts in this area were minimal. This is not to say that Virginia leaders would have approved a federal aid to education program, for the Byrd organization showed little interest in public education at all and reacted almost automatically against federal expenditure for any economic or social program.

Finally, the New Deal as a threat to reform Virginia's established pattern of race relations lay beneath the surface of much of the Old Dominion's chary attitude, and on occasion Senator Glass said it out loud. The Byrd organization would not have tolerated a blatant racist, and appeals to the voters such as those of a Talmadge or a Bilbo had no place in Virginia politics. The incident in Hamilton's 1938 campaign against Darden seems to have been singular, but perhaps indicative of the strength of the submerged race issue in politics. The attitude of white Virginians was generally paternalistic, based upon a conviction of the truth of white supremacy. The erosion of this conviction was beginning during the 1930s, and so also was the racial barrier beginning to erode in places, thanks only in part to the New Deal.

The legacy of the New Deal in Virginia was a general feeling of antipathy. It awakened little desire for reform and social justice. To a much greater extent, the New Deal was remembered as a time when the federal government engaged in deficit spending for dubious purposes with too little restraint, and when it became involved in matters outside its legitimate concern. Time may change this point of view, but the harsher critics of the New Deal in Virginia believed that the New Deal leaders assumed more authority for combatting the depression than they either needed or had thrust upon them by Congress, and that having assumed it they succumbed to the temptation to use power arbitrarily. The depression made reforms of some kind inevitable, but the people of Virginia and their leaders looked upon reform in the style of the New Deal with understandable reluctance.

1. V. O. Key, *Southern Politics in State and Nation* (New York, 1949), pp. 19–35.

2. The most valuable recent study of Virginia politics during the progressive era is Allen W. Moger, *Virginia: Bourbonism to Byrd, 1870–1925* (Charlottesville, 1968). A parallel study of interest is Raymond H. Pulley, *Old Virginia Restored: An Interpretation of the Progressive Impulse, 1870–1930* (Charlottesville, 1968). Pulley interprets the progressive movement in Virginia as the reestablishment of Virginia's traditional political and social system following the threats posed by Reconstruction, the Readjuster movement, and the Populist movement. The response of Virginians to the New Deal seems to be in harmony with such interpretation. J. Harvie Wilkinson's *Harry Byrd and the Changing Face of Virginia Politics, 1945–1966* (Charlottesville, 1968) examines the last years of the Byrd organization, but there is no published study of Virginia and the New Deal.

3. George B. Tindall, "Business Progressivism: Southern Politics in the Twenties," *South Atlantic Quarterly* 62 (1963): 92–106.

4. Alvin L. Hall, "Virginia Back in the Fold: The Gubernatorial Campaign and Election of 1929," *Virginia Magazine of History and Biography* 73 (1965): 280–302.

5. Frank Freidel, *Franklin D. Roosevelt: The Triumph* (Boston, 1956), pp. 306–7.

6. *Richmond Times-Dispatch*, 2 November 1932.

7. Carter Glass to George H. Moses, 14 November 1932, Glass Papers (University of Virginia).

8. Glass to FDR, 7 February 1933, PPF 687, Roosevelt Papers (Franklin D. Roosevelt Library); Raymond Moley, *The First New Deal* (New York, 1966), pp. 80–82; Frank Freidel, *F.D.R. and the South* (Baton Rouge, 1965), p. 55.

9. Harry Byrd to Douglas S. Freeman, 24 December 1932, Freeman Papers (Library of Congress).

10. On Roosevelt's motives for appointing Swanson, see Moley, *The First New Deal*, pp. 75–76. In Moley's opinion, Roosevelt appointed Swanson primarily to clear the chairmanship of the Senate Foreign Relations Committee for Senator Key Pittman. Moreover, Roosevelt believed Swanson would not interfere with his own directing of naval affairs, and that Swanson's prestige would be an asset in obtaining naval appropriations. Roosevelt was well aware that another result would be to clear Swanson's Senate seat for Byrd.

11. *Richmond Times-Dispatch*, 24 December 1936.

12. On Price's governorship, see George W. Spicer, "Gubernatorial Leadership in Virginia," *Public Administration Review*, 1 (1941): 441–57; Herman L. Horn, "The Growth and Development of the Democratic Party in Virginia since 1890" (Ph.D. diss., Duke University, 1949), pp. 127–29, 442–43.

13. All Democrats, they were Schuyler O. Bland of Hampton, Colgate W. Darden of Norfolk, Patrick W. Drewry of Petersburg, Thomas G. Burch of Martinsville, Clifton A. Woodrum of Roanoke, A. Willis Robertson of Lexington, Howard W. Smith of Alexandria, John W. Flannagan of Bristol, and Andrew J. Montague of Richmond. Montague was succeeded by David E. Satterfield, Jr., and Darden was displaced by Norman Hamilton for one term following the election of 1936.

14. Cross reference to letter from Farley to Roosevelt, 6 September 1938, in OF 4400, 300-Va-H, Roosevelt Papers.

15. *Richmond Times-Dispatch*, 20 March 1936.

16. The impact of the depression on Virginia is discussed in Ronald L. Heinemann, "Depression and New Deal in Virginia" (Ph.D. diss., University of Virginia, 1968).

17. *Richmond Times-Dispatch*, 12 July 1933, 7 March 1934.

18. Ibid., 25 November 1934.

19. The source of this interpretation is a professor of economics who was on Hopkins's staff and prefers not to be named.

20. *Richmond Times-Dispatch*, 5 May 1935.

21. Ibid., 2 March 1934, 13 August, 1936. See also J. Kerwin Williams, *Grants-in-Aid under the Public Works Administration* (New York, 1939), pp. 231, 244.

22. *Richmond Times-Dispatch*, 31 March 1934.

23. Ibid., 10, 20, 24 January, 15 May 1934. See also Key, *Southern Politics*, p. 32.

24. *Richmond Times-Dispatch*, 27 January 1935.

25. Ibid., 13 March 1935.

26. Donald S. Howard, *The WPA and Federal Relief Policy* (New York, 1943), pp. 540–43.

27. Lewis Meriam, *Relief and Social Security* (Washington, D.C., 1946), pp. 398–99.

28. Testimony of Hugh S. Johnson before the Senate Finance Committee, quoted in the *Raleigh News and Observer*, 19 April 1935.

29. Louis Galambos, *Competition and Cooperation: The Emergence of a National Trade Association* (Baltimore, 1966), pp. 225–26; Robert Sidney Smith, *Mill on the Dan* (Durham, N.C., 1960), pp. 328, 360–61.

30. Robert R. West to R. M. Marchant, 12 April 1935, quoted in Smith, *Mill on the Dan*, p. 385.

31. Glass to Walter Lippmann, 10 August 1933, Glass Papers; also quoted in Freidel, *F.D.R. and the South*, p. 61.

32. Hugh Johnson to Carter Glass, 16 January 1934, Glass Papers.

33. H. J. Woolfolk to Glass, 22 December 1933, ibid.

34. E. L. Giles to Glass, 19 December 1933, ibid.

35. Richard Eldridge to Glass, 15 August 1934; Glass to Eldridge, 20 August 1934, ibid.

36. J. J. Baecher, Secretary, Norfolk NRA Compliance Board, NRA Progress Report, 10 November 1933, Box 1230, Series 121, Record Group 9, National Recovery Administration Records (National Archives).

37. Brief Résumé of Standard Drug Company Case, Richmond, Virgina, typescript, in Memorandum from Mark Merrill to Harry C. Carr, 11 February 1935, Box 7941, Series 101, ibid.

38. Henry I. Richards, *Cotton and the AAA* (Washington, D.C., 1936), pp. 119–21.

39. Calvin B. Hoover and Benjamin U. Ratchford, *Economic Resources and Policies of the South* (New York, 1951), p. 344.

40. David L. Corbitt, comp., *Addresses, Letters, and Papers of J.C.B. Ehringhaus* (Raleigh, N.C., 1950), pp. 70–72.

41. Ben Kilgore, "Farmers Have Set the Stage for Higher Tobacco Price," *Progressive Farmer*, July 1934, p. 5.

42. Reed to Byrd, 21 September 1933, Harry F. Byrd Papers, (University of Virginia). See also correspondence between Byrd and Reed in Reed Family Papers, Virginia Historical Society (Richmond).

43. Byrd to Reed, 21 June 1934, Byrd Papers.

44. Murray R. Benedict and Oscar C. Stine, *The Agricultural Commodity Programs* (New York, 1956), p. 60.

45. This was a perennial complaint of Clarence Poe, editor of the *Progressive Farmer*, published in Raleigh and widely read by Virginia farmers. "From the very beginning of AAA and crop legislation the *Progressive Farmer* has demanded that first consideration be given the 'right of the little man to live,' " he asserted in criticizing the 1938 farm law. "No man with a base of five acres or less should be required to make any cut whatever if he is planting less than one fifth of his tilled acres in tobacco" (Poe editorial in issue for March 1938, pp. 5, 68).

46. *Richmond Times-Dispatch*, 24 May 1934.

47. Ibid., 28 April 1935.

48. *Raleigh News and Observer*, 15 May 1935.

49. Edwin G. Nourse, Joseph S. Davies, and John D. Black, *Three Years of the Agricultural Adjustment Administration* (Washington, D.C., 1937), pp. 583–84.

50. Murray R. Benedict, *Farm Policies of the United States, 1790–1950* (New York, 1953), p. 350.

51. *Richmond Times-Dispatch*, 18 December 1937.

52. Glass to W. Gordon McCabe, 14 February 1938, Glass Papers.

53. Byrd to Freeman, 2 June 1939, Freeman Papers.

54. *Richmond Times-Dispatch*, 24, 25 January 1935.

55. Ibid., 26 January 1935.

56. Ibid., 16 August 1935, 20 January, 14 February 1936.

57. Ibid., 11, 25 February, 6 March 1936.

58. Ibid., 8 November 1936.

59. Ibid., 10 November, 4, 18 December 1936.

60. Glass to J. H. Carter, 10 November 1937, Glass Papers.

61. *Richmond Times-Dispatch*, 16, 20 December 1937.

62. Price Inaugural Address, 19 January 1938, draft copy in James H. Price Papers (in possession of James H. Price, Jr.).

63. *Richmond Times-Dispatch*, 26 February 1938

64. Clarence Heer, "Financing the Social Security Program in the South," *Southern Economic Journal* 4 (1938): 299. See also James T. Patterson, *The New Deal and the States: Federalism in Transition* (Princeton, N.J., 1969), pp. 99–100.

65. John J. Corson, "Old Age Insurance and the South," *Southern Economic Journal* 5 (1939): 321.

66. Freidel, *F.D.R. and the South*, pp. 71–102.

67. W.P.A. Writers' Project, *The Negro in Virginia* (New York, 1940), p. 273.

68. Charles S. Johnson, *Into the Main Stream* (Chapel Hill, N.C., 1947), pp. 159, 164; Mary B. Pierson, *Graduate Work in the South* (Chapel Hill, N.C., 1947), pp. 153–55.

69. George B. Tindall, *The Emergence of the New South, 1913–1945* (Baton Rouge, 1967), p. 564.

70. Edward Ainsworth Williams, *Federal Aid for Relief* (New York, 1939), p. 172.

71. John A. Salmond, "The CCC and the Negro," *Journal of American History* 52 (1965): 87–88.

72. Wiley A. Hall to Dr. John J. Corson, III, 12 October 1937; Corson to Hall, 26 October 1937, File Folder 530, Box 66,Series 9, Social Security Board Records, Record Group 47 (National Archives).

73. Herbert R. Northrup, "Tobacco Workers' International Union," *Quarterly Journal of Economics* 56 (1942): 616–17.

74. W.P.A. Writers' Project, *The Negro in Virginia*, pp. 244–45.

75. Johnson, *Into the Main Stream*, pp. 42–44.

76. Andrew Buni, *The Negro in Virginia Politics, 1902–1965* (Charlottesville, 1967), pp. 115–30, 143.

77. *Richmond Times-Dispatch*, 3 April 1935.

78. Freeman to Byrd, 19 January 1934, Freeman Papers.

79. *Richmond Times-Dispatch*, 20 November 1934.

80. Ibid., 17 August 1936. See also Paul Conkin, *Tomorrow a New World: The New Deal Community Program* (Ithaca, N.Y., 1959), pp. 200–202.

John Robert Moore

The New Deal in Louisiana

THE GREAT DEPRESSION INVADED LOUISIANA SLOWLY, ALMOST imperceptibly, for like most southern rural-agrarian states, Louisiana had not shared significantly in the prosperity of the 1920s. Nevertheless, Louisiana's per capita income declined from $415 in 1929, to $344 in 1930, to $299 in 1931, to $230 in 1932, and to $222 in 1933.[1] Although this suggests the over-all state of Louisiana's economy, the plight of agriculture provides a more relevant indicator. For the one-third of the state's total labor force employed in agriculture, and for the 39 percent of its total population classified as "rural-farm," declining crop prices and markets spelled ruin for an already economically destitute farmer class. In 1929, Louisiana farmers received $170 million in cash income; but with the depression's onset, that income fell steadily. For the 1932 fiscal year, the total cash income of Louisiana farmers amounted to only $59 million, a decline of 65 percent.[2] These figures, of course, pertain more to the relatively prosperous farmers and planters than to the two-thirds of Louisiana's farmers who were classified as tenants. For over a half-century, Louisiana's tenant farmers had suffered from poor farming practices, limited tenure and credit systems, price fluctuations, ill-health, poverty, insecurity, and other deep-rooted maladjustments. The Great Depression only aggravated an already distressed situation for the largest part of Louisiana's farm population.

Urban workers, of course, felt the depression's pinch early. Louisiana had in 1930 only eight cities with populations above 10,000, but New Orleans's population of 458,762 ranked it as the South's largest city. A minor riot resulted there in March 1930 when three to four hundred men

answered a bogus classified advertisement in the newspapers for employment in Texas. Although unemployed persons still revealed great reluctance to admit their situation, a mayor's committee to register the unemployed reported on 30 March 1930 that 10,395 persons in New Orleans
needed work, with day laborers and construction workers heading the list.
Despite this evidence of job shortages, the city's only action to relieve the
situation in 1930 came in December with an orange-selling campaign
similar to New York's famous apple-vending episode. Early in 1931,
however, the situation had so deteriorated that business and civic leaders
formed the New Orleans Welfare Committee, secured $10,000 from the
city government for initial relief benefits, and within a year raised over
$500,000 in contributions. When by March 1932 it appeared that the
committee would soon exhaust its resources, the New Orleans Commission Council supported a $750,000 bond issue to finance the Welfare
Committee's relief efforts. Overwhelming voter approval of the bond issue
enabled the Welfare Committee to provide part-time work for several
thousand jobless workers and to relieve the worst cases of distress until
federal funds and programs took over in 1933.[3] Other Louisiana cities
apparently lacked either the resources or the interest and leadership to cope
with the depression, for most neglected their unemployed and needy
families until spurred by New Deal initiatives.

Louisiana remained a predominantly rural-agrarian state during the
depression decade. Its population of 2,101,593 increased by only 12.5
percent to 2,363,880 in 1940, as compared with a 16.9 percent increase
between 1920 and 1930. Moreover, the percentage of the population
classified as rural declined by less than two percent, from 60.3 percent in
1930 to 58.5 percent in 1940. Although the official census data on the
occupational status of Louisianans for 1930 and 1940 are not fully comparable, the demographic study of Smith and Hitt indicates little significant
change during the decade.[4] Consideration of the 1940 labor force and its
occupational distribution closely suggests, therefore, the situation of a
decade earlier. The 1940 census classified 884,164 persons (37.4 percent
of the total population) in the labor force. Of these, 71,450 were unemployed, 41,572 labored on emergency public works, and 771,142 had
normal employment. Agriculture (including forestry and fishing) employed 33.2 percent of the normally employed labor force; wholesale and
retail trade, 14.6 percent; manufacturing, 12.9 percent; personal service,
12.2 percent; transportation, communication, and public utilities, 6.6
percent; professional and related services, 6.0 percent; and construction,

government, finance, insurance and real estate, mining, business and repair services, and amusement and recreation accounted for the remaining 14.5 percent.[5] In terms of the total Louisiana population, the "rural-farm" population accounted for 39.0 percent in 1930, but declined to 36.0 percent by 1940.[6] Of Louisiana's land area, 32.2 percent constituted farms in 1930 and 34.6 percent in 1940, although the total number of farms dropped from 161,445 to 150,005. Composing a substantial proportion of the farmers, tenants accounted for 66.6 percent of the "rural-farm" population in 1930 and declined only to 59.4 percent by 1940.[7] Although informative, such figures ignored the complex factors that distinguished and often divided Louisianans.

Louisiana encompassed a diverse people rich in racial, cultural, economic, and religious variety. Anglo-Saxon Protestants dominated the northern part, and French Catholics inhabited southern portions. Yet the state's 37.3 percent Negro population ranked Louisiana third in the nation in proportion of Negro population. The northern area divided generally into cotton planters along the rich alluvial floodplain of the Mississippi and in the valleys of the Red, Ouachita, and Tensas rivers, small commercial farmers on the good soil of northern hill areas, and subsistence farmers and lumber workers on the thin soil of the central, cut-over, "piney woods" region. Negroes tended to be more heavily concentrated in southern Louisiana, where the soils were richer than in the north; but most were agricultural laborers, sharecroppers, or tenant farmers. Southern Louisiana also had rich cotton plantation areas along the Mississippi north and west of New Orleans; but sugar cane cultivation prospered in the south-central bayou region originally settled by Acadian exiles from French Canada, and irrigation of the prairie section of southwestern Louisiana made rice production profitable. Although overwhelmingly rural, Louisiana experienced a sharp urban-rural contrast and conflict because of the city of New Orleans and part of adjacent Jefferson Parish, which made up about 20 percent of Louisiana's population. Most industries processed agricultural products and included sugar refining, lumber, paper, and rice cleaning and polishing. However, Louisiana ranked fifth in the nation in petroleum output, and its oil industry accounted for 25 percent of the state's annual income. Commercial enterprises centered in the three deep-water ports of New Orleans, Baton Rouge, and Lake Charles in southern Louisiana, where they encouraged growth of a wealthy and influential business-professional group.[8] Such diversity encouraged conflict between Catholic and Protestant, planter and dirt farmer, white and black, country and city, and businessmen and laborers. "Against such a background and in such a climate," Charles Dufour noted, "it is perhaps not surprising that Louisiana politics is steeped in easy cynicism."[9]

Farmers and laborers comprised the mass of Louisiana's population, but an economic-political alliance of businessmen and planters ruled the state until 1928. That year, Huey P. Long, a brilliant lawyer and charismatic leader from Louisiana's "piney woods" region, effected a class revolution at the polls based on antagonism between dirt farmers and wealthier planters and between county parishes and the New Orleans Ring (city machine). Government by gentlemen characterized Louisiana until Governor Long's advent, but the gentlemenly "reformers" as well as "conservatives" served business-planter interests far more diligently than the mass's interests. Long was no gentleman, but he instituted an activist, if corrupt and dictatorial, government that satisfied many of the people's frustrated needs and demands. Following Long's death in late 1935, a north Louisiana farmer summarized the situation: "At least we got *something*. Before him we got nothing. That's the difference."[10] The difference was substantial. Long spent more money between 1928 and 1932 than the three previous governors had spent in twelve years. State expenditures increased from almost $29 million in 1928 to over $35 million in 1929, to almost $47 million in 1930, and then in 1931 to over $83 million. Total state spending increased by 189 percent, but the amount expended above revenues soared to 912 percent as Long floated massive bond issues.[11] Although Long had no knowledge of Keynesian economics, he obviously preferred practical results to the balanced-budget principle. Largely coinciding with the onset of the Great Depression, Long's massive spending programs had an immeasurable effect on Louisiana's economy, but some results were clearly visible.

When Long took office as governor in 1928, Louisiana had 6,059 miles of roads, of which 296 were concrete, 35 asphalt, and 5,728 gravel.[12] By late 1931, in which year 66 percent of the state's total spending went for road and bridge construction, Louisiana had an additional 5,117 miles of roads, of which 1,583 were concrete, 718 asphalt, and 2,816 gravel. The largest public works project in the South before the New Deal, Long's road-building program employed 22,200 men in 1931, or about 10 percent of the total working on highways in the United States.[13] A much smaller, but still significant, increase in state spending expanded educational opportunities for Louisiana children and adults. Under Long's proddings, the 1928 legislative session enacted a free textbook law by which the state furnished textbooks to elementary and high school children in public, private, and parochial schools. Long estimated that free textbooks increased school enrollment by over 25 percent.[14] Tackling problems of adult illiterarcy, Long's special programs provided night-school classes three times a week for about a year. He later claimed that 100,000 of the state's 238,000 illiterates had learned to "read, write and cipher." The program became an overnight success, for the 1930 census reported a 3 percent increase in white literacy and a 15 percent increase in black literacy.[15] Although Long added thirty-five new taxes and raised the state debt to the second or third highest in the nation, Louisianans could appreciate his reduction of utility and telephone rates, his taxation of oil corporations, his introduction of the state's first income tax, his elimination of the poll tax, his efforts to improve state hospitals, his success in bringing natural gas to citizens of New Orleans, his humanization of services at state lunatic asylums and at the state penitentiary, and, of course, his construction of needed roads. Gentlemen critics admitted the state's progress under Long but complained of its cost. T. Harry Williams, however, calculated that "of the twenty-four states that kept records on combined costs, Louisiana was third from the lowest, bettered only by Virginia and Oklahoma, neither of which supported such an extensive road, educational, or welfare program."[16] Despite Long's substantial accomplishments in building roads and bridges, expanding and encouraging education, and providing some new services to Louisianans, Harnett Kane observed that "much of these benefits failed to reach down to the lower third of the urban populations, or to the rural tenants," and that during Long's lifetime "the state did little to share in the support of the unemployed, though others were assuming part of this burden."[17] Significantly, not until 1936 (after Long's death) did the Louisiana legislature finally establish a Department of Public Welfare.

The Great Depression exposed the inadequacy of Louisiana's welfare "system" and the necessity of reform. Growing numbers of jobless employables created problems that the existing welfare apparatus could not solve. In 1931, private sources, themselves insufficient, contributed 98.5 percent of all relief expenditures in Louisiana.[18] Lacking the English poor-law background, Louisiana made no provision for social welfare until the late nineteenth century. In 1870, for example, the legislature rejected a bill for poor relief as "calculated to encourage laziness, and make the State of Louisiana a receptacle for the poor of other states." Not until 1880 did Louisiana establish its first statewide poor law. The Pauper Act of 1880 as

well as later supplementary laws entrusted elected parish (county) administrative boards, the police juries, with responsibility for ascertaining and
supporting the destitute and helpless in their parishes. However, the law
expressly forbade parish officials from supporting or aiding at public
expense "any persons as paupers except such as are infirm, sick or
disabled."[19] Louisiana's welfare laws obviously made no provision for
assistance to the able-bodied unemployed. The state itself, moreover,
neither assumed responsibility nor provided basic standards. Inconsistency
and negligence in levying taxes and in distributing aid naturally resulted
throughout the state. For example, the police jury of Washington Parish in
southeast Louisiana, representing 29,904 persons, appropriated only $40
for poor relief in 1931, but the police jury of Calcasieu Parish in southwest
Louisiana, representing 41,963 persons, expended $14,698 from its
pauper funds for relief of the destitute.[20] Under this system, police juries
dispersed funds haphazardly, kept few written records of welfare recipients, rarely determined the needs of potential relief clients, and in some
cases relinquished responsibility to private charities. Saint Landry Parish in
southwestern Louisiana typified the latter category, for it normally provided only an occasional coffin for paupers and, as late as 1934, refused to
appropriate $6,000 for indigent relief.[21]

Louisiana established its first statewide relief system in August 1932,
"to assist in the problem of economic distress and unemployment."
Created by Governor O. K. Allen, the Unemployment Relief Committee
was the state's response to the Federal Emergency Relief and Construction
Act, which authorized the Reconstruction Finance Corporation to loan
funds to states that could verify relief needs. The URC promptly investigated conditions throughout Louisiana, found state and local relief efforts
and funds deficient, and requested financial aid from the RFC. Louisiana
became the first southern state to receive an RFC loan for direct relief to the
unemployed and for work projects. Beginning relief operations in October
1932, the URC expended over $6.5 million by May 1933 and handled an
average case load in excess of 115,000 each month. The URC used over
98.1 percent of the grant to employ workers on small public works
projects, primarily the construction, maintenance, and beautification of
roads. Employment ranged from one to four days a week depending upon
the families' relief needs. The remaining 1.9 percent of the grant provided
direct relief grants, such as the Sustenance Garden program's distribution
of seeds to many farmers. Except for the $750,000 bond issue floated by
New Orleans to assist relief programs in Orleans Parish, federal URC

funds provided the only assistance to the able-bodied unemployed in Louisiana before the advent of the New Deal. Unemployables, of course, still had to seek welfare aid from parish pauper funds and private charities. Louisiana's Unemployment Relief Committee contributed significantly to the state's welfare activities. It initiated investigations into welfare needs, accepted responsibility for unemployment relief, cooperated with national authorities in combatting suffering, and established public works projects as the most desirable method of relieving the unemployed. Following passage in March 1933 of the Federal Emergency Relief Act, which provided $500 million for direct grants to the states for relief, Governor Allen renamed the URC the Emergency Relief Administration and authorized it to operate in accordance with FERA policies.[22]

While Louisiana took tentative steps toward welfare reform, Huey P. Long extended his personal political power over the state. Following his inauguration as governor in May 1928, Long had begun the process of securing control of every state agency and with it the major share of state patronage. Even presumably independent agencies suddenly found themselves "superceded" by new agencies to which Long appointed loyal followers, who in turn submitted signed undated resignations to Long. Using his patronage opportunities to reward and to coerce legislators into approving his program, Long won passage of measures in 1928 providing for a $30 million bond issue to finance road construction, for free textbooks to school children, and for increased funds for hospitals. Outraged by his effective use of patronage, by his domineering and personal command of the legislature, and most of all by his success, Long's conservative opponents abortively attempted to impeach him in 1929. The impeachers' incredible ineptitude plus Long's adroit maneuvering blocked the effort, but the conservative counterattack hardened Long's ruthless determination to have his own way. In 1930, Long ambitiously proposed a major public improvements program that would stimulate Louisiana's economic growth despite the national depression. He called for a $68 million highway bond issue, for a multimillion-dollar new skyscraper state capitol, for debt retirement and improvements to the New Orleans port, and for other measures that would cost the state a total of $100 million. The most important measures required submission as constitutional amendments and, therefore, a two-thirds vote of the legislature. Long easily controlled a majority of the legislators, but against determined conservative opposition, he could not win the necessary two-thirds before the legislature adjourned. Long immediately went to the people for vindication of his program in a campaign for the United States Senate. "In effect," Long announced, "my election will mean that the legislature will submit my plan to the people, or those who refuse to accede to the publicly expressed stand of the voters will be signing their own political death warrant."[23] On 9 September 1930, the people of Louisiana overwhelmingly approved Long and his program. One week later, a submissive legislature met in special session to pass Long's public improvements measures; and in November, the voters favored the constitutional amendments by majorities of twenty and thirty to one. During 1931, the new senator-elect but still governor consolidated and centralized his power over Louisiana until no faction could offer effective resistance. He secured the election of his follower, O. K. Allen, to the governorship in January 1932. Shortly thereafter, Long journeyed to Washington to take his oath of office as United States senator.

An untypical freshman senator, Long broke every tradition from the beginning, insulted the Democratic party leadership, antagonized all conservative senators, spoke expansively and obstreperously on many subjects, and used the Senate floor to capture national publicity. He boldly proposed a radical plan to redistribute wealth by taxation and to prevent any person from receiving annually income over $1 million or lifetime bequests over $5 million. Absenting himself from the Senate almost 60 percent of the 1932 session, Long returned to Louisiana frequently to run the state personally. Since he now controlled two-thirds of the legislature, he pushed all his measures through in record time. Leading the Louisiana delegation to the Democratic National Convention in Chicago in June 1932, Long not only supported Franklin D. Roosevelt's bid for the presidential nomination but also held the wavering Arkansas and Mississippi delegations in line through the crucial third and fourth ballots. Then in August, Long invaded Arkansas, the home of Senate Democratic Leader Joseph Robinson, to campaign on behalf of Senator Hattie Caraway, who did not seem to have a chance against six male opponents. In a one week sound-truck tour of the state, Long rallied sufficient support to give Caraway the election and, thereby, to add another "Share-the-Wealth" voice to the Senate. Returning to Louisiana, Long campaigned for the election of his lieutenant, John Overton, to the Senate against incumbent Senator Edwin Broussard. Again Long appealed to the people for further senatorial support for decentralization of wealth, and again the depression-frustrated masses responded. Campaigning for Roosevelt in October, Long carried the same political style and circus techniques into North and South Dakota, Nebraska, and Kansas. Roosevelt's campaign manager, Jim Farley, assigned these states to Long in the belief that he could do little harm there. Instead, Long enjoyed a triumphant tour through the depressed farm states, which so impressed Farley that he later wrote, "We never again underrated him."[24] The relationship between Long and Roosevelt elicits endless speculation among New Deal writers, but most agree that both sought national power and were certain to clash. Roosevelt early concluded that Long was one of the most dangerous men in the country, while Long became increasingly alienated by what he regarded as Roosevelt's conservative inclinations and by his banker-business–oriented associates.

New Deal relief efforts rested largely on development of a strong federal-state partnership. In Louisiana, however, this development fell victim to the control exercised by Long over the state's government and to the political contention between Long and Roosevelt. Appalled by Long's despotism over the state and distrusting Long's national political ambitions, Roosevelt determined in the spring of 1933 to diminish Long's influence in Louisiana by denying him patronage. He channeled regular patronage appointments through five anti-Long congressmen and consulted only anti-Long leaders, such as former Governor John M. Parker. The appointment of Harry J. Early as state director of the Emergency Relief Administration to handle the distribution of FERA funds exemplified Roosevelt's course. Originally from West Virginia, Early had served successfully as relief director in the federal welfare administration for areas of Alabama. By appointing a nonresident to head Louisiana's relief agency, Roosevelt and Harry Hopkins, the national FERA director, expressed their distrust of a Louisianan handling federal funds and sought to prevent Long from politicizing the relief agency. In addition, Roosevelt reinstituted an income-tax investigation, originated during Hoover's administration, against Long's henchmen and Long himself. Although Long commanded thousands of state jobs for patronage purposes, the income-tax investigation provided Long a constant source of annoyance, and federal patronage denials threatened to erode his power base. In January 1934, Long severed most of his diplomatic relations with Roosevelt and launched his "Share Our Wealth" campaign nationally. His speeches promised assistance for the underprivileged and unemployed, but his obstruction of federal relief operations in Louisiana demonstrated that assistance would have to be on Long's terms or not at all.[25]

Following passage of the Federal Emergency Relief Act by Congress in March 1933, tighter federal standards for distributing relief funds and development of new relief measures promised to make the state ERA much more effective than the former URC in aiding the able unemployed. Ostensibly, the FERA provided $1.00 in federal funds for every $3.00 contributed by the state for unemployment relief programs; but in Louisiana, state officials pleaded insufficient funds. As a consequence, the FERA long carried the full unemployment relief load in Louisiana without requiring any state or parish matching funds.[26] The load was considerable, for in October 1933 the federal government gave unemployment relief to 325,611 Louisianans, or to about 15.5 percent of the total population. Louisiana ranked sixteenth among the states in number of families receiving direct or indirect assistance, having 76,751 relief families, of which 41,642 were white and 34,967 were Negro. New Orleans also ranked sixteenth among the nation's cities in persons receiving aid, with 80,812, or about 17.6 percent, of the city's population on relief.[27] By January 1934, the FERA was aiding almost 400,000 persons in Louisiana, and between May 1933 and March 1934 had granted almost $31.8 million for unemployment relief in the state.[28] Not only did the state not provide funds to match federal grants, but the local parishes exploited FERA generosity by transferring to it support for unemployables. For example, the Mothers' Aid Act passed in 1930 charged the parishes to provide for dependent fatherless families; but negligent parish officials passed responsibility to the FERA, which in April 1934 cared for more than 1,200 mothers and 3,600 children in Louisiana. Speaking to the Police Jury Association, in mid-April 1934, Harry J. Early warned that "no state, however poor, however debt-ridden, can afford to take the position that it can do nothing and make no effort. . . . In no few instances has it become necessary for Mr. Hopkins to require a showing of good faith through special sessions of State Legislatures."[29]

In late May 1934, Harry Hopkins informed Governor Allen that federal support of relief in Louisiana would be withdrawn if the state did not meet its obligations. Specifically, Hopkins requested state appropriations of $100,000 for establishment of a State Department of Public Welfare, $500,000 for parish matching funds for relief of unemployables, $300,000 for parish assistance to dependent fatherless families, $100,000 for parish aid to dependent blind, and $600,000 to compensate FERA—ERA employees in Louisiana.[30] However, Governor Allen did not introduce the federally demanded relief bills until the last day for presentation of appropriation measures in the June legislative session, and Senator Long then allowed the bills to die in committee. The FERA retaliated on 1 August

1934 by removing all unemployables from its rolls. The previous month, the FERA had spent over $65,000 to aid approximately 4,400 unemployables, who as heads of families represented more than 15,000 Louisianans.[31] Soon cries of distress resounded from the parishes. Special sessions of the legislature in August and November further entrenched Long's power over the state, but they also made minor concessions to federal relief demands. The August session earmarked a portion of state franchise tax collections to pay ERA employees and to augment parish pauper funds and authorized parish police juries to allocate any portion of the one-cent gasoline tax for welfare relief. When this proved inadequate, the November session enacted a further one-cent tax on gasoline for exclusive relief of parish unemployables under ERA supervision.[32] By these financial expedients, the FERA continued to function in Louisiana, but federal-state collaboration ended in April 1935 with the complete federalization of the program. Although state ERA director Early took a position temporarily on Hopkins's Washington staff, federal authorities apparently considered him too pro-Long in his attitudes and appointments. Hopkins replaced him with an acknowledged anti-Longite, Frank H. Peterman.[33] Although Peterman served with little distinction as FERA director in Louisiana, Hopkins and Roosevelt so prized his anti-Long antagonism that they continued him as administrator for the Works Progress Administration in Louisiana between October 1935 and February 1936. Unfortunately a poor administrator, Peterman was guilty of "inefficiency from every angle from which a job could be viewed."[34]

The New Deal relief agencies in Louisiana seemed destined for politicalization either by Long or by Roosevelt in their running feud. Political conflict also surrounded the program of the Public Works Administration. As early as October 1933, Secretary of the Interior Harold L. Ickes criticized the state for *not* spending one-half of the federal funds allotted for highway construction. According to Williams, Long "had prevented the state from accepting the money because it would be spent under the supervision of his enemies."[35] In 1934, the PWA threatened to halt $10 million in loans to Louisiana in retaliation for a new state law creating a moratorium on debts except those owed to local, state, and federal governments, but the PWA backed down from its all-too-weak position after Long challenged it. By the spring of 1935, however, when Long's "Share Our Wealth" campaign attracted a national following estimated at between six and eight million persons, the Roosevelt admininstration could no longer tolerate Long's efforts to control federal spending in Louisiana. On the other hand, Long could not endure the use of federal patronage to weaken his state power base. Seeking to negate federal domination of relief programs, Long's subservient legislature created a state "bond and tax board" to approve (or disapprove) debts incurred by any governmental subdivision in Louisiana and to supervise the distribution of all federal grants. The measures demonstrated Long's independence, but served no useful purpose for Louisiana. Hopkins completed the federalization of the FERA–WPA activities, and Ickes cut off an estimated $30 million in PWA funds earmarked for Louisiana. "In the war between the Kingfish and Washington," Kane concluded that "the little Louisianan was the forgotten man."[36]

Louisianans may not have received all the benefits possible from New Deal programs as a result of obstacles thrown up by Long and Roosevelt, but they were not forgotten. New Deal agencies reached into every aspect of Louisiana to touch, albeit sometimes lightly or indirectly, the lives of all. The FERA–ERA provides an obvious example. The FERA's Work Division operated in communities of 500 or more persons to provide unemployment relief projects. FERA-sponsored programs in New Orleans illustrate its nature and success. In February 1935, the FERA in New Orleans employed 20,000 laborers on seventy projects. FERA workers transformed a cut-over cypress marsh of about one thousand acres adjacent to the New Orleans's City Park into a magnificent extension through draining, landscaping, and building recreational facilities; built a concrete promenade and a five-mile scenic highway along Lake Ponchartrain; built additional levees against the threat of disastrous Mississippi River floods; preserved and restored historic buildings and landmarks in the French Quarter; translated, codified, and indexed historic French and Spanish documents from Louisiana's past; and provided directed playground activities for thousands of children in public school recreational projects. The FERA's Transient Division established six work camps for transients in Louisiana, at New Orleans, Baton Rouge, Monroe, Alexandria, Shreveport, Lake Charles, and New Iberia. The camp at Algiers near New Orleans could accommodate as many as 2,500 people. It began operating in May 1934 with ninety men and boys in residence, but by October there were 1,400 transients. They worked thirty hours a week using camp equipment in exchange for shelter, food, medical examinations, hospitalization, and $1.00. Men learned techniques in machine repairs, carpentry, and other crafts, and often received also elementary- or secondary-level academic courses.[37]

The FERA's Division of Self-Help Cooperatives encouraged establishment of associations to barter products and services of participating members. The FERA, for example, provided capital for expansion of the East Baton Rouge Employment Exchange, which originated in April 1933 and liquidated in the spring of 1936. In addition to providing employment, the exchange established a store, garage, canning plant, and chair factory on a barter basis. The exchange issued scrip to members in payment for goods and services. After two months in operation, the employment exchange had negotiated jobs yielding 3,500 total working days for its membership, which had grown from 60 to 500 persons.[38] The Emergency Education Division assisted both jobless teachers and adult illiterates. It also provided nursery schools for preschool children from economically deprived families. In less than eighteen months, some 1,700 nursery centers provided 50,000 children with day care services, including daily meals, immunization, and supervised recreation.[39] The College Student Aid Division made part-time employment available to needy students, thereby reducing the threat of added labor competition from the student sector. Louisiana's ERA funded college student aid in fourteen institutions of higher learning to 1,162 students at a rate of $17,430 per month.[40] The FERA's Rural Rehabilitation Division established a subsidiary agency on 24 July 1934—the Louisiana Rural Rehabilitation Corporation—to coordinate farm relief measures in areas with a population of less than 500 persons. The LRRC provided loans to farmers based on liens on their future crops, gave emergency aid when crops sustained damage from natural disasters, and initiated a beef-canning project when drought killed cattle.[41]

During the winter of 1933-34, FERA–ERA director Harry Early also headed the Civil Works Administration in Louisiana, which provided an exclusively federal program of work relief. Although state and local governments "sponsored" CWA projects by pledging financial contributions, CWA project workers received their pay directly from the federal government. Between mid-November 1933 and 31 March 1934, the CWA provided Louisiana workers with earnings of over $10.8 million. Total costs for wages and materials in Louisiana amounted to almost $14.7 million.[42] Initially, CWA workers received a minimum wage rate of 40 cents an hour for unskilled labor and $1.00 an hour for skilled labor for up to 30 hours of work per week, which might provide a minimum weekly wage of $12.00 for unskilled labor and $30.00 for skilled. However, in January 1934 the work week was reduced to 24 hours in urban centers with more than 2,500 population and to only 15 hours in centers of less than 2,500 population. Then in February 1934, the minimum wage for unskilled labor was reduced to 30 cents per hour, enabling unskilled workers to make only $4.50 per week.[43] Although the CWA originally promised considerable relief, the declining wage and work-week reduced that promise by about 63 percent within three months. Nevertheless, the CWA provided employment for substantial numbers of Louisianans, ranging from 38,636 in mid-November 1933 to 80,372 at its peak in mid-February 1934, to 1,146 in mid-April as the CWA phased out its operations.[44] The largest single construction project of the CWA in Louisiana employed over five thousand men at a cost of $1.4 million to build roads in New Orleans, but the CWA's sanitation and tick and mosquito eradication programs may have proved most beneficial in human terms. By late November 1933, a tick eradication program had begun in several parishes, involving construction of dipping vats and actual assistance in dipping cattle. This program would eventually be picked up by the WPA and extended throughout the state. The mosquito eradication campaign attacked the breeding places of yellow fever, malarial, and "plain pest" mosquitoes through dredging or draining sloughs and ravines in swamp areas. Through the sanitation program, the CWA gave one month's employment to about 23,000 farmers, tenant farmers, and sharecroppers, who were paid in food, clothes, medical care, and supplies for building their own sanitary outhouses, protecting their water supply, draining low areas near farm houses, and disinfecting and screening farm houses.[45] Of the $14.7 million expended by the CWA in Louisiana, federal funds accounted for $14.2 million, local contributions for $1.3 million, and state funds for $190,635. Louisiana's state government obviously contributed little toward relief in the bitter winter of 1933-34, but federal expenditures and programs took up much of the slack.[46]

The war between Roosevelt and Long ended by default on 10 September 1935, when Long died by an assassin's bullet. There followed one of the most bizarre political episodes of the New Deal. According to Kane, "Huey's men proposed an *anschluss* with Washington. They were ready, from the first moment, to give up the political fight to which he had dedicated the major energies of his last years. But Washington declined."[47] Roosevelt's political advisers apparently expected that without Long's personal leadership the Long machine would splinter into dissident factions and that Louisianans would seize the opportunity to elect anti-Long and pro–New Deal candidates in the January 1936 state primary. Claiming pledges of support from Washington, the anti-Long forces, led by Congressman Cleveland Dear as a candidate for governor, ceased their previous reactionary obstructionism and pushed a liberal constructive program that combined the New Deal's plans for social security, old-age pensions, and slum clearance with continuation of Long's measures for good roads, free textbooks, and homestead exemptions. The pro-Long forces, after an initial scramble for the mantle of their fallen leader, supported Richard W. Leche for governor and Earl Long, Huey's younger brother, for lieutenant governor. Pro-Long candidates stressed the martyrdom and sainthood of Huey Long, their faith in Long's "Share Our Wealth" program, and the efforts of Roosevelt to interfere in state politics. Leche charged that "not since Reconstruction days in the South has a national Administration, and particularly one Democratic in name, made such an attempt through the use of all its resources to dictate the policies of a sovereign state."[48] The January 1936 election sustained a firmly pro-Long legislature, removed the five acknowledged anti-Long and pro–New Deal congressmen, and gave Leche over two-thirds of the record vote of over one-half million. A Roosevelt supporter remarked:

> On our side we had only the federal patronage. In a vote-getting sense, this consisted mainly of WPA work orders, which were distributed by the thousands to the anti-Long organizations. They didn't help much. The poor jobless devils took the work orders readily enough, but they didn't vote WPA.[49]

A more sweeping victory than Long had ever enjoyed, the January election marked a major political defeat for the Roosevelt administration and seemingly removed any chance for creation of a loyal New Deal following in Louisiana.

Events soon proved, however, the truth of the ancient adage that "politics makes strange bedfellows." Each side had much to gain from a deal, but even more to lose from continuing enmity. Several of Long's former lieutenants were under federal income tax indictments, and many more had reason to fear federal investigations into their affairs. The Roosevelt administration had to consider the possible political influences of Louisiana's votes in the approaching 1936 Democratic National Convention and of the estimated six million "Share Our Wealth" voters in the nation that Long's heirs might rally. The pressures for rapprochement were apparently sufficient for both sides. Governor-elect Leche and others stilled their anti–New Deal rhetoric, while emissaries suggested that cooperation with New Deal programs might begin. In May, a United States attorney moved for dismissal of the criminal tax proceedings pending against pro-Long associates. Calling the action "The Second Louisiana Purchase," Kane summed up the situation: "Jefferson had paid $15,000,000. The United States bought Louisiana back for the sacrifice of some possible prison terms. The Roosevelt Administration made Jefferson look like a sucker."[50] In early June, the Louisiana legislature convened on foreign soil (Texas) to pay tribute to Roosevelt, who visited the Texas Centennial grounds on the way to Gulf fishing. After praising providence for sending Roosevelt to deliver the nation from ruin, the legislature speedily repealed Long's anti–New Deal measures, created a new Department of Public Welfare, and provided for state compliance with the new Social Security Act. At the Democratic National Convention in late June, the Louisiana delegation supported Rooevelt's move to abrogate the old two-thirds rule and seconded Roosevelt's renomination for president. In the new friendly atmosphere, the Roosevelt administration granted patronage privileges to the Leche regime and dropped anti-Long officeholders from federal agencies in Louisiana. Obstacles that had delayed federal projects in the state for years suddenly disappeared. The arrangement reflected no credit either on the New Deal or on post-Long politics in Louisiana, but it flooded the state with money, jobs, and building projects. As Kane observed: "Evidences of prosperity thrust themselves upward on all sides; parts of Louisiana became gardens of WPA and PWA goodwill."[51]

The expenditures of New Deal agencies in Louisiana indicated the economic and physical impact of the New Deal. From 1933 through 1939, Louisiana received over $465 million (about $221 per person) in federal grants as well as over $290 million (about $138 per person) in federal loans.[52] While probably about forty percent of the federal funds were received before the "Second Louisiana Purchase," and about sixty percent after, the total expenditures represented an enormous pump-priming stimulus for Louisiana's economy and massive relief for the state's poor and unemployed. The $211 per person average in federal grants over the six years, for example, almost matched the $222 per capita income of Louisianans in 1933. More important, of course, the federal grants were expended primarily for wages and the federal loans for public service projects, while per capita income was derived merely by dividing the state's total income by its total population, overlooking inequities in wealth distribution.

Louisiana's agricultural-based economy clearly demonstrated the effects of New Deal recovery measures. From its low point of $59 million in

1932, Louisiana's cash farm income climbed for five consecutive years until in 1937 Louisiana farmers received almost $129.9 million. The unprecedentedly large harvest of 1937 in both state and nation momentarily checked the income rise. Nevertheless, in 1938 farm cash income in Louisiana totaled over $126.4 million, a 114 percent increase over the 1932 figure. Direct government payments of almost $17.6 million in 1938 accounted for only 14 percent of the increase. Farmers in Louisiana, moreover, enjoyed a greater cash income increase than farmers in the nation. The nation's cash farm income in 1938 was only 73 percent larger than in 1932. Louisiana's increased farm income resulted from generally better prices as well as greater productivity. Of Louisiana's three major farm commodities—cotton, sugar cane, and rice—only sugar cane failed to rise in price and actually declined between 1932 and 1938. However, increased sugar cane production brought the farmer over 60 percent more cash income from that product by 1938. Although the average price for rice rose by only about 50 percent, that increase plus greater production gave farmers a cash income over 100 percent higher. Cotton (both cotton lint and cottonseed) continued to dominate the Louisiana farm economy, bringing a slighter greater cash income than rice and sugar cane combined. Cotton lint increased in price by only 30 percent, but prices for cottonseed more than doubled. Louisiana farmers received almost $36 million in cash income from cotton in 1938 as compared with $20.3 million in 1932. New Deal efforts at diversification encouraged Louisiana farmers to increase production of corn and hogs, truck crops, and chickens and eggs. The combined cash income from these farm products had increased by over 160 percent by 1938, putting an additional $10 million in farmers' pockets. Encouragement of these food and feed crops brought not only greater income but also greater home use, which raised farm living standards. Rising real estate values on Louisiana farms also testified to agricultural recovery. By March 1933, farm real estate in Louisiana was valued at only 89 percent of its pre–World War I level, whereas the nationwide figure was 73 percent. Six years later, the per-acre estimated value in Louisiana had reached 117 percent of the prewar base, and national farm real estate values had reached only 84 percent. Thus, Louisiana farm values not only shared in the national increase but also exceeded the national average by 17 percent. Forced sales of Louisiana farms, moreover, dropped from 75 percent for the year ending March 1933 to only 1.2 percent for the year ending March 1939, and the number of farm bankruptcies decreased by one-half.[53]

Louisiana farmers benefited greatly from the Agricultural Adjustment

Administration soil conservation programs, Farm Credit Administration's financing operations, and the Rural Electrification Administration's extension of services. In 1936, about 69 percent of Louisiana's total cropland of about 5 million acres was covered by applications for payments under the Soil Conservation and Domestic Allotment Act. Almost 444,000 acres were diverted from soil-depleting crops, and 808,000 acres received help in building soil fertility through legume seedings, fertilization, tree plantings, and terracing. In 1938, almost one-half of Louisiana's total cropland benefited from federal soil-building programs. The Farm Credit Administration both loaned money to individual farmers and extended credit to privately organized agricultural financing institutions and farmers' cooperatives. The Federal Land Bank of New Orleans and the land bank commissioner provided the chief sources of long-term mortgage loans during the early New Deal years when farmers needed to refinance burdensome farm mortgages and other debts. By 31 December 1939, over $24 million land bank and commissioner loans were outstanding in Louisiana and represented mortgage indebtedness on 13,514 farms, or 44.3 percent of Louisiana's total farm mortgage debt. Following passage of the Farm Credit Act of 1935, increasing numbers of Louisianans used federal loans to finance purchase of farms rather than merely to refinance existing mortgages. Between 1935 and 1939, the Land Bank and the Federal Farm Mortgage extended $3.7 million to 1,900 farmers and former tenants to finance purchase of farms. Credit extended to private financing institutions and farmers' cooperatives vastly increased the volume of short-term loans for farm operation. The largest sources were the eight Louisiana production credit associations, organized in 1933-34, which by late 1939 had loaned more than $28 million. In addition, the New Orleans Bank for Cooperatives, another FCA institution, made loans to fruit and vegetable cooperatives, cooperative sugar mills, and farm supply associations. By late 1938, eleven Louisiana co-ops had secured loans from the New Orleans bank amounting to over $3 million. In 1935, only 1.7 percent of Louisiana's farms (or 2,826 farms) enjoyed electric service. Following creation of the Rural Electrification Administration on 11 May 1935, eleven REA-financed projects in Louisiana received over $2.5 million by October 1939 for construction of about 2,700 miles of rural lines, serving over 9,000 farm homes. Introduction of electricity encouraged poultry-raising, but most important it made possible use of radios, refrigerators, and other household appliances.[54]

The Farm Security Administration, created in 1935 to encourage low-income families to become self-supporting, operated three programs in

Louisiana. The rehabilitation loan program provided loans to farmers for purchase of feed, seed, fertilizer, and equipment, which they needed to continue farming. The homestead program developed a few rural communities to demonstrate more efficient farming methods and economic organization. The tenant purchase program enabled tenant farmers to borrow funds for farm purchases. The FSA had aided over 52,188 Louisiana families by 1 July 1939. Of these, some 49,270 families received rehabilitation loans totaling almost $11 million for equipment and training in sound farm methods. In addition, the FSA granted $298,736 to 10,669 families in extreme need for purchase of food, fuel, and other necessities. Community service loans of $198,456 from the FSA enabled neighboring groups of low-income farmers to purchase cooperatively such expensive farm equipment as tractors and combines. Through FSA arbitration, moreover, 2,958 debt-burdened Louisiana farmers adjusted their debts of $5,390,691 downward by $1,427,690 for a 26.5 percent relief. This not only saved many farmers from foreclosure but also gave creditors substantial payments on seemingly bad debts. The homestead program developed eleven rural communities in Louisiana. Although no two projects were quite alike, each attempted to construct resident houses, schools, cooperative stores, and other facilities such as cooperative cotton gins. The Bankhead-Jones Act of 1937, which attacked the South's perennial problem of farm tenancy, enabled 249 Louisiana tenant farmers to borrow over $1.3 million for farm purchases and building repairs by the end of the 1938-39 fiscal year. During the following year, approximately 300 tenant loans, totaling over $1.5 million, were made.[55] Reaching its peak in 1935, farm tenancy would decline in Louisiana thereafter.

Unfortunately, the New Deal's effort to reduce farm tenancy did not effectively reach the lowest economic level—Negroes. In 1935, Louisiana had a total of 108,377 farm tenants, but the number would decline to 89,167 by 1940 and to 63,541 by 1949.[56] Negroes composed 54.3 percent of Louisiana's tenant population in 1935, 59,456 out of 108,377. However, they also composed 66.7 percent of the croppers, who were the lowest level of tenants. The Farm Security Administration's working policy was to move tenant applicants up the scale of tenancy by using rehabilitation loans until they proved worthy and capable of operating and owning farms. When the tenant had proved that he only needed a chance, then the FSA might consider granting tenant-purchase loans (100 percent loans at 3 percent interest with a 40-year period in which to repay the loan). The FSA's rural rehabilitation program in Lousiana dispensed over $27.5 million between 1937 and 1943. Original or first loans totaled 34,371 with the average loan being $282, and supplemental or second loans totaled 77,639 with an average of $206.[57] However, the FSA lacked sufficient funds to support the tenant-purchase program. Between 1937 and 1941, 14,815 Louisiana tenants applied for tenant-purchase loans, but the FSA made only 941 loans, amounting to almost $2 million. The average loan per farm was $5,153, and the average size of the farms purchased was 74 acres.[58] Both the FSA's insistence upon prior performance and its lack of funds hampered the efforts of Negro sharecroppers at the bottom of Louisiana's agricultural ladder from improving their status. Nevertheless, at least one of the FSA's land-leasing associations—the LaDelta Cooperative Association, Inc., at Tullulah, Louisiana—sought "to resettle low-income and needy Negro farm families on small improved farms." The LaDelta Association comprised 143 families who operated an area of approximately 10,500 acres. By June 1942, the FSA had invested $967,723 in the project to purchase land, build homesteads, establish cooperative business enterprises, and create recreational and educational community facilities.[59]

The urban-oriented Public Works Administration had by July 1939 completed or initiated projects in Louisiana at a total cost of $79,035,909. Of this amount, nonfederal projects accounted for $52,266,479, and federal projects accounted for $26,769,430. The federal projects were already about 99 percent financially complete and the nonfederal projects were about 75 percent financially complete. All told, the projects by mid-1939 had provided almost 26 million man-hours of work for Louisianans. The federal program of the PWA in Louisiana provided funds for flood control, streets and highways, post office and administrative buildings, water navigation aids, and improvements to federal land military facilities. Three-fifths of the funds, or $15,727,519, were spent for extensive flood control work on the lower Mississippi River, especially the Atchafalaya Basin. This included dikes, levees, and channel straightening. Over six million man-hours of site labor were paid for under this program. At the peak of labor in November 1933, flood control work employed 10,280 men. In cooperation with the State Highway Department of Louisiana, the PWA provided over $5.8 million for construction and improvements of roads and highways. The PWA also spent almost $2.2 for construction of officers' quarters, barracks, administration buildings, airport renovations, and other improvements at Barksdale Field, an army aviation post. Almost $200,000 was alloted for construction or improvement of post office buildings at Bastrop, Houma, New Orleans, and Plaquemine, and $340,843 provided for construction of a Marine Hospital at Carville. By mid-1939, the 227 federal projects of the PWA had provided almost thirteen million man-hours of labor.[60]

The PWA's nonfederal projects were financed by a 45 percent grant and often by a PWA loan for the remainder. By mid-1939, the PWA had participated in 228 nonfederal projects in Louisiana, principally the construction of educational buildings, hospitals, courthouses and city halls, sewer and water systems, and streets and highways. PWA allotments of $4,662,203 in loans and $19,722,414 in grants accounted for almost fifty percent of the projects' estimated total costs of $52,266,479. Without the stimulus of PWA funds, most of the projects would not have been undertaken. Louisiana's cities benefited substantially. New Orleans, for example, desperately needed new and expanded medical facilities. The main building of its ancient Charity Hospital had been condemned not only by the New Orleans fire marshall but also by the State Board of Health. With massive PWA aid, a new twenty-story modern hospital with bed accommodations for 2,470 was constructed, and several other small, specialized institutions were improved and incorporated into the Charity Hospital complex. These improvements cost almost $13 million. Construction of educational buildings at a total cost of almost $22 million, however, provided the greatest area of PWA nonfederal allotments. The largest percentage of the funds went into construction on the Baton Rouge campus of Louisiana State University, but other small colleges also benefited. Southwestern Louisiana Institute in Lafayette (now the University of Southwestern Louisiana and the largest university under the State Board of Education) began its rise from the smallest of state colleges thanks to the impact of federal funds. Allotments from the National Youth Administration, the Works Progress Administration, and the Public Works Administration initiated a major building program. The PWA provided for thirteen buildings, a one-story addition to the dining hall, and improvements to recreational and service facilities. The buildings included two girls' dormitories, a fine arts building, clinic and infirmary, elementary training school, library, stadium and dormitory, president's house, industrial arts building, engineering and laboratory buildings, girls' gymnasium, demonstration high school, and recreation center. Built of concrete and brick, all the buildings still serve the university and many in their original capacity.[61]

Between its beginning in October 1935 and 30 June 1939, the Works Progress Administration (later the Work Projects Administration) expended over $80 million in federal funds in Louisiana, of which approximately 85 percent went for wages for Louisiana's able-bodied unemployed. During the four years, the PWA provided a working income for several hundred thousand Louisianans. WPA employment hit a peak in December 1938, when it employed 54,736 persons; but even as late as June 1939, the WPA provided work for 42,225 persons and monthly earnings of over $1.8 million. Local and state governments sponsored WPA construction and service projects, usually by proposing, planning, and then paying most of the nonlabor costs. The WPA substantially expanded and improved Louisiana's public facilities through its construction program. City streets and highways made up over 40 percent of WPA construction projects, which included over 1,200 miles of roads, 2,000 culverts, and 286 bridges. Municipalities benefited from WPA additions of over 115 miles of water mains, aqueducts, and distribution lines, as well as almost 220 miles of trunk and lateral sewer lines. In rural areas, WPA workers constructed farm-to-market roads. Public buildings repair and construction, especially of educational facilities, composed over 12 percent of the total WPA program in Louisiana. By mid-1938, the WPA had constructed 181 public buildings, including schools, auditoriums, stadiums, grandstands, gymnasiums, and office buildings, while modernizing and improving 339 others. About 11 percent of total WPA construction funds went for development of recreational facilities, since hundreds of municipalities sponsored construction of parks, playgrounds, and community centers. The WPA built 22 athletic fields, 4 playgrounds, five parks, 9 swimming pools, and 39 tennis courts, while improving 14 athletic fields, 8 parks, and 36 playgrounds. WPA conservation projects terraced land in north Louisiana, where erosion constituted a serious problem, and installed drainage facilities in swampy southern Louisiana. In New Orleans, the WPA provided surveys of soil foundation, city planning, and traffic control; and for the state, a WPA coast and geodetic survey covered 50 percent of the state's area. Cooperating with other federal agencies, which acted as sponsor, the WPA helped the National Wildlife and Fisheries Bureau to develop game refuges and the Veterans' Administration to improve VA hospitals.

The WPA's Service Program assisted the educational and welfare needs of Louisiana communities. Educational programs varied from instructional classes to research and records projects. The WPA employed hundreds of needy teachers and educated thousands of interested citizens through language classes, home and family living seminars, citizenship training, vocational education, first-aid instruction, and literacy courses. Continuing and expanding the Long-initiated literacy drive, the WPA paid teachers' salaries, while school boards furnished classrooms and materials. By 1939, almost 50 percent of Louisiana's illiterates had received basic instruction in reading and arithmetic at a cost to the WPA of over $500,000. WPA-established nursery schools employed teachers, nurses, and nutritionists to provide children with proper health care, dietary attention, and educational instruction. This aided development of permanent nursery school programs in many Louisiana communities. The welfare phase of the WPA Service Program created a food distribution project that encouraged gardening and canning of produce by the needy unemployed. The WPA provided over four million quarts of milk and almost forty million pounds of foodstuffs to the needy as well as 664,000 hot lunches to undernourished school children. The hot lunch program became so popular that the state legislature appropriated funds for continuation of this WPA-pioneered project. WPA library programs extended library services to rural areas and provided funds for purchase of new books, refurbishing of old ones, and employment of librarians. Over one million public school and library books were renovated, and over one-half million volumes were catalogued by WPA workers. WPA sewing rooms, employing from 10 to 1,000 unskilled women from low-income families, produced wearing apparel, mattresses, and comforters. Over 1,800,000 articles and garments were provided for distribution to needy families. Farmers constituted a special case of WPA employment. Since many farm workers and tenant farmers owned no land and failed to qualify for FSA benefits, the WPA in 1938 instituted a program for landless agricultural laborers. Although the farm laborers received the lowest unskilled pay rates, farm owners complained that WPA employment seriously handicapped the whole agricultural effort and forced them to raise wages for farm laborers. WPA workers gave important emergency aid during natural disasters in Louisiana. They built or reinforced levees during the 1937 flood, saved the sugar cane crop during the hard freeze of 1937, and helped avert epidemic following the 1940 hurricane.[63]

Smaller in scope and funding but important for its job-training opportunities and permanent benefits to Louisiana, the Civilian Conservation Corps compiled an impressive record of achievements. Until the late nineteenth century, virgin pine forests covered most of northern Louisiana, but massive exploitation of the timber resources after 1881 left large areas of cut-over and burned-over lands unable to reproduce naturally second-growth forests. The situation created not only a conservation crisis but seriously depressed the forest industry, including timber-associated manufactures. At its peak in 1913, lumber production amounted to over 4.1 billion board feet; but by 1930, production had dropped to 567 million board feet, for a decline of 86.5 percent. In its first six-month enrollment period in 1933, the CCC employed about 4,250 men in twenty-three Louisiana camps; but by the fourteenth enrollment period, 1 October 1939 to 31 March 1940, the number of enrollees had increased to about 5,800 and the number of camps to twenty-nine. One of the first CCC projects was the development of the Stuart tree nursery in the Kisatchie National Forest near Alexandria, which became the South's largest and which by 1937 produced annually 26 million trees. The CCC planted in Louisiana the second-highest number of trees in federal forests of any state in the country. A 1940 report of Louisiana's Department of Conservation listed the following major accomplishments of the CCC in Louisiana forests: 2,998 bridges, 31 lookout towers, 2,142 miles of telephone lines, 63 cattle guards, 3,070 miles of main roads (truck trails), 23 miles of minor roads, 30 miles of foot trails, 90,301 man-days of fire fighting and presuppression, 3,515 miles of fire breaks, 1,550 miles of roadside and trailside clearing, 10 tower residences, reduction of fire hazards on 9,656 acres, 2 forest administration buildings, and 8 other buildings. The soil conservation activities of the CCC were equally important, for by 1939 Louisiana still had an estimated 13 million acres requiring erosion prevention and 6 million acres with 25 percent of the top soil lost. CCC workers planted 6,285 acres in trees, built 5,646 check dams and 225 miles of outlet channels, and seeded or sodded almost 1.5 million square yards. Primarily responsible for development of Louisiana's state park system, the CCC built picnic grounds, shelters, camping areas, swimming-boating-fishing facilities, and accompanying road, walkway, water, and sanitary systems. Of the six large regional parks that today provide recreation for the state, the CCC developed four. In addition to permanent forestry, soil conservation, flood control, and recreational benefits, the CCC gave each Louisiana enrollee at least ten hours of instruction and on-the-job training each week, enabling many to secure positions in private industry. By mid-1939, the CCC had furnished employment to an estimated 42,000 Louisiana enrollees, most of whom were young men between the ages of nineteen and twenty-one years.[64]

The myriad New Deal programs in Louisiana almost defy enumeration, but the Roosevelt administration's encouragement of home-owning and the Social Security Act deserve notice. Between June 1933 and June 1936, the Home Owners' Loan Corporation in Louisiana provided over $40 million to refinance 14,379 homeowners. Unable to secure private credit and averaging two years behind on principal, interest, and taxes, these borrowers would almost certainly have lost their homes without HOLC assistance. Moreover, the Federal Housing Administration in Louisiana conducted a net volume of business through 30 June 1939 of almost $22 million, of which $14.6 million represented small-home mortgages accepted for insurance, $630,500 represented large-scale housing mortgages closed, and almost $6.6 million represented insured property improvement loans. In order to participate in the United States Housing Authority's slum clearance and low-rent housing program, Louisiana passed its own Housing Authority Law in 1936, amended it in 1938, and secured approval of its constitutionality from the state supreme court in 1938. By late 1939, six low-rent housing projects had begun construction in New Orleans with the assistance of over $25.3 million in USHA loans. Intended to accommodate almost 5,000 families, the projects were required to be financially in the reach of the lowest-income families living in the slums.[65] On 29 June 1936, Louisiana passed its unemployment compensation law in response to provisions of the Social Security Act. Benefits did not become payable until January 1938, but by the end of August 1939, payments totaled over $8.4 million, and about 425,000 workers had qualified for coverage. Under the old-age insurance system, 4,929 single cash payments, totaling $193,496, were made to workers at age 65 and to heirs of workers between January 1937 and August 1939. Under the Social Security Act's program of public assistance, Louisiana between 7 August 1936 and 30 June 1939 received $101,450 for aid to the blind and almost $2.4 million for aid to dependent children. By 31 August 1939, Louisiana had also received $335,074 for maternal and child health services, $52,500 for services for crippled children, $102,593 for child welfare services, and $601,588 for public health services.[66]

By mid-1939, Louisiana had received about $750 million in federal grants and loans; but as the flow of funds increased, so did political corruption in the state. Officials and friends of Governor Leche's administration became spoilsmen on a grand scale. As Harnett Kane testified: " 'Share the Wealth' was a slogan they understood well. There was so much to share that they stuck together, almost to the end, one for all, all for one thing. They knew exactly what they wanted: everything in sight."[67] In June 1939, the national press spotlighted Louisiana's corruption, and Governor Leche resigned in favor of Lieutenant Governor Earl K. Long. Soon Louisiana became the subject of massive federal investigations by the

Department of Justice, the Post Office Department, the Internal Revenue Service, the Securities and Exchange Commission, the Commodity Exchange, the Public Works Administration, a special congressional committee, federal grand juries, and others. Hundreds of indictments were returned against Louisiana officials. In January 1940, in the midst of these revelations, came the primary for selection of the Democratic gubernatorial nominees. Earl Long sought to perpetuate the Long political dynasty, and Sam H. Jones campaigned as a reform (but not an anti-Long) candidate. Despite the scandals, Jones barely won the nomination with 52 percent of the popular vote. He promised to clean up the corruption, but also to preserve the increased state services provided by Longism. Speaking to the legislature in May 1940, Jones declared:

> The principal reason for the revolutionary changes of 1928 was that the great masses of the people were being forgotten. . . . The present regime, at its inception, was ushered in because of the sins and faults and defects of a preexisting group. Many thousands of Louisianans were ready for a change which would dig up by the roots the power then entrenched and give it to the people—benefits of which they were justly entitled.[68]

No one could turn back the clock on Longism in Louisiana. All subsequent governors would extend state services to the people, but most did so with greater economy and efficiency. Corruption also continued, although not on such a grand scale. Louisianans then as today still evaluated their governments not on how much politicians steal but on what benefits the people receive.

In Louisiana, the overlapping, competing, but often complementary forces of Huey P. Long and Franklin D. Roosevelt complicate generalizations about the New Deal's impact. The Louisiana experience offers no support for the claim of William E. Leuchtenburg that "in eight years, Roosevelt and the New Dealers had almost revolutionized the agenda of American politics," or of James T. Patterson that "The New Deal years witnessed neither federal dictation, a complete cooperative federalism, nor a dramatically new state progressivism."[69] In 1928, for the first time, Louisiana's lower classes captured political power in the person of Huey Long. Unlike others appealing for lower-class support, Long fulfilled his promise of benefits to the people. If in the process the people lost various constitutional protections, they also received public services that satisfied some of their deep-rooted frustrations. Between 1930 and 1933, Louisianans felt the impact of the Great Depression, but that impact lessened under the reality of Long's massive building program and the promise of Long's responsive, activist leadership. Huey Long revolutionized the agenda of Louisiana politics, but New Deal funds and programs assisted the completion of that revolution. With the New Deal's advent in 1933, Louisianans received further benefits from federal largess, much of which reached further down the economic ladder than even Long had accomplished. The conflict between Roosevelt and Long may have slowed the flow of federal funds into the state, but Louisiana's masses probably agreed with Long's criticism that the New Deal did not go far enough or fast enough in working for the people's interests. Long's critics, it must be remembered, were persons who already had it made, not the people who had little chance of making it. Certainly the New Deal years witnessed attempts at federal dictation in Louisiana, which were only partially blocked by Long's dictatorial attitude and measures, but to which Long's immediate successors largely submitted. After Long's death, the new "friendly atmosphere" between Louisiana and Washington clearly approximated a completely cooperative federalism. Long's followers accommodated themselves to political realities and thereby primed the federal pump for their own and Louisiana's advantage. The availability of federal funds enabled Long's successors to continue and to expand Long's benefits to Louisiana, and thereby to reinforce their political power base. Criminal greed brought the downfall of Long's successors under the scrutiny of federal investigations and the decisions of federal courts. However, between 1928 and 1940 Louisianans became accustomed to receiving services from the state and federal governments. Their expectations rose so far that no subsequent state government could ignore them with impunity. Huey Long made a sharp break with the past and supplied a dramatically new state progressivism (or perhaps neo-populism). New Deal innovations and funds sustained that new state progressivism in Louisiana and directed it toward the welfare state.

1. Stuart O. Landry, ed., *Louisiana Almanac and Fact Book: 1949* (New Orleans, 1949), p. 355.

2. Office of Government Reports, Statistical Section, Report 10, Vol. 2, "Louisiana," (typescript, Washington, 1940), p. 7.

3. Roman Heleniak, "Local Reaction to the Great Depression in New Orleans, 1929–1933," *Louisiana History* 10 (1969): 289–306.

4. T. Lynn Smith and Homer L. Hitt, *The People of Louisiana* (Baton Rouge, 1952), pp. 112–27.

5. U.S. Department of Commerce, *Sixteenth Census of the United States: 1940* (Washington, 1941), vol. 3, pt. 3: 16–18, 2328.

6. Ibid., vol. 2, pt. 3: 331.

7. Ibid., vol. 1, pt. 5: 114.

8. Smith and Hitt, *The People of Louisiana*; Fred B. Kniffen, *Louisiana: Its Land and People* (Baton Rouge, 1968); WPA Writers' Project, *Louisiana: A Guide to the State* (New York, 1941); Perry H. Howard, *Political Tendencies in Louisiana* (Baton Rouge, 1971).

9. Charles L. Dufour, *Ten Flags in the Wind: The Story of Louisiana* (New York, 1967), p. 5.

10. Quoted in Harnett T. Kane, *Louisiana Hayride: The Rehearsal for Dictatorship, 1928–1940* (New York, 1941), p. 137.

11. T. Harry Williams, *Huey Long* (New York, 1970), p. 550.

12. Allan P. Sindler, *Huey Long's Louisiana: State Politics, 1920–1952* (Baltimore, 1956), p. 103.

13. Williams, *Huey Long*, p. 546.

14. Kane, *Louisiana Hayride*, p. 141.

15. Ibid.; Williams, *Huey Long*, p. 523.

16. Williams, *Huey Long*, p. 550.

17. Kane, *Louisiana Hayride*, pp. 143, 142.

18. Donald Wilson, *Public Social Services in Louisiana* (Monroe, La., 1943), pp. 23–24.

19. WPA Writers' Project, *Louisiana*, pp. 112–13; see also: Louisiana Department of Public Welfare, "A History of Public Assistance Measures in the Past," *Annual Report, 1937* (Baton Rouge, 1937).

20. Lillie H. Nairne, "A Study of the Administration of Relief to the Unemployed in Louisiana with Special Reference to a Future Public Welfare Program" (M.A. thesis, Tulane University, 1935), pp. 4–5.

21. See Pamela Bordelon, "The Works Progress Administration in Louisiana" (M.A. thesis, University of Southwestern Louisiana, 1971); Kathryn Park, "The Federal Emergency Relief Administration in Louisiana, 1933–1937" (M.A. thesis, University of Southwestern Louisiana, 1971).

22. Ibid. See also B. F. Eshleman, "A General Report of the Unemployment Relief Activities in Louisiana" (Louisiana Room, Louisiana State University, 19 January 1938), pp. 1–7.

23. Williams, *Huey Long*, p. 453.

24. James A. Farley, *Behind the Ballots* (New York, 1938), p. 171; sketches of Long's activities rest entirely on the studies of Williams and Kane cited previously.

25. For a detailed treatment of FERA politics, see Park, "The FERA in Louisiana, 1933–1937," chap. 2; I express with great appreciation my indebtedness to numerous graduate students in my New Deal seminar for excellent papers on agencies in Louisiana, but especially to Pamela Bordelon on the WPA, Kathryn Park on the FERA, George Stearns on the banking crisis, Jerry Valentine on WPA educational activities, James Bealer on the Farm Security Administration, and Virgil Mitchell on the Civil Works Administration.

26. *New Orleans Times-Picayune*, 13 November 1933.

27. *Ibid.*, 30 May 1934.

28. Sidney Tobin, "The Early New Deal in Baton Rouge as Viewed by the Daily Press," *Louisiana History* 10 (1969): 313.

29. Park, "The FERA in Louisiana, 1933–1937," chap. 2.

30. Harry L. Hopkins to Governor Oscar Allen, 29 May 1934, File D-50, Works Progress Administration Correspondence, State Archives and Records Commission.

31. Park, "The FERA in Louisiana, 1933–1937," chap. 2.

32. Wilson, *Public Social Services in Louisiana*, p. 28.

33. *New Orleans Times-Picayune*, 19 April 1935.

34. "Final Report of the Louisiana WPA," p. 5, Works Progress Administration Records, Record Group 69, National Archives (on microfilm in University of Southwestern Louisiana Library).

35. Williams, *Huey Long*, p. 639.

36. Kane, *Louisiana Hayride*, p. 128.

37. Park, "The FERA in Louisiana, 1933–1937," chap. 4.

38. Ibid.

39. *New Orleans Times-Picayune*, 14, 16 February 1935.

40. Ibid., 13 August 1935.

41. Park, "The FERA in Louisiana, 1933–1937," chap. 3.

42. Works Progress Administration, *Analysis of Civil Works Program Statistics* (Washington, June 1939), p. 30.

43. *New Orleans Times-Picayune*, 26, 28 November 1933, 19 January, 22 February, 1934.

44. WPA, *Analysis of CWA Program Statistics*, p. 18.

45. *New Orleans Times-Picayune*, 30 November, 21 December 1933, 11 January, 10 March 1934. A Ph.D. dissertation, "The Civil Works Administration in Louisiana," is now in progress by Virgil Mitchell at the University of Southwestern Louisiana.

46. WPA, *Analysis of CWA Program Statistics*, p. 30.

47. Kane, *Louisiana Hayride*, p. 157.

48. Ibid., p. 161.

49. Hodding Carter, "Huey Long: American Dictator," in Isabel Leighton, ed., *The Aspirin Age, 1919–1941* (New York, 1949), p. 357.

50. Kane, *Louisiana Hayride*, pp. 183–84.

51. Ibid., p. 201.

52. Leonard Arrington, "The New Deal in the West: A Preliminary Statistical Inquiry," *Pacific Historical Review* 38 (1969): 311–16.

53. Office of Government Reports, Statistical Section, Report 10, Vol. 2, "Louisiana," pp. 7–10.

54. Ibid., pp. 12, 15, 19.

55. Ibid., pp. 16–18.

56. U.S. Department of Commerce, *U.S. Census of Agriculture, 1959, Louisiana, Parishes*, Vol. 1, Pt. 35, p. 6.

57. U.S. Congress, House, Select Committee of the Committee on Agriculture, *Hearings on the Farm Security Administration*, 78th Cong., 1st Sess., (1943–44), pp. 986–91.

58. Issac Lemon, "A Study of the Tenant-Purchase Program in Louisiana" (M.A. thesis, Louisiana State University, 1942), p. 18, Table 2.

59. *Hearings on the Farm Security Administration*, p. 1063; James D. Holley, "Old and New Worlds in the New Deal Resettlement Program: Two Louisiana Projects," *Louisiana History* 11 (1970): 137–65, provides an informative comparison of the Terrebonne project's experiment with communal living and of the Crew Lake's emphasis on the family farm ideal.

60. Office of Government Reports, Statistical Section, Report 10, Vol. 2, "Louisiana," pp. 32–33.

61. Ibid., pp. 33–34.

62. Ibid., pp. 30–33; "Final Report of the Louisiana WPA," pp. 30–33; Bordelon, "The Works Progress Administration in Louisiana," chap. 2.

63. Ibid.

64. All information on the CCC in Louisiana is drawn from Hubert Humphreys's excellent two-part article entitled "In a Sense Experimental: The Civilian Conservation Corps in Louisiana," *Louisiana History* 5 (1964): 345–67; and *Louisiana History* 6 (1965): 27–52.

65. Office of Government Reports, Statistical Section, Report 10, Vol. 2, "Louisiana," (Washington, 1940), pp. 37–42.

66. Ibid., pp. 25–27.

67. Kane, *Louisiana Hayride*, pp. 6–7.

68. Howard, *Political Tendencies in Louisiana*, p. 265.

69. William E. Leuchtenburg, *Franklin D. Roosevelt and the New Deal, 1932–1940* (New York, 1963), p. 326; James T. Patterson, "The New Deal and the States," *American Historical Review* 73 (1967): 84.

Keith L. Bryant, Jr.

Oklahoma and the New Deal

VIEWING THE NEW DEAL FROM THE SAME PERSPECTIVE—BE IT
Washington or Hyde Park—historians have variously concluded that it
was "revolutionary," a "drastic new departure," a "story of adjustment,"
and "an exceedingly personal enterprise."[1] From the point of view of the
residents of Oklahoma City or Tulsa, or even Seminole, Ponca City,
Tishomingo, or Hollis, the New Deal was none of these things. In
Oklahoma, other factors were of much greater significance than the programs devised in Washington corridors, the Hyde Park study, or Columbia
University seminars. The depression itself was of more immediate concern
because agriculture and the petroleum industry, the two primary economic
endeavors in the state, had been depressed long before the "Great Crash."
Compounding the misery of the state's farmers, the dust storms of the
mid-1930s destroyed croplands and produced major demographic
changes. Poverty and want were the conditions that created the most
profound alterations of the social and economic structures of the state, and
the political institutions failed to meet the challenges these conditions
presented. Even federal programs to alleviate economic distress in Oklahoma proved to be of minimal value to most residents, and few long-
lasting socioeconomic changes were wrought by the New Deal.

Likewise, the New Deal produced only the most modest political
changes in the state. Farmers and small-town conservatives dominated the
legislature, and the governors proved to be either implacable foes of
Roosevelt or inept New Dealers. The segment of the Democratic party in
the state that supported the national administration was poorly led and often
suffered defeat in the party's primaries. In Oklahoma, the elements of the

national electorate that supported the New Deal were largely absent. Without strong labor unions, sizable ethnic blocs, large numbers of Negro voters, or reform-oriented urbanites, a pro–New Deal coalition did not develop. Roosevelt's magnetic appeal did not translate into votes for state candidates who supported his programs. The New Deal was certainly not "revolutionary" in Oklahoma and was, at best, only marginally evolutionary.

Economic misery came to Oklahoma long before 29 October 1929. Throughout the Roaring Twenties, the state suffered a rash of bank failures, retrenchment in agricultural production, and boom-and-bust cycles in the petroleum industry. Eastern Oklahoma was particularly depressed as farm property values declined by one-third to one-half and most counties suffered population declines. Only the urban areas and the southwestern cotton and northwestern wheat counties demonstrated strong economies and population increases.[2] That the state was poor and its services minimal became obvious when comparisons were made with the rest of the nation.

In an attempt to discover the "worst" state, H. L. Mencken and Charles Angoff published a three-part article in 1931 ranking the states on the basis of wealth, culture, services, medical facilities, and other characteristics. Of the forty-eight states, Oklahoma ranked thirty-ninth in tangible property per capita, forty-first in wealth, thirty-second in "culture," thirty-fifth in a "summary of health," and forty-fourth in average length of school sessions. Yet the death rate was very low, literacy was high, and the percentage of the total population in school was third highest. The population was white (only 7.2 percent were Negro), Protestant (57.1 percent were Baptists or Methodists, 1.95 percent Catholics, and .33 percent Jewish), and at least second-generation American (only 1.3 percent were foreign-born). In their summary, Mencken and Angoff concluded that the Sooner State ranked thirty-sixth among the states in their search for the "worst." One of their most telling statistics was that Oklahoma ranked thirty-seventh in state expenditures and services.[3] Those most in need of such services were the farmers, particularly the tenants.

Settled largely after 1889, Oklahoma had been overpopulated, farms were too small, debts were large, and agricultural practices were extractive, wasteful, and careless. Erosion began to occur after the original sod was cut, and one-crop farming without the use of fertilizers produced depleted soils. By the mid-1920s, farm towns were in deep trouble because of the decline of agricultural prices and growing rural poverty. Tenancy, which had always been high, increased. At the opening of the 1920s, some

50 percent of the farmers were tenants; by 1935, this would grow to 60 percent. Migration out of the state began in this period as foreclosures increased and more land fell into the hands of banks and insurance companies. Cash receipts from farming reached a peak in 1925, but the next year saw a drastic decline. Wheat and cotton, the major cash crops, were being abandoned before 1929; Oklahoma farmers shifted to other crops to avoid glutted markets.[4]

After October 1929, with farm prices continuing to fall, Oklahoma farmers refused to curtail production or acreage. Unlike other crops, cotton was clearly overproduced, and farmers could not legitimately complain that underconsumption was to blame. By the spring of 1933, 27 percent of all Oklahoma farm families were on relief, and many more were unable to qualify for aid.[5] But there were voices of hope echoing President Hoover; the *Oklahoma Farmer-Stockman* declared:

> The dry weather and hard times are but temporary. They will pass with the coming of spring when the earth smiles once more; when the gardens are full of tender vegetables, the hens are busy laying, and the cows waddle up from pasture with extended udders.[6]

The bucolic serenity suggested by the editor was only a dream.

The state's other principal economic activity, petroleum, was also rapidly becoming unprofitable for the same reason—overproduction. Since statehood in 1907, Oklahoma had attempted to regulate oil and gas production, and in 1915 passed the first state conservation law. The state had tried to limit crude oil output to market demand, and forbade wasteful production practices. When the great Seminole field opened in 1926, the Oklahoma Corporation Commission established barrel limitations and prorated pipeline runs, but statewide restrictions proved unenforceable.[7] The opening of the Oklahoma City field in 1928 compounded the problem. The state passed a new conservation law, but the market remained glutted, the price of oil fell, and the small independent producers begged for federal legislation against foreign imports.[8]

Black gold proved to be an elusive generator of wealth. The petroleum market collapsed in 1930 under the added weight of the production of the new East Texas field, yet on 3 August 1931 a federal district court ruled against the Oklahoma Corporation Commission's efforts at curtailment. Governor William "Alfalfa Bill" Murray declared martial law the following day, sending the National Guard into the fields to police the wells and pipelines. The Guard tried to prevent the flow of "hot oil," but the administration of its efforts by the governor's nephew led to charges of corruption and inefficiency. In a futile gesture, President Hoover called for voluntary cooperation. The oil fields remained in a state of chaos and violence until 16 May 1932, when the Supreme Court upheld Oklahoma's proration statute.[9]

It became obvious to Governor Murray and to Governor Alfred M. Landon of Kansas, an oilman himself, that state proration policies would fail unless all states agreed to limit production. Although Governor Ross Sterling of Texas had called out the National Guard in the East Texas field, petroleum from that area flooded the already depressed market. Governor Murray then called a series of meetings of governors and representatives of oil-producing states to coordinate their efforts. The Oil States Advisory Committee, as the group became known, functioned for a year with some success, but finally issued a call for federal control despite the opposition of the Texans on the committee. More significantly, the committee also called for an interstate oil compact to regulate petroleum production. Legislation to create the compact was introduced in Congress by Senator Elmer Thomas and Representative Tom D. McKeown of Oklahoma in the summer of 1932, but no action was taken.[10] By the time of the presidential election, the industry faced total collapse; federal inaction, divided industry spokesmen, and the inability of the states to act in concert had produced chaos.

As the industrial sector of the economy collapsed, unemployment in Oklahoma rose drastically. Employment in most aspects of the petroleum industry declined, and 2,500 coal miners and 4,000 lead miners were laid off. Between 1929 and 1933, one-half of all industrial workers in the state lost their jobs. The income decline in Oklahoma between 1929 and 1932 was third highest in the nation.[11] Cries for relief grew as additional workers were fired and tenant farmers were displaced.

Oklahoma's experience in providing relief before 1933 paralleled that of other states. Although the state government was not paralyzed, it found appropriating money for relief purposes most difficult. Sums raised were small, and relief efforts were generally combined with highway construction and maintenance. Constitutional limitations on the debts of counties and municipalities prevented borrowing from the Reconstruction Finance Corporation. Oklahoma's colorful governor, "Alfalfa Bill" Murray, gave ten unemployed men one-half acre each on the gubernatorial mansion lawn for vegetable gardens, but more realistically issued an executive order forbidding police from arresting the unemployed as vagrants and arranged for $160,000 to be appropriated for free seed for farmers.[12] Clearly, state and local efforts to aid the needy and destitute were inadequate. Even Oklahoma's cowboy-philosopher Will Rogers, normally not given to strong comments, denounced relief efforts:

> If you live under a Government and it don't provide some means of you getting work when you really want it and will do it, why then there is something wrong. You can't let the people starve, so if you don't give em work, and you don't give em food, or money to buy it, why what are they to do? What is the matter with our Country anyhow?[13]

Will Rogers had been away from his native state for many years and was perhaps unaware that Oklahomans no longer expected their state and local governments to act in a positive manner.

The political history of the Sooner State since 1907 was a study in growing irresponsibility and sterility. There had been a strong strain of progressivism in the state that produced a reformist constitution in 1907. A coalition of farm organizations, labor unions, and urban reformers dominated the state government and the Democratic party before 1920, providing Oklahoma with a responsive and responsible government. A more radical element also existed based on populism and socialism, with strength in rural counties with high levels of tenancy. World War I and the antiwar Green Corn Rebellion destroyed this left-of-center faction, and many of its former members ultimately entered the Democratic party in the early 1920s as the Farmer-Labor Reconstruction League. The recession after the war, "radicalization" of the Democratic party as seen by many Oklahomans, revival of the Ku Klux Klan, and a national trend to conservatism led to a resurgence by the Republican party.[14]

Although never successful at winning statewide office before 1920, the Republican party had remained competitive with strong support in the northern half of the state. The wheat areas, settled by Kansans and other "Yankees," traditionally voted Republican, but could not offset large Democratic majorities in the southern cotton counties. A legislative minority and a few seats in Congress continued to remain in Republican hands. After 1920, however, the party made widespread gains. Handicapped by separation of state elections from presidential years, the Republicans failed to elect a governor; but in 1920, the state's electoral votes went to Harding, the Republicans gained control of the state House of Representatives, Republican John Harreld won a United States Senate seat from the Democrats, and a majority of the congressional delegation were Republicans. A divided Democratic party enabled the Republicans to win the second Senate seat in 1924, carry the state for Hoover in 1928, and elect Republicans to a few state offices in presidential years. Superficial prosperity, the revival of the Ku Klux Klan, impeachment of two Democratic governors, Al Smith's Catholicism, and the prohibition issue gave the Republican party its first major victories. Although not considered a southern state by V. O. Key, or a western state by Frank Jonas, or even a border state by John Fenton, Oklahoma began to exhibit characteristics of the border states.[15]

The Democratic party in Oklahoma between 1920 and 1930 suffered grave internal divisions, bitter primary elections, and political defeats. Jack Walton, mayor of Oklahoma City, had been elected governor in 1922 with Reconstruction League support, but opposition by the Klan and heavy-handed use of martial law led to his impeachment. Nominated for the United States Senate in 1924, he was rejected by the voters, and W. B. Pine became Oklahoma's second Republican senator. Henry S. Johnston, elected governor in 1926, proved to be capable of consistently wrong decisions and political errors. A Protestant and a "dry," Johnston supported Al Smith in 1928; and after the voters overwhelmingly supported Hoover, the large Republican minority in the legislature joined a few conservative Democrats to impeach him. By 1930, the state government stood stripped bare of progressive leaders and both parties were bankrupt of ideas.

The depression ended the two-party competitiveness of the twenties, and left the state worse off than before. The strong labor unions of the progressive period had become less significant as they declined absolutely and proportionally in the general population; the small Negro bloc clung tenaciously to the party of Lincoln; the farm vote remained divided along traditional voting lines; and the two urban areas of Oklahoma City and Tulsa swung from party to party on the basis of personalities rather than issues.

The structure of the state government was not conducive to strong executive leadership or to sweeping legislative programs. The bed sheet–size ballot acknowledged the limited appointive power of the governor, whose entire "cabinet" was elected. Most executive offices, including the governorship, could be held for only one four-year term. The congressional districts and the state legislature were gerrymandered to provide Democratic victories and rural control. The low quality of men elected to state offices meant the absence of leadership and responsibility, and corruption at all levels was widespread. Heavy state property taxes fell on those least able to pay, and the inadequate income tax protected the prosperous.[16] In 1930, Oklahoma voters decided to elect strong men who promised to do something.

Hard hit by the depression, demanding a change in state government, angry at Hoover and the Republican party, Oklahomans refused to accept the status quo. "Alfalfa Bill" Murray, returning to Oklahoma after a ten-year absence in Bolivia, promised tax reforms, reduced state expenditures, and relief measures if elected governor. Populist-turned-Democrat, former Senator T. P. Gore ran for the Senate seat held by Pine on a similar platform. Running against oil millionaires in the primaries and general elections, Murray and Gore won easily to the dismay of the metropolitan press, the oil companies, and the majority of upper- and upper-middle-class voters.[17] Murray had frightened this segment of the electorate by proclaiming, "The flames ignited by economic errors, now consuming the huts and cabins of the poor, will eventually destroy the mansions and palaces of the rich, and the rich seem not to comprehend the truth."[18] Murray's rhetoric did not translate into a radical program, but he did introduce an unusual approach to government and economics—fighting the depression with the National Guard.

During the first two years of his term, Murray fought the legislature, the state university, the oil companies, the metropolitan press, his "cabinet," and state educational associations. Through legislative action, he obtained property tax relief, reorganization of some state agencies, and free textbooks for school children. Employing the National Guard, he seized control of the state's oil fields, closed state banks, opened free highway bridges, closed toll bridges, and released unemployed workers from jails. Flamboyant, egotistical, picturesque, and unflappable, Murray proved to be excellent copy for journalists and by 1932 was one of the best-known governors in the country.[19] Confusing notoriety with popularity, Murray announced himself a candidate for the Democratic nomination for president.

Murray's personality and misreading of national politics set the stage for the poor relations the state would have with the New Deal. Entering several presidential primaries, Murray attacked Franklin D. Roosevelt and his program.[20] Following losses to Roosevelt in North Dakota, Nebraska, Oregon, and Florida, Murray vituperously assaulted the New York governor, hitting an all-time low in American politics by suggesting that Roosevelt's physical infirmity was the result not of infantile paralysis but of locomotor ataxia.[21] Murray's ridiculous posturing at the Chicago convention embarrassed and angered many Oklahoma Democrats, but the governor firmly refused to allow a switch of votes to Roosevelt until the last ballot. Roosevelt, his aide Louis Howe, and Democratic Chairman James A. Farley would long remember the nomination campaign.[22]

The election of 1932 failed to alter Oklahoma's political structure, although the Negro vote moved slightly from the Republican to the Democratic column. Roosevelt trounced Hoover, who carried not one of the state's seventy-seven counties. Democrat Elmer Thomas, who had been first elected to the Senate in 1926, won reelection, and the lone Republican congressman was defeated by former oilman E. W. Marland. The Republican minority in the legislature was reduced to miniscule size. Also, the voters sent Will Rogers to Washington as congressman-at-large. No, not the entertainer and humorist but a schoolteacher from the town of Moore who happened to share his famous name.[23] After 1932, the crucial political decisions would be made in the Democratic primary and runoff primary, where New Dealers and anti–New Dealers would combat each other in extraordinary contests made complicated by the presence of Bill Murray and others who were able to develop sizable followings based not on significant issues but on personalities.

From the beginning of the "Hundred Days," relations between the New Deal and the Murray administration were difficult, particularly with regard to relief money and federal patronage. One of the major areas of difficulty with New Deal programs was the state's inability to provide matching funds. Oklahoma's constitution set limits on taxes and borrowing, and state and local revenues fell with Murray's property tax–reform program and the sharp reduction in petroleum production. In four years, the state government spent only $1,200,000 for relief.[24] But it was the administration of federal funds that was responsible for the worsening relationship between Washington and Governor Murray.

By the summer of 1933, Murray's use of relief money obtained from the RFC came under attack by New Dealers in Oklahoma, with a spirited defense issued by the governor and his partisans.[25] Murray and his supporters defended the governor's "frugality" and methods; critics complained that the governor's determination of a man's "need" in the distribution of funds tended to be based solely upon political considerations and not on a family's poverty. The governor appointed some of his allies to county relief boards, which prepared lists of "eligibles," and these men received the benefits of relief money or "made-work" jobs. Members of "Alfalfa

Bill's" cabinet, long at odds with the governor, charged that waste and graft were rampant and pleaded with federal relief administrator Harry Hopkins to deprive Murray of this source of money and patronage. Democratic party leaders in Oklahoma wrote Louis Howe that federal funds were being used to undermine Roosevelt and New Deal supporters in the state. In August 1933, Hopkins and his assistant Aubrey Williams came to Oklahoma and worked out a reorganization of Murray's program. They also issued a report that exonerated the governor of accusations of graft and mismanagement. They announced that Murray would bring in professional administrators to dispense relief funds, take the distribution of such monies out of the hands of his political friends, and redefine the basis for eligibility. Oklahoma New Dealers and the State Federation of Labor denounced the report and demanded that Murray be stripped of any control over federal funds.[26]

The controversy refused to be abated, and soon the governor indicated he would not follow the procedures established by Hopkins and Williams. In a heated letter to Henry Morgenthau, who had suggested some names for county relief boards, Murray referred to Morgenthau's associates as "Your Wall Street bunch" and declared he would not be a "cat's-paw" for the bankers trying to "destroy the good beginning of this administration."[27] Murray remained in charge of Civil Works Administration funds until February 1934, when continued charges of corruption, failure to meet employment quotas, and intransigence over appointments led to direct federal control. Despairing of ever having Murray's cooperation and under increasing political pressure, Hopkins took over the administration of relief in Oklahoma.[28] Murray was only one of several governors who frustrated relief efforts, and the decision by Hopkins would be repeated in other states.[29]

Under federal control, relief projects in Oklahoma were expanded, although some reductions were made in the eligibility lists. "Purged" of men ineligible for relief, the CWA and the PWA began the construction of airports, college dormitories, and county courthouses. The PWA had only forty-seven projects in the state, second lowest in the region, and twelve counties had no activities at all. The only large-scale construction operation was the development of Lake Murray near the Texas border. The state purchased the land, and the CWA provided 3,000 men to build the dam and clear the lake bed.[30] Despite these activities, however, relief programs in Oklahoma before 1935 were inadequate, poorly planned, and largely ineffective. The counties, towns, and cities did not have money with which to initiate projects, and local political leaders, faced with declining revenues, favored retrenchment of services, not expansion. Small-town Oklahomans viewed their local government's expenditures in the same way they saw their family budgets; there were no Keynesians on city councils or among county commissioners. Only road-building appeared to be a suitable relief project, and for that purpose earmarked gasoline taxes were available. Between April 1933 and June 1936, most Oklahoma counties received less than $50 per capita in aid, largely because of the absence of relief projects and Murray's "frugality." Only ten of the seventy-seven counties received more than $120 per capita in support, and the urban areas of Oklahoma City and Tulsa were among those receiving the least.[31] The economy of Oklahoma desperately needed "pump-priming," but political problems between the governor and Washington and limited local resources and initiative prevented massive relief efforts.

Another major political question concerned patronage. As early as June 1933, Governor Murray complained to Jim Farley that he was being denied federal appointments and stated he would not name any "dollar a year men" suggested by Harry Hopkins; he took Farley's patronage policy as a "slap at Murray." At the same time, anti-Murray forces in Oklahoma bombarded Farley and Howe with letters urging withdrawal of all patronage from the governor. Oklahoma's attorney general, J. Berry King, told other anti-Murray Democrats that Oklahomans were not getting federal jobs because the governor had stated that Roosevelt had a "loathsome disease."[32] Farley's public statement in answering a reporter's question about Murray receiving a federal appointment supports that view: "Bill Murray has as much chance to be a foreign trade representative of the United States in South America as I have to be Pope in Rome—and I'm not even a priest."[33] Both Murray and Farley made public overtures of friendship, but Farley wrote privately to Marvin McIntyre that "Bill is as crazy as a bedbug."[34] Farley came to Oklahoma in August 1934 to mollify the governor, but a week later Murray again attacked Roosevelt.

To complicate matters for Farley, Howe, and Roosevelt, neither of Oklahoma's senators could be used effectively to block Murray. Senators Elmer Thomas and T. P. Gore did not use the state Democratic organization, which Murray controlled, to dispense patronage, and this caused party officers and the congressional delegation to protest. Gore could not be considered a New Dealer by any stretch of the imagination, and often sided with Murray against Farley and Hopkins. Thomas supported the administration generally, but his demands for inflation and agriculture subsidies caused New Dealers much anguish. The congressional delegation was generally weak, and only first-term Representative E. W. Marland supported the New Deal and the president without reservation.[35] From 1933 to 1935, there was no political New Deal for Oklahoma Democrats.

Effective political leadership was desperately needed in Oklahoma as the economic crisis worsened, particularly in agriculture. Conditions among Oklahoma farmers, deteriorating since the mid-1920s, hit rock bottom in 1932. The previous year had seen a record-breaking harvest and 40-cent wheat and 5-cent cotton. The only area showing an increasing farm population was the southeast, where many sought cheap lands for subsistence farms. The value of farm real estate dropped by almost 50 percent between 1920 and 1933, yet average farm size remained constant.[36] To further complicate the situation, drought followed hard on the heels of falling prices.

The land in the Sooner State varies widely in texture, vegetation, and fertility. The eastern half of the state has a rolling terrain, densely forested in part, and well-watered. The western half is higher in elevation, covered with short grass and scrub trees, and has a thin topsoil. Conditions for wind and water erosion in the west were perfect; and beginning in 1932, nature turned this portion of the state into part of the Dust Bowl. By 1933, farmers were selling their cattle, then their machinery, and then their land—if buyers could be found. The following year brought the most severe drought in modern times. Seeds blew away, and fields were littered with the bodies of dead crows and rabbits. The first of many "Black Blizzards" came on 14 April 1935, and the exodus of farmers began.[37]

Although some farmers would laugh and sing a popular local song "Blowing Away Out On A Wheat Farm," life for most became unbearable. The sun would be shining at 6 A.M., dark clouds would gather by 10 A.M., and by noon you could neither breathe nor see. Drinking water became polluted, wet sheets over doors and windows failed to keep out the dust, and the wind sandblasted paint off cars and even houses. Some said it was the judgment of God for having plowed the plains, others said it was God's response to federal agricultural policies. Regardless, the entire state was designated a drought area.[38]

As the Dust Bowl situation became even more desperate, President Roosevelt decided to proceed with a program in which he had long been interested. He asked the chief forester for an estimate of cost for constructing shelter-belts of trees and shrubs in Oklahoma. The scheme was based on the premise that regular lines of trees would halt drifting soil, slow the wind, and retain moisture. Encouraged by Oklahoma Representative Marland, a program was developed to plant combinations of hardwoods and evergreens along east-west lines in the drought areas. The program began in March 1935.[39] The president continued his interest in the project for several years, but failed to grasp the larger problems caused by the natural disaster. As late as December 1935 he wrote Undersecretary of Agriculture Rexford Tugwell: "That dust storm problem is interesting. Will you and Harry [Hopkins] get together and let me have some kind of recommendation in regard to the program from 1 July 1936 on?"[40]

The shelterbelt, however, was not the primary source of federal aid for drought-stricken farmers. Most farmers received support through the Agricultural Adjustment Act, which proposed to restore farm income through restriction of acreage and direct payments of federal funds. Secretary of Agriculture Henry A. Wallace acted quickly in 1933 to destroy crops and livestock to prevent additional surpluses from entering the market. In a program referred to by critics as "plow up and kill," millions of acres of crops were plowed up and millions of animals were destroyed. In a land ravaged by hunger, the policy, then and now, appears unwarranted and cruel. Because of the drought, it was not necessary to plow up wheat acreage in the Great Plains, but the cotton crop was reduced in this manner. Defenders of the AAA point out that between 1932 and 1936 gross farm income rose 50 percent while farm debts fell by almost a billion dollars.[41] These crude statistics fail to note the personal tragedies such programs produced, the deterioration of the lot of farm tenants, and the maldistribution of this federal largess.

Between 1933 and 1942, the farmers of Oklahoma received from the federal government yearly payments varying from $12,746,000 the first year to $27,731,000 in 1939. The totals in 1936 and 1937 were almost as low as the initial year. At no time did the federal supports amount to more than one-sixth of total farm receipts; and, with the exception of 1937, commodity prices did not rise enough to appreciably increase receipts until 1940. Even the largest sum received, divided among 200,951 farmers and 1,015,562 people, was miniscule in terms of need. Federal payments were not evenly divided, of course, and the bulk of the aid went to cotton farmers. The wheat areas within the Dust Bowl received less support than either the corn and hog counties in the north central portion of the state or the southern cotton counties. Yet the federal program failed to win even the support of Oklahoma cotton growers; only Oklahoma and California of seventeen states failed to approve the Bankhead Cotton Control Act of 1935 by the necessary two-thirds margin.[42] The cotton farmers appear to have been determined to produce bumper crops regardless of the low prices. They, seemingly, could not adjust to the idea of restriction of acreage.

Especially victimized by federal agricultural policies were the tenant farmers of the state. Not only were 61 percent of the state's farmers tenants, but they operated the least valuable properties and were largely to be found in the southern cotton counties; there were few tenants in the wheat or corn areas. The cotton tenants had existed on the edge of poverty for a decade, suffering from a lack of education and high operating costs. Attempts to organize these farmers by the Southern Tenant Farmer's Union had failed largely because of their rapid migration.[43] Many tenants had been "tractored off" the land. One landlord declared: "In '34 I had I reckon four renters and I didn't make anything. I bought tractors on the money the government give me and got shet o' my renters."[44] Among those most affected by the AAA program were Negro tenants and sharecroppers. Between 1930 and 1935, Negro tenants declined by 24.1 percent while the number of white tenants increased. Clearly, landowners were sacrificing Negro tenants to consolidation and mechanization.[45]

As the rate of foreclosure on farm properties continued to rise and the displacement of tenants increased, extensive migration of Oklahoma agriculturalists began. At first, the movement was internal as farmers left the western drought counties for the eastern part of the state; but even there, some 60 percent of the people were on relief. After 1935, the exodus was external. The Sooners of 1889 and their children were simply giving up in the face of natural disaster, economic collapse, and federal programs inimical to their interests.[46]

Although Frances Perkins would write that "the Agricultural Adjustment program was launched to save farmers from extinction," it is clear that the AAA proved harmful to many farmers. Assistant Secretary of Agriculture Rexford Tugwell even proposed that all federal aid to Dust Bowl farmers, including AAA payments, be withdrawn to force them off of the land, which would then be acquired by the government. Such proposals raise serious questions about Arthur Schlesinger, Jr.'s conclusion that "the success of AAA derived above all from a brilliant administrative insight."[47] Senator Thomas, who could have influenced the administration's program, spent his time preaching the gospel of inflation.

Thomas's pronouncements led DuPont vice president R. M. Carpenter to declare that the senator was "even more radical than Lenin." If state politicians could be blamed for the chaos and inefficiency in the New Deal relief programs, blame for the total inadequacy of the administration's agricultural policy rested on the shoulders of the young lawyers and the university professors in the Agricultural Adjustment Administration in Washington. Although one student of the early days of the AAA has called the program "revolutionary," it failed to meet the needs of Oklahoma farmers.[48]

The New Deal response to the crisis in the petroleum industry was almost as ineffective as its approach to agriculture. Within a few days after Roosevelt's inauguration, the president asked Secretary of Interior Harold Ickes to try to obtain the cooperation of Murray and the governors of Texas and California in limiting oil production, but Governor "Ma" Ferguson of Texas failed to respond. Murray, meanwhile, continued to employ the National Guard in the oil fields to enforce Corporation Commission proration orders, but the governor finally asked Roosevelt for federal action. In an exchange of letters, "Alfalfa Bill" told the president he was just a "mate" who wanted the "skipper" to use federal police power to curb production, but allow the states to establish quotas. Roosevelt replied that the states should cooperate in limiting output. A month later Murray and Governor Landon again appealed for federal action.[49]

Part of the difficulty stemmed from the confused federal policies on petroleum. Pressure from state governors, Congress, major oil companies with foreign production, small domestic producers, and the State Department led to conflicting actions. The primary program called for curtailed production and price stability through use of the National Industrial Recovery Act. The NIRA code for petroleum, drafted in September 1933, operated for eighteen months. Section (9c) of the code forbade the shipping of "hot oil," but when enforcement proved lax, Murray and other governors asked for federal enforcement of state proration laws. As administrator of the oil code, Ickes tried to curtail production, but failed to set prices on crude oil. Even these efforts would terminate on 8 January 1935, when the Supreme Court voided the law.[50]

Murray and Governor-elect E. W. Marland continued to press for state cooperation through an oil compact. Marland called the governors of the oil producing states to his home on 3 December 1934, and a draft of an Inter-state Oil Compact was prepared. Congress approved the proposal in

August 1935, after seven states had ratified the agreement. The compact provided a means to coordinate production controls based on market demands. Additional states would ultimately join in this effort.[51]

New Deal petroleum policies were not reformist in nature and offered only modest controls at best. Throughout the period, there were few attempts to enforce antitrust legislation or to alter the depletion allowance. The states remained in control of production and achieved cooperation through their own efforts. Federal activities, ranging from "voluntary cooperation" to the Connally Hot Oil Act, which forbade shipments of illegally produced petroleum in interstate commerce, proved to be of little benefit. The states carried the concept of national petroleum planning and regulation to Washington, not the reverse.

The legislation that poured forth during the "Hundred Days" provoked claims that great reforms were being accomplished, that the social and economic order was being altered, and that prosperity loomed in the immediate future. Many greeted this flurry of activity with enthusiasm and restored confidence, but there were few signs of meaningful changes in Oklahoma. Governor Murray had been among the first governors to close banks before Roosevelt closed them nationally, and the banking crisis was eased in the state as a consequence. Unemployment continued to grow despite the actions of the federal government, and by the fall of 1934, some rural counties in the eastern portion of the state had 70 percent of their families on relief.[52] Business indicators and unemployment figures suggest that some improvement did take place in urban areas after January 1932, but this recovery was not uniform. Mineral production, for example, fell drastically throughout the 1930s, but the construction industry, one of the most depressed sectors of the national economy, did not fare as badly in Oklahoma as in other states. By 1934, building permits issued in the state were increasing; and by February 1936, a major recovery was under way. Construction benefited from public works projects, from road and highway improvements, and from private construction projects, particularly in Oklahoma City and Tulsa. Recovery failed to occur in the meat packing, lead, zinc, and glass industries where unemployment and strikes were rampant.[53]

The spotty nature of the economic recovery was also reflected in demographic changes. During the 1930s, significant population shifts occurred in Oklahoma. The rural population decreased slightly, but many western drought counties suffered large-scale population declines while eastern counties showed significant increases. The entire state had a net population loss of almost 60,000. Oklahoma City, which had an increase of over 100 percent in the previous decade, had only a 10 percent increase in the 1930s. Depending almost entirely on the depressed petroleum industry, the city of Tulsa increased in population by less than one percent in the thirties. The smaller county-seat towns were devastated by closed banks and business failures, and many residents drifted away. Blue Eagles would appear on the windows of those stores remaining open, but neither the NIRA nor the AAA were generally accepted by the people of the smaller towns. The Federal Deposit Insurance Corporation helped to restore confidence in local banks, but housing programs, the National Youth Administration, and other agencies had little or no impact. As Angie Debo has written about "Prairie City," "Depression and 'recovery' were the same so far as Prairie's business was concerned."[54] Claims that the NRA proved effective in ending the spiral of deflation, "civilized" competition, or altered wages, hours, and employment practices simply are not valid in Oklahoma.[55] Perhaps significant alterations failed to occur because of the basically conservative nature of the people of Oklahoma and their political leaders.

In 1934, the state would choose a new governor, presenting supporters of the Roosevelt administration with an opportunity to elect a more cooperative state executive. The Oklahoma congressional delegation was determined to stop Murray from naming his successor and to terminate his control over the party machinery. Congressman E. W. Marland, the staunchest New Dealer in the delegation, decided to make the race, and was supported by the national administration. Using the slogan "Bring the New Deal to Oklahoma," Marland ran against Murray's candidate, state Representative Tom Anglin, as well as former governor Jack Walton and Townsendite Gomer Smith. The principal issue proved to be not the New Deal but Murray himself. In the first primary, Marland led Anglin by a large vote, but failed to receive a majority of all votes cast. Anglin declined, however, to enter a runoff primary, and Marland became the nominee. In the general election campaign, Murray's ire at Marland led him to support Republican W. B. Pine despite a trip to Oklahoma by James Farley to persuade him to aid the Democratic ticket. There was no cause for alarm as Marland won the governorship easily, and the congressional delegation remained solidly Democratic. The 1934 election in Oklahoma fails to suggest any "current of radicalism" and turned almost entirely on state issues and personalities.[56]

Ernest W. Marland became a New Dealer after making and losing a fortune in the oil industry. Born in Pennsylvania in 1874, the son of a wealthy family, he had graduated from the University of Michigan Law School at the age of 19. He came to Oklahoma in 1911, speculated in oil, prospered, and by 1920 was worth $85 million. A humanitarian and benevolent employer, he provided his workers with innovative programs for retirement and recreation. Experiencing financial difficulties in the 1920s, he sold some of his stock in the Marland Oil Company only to see his creation slip from his grasp and become Continental Oil Company in 1929. Embittered by this loss and personally bankrupt, he left the Republican party and entered politics in 1930 as a Democrat, winning a congressional seat long held by the Republicans. A dreamer and a utopian, inept and indecisive, Marland became governor of Oklahoma at a crucial time.[57]

Marland's pledge to "Bring the New Deal to Oklahoma" was based on a program of public works, old age pensions, unemployment insurance, and a revamped tax structure. He called for 100,000 homesteads for the homeless, flood protection, reforestation, and state-owned industries to employ the jobless. The legislature was asked to create a state planning board, a housing board, and a new highway commission. He said that higher income taxes and gross production taxes on petroleum would have to be levied to finance these programs and additional relief activities. "It is the duty of the government," he said, "to provide every man able to work and willing to work with employment, and to take care of those who are unable to work."[58]

The Fifteenth Legislature moved slowly to enact this sweeping program. Marland's call for new taxes on petroleum and natural gas were opposed by these industries, and the increases that were levied were less than the governor asked. A sales tax and higher taxes on cigarettes, incomes, and inheritances raised additional revenues. As Marland pushed harder for governmental reforms and new planning agencies, legislators began to balk; and when the Fifteenth Legislature adjourned, the program remained incomplete.[59]

The Sixteenth Legislature was called into special session in November 1936, and Marland's supporters removed his opponents, particularly conservative rural Representative Leon C. Phillips, from control. His program then moved forward, but a downturn in the state's economy and the need to support weak school districts sapped revenues. The "spending Sixteenth" created the State Planning and Resources Board and a Department of Public Safety. No money, however, was appropriated for state-owned industries or housing, as Marland had asked. Marland raised

$75,000 to pay for a Brookings Institute study of Oklahoma government, but no one paid much attention to the report for the state was bankrupt.[60] Making matters worse, the Marland administration was also racked by scandals over textbook funds and pension frauds.

Although one student of Oklahoma's New Deal has referred to Marland's administration as the state's "contribution to a national movement of reform," it proved to be a failure. The governor was a weak leader surrounded by men of little talent, and demands for assertive leadership came from many quarters. Marland's personal ambitions led to clashes not only with small-town conservatives like Leon Phillips, but also with other New Dealers. The cause of the national administration was harmed almost as much by its friends as by its enemies.[61]

Personalities and factionalism marked the election of 1936 in Oklahoma. Although it was a foregone conclusion that Roosevelt would carry the state, the contest for Gore's senate seat proved divisive. A self-proclaimed "constitutional conservative" who became an anti-New Dealer, Gore was vulnerable, and several Democrats entered the primary against him. Representative Josh Lee, an ardent New Deal congressman, entered the race, as did Townsendite Gomer Smith and Governor Marland. The latter campaigned on the slogan "100 percent for Roosevelt," while Lee, a former university professor of oratory, called for "A farm for every farmer and a home for every family." Aided by a group of young lawyers, "The Rover Boys," Lee campaigned across the state attacking corporate wealth. Smith ran almost entirely on the pension question, and was supported by the left-wing Veterans of Industry of America. The primary election found Lee in front with almost one-third of the vote, Marland second, Smith a very close third, and Gore a distant fourth.[62] The primary was followed by a bitter runoff between Congressman Lee and Governor Marland. Both men sought support from Washington, but the administration remained neutral. Marland lost votes because of the new taxes, and Lee proved to be a very effective campaigner. The congressman won the nomination and the general election with ease. Alfred Landon carried only one county in the state in the presidential election despite support by "Alfalfa Bill" Murray, and the Democrats retained all of the congressional seats.[63]

The strong showing by old-age pension advocate Gomer Smith and the presence on the ballot of a referendum for a state pension plan indicated the growing demand for aid to the aged, the dependent, and the physically impaired. During the Murray administration, an attempt to earmark a one cent sales tax for pensions had failed. In September 1935, a pension had been approved; however, it was soon declared unconstitutional. Demands from the elderly, popular support for the Townsend plan, and the coming of federal social security legislation encouraged yet a third pension proposal. Oklahoma had a higher percentage of elderly in its population than the national average, but assistance in the state had been minimal. In July 1936, voters overwhelmingly approved a new two percent sales and motor vehicle tax to be earmarked for the needy aged, the blind, and crippled and dependent children. A thirty-dollar per month pension for those over 65 years of age was the heart of the program. The law allowed the state to receive matching grants from the newly created Social Security Administration.[64]

Despite the opposition of Senator Gore, social security and the related state pension plan with its earmarked revenue proved immensely popular. It was so popular, in fact, that by 1938 almost 110,000 residents were covered by the program at a cost of $14,000,000. Indeed, many placed on the pension roles were ineligible, and on 2 March 1938 the Social Security Administration cut off federal payments to Oklahoma because of frauds. Blaming Governor Marland's inept, if not corrupt, administrators, the federal investigators found rates of fraud as high as 30 percent in some counties. Clearing the rolls of ineligibles, however, failed to permanently reduce the lists or the cost. Because the sales tax was earmarked, revenues derived could not be placed in the general fund; and as prosperity returned, monthly pension checks were increased. As a result, by 1960 Oklahoma had the highest per capita welfare expenditure and the highest percentage of a state budget committed to welfare in the nation. Pensioners and politicians have prevented any alteration of the earmarked tax other than allowing the transfer of a few state eleemosynary institutions to the Department of Public Welfare. A regressive tax was used to pay relatively large pensions and maintain an ever increasing welfare load.[65] This is one of the most significant and long-lasting legacies of the New Deal in Oklahoma.

Many of those who sought a position on the pension rolls were victims of the continuing Dust Bowl and low agricultural prices. Despite Roosevelt's declaration that these farmers "were a hopeful people" with "courage written over their faces," by 1936 they were desperate.[66] Although Agriculture Secretary Henry Wallace blamed tenants for poor methods that had led to the dust storms, Pare Lorentz's film "The Plow that Broke the Plains" showed that all farmers were at fault.[67] John Steinbeck's *The*

Grapes of Wrath portrayed the plight and flight of the Oklahoma tenants. Although inaccurate in terms of the source of the migrants, the novel's portrayal of their feelings and existence is accurate. The Joads were symbolic of the "okies" who went to California, Texas, Arizona, or the Pacific Northwest; Highway 66 became a twentieth century "Trail of Tears." Oklahoma Congressman Lyle Boren denounced the novel as a "damnable lie," and the *Oklahoma City Times* said the book was "absurd untruthfulness"; but it was only too true. Although future Governor Leon Phillips called the migrants "flotsam and jetsam," some of these families had owned farms before 1933, and many migrants were fleeing the small towns as well. Eric Goldman has written that "there is little evidence that any considerable part of the population gave up faith in America as the land of opportunity," but "Okie" came to mean "you're a dirty son-of-a-bitch," and "you're scum," according to one of Steinbeck's characters, suggesting that hope had indeed dissipated.[68]

When New Deal agricultural programs failed to aid either the tenant farmers or even many agriculturalists who had been able to acquire and retain land, Oklahoma farmers descended upon Governor Marland to plead for help.[69] Marland's answer was to turn to Roosevelt. Meeting with the president in Des Moines in September 1936, their exchange was sharp:

> Mr. President, what are we going to tell the 100,000 hungry farmers in Oklahoma tomorrow when we go home?
>
> You are going to tell them that the Federal agencies are getting busy on it just as fast as the Lord will let them. . . .
>
> That is small consolation for a hungry farmer.
>
> What more can you say to the hungry farmer, Governor?[70]

Roosevelt still did not understand the magnitude of the drought and told Aubrey Williams to popularize the slogan "A Pond For Every Farmer." William Leuchtenburg is correct that though the New Deal did not create the inequities in agriculture, its policies actually worsened the lot of some farmers. The impact of the Bankhead-Jones Farm Tenant Act, the Farm Security Administration, and even the soil conservation program was minimal in Oklahoma. Under the Bankhead-Jones Act, loans totaling only $6.3 million were made to Oklahoma tenants between 1937 and 1941, with many of those most in need having departed the state before 1937, and the sum lent was small in relation to the needs of those who stayed. The Farm Security Administration loaned $29 million to 37,000 Oklahoma farmers before 1941, but the fact that over half of the sum was repaid by January 1942 suggests the borrowers were not tenants or small farmers but probably farmers with relatively large land holdings. Further, many farmers did not want to substitute soil-building crops for staples and thus did not desire to participate in the soil conservation program.[71]

Massive changes in Oklahoma agriculture took place by 1940, but precious little of this alteration resulted from positive New Deal programs. Farm income rose until October 1938 when a sharp drop occurred, and an upward trend was not reestablished until the fall of 1940. While the Soil Conservation and Domestic Allotment Act encouraged landowners to exercise soil-conserving methods, the farmers of Oklahoma defeated in a referendum a proposal to spend $500,000 of state funds for participation in the program. The drought was the primary factor in altering the agricultural portion of the state's economy, and long-lasting economic distress terminated only with America's entry into the World War.[72]

The industrial side of Oklahoma's economy also failed to recover before 1941. As late as 1939, crude oil production remained far below output in 1929. The oil conservation act reduced crude production, affecting the 60 percent of Oklahoma's industrial activity that was related to petroleum. Industrial activity increased from 1935 to August 1937, but from then until April 1940 there was a steady decline. Several hundred miles of railway were abandoned, including one line almost 200 miles in length.[73] State and local efforts to reverse these trends proved futile.

Some attempts were made to provide more money for relief and for public works, but Oklahoma, like other states, simply did not have the resources to fund large-scale projects.[74] Relief and public works in Oklahoma depended almost entirely on the Works Progress Administration. By 1 March 1937, that agency had spent over $43 million in the state and had generated almost $10 million in matching contributions. Employment ranged from 94,821 in January 1936 to 48,045 in February 1937. Schools, armories, and stadiums were constructed, but over 40 percent of all WPA money in Oklahoma went for highway and road building. Projects in the cities of Tulsa and Oklahoma City were few because of the lack of matching funds. The Federal Music Project in Oklahoma was miniscule, but the arts projects were extensive.[75] The WPA became a controversial program in the state with many confusing its program with earlier "made work" projects, others seeing it as a political arm of the New Deal

Democrats, and some simply opposed the "dole," which, of course, the WPA was not.

One federal program that did receive widespread support in Oklahoma was the Civilian Conservation Corps. The corps began with 23 camps and grew to 49; enrollment varied from 5,000 to 6,000 a month. The camps were generally located in the national forests; and although the principal study of the CCC suggests that the New Deal recognized the effect of the drought by allocating additional camps for soil conservation work, very few Oklahoma camps were in the Dust Bowl, and only three worked on the shelter-belts. Claims that the camps contributed markedly to soil conservation work do not appear correct, but major projects in the eastern Oklahoma forests were undertaken and completed. The CCC was segregated in the state, and a separate Indian Division established camps in the western counties and the Quachita mountains. Oklahoma Congressmen Jack Nichols and Jed Johnson fought for large appropriations for the CCC, which may explain why in 1942 the state had more camps than any other.[76]

Oklahoma suffered the third-greatest income decline in the nation between 1929 and 1932 and yet, despite its needs, received only a small amount of federal relief support. In terms of per capita aid between 1933 and 1939, the state ranked twenty-second in the nation. Although Oklahoma ranked higher than most southern and eastern states in per capita aid, compared with all states federal loans for farm and home mortgages and other programs were small, and Reconstruction Finance Corporation loans were few. Per capita support from the CWA, the WPA, and the CCC was near the national average.[77] Ineptitude by federal and state officeholders, the lack of matching funds, poor planning, contradictory programs, and opposition to the New Deal in Oklahoma by Murray and other political leaders prevented additional projects from being developed.

The Democratic primary of 1938 demonstrated the division among Oklahoma New Dealers and the growing opposition to their programs. Governor Marland, unable to succeed himself, sought Elmer Thomas's senate seat as did Gomer Smith. The race for governor turned into a brawl as "Alfalfa Bill" Murray entered the race with Leon Phillips, William S. Key, former governor Jack Walton and Ira Finley, leader of the Veterans of Industry of America. Key had been a general in the state's Forty-fifth National Guard Division, warden of the state penitentiary, and was state director of the WPA. Phillips, a conservative member of the state legislature, had been a thorn in Marland's side and a voice for "economy" in government. Although Key and Phillips publicly supported the New Deal,

Key was obviously Washington's choice, having the active aid of Senator Lee and the state WPA organization.[78]

The WPA in Oklahoma became the central issue in both the senatorial and gubernatorial campaigns and brought President Roosevelt to the state as a consequence. In a blatantly political act, a large wage increase was announced for WPA employees just prior to the primary election. Senator Thomas, taking credit for the raise, asked for the votes of the workers. Governor Marland attacked Thomas, not for having given the workers more money, but for taking political advantage of their plight. Phillips assailed Key, however, for giving higher wages to men on the federal payroll performing, as Phillips saw it, needless and useless jobs. Most of the state's newspapers, blaming Key's allies for the WPA salary hike, endorsed Phillips or Murray. Roosevelt, meanwhile, sent staffman Charles A. West to Oklahoma to help Key and Thomas; and West, who had worked as a congressional liaison for Roosevelt, urged the president to stay out of the controversy.[79]

Despite the contention by James Patterson that Roosevelt and Farley tried to stay out of state factional disputes, the president entered the Oklahoma Democratic primary against the wishes of his political advisers. Roosevelt's incursion came partially as a result of the insistence of Senator Lee, who begged the president to campaign for Thomas and Key, especially the latter; Lee feared that Murray might win the gubernatorial nomination because the runoff primary had been eliminated. The president came in July, speaking at several eastern Oklahoma towns prior to a major rally at the Oklahoma City fairgrounds on the ninth. Over 50,000 people heard him praise the WPA in Oklahoma, and thereby Thomas and Key, and attack Murray, although not by name, as a Republican. The effect of Roosevelt's speech on Murray's campaign was devastating. In the primary, Phillips defeated Key by 3,000 votes, with Murray a weak third. Senator Thomas won renomination easily as Smith came in second with Governor Marland trailing far behind. The general election saw easy victories by the Democrats in all races; there was no Republican resurgence in Oklahoma in 1938.[80]

Roosevelt's intervention in the gubernatorial primary on behalf of Key proved to have been a mistake because after his inauguration as governor, Leon Phillips became widely known as an opponent of the New Deal. The tall, red-faced, redheaded, and enormously fat Phillips had become a power in Oklahoma politics. A small-town lawyer, his political activities before 1932 were in the Republican party, but in that year he won a seat in the state legislature as a Democrat. Elected Speaker three years later, he staunchly opposed Governor Marland's program and deficit spending. In disavowing the Marland "New Deal," he also became an opponent of Roosevelt's New Deal. Under Phillips's prodding, the Seventeenth and Eighteenth Legislatures dismantled Marland's program. A wage and hours law was annulled, state aid to public schools was cut below the 1929-30 level, all of the new agencies except the Planning and Resources Board were terminated, and the state budget was drastically reduced. Higher taxes on cigarettes, gasoline, and inheritances helped balance the state budget. By 1940, Phillips had reduced the state payroll, reorganized the state government, and turned yearly deficits into a $3.4 million surplus. He had become a militant advocate of states' rights, a leader of the anti–third term movement, and at the Democratic convention refused to allow his hand-picked delegation to vote for Henry Wallace for the vice-presidential nomination. During the campaign in 1940, he worked for Wendell Willkie.[81]

Phillips's support of Willkie came not only as a result of his narrow view of the role of government, but also because of two controversies regarding private utilities versus public power. In the early 1930s, several members of the state legislature from northeastern Oklahoma proposed the construction of a large hydroelectric dam on the Grand River. With Governor Marland's support, the legislature created the Grand River Dam Authority in 1935 to borrow money from PWA to construct the dam and a power plant. After construction began, Governor Phillips demanded that the GRDA pay for relocating highways and building new bridges. When the GRDA refused, the governor called out the national guard to block construction. The federal government sided with GRDA, and a favorable court decision allowed completion of the project, which began to sell power in 1940. President Roosevelt praised the GRDA as an example of federal-state cooperation for power and flood control; but in 1941, when the GRDA failed to make payments on its federally bonded mortgages, the federal government took possession of the property. Phillips saw this as additional evidence of intervention in the state by Washington.[82]

The other conflict concerned the proposal of the Corps of Engineers, supported by Texas Congressman Sam Rayburn, to build a hydroelectric dam on the Red River at Denison, Texas. The flood control and power project bordered Oklahoma and Rayburn's district in Texas. The Flood Control Act of 1936 authorized the project, which Phillips condemned. He contended that Rayburn had threatened the Oklahoma congressional delegation if they opposed the scheme, and noted that the land to be inundated was primarily in Oklahoma. Who would pay to relocate highways and roads, he asked? What of the valuable farmland removed from the property tax roll? The Oklahoma legislature, at Phillips's request, protested against the scheme. Phillips waged war on the federal project, and in a long series of suits and countersuits delayed construction for two years. Finally, a Supreme Court decision against Phillips cleared the way for building Denison Dam and Lake Texhoma.[83] The opposition of Phillips was symptomatic of growing distrust of, and negative attitudes toward, the New Deal by Oklahomans.

Like other western states, Oklahoma saw increasing anti–New Deal sentiment after 1936. Few Oklahoma congressmen openly or privately supported the Roosevelt administration, and those who did often lacked influence in Washington. Opposition by the press in Oklahoma also hurt the cause of the president and his program. The *Daily Oklahoman*, the *Oklahoma City Times*, and the *Tulsa Tribune* shifted from tacit support in 1932 to open antagonism by 1934. Democratic leader Eugene Lorton moved his *Tulsa World* from an administration voice to strong opponent in 1937. With the demise of the Scripps-Howard *Oklahoma News* in Oklahoma City in 1938, there was no pro–New Deal metropolitan newspaper in the state. Except for a few small town dailies and rural weeklies, newspapers gave their readers only negative views of the New Deal. The petroleum industry, always a power in Oklahoma, also worked against the New Deal, especially after the CIO began to organize refinery and production workers. Following the institution of oil import restrictions, most of the larger petroleum companies with foreign holdings began to oppose the administration.[84] Equally significant was the opposition of conservative Democrats in the state.

Political opposition appeared with "Alfalfa Bill" Murray's denunciation of the New Deal in 1935. He represented the feelings of many Oklahoma conservatives when he applauded the Supreme Court's decision against the NIRA, and when he proclaimed that the "dole has broken the morale of the people." James Farley kept Roosevelt informed of the growing animosity in Oklahoma, although neither needed to fear loss of the state in 1936, or 1940, or even in 1944. Murray and Phillips aided Willkie in 1940, but the state cast a large majority for Roosevelt. When Governor Phillips verbally assaulted the CCC in 1942, Roosevelt told Paul V. McNutt, head of the Federal Security Agency, that the Oklahoma governor should be called to Washington to substantiate his claims about juvenile delinquency in the program. "This would be fun as well as useful," the president thought. Opposition to the New Deal was stronger, however, than Roosevelt and Farley realized, and in the election of 1942 the conservative current ran deep in the state. Senator Lee lost badly to a reactionary Republican, and Robert S. Kerr barely managed to keep the governorship in Democratic hands. The First Congressional District had returned to Republican control in 1940, and in 1944 the Eighth District was won by a Republican; both were in the traditionally Republican northern part of the state. A variety of issues brought together opponents of the New Deal, with the "court packing" of 1938 a major factor as well as Roosevelt's entry into the Democratic primary that year. Other Oklahomans resented even the minimal aid given to Negroes, and some strongly opposed Roosevelt's increasing internationalism. There had been no "Roosevelt Revolution" in Oklahoma, and the state would exhibit increasing conservatism for the next thirty years.[85] By the 1960s, conservative Democrats would alternate political victories with conservative Republicans, with an occasional moderate-to-liberal Democrat winning a major office.

If, as Thomas Dye has written, "policy outcomes express the value allocations of a society, and these allocations are the chief output of the society's political system,"[86] then Oklahomans before, during, and after the New Deal favored a weak state government, poorly founded, bureaucratically inept, without imagination, and rife with scandal and incompetence. The administrative machinery of the state was enlarged as a consequence of New Deal programs, but it did not become more responsive to the people it was supposed to serve. The state, through the Corporation Commission and the Interstate Oil Compact, increased its regulatory control over the petroleum industry, but taxes on oil and natural gas remained very low. Despite Marland's efforts at planning, only the Resources Board continued to function, and then only as a statistics-gathering and public relations agency. Unlike some other states during the New Deal, Oklahoma did not gain a streamlined government, a meaningful merit system, or see increased voter participation. The state remained politically divided, philosophically conservative, and lacking in effective leadership.[87]

The major changes wrought in Oklahoma between 1933 and 1945 were the tremendous decline in the significance of agriculture, major population losses in rural counties, and the growth of the urban areas. The small population decline from 1930 to 1940 was followed by a loss of 103,000 between 1940 and 1950. More dramatic was the decrease in the rural population by 330,000 in the same period, while Oklahoma City and Tulsa gained markedly. Large areas in the Dust Bowl were denuded of residents, and some counties could not find two lawyers to serve as county attorney and judge. The exodus that began in 1935 accelerated during World War II as Sooners moved to Texas or California to work in defense plants. The population bloc most likely to support a New Deal Democrat, the small farmers and tenant farmers, was diminished by demographic shifts, and the two metropolitan areas with their "clean" industries, few blue-collar workers, and small racial and ethnic group populations would become increasingly conservative in their voting habits. Tulsa's population, swollen by an influx of migrants from the traditionally Republican northern counties, dominated by a conservative press, and economically dependent upon the petroleum industry became increasingly Republican in its voting habits. Oklahoma City's rising prosperity, based on the aircraft industry, banking, insurance, and small factories manufacturing technologically sophisticated goods, led to the development of a large suburban population that increasingly voted like its counterparts in the rest of the nation. The "agenda of American politics" had not been revolutionized in Oklahoma.[88]

There had been no significant cry for progressive legislation in Oklahoma during the thirties, and few reformist groups pressured for change. Politicians were more concerned with personal success than ideologies or allegiance to Washington. The governors proved to be New Deal opponents or inept supporters, and the congressional delegation did not present a leadership alternative. Social and economic changes came, not because of the New Deal, but because of the depression, the World War, and the vagaries of nature. Franklin Roosevelt became the idol of many Oklahomans, the devil incarnate for a few, but rarely did personal respect and admiration lead to strong support for New Deal programs. There was no significant upheaval in state institutions as a consequence of federal programs, and in Oklahoma the New Deal remained the story of what might have been. The New Deal in Oklahoma did not produce a "Third American Revolution," or even a modestly successful attempt to deal with economic deprivation. The long-lasting legacies included a reverence for President Roosevelt and fear and distrust of "federal bureaucrats."[89]

1. Carl N. Degler, *Out of Our Past: The Forces That Shaped Modern America*, rev. ed. (New York, 1970), p. 413; Richard Hofstadter, *The Age of Reform: From Bryan to F.D.R.*, Vintage Books (New York, 1960), p. 303; Dexter Perkins, *The New Age of Franklin Roosevelt, 1932–1945* (Chicago, 1957), p. 2; Paul K. Conkin, *The New Deal* (New York, 1967), p. 1.

2. Edwin C. McReynolds, Alice Marriott, and Estelle Faulconer, *Oklahoma: The Story of Its Past and Present* (Norman, Okla., 1961), pp. 289–90; Judith Anne Gilbert, "Migrations of the Oklahoma Farm Population, 1930 to 1940" (M.A. thesis, University of Oklahoma, 1965), pp. 30–31.

3. Charles Angoff and H. L. Mencken, "The Worst American State," *American Mercury* 24 (1931): 1–17, 175–88, 355–71.

4. Gilbert, "Migrations of the Oklahoma Farm Population," pp. 12–13, 22–25, 33–35; Edward Everett Dale and Morris L. Wardell, *History of Oklahoma* (Englewood Cliffs, N.J., 1948), pp. 396–97; U.S. Department of Agriculture, Bureau of Agricultural Economics, *Cash Receipts from Farming by States and Commodities, Calendar Years 1924–1944* (Washington, 1946), pp. 3, 116–17.

5. Keith L. Bryant, Jr., *Alfalfa Bill Murray* (Norman, Okla., 1968), pp. 196–97, 237–38; Theodore Saloutos, *Farmer Movements in the South, 1865–1933*, Bison Books (Lincoln, Nebr., 1964), pp. 279–80; Gilbert C. Fite, *George N. Peek and the Fight for Farm Parity* (Norman, Okla., 1954), p. 245; Van L. Perkins, *Crises in Agriculture: The Agricultural Adjustment Administration and the New Deal, 1933* (Berkeley, Calif., 1969), p. 13.

6. *Oklahoma Farmer-Stockman*, 15 September 1930, p. 668.

7. Harold F. Williamson et al., *The American Petroleum Industry*, vol. 2., *The Age of Energy*, 2 vols. (Evanston, Ill., 1963), pp. 49–50, 321–27; Gerald P. Nash, *United States Oil Policy, 1890–1964: Business and Government in Twentieth Century America* (Pittsburgh, 1968), pp. 121–23, 93–97.

8. Williamson et al., *The Age of Energy*, p. 542.

9. Bryant, *Alfalfa Bill Murray*, pp. 198–200; Nash, *United States Oil Policy*, pp. 108–17, 124–25.

10. Donald R. McCoy, "Alfred M. Landon and the Oil Troubles of 1930-'32," *Kansas Historical Quarterly* 31 (1965): 113–37; Williamson et al., *The Age of Energy*, pp. 547–48, 550–52; Interstate Oil Compact Commission, *The Compact's Formative Years, 1931–1935* (Oklahoma City, 1954), p. 20; Nash, *United States Oil Policy*, p. 127; *New York Times*, 19 February 1931.

11. Gilbert, "Migrations of the Oklahoma Farm Population," pp. 48–50; Leonard Arrington, "The New Deal in the West: A Preliminary Statistical Inquiry," *Pacific Historical Review* 38 (1969): 311–16.

12. James T. Patterson, *The New Deal and the States: Federalism in Transition* (Princeton, N.J., 1969), pp. 26–40; *Harlow's Weekly*, 18 July 1931; *Muskogee* (Oklahoma) *Times-Democrat*, 26 February 1931.

13. *Tulsa Daily World*, 18 January 1931.

14. See Keith L. Bryant, Jr., "Kate Barnard, Organized Labor and Social Justice in Oklahoma during the Progressive Era," *Journal of Southern History* 35 (1969): 145–64, and "Labor in Politics: The Oklahoma State Federation of Labor During the Age of Reform," *Labor History* 11 (1970): 259–76; Gilbert C. Fite, "The Nonpartisan League in Oklahoma," *Chronicles of Oklahoma* 24 (1946): 146–57; and James Ralph Scales, "Political History of Oklahoma, 1907–1949" (Ph.D. diss., University of Oklahoma, 1949).

15. V. O. Key, Jr., *American State Politics: An Introduction* (New York, 1956), pp. 42–44, 220–22; Ira Sharkansky, *Regionalism in American Politics* (Indianapolis, 1970), pp. 22–23, 178–79; V. O. Key, Jr., *Southern Politics in State and Nation* (New York, 1950); Frank H. Jones, ed., *Western Politics* (Salt Lake City, 1961); John H. Fenton, *Politics in the Border States* (New Orleans, 1957).

16. The changes taking place in some governments in the 1920s were not to be found in Oklahoma. See Patterson, *The New Deal and the States*, pp. 9–21.

17. Bryant, *Alfalfa Bill Murray*, pp. 173–89.

18. William H. Murray, *Memoirs of Governor Murray and True History of Oklahoma*, 3 vols. (Boston, 1945), 3:484.

19. Bryant, *Alfalfa Bill Murray*, pp. 190–213.

20. Ibid., pp. 214–36.

21. *Blue Valley Farmer*, 9 June 1932. This was Murray's personal newspaper, which was widely circulated in Oklahoma.

22. Letters of apology and pledges of support from Oklahoma Democratic party leaders, officeholders, and members of Roosevelt Clubs sent to the nominee are to be found in OF 300 (Democratic National Committee File, Oklahoma, 1928–1933), Franklin D. Roosevelt Papers (Franklin D. Roosevelt Library).

23. Scales, "Political History of Oklahoma," p. 359; Oliver Benson et al., *Oklahoma Votes, 1907–1962* (Norman, Okla., 1964), pp. 49, 65, 120, 122, 144.

24. *Oklahoma City Times*, 2 December 1932; *Harlow's Weekly*, 23 September 1933; Jerry Peyton Simpson, "Oklahoma's State Debt" (Ph.D. diss., University of Oklahoma, 1958), pp. 56–57.

25. *Blue Valley Farmer*, 23 March 1933; *Harlow's Weekly*, 1 July 1933; see also many letters on this controversy in the William H. Murray Alphabetical File, Roosevelt Papers.

26. Frank C. Carter to Harry L. Hopkins, 3 July 1933, and W. C. Fiddler to Franklin D. Roosevelt, 7 September 1933, both in OF 444 (FERA), Roosevelt Papers; *Harlow's Weekly*, 5, 26 August 1933; Mimeographed letter, State of Oklahoma, Executive Chamber, 17 August 1933, William H. Murray Papers (Oklahoma State Historical Society); *Daily Oklahoman*, 15 September 1933.

27. Murray to "Governor Henry Morgenthau, Jr.," 8 November 1933, Murray Alphabetical File, Roosevelt Papers.

28. *Oklahoma News* (Oklahoma City), 22 November 1933; *New York Times*, 26 November 1933; Hopkins to Roosevelt, 3 March 1934, OF 444, Murray to Hopkins, 2 February 1934, Louis Howe to Murray, 12 March 1934, Murray Alphabetical File, Roosevelt Papers.

29. Patterson, *The New Deal and the States*, pp. 53–54, 59–62, 73.

30. *Harlow's Weekly*, 24 February, 10 March, 21, 29 April, 2 June 1934; *Blue Valley Farmer*, 20 April 1934; Simpson, "Oklahoma's State Debt," pp. 157–58.

31. U.S. Works Progress Administration, Division of Social Research, Research Bulletin Series V, No. 1, *Areas of Intense Drought Distress, 1930–1936* (Washington, 1937), pp. 25–27, 49–50. This study included funds spent by the FERA, CWA, AAA, Resettlement Administration, and WPA.

32. Murray to "Colonel" James Farley, 19 June 1933; T. M. Richardson to Howe, 26 June 1933, Murray Alphabetical File, and J. B. A. Robertson to Howe, 3 July 1933, OF 300 (Democratic National Committee File, Oklahoma, 1933–1944), Roosevelt Papers; J. Berry King to Percy L. Gassaway, 6 January 1934, Gassaway Papers (University of Oklahoma Library).

33. *Daily Oklahoman* (Oklahoma City), 15 January 1934.

34. Murray to Farley, 17 April 1934; Farley to Marvin McIntyre, 26 April 1934, Murray Alphabetical File, Roosevelt Papers.

35. *Harlow's Weekly*, 4 February 1933, 25 August 1934; Eugene Lorton to Farley, 16 July 1935, OF 300 (Democratic National Committee File, Oklahoma, 1933–1944), Roosevelt Papers; Searle F. Charles, *Minister of Relief: Harry Hopkins and the Depression* (Syracuse, N.Y., 1963), p. 183; William E. Leuchtenburg, *Franklin D. Roosevelt and the New Deal, 1932–1940*, Torchbooks (New York, 1963), p. 50.

36. Gilbert, "Migrations of the Oklahoma Farm Population," pp. 13, 41–43, 51, 63–67; Tom Moore, "Farm Tenancy in Oklahoma, 1925–1935" (M.A. thesis, Oklahoma State University, 1938), p. 12; U.S. Works Progress Administration, Division of Social Research, Research Bulletin Series V, No. 2, *The People of the Drought States* (Washington, 1937), pp. 51, 76–77.

37. Paul B. Sears, *Deserts on the March* (Norman, Okla., 1940), p. 137; Fred Floyd, "A History of the Dust Bowl" (Ph.D. diss., University of Oklahoma, 1950), pp. 25–95.

38. Works Progress Administration, *Areas of Intense Drought Distress*, pp. 3–33.

39. Edgar Nixon, ed., *Franklin D. Roosevelt and Conservation, 1911–1945*, 2 vols. (Washington, D.C., 1957), 1:224–25; Wilmon H. Droze, "The New Deal's Shelterbelt Project," in Droze et al., *Essays on the New Deal* (Austin, Tex., 1969), pp. 33–34.

40. Nixon, *Franklin D. Roosevelt and Conservation*, 1:457.

41. Leuchtenburg, *Franklin D. Roosevelt and the New Deal*, pp. 49, 72–73; Arthur M. Schlesinger, Jr., *The Coming of the New Deal* (Boston, 1959), pp. 59–71.

42. Bureau of Agricultural Economics, *Cash Receipts from Farming by States and Commodities, Calendar Years 1924–1944*, pp. 4–5, 7–8, 15; U.S. Department of Commerce, Bureau of the Census, *Census of Agriculture, 1935, Reports for States*, 2 vols. (Washington, 1937), 2:718; *Harlow's Weekly*, 10 February 1934; David Eugene Conrad, *The Forgotten Farmers* (Urbana, Ill., 1965), p. 63.

43. Moore,"Farm Tenancy in Oklahoma," pp 19–20, 25–26; O. D. Duncan and J. T. Sanders, *A Study of Certain Economic Factors in Relation to Social Life among Oklahoma Cotton Farmers* (Stillwater, Okla., 1933), pp. 3, 4–5, 7; Conrad, *The Forgotten Farmers*, p. 173.

44. Dixon Wecter, *The Age of the Great Depression, 1929–1941* (New York, 1948), p. 146.

45. Moore, "Farm Tenancy in Oklahoma," p. 30.

46. U.S. Department of Agriculture, *The Farm Real Estate Situation* (Washington, 1935), p. 31; Gilbert, "Migrations of the Oklahoma Farm Population," pp. 70–76, 80–89.

47. Frances Perkins, *The Roosevelt I Knew* (New York, 1946), p. 174; J. T. Sanders, "Tenancy and Our Cotton Programs," *Current Farm Economics* 9 (1936): 56; Nixon, *Franklin D. Roosevelt and Conservation*, 1:456; Schlesinger, *The Coming of the New Deal*, p. 72.

48. Schlesinger, *The Coming of the New Deal*, p. 485; Perkins, *Crisis in Agriculture*, passim.

49. Harold L. Ickes, *The Secret Diary of Harold L. Ickes: The First Thousand Days, 1933–1936* (New York, 1953), p. 6; *Tulsa Tribune*, 4 March 1933; *New York Times*, 14 March, 11 April 1933; Roosevelt to Murray, 1 April 1933, Murray to Roosevelt, 4 April 1933, Roosevelt to Murray, 22 April 1933, OF 56 (1933–34, Oil); Telegram, Murray and Landon to Roosevelt, 16 May 1933, OF 56-A (Oil, 1933–1939), Roosevelt Papers.

50. Ickes, *The First Thousand Days*, pp. 36–37, 41–42, 49–50, 85–86; Nash, *United States Oil Policy*, pp. 128–33, 139–42.

51. Nash, *United States Oil Policy*, pp. 147–48; *The Compact's Formative Years*, pp, 34, 37.

52. Leuchtenburg, *Franklin D. Roosevelt and the New Deal*, pp. 39, 61, 118; *Harlow's Weekly*, 11 March 1933; Dove Montgomery Kull, "Social and Economic Factors Affecting Unemployment in Oklahoma" (M.S.W. thesis, University of Oklahoma, 1940), pp. 58–59.

53. Edward Harvey Landreth, "Business Barometers and Their Fluctuation in Oklahoma, 1932–1949" (M.B.A. thesis, University of Oklahoma, 1950), pp. 17, 140, 146; Conkin, *The New Deal*, p. 70; U.S. Department of Commerce, Bureau of the Census, *Census of Business: 1939*, vol. 4, *Construction, 1939* (Washington, 1940), p. 25; Scales, "Political History of Oklahoma," pp. 392–93.

54. Angie Debo, *Tulsa: From Creek Town to Oil Capital* (Norman, Okla., 1943), pp. 97, 111; U.S. Department of Commerce, Bureau of the Census, *Seventeenth Decennial Census of the United States, Census of Population, Characteristics of the Population, Oklahoma* (Washington, 1952), pp. 6–8; Angie Debo, *Prairie City: The Story of an American Community* (New York, 1944), pp. 197–235, quotation from p. 228.

55. Leuchtenburg, *Franklin D. Roosevelt and the New Deal*, p. 69; Conkin, *The New Deal*, pp. 34, 39–40; Louis Hartz, *The Liberal Tradition in America*, Harvest Books (New York, 1955), p. 263.

56. *Daily Oklahoman* (Oklahoma City), 25 June 1933; Scales, "Political History of Oklahoma," pp. 362–64; 359; *Oklahoma City Times*, 23 August 1934; *Blue Valley Farmer*, 27 September, 1 November 1934; Leuchtenburg, *Franklin D. Roosevelt and the New Deal*, p. 114.

57. Scales, "Political History of Oklahoma," pp. 371–74; John Joseph Mathews, *Life and Death of an Oil Man: The Career of E. W. Marland* (Norman, Okla., 1951), passim.

58. Cecil L. Turner, "Oklahoma's New Deal: Program and Reaction" (M.A. thesis, University of Oklahoma, 1963), pp. 1, 7–9; *Oklahoma News* (Oklahoma City), 8 January 1935.

59. Turner, "Oklahoma's New Deal," pp. 9–40; Scales, "Political History of Oklahoma," p. 379.

60. Dale and Wardell, *History of Oklahoma*, pp. 359–362; Turner, "Oklahoma's New Deal," pp. 55–95; Robert Arthur Bish, "Leon C. Phillips and the Anti-New Deal Agitation in Oklahoma, 1935–1944" (M.A. thesis, University of Oklahoma, 1966), pp. 13–14; Mathews, *Life and Death of an Oil Man*, p. 239.

61. Turner, "Oklahoma's New Deal," p. 113; Scales, "Political History of Oklahoma," pp. 394–95; Simpson, "Oklahoma's State Debt," p. 54.

62. Royden J. Dangerfield and Richard H. Flynn, "Voter Motivation in the 1936 Oklahoma Democratic Primary," *Southwestern Social Science Quarterly* 17 (1936): 97–105; Monroe Lee Billington, *Thomas P. Gore: The Blind Senator from Oklahoma* (Lawrence, Kans., 1967), pp. 159–75; *New York Times*, 26 May 1936.

63. Benson et al., *Oklahoma Votes*, pp. 65, 123–24, 144; *New York Times*, 16 June 1936; Scott Ferris to James A. Farley, 27 July 1936, Democratic National Committee, Correspondence of J. A. Farley, 1936, Oklahoma-Oregon, Roosevelt Library; Eugene Lorton to "Mac" [Marvin McIntyre], n.d., OF 300 (Democratic National Committee Files, Oklahoma 1933–1944), Roosevelt Library.

64. Scales, "Political History of Oklahoma," p. 380; Turner, "Oklahoma's New Deal," p. 53; Dale and Wardell, *History of Oklahoma*, pp. 538–39; Cecil E. Walton, "Public Welfare in Oklahoma" (M.B.A. thesis, University of Oklahoma, 1950), pp. iii, 10–12.

65. Perkins, *The Roosevelt I Knew*, p. 299; Walton, "Public Welfare In Oklahoma," pp. 12, 24; Turner, "Oklahoma's New Deal," p. 84; Beulah Amidon, "Sooners in Security," *Survey Graphic* 27 (1938): 203–7; Walter Richard Shuttee, "Old Age Assistance in Oklahoma" (M.A. thesis, University of Oklahoma, 1953), pp. 1–12, 18, 60; Richard E. Dawson and James A. Robinson, "The Politics of Welfare," in Herbert Jacob and Kenneth N. Vines, eds., *Politics in the American States* (Boston, 1965), pp. 380, 392.

66. Schlesinger, *The Coming of the New Deal*, p. 70.

67. Kull, "Social and Economic Factors Affecting Unemployment in Oklahoma," pp. 34–38; Robert L. Snyder, *Pare Lorentz and the Documentary Film* (Norman, Okla., 1968), p. 39; Stephen B. Plummer, "The New Deal Soil Conservation Movement in the Dust Bowl, 1932–1936" (seminar paper, Department of History, University of Oklahoma, 1970); Caroline A. Henderson, "Letters from the Dust Bowl," *Atlantic Monthly* 157 (1936): 540–51.

68. John Steinbeck, *The Grapes of Wrath* (New York, 1941), passim; Gilbert, "Migrations of the Oklahoma Farm Population," pp. 1, 90–94; Works Progress Administration, *The People of the Drought States*, pp. 26, 45–46; Eric F. Goldman, *Rendezvous with Destiny*, rev. ed., Vintage Books (New York, 1956), p. 287.

69. Schlesinger, *The Coming of the New Deal*, pp. 376–81; Basil Rauch, *A History of the New Deal, 1933–1938*, Capricorn Books (New York, 1963), p. 120; Nixon, *Franklin D. Roosevelt and Conservation*, 1:564–65.

70. James M. Burns, *Roosevelt: The Lion and the Fox* (New York, 1956), pp. 277–78.

71. Nixon, *Franklin D. Roosevelt and Conservation*, 1:578; Leuchtenburg, *Franklin D. Roosevelt and the New Deal*, p. 137; Dale and Wardell, *History of Oklahoma*, pp. 395–96; Kull, "Social and Economic Factors Affecting Unemployment in Oklahoma," pp. 41–43.

72. U.S. Department of Commerce, Bureau of the Census, *Sixteenth Census of the United States: 1940 Population*, vol. 2, *Characteristics of Population* (Washington, 1943), pt. 5, pp. 793, 824, 828; Floyd, "A History of the Dust Bowl," pp. 269–72; Bureau of Agricultural Economics, *Cash Receipts from Farming*, pp. 117–18; Landreth, "Business Barometers and Their Fluctuation in Oklahoma," p. 142; Leuchtenburg, *Franklin D. Roosevelt and the New Deal*, pp. 77–78, 172, 254–56.

73. *Sixteenth Census of the United States, Manufacturers*, vol. 2, pt. 1, pp. 871, 863, 881; Neil Jude Dikeman, "An Index of Industrial Production, Oklahoma, 1935–1948" (M.B.A. thesis, University of Oklahoma, 1950), pp. 23, 28, 54; Charles Gardner, "Railroad Abandonment in Oklahoma" (M.A. thesis, University of Oklahoma, 1958), pp. 78–82.

74. Simpson, "Oklahoma's State Debt," pp. 63–66; Patterson, *The New Deal and the States*, pp. 94–101.

75. *Accomplishments for Oklahoma: W.P.A., July 1, 1935–March 1, 1937* (n.p., n.d.); Merrill Leroy Ellis, "An Evaluation of the Oklahoma Federal Music Project" (M.M.E. thesis, University of Oklahoma, 1940), passim; "Washington Notes," *New Republic* 95 (1938): 279–80; Patterson, *The New Deal and the States*, pp. 83–84.

76. John A. Salmond, *The Civilian Conservation Corps, 1933–1942: A New Deal Case Study* (Durham, N.C., 1967), pp. 56, 84, 66–67; 170–71; George Sterling Brown, "The Educational Program of the Civilian Conservation Corps" (M.E. thesis, University of Oklahoma, 1935), pp. 257, 69; Reid Holland, "Oklahoma's CCC," *Chronicles of Oklahoma* 47 (1970): 224–34; Donald Lee Parman, "The Indian Civilian Conservation Corps" (Ph.D. diss., University of Oklahoma, 1967), pp. 92–99.

77. Arrington, "The New Deal in the West," pp. 311–12, 315–16; Leuchtenburg, *Franklin D. Roosevelt and the New Deal*, pp. 243–44, 256–57; Conkin, *The New Deal*, pp. 76, 96.

78. Bish, "Leon C. Phillips," pp. 27–29, 47–54; Hermione Briscoe, "The 1938 Oklahoma Gubernatorial Campaign as Presented by a Group of State Newspapers" (M.A. thesis, University of Oklahoma, 1939), pp. 21–28, 89.

79. Scales, "Political History of Oklahoma," p. 405, *Tulsa World*, 19 June 1938; *Harlow's Weekly*, 25 June 1938.

80. Patterson, *The New Deal and the States*, pp. 190–93; Josh Lee to Roosevelt, 28 June, 1938, OF 300 (Democratic National Committee Files, Oklahoma 1933–1944), Roosevelt Papers; *New York Times*, 10 July 1938; Bish, "Leon C. Phillips," p. 57; *Harlow's Weekly*, 16 July 1938; Benson et al., *Oklahoma Votes*, pp. 89, 93, 125–26, 144.

81. Bish, "Leon C. Phillips," pp. 4–6, 7–8, 37–42, 114, 125–27; Dale and Wardell, *History of Oklahoma*, pp. 363–65; *New York Times*, 15 January 1939, 8 January 1940; "Sooner Strong Boy," *Time*, 22 January 1940, pp. 20–21.

82. Simpson, "Oklahoma's State Debt," pp. 200–201; Bish, "Leon C. Phillips," pp. 142–74; Nixon, *Franklin D. Roosevelt and Conservation*, 2:246; "Phillips and the Grand River Dam Authority," scrapbook, Leon C. Phillips Collection (University of Oklahoma Library).

83. Bish, "Leon C. Phillips," pp. 72–80, "Denison Dam," scrapbook, Phillips Collection.

84. James T. Patterson, "The New Deal in the West," *Pacific Historical Review* 38 (1969): 319–25; Scales, "Political History of Oklahoma," p. 388; Jean Truman Richardson, "The Oklahoma Press and the New Deal, 1932–1936, As Reflected in Metropolitan Newspapers" (M.A. thesis, University of Oklahoma, 1950), pp. 1–117.

85. *New York Times*, 9 June 1935; Farley to Roosevelt, 3 January 1936, OF 300 (Democratic National Committee Files, Oklahoma 1933–1944), Roosevelt Papers; Bryant, *Alfalfa Bill Murray*, pp. 266–68; Salmond, *The Civilian Conservation Corps*, pp. 214–15; Bish, "Leon C. Phillips," pp. 175–98; Degler, *Out of Our Past*, p. 393.

86. Thomas R. Dye, *Politics, Economics, and the Public* (Chicago, 1966), p. 1.

87. Patterson, *The New Deal and the States*, pp. 195–207.

88. *Seventeenth Decennial Census of the United States . . . Oklahoma*, pp. 6–8, 30; Leuchtenburg, *Franklin D. Roosevelt and the New Deal*, p. 326.

89. Leuchtenburg, *Franklin D. Roosevelt and the New Deal*, p. xii; Conkin, *The New Deal*, p. 73; Degler, *Out of Our Past*, p. 379.

F. Alan Coombs

The Impact of the New Deal
On Wyoming Politics

"WYOMINGITES AS A CLASS ARE TOO SAGACIOUS TO VOTE AGAINST their own interests," the strongly Republican *Wyoming State Tribune* editorialized near the beginning of the 1936 presidential campaign.

> Those of them not misguided by illogical party loyalty, bought with places on the public payrolls or too ignorant to analyze political and economic factors have no sympathy for the Democratic administration which deliberately is attempting to destroy the state's fundamental industry.[1]

Whether they represented a commentary on the sagacity of the Wyoming voter or the *State Tribune*'s propensity for wishful thinking, the election returns some two and a half months later appeared to tell a different story. The incumbent president, Franklin Delano Roosevelt, had captured 60.6 percent of the popular vote in the Equality State in trouncing his Republican rival, Governor Landon; and certainly at that point in history, few observers in either party would have questioned the claim that the impact of the New Deal on Wyoming politics had been enormous.[2] And yet, when reviewing the spotty results of presidential contests since 1944—and especially when noting that Richard Nixon and George Wallace together polled over 64 percent of Wyoming's popular vote in 1968 against the inheritor of the New Deal tradition, Hubert Humphrey—one could be pardoned for wondering.

The published literature concerning Wyoming and its politics during the decade of the 1930s is hardly extensive. T. A. Larson's prize-winning essay on the New Deal's influence on the state, published in the August 1969 issue of the *Pacific Historical Review*, is certainly worthy of notice. Indeed, in many instances Professor Larson dealt so thoroughly and convincingly with matters not directly related to the state's political complexion that it would be superfluous to reexamine them here. It is only in the somewhat more narrow area of the New Deal's effect on the politics of Wyoming that more intensive and extensive analysis will here be attempted. Larson's *History of Wyoming* is the best single source for a broader view of the state's historical development, and other general studies such as Charles P. Beall's chapter on "Wyoming: the Equality State" in Frank Jonas's *Western Politics* also contain relevant material. Gene M. Gressley has focused on one dramatic episode in his treatment of "Joseph C. O'Mahoney, FDR, and the Supreme Court" in the May 1971 *Pacific Historical Review*.[3] But for the most part, historians have not yet delved deeply into the actual political character of the state during the "depression decade" or into the question of what changes—if any—the New Deal wrought in that character.

At the outset, it should be understood that Wyoming was by no means a typical state, even for the 1930s, in terms of its political sociology. Most striking was its rural character. At the time of the 1930 census, only two towns in the state, Cheyenne and Casper, boasted populations as high as 10,000, and ten years later, there were only four such places as Laramie and Sheridan also climbed past the 10,000 mark. Cheyenne, the state capital, was Wyoming's largest metropolitan area in 1940 with a population of 22,474, but almost as remarkable was the fact that only twelve communities in 1940 could be classified as "urban" at all, despite the fact that a population of only 2,500 was necessary for that designation. The state's urban population was growing at a somewhat more rapid rate than the rural population, but in 1940 over 62 percent of Wyoming's citizens still lived on farms or ranches or in settlements of less than 2,500 inhabitants.[4]

Minority racial groups in Wyoming were not only infinitesimal during the New Deal years but were declining as a portion of the state's total population. In 1910, there were 2,235 Negroes living in Wyoming; but by 1930, that figure had dropped to 1,250, and on the eve of the American entry into World War II, there were fewer than 1,000 blacks left in the Cowboy State. As a consequence, the Negro population comprised only 0.6 percent of all Wyoming residents in 1930, and that figure had diminished to 0.4 percent in 1940. The same was true with respect to the state's residents of Japanese ancestry. In the 1910 census, 1,596 Japanese-Americans had been enumerated, but by 1940 that figure had shrunk to 643. Indian Americans were an exception to the rule, having increased their numbers from 1,845 to 2,349 in the decade of the 1930s, but they still constituted less than one percent of the state's total population in 1940. Over-all, the important point is that Wyoming was predominantly "white" and native-born and was becoming more so. For whatever significance it may have, it may also be noted that the state's male population still outnumbered its females by a margin of nearly 117 to 100 in 1940, but that imbalance had also been undergoing a steady decline ever since territorial days.

Wyoming politics, like the politics of so many other states, had its geographical divisions. The northeastern part of the state—Johnson, Campbell, Crook, Weston, Converse, and Niobrara counties—is nominally Republican and not coincidentally the center of the state's cattle industry. Indeed, Johnson County not only voted for Alf Landon in 1936 and Wendell Willkie in 1940, it voted for the Republican congressional candidate every two years between 1930 and 1940. On the other hand, Wyoming's southern tier of counties (Laramie, Albany, Carbon, Sweetwater, and Uinta)—the region along the Union Pacific tracks— is the region of greatest Democratic strength, and it is there that Democratic candidates must win by wide margins if they are to succeed. Each of the counties mentioned plus the somewhat less reliable Natrona (Casper) and Sheridan counties went for Franklin Roosevelt in 1932, 1936, and 1940, and supported the Democratic nominee for Congress in at least four of the six elections from 1930 through 1940.[5] The reason the Democrats normally find support in this area is not hard to perceive; it is in southern Wyoming that organized labor (and especially the railroad brotherhoods and the United Mine Workers of America) wields its greatest power. Moreover, such "ethnic group" voters as Wyoming possesses—Irish- and Mexican- and Italian-American Catholics, Greek Orthodox, and some Jewish Americans—are generally to be found in places like Cheyenne, Laramie, Rawlins, and Rock Springs, rather than in the central and northern parts of the state.

Another way in which Wyoming differs from larger and more populous states is in terms of its major industries. In the 1930s, the livestock industry, with its two major component parts, cattle and wool, was still the single most powerful force, but there were other occupational constituencies that politicians had to take into consideration. The sugar beet growers, located largely on irrigated lands, were numerous enough to demand attention, and many Wyomingites were involved at least tangentially with development of the state's oil and natural gas resources. Coal mining was still important (if depressed), particularly in Sweetwater and Carbon counties, and the influence of the Union Pacific Railroad and its workers has already been suggested. That, however, very nearly exhausts the list of Wyoming industries with enough "clout" to make a difference politically during the New Deal period; and as a result, the political picture was not especially complex. Wyoming did differ from most of its sister states in possessing, at least from the middle 1930s on, a reasonably bipartisan press. This was due almost single-handedly to the aggressiveness and business acumen of one man, Tracy S. McCraken. McCraken himself was a conservative Democrat, but as he constructed his newspaper empire during the 1920s and 1930s he intentionally left some of the journals under Republican editorship. At the same time, Democratic candidates were assured of a fair hearing in at least some of the state's newspapers so that in 1940, the office of Democratic Senator Joseph C. O'Mahoney could count twenty-four different dailies and weeklies in the state (with a composite circulation of 55,000) that it considered "friendly."[6] But this is getting a bit ahead of the story.

It is stating the obvious to say that, in order to assess the New Deal's influence on the political behavior of Wyoming or any other state, one must begin with at least a cursory survey of that political behavior prior to March 1933. The temptation is to sum up the state's political complexion in the first four decades of its statehood by saying it was "Republican and conservative," but that would be too simple. To be sure, the Republican nominee captured Wyoming's electoral votes in seven of the ten elections from 1892 through 1928, but the deviations from the rule may be significant. For one thing, the Populists had considerable strength on the high plains. In 1892, General Weaver had come within 800 votes of taking the state for the People's party against President Benjamin Harrison when Grover Cleveland's name had not even been on the ballot in Wyoming. Then, four years later, William Jennings Bryan from neighboring Nebraska defeated William McKinley by a similar margin while bearing both the Democratic and Populist banners. In the pivotal election of 1912, Woodrow Wilson carried Wyoming by a plurality of less than a thousand votes over President Taft and trailed the combined Republican and Progressive vote by a margin of nearly 8,500—and yet against Charles Evans Hughes in 1916, Wilson won in Wyoming with relative ease. Admittedly, the 1920s were dismal years for Democratic presidential candidates in Wyoming (Harding, Coolidge, and Hoover all polled at least three votes to every two for their Democratic opponents), but that phenomenon was hardly confined to Wyoming in the prosperity decade.

The explanation for this somewhat erratic behavior is not difficult; Professor Charles Beall correctly identified it in the post–World War II era when he observed that the state's political party organizations are weak and often ineffective with the result that "a large segment of the electorate may adhere generally to a party preference, but the character, personality, and campaign effectiveness of individual candidates is the decisive factor and causes many people to cross party lines."[7] That was as true in the pre–New Deal era as it has been since that time, with the result that the story of Wyoming politics in the early decades of the twentieth century was the story of a succession of men and at least one woman with formidable personal followings. On the Republican side, Francis E. Warren occupied one of the state's seats in the United States Senate for a total of thirty-seven years prior to his death in 1929 (establishing a record for length of tenure in the upper chamber not to be surpassed until the twilight of Carl Hayden's career), finally acquiring the chairmanship of the Senate Appropriations Committee. In the House of Representatives, Frank Wheeler Mondell served as Wyoming's sole congressman, rising to the position of majority floor leader before his defeat in the election of 1922. Then there were the Careys: Joseph, the father, United States Senator and progressive governor, active in supporting Theodore Roosevelt's "Bull Moose" campaign in 1912; and Robert, the son, also serving the state as governor between 1919 and 1923 and succeeding to Warren's old Senate seat following the 1930 election.

But the Democrats, notwithstanding their normal minority position, were not without their own great leaders. In 1914, the state elected the handsome and highly respected stock grower, John B. Kendrick, governor and two years later sent him to the United States Senate to serve alongside Warren. Kendrick would remain a fixture in the nation's capital as the "Cowboy Senator" until his death in November 1933. And in 1924, the party made good on Wyoming's early commitment to women's suffrage by electing Nellie Tayloe Ross after the sudden death of her husband, Governor William B. Ross, to be the nation's first female chief executive. The point is that even though there were supporting casts of characters for each of these leaders, a public official with a distinctive personality and reputation could go a long way on his own in a state with fewer than 250,000 residents and roughly 100,000 regular voters, with or without a smoothly functioning party organization.

For the Democrats, building that reputation was the trick. Senator Kendrick was only being realistic when he observed:

> Statewide campaigning, not once but twice or three times, is the price of success for our Party in Wyoming, and the sooner we realize this fact, that any man who wins an office on our ticket must have a strong personal following, the sooner we will come into our own politically in the State.[8]

This highly personalized brand of politics was something that even a political upheaval such as the New Deal was unlikely to change. It remained true, as Professor Beall has suggested, that virtually everyone of consequence in Wyoming politically knew everyone else, and often the leading families in the state had been acquainted for generations. Friendships, predictably, often extended across party lines (a notable case being the bond between Warren and Kendrick), and Wyoming generally accepted the good middle-class assumption that the wise citizen votes for the man and not his party label. A part of this tendency may be traceable, too, to the fact that many of the state's cattlemen and sheepmen had originally migrated north from Texas with a Democratic heritage but were converted to Republicanism in the 1890s as a result of the vulnerability of the livestock industry to foreign competition and the more protective stance of the GOP on the tariff question. The new allegiance was obviously there, but the roots did not go very deep. Still, it was true, as Professor T. A. Larson has pointed out, that the Republican party controlled the Wyoming state legislature from 1893 on through the 1920s and that the average vote in the state's Democratic primaries was less than half that on the Republican side.[9]

Just as difficult to characterize is Wyoming's dominant ideological complexion in the days before the Great Depression. Once again, in surveying the careers of Congressman Mondell and Senator Warren, the temptation is to designate it "conservative" and let it go at that; the reputation of the Cowboy State as one of the last bastions of "rugged individualism" is well established. On the other hand, the early flirtation with Populism has already been noted, and it is probably significant that the La Follette-Wheeler Progressive ticket of 1924 made a very respectable showing in Wyoming.[10] Professor Larson has described Senator Kendrick as a "conservative high-tariff Democrat," but the senator himself might have disagreed with the first part of that label. Although he unquestionably supported high duties on the imports that threatened his state's major industries, Kendrick took pride in his support of the League of Nations, his vote for a child labor amendment to the Constitution, and the congratulations he received from Samuel Gompers's American Federation of Labor for his "100 percent" voting record on labor affairs in his first term in the Senate. In his own view, then, he was "neither a reactionary nor a radical," but "intended to be in truth and in fact a progressive Democrat, with very great regard for both the principles and the traditions of my Party."[11] In any event, it seems fair to conclude that the basis for receptivity to the New Deal reform program already existed in Wyoming prior to 1933, especially when one considers the sluggishness that had marked the state's economy even before the crash of 1929. Agriculture was doing poorly on the high plains as in the rest of the country during the 1920s; petroleum and coal development was far from encouraging; and the rate of bank failures in the state was appreciably higher during the allegedly prosperous Flapper Era than it was to be following the onset of the national depression.[12]

Nevertheless, Wyoming Republicans appeared to be riding high in the wake of the 1928 elections. Al Smith's candidacy had been little short of a disaster in the Mountain West, despite the very energetic efforts of some Democratic leaders in that area to mobilize support. In almost every way, the New York governor seemed less attractive to the average Wyoming voter than did Herbert Hoover. In a state where prohibition sentiment had been strong, Smith was classified as a "wet"; in a state predominantly Protestant, he was recognized as a Roman Catholic (which might be tolerable in a congressman or senator but created doubts when it came to the presidency); in a state that was top-heavily native-born, Smith was felt to represent recent immigrant stock—something not very vaguely alien. In nominally Republican Wyoming, any Democratic candidate might anticipate an uphill battle, but the "Happy Warrior" was identified with *the* big city and an eastern seaboard that had never understood the problems of the West and was habitually viewed with distrust. As a result, he lost Wyoming by over 23,000 of the approximately 83,000 votes cast, and, with the exception of Senator Kendrick (who had won a third term by the relatively narrow margin of 6,000), most of the other Democratic aspirants went down to defeat with him.

Then came the Crash and the Great Depression. In Wyoming, as in all the nation, that was destined to have an influence on the political picture; but perhaps because the worst effects of the depression were slower to be felt in nonindustrial Wyoming than in many other areas, the reaction there was somewhat less immediate. The GOP did quite well in the 1930 elections, with Robert Carey beating his Democratic adversary by a margin of almost three-to-two, Congressman Vincent Carter rolling up an even more impressive total in his reelection bid, and Frank Emerson edging Democrat Leslie A. Miller in the gubernatorial contest by fewer than 1,000 votes. Meanwhile, the Republicans retained the top-heavy majorities they had enjoyed in both houses of the state legislature, 36 to 26 in the House and 21 to 6 in the Senate. The vice-chairman of the State Democratic Central Committee intimated in his own election postmortem that "the result might have been changed somewhat . . . if our candidates had chosen the right issues, but they didn't, and, of course, we were under wraps all the way because of Kendrick's vote for the Tariff bill." Basically, the economic issue in Wyoming was not yet "ripe" in the fall of 1930, and some were still speculating that the principal issue two years hence might be public power or prohibition.[13]

As the economic picture continued to darken, however, Wyoming Democrats began to bubble with enthusiasm over the prospects for 1932. By the spring of 1931, the condition of the economy was very much in the public mind. The Democratic national committeeman for Wyoming, Joseph C. O'Mahoney (the Massachusetts-born journalist and attorney who in the years ahead would serve the state for over a quarter of a century in the United States Senate), was telling the party faithful that their economic policies "must be measured by the progressive or liberal yardstick." "The Democratic party," O'Mahoney argued in a general letter to his coworkers (which he also sent to Governor Franklin D. Roosevelt),

> has . . . no reason for existence if it be not in fact as well as in name a progressive party. It can serve no purpose by trying to make itself a weak imitiation of the party of Mark Hanna, and, of course, it cannot be successful by following that course.[14]

By mid-July, the political columnist of the state's foremost Democratic newspaper, the *Wyoming Eagle*, was informing his readers that it was already safe "to predict that the Wyoming state democratic convention of 1932 will send a delegation to the party's national convention favorable to the nomination of Governor Franklin D. Roosevelt of New York." Both O'Mahoney and Fred W. Johnson of Rock Springs (later to serve as commissioner of the General Land Office during the New Deal–Fair Deal years) were making no secret of their esteem for Roosevelt, and that was doubly important because both men had been among the most fervent backers of Al Smith in 1927-28. When James A. Farley came through Cheyenne that same month, he was duly informed that the Roosevelt organization could consider Wyoming "safe" in the preconvention maneuvering.[15] The assurances were sound; on 9 May 1932, despite FDR's distressing setback in the California primary a few days earlier, the Wyoming State Democratic Convention voted to instruct its delegates to the national conclave to vote for the New York governor. They did so, and shortly after the Chicago convention Senator Kendrick dropped Roosevelt a line assuring him that the state's Democrats were behind him "to the last man."[16]

In view of the fact that Wyoming claimed only three electoral votes, the joy that this communication spread in Albany and Hyde Park was no doubt restrained, but it is evident that the leaders in the state party had come aboard the bandwagon early and were prepared to give the Roosevelt candidacy their most strenuous support. Accordingly, both Joseph C. O'Mahoney and former governor Nellie Tayloe Ross took active parts in the ensuing campaign on behalf of Roosevelt. Before journeying back to New York City to assist in the management of party headquarters in the Biltmore Hotel, O'Mahoney delivered a stinging attack on the Hoover administration's record during the economic crisis before a meeting of Colorado Democrats in Denver on 1 August, charging that

> the depression from which we suffer has been made immeasurably worse by the perverse refusal of the President and his advisers to recognize facts and act in time. . . .
> The truth of the matter is that the chief cause of our sorry situation is to be found in the stubborn refusal of the administration and its "big business" backers to surrender special privileges. It should not be difficult to prove this statement to any audience in an agricultural state.[17]

When the candidate himself came through Wyoming in mid-September, he was greeted by virtually every important Democrat in the state while making stops at Cheyenne, Laramie, Rawlins, and Rock Springs—and when difficulty was encountered in finding an open touring car for Roosevelt in the state capital, one was finally borrowed from one of the Republican presidential electors to be driven by the brother of Senator Carey! After all those lean years, the Wyoming Democracy was unquestionably having a good time.[18]

For the most part, their ecstasy was only heightened by the election returns. In a remarkable reversal from the 1928 contest, the voters of Wyoming chose Roosevelt over Hoover by a tally of 54,370 to 39,583; and in his second try for the governorship, Leslie Miller swept past his Republican opponent by a little less than 3,500 votes. Moreover, the state's Democrats pulled off a "first" by winning solid control of the Wyoming House of Representatives, 42 to 20, while the GOP held onto the Senate 15 to 12. The only real fly in the ointment was Congressman Vincent Carter's success in narrowly winning election to a third term over Paul Greever, a Democrat from Cody. Even John B. Kendrick, who always took pride in the friends he possessed in both parties, allowed himself a bit of partisan exultation over the election of Roosevelt and Miller in a letter to Joe O'Mahoney: "Mine eyes have seen the coming of the Lord."[19]

Nor were the leading figures of the state party ill-rewarded for their assistance in the campaign. Fred Johnson was called to head the General Land Office in the Interior Department; Jim Farley prevailed upon O'Mahoney to come back to Washington as his first assistant postmaster general; and Mrs. Ross was selected to be the new director of the Mint. Additionally, the *Wyoming State Tribune* carried a list of forty-three other Wyomingites, past and present, who were holding down non–civil service jobs in Washington, presumably because they were "deserving Democrats." One can assume that the impact of the New Deal on this small segment of the state's population was immediate enough.[20]

But if, as many have suspected, most people in 1932 voted for Franklin Roosevelt largely because he was not Herbert Hoover, the next and more important question to be considered is how Wyoming reacted to the New Deal when it began to be transformed from a campaign slogan into a legislative and administrative reality. One indication of constituent opinion, of course, may be the actions of a state's congressional delegation, but in the case of Wyoming's representatives in the Seventy-third Congress, the cleavage divided sharply along party lines. Senator Kendrick backed the Roosevelt administration in every one of its major policies prior to his death in November 1933, and Senator Carey and Congressman Carter could generally be found in opposition to the New Deal's proposals. The "Hundred Days" was hardly a week old when Kendrick announced his intention to support the president throughout the financial crisis, explaining that if some assumption of dictatorial powers in order to cut the expenses of government were "the only way out," he was even "willing to grant him that authority."[21]

Carey, on the other hand, had even had the temerity to oppose the emergency banking bill rushed through on the first day of the special session (merely "because nobody knew what was in it") and he told the *State Tribune* the economy bill was "one of the most drastic pieces of legislation" he had ever seen. "This measure," he warned, "puts more power in the hands of the chief executive than ever before." At the conclusion of that amazing flurry of early New Deal activity, Vincent Carter was asked to comment on the work of the Congress just adjourned. "The only comment I can make on the subject," he replied, "is that they spent money like the proverbial drunken sailors."[22]

By that time, the Republican press in Wyoming was taking up the cudgels. On Inauguration Day, the *Wyoming State Tribune* had wished the new president well, saying that it hoped "with all sincerity that four years since [*sic*] it may be said of Franklin D. Roosevelt that he met the test of exalted place in trying times with courage as magnificent, sagacity as profound, devotion as complete as those which Herbert Hoover exemplified during the last four years." And in response to Roosevelt's call for a special session of Congress and the executive order declaring the Bank Holiday, the *Tribune* congratulated the president for "meeting a national crisis with high courage" but warned its readers that he was a mere mortal with no ability "to compel the miraculous."[23] Three days later, when the outlines of the president's economy program had become clear, the same Republican journal pointed out that Roosevelt could "succeed in the thankless and all but impossible task which he patriotically has volunteered to undertake only if he is backed by militant public opinion." He should have that backing, said the *Tribune*, "in no unmistakable terms."[24]

The period of grace was to be short-lived. Before the end of April, the *Laramie Republican-Boomerang* was already suggesting that "the government should lessen its pace somewhat and not attempt too many revolutionary matters at once." Indeed, some proposals seemed to give the federal departments responsible for their execution "such sweeping powers as to be tantamount to that of a dictatorship."[25] In a few more days, the same newspaper was beginning to reflect its growing skepticism in its headlines—one over a picture of Henry Wallace and Henry Morgenthau, Jr., reading "NEW FARM BILL'S TWIN MUSSOLINIS" and another concerning George Peek's prospective appointment as administrator of the new AAA, "PEEK SLATED AS FARM DICTATOR." On 11 May, the *Republican-Boomerang* (which one might have supposed from its name would have found Henry Wallace congenial) borrowed an editorial from the *Chicago Tribune* directing attention to some of Roosevelt's "glib and plausible but radical and heedless advisers to whom an emergency is an opportunity."[26]

By June, the forces of the opposition to the New Deal had definitely begun to regain their footing. The *Wyoming State Tribune*'s publisher, William C. Deming, reported a meeting of a number of the state's Republican leaders in Casper at which "attention was devoted to the paternalistic program of the Roosevelt administration." "One speaker," the account continued, "compared it to the inflation of an old fashioned circus balloon, which sails away gracefully only to collapse tragically in a remote field or woodland when the gas is all evaporated." On 7 June 1933, a meeting of the Wyoming Stock Growers Association adopted a resolution declaring the organization's opposition to a "paternalistic government with politically appointed dictators at the head of every industry." Furthermore, the statement continued,

> this association is of the opinion that it was the rugged individualism of the people of this country that has made the United States the greatest country of the world, and that the unpractical theories of men and women with no experience in business to create a government where people shall only work three hours a day and three days a week, where all is ideal and nothing is real, would reduce the United States in a short time to the condition of a third rate power.[27]

In another year, the resentment of Wyoming Republicans toward the New Deal would be manifest. In an address before the Lincoln Club of Cheyenne in May 1934, publisher Deming argued that in the space of a little more than a year, "the present Democratic administration has gone further in taking from the people of the United States the right to manage their own affairs and carve out their own destiny than any previous administration has ever done." September 1934 found the *Tribune* directing attention editorially to a statement just issued by the new American Liberty League and suggesting that "every property-owning and other citizen who is interested in the preservation of the principles upon which this nation was founded . . . should read that statement." If some were inclined to "laugh off" the new organization, the *Tribune* said, it was probably because "socialistic and communistic factors in the administration" were afraid of anybody that might awaken Americans to the New Deal's assault on their property rights.[28]

So anti–New Deal sentiment in Wyoming was already well developed as the state headed into the 1934 congressional campaign. Three major prizes were at stake that year: the United States Senate seat vacated by John Kendrick's death and subsequently filled via interim gubernatorial appointment by Wyoming's premier New Dealer, Joseph O'Mahoney; the state's lone seat in the House of Representatives; and the governorship itself. Although it is very difficult to determine how much of the apparent Republican optimism amounted to whistling in the dark, the *Wyoming State Tribune* carried an item in its editorial column in June directing attention to the most recent *Literary Digest* poll that showed "only" 58 percent of the straw vote from Wyoming favoring the "Roosevelt revolutioneering" and 42 percent opposed. Putting the best possible face on this news (the dubious quality of which would not be appreciated until 1936), the *Tribune* pointed out that a shift of only one voter in every eleven "would eliminate the national margin of approval." Be that as it may, there is little evidence to support the paper's conclusion that "the margin is so small, and the swing away from approval so obvious, that the Democratic politicians shiver in contemplation of them."[29]

Quite to the contrary, Democratic spirits had seldom been higher. One party worker in Rock Springs was predicting as early as March 1934 that it would be possible to reelect Leslie Miller governor, to send O'Mahoney back to the Senate, and to capture the Republican seat in the House for Paul Greever if he chose to make a run for it. That same month, Governor Miller confided in a letter to O'Mahoney that Democrats along the Union Pacific tracks were enthusiastic and that "all in all things are very much better than the were three or four months ago."[30]

The gubernatorial contest was not an especially good one to use as a test of pro– or anti–New Deal sentiment. Although Leslie Miller had cooperated with New Deal programs since the end of the preceding year, no one was likely to confuse him either ideologically or personally with Harry Hopkins or Rexford Tugwell. He was challenged in the Democratic primary by Tom O'Neil, a rancher from Big Piney who campaigned on the basis of opposition to the "small group of machine politicians" from Cheyenne who he claimed controlled the state party. "As a Democrat," O'Neil proclaimed, "I demand a party organization free from bosses and dictators." In August, Wyoming Democrats opted for the "bosses and dictators" by renominating Governor Miller handily.[31]

Neither O'Mahoney nor Paul Greever were opposed in their primary campaigns for senator and representative, and when the Democratic State Central Committee met in Thermopolis in September, it showed every willingness to have the ensuing campaign fought on the basis of allegiance or opposition to the New Deal. Resolutions were passed by that meeting expressing

> on behalf of ourselves and of the Democrats of the state, our most hearty appreciation of the patriotic, wise, able and courageous administration of the executive department of the federal government by President Franklin D. Roosevelt, and we pledge to him our most hearty allegiance and cooperation in the consummation of his program, which, it is evident, is designed to promote the greater well-being of all the people.

Further recognition was given to O'Mahoney's position as "one of the administration leaders in Washington," and the state's citizens were informed that Greever too was "in thorough accord with the new deal of President Roosevelt." Could Wyoming expect to receive special consideration from the national administration, the committee asked, while sending back to Washington members of Congress out of sympathy with the New Deal?[32]

This particular strategy was well-advised in 1934; the fact was that a large segment of Wyoming Republicans had come to feel it would be useless and quite possibly harmful to the state's interests to send a second GOP senator to deal with the Roosevelt administration.[33] That Wyoming would continue to have at least one ardently anti–New Deal senator was made clear when Robert Carey delivered a devastatingly critical speech to a meeting in Lusk near the end of July. "Those of you who believe in regimentation of agriculture and industry, who believe in the great Russian experiment," Senator Carey warned, "who believe that bureaucracy can run your business better than you can run it yourselves, should support the Democratic candidates in the coming election." The success of the Roosevelt program, he continued, was "dependent upon fastening upon the American people a bureaucracy to direct their lives and fortunes." Special condemnation was reserved for "the two principal measures of those who have partaken of the loco weed but who are known as the brain trusters," the AAA and the NRA. To return to another familiar line, the senator told his listeners he did not know a single New Dealer who had "been successful in business." "Whether we call it a new deal, managed economy, regimentation, or whatnot, it is but a new shuffle of a very old pack of cards."[34] Carey himself, of course, was not a candidate in 1934, but that kind of rhetoric would help color the entire Republican campaign.

The Republicans were not wanting for an attractive senatorial candidate; in a not-unexpected move, the handsome and popular young Republican

Congressman Vincent Carter announced in mid-July his intention to enter the race for Senator O'Mahoney's seat. Reputed to be the "best vote getter in the state," Carter easily put down a challenge from well-known stockman J. Elmer Brock in the Republican primary and appeared to pose a formidable threat to his New Deal opponent in the general election. Carter, himself a Marine Corps veteran of World War I, had voted to override President Roosevelt's veto of an appropriations bill carrying certain veterans' benefits; O'Mahoney, with no military record of his own, had voted to sustain FDR's action, thus risking the wrath of Wyoming's former servicemen.[35] But the main thrust of the Republican attack centered around a dual theme: (1) O'Mahoney, far from demonstrating the kind of independent judgment exemplified by the late Senator Kendrick, had contented himself to serve as a "rubber stamp" for the New Deal administration; and (2) in that capacity he had been compelled to support numerous measures—such as the Taylor Grazing Act and the Reciprocal Trade Agreements Act—that were directly inimical to Wyoming's best interests.

Here, then, was a test case of the New Deal's popularity in Wyoming. Here was a clear-cut contest between a Democratic candidate who placed full-page ads in the state's newspapers with his picture side-by-side with that of the president and ads bearing the slogan: "O'Mahoney Stands With Roosevelt; Wyoming Stands With Roosevelt ELECT O'MAHONEY" and his opponent who told a gathering in Rock Springs: "[O'Mahoney] is close to President Roosevelt—yes, he is the President's favorite yes man. I am Independent—an individual who owes allegiance to no one but the voters of Wyoming. I am not a rubber stamp."[36] E. V. Robertson, a prominent rancher from the northwestern part of the state who would later serve in the Senate himself, was quoted in early October to the effect that Carter's election was "assured" because the Democratic candidate's record had "stamped him as an administration puppet and the people of Wyoming are determined to be represented by a man who has shown that he places the interests of the people of the state of Wyoming first." Two weeks later, Senator Carey spoke to a congregation in Lander of O'Mahoney's "maliciousness to the interests of the state," charging that "O'Mahoney, who arranged his own appointment before Senator Kendrick was buried, has apparently done everything in his power to defeat the best interests of Wyoming."[37]

The incumbent's principal sin, it developed, was his vote for the Reciprocal Trade bill after attempting in vain to secure limiting amendments. His support of the president had been so regular, maintained the *State*

Tribune, that "he must now answer to the sugar, coal and wool industries of the state for going against their interests in order to boast of being a 100 percent 'yes man' for the national administration." Congressman Carter, on the other hand, described himself as a "protectionist in the extreme" and told the Wyoming Wool Growers Association that there was "much cause for concern" in view of Secretary Wallace's suggestion that "woolgrowers might suffer some pain" as a result of the reciprocal trade policy. And who would have the greatest voice in determining revision of tariff levels? Why, "the greatest free trader in the country today," Cordell Hull.[38]

Perhaps because he could not, O'Mahoney did not back away from the issue. Rather, in a radio address from Salt Lake City on 1 October, he argued that "the history of the development of civilization" was "the history of the development of foreign trade," and that "the depression in the United States" had been "co-incident with the loss of our foreign trade." The fact of the matter was, the senator said, that the economic well-being of the stockman and woolgrower depended primarily upon regaining full domestic employment and a healthy domestic economy, and that could only be accomplished by getting goods and merchandise moving again. Besides, the president had personally sent him a letter on 5 June giving assurances that "an administration, the primary object of which is to improve the condition of agriculture," could "be depended upon not to take any action hostile to the wool industry." No such action had been taken, concluded O'Mahoney, "and there is not now and never has been the slightest basis for any prediction to the contrary." He went on to hammer away at opponents of the New Deal's actions with respect to the drought-stricken cattle industry:

> When the purchase of cattle was begun, they said it would ruin the industry. When it was suspended to allow a readjustment of available funds, they said it was a death blow to the industry and thus accomplished the extraordinary feat of riding two horses in opposite directions at the same time.[39]

With respect to the charge that O'Mahoney was unfit to wear the fallen mantle of John Kendrick, it was hard to know what response to make; despite the long and close association between the two men dating back to O'Mahoney's service as the older man's secretary during Kendrick's first term in the Senate, their own backgrounds and mannerisms were poles apart. Mrs. Kendrick took the trouble to write O'Mahoney a letter shortly before the election telling him Kendrick had always considered him one of the family and "unusually well prepared to carry on the policies that Mr.

Kendrick considered vital to the welfare of Wyoming," but the candidate declined to use it prominently in the campaign. His former connection with the late senator was well known, and he may have felt that his association with Franklin Roosevelt was sufficient to pull him through in 1934.[40]

If that was the assumption, it was well-founded, for as Professor Larson has put it, "The Democratic party's star has never ascended higher in the Wyoming heavens than it did in 1934." Not only did O'Mahoney defeat Carter by a 13,000-vote margin out of 84,000-plus ballots cast, but Paul Greever claimed Wyoming's House seat in a contest with former three-term Republican Congressman Charles E. Winter; Les Miller was elected to a new four-year term as governor; and the Democrats swept all of the other state offices while rolling up an impressive 38 to 18 majority in the State House of Representatives and even tipping the balance in the Senate in their favor 14 to 13. How much of this is directly attributable to the influence of the New Deal is impossible to say, but there is simply no plausible reason to suppose that it would have happened without the impact of the Great Depression and the Roosevelt response.[41] In an effort to analyze the results for Mrs. Kendrick, Governor Miller could only point to "about the best organization . . . we have ever experienced and, of course, we were aided by the general trend of support for President Roosevelt."[42]

How long would this marvelous state of affairs last for Wyoming Democrats? No one knew. The *State Tribune* would continue to complain about "bureaucratic tyranny" and that "Mr. Roosevelt and his advisers have not at any time made the effort to write their reforms within the scope of the constitution," but the question was whether or not anyone was listening. Charles Winter, disgruntled over administration charges that the Republicans had no constructive programs of their own, defended his attacks on the New Deal for their own sake: "Is it not constructive to cut out a cancer? to take a cinder from the eye? to reset a dislocated arm?" But Winter had had his chance in 1934.[43]

Meanwhile, the signs of apparent New Deal success were becoming more and more visible. Between 1933 and the early months of 1936, national unemployment fell by some four million, stock prices doubled, and cash income for the country's farmers rose from about $4,000,000,000 in 1932 to nearly $7,000,000,000 in 1935.[44] Wyoming could boast of its own improving conditions: an increase in the average value per head of cattle to $31.70, the highest it had been since 1931; wool clips selling at 24 or 25 cents in place of the eight cents they had brought a few years before; a rise in Wyoming farm income, even exclusive of AAA benefit payments, of 20 percent between 1934 and 1935; greater employment in private industry in the state and an even more substantial growth of industrial payrolls; and a national increase in tourist travel of 42 percent since 1933 that was already bringing more money into the Cowboy State. Indeed, in mid-1935 the president of the Stock Growers National Bank in Cheyenne had written Senator O'Mahoney to report:

> There has been . . . an improvement in business, which I think probably covers a great deal of the country. I know that conditions have improved in this state. The drouth was one of the worst setbacks we had to contend with and that was disposed of by ample moisture this Spring, and has left the people in a very much better frame of mind.[45]

It is not easy to gauge to what extent this optimism was a result of New Deal policies and programs, but it is clear that the Roosevelt administration was giving the state's citizens their share—and more—of assistance. As Professor Leonard Arrington of Bringham Young University has shown in fascinating studies of the New Deal's economic impact on the various states of the union, the West as a region, at least on a per capita basis, benefited more than any other part of the country, and even within that region, Wyoming did quite well. More specifically, Wyoming ranked third in the nation, behind only Nevada and Montana, in per capita expenditures for the period 1933 through 1939 by a selected group of New Deal agencies including the Reconstruction Finance Corporation, Federal Emergency Relief Administration, Civil Works Administration, Works Progress Administration, Civilian Conservation Corps, and Rural Electrification Administration. This may be considered especially significant when it is noted that the state's per capita personal income at the height of the depression in 1932 was not exceptionally low—ranking thirteenth in the nation—and the decline in that income since 1929 had not been exceptionally large (ranking roughly in the middle of the forty-eight states).[46]

Although relief was never quite so tremendous an undertaking in Wyoming as it was in more heavily urban and industrial states during the 1930s, the *Wyoming State Tribune* estimated in April 1934 that unemployment in the state approximated 25,000, and 10,760 people were on Wyoming's relief rolls in March 1935, with large numbers from the "manufacturing and mechanical industries" and another sizeable contingent from the transportation and communication trades.[47] After the expiration of the CWA and FERA programs in 1933-34, the new Works Progress Administration became the primary federal agency concerned with the relief effort, expending nearly $10,500,000 in Wyoming by the middle of 1939. In the WPA program, the emphasis was always on getting money into the workers' pockets rather than on building great visible, enduring edifices, so that roughly 86 percent of this figure went into nonadministrative wages. Still, the Wyoming WPA, by the end of June 1938, had constructed 122 and modernized or improved 219 public buildings, completed 113 miles of new roads and streets while improving another 2,611 miles, built 375 bridges and 711 culverts, six athletic fields, three playgrounds, eleven swimming and wading pools, three golf courses, and four parks, with the result that its influence was felt beyond the circle of workers and their families.[48]

Meanwhile, the National Youth Administration was spending nearly $450,000 in Wyoming on projects for the employment of out-of-school youth and for wages required to keep needy students in school at various levels. In August 1939, 491 such young people (18–24 years of age) were employed on NYA projects in Wyoming. The Civilian Conservation Corps was similarly active in the state, operating twenty-seven separate camps for over 5,500 enrollees in the winter of 1939–40. Eight of these camps were located in the state's national forests, nine on the public domain (undertaking range rehabilitation projects), five on various federal reclamation projects, and two in Yellowstone National Park.[49]

In Wyoming, as elsewhere, the charge was made "that the federal relief set up—which should be as non-partisan as the sweet spirit of individual charity—has been made a part of the immense patronage machine which the Washington administration has been busily fabricating." For Wyoming, at least, the evidence to support such a charge is not at all persuasive. Not only were WPA workers sometimes hostile to the political fortunes of leading Wyoming Democrats, but so long as Will G. Metz occupied the position of federal relief administrator in the state, the administration of the government's relief programs, far from being political, was often *im*politic because of Metz's rigorous personal code. A controversy arose in the spring of 1934 over the pay formula for FERA workers. Should they be paid the prevailing wage in their communities (as the national policy guidelines indicated) or a flat rate of 45 cents an hour for unskilled labor, 70 cents for semiskilled labor, and 90 cents for skilled labor, as Metz (who was concerned with stretching limited funds as far as possible) had directed? As the pressure on the administrator mounted, he issued a sharp statement saying:

> I am not interested in political office, and I don't care a tinker's dam what anybody thinks of me from an organization standpoint or otherwise; but I do wish all your workmen to know that we have been using a little judgment and an awful lot of midnight oil for the purpose of giving every possible man a chance to get the benefit of the work program instead of being excluded therefrom.

Metz, himself a Democrat, was overruled in this instance by his superiors in Washington after Governor Miller had intervened, but in the process he had made it abundantly clear that partisan politics played no part in the way he ran his office. "I have been criticized," he told one reporter, "but in my administration I have not been swayed by the political affiliation of any person."[50]

Two years later, when the chairman of the Republican National Committee charged in the early stages of the 1936 campaign that Leslie Miller had injected politics into the Wyoming relief program, Senator O'Mahoney sprang to the governor's defense:

> I can say without any equivocation or reservation that there has been no politics in the administration of relief in Wyoming. . . .
> I know the instructions Mr. Hopkins has given to his subordinates have always been to exclude all political considerations.
> This administration has been more free from politics as the word is generally used than any administration of which I have had any knowledge since I first became interested in politics.

A survey of the senator's other correspondence shows more exactly what he meant. More often than not, he was the man to whom local Democrats complained when appointments to field offices of the various New Deal agencies were made without their advice and consent—appointments that in some cases even went to political enemies. The naming of the Republican county chairman to be secretary of the Carbon County Farm Loan Association in 1940 provided an illustration, O'Mahoney said,

> of the headaches with which we have had to contend from the beginning. Very few of the agencies which have been set up under this administration seem to have any comprehension of the political difficulties which are involved in appointments. Paul Greever, Harry Schwartz and I have . . . learned about problems only after they had arisen.[51]

But whereas O'Mahoney might have desired at least a veto power with respect to appointees in many agencies, even that was not the case with the Works Progress Administration. "One rule I have had from the beginning has been not to mix into the relief set-up," he told one correspondent. "I have religiously refrained from making recommendations for jobs on the WPA because from the very beginning I have believed that the WPA method of solving the unemployment problem could not be successful."[52] So aside from the general sense of indebtedness or gratitude that relief recipients might be expected to feel toward a national administration and a political party that had shown it cared, the political impact of the New Deal's relief operations in Wyoming appears to have been slight.

More salutary in its effects, in the eyes of Senator O'Mahoney and, no doubt, most of the other leaders of Wyoming Democracy, was the Public Works Administration's approach to recovery. Perhaps partly for this reason, the PWA was highly active in Wyoming during the depression, sponsoring 374 different projects at a total cost of nearly $28,600,000. Of this figure, some $8,547,000 went for street and highway construction, and, under the "Non-Federal" program (which called for the PWA to pay 45 percent of the bill if the local body would fund the remaining 55 percent), approximately $1,445,000 was spent on construction of water-works and sewer projects. The most impressive PWA endeavors in Wyoming were the Kendrick (or Casper-Alcova) irrigation and hydroelectric power project on the North Platte River, costing around $6,730,000 and supervised by the Bureau of Reclamation, the Heart Mountain reclamation project near Cody, and the Riverton project in Fremont County. Hundreds of thousands of dollars of federal money were pumped into a new Supreme Court building and law library in Cheyenne, a liberal arts building and auditorium, and a student union building at the University of Wyoming in Laramie. One important objective of the PWA program, of course, was to put men back to work while stimulating the economy; and in Wyoming, the peak employment of PWA work sites was reached in August 1934, when some 6,300 workers were employed for a total of over 640,000 man-hours.[53] At virtually the same time, the impact of the New Deal was being felt in the rural sector of Wyoming's economy. The emergency sheep and cattle purchase program implemented in response to the severe drought of 1934 through the Agricultural Extension Service, as Professor Larson has pointed out, no doubt stood the Roosevelt administration in good stead with the livestock industry. Roughly a quarter of the state's cattle and approximately one-seventh of its sheep were purchased through this program—nearly all of them animals that would otherwise have been written off as a total loss.[54] The signs of tangible New Deal activity in Wyoming in the middle 1930s were inescapable.

In a more personal vein, Wyomingites may have been flattered by the attention they received periodically from Franklin D. Roosevelt. He had gone through the state during the 1932 campaign, but during the last week in September 1935, the president's special train again came through Cheyenne, stopping for fifteen minutes so that the chief executive might say "hello" to the assembled throng. Then, eleven months later, FDR paid a similar visit to the state's capital city while returning to the middle west after attending the funeral of his secretary of war, George Dern, in Salt Lake City. In mid-October, the president was back in the state again, going to worship services at St. Mark's Episcopal Church in Cheyenne, having lunch at Fort Francis E. Warren, touring a local CCC camp, and delivering a brief speech at the military post's parade ground. To thousands of Wyoming residents, it all seemed just one more proof that Roosevelt cared about them.[55]

Wyoming's Democrats entered the 1936 election in a basically harmonious mood, at least with respect to the president's candidacy. A possible exception to the rule was Dr. John D. Clark of Cheyenne, a leading attorney, educator, businessman, and Democratic political figure who also happened to be a close personal friend of Governor Miller and Senator O'Mahoney. Clark had reacted negatively to a number of early New Deal measures, most notably the NRA experiment. As the years rolled by, he found himself increasingly disturbed by what he deemed to be the creation of a "vast, sprawling bureaucracy," excessive government spending, and measures that tended to take the freedom out of the free enterprise system, especially for the small businessman.[56] The remainder of the Wyoming Democracy, however, seemed undisturbed by Clark's apostasy; and in October 1935, Senator O'Mahoney was reporting that FDR was "just as strong here as he was in 1932." He went on to say to Mrs. Kendrick:

> Confidentially I can say that this also seems to be Senator Carey's opinion because he remarked to me only last Saturday that in his opinion, to use his own words, "Nobody has a chinaman's chance to beat Roosevelt with the possible exception of Borah".

That delighted O'Mahoney because he knew "conservative Republicans could find no solace in the candidacy of the Idaho Senator for his monetary policies are far more unacceptable to the business interests than anything President Roosevelt has planned or undertaken."[57]

Despite the Democratic optimism, the *Wyoming State Tribune* engaged in its quadrennial exercise in self-delusion. After beginning in early August with reports from the American Institute of Public Opinion (George Gallup's organization) that showed Governor Landon leading the incumbent president by a margin of 54 percent to 46 percent in Wyoming, the Republican newspaper gradually shifted its focus as the Gallup surveys showed Roosevelt gains. By election eve, the *Tribune* was far more interested in the ill-fated *Literary Digest* presidential poll and David Lawrence's speculations, both of which continued to put Wyoming solidly in the Republican camp. As it turned out, of course, Alf Landon captured roughly 38 percent of the popular vote in Wyoming while the president won in a romp. The successful Democratic senatorial candidate, Casper attorney Harry Schwartz, felt it was "an overwhelming victory for the Democratic party in general, and for the President in particular." In his view, "those prominent Democrats who could not see their way clear to support the President can no longer complain that we had no mandate for his general program."[58]

In some respects, Schwartz's own candidacy for the United States Senate was an even better test of the New Deal's standing in Wyoming than was the presidential race; Alf Landon was hardly an archconservative, but Senator Robert Carey had shown little but hostility for the Roosevelt administration and its programs since its first weeks in office. In June 1935, he undertook another scathing denunciation of New Deal policies in an address before the Wyoming Wool Growers, claiming that the destruction of the United States as a self-sustaining nation was imminent because "what the AAA failed to do in destroying markets, the reciprocal tariff pacts are now accomplishing." When Jim Farley visited Wyoming in the summer of 1935 and indicated that Carey would be one of the Democratic party's primary targets when he came up for reelection the following year, the *State Tribune* howled its indignation. "A Wyomingite for Wyoming" was what the state's voters would demand, and neither Farley nor his "political catspaws" could tell them where to "head in."[59] Carey had no difficulty in disposing of his opposition in the Republican senatorial primary in August 1936, but Harry Schwartz had to be content with a plurality in a hard-fought primary race against four other Democrats, the strongest of whom was none other than John D. Clark. Still, his triumph in the face of such adversity merely served to reinforce his identification with the national administration and the New Deal, and he quickly announced in no uncertain terms: "I am 100 percent for Roosevelt."[60]

To the *Wyoming State Tribune*, of course, that also meant that Schwartz was "100 per cent for each and all of the following things":

1. Communism—Comrades Tugwell, Wallace, Hopkins.
2. Bureaucratic dictatorship—Farley and Ickes.
3. Regimentation of farmers and of cattle and sheep men.
4. Destruction of agricultural products, including livestock.
5. Drastic reduction of grazing lands and unreasonable increase of grazing fees.
6. Importation of millions of pounds of canned beef.
7. Importation in 1935-1936 of live hogs and pork products—a loss to the American farmers of $10,718,602—and of cattle—a loss to the cattleman of $28,110,636.
8. Importation of agricultural products from 33,700,000 acres of foreign land by peasant labor.
9. Importation of Cuban sugar in the interest of Wall Street—a loss to the American sugar beet farmer of $83,000,000.
10. The greatest increase in the world's history of the cost of government.
11. Increase of government debt by over fifteen billion dollars, which will be a burden on the next three generations.
12. Increase by 105 percent of the tax burden, 85 percent of which is paid by the farmer, the working men and women, the clerk and the widow.
13. Wasteful and useless expenditures of billions of dollars of the taxpayer's hard earned dollars.
14. Repudiation by the government of its contracts.
15. A rubber stamp congress, wherein Schwartz seeks to be a Roosevelt "yes man."
16. Destruction of state rights.
17. Government in business as a competitor with private enterprise.
18. Monopoly.
19. Rooseveltian hypocrisy.
20. Creation of class hatreds—a principal [*sic*] most inimical to domestic tranquility and welfare.
21. Use of federal tax and borrowed funds for political purposes.

Probably nowhere in the entire decade was the list of things that some Wyomingites found distasteful about the New Deal spelled out in greater detail. Being "100 per cent for the New Deal," the *Tribune* explained with another salvo, meant that Schwartz in "his supine acceptance of Rooseveltism in each and every phase gives approval to the tremendous waste of public funds on demonstrated fallacies and grotesqueries which a host of New Dealers have rejected. Being '100 per cent for the New Deal' he is

100 per cent for—Wallace, Tugwell, Frankfurter, Farley, Ickes." Senator Carey, on the other hand, was not "100 per cent for the New Deal" but rather "100 PER CENT FOR WYOMING."[61]

That kind of political dialogue drew the battle lines about as clearly as they could be drawn; Wyomingites in 1936 did not have to worry, as some later Republicans would, about having a "choice" instead of a mere echo. And the significant thing, therefore, is that the New Deal candidate prevailed so easily against a well-known incumbent from one of Wyoming's most prestigious Republican families—and a man who had trounced him for the same office six years earlier. Topping Carey by a popular-vote majority of 53,919 to 45,483, Schwartz managed to beat his opponent in only twelve of the state's twenty-three counties. More significant was the fact that of the eight counties in Wyoming casting over 5,000 votes in this contest, the Casper Democrat won all eight, leaving Carey only the more sparsely-settled northeastern part of the state plus Sublette and Teton counties. All of the major urban centers—Cheyenne, Casper, Sheridan, Rock Springs, and Rawlins—merely swelled Schwartz's total, indicating that outside of the stockmen and woolgrowers, Senator Carey had few strong adherents.

Why did it happen? The simplest explanation is probably also the most accurate: Robert Carey was badly out of touch with the times, even in Wyoming. In fact, that in itself might not necessarily have been politically fatal had he exercised more discretion in his attacks on the Roosevelt administration and its programs. John B. Kendrick had managed to survive as a Democrat—and even a reasonably progressive one—in the Republican and conservative 1920s by limiting his public disagreements with the majority party and even supporting a few of the GOP measures (notably high tariff legislation) that he could accept in good conscience. But 1936 was not a year in which any candidate could profit from either doctrinaire conservatism or partisan Republicanism, and Senator Carey was guilty of both. In Wyoming, as throughout the land, the New Deal was running at high tide.[62]

But almost as amazing as the size and strength of that tide was the rapidity with which it receded in the next two years. It is not easy to sort out all of the reasons for this dramatic reversal, but some are perfectly easy to discern. The controversy over President Roosevelt's proposal to reorganize the federal judiciary in 1937 is obviously one of the most important factors. With the exception of the membership of Wyoming's labor unions (which were not yet especially well-organized or vocal in a political sense), and a few ardent New Deal attorneys, hardly anyone in the state was in sympathy with the "Court-packing" plan. Wyomingites reacted vigorously against the Court bill, almost from the beginning. The fact that Justice Willis Van Devanter, one of the "nine old men," was a native son could have influenced some people. And millions of Americans, mistaken or not, thought they could perceive a connection between the spread of totalitarianism in Europe and Asia and FDR's apparent quest for a more amenable Supreme Court. Whatever the cause, the Court fight afforded many of the state's citizens the perfect excuse to return to the Republican and conservative allegiances with which they felt more comfortable in somewhat the same way that it gave many members of Congress the ideal issue upon which to part company with a New Deal philosophy to which they could not subscribe. Joseph C. O'Mahoney had compiled a record as one of the most regular New Dealers in the United States Senate, but he felt compelled to break with the administration over this issue; and after he did so in most emphatic fashion, no state in the union was more intimately concerned with the fate of the Court bill than was Wyoming.[63] As the mail poured into O'Mahoney's office (most of it condemning the suggested expansion of the Supreme Court and congratulating the Wyoming Democrat for his courageous stand), Cheyenne's Democratic newspaper, the *Wyoming Eagle*, commented on the curious effect the battle had on normal political alignments:

> Nothing better illustrates the scrambled condition of present-day politics than the unanimity with which the Democratic press opposes the president's attempt to reorganize the judiciary, and the equal unanimity with which the Republican press praises those Democratic senators who have the courage to resist the appeals and the commands which emanate from the White House.[64]

The *Eagle* and its publisher, Tracy McCraken, were now regularly finding fault with Franklin Roosevelt's Court bill while Wyoming's leading Republican journals paid homage to their old enemy, Senator O'Mahoney. It was all very strange.

Had it been an entirely isolated incident, the Court fight might not have been so damaging to the president and his party, but in the public mind—at least in Wyoming— it soon blended in with a number of other items of concern. The plan to "pack" the Court with its implied threat to the separation of powers doctrine created at least a modicum of doubt in many honest minds about Roosevelt's purposes and the means he was willing to adopt to achieve his ends. Could it be that all those silly things the

Republican politicians had been saying about "dictatorship" for the past four years were at least a little bit true? After all, wasn't the administration also pushing for an executive reorganization bill involving a massive grant of authority to the president to shuffle government bureaus and public officials any way he saw fit? "We like F.D.R. personally, mind you," many Wyomingites seemed to say, "but isn't 'eternal vigilance' the price of liberty?"

Besides, things had changed since the darkest days of 1933. One could forgive a president even certain authoritarian inclinations if they were absolutely necessary in order to save the nation's economy—and *if* he seemed to have the answer to the dilemma of stagnation in which the country found itself. But by 1937, most people in Wyoming, like their counterparts in other states, had concluded that the country had been saved, that it would "endure as it has endured." Then, suddenly, came the "Roosevelt Recession," which one scholar later termed a "nine-month decline from September, 1937, to June, 1938, . . . [of severity] without parallel in American economic history."[65] The slump may not have been felt as sharply in Wyoming as in the more heavily industrialized states, and it was at least partially offset by a new local "boom" in the petroleum industry; but Wyomingites were well aware of the unfortunate development. A table of new passenger car registrations for the state shows that whereas they had climbed from 2,945 in 1933 to 7,170 in 1935 and on up to 9,693 in 1936, they slipped back to 9,000 in 1937 and then plunged to 5,136 the year after that. The unhappy fact was that during the readjustment many of the gains of the period from 1933 through the first half of 1937 were eliminated and predepression levels of production and employment would only be achieved again under the impetus of accelerated defense spending. Meanwhile, the abrupt reversal helped shatter the aura of economic infallibility that had previously surrounded the president and his advisors.[66]

Add to these occurrences the backwash that so frequently seems to follow an unnaturally large victory by one or the other of the two major political parties in recent American presidential elections and perhaps it should not have been surprising that a Republican resurgence manifested itself in 1938. So far as Wyoming was concerned, some notable assistance was rendered by local Democrats who had taken to quarreling among themselves. A sizeable portion of the state's Democrats—and especially those with labor union affiliations—were sorely displeased with Senator

O'Mahoney's abandonment of the president during the Court fight, or at least regretted that he had felt it necessary to play such a prominent role in defeating the administration's bill. Attorney T. S. Taliaferro of Rock Springs, from one of the leading Democratic families of the southwestern part of the state, even felt strongly enough about O'Mahoney's alleged defection that he criticized the Wyoming-Montana Bar Associations for inviting the senator to speak to their joint state convention in early September 1937.[67] But when Senator Joseph Guffey of Pennsylvania attempted to reprimand O'Mahoney in a nationwide radio broadcast late that same summer, suggesting that "when the voters of Wyoming next cast their ballots in the Democratic primaries of 1940, the new senior senator from Wyoming will be returned to his home on the range," he did the dapper Irishman a greater favor than he could have known. Political parties during the New Deal years, as later, operated with a considerable amount of state autonomy—as Franklin Roosevelt was soon to discover during the Democratic primaries of 1938. The almost instinctive impulse of most Wyoming Democrats, when confronted with Guffey's attack on one of their own, was to spring to O'Mahoney's defense. To the extent that this reaction served to widen the breach between party members in Wyoming and the leaders in the administration, it too boded ill for the New Deal in the Cowboy State.[68]

When Professor James T. Patterson, in his trail-blazing study *The New Deal and the States*, writes of many state political organizations being "preoccupied with state events and more often than not hampered by party factionalism," he could very well have Wyoming in mind.[69] Probably the most serious personal disagreement arose between Governor Miller and Representative Greever concerning the gubernatorial nomination in 1938. The two men had discussed the matter in the fall of 1937, and, as Leslie Miller recalled it three decades later, he had informed Paul Greever that he would like to seek one more term for personal reasons but that he understood that whenever he was ready to lay down the job, Greever "would like to take a try at it." Then, a few months later, the state Democratic chairman, L. G. "Pat" Flannery, sensing impending difficulty and himself aspiring to a seat in Congress, conducted a survey of Democratic opinion in an effort to demonstrate that Greever would be the stronger gubernatorial nominee. Miller's inference was that the congressman had changed his mind and wanted to run for governor at the earliest possible opportunity.[70]

By March 1938, the correspondence between the state's Democratic chieftains in Washington and those in Cheyenne was filled with extended discussion of the problem. It soon became more than a personal matter with rumors circulating that Greever, Flannery, and their friends were contemplating an intraparty campaign based on complete and undying loyalty to President Roosevelt and the New Deal and presumably in opposition to the conservatism of a Leslie Miller or the infidelity of a Joe O'Mahoney during the Court fight. Apparently assuming that the best defense was a good offense, the governor and John D. Clark were seriously considering some sort of preemptive strike against Paul Greever.[71] O'Mahoney responded by doing everything he could to quell the disagreement between his political allies before it became a full-fledged feud. In a letter to Clark, he said he thought it "would be a mistake for Les to open an active campaign because, unless I am very much deceived by Paul's attitude, he does not intend to become a candidate" and that although he was sure Greever wanted to be governor, he did not think it was "in his character to open a fight within the Democratic Party." Moreover, in the senator's view, Greever's comments with respect to a "loyalist" campaign aimed at 1940 were probably not that significant.

> Paul has spoken to me about 1940 but his thought which, by the way, seems to me to have no foundation was that with Les serving a third term resentments would have accumulated to such a degree by 1940 that with an almost inevitable intra-party fight throughout the country, the situation in Wyoming would be more difficult than otherwise. To this I have expressed my own view to him that the best way to protect the Democratic Party is for himself and Les to hold the positions which they now have.
>
> In these discussions I have pointed out to him that if there should be a Democratic split in 1940 he and Les and I would probably be on the same side and in these conversations he frankly stated that I am probably more radical than either himself or Les.[72]

The upshot of it all was that Greever, without enthusiasm and practically conceding defeat, ran for Congress again while Miller made an effort to be Wyoming's first third-term governor. Both men, in a shocking turn of events, lost badly in November to opponents who subsequently added little luster to the annals of Wyoming politics and government, Governor Nels Smith and Congressman Frank O. Horton. The Republicans also recaptured both houses of the state legislature by healthy margins.

Leslie Miller, who years later still regarded Paul Greever as "a fine character" who had done a good job in the House of Representatives, was of the opinion that "rising resentment against the New Deal" played an important role in Greever's defeat. In fact, there are several identifiable elements in the Democratic reversals in Wyoming in 1938. Commodity prices were off, especially on wheat and beans, and unemployment had risen during the "Roosevelt Recession" of 1937-38. The incumbent congressman had made little effort to woo the followers of Dr. Francis E. Townsend and his old age pension plan and that may have cost him thousands of votes, particularly in the Big Horn Basin region. The Townsend organization was especially strong in the West, and though there was little evidence that Greever's opponent would be more enthusiastic about their visionary scheme, the Townsendites were feeling their political strength and had no hesitation in trying to punish officeholders who failed to pay proper respect to their needs. Then there was the so-called WPA vote, which had gone almost solidly Democratic in 1932, 1934, and 1936, and which now suddenly deserted both Greever and Miller. Actually, "blue collar vote" might be a more accurate description, for the attitudes of those on WPA rolls undoubtedly overlapped to a considerable extent those of organized labor in the state. Both groups deeply resented Greever's less-than-perfect support of the New Deal and the sales tax implemented by Governor Miller during his second term.[73]

On the other hand, it must be remembered that the Republican resurgence of 1938 was by no means limited to Wyoming. There, as elsewhere across the nation, local candidates found themselves in a vulnerable position without the assistance of a presidential contest. One of the great ironies of this election was that a man like Leslie Miller who was obviously honest and industrious but who was not far removed from the national Republican administrations of the 1920s with respect to his distaste for burgeoning federal bureaucracy and government spending at any level lost partly because he was a Democrat. He had not yet publicly criticized the Roosevelt administration, and normally Republican voters were growing increasingly disenchanted with the New Deal.[74] Senator O'Mahoney felt the significance of the outcome was clear:

The election of 1938 surely teaches us what happens to the Democratic candidates when the votes of Independents and Republicans are lost. The only way to win an election is to hold your own lines and draw support from the opposition and from the Independents and unless the Democrats of Wyoming and of the country realize this, we shall be in grave danger of presenting the Republicans with a national election.[75]

Translated somewhat differently, this amounted to a confession that the New Deal had not resulted in a shift of the basic partisan loyalties of any sizeable portion of the Wyoming electorate.

The problem with drawing hard-and-fast conclusions on the basis of the 1938 election results, to be sure, is that the fate of the New Deal was not directly on the line; even in Congressman Greever's reelection battle, other factors muddied the picture. Unfortunately for purposes of analysis, the same thing was true two years later when Senator O'Mahoney and Representative Horton as well as the president himself came up for reelection. Most notably, the international situation conspired to decrease interest in the advocacy of, or opposition to, domestic reform. In 1940, however, the Democrats were taking nothing for granted. Precisely because he had asserted his independence from the national administration during the Court fight, Joseph C. O'Mahoney had become almost a folk hero to many Wyomingites (including a fair number of Republicans); but John D. Clark remained "fearful that an electorate which would trade Les Miller for Nels Smith could very easily send another senator to Washington." Yet O'Mahoney's situation bore little similarity to that of either Miller or Greever two years earlier. Unlike Greever, he had managed to ingratiate himself with the followers of Dr. Townsend (while avoiding an outright endorsement of their dubious pension plan) by voicing deep concern for the plight of older Americans and speaking at their national convention. He was also assured of far more support from stockmen and the rural areas in the state than were most of his Democratic coworkers owing to his role in the Court fight and his close identification with Senator Kendrick. Especially telling, however, was the senator's gentle-but-persistent effort to dissociate himself from his party label and especially from Franklin Roosevelt and the New Deal—certainly an abrupt change of tactics since his first major campaign in 1934. In July 1940, he explained to the National Townsend Club Convention in Saint Louis that "party lines mean little nowadays because the problem with which we are dealing rises above more partisan labels and frankness compels the acknowledgement . . . that the old political formulas have not been at all successful in meeting the needs of our time."[76] At the same time, the senator was not willing to turn his back on groups that had supported him six years earlier; and as a result, wide distribution in Wyoming was given to letters endorsing his candidacy from President William Green of the American Federation of Labor, Senator Robert F. Wagner of New York, and David Lasser, national president of the American Security Union ("It is our conviction that the interests of the unemployed and the WPA workers demand the re-election of Senator Joseph O'Mahoney. His record in Congress has been one of uniform support of the New Deal and support for legislation in the interests of those we represent").[77]

For his part, O'Mahoney's Republican adversary, the Cody attorney Milward Simpson, did his best to identify the senator with the least savory elements of the New Deal. Quoting Hugh Johnson, Simpson intimated that the Wyoming solon was "being manipulated by the White House inner circle for a Communistic or Fascist control of American business" while acting as chairman of the Temporary National Economic Committee. Under the New Deal, the challenger insisted, "key" positions in the federal establishment had been occupied by Communists and fifth-columnists.[78] If that meant that a vote for Milward Simpson was obviously a vote *against* the New Deal, it was no longer certain by any means that a vote for Joe O'Mahoney was necessarily a vote *for* it. Much was said in 1940 about the incumbent's independence and devotion to the interests of Wyoming, but virtually the only words of praise directed specifically toward the president or his administration concerned Roosevelt's great foresight in perceiving as early as 1937 the distressing course of world affairs.[79]

If any real significance is to be attached to the balloting in Wyoming in 1940, it must focus on the comparative strengths of Senator O'Mahoney and President Roosevelt. Both men won, revealing in itself that the average voter in the state was not yet antagonistic toward FDR personally, even if he had trouble marshaling enthusiasm for the president's domestic program. The noteworthy item, however, is that O'Mahoney snowed under Mr. Simpson by over 19,300 votes (collecting approximately 58.7 percent of the total) while Roosevelt topped Willkie by only 6,654 and picked up a little less than fifty-three percent of the popular vote. In the third race of national importance, Republican Congressman Frank O. Horton was unseated by the young Converse County lawyer John J. McIntyre, in a contest which very closely paralleled the voting in the presidential race. (Both Roosevelt and McIntyre carried twelve of the state's twenty-three counties—and indeed, the same ones with two exceptions. The president took Teton County, which McIntyre lost, and McIntyre won a narrow victory in Big Horn County, which ended up in the Willkie column.) When both McIntyre and Senator Harry Schwartz went down to defeat before their Republican opponents in November 1942, it may be said that the time for measuring whatever impact the New Deal had had on Wyoming politics had effectively come to a close.[80]

In searching for an explanation of that impact, it is only prudent to return to the basically agricultural character of the state. It would be tempting to suggest that the apparently limited influence of the New Deal on the political situation in Wyoming can be traced to the paucity or ineffectiveness of economic assistance rendered to the farmers and ranchers by the various New Deal agencies during the 1930s. After all, why should a Democratic administration spend much time, money, and effort on a voting group that considered itself less severely affected by the depression than many others and that was strongly Republican anyway? Yet the fact of the matter is that the New Deal was quite active in the agricultural sector, and it was in that area that the advances made under the aegis of its recovery programs was most striking. This is not to suggest that all the ground lost since 1929 was made up; the figures do not bear that out. But in 1938, after the impact of the 1937-38 slump was being felt, farmers in Wyoming had an aggregate cash income 102 percent higher than that which they had possessed in 1932. The total cash income received from sales of cattle and calves had risen nearly $6,000,000 for the state during that period; for sheep and lambs it had gone up over $5,000,000 (an increase of 130 percent); for wool the advance had totaled over $3,100,000 (or 124 percent); and the progress was even more impressive for some less vital commodities. Due largely to the advent of more potent federal farm loan and credit programs, the volume of forced farm sales in Wyoming dropped from 41.3 per thousand for the year ending March 1933 to a mere 16.7 per thousand in the year ending March 1939—and the average Wyoming farmer found his real property worth roughly six percent more by early 1939 than it had been six years earlier. He may have chafed under a degree of federal regulation that he had not previously been accustomed to, and he may have enjoyed taking verbal pot-shots at Henry Wallace and Rexford Tugwell; but he participated actively in their programs and was considerably better off at the end of the New Deal years than he had been when they began.[81]

So how can one account for the fact that, from 1938 on, it was clearly the most rural parts of Wyoming that reverted most quickly to their original Republican voting habits? H. L. Mencken might have argued that husbandmen are always the last people to perceive their own best interests; others could contend that in the day of the secret ballot, votes cannot be bought, even with largesse on the scale of the New Deal's. In a more serious vein, it was probably inevitable that the opposition to the Roosevelt administration would be led by the leading cattlemen in the state. Senator O'Mahoney was warned even before he took office that "Senator Carey has about taken over the Wyoming Stock Growers Association, body and breeches." "The Republicans hope to use this organization to defeat you," his long-time friend Carl Sackett told him in December 1933, "and to defeat the President ultimately." As O'Mahoney himself later recounted:

> The administration has been represented as hostile to the best interests of the livestock industry. Sometimes it was charged that the acts and policies would destroy the wool industry. . . .
> Of course, the predicted disasters never actually came. Conditions in the West have constantly improved as they have in every other section of the country, and the people of the far West are now [in 1936] in much better position than they were at the beginning of the administration.
> There has been some suspicion that the purveyors of these charges were more interested sometimes in partisan advantage than they were in the advantage of the industry itself.[82]

The Reciprocal Trade Agreements Act and the "life or death" power it seemed to give the president over the domestic cattle and wool industries was the most frequently complained-about measure; but in 1934, considerable unhappiness was being expressed over the administration-supported Taylor Grazing Act, providing for the leasing of grazing lands on the public domain to ranchers under government supervision. Congressman Vincent Carter, feeling that "90 percent of the people of Wyoming are opposed to the Taylor bill," fought it strongly in the House of Representatives; Senator Carey deemed it to be not in the best interests of his state and voted against it when it came up for passage in the Senate; even Governor Miller expressed misgivings about the bill because it appeared to eliminate "the passage of land into private ownership" and quite possibly invaded the rights of the states.[83]

Notwithstanding this opposition, a modified version of the bill passed anyway after Senator O'Mahoney had worked quietly but effectively to soften some of its provisions with a view toward lessening the discretionary authority of officials in the Departments of Agriculture and Interior, thus giving the prospective grazers greater freedom. Some of the most vocal stockmen were still unappeased, but most learned to live with the new legislation; it is significant that the 1935 meeting of the Wyoming Stock

Growers Association approved a resolution opposing "unalterably" any changes in the Taylor Grazing Act and urging that *all* of its provisions be made effective immediately.[84] It should not be assumed, however, that that served to make good New Dealers out of the state's cattlemen and wool growers.

The same general story was true with respect to the framing of the sugar quota system in the Jones-Costigan Act of 1934 and the O'Mahoney-Greever bill concerning prospecting for oil and gas on the public domain. The Jones-Costigan bill had endeavored to introduce greater stability into the sugar market by establishing annual quotas for each of several different groups of sugar producers: domestic beet growers, domestic sugar cane growers, cane sugar producers from the country's insular possessions (Hawaii, Puerto Rico, the Philippines, and the Virgin Islands), and foreign sources (especially Cuba). The problem in Wyoming was that many beet growers had first entered the industry in response to government invitations to settle on reclamation projects following World War I, and now they resented any limitation on their right to produce, feeling it amounted almost to an act of bad faith on Washington's part. It is hard to say just how widespread unhappiness over this legislation was among Wyoming's beet growers, but it may be significant that Goshen County, an area with a substantial sugar industry on reclaimed land, voted for the Republican opponents of both Congressman Greever and Senator O'Mahoney in 1934 and gave Senator Carey the nod over his New Deal challenger two years later.[85]

The O'Mahoney-Greever Act of 1935 was designed to remedy some of the defects in the old permit system that had governed the drilling for oil and gas on public lands since passage of the Mineral Leasing Act of 1920. Among other things it provided that these permits should gradually be replaced by leases on tracts of 640 acres and that the rate of the federal government's royalty should be boosted from a flat 5 percent to a graduated scale beginning at 12.5 percent on wells producing an average of fifty barrels or less of oil per day and rising to 33.33 percent for the largest producers. There was the rub, partly because of the increase in the minimum royalty rate and partly because even the wildest of wildcatters cherished the hope that someday he would be a big producer—and thus might be penalized by the sliding royalty scale. Paul Greever was more than a little bitter about the rough treatment he received at the hands of the Public Lands Oil and Gas Protective Association during the 1936 campaign, declaring after he was reelected despite the efforts of some oil men:

"I will now do as I damn please." That may have been an unfortunate attitude for the congressman, for there is a suggestion that the petroleum industry played a role in Greever's defeat in 1938.[86] Furthermore, most oil and gas prospectors understood that the real culprits (from their vantage point) were the overzealous conservationists in Harold Ickes's Interior Department—so once again, a generally pro-Republican interest group found its own particular reasons for disliking the New Deal. In many ways, both the Jones-Costigan Act and the O'Mahoney-Greever Act were sound pieces of legislation that ultimately profited those most concerned; but they did entail closer regulation and federal supervision, and that was still anathema to many Wyomingites. Henry Wallace knew what he was talking about when he remarked in mid-1934 after a tour of the country:

> Nowhere—except among the Wyoming group—did I find the people frightened about planned agriculture, nowhere had fears of "regimentation" sunk in. Wyoming seemed to be the only fortress of "rugged individualism," but the walls were manned by a rather limited group.[87]

Apparently that "rather limited group"—described by the secretary as "the governing class of Wyoming cattlemen" as distinct from the rank and file—was enough to stave off the liberal invaders, even after they had breached the walls on several occasions in the 1930s.

It is now commonly acknowledged that in order to alter the basic voting habits and partisan allegiances of great numbers of voters, a truly momentous psychological shock is required.[88] Although it is evident that the Great Depression and the New Deal occasioned such an emotional realignment in many parts of the United States among a number of segments of the electorate, it is impossible to perceive any comparable development in the state of Wyoming during those years. The predominantly rural political culture dictated that the effects of the nation's industrial depression—as serious as they may have seemed—would not be so traumatic for Wyoming as for many other areas. Nor, for that matter, would the contrast between the 1930s and the preceding decade be so sharp.

There is simply no denying that, at least in a relative way, Wyoming was a normally conservative and Republican state in the 1920s and was *still* a normally conservative and Republican state in the 1940s and the post–World War II period. T. A. Larson has postulated that Republicans in Wyoming did not outnumber Democrats as decisively in the period since 1945 as they had before the Great Crash, pointing especially to the narrowing gap in turnout between the two parties in the state's primary elections. He may be correct in that assumption, and in the absence of voter registration by party in Wyoming prior to 1967, there are no grounds for dogmatism on the subject. But another possibility presents itself, namely, that lower-income groups in Wyoming (one thinks of blue collar workers and marginal farmers) that might normally be expected to vote Democratic have become sufficiently "middle class" in their attitudes in the past three decades to decide that voting in primary elections was a requirement for "good citizenship"—thus creating a shift in voting statistics for primary elections that was more apparent than real. Moreover, to the extent that the Democratic party offers more complete slates of candidates at the local level, voters are no longer forced to vote in the Republican primary to take part in the real decision-making process. It would have been surprising if the Cowboy State had managed to remain entirely immune to the rising Democratic tide in the country at large, but compared to most other states, the impact of the New Deal on Wyoming politics seems to have been minimal.[89]

So when Professor Larson suggests that, in recent years, "a candidate's personality [has] counted for as much as his party affiliation and his stand on issues," he is stating a truism that would apply with nearly equal force to the first thirty years of the century in Wyoming. When he writes that "attractive, well-qualified Democrats have won major offices more often than was possible before 1932" and argues that "the New Deal must be given some of the credit for this change," the reader's mind flashes to Lester Hunt, Gale McGee, and Teno Roncalio and he is tempted to agree—until he remembers John B. Kendrick and the two Governors Ross. The interpretive difference is obviously one of degree, but if measured on a relative instead of an absolute scale of conservatism versus liberalism, Republicanism versus Democracy, it is difficult to detect any substantial shift.[90]

The question of *why* there was so little realignment is a knotty one. For one thing, basic assumptions and attitudes are remarkably durable and even sharp economic reverses could hardly eliminate the old Jeffersonian feeling that that government was best which governed least. In some states, political patterns were altered or "warped" by the New Deal's appeals to previously ignored groups in the electorate, but Wyoming was little affected by that kind of phenomenon. The high plains did not possess underprivileged and minority-group citizens in sufficient quantities to carry much political weight. But at least one other answer deserves consideration. Obviously, Wyoming was not *like* much of the rest of the nation.

Often its basic economic interests did diverge from those of, say, the eastern seaboard. Is it possible that a majority of the state's voters understood that, and that understanding curtailed their conversion to the party of Franklin D. Roosevelt because the New Deal was addressing itself to the needs and interests of the nation as a whole? Some persuasive recent studies have indicated that the ability of the American voter to render a rational (if not disinterested) decision has too long been underestimated.[91] In any event, some other, more profound crisis (one shudders to think what might be needed) would be required to change the basic character of Wyoming politics.

The research for this study was made possible in part by a grant from the University of Utah Research Committee.

1. (Cheyenne) *Wyoming State Tribune,* 14 August 1936.

2. Any student of Wyoming politics who delves very deeply into election returns will almost certainly find Marie H. Erwin's *Wyoming Historical Blue Book: A Legal and Political History of Wyoming, 1868–1943* (Denver, 1946) an extremely valuable source. The reader may assume, unless otherwise informed, that all of the election results and vote counts mentioned in this study are drawn from Mrs. Erwin's compilation.

3. See T. A. Larson, "The New Deal in Wyoming," *Pacific Historical Review* 38 (1969): 249–73; Larson, *History of Wyoming* (Lincoln, Nebr., 1965); Charles P. Beall, "Wyoming: The Equality State," in Frank H. Jonas, ed., *Western Politics* (Salt Lake City, 1961); and Gene M. Gressley, "Joseph C. O'Mahoney, FDR, and the Supreme Court," *Pacific Historical Review* 40 (1971): 183–202.

4. All of the census figures referred to are drawn from U.S. Department of Commerce, Bureau of the Census, *Sixteenth Census of the United States, 1940: Population*, Vol. 2, *Characteristics of the Population*, pt. 7: Utah-Wyoming, 4 vols. (Washington, 1943).

5. See applicable election tables in Erwin, *Wyoming Historical Blue Book.*

6. See John D. Clark's letter to the editor, (Cheyenne) *Wyoming Eagle,* 8 November 1940, and telegram and list from Julian Snow to Mills Astin, 4 October 1940, Box 38, O'Mahoney Papers (University of Wyoming Library).

7. Beall, "Wyoming: The Equality State," pp. 344, 347.

8. John B. Kendrick to Theodore G. Diers, 16 August 1917, Box 22, Kendrick Papers (University of Wyoming Library).

9. Larson, "The New Deal in Wyoming," pp. 250–51.

10. La Follette received 25,174 votes in Wyoming compared to 41,858 for the victorious Coolidge and only 12,868 for Democrat John W. Davis.

11. Larson, "The New Deal in Wyoming," p. 251; Kendrick to Mildred H. Bemis, 4 February 1927, Box 45, Kendrick Papers. Beall ("Wyoming: The Equality State," p. 337) also describes both major parties in Wyoming as "dominantly center to right-of-center on major political issues," but the most logical explanation is simply that ideology plays a very minor role in a state where the personality and reputation of the individual candidates are of such consequence.

12. Larson, "The New Deal in Wyoming," p. 251.

13. Joseph C. O'Mahoney to Michael A. Rattigan, 9 November 1930, Box 1; George B. Kerper to O'Mahoney, 22 April 1931, Box 3, O'Mahoney Papers.

14. O'Mahoney to Democrats of Wyoming, 20 March 1931, Box 1, ibid.

15. *Wyoming Eagle*, 10 July 1931; Earland Irving Carlson, "Franklin D. Roosevelt's Fight for the Presidential Nomination, 1928–1932" (Ph.D. diss., University of Illinois, 1955), p. 146.

16. Frank Freidel, *Franklin D. Roosevelt: the Triumph* (Boston and Toronto, 1956), p. 288; Kendrick to Roosevelt, 4 July 1932, Box 55, Kendrick Papers. For O'Mahoney's role at the convention, see also James A. Farley, *Behind the Ballots: The Personal History of a Politician* (New York, 1938), p. 107, and *Jim Farley's Story: The Roosevelt Years* (New York and Toronto, 1948), p. 15.

17. Unlabeled, undated MS of O'Mahoney address to Colorado Democrats in Denver, 1 August 1932, Box 5, O'Mahoney Papers.

18. *New York Times*, 17 September 1932.

19. Kendrick to O'Mahoney, 11 November 1932, Box 55, Kendrick Papers. See also Larson, *History of Wyoming*, p. 463.

20. *Wyoming State Tribune*, 6 May 1934. Farley had described Johnson during the campaign as "one of our under cover men" in the West (see Farley to Roosevelt, 10 May 1932, OF 300, Democratic National Committee, Wisconsin, 1938–45 Wyoming, Box 68, Roosevelt Papers [Franklin D. Roosevelt Library]).

21. Agnes V. O'Mahoney to Eula W. Kendrick, 31 October 1934, Box 60, Kendrick Papers; *Wyoming State Tribune*, 16 March 1933.

22. *Wyoming State Tribune*, 30 June 1934.

23. Ibid., 4, 9 March 1933.

24. Ibid., 12 March 1933.

25. *Laramie* (Wyoming) *Republican-Boomerang*, 24 April 1933.

26. Ibid., 29 April, 4, 11 May 1933.

27. *Wyoming State Tribune,* 2 June 1933; *Laramie Republican-Boomerang,* 8 June 1933.

28. *Wyoming State Tribune*, 9 May, 8 September 1934.

29. Ibid., 17 June 1934.

30. Dan Prentice to Fred W. Johnson, 27 February 1934, Box 11; Leslie A. Miller to O'Mahoney, 28 March 1934, Box 9, O'Mahoney Papers.

31. *Wyoming State Tribune*, 19 August 1934. O'Neil's reference was obviously to what Wyoming Republicans and some disgruntled Democrats like to call the "M-O-M Machine" with its power base in Cheyenne. "M-O-M" stood for "Miller-O'Mahoney-McCraken," referring to the governor, the United States senator, and the astute and powerful Cheyenne newspaper publisher.

32. *Wyoming State Tribune*, 13 September 1934.

33. Miller to O'Mahoney, 28 March 1934, Box 9, O'Mahoney Papers.

34. *Wyoming State Tribune*, 25 July 1934.

35. Ibid., 13 July 1934; Julian Snow, "Joseph C. O'Mahoney: His Answer to the Enigma," in J. T. Salter, ed., *Public Men In and Out of Office* (Chapel Hill, N.C., 1946), p. 111; *Wyoming State Tribune*, 6 May 1934.

36. *Wyoming State Tribune*, 4 November, 27 September 1934; *Wyoming Eagle*, 12 October 1934.

37. *Wyoming State Tribune*, 6, 18 October 1934.

38. Ibid., 23 October, 22 September 1934.

39. Press release of O'Mahoney radio address, Salt Lake City, 1 October 1934, Box 5, O'Mahoney Papers.

40. Eula W. Kendrick to O'Mahoney, 18 October 1934, Box 60, Kendrick Papers.

41. Larson, *History of Wyoming*, pp. 464–65. Another factor worth noting in the O'Mahoney-Carter race is the role of organized labor. Congressman Carter has suggested to the author that his own campaign in 1934 was not adequately financed and that "the labor vote that was favorable to me in past elections, forsook me, the reason for which I have no personal knowledge. Senator O'Mahoney's campaign was well financed—it was a Democratic year; and above all he was an astute

politician" (Vincent Carter to the author, 26 January 1968, in author's possession). The shift of labor union support from Carter to his Democratic opponent was no doubt connected in part with the New Deal's efforts on labor's behalf—and with a letter endorsing O'Mahoney's candidacy sent to the State Federation of Labor by AFL President William Green in October. But Joseph O'Mahoney had long been friendly toward organized labor in Wyoming, often supporting its cause and rendering legal assistance throughout the decade of the 1920s, so perhaps too much can be made in this instance of the influence of the national picture. For a remarkable campaign document, however, see the special 30 October 1934, Wyoming Edition of the newspaper *Labor*, circulated widely in Cheyenne and along the Union Pacific tracks.

42. Miller to Eula W. Kendrick, 10 November 1934, Box 61, Kendrick Papers.

43. *Wyoming State Tribune*, 1, 2 August 1935.

44. See James McGregor Burns, *Roosevelt: The Lion and the Fox* (New York, 1956), pp. 266–67.

45. *Sheridan* (Wyoming) *Press*, 23 February 1936; A. H. Marble to O'Mahoney, 13 July 1935, Box 15, O'Mahoney Papers.

46. Leonard Arrington, "The New Deal in the West: A Preliminary Statistical Inquiry," *Pacific Historical Review* 38 (1969): 311–16.

47. *Wyoming State Tribune*, 13 April 1934; Paul Andrew Hassler, "Some Effects of the Great Depression on the State of Wyoming, 1929–1934" (M.A. thesis, University of Wyoming, 1957), p. 81.

48. U.S. Office of Government Reports, Statistical Section, Report No. 10: *Wyoming*, Vol. 2 (State Data) (1940), p. 36. The author is deeply indebted to Professor Leonard Arrington of Brigham Young University for providing him with a photocopy of this valuable fifty-page document, hereafter cited as U.S., Office of Govt. Reports, *Wyoming*.

49. Ibid., pp. 23, 21.

50. *Wyoming State Tribune*, 10 May, 10, 17, 25 April, 11 May 1934.

51. Ibid., 22 July 1936; O'Mahoney to Eph U. Johnson, 26 July 1940, Box 48, O'Mahoney Papers.

52. O'Mahoney to G. O. Housley, 12 August 1940, Box 50, ibid.

53. U.S., Office of Govt. Reports, *Wyoming*, 2:31-33; O'Mahoney to Charles M. Smith, 1 June 1938, Box 31, O'Mahoney Papers. See also State Director, Public Works Administration, Cheyenne, Wyoming, Press Release of 16 June 1936 (copy in Box 62, Kendrick Papers).

54. See Larson, "The New Deal in Wyoming," p. 269.

55. Memorandum signed "A.S.K." for O'Mahoney entitled "Cheyenne—September 25, 1935," Box 15, O'Mahoney Papers; *Wyoming State Tribune*, 3 September 1936; *New York Times*, 12 October 1936.

56. *Laramie Republican-Boomerang*, 5 June 1933; *Wyoming State Tribune*, 20 June, 1 August 1935.

57. O'Mahoney to Eula W. Kendrick, 9 October 1935, Box 61, Kendrick Papers.

58. *Wyoming State Tribune,* 9 August, 6, 10, 20, 26 September, 31 October, 1 November 1936; Harry H. Schwartz to Eula W. Kendrick, 12 November 1936, Box 62, Kendrick Papers.

59. *Wyoming State Tribune*, 20 June, 31 July 1935.

60. Ibid., 30 September 1936.

61. Ibid. 11, September 1936.

62. Miller to Eula W. Kendrick, 10 November 1936; O'Mahoney to Eula W. Kendrick, 1 December 1936, Box 62, Kendrick Papers. Also noteworthy in the Democratic sweep was Representative Greever's easy reelection over a future congressman, governor, and U.S. senator, Frank A. Barrett, and the continuance of Democratic control of both houses of the state legislature, 16 to 11 and 38 to 18.

63. The entire affair from Wyoming's standpoint is covered in F. Alan Coombs, "Joseph Christopher O'Mahoney: The New Deal Years" (Ph.D. diss., University of Illinois, 1968), pp. 242-86. See also Gressley, "Joseph C. O'Mahoney, FDR, and the Supreme Court."

64. *Wyoming Eagle*, 23 July 1937.

65. Kenneth D. Roose, "The Recession of 1937–38," *Journal of Political Economy* 56 (1948): 241.

66. See Larry J. Krysl, "The Effects of the Great Depression on the State of Wyoming, 1935-1940" (M.A. thesis, University of Wyoming, 1960), especially pp. 17, 44; U. S., Office of Govt. Reports, *Wyoming*, 2:5–6.

67. *Wyoming Eagle*, 20 August 1937.

68. Ibid., 21 August 1937; O'Mahoney to James W. Barrett, 7 September 1937, Box 25, O'Mahoney Papers.

69. James T. Patterson, *The New Deal and the States: Federalism in Transition* (Princeton, N.J., 1969), p. 159.

70. Typescript of author's tape-recorded interview with Leslie A. Miller in Cheyenne, 6 July 1967, in author's possession. See also miscellaneous correspondence in Box 2-A, O'Mahoney Papers.

71. T. K. Cassidy to O'Mahoney, 17 March 1938, Box 4, O'Mahoney Papers.

72. O'Mahoney to John D. Clark, 18 March 1938, ibid.

73. Leslie A. Miller interview; Paul Greever to Eula W. Kendrick, 14 November 1938; Leslie Miller to Eula W. Kendrick, 14 November 1938, Box 63, Kendrick Papers.

74. Larson, *History of Wyoming*, pp. 466–67; James T. Patterson, "The New Deal in the West," *Pacific Historical Review* 38 (1969): 322. The observation about the importance of the labor vote is supported as well by John J. McIntyre, U.S. representative from Wyoming (1941–43) and later chief justice of the Wyoming Supreme Court, in a tape-recorded interview with the author in Cheyenne, 12 August 1970 (tape in author's possession). See also Larson, "The New Deal in Wyoming." p. 259n.

75. O'Mahoney to Bayard C. Wilson, 5 April 1940, Box 54, O'Mahoney Papers.

76. Clark to Julian Snow, 4 March 1940, Box 59; J. F. Paulson to O'Mahoney, 3 June 1939, Box 46; Fred D. Boice to O'Mahoney, 15 August 1939, Box 45; Frank J. McCue to O'Mahoney, 4 March 1940, Box 50; and text of O'Mahoney address, "The Significance of the Monopoly Committee," to the National Townsend Club Convention, St. Louis, Missouri, 1 July 1940, Box 37, ibid. Political allies back in Wyoming had warned the senator that "the Townsendites now hold the balance of the voting power in the state and . . . will do so in 1940" (see Thomas K. Cassidy to O'Mahoney, 16 June 1939, Box 46, ibid.).

77. (Cheyenne) *Wyoming Labor Journal*, 1 November 1940; David Lasser to J. Claude Davis, 14 October 1940, Box 47, O'Mahoney Papers.

78. *Wyoming State Tribune*, 6 October 1940; Larson, *History of Wyoming*, p. 451.

79. *Wyoming Eagle*, 15 October 1940.

80. One hardly knows how to treat the apparent anomaly of the majority of Wyoming voters continuing to support with some enthusiasm both Franklin D. Roosevelt and the senator who had established his reputation for independence from the Roosevelt administration (although in 1944, Wyoming finally abandoned FDR for Thomas E. Dewey by a narrow margin). It is conceivable that what seems to be electoral schizophrenia was no more than a case of the state's voters exercising their dual citizenship. Consciously or unconsciously, they understood that the president had to be responsible for the entire nation and that the national interest did not always coincide with Wyoming's peculiar state interests. It was Roosevelt's *job* to be president of *all* the people. But Wyoming's senators and representatives were a different matter; Carey, O'Mahoney, Schwartz, Greever, Horton, and McIntyre were elected solely by Wyoming to represent that state's vital interests, and when they failed to do so with sufficient vigor, their political lives might be forfeit. To be sure, in time even a president who seemed to pursue policies hostile to Wyoming's needs might incur the voters' wrath. Another explanation, of course, is simply that O'Mahoney's voting record, despite his efforts after 1937 to keep his identification with the New Deal faint, remained liberal enough to attract those who still admired the president.

81. U.S., Office of Govt. Reports, *Wyoming*, 2:7–14, passim. For pointed criticism of Tugwell and Wallace, see *Wyoming State Tribune*, 6, 7 June, 29 July 1934.

82. Carl L. Sackett to O'Mahoney, 21 December 1933, Box 11, O'Mahoney Papers; U.S. Congress, Senate, *Congressional Record*, 74th Cong., 2d Sess. (1936), 80, pt. 7, p. 7878.

83. *Wyoming State Tribune*, 27 April, 21 June, 3 May 1934. The president of the Wyoming Stock Growers in June 1934 termed the Taylor bill "a most iniquitous measure" and, speaking for his organization, said, "There is no doubt that we are strongly opposed to the Taylor bill" (ibid., 6 June 1934).

84. Ibid., 11 July 1934, 21 June 1935.

85. See miscellaneous correspondence in the sugar legislation files, Box 15, O'Mahoney Papers.

86. Greever to O'Mahoney, 23 November 1936, Box 16, O'Mahoney Papers; miscellaneous materials in "O'Mahoney—Leasing Law Amendment S. 3311" file, ibid.

87. *Wyoming State Tribune*, 19 June 1934.

88. See, for example, Samuel Lubell, *The Future of American Politics*, 2d ed. rev. (New York, 1956), p. 7; V. O. Key, Jr., "A Theory of Critical Elections," *Journal of Politics* 17 (1955): 3–4; and Angus Campbell et al., *The American Voter*, Abridged Edition (New York, 1964), p. 276.

89. Larson, *History of Wyoming*, p. 506; Larson, "The New Deal in Wyoming," p. 272n.

90. Larson, *History of Wyoming*, p. 507.

91. See Patterson, *The New Deal and the States*, p. 192, and Martin Fishbein and Fred S. Coombs, "Basis for Decision: An Attitudinal Approach toward an Understanding of Voting Behavior," paper prepared for delivery at the Sixty-seventh Annual Meeting of the American Political Science Association, Chicago, Illinois, 7–11 September 1971, in author's possession.

Michael P. Malone

The Montana New Dealers

MONTANA IS A STATE OF RUGGED, SPECTACULAR BEAUTY AND OF remote, sparsely populated expanses. Encompassing the jagged ranges of the Northern Rockies in the west and the undulating upper Great Plains in the east, the "Treasure State" has existed for little more than a century as a political unit. Yet during that time, it has produced a colorful and fascinating heritage. History to most Montanans means the frontier; homesteaders came here, after all, in Model T's. Amateur and professional historians alike have pored over the various frontier movements into Montana and have dwelt at length on the amazing "Wars of the Copper Kings," which occurred at the turn of the century. The state's history since 1900, however, remains largely unexplored.[1]

The student of Montana society thus finds that modern scholarship has barely touched the crucial decade of the 1930s. Considering the disastrous local results of the post-1919 and post-1929 depressions, this neglect seems especially serious. The purpose of this essay is to focus upon the 1930s, particularly the impact that the Great Depression and the New Deal had upon Montana *political* affairs. What effect did the New Deal have upon the Montana political culture? Did it, or did it not, work an authentic revolution in local political attitudes and organization?

In 1932, as the economy fell to its nadir in Montana, the state's political order revealed its classic twentieth-century posture—liberalism in Washington, D.C., conservatism in Helena. As usual, personalities and personal loyalties overshadowed political parties and their organizations.

Montana's two prestigious Democratic senators, Thomas J. Walsh and Burton K. Wheeler, had become liberal favorites during the twenties, Walsh for his role in exposing the Teapot Dome scandal and Wheeler for his crusade against President Harding's attorney general, Harry Daugherty.

Ironically, Montana's liberal image in Washington found little reflection at home. Since the turn of the century, when the Anaconda Copper Mining Company[2] had enormously expanded its statewide economic and political power, local debate had centered around "the Company" and its role in affairs of state. Indeed, the central purpose of Montana progressives had always been to break the hold, as they saw it, that the Anaconda, its corporate twin the Montana Power Company, and its powerful string of newspapers had upon the state's governmental structure. The climax of this struggle came during the administration of liberal Republican Governor Joseph M. Dixon (1921–25), who had served as Theodore Roosevelt's campaign manager in 1912. Dixon won the greatest symbolic victory of local progressivism by imposing an effective mine tax on "the Company" in 1924, but in the election of that year he was defeated for reelection by Company and conservative onslaughts and by the devastating impact of the post–World War I depression.[3]

After 1924, the passions of Montana progressivism rapidly cooled. Governor John E. Erickson (1925–33), the Democrat who defeated Dixon, was a conservative friendly to the corporate "interests" in Montana. Powerful Senators Walsh and Wheeler seldom involved themselves in local political struggles. Some liberals accused them of "selling out" to the Company, a familiar refrain; but that charge seems largely unfounded. More likely, both Walsh and Wheeler had learned to keep their fences mended by avoiding confrontations with the established powers at home. Certainly, both men were becoming increasingly preoccupied with national rather than state issues.[4]

By the early thirties, the Anaconda Company too was lessening its overt political involvement, in part, it would seem, as a result of its increasing reliance on Chilean and Mexican sources of copper. The changing policy of the Anaconda newspapers, which included eight of the state's major dailies, indicated this shift. Earlier, the Company papers had lashed out vehemently at their political enemies; now they simply ignored them and dwelt instead on far away, remote issues, a tactic that their exasperated foes appropriately referred to as "Afghanistaning."[5]

Thus by 1932, both the forces of liberalism and those of conservatism had retreated from the wide-open confrontations of the pre–1924 progressive era. State politics seemed to rest on dead center. In their political attitudes, Montanans revealed a certain ambivalence. They showed a lively interest in, and awareness of, national politics and government. And, since Montana is a large public domain state, heavily reliant upon the federal government, this is hardly surprising. After the defeat of activist Governor Dixon, though, Montana citizens appeared apathetic toward state government. They seemed to expect little more than fiscal integrity from Helena.

By 1932, forces were at work that would break the political calm. Depression in Montana was nothing new. This state's homesteading boom peaked just prior to and during World War I. Then came the spectacular crash of Montana agriculture when, during 1919–25, the state's heavily indebted wheat farmers and its badly overextended banking and credit structure collapsed. Between 1921 and 1925, 20,000 Montana farmers fell victim to mortgage foreclosure, two million acres went out of production, and 11,000 farms (one-fifth of the state's total) disappeared. Nationally prominent Montanans like economist M. L. Wilson voiced the local demand for federal farm relief. As the postwar depression also hit the copper and lumber industries, 60,000 people left the state, and Montana became the only state in the nation to lose population during the "prosperity decade" of the 1920s.[6]

Rains and a fleeting prosperity returned in the mid-twenties, but the drought and winds hit again in 1929. They would last intermittently for almost ten years. As it barely began to recover from the postwar collapse, Montana agriculture was staggered again. In 1931–32, as cutbacks in American production reached out to areas supplying raw materials, Montana's extractive industries also felt the squeeze. The mining and smelting centers of Butte-Anaconda, Great Falls, and Helena and, to a lesser extent, lumber towns like Missoula and Libby witnessed scenes of unemployment, deprivation, and despair that equaled or exceeded those of most major industrial areas throughout the country.

As the depression widened and deepened in 1931–32, conditions became critical. Employment in Montana's manufacturing industries fell from 14,860 in 1929 to 6,224 in 1933. Wheat prices plummeted to such depths that wheat worth $100 in 1920 brought only $19.23 in 1932.[7] In the northern Montana town of Scobey, Daniels County, which a few years earlier had billed itself as the nation's largest primary wheat shipping center, 1933 found 3,500 of the county's 5,000 inhabitants on federal relief. During 1933–35, approximately 25 percent of all Montanans were on some form of federal relief assistance. Hardest hit were the mining counties of Silver Bow, Deer Lodge, and Cascade and the agricultural counties along the state's eastern border, where population percentages on relief remained at 31–40 percent in early 1935.[8]

Politically, Montanans, like most Americans, blamed the incumbent Republicans and President Hoover for the hard times; and they drifted less toward radicalism than simply toward the "out" party, the Democrats. Regardless of personal leanings toward the right or left, Montana's Democratic leaders were among the first to support the presidential candidacy of New York Governor Franklin D. Roosevelt. Senator Wheeler endorsed FDR's candidacy in April of 1930, one of the first nationally prominent Democrats to do so. Senator Walsh, the old Wilson Democrat, followed later. Even J. Bruce Kremer, veteran conservative and Anaconda ally, lent his influential support to the Roosevelt cause from the position that he had held on the Democratic National Committee since 1908.[9]

By the spring of 1932, Governor John Erickson reported FDR to be "the outstanding candidate in Montana." In May, state Democrats met and followed the lead of Walsh and Wheeler by instructing their delegates to support the Roosevelt candidacy at the national convention.[10] At the Democratic convention in Chicago, Montanans played a major role in securing the nomination for FDR. On 28 July, the convention chose Senator Walsh as its permanent chairman, a major victory for the Roosevelt forces. J. Bruce Kremer, serving as chairman of the rules committee, worked effectively for the New York governor. And Senator Wheeler assisted Arthur Mullen of Nebraska as FDR's floor leader at the convention.[11] Probably no western state played a greater role than Montana in gaining the first Roosevelt nomination.

In contrast to the exciting developments on the national stage, Montana's 1932 political campaign generated little enthusiasm. Since there was no senate race this year, attention focused upon the presidential and gubernatorial contests. Completing his second four-year term as governor, conservative Democrat John E. Erickson barely salvaged a third-term nomination in the July primary; the combined vote of his three progressive opponents actually exceeded his own. Democrat John Evans, an eighteen-year veteran congressman from the state's western district, narrowly lost renomination to a young and ambitious upstart, Joseph P. Monaghan from Butte.[12]

The state Democratic party was well united in 1932. Its liberal wing supported, without noticeable enthusiasm, a gubernatorial candidate who was fiscally very conservative and politically a well-known friend of "the Company." Governor Erickson's Republican challenger, Frank Hazelbaker of Dillon, based his attack upon demands for retrenchment and paring down the state bureaucracy. Like many other Democrats in 1932, Erickson followed the same tack. Time and again, he argued that his administration had held expenditures at least $100,000 below appropriations and that he had cut the actual costs of government below the levels of his Republican predecessor. The other leading Democratic aspirants, especially congressional candidates Joseph Monaghan and Roy Ayers of Lewistown, followed the standard 1932 line of assailing Hoover for the hard times. The one enthusiastic episode in a generally humdrum campaign was FDR's train trip through Montana in September. Speaking to a large, excited crowd in Butte, Roosevelt voiced his commitment to agriculture and mining and emphasized his plans to take the initiative in international efforts to remonetize silver.[13]

The 8 November 1932 election returns in Montana mirrored the nationwide Democratic sweep. Roosevelt carried all but one of the state's 56 counties and trounced Herbert Hoover, 127,286 to 78,078. Two freshman Democrats easily won election to Congress, Joseph Monaghan in the western district and Roy Ayers in the east. Although the Republicans maintained majority control in the State Senate, the Democrats won the House of Representatives and took every major state administrative office except one. Governor Erickson, sagging in popularity after eight years in office, barely rode back into the governorship on the Democratic tidal wave. His margin over Hazelbaker was a bare 3,844 votes.[14] Obviously, Montana joined in the 1932 national repudiation of Hoover Republicanism. The Roosevelt landslide had swept across the state, drawing Montana issues and Montana politicians in its wake. The future of the state's Democratic party seemed fair indeed.

A hectic series of events followed the 1932 election that, quite without plan, recast the political scene in Montana. In view of Montana's contributions to the Roosevelt victory, many people assumed that the state would be represented in the new cabinet. As National Committeeman Bruce Kremer saw it, Montana seemed entitled "above any other state in the west" to a cabinet spot. The president-elect made the obvious selection and offered the position of attorney general to Senator Thomas Walsh, famed investigator and one of the great legal minds in public life. Reluctant to leave the Senate and apprehensive about whom Governor Erickson might appoint to succeed him, Walsh hesitated. Apparently, his greatest fear was that the ubiquitous Bruce Kremer, a close friend of the corporate "interests" in Montana, might be named as his successor.[15] Walsh finally put his doubts aside and accepted, and Roosevelt named him to the cabinet on 28 February 1933.

The Walsh appointment evoked widespread praise and enthusiasm. But on 2 March 1933, while en route by train to Washington, D.C., from Havana, where he had just married for a second time, the 73-year-old Walsh suffered a heart attack and died. The shock produced by his death, and the eulogies that followed, gauged the former senator's towering prestige. As the *Nation* remarked: "The outstanding figure in the newly appointed Roosevelt Cabinet, his nomination was the guaranty of the Administration's integrity of purpose and an augury of its progressivism."[16] In the death of Walsh, the United States lost one of its outstanding public men, and Montana lost its most imposing statesman.

The loss of Walsh immediately complicated political affairs in Montana. Even before Walsh's death, news of his impending resignation set off a mad scramble for his seat in the Senate. Among the contenders, the most powerful was the man whose appointment Walsh had apprently most feared—J. Bruce Kremer, who enjoyed Anaconda and Montana Power support. Since Governor Erickson, who held the appointive power, was favorably disposed toward "the Company," that might have decided the issue. But Kremer had one obstacle to overcome: the enmity of his old foe Burton K. Wheeler, now Montana's senior senator.

In his autobiography, Wheeler recalls how he and Walsh's daughter, Mrs. Genevieve Gudger, tried to dissuade Erickson from making the Kremer appointment. Senator Wheeler was so adamant about Kremer and his corporate connections that he forced a confrontation over the matter with the "interests" directly. As the senator recalled it, he met Frank Kerr, the president of Montana Power, one day in a hotel lobby and warned him that, if the company continued to support Kremer for the Senate, he would challenge them in the forthcoming election campaign of 1934.[17] Evidently, the Anaconda–Montana Power forces chose to avoid a showdown with the popular Wheeler. According to the senator's account, company spokesmen assured him that they had withdrawn their support of Kremer and had explicitly delivered this news to Governor Erickson.

This left the problem of Walsh's successor unsolved. Erickson, besieged from all sides, apparently decided to follow the advice of Wheeler. On 13 March 1933, in a prearranged maneuver, Erickson resigned as governor, and Lieutenant Governor Frank H. Cooney became his successor. Cooney then appointed Erickson to succeed Walsh in the Senate. As usual in such ploys, Erickson's "self-appointment" brought an indignant outcry and charges of an unseemly "deal." The *Sidney Herald* voiced a common sentiment in finding Erickson an unworthy replacement of Walsh, "whose shoes he can no more fill in these trying times than could a child."[18]

The Erickson-Cooney "deal" marked an abrupt departure in Montana affairs of state. It sapped the popularity of both men. It also reversed the ordinary Montana pattern by placing a conservative in the Senate and a liberal—Cooney was a progressive favorite—in the governor's mansion. Most significantly, the whole series of events since Walsh's death marked the rising star of Burton K. Wheeler, who would dominate the Montana scene for the next dozen years. Walsh was dead and Erickson's influence declining. Kremer, whose advancement Wheeler had just blocked, resigned from the Democratic National Committee in early 1934, when President Roosevelt attempted to reform that body. Although Kremer remained an influential lobbyist in Washington, due mainly to his close friendship with the new attorney general, Homer Cummings, his political power in Montana waned.[19] In short, as the New Deal era opened in 1933, Wheeler's stature at home was unmatched and momentarily unchallenged. His role in selecting his Senate colleague marked the dawning of what might well be called "the Age of Wheeler" in the Treasure State.

As political excitement abated in the spring of 1933, local attention focused on the New Deal program now emerging from Congress. An extensive analysis of the myriad New Deal agencies and their activities lies beyond the scope of this essay. But beyond dispute, the various relief, reform, and recovery efforts of the first Roosevelt administration had an enormous political impact.[20]

From 1933 through 1939, the federal government spent $381,582,693 and loaned another $141,835,952 in Montana. This amounted to a per capita expenditure of $710 and a per capita loan expenditure of $264, ranking Montana second in the nation in federal investment thus computed.[21] Like most public domain states of the west, Montana benefited greatly from New Deal spending.

Among the key Roosevelt programs, the Agricultural Adjustment Administration was probably the most important to Montana. The AAA negotiated 137,748 crop adjustment contracts with state farmers during 1933–37, most of them for wheat, and poured from $4,500,000 to almost

$10,000,000 yearly into Montana's dormant economy.[22] Various relief agencies, like the Public Works Administration, the Federal Emergency Relief Administration, the Civil Works Administration, and finally the Works Progress Administration, contributed most of the support for the 110,000 Montanans dependent on relief during 1933–35. The WPA alone spent $44,454,974 during 1935–39 and left behind an impressive number of useful public projects. Some minor New Deal efforts also had great local significance. The Civilian Conservation Corps, for instance, was operating 27 camps in Montana during 1937–38 and had by then employed almost 14,000 local youths. By 1938, the new Rural Electrification Administration had 756 miles of rural electric line under construction, bringing a new way of life to 2,463 farm families.[23]

The over-all effect of this massive federal spending will, of course, always be disputed; but by the later thirties, Montana's economy was undeniably on the upswing. Manufacturing employment climbed from 6,224 in 1933 to 11,268 in 1937, corresponding annual payrolls from $8,800,112 to $15,757,784 in the same period. Internal revenue collections rose from $3,959,000 in 1934 to $5,898,000 in 1939, and bank deposits climbed from $85,927,000 in mid–1933 to $123,394,000 in March of 1939. By 1936–37, the mining and oil industries were again operating at near-capacity, but severe drought still afflicted northern and eastern Montana. The 1937–38 recession brought brief but large-scale shutdowns in mining while, ironically, the rains returned to the stricken plains areas. By 1939–40, Montana, like the nation at large, was climbing toward the wartime prosperity that would truly end the hard times.[24]

Some New Deal efforts caused perplexing problems in Montana, such as the federal demands for state matching funds that so harried the legislature in 1933 or the jarring requirements for new state efforts in relief and public welfare that preoccupied the 1935 and 1937 legislative assemblies. But more importantly, the New Deal also created a great sense of renewed vitality and civic accomplishment. The great symbol of New Deal achievement in Montana was Fort Peck Dam on the Missouri River. FDR made the initial investment of $75 million for this massive project in 1933, mainly, it would seem, to pay off his political debts to Senator Wheeler. Throughout the New Deal era, the Public Works Administration, Army Engineers, and other agencies supervised the huge work project. Ten thousand workers and their dependents clustered around the site in squalid little hell-for-leather cities like New Deal, Square Deal, Wheeler, and Delano Heights.[25] At the close of the depression decade, the dam stood as a monument to New Deal aspirations and values, the greatest alteration man had yet made in the Montana landscape.

In the midterm elections of 1934, the American people received an opportunity to voice their opinions on the virtues and vices of the New Deal. Local circumstances in Montana served especially to make this election a "mandate": since the Walsh seat had been vacated in 1933, both Senate positions were now up for election, and the political parties in Montana divided for once along fairly clear lines—for or against the Roosevelt program.

In the Democratic primary, the results clearly revealed the rise of New Deal liberalism. Incumbents Senator Burton K. Wheeler and Congressmen Roy Ayers and Joseph Monaghan all ran as Roosevelt loyalists, and all triumphed easily. Standing for a short, two-year term in order to complete the unexpired Walsh tenure, Senator Erickson failed. His popularity had languished since his "self-appointment" to the Senate in 1933, and his brief service there had been largely undistinguished. In the extremely close, six-man race for the Erickson seat, the winner was James E. Murray of Butte, wealthy attorney, longtime party stalwart, and spokesman for the vocal Butte Irish. Even in the contests for lesser state offices, the leftward trend was unmistakable. Jerry J. O'Connell, a twenty-five-year-old Butte lawyer and a fiery, outspoken foe of the corporate "interests" in Montana, surprisingly won nomination to the important Railroad and Public Service Commission, which supervised railroad and utility rates. Since the Republican candidates generally stood categorically against the New Deal, a direct confrontation over the issues loomed in the general election. The liberals were jubilant. The *Western Progressive* of Helena crowed that the primary "marks the passing of corporation control and the age-long domination of seekers for special privilege."[26]

Attention in the 1934 campaign centered on the two Senate races. Wheeler and Murray often campaigned together, and they joined in grandiose claims about the benefits of New Deal spending and about how Montana had been especially favored by the federal government. Their Republican opponents were, respectively, Judge George M. Bourquin and former Congressman Scott Leavitt, both leaders of the GOP's conservative wing. Swimming against the tide, Bourquin and Leavitt leveled their attacks directly against the New Deal and especially against that great New Deal symbol, the Fort Peck project.

Bourquin, a handsome, imposing man and flamboyant orator, dwelt at length on Fort Peck. In countless talks, he scored Wheeler, Roosevelt, public spending, and especially the dam, which he dismissed as a useless "duck pond." "As by a trumpet blast," thundered Bourquin, "I would arouse the outraged citizenry of the State, irrespective of party, to pour the vials of their wrath upon these hucksters until they call upon the mountains to fall upon and cover them and their shame."[27] President Roosevelt personally helped make Fort Peck the central issue by visiting the dam site in August. Assiniboine and Sioux Indians, apparently taken with the National Recovery Administration, made him an honorary chief with the name "Fearless Blue Eagle."

In a state as hard pressed as Montana, a state so handsomely treated by the federal government, the Republican tactics could have only one result. The Democrats won a staggering victory. Senator Wheeler crushed Judge Bourquin by an 84,304-vote plurality, 142,823 to 58,519, and carried every county in the state. James Murray, a newcomer, beat Leavitt by an easy 39,658 plurality. Both New Deal Congressmen, Ayers and Monaghan, coasted to comfortable victories; and the young radical, Jerry O'Connell, won a berth on the Railroad and Public Service Commission.[28] For old-style progressives like Burton Wheeler, now at the pinnacle of his local popularity, this was the golden hour. For newly emerging liberals like Murray and O'Connell, it was the dawning of a new era. For all Democrats in Montana, well united in 1934, it seemed that the New Deal was crumbling the foundations of the old political order and opening a bright, new future for their party.

The impressive consensus of 1934 could not, in any case, have lasted long. Even by 1935, too many centrifugal forces worked against it. A multitude of eager, young New Dealers looked longingly at higher positions. The Townsend Movement spread rapidly throughout the state, offering chimerical promises of abundant pensions to Montana's many old folks. Stimulated first by the National Industrial Recovery Act of 1933 and then by the Wagner Act of 1935, unionism enjoyed a renaissance in Montana after 20 years of the open shop. In mid-1934, the Mine, Mill, and Smelter Workers Union struck in Butte and regained the closed shop. Thereafter, union power in politics rapidly expanded.[29] All these developments would now drive factional fissures into the Democratic party. So, especially, would the combustible issue of unemployment relief.

Montana, like most states, lacked an adequate welfare system when the depression began. But unlike many rural states, Montana had a traditional commitment to caring for its needy. It was one of the first states to experiment with workmen's compensation; and along with Nevada in

1923, it was the first to provide state old-age pensions.[30] Nevertheless, swelling ranks of the unemployed placed impossible demands upon the state government for aid by 1933; and Montana welcomed the New Deal's Federal Emergency Relief Administration, which poured massive federal aid into the states to care for the unemployed. This spending proved to be beneficial but politically explosive.

Federal Emergency Relief Administration (FERA) allotments to the states carried strong federal guidelines, of course, but the state governments formally administered them. In Montana, this operation was entrusted to an appointed relief commission, which supervised the state relief office. The problem arose, initially, from the fact that Governor Erickson had appointed a number of his political allies to the Montana Relief Commission before he resigned. When the more progressive Frank Cooney became governor, he soon clashed with the Erickson appointees. Cooney felt—and field agents of the FERA agreed—that the state relief office, especially the Butte operation, was too closely tied to the business community and that, at least on occasion, relief spending was being used to further the interests of the Company.[31]

After a series of investigations in early 1934 by agents of the FERA, federal authorities forced the resignation of Relief Administrator Thomas C. Spaulding and the resignation from the relief commission itself of certain individuals whose ties to the corporate interests they found questionable. This federal "housecleaning" of the Montana relief operation did not end all problems. Political factions continued to quarrel over the allocation of the funds, and the FERA remained perplexed at the local situation. The relief situation remained unsettled until 1935, when the legislature created the more efficient State Department of Public Relief and when the Works Progress Administration brought relief projects under more direct federal control.[32]

By 1935, however, relief had played a major role in whipping up the winds of politics, and in the eye of the storm stood Governor Frank Cooney. Cooney had come into office under the cloud of his "deal" with Erickson, but he did not hesitate to assert the powers of his new office. In addition to his relief problems, Cooney soon found himself in one political scrape after another. By favoring a state monopoly on liquor sales and keeping a tight rein on the patronage thus created, he offended many people, especially those favoring a system of privately owned stores. His renegotiation of state insurance policies angered local firms, and sportsmen attacked him for his efforts to overhaul the Fish and Game

Commission. By working against his Democratic enemies in the 1934 primary, he widened the fissures within his own party.

During a marathon special session of the legislature, called in late 1933 to raise state matching funds for relief, Cooney's political fortunes fell to their lowest ebb. The governor had resisted calling the legislature into special session, well knowing the dangers of seeking increased taxes, but federal threats to cut off relief funding forced him to do it. At the climax of the special session, Cooney's enemies narrowly failed in an attempt to file charges of impeachment against him. Although the charges were mostly minor, involving the improper awarding of contracts, the misuse of travel funds, the alleged browbeating of subordinate officials, and so on, they dealt a near-lethal blow to the governor's prestige and political power. Failing in health, Governor Cooney had apparently decided to retire after his term expired, but he died of a heart ailment in December 1935. W. Elmer Holt of Miles City, president pro tem of the State Senate, then became acting governor, and the reins of state government passed back to customary, conservative hands.[33]

The wide-open Democratic primary election revealed in July 1936 that the volatile New Deal coalition in Montana had by then reached the boiling point. Political energies generated by the New Deal cracked open the party unity of 1932 and 1934. By 1936, Senator James E. Murray had emerged as a solidly loyal New Deal senator, closely allied to organized labor. But Murray faced a dangerous challenge in the 1936 primary from young Representative Joseph P. Monaghan, a champion of old-age pensions who ran with potent support from the Townsend organization. As a result of Governor Cooney's death, the gubernatorial primary was even more heated. Incumbent W. Elmer Holt, a conservative, faced stiff challenges from moderate New Deal Congressman Roy Ayers and from the outspokenly liberal newspaper publisher from Hamilton, Miles Romney.[34]

Both the senatorial and gubernatorial primary contests were hard fought and bruising. Running against three contenders, Senatory Murray barely held on to his Senate berth of two years, beating Monaghan by only 2,000 votes. Representative Ayers won the gubernatorial nomination from Elmer Holt and three other Democratic candidates, but only by a narrow margin. His Republican opponent would be the same Frank Hazelbaker, a conservative, who ran in 1932. Since both Democratic incumbents in the House, Monaghan and Ayers, had vacated their positions to seek other offices, two new nominees appeared for these offices: Jerry J. O'Connell in the western district and James F. O'Connor of Livingston in the east.[35]

Democrats found one very encouraging omen in the primary: whereas they had registered only 53.3 percent of the total vote in the 1932 primary, they received 75 percent in 1936. But as the general election campaign began, the factional divisions within the party quickly became pronounced. The embittered Elmer Holt first filed a libel suit against several individuals who, he said, had defamed him during the gubernatorial primary campaign. Then Holt, a solid conservative, announced that he would not support Democrat Ayers for governor and came out instead for his Republican opponent Hazelbaker. In the Senate contest, the ambitious Joseph Monaghan announced his independent candidacy, based upon Townsend Movement support, for Murray's post.[36]

Although factional chasms widened in the Montana Democratic party, the great popularity of President Roosevelt and the New Deal gave all Democratic candidates an enormous boost. While the Republicans kept up their onslaughts against the New Deal, Ayers and Murray played up their own progressivism and constantly talked about drought relief and other locally beneficial programs. Party regularity blurred as Republican progressives backed Democrats, Democratic conservatives like Holt supported Republicans, and thousands of unpredictable voters voiced their admiration for such independents as Monaghan.

In the last analysis, though, New Deal popularity overcame all other factors. President Roosevelt carried every Montana county and beat Alf Landon by 159,690 votes to 63,598. Roy Ayers overcame Democratic defections and defeated Hazelbaker by a lean 6,396-vote plurality, obviously owing his victory to the Roosevelt landslide. Senator Murray, who was not an effective campaigner, carried all but two counties; and his tally of 121,769 votes exceeded the combined total of his opponents, Republican T. O. Larson and independent Monaghan. Both Democratic congressional aspirants, O'Connell and O'Connor, ran liberal campaigns, and both swept to easy victories. Democrats held majority control of both houses in the state legislature and won every major state administrative office.[37] Montana obviously remained a heavily New Deal–Democratic state in 1936. Despite the considerable fragmenting of the local Democratic party, the national landslide carried the day.

As the New Deal entered its final phase after the 1936 landslide, the Montana Democrats were, even more so than usual, a heterogeneous lot. There were the conservatives or "bourbons" like John Erickson and Elmer Holt, who had always worked easily with the corporate interests in Montana. The mass of moderately liberal New Dealers, like Senator James Murray and Congressman James O'Connor and, to a lesser extent, Governor Roy Ayers, molded themselves to fit the presidential pattern. On the far left, a growing minority moved beyond the New Deal mainstream toward a genuine, class-conscious radicalism; their most visible leader was freshman Congressman Jerry O'Connell. Then there were the older progressives like Burton K. Wheeler, locally numerous and mixed in their reactions to the New Deal. Altogether these ideological groups formed a highly unstable compound, and in 1937–38 it decomposed.

The key figure on the Montana political horizon was Senator Burton K. Wheeler. Few senators of the interwar period could boast of more impressive progressive credentials than those of Wheeler. He had risen to local renown during World War I as a defender of minority rights; in 1920, he ran unsuccessfully for the governorship in a bitter anti-Company campaign in which he was branded "Bolshevik Burt." After going to the Senate in 1922, Wheeler caught the eye of liberals throughout the country when he "exposed" the machinations of Harding's attorney general, Harry Daugherty, and when he ran for the vice-presidency with Robert LaFollette on the Progressive party ticket of 1924. By the mid-1930s, Wheeler was, according to Arthur M. Schlesinger, Jr., "plainly the most formidable of the Senate radicals."[38]

As noted previously, Senator Wheeler played an important role in Franklin D. Roosevelt's 1932 campaign. In general, he enjoyed friendly relations with the White House during FDR's first term. The senator supported the major administration measures, and he personally shepherded two significant administration bills through the Senate—the Wheeler-Howard Indian Rights Act of 1934 and the bitterly fought Utility Holding Company Act of 1935.[39] In turn, Wheeler had been nicely rewarded by the administration, especially with the Fort Peck project. He became chairman of the Senate Interstate Commerce Committee in 1935, and his prestige rose accordingly.

Well before 1937, however, differences arose between the president and the Montana senator. As an inflationist in the old Populist tradition, Wheeler battled vociferously for the remonetization of silver at a 16/1 ratio with gold, a policy FDR effectively opposed. Like other western progressives, Wheeler distrusted those New Deal programs that most tended toward increasing centralized governmental power, such as the National Recovery Administration. The Montana senator frowned upon Roosevelt's appointment of Homer Cummings to succeed Walsh as attorney general, and found that his old foe J. Bruce Kremer now carried considerable weight in the Justice Department. Considering Wheeler's important support of Roosevelt, the president seemed to pay him little heed in return, and Wheeler found this galling. "Who does Roosevelt think he is?", he asked a White House aide in 1938. "He used to be just one of the barons. I was baron of the Northwest. Huey Long was baron of the South. He's like a king trying to reduce the barons."[40]

The famous break between Roosevelt and the Montana senator came, abruptly, in 1937, as a result of the president's attempt to "pack" the Supreme Court. Like other old progressives who had generally backed the New Deal, Wheeler sharply opposed FDR this time and denounced the Court maneuver as a threat to the constitutional separation of federal powers. Always outspoken and flamboyant, Wheeler effectively led the bipartisan coalition in the Senate that defeated the administration's Court bill. His well-publicized role in handing FDR his most stinging defeat was especially galling to the White House because Wheeler was clearly no conservative but an old-fashioned radical, to the left of the president himself on some issues.[41]

At first, it seemed as though Senator Wheeler had destroyed himself politically by fighting the administration on the court issue. Discontent rumbled through the ranks of the labor unions and small farmers who had always provided the bulwark of his support. Democratic papers in Montana openly criticized him. Patronage from the federal government flowed increasingly away from Wheeler and toward the Roosevelt loyalists —Senator Murray and Congressmen O'Connor and O'Connell.[42]

Among the latter, Senator James E. Murray was the key figure. Murray was the complete New Dealer. Born in Canada, he established a Butte law practice at the turn of the century and later inherited a fortune from his picturesque uncle, James A. Murray. Prior to 1933, although Murray had been known as a Democratic party stalwart, his only real claim to fame had been as a champion of Irish independence during the war years. After his Senate debut in 1935, Murray pursued an almost 100 percent Roosevelt line in both foreign and domestic affairs. As a devoted champion of labor especially, he resembled such "urban" liberals of the 1930s as Senator Robert Wagner of New York.

Senators Murray and Wheeler soon clashed, personally and politically, and by 1937 their feud became well known publicly. During the 1937–38 recession, Murray became noticeably more outspoken in his liberalism and began advocating the planned society and advanced welfare state. Cynical critics said that, as Wheeler moved to the right, Murray was simply courting the favor of the White House; the sincerity of this "Millionaire Moses," however, seems to have been genuine.[43] At any rate, as Wheeler abandoned the Roosevelt camp, Murray moved into it more solidly.

Following the Court fight, though, the immediate challenge to Wheeler's Montana hegemony came, not from Murray, but from freshman Congressman Jerry O'Connell. Only twenty-eight years old in 1937, O'Connell had grown up in Butte nurtured on anti-Anaconda radicalism. His father had died of silicosis, a miners' disease, and of wounds suffered in the famous Butte strike of 1914. During his spectacular political rise, O'Connell moved to the far left—first in the state legislature, then on the Railroad and Public Service Commission, then in Congress in 1937. He became something of a boy wonder in the House of Representatives. O'Connell applauded every leftward move of the New Deal, spoke out against Mayor Hague of Jersey City so heatedly that Hague expelled him from that city, and championed the cause of the loyalists in the Spanish Civil War, an unpopular move in heavily Catholic western Montana.[44]

Recklessly ambitious, Representative O'Connell threw down the gauntlet in the fall of 1937. He publicly attacked Senator Wheeler for opposing the president, and he soon announced that he would run for Wheeler's Senate berth in 1940. Senator Murray joined O'Connell in denouncing the president's foes, but avoided mentioning his Senate colleague by name. O'Connell apparently had some administration backing. Although FDR never openly endorsed him, the congressman claimed openly that the president had told him to "go out there and fight like hell to defeat Senator Wheeler's machine so he wouldn't be back in 1940."[45] Roosevelt indisputably sought vengeance against Wheeler. When the president visited Fort Peck in October 1937, he surrounded himself with and praised Montana's congressional delegation, but he completely snubbed the man most responsible for getting the project. Senator Wheeler hurriedly left the state "on business" to avoid further embarrassment.[46]

Jerry O'Connell's challenge to Burton Wheeler split the Democratic party wide open, into a liberal, New Deal wing and a pro-Wheeler faction. This was the first time since 1920 that the party had truly split apart. Then, a young radical named Burton K. Wheeler had run for the governorship with Non-Partisan League support, and conservatives had bolted the party, branding him a subversive. Now, for the first time, Wheeler had been challenged from the left, by another ambitious young man who was often accused of un-American leanings.

No stranger to intrigue, Wheeler moved to thwart O'Connell's challenge by plotting his defeat in 1938—before the young congressman could run against him in 1940. In the 1938 Democratic primary, Wheeler and his associates worked for the nomination of O'Connell's leading opponent, Payne Templeton. Representative O'Connell stressed his New Dealism and launched a bruising attack against the "Montana Twins" (the Anaconda Copper Mining Company and the Montana Power Company). In this first attempt to down his challenger, Wheeler failed; O'Connell won handily against four contenders.[47]

The showdown came in the general election campaign. In opposing O'Connell, the Wheeler forces could count, obviously, on the support of the Republicans and the Anaconda newspapers; they could also rely upon at least the passive support of Governor Ayers, who was, by 1938, under increasing attack from the liberals for his alleged desertion from their side. At the party's state convention in September, the Wheeler and Ayers Democrats dominated the proceedings, controlled the writing of the platform, and elected their favorite, Arthur Lamey, as state chairman. Then they moved, quietly, to the support of the Republican congressional candidate, Dr. Jacob Thorkelson, an eccentric archconservative.

Senator Wheeler personally stayed out of the limelight, but worked effectively behind the scenes to undercut O'Connell. Even though O'Connell was an ardent supporter of labor unions, Wheeler, a long-standing and highly influential friend of the national unions, apparently convinced the national rail brotherhoods to oppose the congressman's reelection. Although O'Connell was an outspoken advocate of old-age pensions and the Townsend Plan, Dr. Townsend himself came to Montana, reportedly at Wheeler's instigation, and endorsed Thorkelson. Opponents of O'Connell reminded Catholics of the congressman's recent divorce and charged the WPA with political involvement on his behalf. And throughout the campaign, the Anaconda papers blacked out O'Connell's speeches while featuring Thorkelson's accusation that he was sympathetic to communism.[48]

Montana Democrats generally did well in 1938. New Deal Congressman James O'Connor won reelection, and the Democrats held control in both houses of the state legislature. But in the western congressional district, one of the safest Democratic areas in the west, Jerry O'Connell went down to defeat. Dr. Thorkelson, who had mustered only 5,850 votes in the primary, beat him in the general election by a margin of 49,253 votes to 41,319. There can be little doubt that Wheeler Democrats played a decisive role in achieving this result. Momentarily at least, the Montana senator had routed his leftist opposition, had protected his state base, and had foiled the president's attempt to intervene in Montana politics. FDR learned here, as in other states during the 1938 campaign, the futility of local political involvement. For now, it seemed that Wheeler reigned supreme in Montana. His biographer, Richard Ruetten, seems correct in concluding that Wheeler had proven himself "the most powerful politician Montana had ever seen."[49]

Historians generally agree that the New Deal ended with the 1938 elections, which produced a decisive number of Republican and conservative Democratic victories. In Montana, the Democratic New Deal coalition broke apart in the Wheeler-O'Connell struggle. Conservatives and Wheeler-style progressives parted company with the New Deal liberals.[50] Following 1938, the splintered Democratic party declined rapidly as an instrument of reform, but the volatile liberalism that had emerged since 1933 lived on.

Aside from Jerry O'Connell's personal career, the chief casualty of 1938 was party regularity itself, never one of Montana's more abundant resources. Wheeler Democrats tended now, in the aftermath of the senator's break with the president, to align more frequently with moderate Republicans, many of whom had always supported Wheeler anyway. The newly arisen Democratic left wing similarly tended to ignore party status and to distrust more conservative members of their own party.

Burton Wheeler himself rose during 1939–41 to the peak of his national renown. Contrary to many charges, the Montana senator did not suddenly abandon liberalism, and many old progressives such as Senators William E. Borah and George Norris spoke of him as a presidential possibility. But Wheeler never fully mended his fences with the Roosevelt administration, and as foreign affairs moved to center stage on the eve of World War II, the Roosevelt-Wheeler feud flared again. A longtime isolationist, Wheeler became increasingly outspoken as a critic of FDR's internationalism and eventually became a favorite speaker for the America First movement against involvement in foreign war. The climax of his isolationist crusade came during the 1941 debate over Roosevelt's "lend-lease" policy, when Wheeler denounced the program as "the New Deal's triple-A foreign policy; it will plow under every fourth American boy." The president hotly retorted that this remark was "the most untruthful, the most dastardly, unpatriotic thing that has been said in public life in my generation."[51] Senator Wheeler's campaign against foreign entanglement kept him in the headlines until the Pearl Harbor attack, after which isolationism and its advocates faded from view.

Following O'Connell's defeat, the Democratic left wing attempted to regain its lost initiative. In 1938, representatives of labor and agricultural organizations, the unemployed, and pension advocates united and formed the Montana Council for Progressive Political Action to pursue their political ends. A year later, the same groups, especially representatives of the Farmers' Union, the American Federation of Labor, and the Congress of Industrial Organizations, began publication of a weekly newspaper, *The People's Voice,* which would remain the key spokesman of Montana liberalism for the next thirty years. Jerry O'Connell was still the most vehement and visible of the Montana radicals. He established his own newspaper, the *Montana Liberal,* lashed out at his Democratic foes, and began building for a comeback. The Ayers administration he denounced as "the most corrupt, most disgraceful, most scandalous administration the state has even known." Wheeler, he concluded, had abandoned liberalism completely: "Now, Bertie, old boy, . . . Are you with us agin' us?" "Where is our wandering boy tonite?"[52]

The political campaign of 1940 revealed how jumbled party lines had become. Before the primaries, the Montana Council for Progressive Political Action endorsed all Democratic candidates except Governor Roy Ayers and Senator Burton Wheeler.[53] The liberals were especially vehement against Ayers, who had sought the governor's chair in 1936 as a progressive. As a result of passage of House Bill 65, the so-called "Hitler Bill," in the 1937 legislature, Ayers had gained considerably increased power over the hiring, firing, and supervision of many state employees. By 1939-40, Democrats and Republicans alike were hotly accusing Ayers of building a powerful political machine within the state bureaucracy and of fostering corruption in government. Ayers had, by 1940, alienated many elements within the Democratic party and left himself highly vulnerable.[54]

In the Democratic primary, the liberals failed to unseat either Wheeler or Ayers, but they did manage to nominate O'Connell again for Congress. In the Republican primary, Representative Thorkelson, who had embarrassed many of his 1938 supporters by his rightist extremism and anti-Semitic remarks, was defeated. The nomination went instead to Miss Jeannette Rankin, Montana's legendary pacifist, who had become the first female member of Congress long ago in 1916. Since the Republican gubernatorial nominee, Sam C. Ford, had a past record of liberalism, the Montana Council for Progressive Political Action supported him against Ayers. On the other hand, E. K. Cheadle, the GOP Senate nominee to oppose Wheeler, was a party stalwart; so the liberals shied away from both candidates and skirted the Senate race.[55]

The prime local issue in 1940 was Ayers, and liberals continued their onslaughts against the alleged corruption and machine domination of his administration. Since Wheeler faced only nominal Republican opposition, he did not actively campaign in Montana but rather focused his attention on his short-lived bid for the presidential nomination. In Montana, as in the nation at large, attention in the campaign centered mainly on foreign affairs and the threat of war.

The results of the 1940 election showed clearly, on the one hand, how popular President Roosevelt still was locally; he carried Montana by a whopping 46,119-vote plurality. But the election showed even more graphically how the New Deal coalition, and how party regularity itself, had disintegrated. Senator Wheeler, a prominent critic of the president, scored one of the great landslide victories in the state's history. He carried every county and beat his opponent by a staggering margin of 176,753 to 63,941. Congressman O'Connor, who remained loyal to the President on domestic issues but followed Wheeler's isolationist line on foreign affairs, won again in the eastern district; and isolationist Republican Jeannette Rankin beat Jerry O'Connell in the west. Miss Rankin would soon become the only member of either house of Congress to vote against war in December 1941. Just as moderate Republicans helped reelect Wheeler, thousands of liberal Democrats helped Republican Sam Ford defeat Roy Ayers in the gubernatorial contest. In every respect the two parties in Montana were now closely—and loosely—divided; they shared possession of the major state offices and of the legislature, with a Republican Senate and a Democratic House.[56]

The 1940 election, then, was both an end and a beginning. It marked the end of the Democratic–New Deal coalition. It also began a curious, six-year period of extreme party irregularity and bipartisan alliances that Montana progressives characterized as the "Wheeler-Ford-Rankin Axis." The "Axis" was not a "machine" in any precise sense but rather an informal, working friendship between Wheeler and his old Republican allies Sam Ford and Wellington Rankin (Jeannette's brother), all of whom were by now tending increasingly toward conservatism. Some important Wheeler Democrats held posts in the Ford administration.

Naturally, this bipartisan "friendship" could not remain in blissful equilibrium for long. Progressive spokesmen, like the *People's Voice* or the articulate Great Falls liberal Joseph Kinsey Howard, railed against it from the left; conservative Republicans alarmed about the unity of their own party, like Dan Whetstone, the intelligent national committeeman from Cut Bank, criticized it from the right. Democratic liberals angrily abandoned Governor Ford in 1944, as they had earlier abandoned Ayers. They denounced him for "selling out" and for working against the proposed Missouri Valley Authority, the highly controversial plan for a TVA-style federal development of the huge Missouri basin. The MVA issue was bitterly divisive in Montana, and conservative stockmen and business groups hotly opposed it. So did Governor Ford, but he survived the liberal effort to defeat him.[57]

The New Deal liberals also focused their anger upon Senator Wheeler during the war. After his 1937 break with the president, Wheeler had seemingly confounded those who had predicted the fall of his political bastion in Montana. He had, after all, won a smashing reelection victory in 1940, and thereafter he seemingly dominated both Montana congressmen and worked well with the Republican governor. Actually, though, the early predictions were not so far wrong. Wheeler's prewar and wartime strength, though impressive, rested precariously on bipartisan support. Throughout the war years, more and more local liberals deserted him, criticizing his now unpopular stand against foreign involvement, his disregard of party lines, and his conservative stands on such pressing domestic issues as the Missouri Valley Authority plan. Whether Wheeler actually abandoned liberalism, as his enemies claimed, or whether he remained consistent with his progressive principles, as he has always argued, the fact remains that he stood at sword's point with the Montana liberals by the early 1940s.[58]

When Burton Wheeler came up for renomination in the 1946 primary, he faced a formidable opponent in young Leif Erickson, who challenged him on a platform of progressivism at home and internationalism abroad. Although President Truman and other prominent figures spoke out in Wheeler's favor, the ranks of small farmers and organized labor in Montana turned against him. Failing in the large labor counties of Silver Bow, Deer Lodge, and Cascade, Wheeler lost to Erickson by 5,000 votes, and his twenty-four-year tenure in the Senate drew to a close. The senator's isolationism, his long tenure in office, and especially his post–1937 break with New Deal liberalism led to his defeat.[59] Without exaggeration, Wheeler's fall signified the end of an era in Montana. He was the last of the old progressives who had risen in the days of open warfare against the state's corporate "interests." No man before or since has ever so dominated the political life of Montana.

The New Deal farmer-labor coalition that defeated Wheeler remained a potent force in the Democratic party well into the postwar era, but it mellowed over the years. Leif Erickson, who defeated Wheeler, lost in the 1946 general election to Zales Ecton, the only Republican, incredibly, that the people of Montana have ever voted to the U.S. Senate. Following unsuccessful attempts to regain his House seat in 1938, 1940, and 1942, Jerry O'Connell, the erratic key figure among the post–1937 radicals, gradually lost his local influence. Interestingly, young Mike Mansfield, who defeated him in the 1942 congressional primary, espoused a mellower brand of liberalism and carefully skirted the furious Democratic factional wars of the early 1940s. Although O'Connell was later active in the leftist Washington (State) Commonwealth Federation and in the 1948 Henry Wallace presidential campaign, his brand of radicalism faded in Montana during and after the war.[60]

Most of Montana's other leading New Deal personalities had left the political arena by 1945. Governor Roy Ayers, who had started as a Roosevelt man and had been defeated, partially at least, by liberal opposition in 1940, never rose to the forefront again. Joseph P. Monaghan, the young New Deal congressman who attempted unsuccessfully to unseat Senator Murray in 1936, failed again in a 1942 contest against Murray, and that ended his active political aspirations. Representative James O'Connor followed the safe political course throughout his career, withdrawing from factional fights, endorsing New Deal liberalism, espousing locally popular isolationism. He died while still in office in 1945.[61]

The most durable of the Montana New Dealers, politically, philosophically, and physically, was Senator James E. Murray. Throughout his Senate tenure (1935–61), the longest in Montana's history, the aging but active Murray pursued a course of New Deal–Fair Deal liberalism. In the Senate, he championed such liberal innovations as the unsuccessful Missouri Valley Authority, national health insurance, and the Employment Act of 1946; he consistently advocated the causes of organized labor and internationalism. Never an inspiring campaigner, Murray relied on the strong liberal voting blocs in Montana to pull him through several narrowly won elections, especially the close call of 1942 when Wheeler opposed him. Murray retired from the Senate in 1961 and died later that year, at the age of 84.[62]

Viewed from thirty years' perspective, what then has been the New

Deal's political effect? In his recently published book *Twentieth Century Montana: A State of Extremes*, Professor K. Ross Toole dismisses the depression and war years as a period of "deep somnolence" in Montana, which produced little of significance. Quite the contrary, in Montana as in every other state, these turbulent years witnessed great social and economic dislocation and change. Clearly, the New Deal had a major impact upon Montana's political order. It produced an eight-year period of Democratic hegemony and promoted a powerful liberal coalition of farmers and workers that shook the state's political structure and endured until after World War II. Yet, significant as it was, the New Deal's over-all effect seems obviously less than "revolutionary." As James T. Patterson notes in his *The New Deal and the States*, most states fluctuated leftward in political attitudes and organization during the 1930s, but they usually returned to near "normal" by the decade's end. The Treasure State seems, generally, to have been no exception.[63]

The New Deal did not produce in Montana any genuine "renaissance" of state government. The guidelines of newly enacted New Deal legislation and the lure of federal matching funds, it is true, did stimulate the state legislature to enact badly needed planning and welfare measures. The 1935 session produced a renovated State Department of Public Relief, an elaborate Water Conservation Board, a Montana Grazing Commission, and an old-age assistance system to match the New Deal's Social Security program. The 1937 legislature again renovated the welfare system, creating the State Department of Public Welfare, established an Unemployment Compensation Commission, and revamped the Liquor Control Board and the Highway Patrol. Retrospect shows, however, that this new activism in state government, which so vastly expanded the state bureaucracy, was mostly a response to federal stimuli. By the late thirties, as the New Deal ground to a halt, so too did reformism in Montana. The Ayers and Ford administrations (1937–49) both began with progressive support and ended under liberal attack.

The New Deal had a more profound, but still less than revolutionary, impact upon the political attitudes and loyalties of Montanans. As noted earlier, Montana, a thinly populated, public domain state, had always been heavily reliant upon the federal government. It had usually shown more interest in affairs in Washington than in those at Helena. The New Deal's vast expansion of federal authority did not reverse this trend—it intensified it. By 1940, Roosevelt programs like the Agricultural Adjustment Act, the Rural Electrification Administration, and the Taylor Grazing Act had brought the state's economy much more directly under federal sway. In their political attitudes, most Montanans accepted the new federal role, but they did not necessarily applaud it. Many local farmers and stockmen enjoyed the benefits of New Deal subsidies while continuing to maintain their conservative political philosophy, distrusting and criticizing the federal government. Apparently, a Montana conservative of 1930, no matter how his livelihood may have changed, probably remained a conservative in 1940.

The election maps in Professor Ellis Waldron's valuable *Montana Politics since 1864* show very clearly the continuity in voting behavior of twentieth-century Montana. New Deal Democrats received their main support from the traditional centers of progressive and Democratic strength: the mining and lumber counties of the south and west and the farming region north of the Missouri River. The dry land farming and ranching areas of central and eastern Montana were far less friendly to Democrats then, as they still are today. In other words, small farmers and workers filled the ranks of the Montana New Dealers; stockmen and businessmen led the opposition. This had been the normal political balance in Montana before the New Deal; it has been the normal situation since.

In Montana, therefore, the New Deal ended in 1938–40 with a scrambling of party lines. Democratic conservatives and old-fashioned progressives combined with the Republicans, in effect, to restore political normality. The advanced New Deal liberals were well organized through the war years, and they exerted considerable sway in state affairs. But they proved much more powerful in Democratic primaries, where farm and labor organizations could prevail, than in the larger arena of general election campaigns. Since 1945–46, their reformism has mellowed, and they have generally operated quietly in the normal two-party system, with few state controversies reminiscent of those in 1938, 1940, or 1946.

The continuity of Montana's twentieth-century political history, its even flow, seems much more impressive than the abruptness of such departures as the New Deal. Since World War II, Montana has returned to its familiar patterns of party irregularity and of conservatism at the local and liberalism at the national levels. Montanans have sent liberals like James Murray, Mike Mansfield, and Lee Metcalf to the Senate; yet they have favored conservative Republicans such as J. Hugo Aronson, Donald Nutter, and Tim Babcock in Helena. There are several explanations for this "political schizophrenia"—the influence of a few powerful corporations in state government, for example, or the responsible electorate's "wise" preference for parsimonious conservatives at home and free-spending liberals in Washington, D.C.[64] No single answer seems entirely convincing. The important point is that the New Deal altered but did not permanently reshift the main currents of Montana's political history.

1. Montana's historiography is assessed in Michael P. Malone and Richard B. Roeder, eds., *The Montana Past: An Anthology* (Missoula, Mont., 1969), pp. v-viii. I have explored some of the following themes more briefly in "Montana Politics and the New Deal," *Montana: The Magazine of Western History* 21 (1971): 2-11.

2. The Anaconda Copper Mining Company was founded during the 1880s and became an open-stock corporation in 1895. In 1899, Standard Oil purchased control of the Anaconda Company and made it the keystone of its holding company, the Amalgamated Copper Company. The Amalgamated was dissolved in 1915, as Standard Oil moved out of the copper industry, and the "Anaconda Copper Mining Company" then reappeared. By 1915, of course, control of the Anaconda Company had passed to New York, where it remained. Also by 1915, the firm had acquired control of a number of Montana newspapers and had invested heavily in electric power (forming the Montana Power Company in 1912), lumber, and other fields. A laudatory study of the firm is Isaac F. Marcosson, *Anaconda* (New York, 1957); critical of the firm's local political involvement is K. Ross Toole, "A History of the Anaconda Copper Mining Company: A Study in the Relationships between a State and Its People and a Corporation: 1880–1950" (Ph.D. diss., University of California, Los Angeles, 1954).

3. K. Ross Toole argues in *Montana: An Uncommon Land* (Norman, Okla., 1959), chap. 10, that progressivism in Montana amounted to little; his argument has been sharply challenged by Richard B. Roeder, who closely analyzes progressive activities and attitudes in "Montana Progressivism: Sound and Fury—and One Small Tax Reform," *Montana: The Magazine of Western History* 20 (1970): 18–26. Professor Jules Karlin of the University of Montana is presently completing a biography of Joseph Dixon; see also his "Progressive Politics in Montana," in M. G. Burlingame and K. R. Toole, eds., *A History of Montana*, 3 vols. (New York, 1957), 1:247–80.

4. J. Leonard Bates is currently preparing his full-scale biography of Walsh; see his "Senator Walsh of Montana, 1918–1924: A Liberal under Pressure" (Ph.D. diss., University of North Carolina, 1952), esp. chaps. 2, 8, 13; on Wheeler, see Burton K. Wheeler and Paul F. Healy, *Yankee from the West* (New York, 1962). Richard T. Ruetten is now completing his biography of Wheeler; see his "Burton K. Wheeler of Montana: A Progressive between the Wars" (Ph.D. diss., University of Oregon, 1961).

5. Cf. Richard T. Ruetten, "Anaconda Journalism: The End of an Era," *Journalism Quarterly* 37 (1960): 3–12; Oswald Garrison Villard, "Montana and 'the Company,' " *Nation* 131 (1930): 39–41.

6. Joseph Kinsey Howard, *Montana: High, Wide and Handsome,* 2d ed. (New Haven, 1959), chaps. 17-21; these statistics are from pp. 207-8. See also K. Ross Toole, *Twentieth-Century Montana: A State of Extremes* (Norman, Okla., 1972), chaps. 2 and 3.

7. Toole, *Montana*, p. 240; "Report No. 10, Volume II, Montana: Federal Loans and Expenditures 1933–1939 . . . Work Accomplishments," mimeo. copy (Washington, D.C., 1940), p. 6. I wish to thank Professor Leonard Arrington for providing me with this valuable report (cited hereafter as "Report No. 10, Montana").

8. J. V. Brumehl to Henry Wallace, 7 March 1933, File E-25, M. L. Wilson Papers (Montana State University Library, Bozeman); Carl F. Kraenzel, "The Relief Problem in Montana," *Montana Experiment Station Bulletin*, June 1937, pp. 3, 9–11.

9. Wheeler, *Yankee from the West*, pp. 294–95; Ruetten, "Burton K. Wheeler," pp. 79–86.

10. John E. Erickson to Thomas J. Walsh, 14 March 1932, Box 382, Thomas J. Walsh Papers (Library of Congress); *New York Times*, 15, 18 May 1932; James A. Farley to Franklin D. Roosevelt, 12 May 1932, OF 300-Montana, Roosevelt Papers (Franklin D. Roosevelt Library).

11. James A. Farley, *Jim Farley's Story* (New York, 1948), p. 16; *New York Times*, 29 July 1932; Ruetten, "Burton K. Wheeler," pp. 95–107; Wheeler, *Yankee from the West*, pp. 285–87, 297–98; T. Harry Williams, *Huey Long* (New York, 1969), pp. 572–73.

12. Ellis L. Waldron, *Montana Politics since 1864: An Atlas of Elections* (Missoula, Mont., 1958), p. 239; *Hamilton Western News*, 11 August 1932; *Helena Western Progressive*, 22 July 1932. All city names in newspaper titles indicate Montana cities, unless otherwise indicated.

13. *Billings Gazette*, 18, 29 October 1932; *Butte Montana Standard*, 20 September, 11 October 1932.

14. Waldron, *Montana Politics since 1864*, pp. 240–52; *Great Falls Tribune*, 10 November 1932; *Butte Montana Standard*, 10 November 1932; *Helena Daily Independent*, 9 November 1932.

15. J. Bruce Kremer to Walsh, 10 December 1932; Walsh to Kremer, 16 December 1932; Walsh to Erickson, 31 January, 22 February 1932, Box 383; Walsh to FDR, 24 January 1933, Box 384, Walsh Papers; Wheeler, *Yankee from the West*, pp. 298–99; *New York Times*, 1 March 1933.

16. *Nation*, 136 (1933): 273; *New York Times*, 3, 10 March 1933; *Christian Century* 50 (1933): 348; *New Republic* 74 (1933): 185; *Helena Daily Independent*, 2, 3, 7, 10 March 1933.

17. Wheeler, *Yankee from the West*, p. 301; interview with Burton K. Wheeler, 23 May 1970.

18. *Sidney Herald*, 23 March 1933; *Great Falls Tribune*, 14 March 1933; *New York Times*, 14, 19 March 1933; Wheeler, *Yankee from the West*, p. 301.

19. On Kremer, see Kenneth G. Crawford, *The Pressure Boys* (New York, 1939), pp. 8–9; *Hamilton Western News*, 11 January 1934.

20. See James T. Patterson, *The New Deal and the States: Federalism in Transition* (Princeton, N.J., 1969); and Patterson, "The New Deal in the West," *Pacific Historical Review*, 38 (1969); 317–27.

21. Leonard Arrington, "The New Deal in the West: A Preliminary Statistical Inquiry," *Pacific Historical Review* 38 (1969): 314–15, tables II and III; cf. *Butte Montana Standard*, 14 October 1938.

22. "Report No. 10, Montana," pp. 2, 44; on New Deal spending in Montana and agency activities, see Richard D. Seibert, "New Deal Expenditures in Montana: 1933–1939" (Master's thesis, Utah State University, Logan, 1970).

23. W. J. Butler to F. H. Cooney, 31 January 1935, Box 1, Erickson-Cooney Papers Montana State Archives, Helena); Seibert, New Deal Expenditures in Montana," p. 29; "Report No. 10, Montana," pp. 44-46.

24. "Report No. 10, Montana," pp. 4–6; Federal Writers' Project of the Montana Works Progress Administration, *Montana: A State Guide Book* (New York, 1939), pp. 6, 56.

25. Wheeler, *Yankee from the West*, pp. 304–5; "10,000 Montana Relief Workers Make Whoopee on a Saturday Night," *Life*, 23 November 1936, pp. 9–17; James Rorty, "Fort Peck: An American Siberia," *Nation* 141 (1935): 300–301; John T. Ryan, "Chapters on the Fort Peck Development" (Master's thesis, University of Montana, 1961).

26. Waldron, *Montana Politics since 1864*, p. 253; *Helena Western Progressive*, 20 July 1934.

27. Quote in *New York Times*, 11 October 1934; *Miles City Star*, 8 August 1934; *Lewistown Democrat-News*, 6, 21 October 1934; *Helena Daily Independent*, 4 November 1934; *Great Falls Tribune*, 30 October, 1 November 1934.

28. Waldron, *Montana Politics since 1864*, pp. 254–62.

29. Montana Writers' Project, *Montana: A State Guide Book*, pp. 68–78; Ward Kinney [Joseph Kinsey Howard], "Montana Challenges the Tyranny of Copper," *Nation* 139 (1934): 86–87, 98–99; Charles E. Sebold, "No Troops—No Violence," *Christian Century* 51 (1934): 1310–11; *Butte Eye Opener*, 15 September 1934; Irving Bernstein, *Turbulent Years: A History of the American Worker, 1933-1941* (Boston, 1970), pp. 106-9; Vernon H Jensen, *Nonferrous Metals Industry Unionism, 1932-1954* (Ithaca, N. Y., 1954), chap. 1.

30. Montana Writers' Project, *Montana: A State Guide Book*, pp. 100–101.

31. R. E. Miller in *New York Times*, 26 August 1934; *Libby Western News*, 12 July 1934; Clarence King to Harry Hopkins, 20 January 1934, State Files: Montana, Box 167, Federal Emergency Relief Administration Records, Record Group 69 (National Archives).

32. R. E. Miller in *New York Times*, 26 August 1934; King to Hopkins, 9 February, 7 March 1934; Pierce Williams to Hopkins, 20 March 1934; T. J. Edmonds to Aubrey Williams, 5, 14 March 1935, Box 167; R. S. Olson to Corrington Gill, 11 March 1935, Box 168, State Files: Montana, FERA Records; *Laws, Resolutions and Memorials of the State of Montana Passed by the . . . Legislative Assembly . . . 1935* (Helena, 1935), pp. 183–95.

33. *Great Falls Tribune*, 17, 19 January 1934, 16 December 1935; *New York Times*, 17 January, 26 August 1934.

34. F. L. Fljozdal to James E. Murray, 12 September 1935; Murray to Fljozdal, 23 September 1935; Murray to Jack Pettinger, 1 October 1935; Murray to M. S. Gunn, 24 October 1935, Murray Papers (University of Montana Archives).

35. Waldron, *Montana Politics since 1864*, p. 263; *Cut Bank Pioneer Press*, 24, 31 July 1936; *Havre Daily News*, 19 July 1936; *Helena Western Progressive*, 29 May, 5 June, 24 July 1936.

36. *Billings Gazette*, 7, 23 October 1936; *Butte Daily Post*, 13 October 1936; *New York Times*, 27 July, 11 August 1936; G. C. Cisel to James A. Farley, 23 July 1936; Murray to Farley, 27 July 1936; Thomas J. Walker to Farley, 27 July 1936, OF 300-Montana; Murray to FDR, 27 July 1936, PPF 2534, Roosevelt Papers.

37. Waldron, *Montana Politics since 1864*, pp. 264–74; *New York Times*, 1, 6 November 1936; *Shelby Promoter*, 10 September, 8 October 1936; *Great Falls Tribune*, 5, 6, 8 November 1936; *Billings Gazette*, 25, 27, 28, October, 3, 8 November 1936.

38. Arthur M. Schlesinger, Jr., *The Politics of Upheaval* (Boston, 1960), p. 142; on Wheeler's pre–New Deal career, see his autobiography, *Yankee from the West*, chaps. 2–13; and Ruetten, "Burton K. Wheeler," pp. 3–77.

39. Wheeler, *Yankee from the West*, pp. 294–318; Ruetten, "Burton K. Wheeler," chap. 5; interview with Burton K. Wheeler, 23 May 1970.

40. Quoted in James M. Burns, *Roosevelt: The Lion and the Fox,* Harvest Books ed. (New York, 1956), pp. 341–42; Ruetten, "Burton K. Wheeler," pp. 109–44, 204–7; Richard L. Neuberger, "Wheeler of Montana," *Harper's Magazine* 180 (1940): 609-18; "T.R.B.," "Washington Notes," *New Republic* 90 (1937): 261–62; Joseph Kinsey Howard, "The Decline and Fall of Burton K. Wheeler," reprinted from *Harper's Magazine* 187 (1947), in Malone and Roeder, eds., *The Montana Past*, pp. 269–85.

41. On Wheeler's Senate leadership in defeating the Court bill, see James T. Patterson, *Congressional Conservatism and the New Deal* (Lexington, Ky., 1967), pp. 114–21; see also Ruetten, "Burton K. Wheeler," chap. 7; Wheeler, *Yankee from the West*, pp. 319–40; Burton K. Wheeler, "First Member of Senate to Back the President in 1932—," *Vital Speeches* 3 (April 1937): 404-8; Catherine C. Doherty, "The Court Plan, B. K. Wheeler, and the Montana Press" (Master's thesis, University of Montana, 1954).

42. Richard L. Neuberger, "Senator Wheeler's Plight," *Current History*, August 1937, pp. 29–31; Ruetten, "Burton K. Wheeler," pp. 230–34; Burton K. Wheeler to Farley, 10 May 1937; Farley to FDR, 16 June 1937, PPF 723, Roosevelt Papers.

43. Murray is well assessed in Forrest Davis, "Millionaire Moses," *Saturday Evening Post*, 8 December 1945, pp. 9–10, 103–4, 106.

44. On O'Connell, see *Great Falls Tribune*, 17 January 1956; "Why They Don't Like O'Connell," *New Republic* 95 (1938): 115.

45. Richard T. Ruetten, "Showdown in Montana, 1938: Burton Wheeler's Role in the Defeat of Jerry O'Connell," *Pacific Northwest Quarterly* 54 (1963): 19–29; Ruetten, "Burton K. Wheeler," chap. 8; *New York Times*, 2 September 1937, 20 July 1938.

46. On the Fort Peck episode, see *Glasgow Courier*, 5 October 1937; *New York Times*, 2, 3, 4 October 1937; Wheeler to FDR, 2 October 1937, PPF 723, Roosevelt Papers.

47. Ruetten, "Showdown in Montana," pp. 23–25; John E. Kennedy, "Confidential Report of Campaign of Congressman Jerry J. O'Connell of Montana for Re-election at the Primary Election July 19, 1938," typescript in OF 300-Montana, Roosevelt Papers.

48. Ruetten, "Showdown in Montana," pp. 26–28; *Cut Bank Pioneer Press*, 16 September 1938; on the unions, see Kenneth Crawford, *The Pressure Boys*, pp. 29–30; on Townsend, *Billings Gazette*,

6 November 1938; *Helena Daily Independent*, 29 October 1938; *Butte Montana Standard*, 26, 27 October 1938; Mrs. Lulu Wheeler to C. H. McLeod, 21 October 1938, Box 60, McLeod Papers (University of Montana Archives); on Wheeler's airing of the WPA political issue, see the correspondence in File 610, State Series—Montana, Works Progress Administration Records, Record Group 69 (National Archives); and Burton K. Wheeler, "W.P.A. and Politics: Abuses in Government Aid," *Vital Speeches* 4 (1938): 681–83.

49. Ruetten, "Showdown in Montana," pp. 28–29; Waldron, *Montana Politics since 1864*, pp. 275–83; assessments of O'Connell's defeat are Kenneth Romney to Marvin McIntyre, 17 November 1938, OF 300-Montana, Roosevelt Papers; John E. Kennedy, "Liberal's Defeat—a Case History," *Nation* 147 (1938): 564–65; John W. Nelson, "Behind O'Connell's Defeat," ibid., 148 (1939): 47.

50. In *An Encore for Reform* (New York, 1967), his superb study of the old progressives and their responses to the New Deal, Otis L. Graham, Jr., regrettably did not include Wheeler in his "sample"; but see his cogent remarks concerning the Montana senator's abandonment of New Dealism on pp. 115 n and 147 n.

51. Wheeler, *Yankee from the West*, pp. 17–36, 353–68; the quote is on p. 27; on Wheeler as liberal and as isolationist, 1937–41, see especially Neuberger, "Wheeler of Montana," pp. 609–18; Oswald Garrison Villard, "Issues and Men," *Nation* 149 (1939): 72; Robert Bendiner, "Men Who Would Be President: Burton K. Wheeler, *Nation* 150 (1940): 532–36; Hamilton Basso, "Burton the Bronc," *New Republic*, 102 (1940): 527–30; Hubert Kay, "Boss Isolationist: Burton K. Wheeler," *Life*, 19 May 1941, pp. 110–12, 114, 117–19; "Men A-Plenty," *Time*, 15 April 1940, pp. 19–22.

52. *Hamilton Montana Liberal*, 14 March, 4 July 1939; Karlin, "Progressive Politics in Montana," p. 271.

53. *Cut Bank Pioneer Press*, 14 June 1940; Karlin, "Progressive Politics in Montana," p. 272; *Helena People's Voice*, 19 June 1940; on Thorkelson's rightist extremism, see George Wolfskill and John A. Hudson, *All But the People: Franklin D. Roosevelt and His Critics, 1933-1939* (New York and London, 1969), pp. 56, 75, 116; and *Time,* 30 October 1939, p. 10.

54. *Helena People's Voice*, 3 July 1940; *Plentywood Producers' News*, 8 January 1937; for Democratic assessments of Ayers and his predicament, see George Fowlie to James F. O'Connor, 22 June 1940, Campaign file; George E. Hard to O'Connor, 16 November 1940; O'Connor to Tom Stout, 3 December 1940, Congratulations-1940 File, O'Connor Papers (Montana State University Library); Bailey Stortz to Joseph Kinsey Howard, 29 October 1941, B. K. Wheeler File, Howard Papers (Montana Historical Society Library); on Ayers and the liquor board, see Larry D. Quinn, *Politicians in Business: A History of the Liquor Control System in Montana* (Missoula, Mont., 1970), pp. 32–58.

55. *Helena People's Voice*, 17 July 1940; *New York Times*, 6 June, 18 July 1940.

56. Waldron, *Montana Politics since 1864*, pp. 285–96; Ruetten, "Burton K. Wheeler," chap. 9; *New York Times*, 6, 7 November 1940; *Helena People's Voice*, 6 November, 11 December 1940; Miles Romney to Murray, 5 August 1940, Murray Papers; Murray to FDR, 26 October, 2 November 1940, PPF 2534, Roosevelt Papers.

57. For examples of liberal criticism of this arrangement, see Joseph Kinsey Howard's essays "Montana, Political Maverick" and "Influence of Business on State Government and Political Affairs in Montana," typescripts in Box 6, Howard Papers; see also Howard's "Decline and Fall of Burton K. Wheeler," in Malone and Roeder, eds., *The Montana Past*, pp. 269–285; *Helena People's Voice*, 29 September 1944; for Whetstone's thoughts on Ford and Wheeler, see Dan Whetstone to Senator Zales Ecton, 10 May 1947, "P & P-W" File, Ecton Papers (Montana State University Library); and *Cut Bank Pioneer Press*, 18 August 1944; on the Missouri Valley Authority issue, see J. K. Howard, "Golden River," *Harper's Magazine* 190 (1945): 511–23.

58. Wheeler argues in *Yankee from the West*, chap. 18, that he remained true to his earlier liberalism; Joseph Kinsey Howard, in "The Decline and Fall of Burton K. Wheeler," reasons that the senator drifted to the right and that his lust for power led to his rejection in Montana; on Wheeler's wartime decline, see also "Wheeler Rides the Storm," *Collier's*, 18 July 1944, pp. 10–11, 72–73; "Potomacus," "Wheeler of Montana," *New Republic* 109 (1943): 390-92.

59. On Wheeler's defeat, see Joseph P. Kelly, "A Study of the Defeat of Senator Burton K. Wheeler in the 1946 Democratic Primary Election" (Master's thesis, University of Montana, 1959), esp. pp.

80–86; Dan Whetstone in *Cut Bank Pioneer Press*, 26 July 1946; *Newsweek*, 29 July 1946, pp. 20–21; *Nation* 163 (1946): 99–101; *St. Louis Post-Dispatch*, 18 July 1946, clipping in "newspaper articles" file, Howard Papers; Howard, "The Decline and Fall of Burton K. Wheeler"; on the Erickson-Ecton contest, see Timothy J. Carman, "Senator Zales Ecton: A Product of Reaction" (Master's thesis, Montana State University, 1971).

60. Earl Pomeroy, *The Pacific Slope: A History of California, Washington, Idaho, Utah, and Nevada* (New York, 1965), p. 321; *Hamilton Montana Liberal*, 12 November 1940; *Great Falls Tribune*, 17 January 1956.

61. *Biographical Directory of the American Congress: 1774-1961* (Washington, D.C., 1961), pp. 498, 1343; *Washington Evening Star*, 15 January 1945, clipping in PPF 4836, Roosevelt Papers.

62. See the extensive obituaries of Murray in *Great Falls Tribune*, 24 March 1961; *New York Times*, 24 March 1961; see also Davis, "Millionaire Moses," pp. 9–10, 103–4, 106; "Murray —Wealthy Champion of a Newer Deal," *Business Week*, 10 February 1945, p. 22; Ralph Robey, "Senator Murray as a Social Problem," *Newsweek*, 25 March 1946, p. 76; and the data in "Mr. Murray—Releases" File, Murray Papers.

63. K. Ross Toole, *Twentieth Century Montana: A State of Extremes* (Norman, Okla., 1972), p. 271; Patterson, *The New Deal and the States*, chaps. 6–8; and Patterson, "The New Deal in the West," pp. 319–20, 325–27.

64. Cf. Thomas Payne, "Montana: Politics under the Copper Dome," in Frank H. Jonas, ed., *Politics in the American West* (Salt Lake City, 1969); reprinted in Malone and Roeder, eds., *The Montana Past*, pp. 298–332, esp. p. 332.

James F. Wickens

Depression and the
New Deal in Colorado

AMONG THE WESTERN STATES, FEW OFFER THE HISTORIAN A BET-
ter opportunity to study the impact of the New Deal on the region than does
Colorado. Because of the state's diverse environment and economy, in one
way or another it encompassed in the thirties much of what was typical of
western America and shared in most of the region's problems that the New
Deal attempted to resolve.[1] Largely agricultural, Colorado supported
federal programs of mortgage moratoriums, low-interest farm loans, resettlement and land-purchase schemes, and Dust Bowl abatement. The state
initially balked at, but eventually went along with, crop reduction proposals. Beyond the farm lands, in the thickly forested mountains that covered
one-third of the state, possibilities to develop and perfect projects in
conservation and reclamation abounded. Nestled against these mountains
were the state's two primary urban centers, Denver and Pueblo, which in
the thirties cried for creative experimentation to alleviate the depressed
conditions of their industry and commerce.

A generation earlier, Colorado along with other Rocky Mountain states
had shared in the flush times of World War I. High commodity prices
during the war years had stimulated farmers to convert their dry lands into
plowed fields, often recklessly in search of quick profit. Acreage in wheat,
for example, tripled in Colorado between 1913 and 1919, from 465,000
acres to 1,329,000. But when commodity prices fell after the war,
Colorado's farming bonanza quickly dissipated into agricultural distress.
Similarly, in the plateaus and mountains of Colorado, high wartime prices

had encouraged certain types of metal mining. The price of silver, for example, doubled to $1.11 an ounce. Three rare metals in particular had enjoyed boom conditions because of their high demand as steel alloys: molybdenum, from the Continental Divide near Leadville; vanadium, from the Paradox Valley region of western Colorado; and tungsten, particularly in Boulder County. All had flourished before foreign competition and the decline in prices after the war ended their brief heyday. Similarly, coal mining, once an important contributor to Colorado prosperity, had fallen into decline after the war.[2]

As a result of this postwar depression in Colorado's two major economic interests, agriculture and mining, the state was never able to reach the level of prosperity the nation as a whole enjoyed during the twenties. Smelters closed, and mine laborers were unemployed. Farm returns declined, and farm tenancy rose. At first, the formation of farm marketing cooperatives softened the blow to rural inhabitants, as did a limited shift from raising staple crops to growing fruits, melons, and vegetables. Only in 1929, when agricultural returns approached those of 1920, when wholesale and retail trade broke a few records, when the state's tourist trade boomed, and when crude oil production reached a record of more than 1,000,000 barrels annually, did Colorado experience near-recovery. But it was limited and only temporary. Except for this one year, Colorado generally followed the economic cycle of its Rocky Mountain sister states, Utah, Wyoming, Idaho, and Montana. From the turn of the century, these five states had experienced relative economic retrogression. Their per capita income had declined from a position second only to the Far West in 1900, and well above the national average, to a position barely above it in 1920. By 1930, their average annual per capita income of only $551 was well below the national average of $640.[3]

Thus, when the Great Depression of the thirties descended upon Colorado, hard times was no stranger to the state. Unruffled but aware of his state's condition, William "Billy" Adams, Democratic governor since 1927, commanded public trust in such adversity. He had overcome the Ku Klux Klan's grip on the state in 1926 to capture the governorship, and then went on to win reelection in 1928 and an unprecedented third successive term in 1930. Simple in taste and manner, this self-made millionaire rancher from Alamosa had won the hearts of the voters in each of these elections without ever actively campaigning for office. And he remained cautiously optimistic about the problem of depression before 1932. He assured Colorado citizens that their state's "resources and its climatic advantages" would protect them from national economic problems, so long as he continued his program of reducing public expenditures and taxes. In fact, a national survey ranked Colorado's level of unemployment before early 1932 as lower than that of the nation as a whole. Indeed, the traditional heading of the *Denver Post*, " 'Tis a privilege to live in Colorado," now appeared almost prophetic.[4]

Nevertheless, such confidence belied the truth. Colorado entered the Great Depression in 1930 with a level of unemployment that was higher than the national average. Thereafter, between 1930 and early 1932, the state's unemployment increased much more slowly than that of the nation as a whole, thus giving the appearance that Colorado was fending off the depression. The national census taken in April 1930, for example, had reported 22,696 persons unemployed in Colorado, or 5.6 percent of the state's employables, as opposed to a 5.0 percent average for the United States as a whole. Only one other neighboring state, Utah with 5.1 percent, approached the higher Colorado rate. Within Colorado itself, its two largest cities suffered the most. Denver with 7.2 percent and Pueblo with 6.2 percent unemployed accounted for nearly half of the state's total unemployed at that time.[5]

Although, until 1932, the depression had produced only a mild increase in unemployment and decrease in industrial wages, Colorado's metropolitan charities felt a growing strain as the rural jobless began to stream into the cities, compounding the problem of caring for the unemployed. Assistance in the form of food and clothing was modest, though a few municipalities provided temporary work projects that allowed a man to earn from one to two dollars per day. Having the most extensive program of assistance was Denver, the largest city in the Rocky Mountain region and the one that attracted the greatest number of unemployed. Through the coordinated efforts of various charities organized into the Citizens' Unemployment Committee, Denver was able to pull through 1931. During 1932, however, as unemployment increased, relief needs tripled over the previous year, rising from about 153,000 requests in 1931 to almost 460,000 in 1932. Simultaneously, as business activity waned, charitable contributions declined along with personal income and taxes. As a result, charities in Denver, as did those throughout the state, collapsed in financial exhaustion. In reaction, some unemployed citizens formed cooperative groups that, among other activities, shared living accommodations, harvested crops rotting in nearby farmlands, salvaged edible food from merchants, organized drives to provide housing, clothing, and transportation for their members, exchanged labor for goods, and conducted social events to raise funds.[6]

Contributing substantially to these urban difficulties was rural distress. Declining farm prices, drought in southeastern Colorado, and grasshopper infestations throughout the state reduced farm income in 1931 by one-third of that in 1930, which was already 14 percent below the $212,958,000 total for 1929. Violent spring hailstorms, a late freeze, an invasion of cutworms, and a second year of drought, in addition to plunging prices for farm products, reduced farm income in 1932 even more, to only $81,756,000, or 38 percent of that in 1929. The Great Depression had finally crushed rural Colorado's long-standing expectations of imminent recovery.[7]

Between 1929 and 1933, per capita income for the state declined about one-third. This proportion paralleled the national average, but among the western states Colorado's decline was one of the least severe. Though no two studies agree exactly, the average annual income of a Coloradan dropped roughly from $630 to $360. This decline was not so steep as that in the Plains states, and thus probably Colorado farmers on the plains, where protest was the strongest, suffered more than the state's residents in general. Denver, on the other hand, with a population constituting one-quarter of that of the state, had an income decline of only about 18 percent for full-time employed heads of families during the same general period.[8] Granted that the two income categories, per capita and full-time employed heads of families, are not identical, the figures give enough of an indication to support the premise that distress among plains farmers was greater than among urbanites, and that all were in serious economic difficulty by early 1933.

With economic conditions deteriorating badly after 1931, Governor Adams formed a fact-finding committee to survey the state and report the amount of unemployment in March 1932. The results revealed that unemployment had swelled to at least 55,000, roughly three times that of early 1930. Actually, unemployment was greater, for the state report did not include 4,000 railroad employees and 3,421 members of organized labor, all of whom shared work loads and relief benefits. Nor did it include itinerant farm laborers, whom the report had categorized as "destitute" rather than unemployed. Moreover, "some of the counties were very slow to recognize the problems in their own community." Frequently they refused "to face the facts," as one state study concluded, "on account of a natural pride, as expressed by one of the counties reporting—'We will not need nor ask for any help outside our county as we have a great deal of local pride and will not ask for outside help as long as we can help ourselves.' "[9]

By the summer of 1932, Colorado was feeling the full impact of economic decline. "Unemployment conditions in Colorado," admitted Lieutenant Governor Edwin C. Johnson, "are very serious and rapidly becoming acute." A "conservative" estimate of unemployment at this time was 65,000 persons, or about one-sixth of the entire Colorado working force.[10] Bankrupt and exhausted, private charities closed their doors. County poorhouses strained under mounting applications from the unemployed. Banks and businesses collapsed. Stunned farmers, shaken by precipitously declining commodity prices, pleaded in vain for local and state government intercession to halt foreclosures.[11]

Angry and frustrated, several groups of citizens protested. A mass march of Denver's unemployed in January 1933 dispersed without incident after they demanded unemployment insurance and a debt moratorium. More aggressive was unrest in northeastern Colorado, where the Farm Holiday Association was active. For example, in January 1933 a small band of irate farm women stormed the Larimer County Courthouse to demand a reduction in taxes and government spending. Two months later, 200 militant farmers with similar requests attacked the Sedgwick County Courthouse. At about the same time, 1,500 farmers from the northeast descended upon the state capitol "to encourage" a state reduction in assessments on their land.[12]

Facing the worst crisis in state history during the winter of 1932–33, Coloradans looked to the federal government for help as they had since territorial times. For years, they had pleaded for, and received, federal aid to remove Indians, build railroads, determine land policy, peg the price of silver, and pass protective tariff legislation, among other things; so it was reasonable for them to expect Washington to reduce unemployment, provide the state with means to care for the needy, and even end the depression.[13]

They were not disappointed. President Franklin D. Roosevelt introduced a wide variety of relief and recovery measures under his New Deal program, which Coloradans eagerly anticipated. Before this time, the only assistance that Washington had provided for the unemployed were five Reconstruction Finance Corporation (RFC) loans, their total with matching state funds amounting to $2,191,048. These had come during the fall and winter of 1932–33. In order to raise state funds to match federal loans, since the state constitution prohibited bonded indebtedness, Governor

Adams shifted money allocated for federal emergency road construction to this RFC loan program. Counties utilized this money as they saw fit, for poorhouses, hospital charity wards, and doles of commodities to families on an uncoordinated first-come, first-served basis. Colorado had formed a State Relief Committee in July 1932, clothed with vague authority and lacking precedence, procedures, and power to step directly into the counties and resolve such problems as political favoritism and illegal relief requests. As a result, the only time this committee ever involved itself directly in local relief before the New Deal was in cooperation with the American Red Cross, which offered surplus goods to the needy in drought-stricken areas.[14]

Thus, when the Federal Emergency Relief Administration (FERA) began in May 1933, Coloradans rejoiced that the federal government was going to care for the state's unemployed. "The day after he took office," President Roosevelt later wrote of FERA Administrator Harry Hopkins, "he telegraphed his first communication to the Governors of the respective States; and before nightfall he had made grants of money to Colorado [and six other states]." Thereafter, Hopkins doled out to Colorado one-third of a million dollars each month throughout the year while he awaited the appropriation of state matching funds. Legal provisions provided a $1 federal grant for every $3 of state and local funds spent on relief. While awaiting the state funds, the federal government carried Colorado's relief burden, contributing 85 percent of the funds, with local communities furnishing the remaining 15 percent.[15]

Reluctant to commit the state to a large spending program for relief, the Colorado state legislature adjourned in May 1933 without providing the new Democratic governor, Edwin C. Johnson, with any means of raising funds to match FERA grants. A special session three months later, in August, passed an automobile users' tax, but in October the Colorado State Supreme Court invalidated it as unconstitutional by a four-to-three decision. The court also prohibited by the same margin an increase of one cent per gallon on gasoline, which the governor had requested for a $20,000,000 public works highway construction program. The repeated negative decisions of four to three on political issues at this time reflected the political affiliations of the judges. The high court consisted of four Republicans, all joining the bench during the twenties, and three Democrats, all becoming justices in the early thirties.[16]

Because Colorado failed to provide its share of FERA matching funds, Harry Hopkins federalized the Colorado relief program in November and administered from Washington care for the needy. This action offended the states' rights philosophy of the governor, who then called the state legislature into a second special session that December. But that body adjourned for Christmas vacation without taking any action. Frustrated, and as a last resort, Hopkins announced the termination of all FERA grants to the state after 31 December 1933, an extreme measure he used with only a half-dozen states.[17]

Colorado's unemployed had subsisted earlier without federal assistance; but once Washington took over responsibility for their care, most assumed that the federal government would continue such support for the duration of the depression. That is why just prior to the New Year's Day deadline, violence erupted in Denver. Unemployed men staged two riots to demonstrate their opposition to the threatened cut in aid. Another mob nearly killed a federal agent investigating these disturbances. Civil insurrection had begun to threaten Colorado.[18]

To prevent further incidents, including a planned pillaging of Denver food stores, the chaplain of Denver's Grace Community Center, Reverend Edgar M. Wahlberg, pleaded with the discontented to assemble at the state capitol on 3 January 1934 to pressure the needed legislation from the "Twiddling Twenty-Ninth," as some called this session of the General Assembly. Throughout the two preceding sessions in 1933, Reverend Wahlberg had implored the obstinate legislature to pass relief measures on behalf of the needy. At one legislative invocation, his prayer had been so frank that the assembly charged the reverend with lobbying. He had prayed:

> O God, make the more intelligent among us strong to lead. Give those who are afraid, courage. Save us from the temptation and sin of selfishness. Make us see the foolishness of dodging the real issue with petty interests and practices.[19]

The lawmakers returned from their two-week Christmas vacation to face the angry shouting throng. Much to the chagrin of Reverend Wahlberg, as journalist Frank Clay Cross reported it, "Communist leaders had seized control of the mob." Persuaded to storm the state capitol, the rioters poured into the senate chamber as panic-stricken senators fled before them. "A genuine Communist meeting followed," Cross asserted, "the first Communist controlled meeting ever held under the dome of any state capitol in the United States."[20]

Although such an event might have constituted front-page news in some areas, newspapers in Denver said nothing about the incident.[21] Neither did the state legislature acknowledge the occurrence. The official minutes of the senate do not indicate a disturbance, and the house journal records only a recess at the critical hour.[22] All apparently did not want to admit the extent of growing discontent among the unemployed or justify the need for greater federal involvement.

In the two weeks that followed the insurrection, unprecedented suffering prevailed throughout the state. For a second time, Reverend Wahlberg persuaded Denver's poor not to pillage food stores. By then, some Coloradans initially oppposed to increased taxation had changed their minds, and a few even threatened to join the rebellion.[23] Finally, on 22 January 1934, the legislature passed an excise tax on gasoline with a specified fraction of the proceeds designated for relief. For some reason, no one challenged the constitutionality of this measure. The state also diverted highway funds to match FERA grants. When the *Denver Post*, a rabid opponent of any increased taxation, attacked this new measure, an angry mob marched on the newspaper's office. The police barely prevented the group from lynching members of the *Post* staff. Thus, the influence of antitax interests buckled under the pressure of Colorado's poor, who threatened the very viability of state government.[24]

The next day, the FERA forwarded $500,000 to Colorado for the resumption of the relief program in the state. This grant provided each case—a case equaled a family of four—a total of $5.20 for January, or about one-half of that offered in previous months. Thereafter the amount gradually rose, until by May it totaled more than $20 per month, where it remained throughout the duration of the program. By its demise in mid-1935, the FERA had expended in total nearly $40,000,000 worth of federal funds, or 84.5 percent of all direct relief granted in the state between 1933 and 1935.[25]

In addition to providing a dole, the FERA offered three special forms of assistance. One of these was the Federal Surplus Relief Corporation, which in October 1933 took over the Colorado State Relief Committee's program of distributing surplus farm products to the needy. Farmers had been donating their surplus goods to the state, especially for victims of the continuing drought. The federal program of food grants had had a rocky start in Colorado. Delays had resulted with exposés of food spoilage and businessmen's grumblings about FERA shipments of surplus goods into the state, which conflicted with their "Buy-It-In-This-State" campaigns. Eventually, in 1935, the State Relief Committee once again resumed control of surplus food distribution, after the FERA had administered over $3,000,000 worth of goods. Thereafter, until 1943, Colorado's needy received an additional $10,000,000 worth of federal surplus food.[26]

Another early FERA program was assistance to cooperative associations. These had begun in 1932 when individuals voluntarily grouped together for survival. They struggled along until mid-1933 when they either died out or, as in the case of five large cooperatives, came under FERA subsidization and direction. In 1934, these five united to form the State-wide Cooperative Organization, with a membership of over 1,500 members. The next year the Colorado organization joined the Cooperative League of the United States, to become a link in the national system. During these two years, FERA financial assistance to Colorado cooperatives totaled nearly $200,000. With the money, the cooperatives were able to operate a coal mine for fuel, improve their machinery to produce needed goods, and implement a vocational educational program for their members. When this federal aid ended in mid–1935, so too did the remaining cooperatives, unable to maintain themselves independently.[27]

A third FERA activity was the care of Colorado's transients. The state had become a tourist mecca; and with all the propaganda that accompanies such an industry, it was only natural that in hard times some would head for what they thought was the end of the rainbow, Colorado. During the early years of the depression, thousands of America's unemployed, male and female, "took to the road," and many stopped off in Colorado. Indeed, by the thirties transients looked upon Denver as a key resting spot on the path of transcontinental travel. During one ten-month period of 1931–32, for example, the city offered transients nearly 100,000 individual grants of assistance in the form of meals and a bed in exchange for labor on city work projects. The burden of Denver Welfare Department expenditures for this aid grew so rapidly that when its share of RFC loan money dwindled away, the agency initiated a campaign to rid the city of what it termed "moochers." Transients faced rough going until mid-1933, when the FERA assumed the financial burden. Its Transient Division removed migrants from public and private charity wards and housed them in temporary mountain shelters away from the cities. Eventually five of these areas turned into permanent camps, each with a capacity of 2,000 men. In addition, the division maintained two reference centers, an infirmary, three registration shelters, and a housing compound for families and unmarried women, all in Denver. Most unique, however, was the special camp near

Colorado Springs for tuberculosis cases, since 6 percent of all transients entering Colorado came in hope of finding a cure in the state's high altitude and dry air.[28]

No matter where the transients went in Colorado, the FERA tried to persuade as many as possible to return home. For those who remained, the division offered vocational training in construction and conservation projects. By the time the FERA terminated its Transient Division in 1935, it had expended over $2,000,000 in the care of transients in Colorado. Thereupon, the FERA urged all transients to apply for work in the newly created federal work programs. Most refused and resorted to begging for a livelihood.[29]

Closely allied to, but separate from, the FERA, was the experimental Civil Works Administration (CWA), a program that employed nearly 33,000 Coloradans during the winter months of 1933–34. Scheduled to begin in November 1933, the state program failed to get under way for over a month due to delays. The CWA had to persuade cities to provide necessary equipment and materials, since nearly all of its funds had to go for salaries; and the agency became ensnarled in local complaints over hiring procedures, which eventually ended when the CWA arranged with the United States Employment Service to register and employ all applicants. Two sorts of discontent never did end, however. One pertained to Spanish-speaking Americans. They charged the CWA with discrimination in hiring practices. Unlike non-Spanish-speaking individuals, they had to prove their American citizenship, an impossibility in a large number of cases. Many had not been born in a hospital, and thus were not registered, and others were migrants from Mexico. The other continuing dissatisfaction was the fact that the CWA funds were only sufficient for the agency to absorb one-third of its applicants.[30]

Despite these complaints, the CWA participated in a wide variety of projects during its ninety-day duration. CWA employees repaired municipal property and streets; worked on Denver's flood control project for the South Platte River; and completed local surveys and census reports on wages, purchasing power, farm prices, rural housing, tax delinquencies, and parking and traffic problems. Specialized projects included paintings for public buildings, health examinations for children, concerts for the public, and, the first of its kind, the gathering of local history, under the guidance of State Historian LeRoy R. Hafen.[31]

Although the CWA terminated its program in Colorado in April 1934, the FERA did continue a few of the work projects. One of these, flood control construction, drew national attention in late October 1934. When, for lack of funds, the FERA reduced appropriations for work projects in Colorado during a period of rising unemployment, a thousand Denver laborers struck, demanding more work. Threats against FERA "scabs," police interference, a riot, and unfounded charges of a Communist conspiracy made headlines. Harry Hopkins's emergency expansion of FERA work projects immediately cured the strike fever.[32]

Hopkins was not so adept at quelling friction between him and Governor Edwin C. Johnson. A year earlier, when Hopkins federalized relief in Colorado, he inadvertently initiated an intense power struggle with the governor. Issue by issue, the two men locked horns in a political battle that lasted throughout much of the depression. Hopkins wanted to professionalize and federalize Colorado's social welfare; Johnson sought to protect his patronage and further his political ambitions.

Groomed for state leadership by Governor Billy Adams, "Big Ed" Johnson, as Coloradans called him, had become immensely popular by 1932.[33] He had come from Kansas years earlier and settled near Craig, where he became a wealthy rancher. A member of the state legislature during the twenties, Johnson served as lieutenant governor under Adams during the early years of the depression. When the 72-year-old Adams stepped aside in 1932 to prevent any charges of nepotism against his nephew, Alva B. Adams, then running for the United States Senate, "Big Ed" Johnson won the Democratic nomination virtually unopposed. Thereafter, without owing any political debts to Franklin Roosevelt and the New Deal, Johnson succeeded in Colorado politics for a quarter-century. "As long as Ed Johnson retained his personal popularity," contended Curtis W. Martin, Colorado political scientist, "he was subject to no discipline from the state party, much less any national party organization." Indeed, he outpolled Roosevelt in 1932 to become governor, won reelection over established New Dealers in 1934, and gained a United States Senate seat two years later. By this time he had become the most powerful politician in the state, and in time he would rank among the strongest in its history.

In 1932, Colorado voters chose three new congressmen, all Democrats, who would represent the state throughout the depression years, and returned to office another Democrat, Edward T. Taylor, a veteran of 34 consecutive years in the House by the time of his death in 1941.[34] All four men usually voted together in favor of New Deal legislation. The electorate also chose Democrat Alva B. Adams, son of former governor Alva Adams (1897–99, 1905), as their new United States senator. Of him,

Secretary of the Interior Harold L. Ickes later noted: "Senator Adams is one of the most effective men in the Senate and is on the conservative side." By that statement, Ickes meant that Adams was only a partial backer of the Roosevelt administration. Throughout the depression years, Adams was constantly at odds with Roosevelt over the subject of federal expenditures. As chairman of the Senate Appropriations subcommittee for federal relief, he openly rebuked the president during debates over relief appropriations. In 1935, for example, Adams chided, "I want it written that Roosevelt led the country out of the depression rather than into further catastrophe and calamity." In another instance, during 1939, when Adams personally brought defeat to a relief measure, he wrote a Pueblo constituent, "You will readily recognize that a rough road is laid out for those who seek to protect the government against waste and extravagance."[35]

Opposed to Adams's view was Colorado's other United States senator, Edward P. Costigan.[36] Founder of the Colorado Progressive Party and then a Wilsonian Democrat, Costigan had gained a national reputation by the time of the New Deal for his vigorous demands that the federal government initiate work relief. Under Franklin Roosevelt, he helped to develop such a program, and it was upon his influence in Colorado that Harry Hopkins relied for implementation of federal relief. Costigan viewed his state and others as failing in their responsibilities to care adequately for the unemployed, and therefore creating by default the need for federal intervention. Governor Johnson, on the other hand, came to view the program of New Deal relief as detrimental to his political power and a waste of state matching funds. Indeed, men like Hopkins, contended the governor, were "full of theories on humane welfare of the parlor socialist type."[37] Johnson's opposition to Costigan was more than a mere jostling for control of the state Democratic party and an ultimate bid for a Senate seat in 1936. It was a much deeper fight, one that pitted the federal government against the state in a redefinition of federalism.

Thus, not surprisingly, in the years after the demise of the FERA in 1935, problems associated with caring for Colorado's needy did not end, and neither did the conflict between the federal and state personalities. No sooner had Harry Hopkins organized the Works Progress Administration (WPA) than the old Johnson-Hopkins feud erupted once again. When the program was slow to begin, due to administrative delays, the recipients of relief demanded that Governor Johnson act in their behalf. Requests to Washington for continued FERA grants to care for the unemployed met with rejection. Even worse for the governor, Hopkins selected as Colorado

WPA administrator Paul Shriver, secretary of the Colorado Democratic Committee and a strong supporter of Johnson's antagonist, Senator Costigan. Fearful that Costigan's influence would grow through WPA appointments, thus reducing the governor's chances of winning Costigan's senate seat in 1936, Johnson attacked the WPA as an engine of political corruption. He claimed that Shriver was "building a Tammany Hall in Colorado for the benefit of Senator Edward P. Costigan." Charges and countercharges raised public eyebrows, but investigations proved unfounded Johnson's allegations of political favoritism. The antagonism between Johnson and Costigan faded slowly thereafter. When serious illness prevented Costigan from seeking reelection in 1936, Johnson replaced him.[38]

Meanwhile, it took five months after the creation of the WPA in July 1935 before full-scale operations got under way. Its immediate objective was to provide jobs for those unemployed persons who were capable of working, leaving the others to state care. To this goal, the agency employed a total of about 150,000 Coloradans and expended nearly $142,000,000 in federal and local grants.[39] The WPA comprised a variety of projects, which fell into four general categories. One was construction. WPA employees built or repaired thousands of miles of highways and streets; thousands of culverts, bridges and viaducts; nearly two thousand community buildings; and worked on hundreds of projects involving flood control, water conservation, storm and sanitation sewers, and provided assistance to soil and forest conservation efforts. Notable, too, was the $7,000,000 for construction and improvement of airport facilities throughout the state at a time when air traffic in Colorado had begun to expand.[40]

Another category of WPA projects was work for women, who constituted 20 percent of the Colorado WPA labor force. Women sewed and repaired over 7,000,000 garments, quilts, and other clothing accessories, and Spanish-speaking women with special skills wove thousands of rugs. Other WPA women canned over 5,000,000 quarts of preserves and served over 21,000,000 school lunches, utilizing federal surplus foods. Still others worked as nurses who tended sick relief patients, provided day care for the children of WPA parents, and trained to become domestic servants in motherless homes.[41] Women joined men in a third category of WPA projects, the white-collar program. Projects in this category included extensive library work for public and private institutions in research, indexing, and book repairs. Men and women also completed various types of surveys, conducted adult and special education programs, and participated in recreational projects. Disabled war veterans located and recorded military graves dating back to John C. Frémont's expedition through Colorado in 1842.[42]

Closely allied to the white-collar projects was the fourth category of WPA programs, the Federal Arts Projects, which evolved out of the CWA experiment. Unemployed artists, actors, musicians, writers, archivists, and historians spent four years, until 1939, in a variety of endeavors. Artists produced works of art depicting Colorado life, which eventually decorated museums, public offices, schools, military posts, and hospitals. The WPA Federal Theater Project provided performances throughout the state, as did the Federal Music Project. The Federal Writers' Project resulted in the preparation of a comprehensive guidebook to the state, one of a series covering states in the nation, as well as books on Colorado ghost towns, personalities, folklore, and place names. Originally part of the Writers' Project in Colorado, the Federal Archives and Historical Survey Project became independent in July 1936. With 80 professional workers, this project compiled for public use lists of federal and nonfederal documents and records within the state. They also gathered information on the state's resources for the purpose of long-range planning and expanded the State Historical Museum and its library collections by gathering thousands of early photographs and recording hundreds of oral history interviews.[43]

These activities successfully overcame the initial adverse reaction to the WPA in Colorado, and by the end of the thirties, Coloradans looked with favor upon the agency. In a national survey of WPA popularity, Colorado placed among the twenty states in the Union that were "Outspokenly in favor of the WPA."[44]

Akin to the WPA was its junior partner the National Youth Administration (NYA). In Colorado, the NYA ministered to the monetary and educational needs of youth upon the termination of the FERA youth programs. About one-fifth of those Colorado young people seeking work during the depression received NYA assistance in one form or another. In general, the agency emphasized aid to high school dropouts, for whom the NYA expended two-thirds of its funds.[45]

What was rather notable about the NYA was not so much its achievements in Colorado as the influence certain Coloradans had on administering the national agency. Under NYA Executive Director Aubrey Williams, a soft-spoken Alabama social worker, various departmental officials formed a national executive committee. Josephine Roche, a quiet but ambitious middle-aged Colorado woman, headed this body. She was a director of the Rocky Mountain Fuel Company, a member of the Colorado PWA advisory board, and, as a representative of the Costigan faction in state politics, had been an unsuccessful opponent of Colorado Governor Edwin C. Johnson in the 1934 gubernatorial primary election. From that time until 1937, Josephine Roche also served as assistant secretary of treasury.[46]

When Williams resigned his position as national executive director of the NYA in 1935, Richard R. Brown, Colorado youth director, succeeded Williams, and Brown's administrative assistant was Mabel Cory Costigan, wife of the ailing former senator from Colorado. After two years in his post, Brown resigned, handing his position over to another Coloradan, Oren H. Lull, former emergency relief commissioner in Colorado and director of the Colorado Transient Bureau of the FERA. Lull administered his NYA duties until 1939, when Aubrey Williams returned to lead the agency through to its demise in 1943.[47]

Also of assistance to youth, and meeting with widespread support throughout its existence, was the Civilian Conservation Corps (CCC), a special relief program mainly for young men from relief families. Two reasons surfaced for this enthusiasm in Colorado. First, CCC projects required no matching state funds and thus were of unequivocal financial benefit to the state. And second, the concept of conservation was an old and favorite one with Colorado citizens. Their constitution, in fact, was the first in the nation to recognize the need for proper forest management, and the state's forestry interests provided active leadership in national issues over forest management.[48]

During the nine years that the CCC worked in Colorado forests, as well as elsewhere in the state, the program employed a total of some 30,000 men, generally about 3,000 volunteers in the summer months and 2,000 during the winter. More than 75 percent of them were either native sons or long-time residents of the state, and those who were not, frequently came from neighboring states, especially Kansas and New Mexico. Colorado shipped its few black volunteers to New Mexico, where they served in a segregated camp. Although national policy normally dictated that a state's population determined the allotment of camps, projects, and men, in the case of Colorado, which had such an abundance of conservation opportunities, the state received allotments disproportionate to its small population. As a means of supplying men for these projects, the CCC sometimes transferred youthful volunteers from densely populated areas in the East to Colorado. When it did, mild protests arose against the federal government from Colorado residents and politicians who expressed resentment that nonresidents worked in "their" forests while residents went unemployed.[49]

Minor problems of other sorts also surfaced during these years. One, the inability of some CCC project supervisors to administer the program well, arose partly from the method of their appointment. Congressmen from those districts that contained CCC camps forwarded a list of the names of prospective appointees to Julian N. Friant, special assistant to the secretary of agriculture, who in turn selected CCC supervisors from it. As one might expect under such circumstances, congressmen obtained these names from Colorado politicians, who suggested only those persons whom they considered "ardent and consistent" Democrats. This method of selection sometimes provided poor camp leadership. Administrative incompetence became so noticeable by 1935, for example, that one of the state's regional foresters, John W. Spencer, publicly charged that political appointees had "left a wake of waste, drunkenness and even crime" throughout the state's forested areas. Difficulties of this sort recurred throughout the entire period of CCC operations in the state, as they did elsewhere.[50]

The CCC had other personnel problems, too. Although the agency offered its members a wide variety of educational, vocational, and recreational opportunities in camp, not all CCC volunteers adjusted well to their new life. Homesickness and hard work led to desertion, and in one case 100 CCC enrollees went out on strike over job conditions. All received an immediate discharge.[51] More lasting as a controversy within Colorado was the disapproval by pacifists of CCC militarism. They were angry that Colorado boys lived in a military manner and drilled like soldiers.[52]

Despite these shortcomings, the CCC continued to gain in popularity with Colorado residents, particularly as it completed numerous projects throughout the state. From early May 1933, when CCC enrollees opened their first camp high in the Rocky Mountains near Buena Vista, to the closing of their last camp in 1942, CCC men from more than forty permanent camps fought and prevented forest fires, controlled forest pests and noxious plants, involved themselves in water reclamation projects, cleaned lakes and rivers, and conducted surveys in the state's national forests, parks, and monuments. The most publicized achievement of the CCC in Colorado was the construction of the nationally acclaimed Red Rocks Amphitheater near Denver, used ever since for public events. In addition to these projects, beginning in 1935 the CCC practiced soil conservation to improve lands affected by overgrazing, drought, and dust storms. The agency established twelve permanent camps in eastern Colorado's plains, where it joined with the Soil Conservation Service to educate farmers in the proper use of their soil.[53] The Colorado Soil Conservation Act of 1937 helped the CCC with this work. The new law, aside from one in Nevada, was the only satisfactory legislative attempt by a western state to assist the federal effort.[54]

Successful as these programs of work relief were, be they the WPA, NYA, or CCC, all provided assistance only for employable persons. For those deemed unemployable at the demise of the FERA in mid-1935, they became wards of the state. That is, at this time Colorado had to assume the care of an estimated 30,000 indigents, or one-sixth of the state's relief recipients. Reluctantly the state legislature passed a sales tax specifically to provide revenue for a state welfare program and in early 1936 replaced the State Relief Committee with the Department of Public Welfare to coordinate and direct these operations. The state and the counties shared this burden thereafter, expending about $4,000,000 per year during the depression on direct relief.[55]

At the same time, in mid-1935, Colorado passed the necessary enabling laws to qualify for federal benefits deriving from the newly passed Social Security Act. Among other things, this law provided for federal aid to states for the care of the aged and destitute blind, and of homeless, dependent, crippled, and delinquent children. Furthermore, the act assisted in public health work, maternity and infant care, and vocational rehabilitation. For its part, Colorado had to provide a source of matching funds, which initially came from the new sales tax, and cooperate in setting up the program within the state. The Department of Public Welfare served as the permanent statewide organization to administer social security. Coloradans apparently received the new program with favor, though at first Governor Johnson resisted its federal features, claiming them an invasion of state power.[56]

In order to determine how effective this new social welfare program was in Colorado, one must consider two difficult questions. Did Colorado provide its welfare dependents with at least the minimum necessities? And did Colorado spend all that it could for their care?

An insight into the answer to the first question appears in a 1938 study of Denver welfare cases. It revealed undue suffering among the needy, for those receiving aid did not gain enough for the necessities of life. The dole averaged $7 per month per person, whereas a minimum budget required about $27 for a single person and $53 for a family of three. Nearly two-thirds of all alien heads-of-family, many single persons, and most jobless "employables" did not receive any assistance. Instead of devising effective aid measures, the state contented itself with the "ferreting out of relief chiselers" to reduce expenditures. Many of those disqualified were not imposters but jobless people desirous of work. The study also noted that malnutrition, mental illness, and stomach disorders among the needy contributed to a rise in family tensions and juvenile delinquency. Although relief investigators had reduced Colorado's welfare costs, they had inadvertently increased expenditures for police protection, court procedures, hospital welfare wards, and mental institutions.[57]

One reason Colorado failed to provide funds to alleviate such suffering was the state's legal responsibility to balance its budget and its inclination to reduce its debts. When he took office, Governor Teller Ammons (1937–39) inherited from Governor Johnson's administration a $1,000,000 deficit, which led to a state fiscal crisis.[58] To resolve the problem, the young Democratic governor pushed through the legislature a 2 percent tax on the value of services rendered and attempted to reorganize the state government. Both moves proved unpopular. Businessmen opposed the tax, and state bureaucrats feared for their jobs. With recession hurting many and the budget still unbalanced, Coloradans voted in a new governor in the next election, Republican Ralph C. Carr (1939–43). He promptly balanced the budget by sacrificing public education. Carr shifted most revenues from the schools into the general fund to help offset the deficit and to provide money for the "unemployables." The return of business prosperity resulting from economic stimulus growing out of World War II also helped Carr achieve a balanced budget in a decade of growing state expenses.[59]

The cost of state government during the depression years had increased alarmingly. Colorado state expenditures rose 200 percent in the thirties, as opposed to 54 percent in the twenties and 120 percent in each of the two postdepression decades.[60] Because deficit financing was unconstitutional, the state had to raise this income before spending it. The increased funds came from two sources: new forms of taxation and federal grants. In addition to the 2 percent sales tax enacted in 1935, the state initiated in 1937 a 2 percent service tax and a personal income tax. These new taxes did not lessen Colorado's dependence on property taxes but supplemented existing revenues. Thus, during the depression decade, total state revenues doubled, as they had already done in the twenties and would do again in the forties.[61]

Federal grants benefited Colorado, too. Between 1933 and 1940, Colorado received over $92,000,000 for various federal programs in addition to funds for relief and recovery. This amount was more than double the combined appropriations during the preceding three decades. Considering that New Deal relief and recovery agencies expended approximately $396,000,000 in Colorado, it becomes apparent that, along with the above $92,000,000, the state received twice as much as it sent to a government that some state officials believed meddlesome and constitutionally threatening.[62]

This assistance, plus the state's penurious welfare contributions, help explain why the state was able to continue reducing state and county government debts. These debts declined during the depression years from a high of $123,253,000 in 1929 to $100,708,590 in 1940, a decrease of 19 percent. In fact, by late 1941, Colorado turned the deficit in its general fund into a $761,000 surplus.[63] Such fiscal success suggests that the state might have been able to reduce the suffering of those in want if it had emphasized a social conscience over a sense of constitutional duty to financial solvency.

The other reason that the state neglected the "unemployables" had to do with the Colorado old-age pension system. By 1934, the aged, who numbered about 100,000 in Colorado, had jelled into a powerful political force.[64] In the gubernatorial race of that year, for example, Governor Johnson jumped on the Townsend bandwagon early, knowing full well that the first candidate to do so would receive the vote of the elderly. Dr. Charles F. Townsend, a former Colorado resident, had come to the state earlier that year and received a tremendous reception for his plan to pay all persons over 60 years of age a pension of $200 a month. Despite its infeasibility, three of Colorado's four congressmen voted for the doomed scheme the next year, more in fear of their political future than as converts to the plan.[65]

Rejecting Townsend's plan after its defeat in Congress, a group of Colorado rebels within the organization broke away to form their own pension organization, the National Annuity League. Under the capable leadership of O. Otto Moore, a colorful Democratic lawyer who was later a justice on the Colorado Supreme Court, the league sponsored a state constitutional amendment for a pension to supplement social security benefits for the aged. In 1936, Coloradans voted two to one to approve a $45 per month pension, the most liberal in the nation.[66] The state, however, was able to pay this full amount only once before 1941—in January

1938—because the law provided no separate means of raising money for such a payment other than tapping existing revenues. Thus, the pension consumed about three-quarters of all relief expenditures in the state, which was twenty times as much in 1940 as Colorado paid its younger relief recipients. The state had simply decided to sacrifice the welfare of its younger generation in order to cater to the aged.[67]

The conflicts and failures in providing relief to the state's needy during the thirties should in no way obscure the efforts of some in Colorado, at least at first, to support New Deal programs designed to return prosperity. After the creation of the National Recovery Administration (NRA), Coloradans enthusiastically glued blue eagles in their windows, formed committees to publicize "blanket code" compliance, and even encouraged Boy Scouts to earn merit badges recruiting NRA pledges. State residents watched hopefully as wages and employment rose in the summer of 1933. But when this improvement did not continue into the fall, enthusiasm waned, promotional support faltered, and code infractions increased. Within a short time, Colorado drew national attention because of several cases of early noncompliance with the codes.[68]

In Colorado, small businesses generally were the ones that failed to comply with NRA codes. From the very beginning, many rejected the concept of a government-business partnership. Since big business and industry frequently drew up the codes, small businessmen believed themselves to be the victims of discrimination. Their struggle against compliance grew during 1933 and 1934. Denver merchants threatened mass disregard of codes until the NRA removed all retail code exemptions for small businessmen near large cities. Soon after, a Denver laundry abandoned the code because its owner claimed that he could not afford to pay the minimum wage of 25 cents per hour. This company was the second in the nation to disregard NRA codes openly, the first being a Tennessee grocer. Within a few months, another Colorado business followed suit. In early 1934, a Pueblo cleaning and dyeing establishment disregarded NRA codes and undersold its business rivals. Hearing of the violation, and perhaps hoping to intimidate others by example, NRA chief Hugh S. Johnson ordered the Pueblo firm to surrender its Blue Eagle in the manner of a defeated general handing over his sword. In the legal melee that followed, the Pueblo company flaunted NRA threats to enforce rigidly all small business codes in Colorado. Two weeks after its announcement, the NRA sheepishly abandoned all attempts at price-fixing in service industries. "Johnson," asserted the historian Arthur M. Schlesinger, Jr., "who estimated that 90 percent of the complaints on noncompliance arose from the small service establishment, later felt that the Cleaning and Dyeing Code had singlehandedly killed the Blue Eagle."[69]

Its small-business codes discredited and its pride tarnished, the NRA had met its first big public defeat in Colorado. Taking the cue to act, small bituminous coal firms in the southern part of the state, the most numerous abusers of the codes, began a price war. NRA threats of prosecution led to an August 1934 federal district court decision in favor of the coal operators. This decision gave the NRA its first legal setback in Colorado. Thereafter, Coloradans paid more interest to wild eagles in their beloved Rocky Mountains than they did to blue eagles flying out of Washington, D.C.[70]

While Coloradans were losing confidence in the NRA, the state government's support for the agency was gaining. With no federally appointed state director, a State Recovery Board, chaired by former Governor Billy Adams, served as the only statewide NRA agency. Its main function was to give advice for the drafting and enforcement of the codes. Governor Johnson issued several proclamations urging compliance and appeared to have taken the NRA concept seriously. He not only encouraged the state legislature to suspend antitrust laws, but he also strongly supported the Colorado State Industrial Recovery Act (CIRA), commonly referred to as Colorado's "little NRA".[71]

Designed to harmonize state laws with the NRA program, the CIRA met with stiff opposition. Denver District Judge Frank McDonough invalidated the first CIRA, passed in January 1934, as an illegal delegation of legislative power. In April 1935, one month before the United States Supreme Court killed the NRA, the state legislature passed the second CIRA. This measure created a state Industrial Recovery Board to govern the approval and maintenance of fair competition codes. Governor Johnson defended it, too; but in October 1935, the Colorado Supreme Court declared this law unconstitutional as well.[72]

The NRA's demise in 1935 did not affect the other aspect of the recovery program, the Public Works Administration (PWA) plan of "pump priming." Aside from minor patronage squabbles within the state, Colorado generally supported the PWA throughout the thirties. Of the few difficulties that did arise during this time, the most controversial, though not bitterly so, revolved around the PWA's refusal to sponsor special projects to assist metal mining. During the decade that preceded the New Deal, western mining interests had failed in their effort to gain federal legislation to stimulate production. The early years of depression saw a few unemployed individuals take to the hills in hope of striking it rich by panning for gold. Even some Denver society matrons waded in local streams on Sundays, pans in hand, more as a fad than for a need. Few received much reward for their labor.[73]

Meanwhile, the state government made every effort to get Washington to stimulate metal mining as a means of ending the depression. Governor "Billy" Adams and William Jennings Bryan, Jr., organized a Denver conference in 1932 to drum up the old chant of bimetallism at a ratio of 16:1. But not all silverites still favored this panacea. The governor's own nephew, Senator Alva B. Adams, for example, supported another faction's solution, an international monetary conference to stabilize the world price of silver. Not until the passage of the Gold Reserve Act of 1934 did the silver interests find enough unanimity to act. In that same year they succeeded in obtaining passage of the Silver Purchase Act.[74]

All of this activity in Washington sent shock waves of hope throughout Colorado. "Recently I was in Cripple Creek," wrote a writer on tourism. "The town thronged. A buoyant optimism has replaced the vacant retrospection of yesterday." Production in gold did double that year, in fact, but metal mining production never approached the prosperous years before World War I. The Silver Purchase Act, for example, provided a wide latitude for presidential action, and Roosevelt acted far more conservatively with purchases than silver interests had expected. The act had failed to achieve its objective of recovery in silver mining. Not until after 1935 did metal mining begin to recover, and that was a direct result of the world armament race, which created a demand for copper, lead, zinc and molybdenum.[75]

Despite the difficulties Colorado metal mining faced, not all mining suffered so badly during the depression years. Colorado benefitted from increased demand for base and nonferrous metals and nonmetallic minerals, which the various public works programs used. For the most part, however, the PWA provided too little too late in Colorado to initiate economic recovery. Before mid-1936, the state received only a slight stimulus to its economy because of PWA director Harold Ickes's penurious handling of project applications. Apparently the influence of Colorado-born PWA Executive Secretary Oscar L. Chapman carried little weight. Only after the mid-thirties did contractors complete any major projects, and some did not become a reality until the postwar era. The most spectacular of these was the Colorado–Big Thompson project, the transmontane diversion of water under the Continental Divide. As a result of this time lapse, therefore, the PWA was not able to prime the state's economic pump during the Great Depression.[76]

On the other hand, the federal government was not solely responsible for the PWA failure. Colorado itself contributed stumbling blocks. State laws, for example, prohibited towns and cities from using deficit spending to fund PWA projects. Since these municipalities refused to increase taxes to pay for such work, they had to go through the slow process of amending their local laws to fit project needs. It took time, as well, for Governor Johnson to obtain constitutionally acceptable financing for his pet $25,000,000 highway construction plan. The project did not get under way until 1939, six years after he had offered it as "the greatest relief to unemployment."[77] To provide long-range planning for other large-scale projects under the PWA, Governor Johnson, by executive order in January 1934, and the state legislature, by a special measure in 1935, created the Colorado State Planning Board. This new agency tried to promote "conservation and an orderly development of natural resources in Colorado" by coordinating public works programs. The Planning Board helped local governments develop industry, agriculture, electric power, conservation, mining, and military projects. Since extensive planning was absent in many states, Colorado became a leader in this field.[78]

The major achievement of the State Planning Board and the PWA in the depression years was a ten-year building program, which began in 1937. By this time, the shortage of state funds for construction had forced expanding agencies and institutions to house themselves in antiquated buildings, some of them erected before Colorado achieved statehood in 1876. To meet this problem, the state issued anticipation warrants on expected income tax levies and persuaded the PWA to grant $4,000,000 of an estimated $12,000,000 necessary for the expansion program of state buildings. The PWA and WPA cooperated in the construction. Despite wartime delays, Colorado accomplished its goal of building facilities for penal institutions, charitable agencies, and administrative services during the first five years and educational institutions, which absorbed one-third of the funds, during the second five.[79]

Simultaneously with its attempts to promote relief and recovery in urban areas, the Roosevelt administration was endeavoring to provide the countryside with similar programs of assistance. Drought and insect infestation continued their seasonal devastation throughout the New Deal years, little impressed by changes in Washington's political scene. The spring that

Roosevelt took office, however, abundant rains made some wonder if the new president was omnipotent. Scant rain thereafter, except for one downpour in late summer, and the blowing of hot dry winds during the summer transformed that hopefulness into despair.[80]

In the 1930s, many of the inhabitants of southeastern Colorado were recent settlers from neighboring states.[81] Most were in the process of either buying farms or working as tenants with expectations of purchasing the land in the future. Their method of cultivation was dry farming, to grow crops without irrigation and depend upon adequate rain. They plowed under the natural grass that had covered much of the plains and had kept the soil intact. Uprooted, the grass oxidized into organic matter, and the rich topsoil lay loose without any adhesiveness. During the dry periods of 1931 and 1932, winds blew around small clouds of this topsoil, or dust. But during 1933, dust storms so increased in intensity as to make living difficult for both people and livestock in eastern Colorado, as well as to damage severely crops, pasture lands, roads, railroads, and farm lands. What in fact had developed was the "Dust Bowl," an ever shifting area in southeastern Colorado and its neighboring states of Kansas, Oklahoma, and Texas. In this region, Baca County was the most severely affected part of Colorado. During 1933, about one-third of that county's 10,000 residents became dependent upon federal relief; and by the end of the decade, roughly forty percent of the county's population had moved away, either to other areas of Colorado or to other states.[82]

If the "dusters" of 1933 were bad, the "black blizzards" of 1934, 1935, and 1936 were catastrophic. Hundreds of millions of tons of Colorado lifted into the air and blew away, some of it landing as far off as the East Coast and the Gulf of Mexico. When it met with rain clouds, as it sometimes did over the Rocky Mountains, the two combined to form mud that pelted down on the inhabitants below. Without rain, as on the Plains, the air choked with dust. Some people contracted "dust pneumonia," a new disease that resulted from too much dust filtering into the lungs. The vegetation that did survive the drought served as salad for an army of hungry grasshoppers. So severe was their infestation in 1934, the worst in decades, that the Colorado State Agricultural Extension Service borrowed airplanes from the United States Army to bomb the insects with pesticides.

The rain that did occur in these tragic years sometimes produced ironic results. In May 1935, for example, the brief downpour was so heavy and the parched land so dry that the earth could not readily absorb all the water, resulting in the worst floods in the area's history. One and a half years later, while the federal government was mapping the western drought area for purposes of relief classification, the rain was so heavy that officials moved on to Nebraska after disqualifying many portions of Colorado from assistance. As soon as the survey team left the state, the drought returned and remained for the rest of the year. The changed classification pleased many Colorado urban chambers of commerce. All along they had insisted to prospective tourists that Kansas, Nebraska, and the Dakotas contained the Dust Bowl, not "Colorful Colorado."

Up until this time, relief assistance for rural Colorado had come in various forms. At first, the Colorado State Relief Committee financed the purchase of feed for livestock, and the Colorado Rural Rehabilitation Corporation provided loans for several thousand farmers to improve their productivity. In many cases, the net effect of this assistance was to work at cross-purpose with long-range needs, for loans merely prolonged residency in marginal farm areas. They did not solve the problems of drought, depressed prices, or inefficient land utilization. Nor did initial proposals to resettle the destitute on subsistence homesteads prove fruitful. When the federal government purchased two sites for this purpose, the project generated local enthusiasm. As Governor Johnson expressed it to Washington: "There is a surprising demand all over the state for these homesteads." But Washington never followed through with the homesteads. Rather, in 1936, a newly organized Resettlement Administration established three cooperative farm communities in southwestern Colorado. Due to their qualified success, these settlements continued until 1945 when the federal government sold these lands on the open market.[83]

Another way in which the federal government attempted to provide aid to rural inhabitants in drought-stricken areas was through the purchase of surplus cattle. During the early depression years, ranchers in the plains had held on to their cattle to await the return of high prices. When drought and dust storms came instead, and natural vegetation and feed grew scarce, many cattle, sheep, and goats starved to death or died from the dust. The New Deal program to purchase sick and emaciated animals seemed a generous solution. Prices and meat consumption in the United States had declined drastically by this time, and Colorado ranchers were hard put to find a path out of their plight. Nevertheless, the federal program enraged cattlemen and meat processors at first, because the Federal Surplus Relief Corporation shipped the cattle to other states, slaughtered and processed them there, and then reshipped the meat back into Colorado to feed those on relief. The meat industry bellowed about unfair competition. "Buy-It-

In-This-Market" campaigns and threats of retaliation by boycott reverberated throughout the state. In the face of this uproar, Washington stopped shipping the meat back into the state and extended the purchase program until early 1935.[84]

Paralleling these relief measures were New Deal efforts to promote recovery in the countryside. One agency, the Agricultural Adjustment Administration (AAA), attempted to raise farm income by reducing crop surpluses and thus raise commodity prices. Its program provided federal subsidies for the voluntary limitation of acreage cultivation, the purchase of surplus crops, and the promotion of cooperative marketing. From its very beginning, aspects of the AAA caused Colorado farmers to voice strong disapproval. They stiffly opposed AAA acreage allotments for wheat, the first commodity to come under control. Since the AAA set its production quotas on the average of acreage cultivated after 1930, when many Colorado farmers had abandoned large tracts of land because of drought, they felt cheated by the relatively small quotas the AAA allotted them. Not until the agency adjusted its quotas upward for Colorado did the state's wheat farmers join the program, which eventually included nearly 90 percent of these growers.[85]

The other agency, the Farm Credit Administration (FCA), liberalized credit to farmers by reducing interest rates and consolidating into one unit all existing federal farm credit organizations. This agency also aroused initial controversy because of its rigid loan policy regulations. During the original settlement of Colorado, many farmers, especially those in the eastern counties, had acquired their land either from the federal government through homesteading or by purchase from the Union Pacific Railroad. In both cases, the seller retained the subsurface mineral rights. This situation created difficulties because before granting a loan the FCA required ownership with unrestricted rights of disposition. When the FCA revised its loan policy in 1934 to include landowners without subsurface rights, many farmers in debt, particularly those residing in eastern Colorado, rushed to FCA centers and filed for assistance. Ultimately, the FCA helped Colorado farmers scale down their debts by nearly $1,000,000 and won their strong support of the program.[86]

By this time, Congress had expanded the AAA program of production control with two new pieces of legislation. The first of these, the Jones-Connally Act, added a variety of new commodities to the original list, all of which Colorado farmers and ranchers generally supported. The second change, the Jones-Costigan Sugar Act, placed sugar, the state's leading cash crop, under AAA control. In this sense, the act had a powerful influence on the state's economy, for sugar production not only affected the entire pattern of economic life in its areas of cultivation, refining, and distribution, but it contributed markedly to the state's economic well-being as a whole. By 1933, depressed prices, a glutted international sugar market, and drought spelled disaster for the industry. Consequently, Colorado sugar producers at first rejected the concept of acreage restriction, believing that it would further diminish their incomes. Eventually, however, as drought reduced their productivity, they saw an advantage in receiving AAA benefits for that which they could not grow. Why Colorado sugar producers became the AAA's strongest supporters is understandable; they were the state's largest beneficiaries, receiving 40 percent of the $15,526,943 that the AAA paid to farmers in Colorado.[87]

While the producers were striving to earn profits, sugar beet workers were struggling to survive. Soon after the establishment of the FERA, Harry Hopkins learned that, during the spring of 1933, almost one-half of all relief expenditures in Colorado went to the sugar beet counties. An investigation revealed that migrant beet workers needed the dole at least half a year for survival and during the other half, when employed, to supplement their meager wages. So he allowed the beet laborers to collect both the dole and their wages in 1933. But in 1934, when the pattern persisted, he cut them off FERA rolls and denounced the sugar producers for maintaining their stock dividends without improving the workers' low wages, then averaging $78 per year, or one-quarter of the minimum amount needed to support a family of four. Governor Johnson agreed that working conditions in the fields approached "industrial slavery," but he bitterly assailed Hopkins for cutting the migrants off from the FERA dole.[88]

Just such conditions drove Senator Costigan to include in the act that he and Senator Jones had coauthored a section that raised wages, reduced hours, and prohibited child labor in sugar beet production. Those growers who participated in the AAA obliged themselves to contribute to improved working conditions. When the Supreme Court invalidated the AAA in 1936, however, the migrants lost any benefits they had obtained from the new law. Not until 8,000 workers joined the Congress of Industrial Organizations' United Cannery, Agriculture, Packing, and Allied Workers of America and federal hearings took place in 1940 did the situation improve. By then, however, the growers had replaced much of the hand labor with machinery that unskilled migrants could not operate.[89]

Akin to the problems of farming were those of ranching. In 1934, Congressman Edward T. Taylor, conservative Democrat from Grand Junction, Colorado, was able to obtain the passage of an act that withdrew from public sale all unappropriated and unreserved federal land in the nation. For Colorado, the Taylor Grazing Act placed about one-ninth of the state's total acreage, scattered and heterogeneous as it was, under the Department of Interior's Division of Grazing. With an approving nod from Assistant Secretary of Interior Oscar Chapman, himself a Coloradan, Farrington R. Carpenter of Hayden, Colorado, a Republican lawyer and large cattle rancher, headed the Grazing Division.[90]

Although the State Land Board strongly but privately opposed the Taylor Grazing Act as an invasion of its power, state representatives in Washington as well as large cattlemen supported the new law. They, too, believed in states' rights, but economic necessity overruled political philosophy. "Apparently Taylor [himself] was a strong states' rights man," Phillip O. Foss later concluded, "but he realized the futility and impracticality of attempting to transfer the public range lands to the states." What seems to have motivated acceptance of the law by those involved with the range-cattle industry in this period, at least in western Colorado and much of Utah, was the growing intrusion of itinerant sheepherders who roamed widely and competed seriously for grass. Federal enforcement of grazing would, and in fact eventually did, stop this practice, as cattle ranchers had hoped. That is one reason why they supported Farrington Carpenter so strongly once he explained his grazing program to them. He was one of them, and his reputation as an "anti-sheep" man preceded him. Moreover, Carpenter charged a grazing fee only half that of the Forest Service. And each summer he even obtained the services of from five to eight CCC camps to improve grazing conditions on western federal lands.[91]

During the last half of the thirties, events in Colorado agriculture often paralleled those preceding this time.[92] Each year, for example, the drought reappeared, turning hopeful expectations into pessimism. With similar regularity, a horde of grasshoppers showed up and, in 1937, caused record-breaking destruction. That year they devoured about one-fifth of the state's crops and rangeland. So serious was their invasion that Congress appropriated over $1,000,000 to Colorado to eradicate them. The state's poorly directed campaign provided little relief from the insects.

Also persisting were Roosevelt's efforts to promote his programs aimed at agricultural recovery. Though Colorado farmers and ranchers participated in the federal programs, for varied reasons they were reluctant to join programs developing out of the Soil Conservation and Domestic Allotment acts and the second AAA. Sheep ranchers, for example, disliked the conservation program of rodent control. With fewer prairie dogs and rabbits as prey, they feared, coyotes might turn upon their sheep for food. Nevertheless, most sheepherders joined the new programs anyway, as did most ranchers and farmers. As for tenant farmers, the new Farm Security Administration program of providing loans to purchase land benefited few of them in Colorado. Though fully one-third of these tenants qualified for such loans, only 35 of them received one because of the program's limited funds. Moreover, some tenants were members of landlord families, and they had an agreement with the owners to acquire the land through working it. At any rate, agricultural specialists in the state opposed such purchases on the ground that the West needed greater farm consolidation, not more small farm holdings.[93]

More acceptable to farmers in the state was the Rural Electrification Administration (REA) program. When it began in 1935, electricity was available in only one out of nine Colorado farm homes. Five years later, that ratio had increased to one out of four, after the REA had expended over $3,000,000 in grants and loans to local cooperatives within the state that eventually formed the Colorado State Rural Electrification Association. During the decade that followed, nine out of ten rural homes had electricity. Private power firms had fought this change all the way.[94]

Whether supported or not, New Deal programs in agriculture failed to bring the state's economic recovery up to the 1929 level, let alone to the prosperity of World War I. Colorado had to wait until World War II for rising farm prices and profits. With the beginning of a new decade, too, the end of exceptional aridity also helped to remove the state slowly from the depths of depression. But Colorado unemployment remained high, declining more slowly before 1943 than the national average. This slowness was characteristic of the entire Rocky Mountain region.[95]

With the return of prosperity, the question arises as to the extent of change that the New Deal brought to Colorado during its depression. Colorado historian Carl Ubbelohde suggests:

> Probably no twenty-year period in the history of Colorado witnessed as little change in the social scene as did the two decades from 1920 to 1940. Compared with previous eras, or with the years that followed the Second World War, these decades were a time of very slow growth and relatively little change.

In Professor Ubbelohde's view, World War II ended Colorado's period of uneasy adjustment and marked a watershed in state history:

> No other single event in its history and no other national crisis — not the Civil War, nor World War I, nor the Great Depression—brought Colorado such great change as did the Second World War. Much of what contemporary Colorado is, and what the state will become in the future, results from the events of the years from 1940 to 1950.[96]

Such a statement oversimplifies the complexities of life during the thirties, particularly if one analyzes separately various aspects of the depression in Colorado. There is no denying that the Colorado economy changed dramatically some time after, not during, the New Deal era. That World War II was a watershed in the state's economic history, on the other hand, is open to debate. Further investigation might well reveal that the late forties–Korean War era was the turning point in Colorado economic history. There is much more certainty, however, that the New Deal did affect the state's social scene to a far greater extent that Ubbelohde admits. Though state care for the indigent during the thirties was often meager, Colorado did accept federally established welfare measures that still exist. Also, one might point out the continued impact of subsidies for crop reduction on Colorado farm income and the difference that electrification brought to rural areas. Memorable, too, are the many recreational facilities still in use that various federal works programs provided, as well as the many modifications to the Colorado landscape, whether water diversion projects that permitted an acceleration of urban growth or state programs that increased the number of public buildings to facilitate the handling of expanded government.

In the realm of politics, however, the New Deal seems to have had little impact on Colorado, for the state came through the "Roosevelt Revolution" with much of its states' rights philosophy intact. In this sense, the New Deal failed to mark a watershed in Colorado history. Rather, the scene revealed a great deal of continuity between the era of Democratic Governor "Billy" Adams (1927–33), whom some wanted to elect to the Cowboy Hall of Fame, and Republican Governor John C. Vivian (1943–47), whom writer John Gunther described as "one of the dullest American governors I met."[97] Indeed, Governor Edwin C. Johnson (1933–37) himself symbolized the bridge between the years preceding and those following the depressed thirties. As the "Grand Old Man" of the Colorado Democratic party, he returned home after eighteen years of service as United States senator, his basic states' rights views unchanged, to sit once again in the governor's chair (1955–57).

Throughout the depression years, as it did earlier, the states' rights wing of the Democratic party drew upon votes outside the city and county of Denver and outside organized labor in Pueblo. Within these urban centers, New Deal–oriented Democrats had control, first under the leadership of Edward P. Costigan, until illness forced him out of politics in 1936, and then under the long-time powerful Denver mayor, Benjamin F. Stapleton. Looming in the background, always, was former Governor "Billy" Adams. In many a state contest, Adams's nod proved the margin of success for an aspiring office seeker.[98]

Within the heavily Democratic-dominated legislature of the depression years, individualism was rife and factionalism rampant, making generalizations difficult and party discipline often impossible. An issue like the repeal of prohibition in 1933, for example, revealed no clear-cut party pattern. Denver and the mountain counties supported the measures, as did their representatives, and most rural areas opposed the measure. Yet, rural-oriented "Big Ed" Johnson, himself a Christian fundamentalist and teetotaler, supported repeal as a matter of political expediency. And his political astuteness proved him correct. The state's prohibitionist vote dwindled thereafter, giving Johnson and most other politicians little opposition. In time, the public turned much more of its attention to the question of political corruption concerning the enforcement of liquor laws once prohibition ended than it did to the question of local option and repeal. In one sensational case, Secretary of State James H. Carr, a colleague of Ed Johnson's, resigned under pressure as a special session of the state legislature debated impeachment charges against him for bribery in connection with liquor permits. And old-age pensioners successfully lobbied for a large share of the receipts from state liquor taxes.[99]

Democrats continued to dominate state government after Costigan resigned from politics and Johnson went to the Senate in 1937. By this time, political power had shifted to Major Benjamin Stapleton and his Denver stronghold. In fact, his protégé, Teller Ammons, became governor in 1937 and served a two-year term. The first Colorado-born governor and, at 39 years of age, the youngest man ever to hold that office, Ammons was the son of former Governor Elias N. Ammons. The new governor faced a headstrong Democratic legislature that appropriated more money than the state could afford, ultimately raising his inherited $1,000,000 debt to a deficit of $3,600,000. Shackled with earmarked funds for various agencies, in addition to the drain of tax dollars represented by the $45-a-month old-age pension, Ammons retrenched state government expenses, increased taxation, and attempted to reorganize state government. His inability to solve the "fiscal crisis," as some called it, proved his undoing; and in 1938, the electorate replaced Ammons with a small-town Republican lawyer, Ralph L. Carr. The governorship was his first elective office, and he won it by advocating tax reductions and a balanced budget. He succeeded in achieving both by 1941.[100]

Not surprisingly, therefore, by the election of 1940, popular sentiment in Colorado had clearly turned against another Democrat, Franklin Roosevelt.[101] The Republican presidential candidate, Wendell Willkie, swept the state with the aid of a close Republican associate, Governor Carr, and Democratic Senators Ed Johnson and Alva B. Adams. These and other leading Colorado Democrats vehemently opposed President Roosevelt's bid for a third term.[102] In voting, nonetheless, the state followed its established pattern, which paralleled the national trend that year. The city of Denver, organized labor in Pueblo, and southern Colorado, populated with many Spanish-speaking Americans, all supported Roosevelt. Rural and small-town Colorado backed Willkie. They also gave Colorado Republicans two congressional seats and strenghtened the Republican hold on state offices. This Republican surge eliminated virtually all Democrats from higher office by 1942 and persisted throughout the war years.[103]

Republican success in Colorado after 1938 did not mean, however, that voters sought to repudiate all federal activity within their state. The federal government had long been present in Colorado and had supplemented its wealth. "Denver is called the little capital of the United States," the Denver Chamber of Commerce boasted in 1935, "because it has more Government offices than any other city save Washington." And that meant millions of federal dollars each year for salaries and supplies expended in a state desperately in need of an economic stimulus.[104] The acceptance of federal spending in Colorado, therefore, proved to be extremely important in the state's economic history. Just as precious metals contributed so much to prosperity before World War I, federal expenditures for military and scientific purposes have been the mainstays of the state's economy since the depression. This development has attracted industry and thousands of skilled workers to the state's urban areas, especially Denver. Today, that city and its nearby communities compose approximately half the Colorado population.

On the other hand, the state's support of federal expenditures had little to do with acceptance or rejection of the New Deal or any reinterpretation of federalism. In 1933, Colorado was desperate for immediate and temporary help in the areas of relief and recovery. Acceptance of this federal assistance did not imply a relinquishment of state power. The question of federal power was seldom a campaign issue. "Principles and issues are fine," Ed Johnson once mused, "but they don't win elections."[105] Carl Ubbelohde has reached somewhat the same conclusion. "Probably not one of these elections from 1938 to the present [1965] was actually decided on the issue of growing centralization of authority and control by the federal government; in fact, for almost any election, some other, usually local element was probably more significant in determining results."[106] Certainly that situation held true during the thirties. In the 1934 election, for example, there was evidence of confusion in the electorate's mind. To aid them in their choice for governor, one humorous editorial suggested the following: "In Colorado we have a Republican gubernatorial candidate favoring the New Deal and a Democratic candidate whose stand is just the opposite. Things are balled up. If you are a Republican or a Democrat and want the New Deal, vote for Nate [Warren]. If you want to be a reactionary and a liberal at the same time, for Ed [Johnson]."[107]

That advice was more than rustic humor, for it captured the essence of Colorado's political philosophy. From hindsight, success would come to anyone shrewd enough to knit specific aspects of both states' rights opposition and federal cooperation into a pattern that reflected the interests of the electorate. Ed Johnson did just that. On the one hand, he was flexible enough to accept New Deal assistance when it served Colorado's parochial ends. On the other hand, when federal agencies directly intervened in state decision-making, as the FERA did, Johnson was defensive enough to interpret this action as a threat to Colorado's rights. The Costigan-Stapleton faction of the Democratic party in Colorado was more consistent. It emphasized federal expansion and generally sided with the Roosevelt administration in its conflicts with the state. The failure of this faction to purge Ed Johnson in 1934 and its inability to replace Alva B. Adams in 1938 must have reinforced the beliefs of states' rights Democrats that to defy Roosevelt and yet win reelection was possible. In fact, the independence of Johnson-Adams Democrats often made it difficult to distinguish them from their Republican counterparts. Certainly, Ed Johnson's philosophy sounded closer to that of Hoover than that of Roosevelt when he declared in his 1934 candidacy for reelection:

Colorado has had a sound, thorough going, common sense business administration, second to none for efficiency, economy and effective government. Taxes for State purposes on farms and homes have been reduced 25% and every state agency and institution is now operating with greater efficiency than ever before upon a severely reduced revenue. The State Budget is balanced, and our fiscal condition is excellent.[108]

Four years later, as United States senator, when he fought to balance the national budget, Johnson had not changed his view: "I hope that Congress will go much further than the President advocated in balancing the budget and encouraging business."[109]

Opinions such as these, added to the lack of dramatic economic changes, thus lead one to question the validity of the thesis that Roosevelt and the New Dealers were able to revolutionize American politics during the depression. Political philosophy among successful leaders in Colorado remained much the same as it had been since the progressive movement. Characteristics of that era, such as progressive sentimentality, "Methodist-parsonage morality," individualism, rigid utopianism and anti-intellualism, persisted beyond the Great Depression as the marrow of the Colorado political personality.[110] These attitudes were basic to nineteenth-century frontier thinking. By no means did the end of that frontier in 1890 or the beginning of a "new frontier" in 1961 extinguish them in the state.

This exception represented by Colorado, and perhaps other western states, should temper the broader interpretations of the impact of the New Deal. It also helps to explain the modern western political rationale that exhibits such close ties with the past. And it gives an insight into why Colorado's leading Democrat during the Great Depression, "Big Ed" Johnson, could reminisce in late 1944: "As I see it, the New Deal has been the worst fraud ever perpetrated on the American people."[111]

1. On the New Deal and the West, see the August 1969 issue of the *Pacific Historical Review* (vol. 38). My own coverage of Colorado in that issue is herein modified and expanded. For the West as a region, see Gerald D. Nash, *The American West in the Twentieth Century* (Englewood Cliffs, N.J., 1973), chap. 3.

2. Robert G. Dunbar, "History of Agriculture," in LeRoy R. Hafen, ed., *Colorado and Its People: A Narrative and Topical History of the Centennial State*, 4 vols. (New York, 1948), 2:133–40; Carl Ubbelohde, *A Colorado History* (Boulder, 1965), pp. 278-80, 283-85, 290-91.

3. Harvey S. Perloff et al., *Regions, Resources, and Economic Growth* (Baltimore, 1960), pp. 27, 591; Colorado Co-operative Crop Reporting Service and United States Department of Agriculture, *Agricultural Statistics, Crops, and Livestock of the State of Colorado, 1942* (Denver, 1942), p. 10 (hereafter cited as *Colorado Agricultural Statistics*); Colorado State Board of Immigration, *Year Book*

of the State of Colorado, 1932 (Denver, 1933), pp. 344, 348 (hereafter cited as *Colorado Year Book*); "Where the Tourist Dollar Goes" (Conoco Travel Bureau, 1933), Records of the Office of the Governor: Edwin C. Johnson, 1933–1937, "Correspondence, 1936" (hereafter cited as Johnson Correspondence), RCC: 12 (Colorado State Archives and Records Service; hereafter cited as CSARS).

4. "Executive Record Book," 30:160, 199, CSARS; "Biography: Adams, W. H. 'Billy,' " Clippings Collection (Western History Department, Denver Public Library).

5. U.S. Department of Commerce, Bureau of the Census, *Fifteenth Census of the U.S., 1930, Unemployment* (Washington, D.C. 1933), pp. 15, 25, 175.

6. James F. Wickens, "Colorado in the Great Depression: A Study of New Deal Policies at the State Level" (Ph.D. diss., University of Denver, 1964), chap. 1. Two secondary works survey the state in the thirties: Ubbelohde, *A Colorado History*, chap. 28, offers a summary of the decade; Hafen, *Colorado and Its People*, vol. 1, chap. 29, provides an analysis of a historian contemporary to the period. In volume 2, information of a topical nature sometimes touches upon the thirties. Much valuable primary material is available in the Colorado State Archives and Records Service. Of some aid, too, is the Western History Section of the Denver Public Library.

7. Charles C. Gates to William H. Adams, 14 November 1931, Records of the Office of the Governor: William H. Adams, 1927–1933, "Correspondence, 1932" (hereafter cited as Adams Correspondence), RCC: 7 (CSARS); *Colorado Agricultural Statistics, 1931*, pp. 1–7; ibid., *1932*, pp. 1–2; ibid., *1942*, p. 10; *Denver Post,* 9 June, 22 October 1932.

8. Conflicting per capita income statistics are found in Frank A. Hanna, *State Income Differentials, 1919-1954* (Durham, N.C., 1959), pp. 28–29; Office of Business Economics, U.S. Department of Commerce, C. F. Schwartz and R. E. Graham, Jr., *Personal Income by States since 1929* (Washington, D.C., 1956), pp. 192–97; National Bureau of Economic Research, Conference on Research in Income and Wealth, *Regional Income*, vol. 21: *Studies in Income and Wealth* (Princeton, N.J., 1957), pp. 256–57; Frederick M. Cone, "Income Payments by States," *Survey of Current Business* 21 (1941): 14. For Denver, see "Employment and Earnings of Heads of Families in Denver, 1929 and 1933," *Monthly Labor Review* 39 (1934): 1230.

9. The committee never printed its findings. For some information on what it reported, see "Replies from County Commissioners and Others in Regard to Unemployment Conditions, in Answer to Governor Adams' Inquiries of December, 1931," p. 1, Adams Correspondence, 1932, RCC: 8, "The Unemployment Emergency in Colorado," 2 February 1933, Johnson Correspondence, 1933, RCC:13.

10. Johnson to Keith E. Boltz, 21 June 1932; "What Are Unemployment Conditions in Colorado?" (n.p., n.d.), Adams Correspondence, 1932, RCC: 6.

11. "What Are Unemployment Conditions in Colorado?", ibid.; "The Present Status of Emergency Unemployment Relief in Colorado, Radio Talk by John E. Gross over KOA, 23 March 1933," pp. 1-2, and "House Journal Resolution, #8 Report," Sec. 2, pp. 1-3, Johnson Correspondence, 1933, RCC: 13; Fred R. Niehaus, *Seventy Years of Progress: History of Banking in Colorado, 1876-1946* (Denver, 1948), p. 56.

12. See the large exchange of correspondence between Johnson and Colorado members of the Farm Holiday Association, dated February-March 1933, under file entitled "Farmers Union," and Niel Kimball to Edward Costigan, 3 February 1933, Johnson Correspondence, 1933, RCC:14; *Denver Post*, 19, 24, 28 January, 21 February, 10, 24 March 1933.

13. For a description of the crisis, see Wickens, "Colorado in the Great Depression," chap. 2.

14. "The Present Status of Emergency Unemployment Relief in Colorado"; "House Journal Resolution, # 8 Report"; "Minutes, Official Colorado State Relief Committee. February 1, 1933," Johnson Correspondence, 1933, RCC:13.

15. Robert E. Sherwood, *Roosevelt and Hopkins: An Intimate History* (New York, 1948), p. 44; *Colorado Year Book*, 1935–1936, pp. 290–91.

16. "Executive Record Book," 31:226–30; *Colorado Laws* (1933), pp. 60–65, 94–98; Walker *v.* Bedford, State Treasurer et al. (1933), 93 Colo. 400, 26P (2d), p. 1051; In re Senate Resolution No. 2, Concerning Constitutionality of House Bill No. 6 (1933), 94 Colo. 101, 31P (2d), p. 325; *Colorado Year Book, 1959-1961*, p. 189.

17. Harry Hopkins to Edwin C. Johnson, 18 December 1933, Johnson Correspondence, 1933, RCC: 16; "Executive Record Book," 31: 297–98; *Colo. Senate Journal*, 29th Gen. Assem., 2d Extra Sess. (19 December 1933), pp. 98–99; James T. Patterson, "The New Deal and the States," *American Historical Review* 73 (1967): 75.

18. Frank C. Cross, "Revolution in Colorado," *Nation* 138 (1934): 152–53.

19. Patrick F. McCarty, "Big Ed Johnson of Colorado: A Political Portrait" (M.A. thesis, University of Colorado, 1958), p. 27. Frank C. Cross suggested that the delay was due to a powerful antitax lobby (Cross, "Revolution in Colorado," pp. 152–53).

20. Cross, "Revolution in Colorado," pp. 52, 53; Cross does not specify the size of any mob actions before 14 January 1934, when Reverend Wahlberg stopped "400 desperate men . . . at 4 o'clock in the morning, ready to loot the chain stores for food." Vere V. Loper, "Hunger Threatens Denver's Poor," *Christian Century* 51 (1934): 164, also reported the above incident. As for the 3 January event, he noted: "The legislature is invaded by crowds of the unemployed." McCarty, "Big Ed Johnson," pp. 27-32, adds a few details about the events in January 1934. Personal correspondence, dated January 1969, between the author and several state officials of that time adds little to the story of the revolt. All replied with evasive or conflicting answers, specifying few details. Recent correspondence, dated July 1974, between the author and Reverend Wahlberg, who was on the outside of the capitol building at the time, verifies the event but discounts an actual Communist takeover. Wahlberg did read Cross's article and inquired about the authenticity of activities within the capitol building. Of the crowd of "over 2,000 people," Wahlberg estimates, "some . . . . entered the chambers and sat in the vacated chairs. Nothing much was done because there wasn't anyone there to talk with so they soon departed." And, he adds, "I talked with a Communist, named William Deiterick . . . . He discounted the story [of a takeover]."

21. John Gunther considered this type of omission a favorite game of the *Denver Post*; see his *Inside U.S.A.* (New York, 1947), p. 225. According to Cross, the *Denver Rocky Mountain News* and all other Denver papers joined in a conspiracy of silence concerning the riot ("Revolution in Colorado," p. 153).

22. *Colo. Senate Journal*, 29th Gen. Assem. 2d Extra Sess. (3 January 1934), pp. 100–105; *Colo. House Journal*, 29th Gen. Assem., 2d Extra Sess. (3 January 1934), p. 195.

23. Loper, "Hunger Threatens Denver's Poor," p. 164; Herbert Fairall to Johnson, 17 January 1934, Johnson Correspondence, 1934, RCC: 9.

24. McCarty, "Big Ed Johnson," p. 32.

25. Ibid., p. 33; United States Federal Works Agency, Works Projects Administration, *Final Statistical Report of the Federal Emergency Relief Administration* (Washington, D.C., 1942), pp. 103, 169, 254.

26. "Minutes, Official Colorado State Relief Committee, 1 March 1933," Johnson Correspondence, 1933, RCC: 13; William D. Tidwell to Johnson, 13 March 1935; Ralph O. Baird to Johnson, 12 July 1935; and Bernice Jackson to Johnson, 26 August 1935, Johnson Correspondence, 1935, RCC: 13; Colorado State Department of Public Welfare, *Quarterly Bulletin* 2 (1938), no. 2, p. 28, and no. 4, pp. 37–39 (hereafter cited as *Colorado Welfare Bulletin*). Federal expenditures estimated from *Colorado Year Book, 1937–1938*, p. 348; ibid., *1943–1944*, p. 417; *Final Statistical Report of the FERA*, pp. 107, 109.

27. "Minutes, Official Colorado State Relief Committee, September 17, 1933" and "October 25, 1933," Johnson Correspondence, 1933, RCC: 13, "Application for a Federal Grant, from the Federal Emergency Relief Administration, for Cooperative and Self-Help Groups of the State of Colorado," n.d., Johnson Correspondence, 1935, RCC: 15; Colorado Emergency Relief Administration, *Official News Releases* (hereafter cited without agency), 17 December 1934, p. 2, 14 January 1935, p. 1, 4 November 1935, p. 1; *Final Statistical Report of the FERA*, p. 115.

28. Edmond C. Young to Johnson, 7 February 1933, Johnson Correspondence, 1933, RCC: 13; *Official News Releases*, 7 January 1935, p. 3, 14 January 1935, p. 1, 18 February 1935, p. 3, 8 April 1935, p. 1, 5 August 1935, p. 1; *Denver Rocky Mountain News*, 7 May 1933, 1 January 1936, 14 March 1940.

29. Colorado State Relief Committee to Harry Hopkins, 26 September 1935, Johnson Correspondence, 1935, RCC: 15; *Final Statistical Report of the FERA*, p. 297; *Official News Releases*, 10 June

1935, p. 3, 23 September 1935, p. 2; *Denver Post*, 16 August, 16 September 1935; *Denver Rocky Mountain News*, 14 March 1940.

30. "C.W.A. Rule and Regulations, No. 1," 15 November 1933, and Johnson to H. D. Barnhart, 26 December 1933, Johnson Correspondence, 133, RCC: 16; Ralph O. Baird to Niel Kimball, 5 January 1935; "A Petition for a Redress of Grievances," 10 January 1934; E. E. Adams to Johnson, 19 February 1934; Baird to Johnson 20 February 1934; and Johnson to Benjamin Glassberg, 19 April 1934, Johnson Correspondence, 1934; RCC: 9; *Colorado Year Book, 1935–1936*, p. 288.

31. United States National Emergency Council, Colorado Division, *Report of the Proceedings of the Statewide Coordinating Meeting of Federal Agencies Operating in Colorado, Held April 13, 1936* (Denver, 1936), p. 1-C (hereafter cited as *Proceedings, Statewide Meeting*); Colorado State Relief Committee, *News Releases . . . .* 18 June 1934; p. 1; *Denver Post,* 30 November, 26 December 1933; 12, 15 January, 11 February, 1 April, 22 August 1934. Results of the historical endeavors are available in the Colorado State Historical Society Archives. LeRoy R. Hafen, "History of the State Historical Society of Colorado: III, 1924–50," *Colorado Magazine* 31 (1954): 45–47.

32. "Relief: Cold Weather," *Time*, 12 November 1934, p. 17; *Denver Post*, 29, 30, 31 October 1934.

33. McCarty's "Big Ed Johnson," based primarily upon scrapbook clippings, provides the only biography of a Colorado political figure in the depression years (Curtis Martin, "Introduction," ibid.).

34. "Biography: Cummings, Fred; Lewis, Lawrence; Martin, John A.; and Taylor, Edward T.," Clippings Collection (Western History Library, Denver Public Library).

35. "Biography: Adams, Alva B.," ibid.; Harold L. Ickes, *The Secret Diary of Harold L. Ickes,* 3 vols. (New York, 1953–54), 3:618.

36. "Biography: Costigan, Edward P.," Clippings Collection (Western History Department, Denver Public LIbrary); *Denver Post,* 31 July, 17 August 1934; *New York Times*, 15 July, 23 September 1934; McCarty, "Big Ed Johnson," pp. 40–60.

37. Johnson to Philip D. Norvell, 24 March 1934, Johnson Correspondence, 1934, RCC: 10.

38. Johnson to Franklin D. Roosevelt, 14 October 1935, Johnson Correspondence, 1935, RCC: 3; clipped correspondence to Johnson under "FERA, No. 2;" Johnson to Harry Hopkins, 21 June 1935; Johnson to Alva B. Adams, 16, 17, 18 July 1935; Johnson to F. M. Vaugh, 2 July 1935; Johnson to Shriver, 18, 19 November 1935; and Shriver to Johnson, 19 November 1935, Johnson Correspondence, 1935, RCC: 13; John Martin to Johnson, 29 November 1935, and reply, 3 December 1935, Johnson Correspondence, 1935, RCC: 11; McCarty, "Big Ed Johnson," p. 62, *Pueblo Star Journal*, 9 December 1935; *Denver Post*, 1, 6 October, 27 November 1935, 25 September 1936, 2 November 1938, 1 November 1940.

39. *Colorado Year Book, 1943–1944*, pp. 488–89; *Denver Rocky Mountain News*, 28 March 1943.

40. Colorado Works Progress Administration (hereafter cited as CWPA), *Permanent Achievements* (Denver, September 1936), pp. 1–5; *Colorado Year Book, 1943–1944*, p. 489; CWPA, Division of Information Service, *Official News Letter and Clip Sheet* (Denver 1936–37), no. 2, pp. 3, 6; no. 11, p. 2; no. 14, p. 3; no. 15, p. 4; no. 17, p. 5; no. 23, p. 3; no. 26, p. 1; no. 27, p. 5; and no. 55, pp. 1, 4.

41. CWPA, Division of Women's and Professional Projects, "Accomplishments," by Mary H. Isham, typed manuscript, Denver Public Library (Denver, n.d.), pp. 3–5; *Colorado Welfare Bulletin*, (1940), vol. 4, no. 2–3, p. 29; *Denver Rocky Mountain News*, 5 December 1937; *Denver Post*, 31 August 1936.

42. CWPA, "Accomplishments," pp. 1–2, 32–37, 49–55; *Official News Letter and Clip Sheet*, no. 26, p. 3; no. 36, p. 5; no. 39, p. 1; *Final Report of the FERA*, pp. 59–63, 228, 297; "Relief Projects-WPA," Clippings Collection (Western History Department, Denver Public Library).

43. "Relief Projects-WPA Art," Clippings Collection (Western History Department, Denver Public Library); CWPA, Division of Information, *The Professional WPA Worker and His Contribution* (Denver, 1937), pp. 2–5; *Proceedings, Statewide Meeting*, pp. 47D and E; CWPA, *The Writers' Program* (Denver, 1941), annotated descriptions; CWPA, Division of Professions and Services, Historical Records Survey, *Inventory of Federal Archives in the States* (Denver, 1938–40), preface; CWPA, Division of Women's and Professional Projects, *Inventory of the County Archives,*

(Denver, 1939–41), preface; Hafen, "History of the State Historical Society of Colorado: III," pp. 45–52.

44. United States National Appraisal Committee, *U. S. Community Improvement Appraisal: A Report on the Work Program of the Works Progress Administration* (Washington, D.C., 1939), pp. 3, 23.

45. United States Federal Security Agency, War Manpower Commission, *Final Report of the National Youth Administration, Fiscal Years 1936–1943* (Washington, D.C., 1944), p. 242; *Denver Post*, 11 May 1939.

46. For an analysis of Miss Roche's background and the events of the 1934 primary election, see: McCarty, "Big Ed Johnson," pp. 42–50; Oswald G. Villard, "Issues and Men: Josephine Roche for Governor of Colorado," *Nation* 138 (1934): 665.

47. "Biography: Costigan, Edward P.," Clippings Collection (Western History Department, Denver Public Library); *Final Report of the NYA*, p. 28; *Denver Post*, 17 July 1935, 8 July 1936.

48. Written in 1876, the Colorado Constitution in part states: "The general assembly shall enact laws in order to prevent the destruction of, and to keep in good preservation, the forests upon the lands of the state, or upon the lands of the public domain, the control of which shall be conferred by congress upon the state" (*The Constitution of Colorado* [1876], Art. 18, Secs. 6, 7). For the general story of forest conservation in Colorado, see: W. J. Morrill, "Forestry," in James H. Baker and LeRoy R. Hafen, eds., *History of Colorado*, 5 vols. (Denver, 1927), 2: chap. 14.

49. *Colorado Year Book, 1941–1942*, p. 464; *Colorado Welfare Bulletin*, 1940, vol. 4, no. 1, p. 13; vol. 5, no. 4, pp. 33–34; and vol. 6, no. 2, p. 5.

50. Although slim in its description of the CCC in the states, a survey of problems nationally is available in John A. Salmond, *The Civilian Conservation Corps, 1933–1942* (Durham, N.C., 1967). For the Colorado side of these conflicts, see: *Denver Post*, 4 December 1935; Lawrence Lewis to William C. Danks, 9 May 1934, and enclosures, Johnson Correspondence, 1934, RCC: 8; Johnson to John A. Martin, 21 June 1935, Johnson Correspondence, 1935; RCC: 14; Johnson to Alva Adams, 14 July 1936; Lewis to Danks, 13 June 1934, and enclosures, Johnson Correspondence, 1935, RCC: 12; Danks to Julian N. Friant, 14, 15 August 1934, Johnson Correspondence, 1936, RCC: 12.

51. *Colorado Welfare Bulletin* (1937), vol. 1, no. 2, p. 1; vol. 2, no. 1, pp. 32–33; and vol. 5, no. 4, p. 33; *Montrose* (Colorado) *Daily Press*, April 1939, in "Relief Work: Colorado, C.C.C.," Clippings Collection (Western History Department, Denver Public Library); *Denver Post*, 2 October 1934, Johnson Correspondence, 1936, RCC: 12.

52. "Arrangement Memo," 20 October 1933, Johnson Correspondence, 1933, RCC: 14; American Youth Commission of the American Council on Education, *The Civilian Conservation Corps* ([Washington,] 1941), pp. 8–10, Records of the State Department of Public Welfare: Civilian Conservation Corps, "Correspondence, 1933–1942," RCC: 1 (CSARS); *Denver Rocky Mountain News*, 17 April 1938.

53. L. A. Gleyre and C. N. Aleger, comps., *History of the Civilian Conservation Corps in Colorado, Littleton District–Grand Junction Distrist; that the Work of Young America May Be Recorded* (Denver, 1936), pp. 10–11, 149–52; *Colorado Year Book, 1943–1944*, p. 489; J. G. Lindley, "Protecting Colorado Range Lands," *Soil Conservation* 1 (1936): 12–13; J. G. Lindley, "Soil Conservation and the C.C.C.," ibid., 2 (1937): 285; *Colorado Laws* (1937), pp. 1169–93; *Denver Post*, 30 March 1948. Statistics and types of work projects conducted in Colorado appear in the appendixes of annual reports by the director of the Emergency Conservation Corps and Civilian Conservation Corps (Washington, D.C., 1933–42).

54. *Colorado Laws* (1937), pp. 1169–93; Robert J. Morgan, *Governing Soil Conservation: Thirty Years of the New Decentralization* (Baltimore, 1968), p. 72.

55. Johnson to Hopkins, 15 January 1935, Johnson Correspondence, 1935, RCC: 13; *Colorado Laws* (1935), chap. 171; *Colorado Laws* (April 1936), pp. 27–35; *Colorado Laws* (1936), pp. 1000–1021; *Colorado Year Book, 1948–1950*, p. 496; Colorado State Department of Public Welfare, "Historical Background of Public Welfare in Colorado," by Blanche E. Caldwell (Denver, mimeo., 10 December 1947), p. 2; *Denver Post*, 17 June, 7 November 1935.

56. "Executive Record Book," 32: 181–82, 308; *Colorado Laws* (1935), pp. 972–78; *Colorado Laws* (April 1936), pp. 27–35; *Colorado Laws* (November 1936), pp. 13–59; *Denver Post*, 11 August, 29, 30 December 1935.

57. Colorado State Department of Public Welfare, Denver Public Welfare Bureau, *The Denver Relief Study*, by Jean Simmock and Associates (Denver, 1940), pp. 5–6, 34–39, 46, 49, 56–57; Donald S. Howard, *The WPA and Federal Relief Policy* (New York, 1943), pp. 63–66, 73; Earl Knous to Ralph Carr, 2 January 1940, Records of the Office of the Governor: Ralph C. Carr, 1939–1943, "Correspondence, 1940" (hereinafter cited as Carr Correspondence), RCC: 6 (CSARS).

58. An analysis of this fiscal "crisis" compared to two other deficit situations in the interwar era, as well as their political implications, are available in James F. Wickens, "Tightening the Colorado Purse Strings," *Colorado Magazine* 44 (1969): 271–86.

59. "Legislative Interviews," 22 February 1939, pp. 1–9, Carr Correspondence, 1939, RCC: 7; "Finances," Clippings Collection (Western History Department, Denver Public Library).

60. Excluding federal spending, state disbursements in millions of dollars were as follows: $13 (in 1920), $22 (in 1930), $67 (in 1940), $151 (in 1950), $381 (in 1960). *Colorado Year Book, 1948–1950*, p. 521; ibid., *1959–1961*, p. 233. The increase in Colorado was much greater than that in other states (Patterson, "The New Deal and the States," p. 74).

61. *Colorado Laws* (1937), pp. 1144–68; Earl C. Crockett, *Taxation in Colorado*, "Report Number One, The Colorado Income Tax" (Boulder, 1946), p. 11; ibid., "Report Number Three, The Colorado Property Tax" (Boulder, 1947), pp. 1, 6, 8.

62. For the figure $396,000,000, see Wickens, "Colorado in the Great Depression," chap. 13. For nonfederal relief and recovery appropriations and federal tax returns, see: *Colorado Year Book, 1948–1950*, pp. 490, 496, 519, 604.

63. Colorado State Planning Commission, *A Report in Three Parts by the Committee on Government and Finance of the State Planning Commission* (Denver, 1950), p. 22. Colorado's reduction was not out of step with that of other states; see: Patterson, "The New Deal and the States," p. 74; *Federal, State and Local Government Fiscal Relations*, 78th Cong., 1st sess., Senate Doc. 69 (1943), p. 324.

64. The number of persons over 60 years of age rose from 97,114 in 1930, or 9.5 percent of the total population, to 129,918 in 1940, or 11.6 percent (United States Bureau of the Census, *Sixteenth Census of the United States: 1940. Population*, 4 vols. [Washington, D.C., 1943], 2: 701).

65. J. Frank Coss to Johnson, 10 August 1934; Danks to M. E. Hagen, 16 August 1934; Danks to Benjamin L. Wright, 17 September 1934, Johnson Correspondence, 1934, RCC: 8, *Colo. House Journal*, 30th Gen. Assem. (1935), p. 1685; Richard L. Neuberger and Kelley Loe, *An Army of the Aged* (Caldwell, Idaho, 1936), pp. 37–39, 78–79, 84, 95, 108, 258; O. Otto Moore, *Mile High Harbor* (Denver, 1947), p. 13.

66. "Old Age Pensions in Colorado, by Earl O. Crockett, University of Colorado, Department of Economics, August, 1947," typed manuscript, pp. 9–12, Records of the Office of the Governor: Reports Section (CSARS); *Abstract of Votes, 1936; Colorado Laws* (1937), pp. 881–89; *Denver Post*, 23 October 1958. For more details on the schism, see Neuberger and Loe, *Army of the Aged*, pp. 141–50. For the reasoning and mathematical calculations behind the choice of $45 as the amount of the pension, see Moore, *Mile High Harbor*, pp. 82–87.

67. *Colorado Welfare Bulletin*, 1941, vol. 5, no. 4, pp. 43–45; *Colorado Year Book*, 1948–1950, pp. 484–85; *Denver Post*, 5 February 1941, 28 January 1943; *Denver Rocky Mountain News*, 4 December 1942.

68. The only written account of the NRA in Colorado is in Wickens, "Colorado in the Great Depression," chap. 6.

69. *Denver Post*, 1 August, 26 October, 15 November 1933, 12 March, 16 May, 1934; Arthur M. Schlesinger, Jr., *The Coming of the New Deal* (Boston, 1959), p. 161.

70. "Hearings, September 14, 1934, re Code Violations, Fremont Co., Colorado," Records of the Office of Attorney General: Paul P. Prosser, 1933–1936, Correspondence, 1933–1936, RCC: 104 (CSARS); *Denver Post*, 2 February, 22 April, 24 May, 24 June, 9 August 1934.

71. Roosevelt to Johnson, 9 August 1933, and "District Office Territories for NRA Activities" (n.p., n.d.), Johnson Correspondence, 1933, RCC: 14; "Executive Record Book," 31: 243, 265, 274, 333, 348, 350; *Colorado Laws* (August 1933), pp. 29–31, 49–50; *Colorado Laws* (1933–34), pp. 78–83.

72. *In re Interrogatories of the Governor Concerning Chapter 89 Session Laws 1935* (1935), 97 Colo. 528, 51P (2d), p. 695; *Colorado Laws* (1935), pp. 298–311; Hartley J. Murray, "Has the Colorado IRA Met an Advisory Death?", *Rocky Mountain Law Review* 8 (1936): 141–43; *Denver Post*, 4 February, 28 May, 8 October, 1 November 1935.

73. Colorado Mining Association, *The Mining Year Book, 1935–1936* (Denver, 1936), pp. 33–34; *Denver Post*, 1 February 1930, 16 May 1932; *Denver Rocky Mountain News*, 15 March 1931.

74. For the story of silver, in which Colorado's role appears less significant than that of other silver-mining states, see John A. Brennan, *Silver and the First New Deal* (Reno, 1969).

75. David Lavender, "Back to the Hills Again! New Gold Rush in Colorado," *Travel*, June 1934, p. 20; Colorado State Bureau of Mines, "Annual Report for the Year 1936" (Denver, 1937), typed manuscript in possession of the Bureau, pp. 11–13.

76. Colorado State Bureau of Mines, *Annual Report for the Year 1935* (Denver, 1936), p. 8; Donald Barnard Cole, "Transmountain Water Diversion in Colorado," *Colorado Magazine* 25 (1948): 49–65, 118–35. For an analysis of the PWA's failure to pump prosperity into Colorado, see Wickens, "Colorado in the Great Depression," chap. 7.

77. Johnson to Roosevelt, 28 April 1933, Johnson Correspondence, 1933, RCC: 4; Johnson to Roosevelt, 31 December 1934, and reply 18 January 1935, Johnson Correspondence, 1935, RCC: 15; Johnson to Harold Ickes, 18 March 1935, Johnson Correspondence, 1935, RCC: 5; McCarty, "Big Ed Johnson," pp. 94-97. For an examination of the legal impediments, see Wickens, "Colorado in the Great Depression," chaps. 1 and 7.

78. Patterson, "The New Deal and the States," p. 77. The Colorado State Planning Board superseded the Colorado State Board of Immigration, which began in 1909 with the purpose of attracting settlers and investments to Colorado (Colorado State Planning Commission, *Ten Years of State Planning in Colorado*, ed. Elmore Peterson [Denver, 1945], pp. 3-14).

79. Colorado State Planning Commission, *The Ten-Year Building Program of the State Institutions of Colorado: Report of the Colorado State Planning Commission to the Governor and the Thirty-Third General Assembly* (Denver, 1941), p. 4; ibid., *Thirty-Fifth General Assembly*, 2 vols. (Denver, 1945), 1:8; ibid., *Thirty-Sixth General Assembly* (Denver, 1947), pp. 10–13.

80. *Colorado Agricultural Statistics, 1933*, pp. 1–8; *Denver Post*, 23 April, 4 May, 18 June, 17 September 1933.

81. The following discussion of drought summarizes an analysis of the subject in Wickens, "Colorado in the Great Depression," chap. 8.

82. Of the 110,000 people who left Colorado during the thirties, and not all involved were drought-stricken farmers, about 30 percent moved to California, 10 percent to the Pacific Northwest, 20 percent to the Rocky Mountain area, 20 percent to the Midwest, and the remainder scattered throughout the nation (U.S. Bureau of the Census, *Sixteenth Census of the United States: 1940. Population, Internal Migration 1935 to 1940* [Washington, D.C., 1943], pp. 3, 17, 45, 69, 92, 115; *Colorado Year Book, 1959-1961*, p. 497).

83. Johnson to all Colorado Representatives in Congress, 10 April 1934, Johnson Correspondence, 1934, RCC: 10; *Colorado Year Book, 1941–1942*, p. 97; *Denver Post*, 2 September 1937, 29 September-4 October 1940; *Denver Rocky Mountain News*, 11 June 1945.

84. Attached correspondence and newspaper clippings dated July through August, 1934, and "Cattle Slaughter Regulations," Johnson Correspondence, 1934, RCC: 1; Johnson to Harry Petrie, 5 October 1934, and Johnson to Alva B. Adams, 8 December 1934, Johnson Correspondence, 1936, RCC: 11; *Colorado Year Book, 1935–1936*, p. 284; John T. Schlebecker, *Cattle Raising on the Plains, 1900–1961* (Lincoln, Neb., 1963), pp. 133–35; *Denver Post*, 18 July, 20 July 1934.

85. *Proceedings Statewide Meeting*, pp. 1-A and 1-B; *Denver Post*, 28 June, 25 September 1933.

86. Lawrence Lewis to Henry Morgenthau, Jr., 19 October 1933; Lewis to Johnson, 23 October 1933; and J. H. Guill to Johnson, 24 October 1933, Johnson Correspondence, 1933, RCC: 13; "Press

Release, Farm Debt, Colorado," 13 May 1936, Johnson Correspondence, 1936, RCC: 9; "Report of Farm Debt Adjustment in Colorado, Colorado Advisory Council and County Debt Adjustment Committees," 1 December 1934, pp. 1–7, Johnson Correspondence, 1935, RCC: 12; Johnson to E. A. Starch, 23 December 1935, Johnson Correspondence, 1936, RCC: 13.

87. United States Department of Agriculture, Agricultural Adjustment Administration, *Agricultural Adjustment, 1933·to 1935* (Washington, D.C., 1936), p. 296; Charles M. Kearney to Johnson, 14 February 1934, Johnson Correspondence, 1934, RCC: 11; R. T. Burdick, "Economics of Sugar Beet Production in Colorado," *Agricultural Experiment Station Bulletin* (Ft. Collins, Colo.), No. 453 (June 1939), p. 40; *Proceedings Statewide Meeting*; p. 1-A; Floyd E. Merrill, "Colorado's Silver, Beets, and Factions," *Review of Reviews*, April 1936, p. 57; "Agriculture, Colorado, Beet Sugar, AAA," Clippings Collection (Western History Department, Denver Public Library).

88. "Statement of Conditions Relating to Sugar Beet Workers in Colorado, August 11, 1933," pp. 1, 8, 10–12, Johnson Correspondence, 1935, RCC: 15; "Minutes, Official Colorado State Relief Committee, July 24, 1933," p. 1, Johnson Correspondence, 1933, RCC: 13; Frank Clay Cross, "Pity the Poor Sugar Trust," *Nation* 138 (1934): 16; Burdick, "Economics of Sugar Beet Production in Colorado," pp. 33–34.

89. United States Works Progress Administration, Writers' Program, *Colorado: A Guide to the Highest State* (New York, 1941), pp. 66–67; Elizabeth S. Johnson, "Wages, Employment Conditions, and Welfare of Sugar-beet Laborers," *Monthly Labor Review* 46 (1938): 327–31, 338–39; Edwin G. Nourse, Joseph S. Davis, and John D. Black, *Three Years of the Agricultural Adjustment Act* (Washington, D.C., 1937), p. 319.

90. *Colorado Year Book, 1935–1936*, pp. 308–11; Phillip O. Foss, *Politics and Grass: The Administration of Grazing on the Public Domain* (Seattle, 1960), pp. 78–79.

91. Foss, *Politics and Grass*, pp. 5, 49–59; Schlebecker, *Cattle Raising on the Plains*, pp. 143–60; Virginia N. Price and John T. Darby, "Preston Nutter: Utah Cattleman, 1886–1936," *Utah Historical Quarterly* 32 (1964): 249–50; Johnson to Arthur H. King and enclosed "confidential notes," 23 May 1934, Johnson Correspondence, 1934, RCC: 5; *Colorado Welfare Bulletin* (1940) vol. 4, no. 1, p. 23.

92. For a detailed analysis of Colorado's agricultural problems during the late thirties, see Wickens, "Colorado in the Great Depression," chap. 9.

93. *Colorado Welfare Bulletin*, 1939, vol. 3, no. 1, p. 20; *Colorado Year Book, 1941–1942*, p. 97; ibid., *1959–1961*, p. 500; R. T. Burdick, "Landlord Tenant Income," *Agricultural Experiment Station Bulletin*, No. 451 (October 1938), pp. 5–7, 29, 52–53.

94. *Colorado Year Book, 1939–1940*, p. 339; *Denver Post*, 21 June 1936, 22 August 1938, 1 January, 28 November 1940, 17 November 1942.

95. *Colorado Agricultural Statistics, 1942*, p. 10; *Colorado Year Book, 1948–1950*, pp. 361–63; ibid., *1943–1944*, p. 145; *Denver Rocky Mountain News*, 3 January 1942; University of Denver, *Employment Trends in Relation to the Post-War Economy of the Denver Area*, Publication No. 2 of the Denver Regional Association (Denver, 1943), 19:3–5.

96. Ubbelohde, *Colorado History*, pp. 303, 313.

97. Gunther, *Inside U.S.A.*, p. 213.

98. Thomas C. Donnelly, ed., *Rocky Mountain Politics* (Albuquerque, 1940), pp. 84–85.

99. McCarty, "Big Ed Johnson," pp. 32–35, 55–56, 104–5; Johnson to Foster Cline, 19 August 1933, Johnson Correspondence, 1933, RCC: 16; "Executive Record Book," 32:102, CSARS; Leah M. Bird, "The History of Third Parties in Colorado" (M.A. thesis, University of Denver, 1942), pp. 112–23; Benjamin S. Galland, "Impeachment of a State Official," *Rocky Mountain Law Review* 8 (1935): 50–58; *Denver Rocky Mountain News*, 23 March 1937.

100. For a synopsis of these problems, see Wickens, "Tightening the Colorado Purse Strings," pp. 278–83.

101. A surface check of ten Colorado newspapers revealed over-all anti-Roosevelt feelings on the issue of a third term and deficit spending by November 1940. Eight of these papers voiced strong anti-Roosevelt and anti-New Deal sentiments. They were as follows: *Denver Post, Denver Rocky Mountain News, Gunnison News Champion, Glenwood Post, Cheyenne County News, Colorado*

Springs Gazette, Grand Junction Daily Sentinel, Trinidad Chronicle-News. Only one newspaper, the *Greeley Booster*, supported Roosevelt, claiming that the president had kept the nation out of war. The tenth newspaper, *Boulder Daily Camera*, did not openly commit itself.

102. McCarty, "Big Ed Johnson," pp. 151–52; *Denver Post*, 4 May, 28 June, 31 October, 6, 10 November 1940; *Denver Rocky Mountain News*, November 7, 1940.

103. Colorado State Office of the Secretary of State, *Abstract of Votes Cast at the Primary and the General Election, 1940* (Denver, 1940); ibid., *1942* (Denver 1942); Donald B. Johnson, *The Republican Party and Wendell Willkie* (Urbana, Ill., 1960), p. 163.

104. "Distinctive Denver, The Residential City" (n.p., n.d.), p. 5, Johnson Correspondence, 1935, RCC: 14.

105. Quoted in McCarty, "Big Ed Johnson," p. 64.

106. Ubbelohde, *Colorado History*, p. 326.

107. *Denver Rocky Mountain News*, 6 November 1934.

108. Johnson to James A. Marsh, 26 May 1934, Johnson Correspondence, 1934, RCC: 9.

109. *New York Times*, 4 January 1938, p. 17.

110. William E. Leuchtenburg, *Franklin D. Roosevelt and the New Deal* (New York, 1963), pp. 326, 338–44.

111. *Denver Rocky Mountain News*, 23 October 1944, as quoted in McCarty, "Big Ed Johnson," pp. 187–88.

William Pickens

The New Deal in New Mexico

THREE SHOTS CRACKED THE CALM OF THE AMERICAN LEGION
hall in Gallup, New Mexico, and the evening's principal speaker stood up
to see what had happened. Former governor Richard Dillon then helped to
calm the crowd and soon heard that a scuffle had occurred under the
Republican banner on the outside steps. A family quarrel had exploded as
Joe Baca, an unemployed teacher drifting from Oklahoma, had pressed a
pistol to the chest of his uncle. After a few nervous moments, the Republican affair proceeded. Two hours of speeches later, the formalities of that
memorable election eve, 7 November 1932, drew to a close. The crowd
disappeared into the dark streets, and the candidates stood talking with
party organizers. That same night, the elder Baca died with a bullet in his
heart. To the *Santa Fe New Mexican,* it seemed a tragic though appropriate conclusion to the 1932 Republican campaign in New Mexico.[1]

Certainly the results were tragic for Republicans. Exceeding even the
expectations of Democrats, Franklin Roosevelt carried New Mexico with
an unprecedented 63.7 percent of the votes. Democratic Congressman
Dennis Chavez won by an even larger majority. Republicans won only
four of the twenty-four seats in the state Senate. All statewide offices were
captured by Democrats in a victory reminiscent of the Republican triumph
of 1928. Here seemed the beginning of the monumental shift away from
conservative Republicanism toward the liberal persuasion of Franklin
Roosevelt and those identified with him in New Mexico. By 1938, state
government appeared to have a strikingly different attitude toward its
social responsibilities than Republican dominance had allowed during the

twenties. By then, Democrats enjoyed a political monopoly, and New Mexico was classified as a "One Party State."[2]

Certainly the government in Santa Fe was reformed by the New Deal. From a small institution directed by conservative political "barons" and a handful of bosses, it became a vital force for economic reconstruction. Social service boards blossomed into professional agencies with substantial support from state revenues. Large matching-fund programs tied Santa Fe to Washington with efforts ranging from unemployment relief to old-age pensions. Within a few short years, government in New Mexico became an institution that could meet many of the problems grown acute during the depression decade. These changes, however, reflect little credit on state Democrats. It will be one of the purposes of this essay, beyond descriptions of the major reforms, to show that most came from the pressure of national New Dealers who needed effective administration of federal money at the local level.

Nor were Democrats at the vanguard of progressivism during these years. It was a faction within the Republican party between 1929 and 1935 that consistently supported an active state government. The GOP, not the Democrats, first mobilized the "Forgotten Americans" to whom Roosevelt appealed so strongly. A fight within the Republican ranks was the first indication of demands that government should not be allied with powerful private interests. Throughout the Great Depression, state Democrats remained the party of the "middle," understanding few of the deeper changes caused by the crisis. They showed little imagination or willingness to deal with new economic and social realities. The political dominance of state Democrats came through pragmatic use of the national New Deal based on old formulas of patronage and through the death of the Republicans' progressive leader. It should become clear that the political struggles of the twenties and thirties in New Mexico are quite different than the traditional descriptions of a "Democratic revolution."

After the Civil War, Republican administrations in Washington guaranteed a strong hold for that party over the territory. But through the influence of President Woodrow Wilson and migrations from Texas, Democrats ended the domination of the entrenched Republicans. The two parties elected four governors each between 1913 and 1930. Democrats served most often in Congress but consistently lost the legislature.[3] During the early twenties, eleven "Spanish-American" and five "Anglo" counties usually favored the GOP, and thirteen heavily Anglo counties could be counted in opposition. This balance tended to strengthen party discipline and ruin independent politicians. Republican Governor Octaviano A. Larrazolo (1919–21) was the most famous casualty of this political balance. His administration achieved national prominence through substantial assistance to education, renewal of bilingual teaching, and restrictions on child labor. Larrazolo took leadership among western governors demanding that Washington donate the public domain to local governments. He seemed popular enough for victory over any Democrat in 1920, but his endorsement of an income tax and a direct primary (examples of a "radical state legislative program") doomed his renomination at the GOP state convention. Because factions within each party had to be united, undistinguished candidates often prevailed.[4]

Until the late twenties, few public issues could separate the parties. Because the state and its government were so poor, politicians offered insignificant services other than employment for party faithfuls. The two political parties were dominated by cliques of men, separated mainly by party label, who had the means to support campaigns and newspapers. Until the late twenties brought demands from lower economic groups, private bargaining followed even the most inflammatory political rhetoric. The 1928 election in New Mexico was the twilight of this political system. The twenties had loosened the grip of the old leaders. *Patrones* such as Solomon Luna and Thomas Catron were in the grave at the decade's start. Charles Spiess, the fiery "Black Eagle of San Miguel" who chaired the Constitutional Convention, was inactive at sixty-one. George Curry, whose skill had united Republicans before statehood, became an elderly soldier of fortune. Young and liberal Sam Bratton had taken a United States Senate seat away from Holm Bursum in 1924, a man whose conservatism was a pillar of the Republican party. Finally, Secretary of the Interior Albert Fall, once the king-maker in politics, faced charges of misconduct and was later sentenced to a year in the federal penitentiary.[5]

The twilight of the "old politics" was also evident in the Republican coalition of 1928. Three men—Charles Springer, Richard Dillon, and Bronson Cutting—represented the components of Republican strength that crushed Democrats a year before the Great Crash. On the right stood Springer. Arriving in Cimmarron in 1878, he had bought a sprawling ranch, purchased mining interests, practiced law, and served in the Constitutional Convention of 1910. He was an expert draftsman whose pen had produced more laws and party documents than any other. He was prominently mentioned for the United States Senate when A. A. Jones died in

1927. Springer "was one of the most brilliant men I have ever met in political life," wrote Democrat Arthur Hannett.[6] Such stature enabled Springer to speak for the "barons" of New Mexico. Baron membership was informal but well understood. Their ranks included Spiess, Curry, Bursum, and Fall as well as such private citizens as Frank Hubbell (the largest sheep rancher in America, according to Ralph Twitchell), the Democrat Harry Daugherty of Socorro, Hugh Woodward of Albuquerque, and later Albert and Ruth Hanna McCormick Simms. As the statewide political elite, these men and women shared attitudes bred by an agrarian, semicolonial society. They devoted much time to public service without immediate financial gain. Although they often disagreed, "even during the bitterest factional wars, they readily cooperated with one another to curb liberal ideas."[7] They were formal, meticulous, distinguished, and above all certain of the eternal wisdom in their conception of government.

Though accused of being reactionary, the barons were not averse to social reforms. They insisted only that changes should come from the private sector and then be institutionalized through law. Ideally, government was an evolving institution that reflected decisions made first in the larger community through competition of various groups and enterprises. State officials should act in accord with the collective judgment of community leaders. Government should preside, benignly and justly, over the competing elements in society. Unlike many industrialists and financiers in the urban East, the barons believed that no private interests, especially interests they disliked, should use the government for narrow benefits.

In an agricultural New Mexico controlled by such barons, state government performed services that were clearly unsuited to private enterprise but ones that contributed to "the general welfare."[8] The government in Santa Fe included a weak corporation commission, a bank inspector, various licensing boards, and revenue agencies. In 1927, the state maintained fifteen penal, charitable, and educational institutions. The total expenditure of all state and local governments was $16 million in fiscal 1927, 65 percent of which went toward education and highways. Despite the fact that two out of every five New Mexicans lived on farms during the twenties, no state agency had direct responsibility for agriculture. New Mexico was among the handful of states with neither an industrial accident board nor a labor commission, even though oil discoveries on the east side were beginning to create a substantial force of wage laborers. The Board of Public Welfare was the clearest "social service" agency in state government, but it directed only a small Child Welfare Service and a Bureau of Public Health. Margaret Reeves, head of the Child Welfare Service, ran a small operation ($27,000 annually) that served the most needy orphans, illegitimates, and delinquents. The service had responsibility for enforcement of the state's child labor law but received no funds for an inspector. Its suggestions, such as a mother's aid law, were usually ignored. The only government assistance to the unemployed was the minimal county indigent funds. The state contributed $49,977 to these in fiscal 1927. The barons insisted that such aid should be kept to a minimum by government. All these conceptions that limited the state's role found expression in New Mexico's constitution and in the philosophy of Charles Springer, Dillon's chief highway commissioner.[9]

Even though Springer and other barons dominated state government, they rarely ran for high office. With more appeal among a variety of voters were candidates like Richard Dillon, a moderately wealthy storekeeper from Encino. "Picnic Dick" became a symbol of Coolidge prosperity through his rise from poverty and his strict moral code. He was a product of the tradition of hospitality associated with the western cattle ranges. "New Mexico has a normal human being as governor," the *New Mexican* proclaimed in 1927. "He is a simple, plain, honest, American businessman. . . . The Governor makes no pretenses of being a reformer or a politician. We have had enough of them." In Dillon's mind, American progress had solved major social problems. Since society was healthy, he was not as concerned with the substance of governmental activity as with its procedure. Government should imitate the successful techniques of private organizations. He advocated efficiency and "sound business principles" as the highest values of administration. Such attention to details of government was possible because of the class harmony and economic progress he believed to exist in New Mexico. "Cooperation," he remarked during the 1928 campaign, "is becoming more and more the watchword between individuals and communities, states and nations. . . . [New Mexico employers] believe in justice, fairness, and cooperation." When cooperation failed, Dillon blamed selfish individuals.[10]

In January 1929, New Mexico seemed to prove the success of the barons' government and Dillon's ideas of common progress. "I know of [only one other] state in which the budget is handled as intelligently," wrote a prominent New York tax consultant.[11] According to federal statistics, net personal income for 1928 was $29,995,501, an increase of $5 million since 1926. Five hundred forty-one corporations reported a gross income of $70,297,472 for 1928 compared with a 1926 income of $57,107,624. Total cash receipts from farm marketings had increased 40 percent since 1924, and cattle, cotton, and wheat sales had doubled. The value of all livestock was $79,796,000, twenty-five million more than 1924. The value of coal mined in 1928, although less than in 1921, was a substantial $8,864,923, with 3,522 full-time employees. Discovered in 1924, oil increased from one million barrels in 1927 to 10,377,415 by 1930. "Wheels of Industry Spinning, New Mexico All Prosperous," the *New Mexican* announced in October 1928. "Plenty of Work for Labouring Men at Good Wages."[12]

Despite prosperity, a strong protest arose over its distribution. Leader of the protest was United States Senator Bronson Cutting, who was appointed to his seat in 1927. An aristocrat by Long Island wealth and Harvard breeding, the owner of the Santa Fe *New Mexican* disagreed that government should be small. Since his days as state secretary of Theodore Roosevelt's Bull Moose party, Cutting had advocated a larger role for the public authority. World War I convinced Captain Cutting that government could use the nation's most important resources to insure social justice in ways private efforts could not. During the late twenties, he argued that New Mexico's unique situation required more government.[13] Competing groups left to their own devices meant disaster. The state was fragmented in a thousand ways: by ethnic background, language, and religion; by the gulf between great estates and hideous agrarian poverty; by eastern farmers and cattlemen who joined in dislike for the oil workers and derricks invading their countryside. Of course, none of these groups felt at ease with the Hispanic farmers who scratched the eroded soil along the Rio Grande and its tributaries.

These Spanish-speaking New Mexicans had few opportunities. Frequently they clung to farms that were cultivated in ways their colonial ancestors would have recognized. Many of their land grants had shriveled through court decisions, sale, or fraud. One-third of the 31,404 New Mexico farms in 1930 had less than fifty acres, and most were in the Spanish counties. What alternatives were there? The towns were growing but offered few jobs for Spanish-American laborers. In 1929, the most prosperous year, only 4,479 New Mexicans were classified as permanent wage earners. Other doors were also closed: formal education was haphazard, vocational education almost nonexistent. Illiteracy in New Mexico was 15.6 percent compared with 6 percent nationwide in 1920. Ten of the twelve most illiterate counties were highest in Spanish-speaking citizens. Regardless of literacy in Spanish, their chief handicap was that they communicated poorly in English, the language of the American economy. A decade later only South Carolina and Louisiana ranked lower in literacy.[14]

It was clear to Cutting that opportunities in New Mexico were unequal and that time served to make them more so. Government was the only social institution that could ensure opportunities for all New Mexicans. Since Washington seemed unwilling in 1929, state government had to intervene with direct benefits for dispossessed citizens. Only a government that would "look out for the underdog and the underprivileged man" might ensure justice.[15] In 1929, Cutting saw an opportunity for such a government in Santa Fe.

In spite of substantial differences, Cutting joined Springer and Dillon to rout the Democrats in 1928. From all over New Mexico had come support for Republicans because of these three men. Cattle growers, sheep ranchers, and commercial owners voted with railroad workers and struggling farmers on the eastern plains. "He sido Republicano y siempre lo espero ser," wrote Próspero Baca, a poet in northern New Mexico who spoke for thousands of his people.[16] Even most of the coal miners in Colfax County, where Dillon helped to break a strike in 1927, supported the GOP ticket. Chief Justice Bickley of the Supreme Court remained the only Democrat in statewide office. Dillon was the first governor to succeed himself. The 1929 legislature was dominated three-to-one by Republicans, and Cutting supporters seemed to dominate the Republicans. A broader workmen's compensation law was passed. Complaints from Spanish American farmers about assessments for the Rio Grande Conservancy District (which erupted into riots a year later) were met by increased appropriations for irrigation projects. Although the state budget held most departments at about the same level, highways and education received healthy increases. Cutting liberals, however, lost a free-textbook measure and a proposed income tax.[17]

The real test of Cutting's strength came over a labor commission bill. Cutting had been organizing support for the proposal for months. Even Dillon mildly endorsed it. The bill authorized a labor commission empowered to inspect factories and mines for safety devices, encourage organizations of workers, enforce employer liability laws, and maintain an employment bureau. Legislators of Springer's persuasion were incensed. Publicly they contended that such a commission was favoritism by government and privately that GOP donations from wealthy employers would cease. The battle consumed six weeks of the sixty-day session. Newspapers reprinted debates and poured out violent editorials. Cutting's paper charged "the Republican Old Guard [with] keeping the lower class in a state of serfdom."[18] Finally, the House of Representatives passed the bill, and it came to the Senate on the session's last day. Cutting himself was present, having missed Herbert Hoover's inauguration for the occasion. Cutting's followers, including all but one of the Spanish-American senators, fought bitterly for the commission through hours of shouts and impassioned pleas. Opponents, however, mustered the votes. But defeat for the commission was more than a slap at workers; it ended the Republican coalition and split the GOP for twenty years. "The Republican Party in New Mexico was butchered by its own leaders," wrote Professor Charles Judah.[19]

So stood politics as the New Era of the twenties closed. Domination by the barons was possible only so long as the parties were competitive. Prosperity gave the Republicans an enormous victory in 1928, but this in turn raised the expectations of Spanish-Americans and lower-class Anglos. Through Cutting and his allies, these disadvantaged groups began to demand an end to passive.government even before the depression struck. The Democrats in 1929 tended toward the view of Charles Springer. In view of these origins, the Great Depression and the national New Deal would twist this movement for state action—initiated by the Cutting Republicans—into strange shapes.

Despite a veneer of prosperity, New Mexico had many of the economic illnesses of America in 1929. Labor was organized in only five communities and was pitifully weak even there.[20] As a commercial operation, agriculture in New Mexico was a disaster. Dry farming on the east side was the most successful, but a five-year study of 125 farms in two prosperous counties showed the average family income at $1,147. Farm tenancy had increased there by 131 percent during the twenties. Perhaps the real tragedy was not that most rural New Mexicans lived in poverty but that periodic fluctuations gave many of them enough hope to continue farming. Farm values had dropped disastrously from $224 million in 1920 to $174 million in 1925, but they edged upward to $207 million by 1929. The wet year of 1926 brought a New Mexico winter wheat crop of 4,876,000 bushels, but a dry 1927 left only 150,000 bushels. Ninety-nine percent of the state's arrable land was "affected by accelerated soil erosion" so that cloudbursts ate deep arroyos into topsoils. The value of all livestock had increased little since 1880, and in 1929 was one-half of the 1918 "boom" value of $132,652,000. The assessed value of all property was two million dollars less than it had been in 1915. "Within the past year two men have died in New York," the *New Mexico Tax Bulletin* announced sourly in December 1928, "the combined cash assets of whose estates is half again as much as the total assessed valuation of all property in New Mexico."[21]

The depression sharply accentuated these weaknesses. By 1931, the value of important crops in New Mexico was about 50 percent less than in 1929. Agriculture collapsed as the total value of crops reached bottom in 1932 at $9,537,000, a sharp drop from its high of $40 million. By 1932, the state's livestock valuation was one-half of the figure just two years before. The assessed value of minerals produced fell to $20,265,442 in 1932 from a high of $37,147,642. Mines closed everywhere. The fall of copper, once the biggest money producer, was typical: by 1932 only 28,419 pounds worth $1,790,397 were processed, one-third of the 1929 pounds that brought $12,939,069. By 1931, the price of coal had dropped by 30 percent from its 1929 level.[22] The Charles Ilfeld Company, in New Mexico for eighty years, lost $4,300 in 1932—it had never been in the red before.[23] "We have little or no manufacturing for the time being," reported Herbert J. Hagerman, president of the Taxpayers' Association:

Most of our mines are wholly or partially shut down and our principal remaining sources of outside income—wool, sheep, cattle, cotton, alfalfa, and a few other items are so low in price that practically all the net received for them goes for interest and taxes.[24]

These statistics are augmented dramatically by individual testimony. The State Archives in Santa Fe include scores of letters, scrawled on any paper handy, telling Governor Arthur Seligman about the misery of permanent unemployment or about the dry earth. The director of the Child Welfare Service, Margaret Reeves, reported that "the situation is rather critical in Dona Ana County" in the middle of 1932. A few months earlier, she had said that the problem was "acute, verging on starvation" in Rio Arriba County. Petitions jammed the governor's office: one signed by seventy-five citizens of Lumberton stated that they were "completely out of the needs of life." Seligman replied that no welfare worker could be sent and that "Red Cross work has now been closed."[25] On 9 August 1932, the State Delinquent Tax Collector filed property confiscation suits against 2,400 of the 4,000 taxpayers in Rio Arriba.[26]

In many ways, however, New Mexicans escaped the tragedy that stalked industrial centers. Most had never been affluent, and living on the land allowed many to remain nourished in some measure. The most burdensome problems of the early depression were the indigents who took up residence in the small towns or threw up shanties on someone's land. By 1935, New Mexico had the second highest number of migrant families per one thousand resident families in the nation. As early as January 1931, officials in Hobbs wired Santa Fe that seven hundred indigents would receive $150 altogether from the annual indigent fund. Raton later reported nine hundred transients on relief, and Clovis declared seven hundred had arrived in one month. The search for assistance with indigents led Margaret Reeves in late 1931 to a Los Angeles conference for welfare representatives that finally recommended creation of a federal training camp for migrants in El Paso. The request to President Hoover died, but the migrant problem did not.[27]

If federal officials did little, state government did even less. The campaign of 1930 was uninspiring. The national financial panic and the Republican split were sufficient to elect Democratic Governor Arthur Seligman and his entire ticket, some by narrow margins. Since the crisis had not yet awakened Democrats to the new realities, they continued most of the old practices. New leaders carved out spheres of influence in the government and promptly set to feuding. Congressman-elect Dennis Chavez and former governor Arthur Hannett opposed the followers of Seligman. In Bernalillo County, State Chairman Ed Swope and Edmund Ross fought with Mayor Clyde Tingley and D. K. B. Sellers. Charges of corruption were constant; patronage flared up as the major issue. Seligman demanded resignations from all state employees during December 1930, presumably to replace them with his own followers.[28] "I remember when Governor Seligman first took office," a housewife wrote the next chief executive, "[his people] thought that Miss Reeve's position should be made appointive, in other words a political plum."[29] Until the economy worsened, Democrats seemed more interested in the Santa Fe spoils than in any positive antidepression program.

When Democrats did respond to the crisis, their actions were weak and confused. The governor did little more than urge legislators to centralize tax collection in the hands of the State Treasurer and "to streamline state government." Though passing the governor's recommendations for tax reform, the legislators refused to cut budgets drastically and allowed state and local spending to rise to a record $23,711,000 for fiscal 1932. Still, except for a limitation on property taxes, some provisions for more equitable assessments, a modest income tax, and a compromise labor commission bill, little was done to meet the distress of New Mexicans.[30]

The Democratic leadership prevented bold initiatives. The new governor was a New Mexico baron who had spent his life in the family's mercantile firm, banking, social events, and politics. A short man with white hair over a stony face, Arthur Seligman was unlikely to inspire public confidence. His money and political allies, however, allowed him to dominate Democratic politics. He had long been friends with conservatives like Charles Springer, Judge Edward Wright, and Levi Hughes, and his ties with Bronson Cutting brought him the senator's private support in 1930. According to Jack Holmes in *Politics in New Mexico*, Seligman's position between the groups was his weakness:

> The man who . . . had built the Democratic Party through the use of factions was bound by factions. . . . The alliances which had put Seligman into office prevented him from developing or enacting the legislative fiscal program which the times demanded.[31]

Throughout the depression, Seligman tried to convince Democrats that retrenchment was the way back to prosperity. "There is a need for still further curtailment of expenditures . . . and the greatest possible economy," he told the 1933 legislature. Although constituents demanded some action, Seligman pointed out that the shrinking tax base simply could not support new programs. What can we do, he asked legislators, borrow money we cannot repay? Initiate programs that generate no tax revenues? Seligman was a financier, a man "to whom money was an important commodity . . . the spending of which had to be carefully planned and even more carefully executed. . . . Relief was a by-product of fiscal responsibility, not an end in itself." For two years, Seligman conducted the affairs of government in a manner that warmed the most conservative hearts. Writing after the governor's death, a friend recalled that "his endeavor to balance the budget was almost fanatical in its zeal. . . . [Seligman] looked with doubt upon the vast expenditures authorized by Washington [during the Hundred Days]."[32]

The Democrats also failed to develop a more liberal program because the party was "pushed" to the right in New Mexico. The left was increasingly dominated by Cutting Republicans or "Progressives" as they came to be known after 1929. Even though the Progressives had supported the Roosevelt-Seligman ticket in 1932, Cutting and the governor could not agree on a comprehensive package for the 1933 legislature. Democrats, having solid control of state government, would not agree to the Progressives' program of expanded government supported by high income taxes. Only four GOP senators survived the Roosevelt landslide, and although they (and many Democratic senators) supported Cutting's ideas in some measure, the state House of Representatives did not. Liberal triumphs came with improvement of the labor commission law, narrow defeat of a sales tax, employee hour regulations, and a few other measures that gave this legislature "the best record" in legislation, according to a student of New Mexico labor.[33] The rest of the session was a disaster for the Progressives. Cutting seemed disinterested in legislative matters as the flurry of the New Deal began in Washington. His *New Mexican* suggested, only half in jest, "abolishing the state legislature." Democrats cut the budget in every feasible way such as abolition of deliquent tax collectors, whose duties were assumed by the overburdened county treasurers. Higher severance taxes on minerals never reached the floor. Further limitations on property taxes passed easily. In fact, relief for property owners emerged as the most important issue during the session. The ambition of the Progressives to coordinate New Mexico's resources in a positive attack on suffering was abandoned. Legislature Democrats, though confused and bickering, agreed that state government should return to taxpayers as much income as possible.[34] In the opinion of a student of his administration, Seligman's concern during these years was "to save the taxpayers the money they needed to invest in their own farms, ranches, and businesses."[35]

Such an ambition failed miserably in New Mexico. One economic bottom gave way to another, and the public sank into common despair. Perhaps the most frightening part of these days was that the people could turn to no one. The barons were powerless and silent. Large landowners, men respected throughout the state, offered little advice except sentences punctuated with a rifle when indigents invaded their property. The few powerful businessmen in New Mexico were crushed and hopeless; some of their counterparts in the East called for a dictatorship. Left without institutional leadership, small communities were drawn together as never before. Many experienced demonstrations such as the day twenty cars jammed with veterans en route to the Bonus March "invade[d] Raton."[36] Some damage was done, but citizens paid little mind. The town gave them food, shelter, entertainment, road maps, and best wishes.

State government touched the lives of few people. Officials in Santa Fe simply ceased to plan programs. Tax collection was sporadic and usually resisted.[37] Many departments did little except draw up budgets. The government in Santa Fe sat, much like the giant corporations in America, waiting for some kind of change. Even for agrarian New Mexico, the end had been reached in early 1933. One-third of all New Mexicans required some governmental relief to approach subsistence living when Franklin D. Roosevelt became the thirty-second president.[38]

On 25 September 1933, Governor Arthur Seligman died of a heart attack after meeting with the New Mexico Bankers Association. Only meager funds had come from Washington before the governor's death: $100,000 found its way to self-help cooperatives for transients under the Emergency Relief Act of May 1933. Then, in what must have appeared to New Mexicans as a deluge in the desert, the money poured down. By the end of 1933, the Federal Emergency Relief Administration had given $594,947 in unemployment grants to the state. The problem during these months increasingly became one of organization. The federal government had to rely on local institutions and personnel to administer the grants. In July, Margaret Reeves of the Child Welfare Service was named state relief administrator under the supervision of the FERA state organization, the Bureau of Public Welfare. As the money increased, so did the confusion. Child welfare workers hurried to determine the state's most pressing needs. Plans and specifications were scattered all over their office. Everyone had ideas and wanted money. "Hundreds of work relief projects of value to the public generally have been planned and carried out by our local commit-tees," Margaret Reeves announced in late September. The FERA had ruled, however, that none of its funds could be used to purchase equip-ment, so large-scale construction was impossible. Even though there was "widespread evasion of the [no equipment] regulation," the FERA in New Mexico gradually began in mid-autumn to give direct relief to those not taken care of by the work projects.[39]

In November, more shape was given to the federal efforts. Harry Hopkins, administrator of the new Civil Works Administration, called the Board of Public Welfare and asked officials to initiate projects from school-remodeling to sewing circles. New Mexico's first quota for CWA employment was 8,250 persons. Before the CWA ended in March 1934, it had spent $2,356,221 in New Mexico and at its peak had employed 11,992 persons. In spite of its "works projects" thrust, the CWA completed few of lasting benefit. Workers stood in CWA offices for weeks waiting for tools and equipment. Corrington Gill, a national administrator, later admitted that it was "virtually impossible to plan programs adequately." Only the

1,800 men on drought programs made substantial contributions to the welfare of other New Mexicans.[40]

On the national level, the FERA took responsibility for most of the unemployed after the CWA was terminated. Again, the Board of Public Welfare, acting through the Child Welfare Service, assumed responsibility for local administration. One change was significant. At the beginning of federal relief in 1933, local officials had felt that work should precede relief payments: "[We believe] firmly that it is better for an able bodied man to work than to receive charity." By the middle of 1934, Margaret Reeves changed her mind: "The new work program is not an employment measure, it is a relief measure. . . . Naturally the relief rolls, especially in rural communities, do not always provide a sufficient number of skilled workmen. Under the new work program it is distinctly not the purpose of the Federal Relief Administration to erect a building or build a road as such."[41] This approach—and an accompanying emphasis on training —more closely fit the depressing realities of New Mexico in 1934. For instance, a federal report in 1936 found that 195 out of 890 heads of families had no training or work experience in as "cosmopolitan" an area as Albuquerque. This was far above the average of the seventy-nine cities surveyed. Most of the unemployed in New Mexico were not trained for beneficial public work, yet state officials found it difficult to provide extensive training under the crash programs. By January 1935, fifty percent of all FERA clients were doing no work at all.[42]

Although state responsibility for relief administration allowed more responsiveness to local situations, problems soon developed. In 1933, the state administrator was given power to declare a "fair wage" on a daily or hourly basis. This lack of standards caused bitterness throughout the relief structure. After the demise of the CWA in early 1934, the FERA tried local wage-rate committees and budgetary deficiency plans that allowed enough relief (above other sources of income) for a family to reach a monthly budget minimum. Since needs differed widely, so did work hours and wages per hour. The whole system became unwieldy because investigations to determine budgetary deficiencies were burdensome, the amount of paperwork was enormous, and the privacy of clients was invaded with regularity.[43] Few were happy with this plan in 1934.

State responsibility also led to partisan manipulation. Although the evidence indicates that federal officials tried to enforce regulations against blatant political use of relief, safeguards were impossible when new programs mushroomed overnight: in one instance, the number of employees on drought-irrigation projects increased from 1,300 to 5,200 during five days. It was a strong tradition in New Mexico politics that such opportunities should be used as rewards to party faithfuls. Nevertheless, the appointment in 1933 of a Republican like Margaret Reeves as state administrator indicates some attempt at nonpartisan employment. So do the complaints of some Democrats at this time. In early 1934, State Chairman Ed Swope wrote bitter letters to Governor Andrew Hockenhull that the PWA was employing Republicans. Rio Arriba Democrats were angry at the Reemployment Commission for similar breaches of political sense.[44] By 1935, however, the situation had changed. In January, Major Ellis Braught, regional FERA representative, came down to Denver for "a complete overhauling of the entire FERA set-up, state and county units." Rumors circulated that "a great deal of information is either being destroyed or being removed from the [Bureau of Public Welfare's] office." After suspending relief administrators, Braught called a dramatic meeting of all welfare workers. "Get this and get it straight," he told them. "There is to be no political office holder as foreman of any project no matter how small, no office seeker over any men, no one, not even a Justice of the Peace, in any official capacity and giving orders."[45] The speech was impassioned but, as we shall see, ineffective.

Although much state responsibility existed for relief administration and governmental reorganization, federal administrators tended to reserve major policy decisions for themselves. Local representatives were rarely consulted on major changes, and scant interchange of ideas occurred between the two levels of government. For instance, several prominent New Mexicans of the Southwest Conservation League drew up an elaborate scheme for a quasi-public agency of district organizations to promote conservation, agricultural education, long-range land planning, lobbying, and determination of grazing fees. All this machinery would operate under provisions of the 1934 Taylor Grazing Act. Advocates hurried to Washington with this well-publicized "New Mexico Plan" but met an unenthusiastic reception from the secretary of the interior. They then saw their grand ideas shuffled under an ineffective State Planning Board. "A refusal on the part of those who had the authority to permit it to be tired out," wrote a University of New Mexico professor, " . . . was a shock to everyone."[46]

These are characteristic examples of the difficulties with administration of federal programs that developed when fairly well-established state institutions received control over them. The results were even more disappointing when no state agency existed to implement the federal programs. New Mexicans welcomed the Federal Transient Service with great fanfare since no local agencies had ever dealt seriously with the indigent problem. The director of the New Mexico Transient Service, Riley Mapes, compiled comprehensive plans for resettlement and training for his many wards in early 1934. Federal officials rejected his plans and sent little money. Mapes finally had to settle for temporary employment of eight hundred transients by the Forest Service. Without a network of local contacts, there was little success in creating permanent employment for these people. Through the Transient Service and several other programs, however, at least responsibility for them was partially taken from the vanishing indigent funds.[47]

The clearest example of the New Deal's failure when local institutions did not exist can be seen in northern New Mexico. All the crash programs for agricultural payments, for direct and work relief, for loans and interest moratoriums, did not rescue impoverished Spanish-Americans in this area. Eshrev Shevky, a soil conservation official, discussed the unique problems in his report on the Santa Cruz River valley. About 3,900 Spanish-speaking citizens lived in this area of fertile soil and ample water. "The present use of this land," Shevky wrote, "centers around a household type of agriculture, each household cultivating a limited number of crops on small parcels of land [rarely more than eight acres]." Before the depression, families had supplemented their incomes with wage work because they had "not been able to sustain themselves through agricultural production for a period of sixty years or longer." Only relief from the FERA kept them at subsistence level during the New Deal. Shevky admitted that the WPA and the Resettlement Administration were doing little to train these people or to establish them in the state's economy. With the exception of a hydrator plant, "all of the work of the Resettlement Administration is in the nature of loans." Yet, Shevky concluded that such loans would not help families become more productive:

> It has so far not been possible to change the working of the present economy in order to alter its structure. If every individual family from Santa Cruz to Truchas were extended credit but the basic resources were not enlarged and the methods of production and certain characteristics of the economy had not changed, the area still could not support itself.[48]

This tragedy was reenacted throughout northern New Mexico. For years, the federal agricultural agents in these counties had provided the major link with modern agriculture. Their job, according to Professor George Sanchez, had been one "in which the social rehabilitation is at least as important as economic reconstruction." The agricultural agent was frequently pushed into the background as New Dealers swept into this wilderness with bureaus, application forms, and progress reports. National officials were, according to Sanchez, "overly impressed with filling quotas and with immediate relief without due regard for the long time effects of their action." In *Forgotten People*, a classic in New Mexico historiography, Sanchez bitterly assessed the New Deal:

> The situation in Taos County is not simply one of "emergency relief." It is not a product of the economic depression. Relief measures . . . [must] realize that the formulas which apply elsewhere must be conditioned to this highly qualifying factor.

To be successful in Spanish-speaking New Mexico, agricultural programs needed a strong state agency and continuous efforts by people who understood the ethnic characteristics of these farmers. Although the federal government extended thousands of dollars to grateful hands in northern New Mexico, this area had little resemblance to the agricultural problems as defined in Washington.[49]

Not all New Deal programs had either corrosive effects on existing state agencies or superficial results when agencies were lacking. Accomplishments were most positive when federal officials found a state institution designed for the purpose of the specific New Deal measure. The State Highway Commission was one such institution. Under the able leadership of Charles Springer, the department avoided major scandals during Dillon's administration. In fact, Springer was so successful that the *New Mexico Tax Bulletin* complained he "was probably overzealous in his planning and too big in his visions." Induced by federal matching funds during the Hoover years, the state made large commitments for roads that the Tax Bulletin termed "too ambitious" in 1931. The state and federal share of highway costs had been roughly equal until then, but the state's portion dropped to twenty percent during the next two years. In 1932, Governor Seligman insisted that "highway construction is the only employment relief agency in the state."[50] The matching funds program had long been under supervision by the Federal Bureau of Public Roads. Its pressure had helped to force the resignation of R. L. Rapkoch, a notorious political figure, from the chairmanship of the commission in 1932. Consequently, many of the worst abuses of crash programs were avoided.

Expenditure of the initial grant of $5,792,935 from the National Recovery Administration was quite orderly. Although never free from accusations of misconduct, the highway department was among the least criticized. Democratic Governor Clyde Tingley heard from a private correspondent in 1935 that the state highway engineer was intransigent about being nonpartisan. As the New Deal gained momentum, the federal government spent about $5 million annually and often completed five hundred miles of new highways per year. By 1936, New Mexico had spent more money for highways than any Rocky Mountain state except Colorado and was first in roads built. The maturity of the State Highway Commission before and during the New Deal certainly contributed to this achievement.[51]

Federal money often improved the conduct of state agencies in other ways. During the twenties, there had been few attempts to solicit honest opinions about government or to cultivate support for state services. "In this state, the people seem resigned to make the best of what they consider an evil, namely public service," wrote a professor at a New Mexico junior college.[52] During the New Deal, public understanding and support were crucial to these agencies, so state administrators became skillful in communications with citizens. The mimeographed *Health Officer* of the state Bureau of Public Health was replaced by a sleek, printed publication. The Health Education Committee, an entire division for publicity, came out of New Deal reform. Almost fifty thousand pieces of health literature were distributed at 491 public lectures, and 2,575 talks were given by health experts in 1936. The *New Mexico Relief Bulletin*, the publication of the FERA, displayed sensitivity to public sneers about "the dole" and so used patriotic and military imagery for the FERA's assault on distress as well as "before and after" pictures of the few work projects.[53]

Another improvement was that many state personnel were protected from local political interference. State politicians and professionals like Margaret Reeves viewed each other with deep distrust. Without strong federal backing, social service personnel would have been left alone to face the crudest sort of political pressure.[54] Further, the federal programs gave such personnel the leverage for pressuring local politicians for more support and reforms. Even though New Mexico was among the five states lowest in local contributions for relief (the federal government contributed 94 percent of the $15,656,751 spent between 1933 and 1935), elected officials would have preferred to do even less in this area. "The FERA expects every state to do its part in helping," Margaret Reeves wrote to the state treasurer in 1934. "They have advised us that they expect New

Mexico . . . to make available the full amount appropriated to the Bureau of Child Welfare." "Under these circumstances," she later told the governor, "I feel that FERA authorities in Washington would take a most decided objection to any of our small [state] appropriation reverting to the state rather than being made available for relief purposes." Conservative Governor Hockenhull, Seligman's successor, wrote all county commissions to curtail other activities before reducing their half-mill levy for indigent funds. "The Federal Government will likely call on us to match dollars with them," he told them, "and as you know it will be impossible for your county to match money" unless the maximum local levy was maintained. Although substantial reforms in the structure of state government came later in the New Deal, professional state administrators used federal leverage from 1933 to induce more state responsibility and a rearrangement of priorities.[55]

Many of the emergency measures and crash programs of the early New Deal ended in 1935. Throughout the first two years, New Dealers in Washington seemed to view these measures as extraordinary. Although recognizing that the crisis required an unprecedented peacetime effort by the federal government, most national officials, and New Mexico Democratic leaders especially, agreed that the economic system was fundamentally sound. Once the depression ended, government should return to its predepression size and practices with minor modifications. A resurgence of purchasing power with some safeguards could create secure affluence. Large projects like the CWA and the AAA, then, were attempts to re-create the former prosperity and to reestablish full employment that could be transferred into the private sector.[56] In a state with the afflictions of New Mexico, such aspirations were unrealistic. By 1935, more New Dealers started to insist that government should coordinate the most important resources, natural and human, in order to meet the challenge of poverty in a technological society. A 1935 FERA monograph declared that problems in the winter wheat area of eastern New Mexico were "prime examples of the sort of economy which can develop under individual initiative with no thought of social and economic consequences."[57] Such thought became more characteristic in the state and federal governments after the first two years of the New Deal.

"In the spring of 1933 the issue of destitution seemed to stand apart," President Roosevelt told Congress in January 1935. "Local agencies of necessity determined the recipients of [the $2 billion spent for] relief."

Calling such grants "a narcotic," Roosevelt maintained that "continued dependence upon relief induces a spiritual and moral disintegration fundamentally destructive to the national fibre." "The Federal government," he concluded, "must and shall quit this business of relief." Even so, the president insisted that government had new responsibilities for the public's welfare. Federal and state authorities had to ensure: (1) security of a livelihood through better use of the national resources; (2) security against the major vicissitudes of life; and (3) security of decent homes. It soon became clear that Washington would assume responsibility for public employment in large work projects and a massive social security program, while returning the burden of looking after "unemployables" to the state.[58]

This new approach can be seen in New Mexico with the end of the FERA on 1 December 1935 and the subsequent rise in importance of the Works Progress Administration. As FERA relief diminished, the 184 WPA projects in September 1935 rose to 453 by the next February, employing over 10,000 workers. The WPA differed from earlier emergency relief programs in several ways. First, employment on public works in New Mexico hovered around 20,000 throughout 1936, a substantial increase over earlier years. Second, there was more training and planning for WPA projects than for others before. The qualifications for employment were more substantial since the cost-per-worker was higher than in other projects. All applicants not only had to register with state employment centers and accept private employment if offered, but they also had to be on the general relief rolls. Equipment purchases were made by a national bid system. Such changes angered many businessmen and unions accustomed to providing materials and men, resulting in several mass protests over the tighter restrictions. In spite of such restrictions, federal spending remained about the same under the WPA: New Mexicans received over $9 million from the WPA alone through December 1936. Finally, the WPA asserted federal control over public works. FERA projects and most begun by the CWA had required only local approval in distinction to the WPA's insistence on confirmation by Washington. Local determination of wages was abandoned. Employees were under federal regulations. Despite this centralization, the WPA tried to tailor itself to local resources. "Almost an entire New Mexico village went 'off relief,'" Harry Hopkins reported, "because of the demand for Moorish period furniture produced in its WPA community workshop."[59] The WPA represented a commitment for a large and continuous presence of federal employment in New Mexico.

Another significant change away from emergency measures was evident in the National Youth Administration, also part of the WPA. The NYA had learned lessons from the Civilian Conservation Corps, an agency that employed young men and women for work on the land. "The CCC's failure to develop wider aims . . . [and] its inability to shake off the relief stamp" were major reasons for its decline during Roosevelt's second term, according to John Salmond's recent account of that agency. In contrast, the NYA was designed to encourage youths to continue in school and earn a diploma, which could mean substantial employment later. The National Emergency Council estimated that $94,000 had gone to New Mexico students from the NYA during academic 1936. Through this program, the New Deal was trying to lay a foundation for prosperity through training rather than merely augmenting incomes.[60]

The New Deal, then, came to mean large federal employment in New Mexico (later military and atomic research) augmented by aid for the special training of various groups. Equally significant were the New Deal efforts to reform state government. Far from usurping authority from the states, federal officials begged them to assume more responsibilities. National administrators began to stress integration of the scattered relief efforts at the state level. Such integration was obvious in the creation of the New Mexico Relief and Security Authority by the 1935 legislature. Such reorganization had become a necessity in New Mexico as federal money poured into social and relief programs scattered among several agencies. Even excluding federal grants, the Bureau of Public Welfare had risen from the stepchild of state government during the twenties to third place in expenditures by 1934. Only highways and education, two traditional state activities, received more money. Because major social legislation was expected from Washington, the 1935 legislature passed the Relief and Security Authority Act, "broad in its powers and designed to place the state of New Mexico in a position to cooperate with the Federal government in any program that might be advanced."[61] Two problems became immediately apparent. First, although the NMRSA was responsible for most federal money granted for welfare purposes, the Board of Public Welfare continued in existence. Many services were obviously duplicated. Governor Clyde Tingley attempted to remedy this situation by making the two boards of directors interlocking and ensuring that the full-time administrator of the NMRSA was the same person as the executive secretary of the Bureau of Child Welfare. Nevertheless, the relief structure was ill-defined and unwieldy. The second problem involved the state's continuing reluctance to finance social services. "March first it will be necessary that New Mexico make available its fair share of the cost of unemployment relief," Harry Hopkins insisted in a telegram during the 1935 legislature's deliberations. "I regard five hundred thousand dollars the minimum amount." Forced in this way, legislators appropriated the minimum by raising liquor taxes and passing a new corporation tax.[62]

On 1 November 1935, the New Mexico Authority began operation. One month later, the FERA transferred responsibility for all unemployables to it. On 15 December, the WPA designated the Authority as the certification and liaison agency for all social service activities of federal work-relief agencies. Later, it received administrative supervision over all money given to the state under the Social Security Act. For its first eight months, the Authority received $669,080 from various sources. Encouraged by this, its administrators prepared plans for social security monies that committed the state to matching funds for old age assistance, dependent children's benefits, and aid to the blind. The total came to $362,384 out of a state budget of about $18 million. On 3 April 1937, the Social Security Board in Washington announced approval of the plan and complimented the state's efforts. The legislature was virtually forced to comply. No agency before the NMRSA had ever received such extensive responsibility or more money for social services.[63]

By 1937, no one could doubt that such services would remain a major responsibility for state government. The legislature then approved a permanent State Department of Public Welfare. Replacing the NMRSA and other relief agencies, the department was to handle all federal and state welfare monies. Funds under the Social Security Act would be administered by this department. Federal law insisted that traditional employment practices in New Mexico be abandoned: every employee below the director had to be chosen on a federally certified merit system. The department's first director, Fay Guthrie, began an elaborate arrangement of professional training for workers, group institutes, and a circulating library. The department hired a staff ten times the size of the Child Welfare Service during the twenties. By April 1938, it had 17,949 cases and spent $106,073 for indigents alone that month. In spite of its size, the department remained free from the charges of corruption usual in New Mexico. By 1938, welfare and relief at the state level reached a level of professionalism inconceivable ten years before.[64]

Encouraged by federal examples and pressure, legislatures adopted other reforms between 1934 and 1938, so many that Jack Holmes concluded they "set the course of government and administration for nearly twenty years."[65] Debates about revenue consumed most of the 1934 special session. In spite of opposition by Bronson Cutting, legislators passed a sales tax that gathered $4,244,263 for the schools during its first two years. Some tax relief was given to farmers along with a prohibition on mortgage foreclosure until after harvests. At the insistence of federal officials, legislators established employment agencies and an Industrial Recovery Act "for the purposes of cooperation with the recovery agencies of the federal government."[66]

The New Mexico Taxpayers' Association reported that the 1935 legislature passed "numerous acts which should have the effect of materially increasing the efficiency" of state government. The association cited creation of central tax collection under a Bureau of Revenue, a new state police and park commission, and consolidation of the Board of Finance with control over all purchases. The legislature adopted a special assessment for irrigation projects in the Rio Grande valley and gave power to the Rural Electrification Authority to issue revenue certificates. Legislators created a strong Oil Conservation Commission that, said Governor Jack Campbell much later, "has been used as a model in a number of states."[67] The 1935 District Health Act combined counties into units with full-time health officers. The act testified to the influence of J. Rosslyn Earp, director of the Public Health Bureau, and to the fact that the United States Public Health Service was directing grants away from the counties toward the state agency. The 1937 legislature reformed the health structure to the point that Professor Thomas Donnelly, an expert in the field of public health, could say "there is no other state comparable in size, area, population, and wealth which is doing as much."[68]

The 1936 special session took an obscure Employment Security Service out from under the New Mexico Labor Commission. The new agency, titled the New Mexico Employment Security Commission, received extensive powers, including the charge to "promote the reemployment of unemployed workers . . . in every way that may be feasible." Under Clinton P. Anderson, the commission began "the first real merit system in connection with the public service in New Mexico." Although its financial weakness forced the commission to rely on federal funds, it indicated that legislators were willing to face unemployment problems with positive legislation.[69]

The 1937 legislature turned to the problems of farmers. The land in New Mexico was called "enchanted" in publicity releases, but its chief characteristic was erosion. The United States Soil Conservation Service was created by President Roosevelt in 1933, and a few representatives fanned out across New Mexico. Demonstrations and advice, however, could hardly heal centuries of neglect. During the late thirties, an agricultural agent in Taos estimated that proper conservation practices could double crops in his county. National New Dealers, plagued with surpluses already, adopted no comprehensive programs for soil erosion. Assistance to New Mexican farmers was minimal. Twenty-five members of Congress in 1935, including New Mexicans, asked Roosevelt for $150 million for soil work in their states. The White House politely said no. Forced into state action, the legislature adopted the Soil Conservation Act of 1937, which split New Mexico into districts with five supervisors each. Three were elected by the farmers, who then organized the district with regulations and voluntary assessment schemes. Farmers in the southeast corner first created the Mesa Soil Conservation District in early 1938. Unfortunately, the success of the Mesa District was limited. Although the plan seemed advanced for New Mexico, the worst aspects of decentralization prevailed. What the districts gained from individual initiative and personal contacts, they more than lost through amateur efforts and a lack of funds.[70]

Although New Dealers in New Mexico wanted a state government with new responsibilities, their efforts often reflected values of the business world. The success of the Tourist Bureau and failure of the State Planning Board are good illustrations. In 1925, a Publicity Bureau had received $4,735 to enhance the state's image. Even with Governor Dillon's support, the bureau died two years later. Critics, especially those with the barons' conception of government, argued that the bureau was a replacement for the obligations of private advertisers and an extravagant use of public money. The depression, however, brought demands from businesses and other groups for government action, and the increase in middle-class travelers made the Publicity Bureau attractive again. As a result, the 1935 legislature created a state Tourist Bureau. Its funding was sharply increased since its predecessor's days, and $41,219 was spent for advertising alone in 1936. Such activity appeared to pay well. In 1938, the peak year of the thirties, 1.6 million cars passed through New Mexico, bringing $80 million to the state.[71] The promotion of private enterprise through advertising thus became firmly established in state government.

The State Planning Board did not fare so well. Federal officials organized the board and funded it in 1934, but it came to the 1935 legislature for more support. Based on the assumption that uncoordinated economic activities by government and private enterprise had to stop, the State Planning Board had been drawing a model economy for New Mexico in cooperation with the National Resources Planning Board. Studies completed or planned by the state board involved mineral resources, power, scenic resources, economic planning, social planning with education studies, methods for unemployment relief, federal and state policies on major social issues, land utilization in New Mexico, land grants, and the Rio Grande basin. Its analysis of erosion patterns provided guidelines for the soil conservation activities of the United States Resettlement Administration.

Still, the legislature granted only $1,000 to the board. Critis complained that its membership consisted of such busy people as the governor and presidents of colleges and that its goals were vague and specific accomplishments few. But their major criticism centered on the "planning" thrust of its activities. Such a distrust of private efforts motivated by profit, they argued, could lead to centralized direction over the private sector that could become coercive and socialistic. "Under our current system, labor and capital may move freely from one industry to another, and the tendency is for an automatic balance . . . for goods and services to be supplied in the right proportions," said C. W. Carson, president of Albuquerque's First National Bank. "Economic planning would substitute for this system a central brain of vast wisdom, wholly disinterested, free from political influence, and able at all times to resist temptation."[72] Fears essentially of this sort insured that the State Planning Board would not play a determining role in New Mexico's economy and that government would do little to direct private enterprise.

It is clear that New Mexico profited enormously not only in terms of improvements for state government but in dollars because of the New Deal. Even in 1932, Herbert Hagerman "conservatively estimated that for each dollar we pay to Washington, Washington pays us ten dollars."[73] From a figure over $18 million in fiscal 1932, federal expenditures rose to at least $75 million annually after 1933. In July 1935, 28 percent of all New Mexicans were on relief, by far the highest percentage in the nation. Though other states in the Rocky Mountains received more money, their local governments were more generous in contributions for social programs. More than for other states in the region, the government in Washington assumed responsibility for the permanent employment and support of many New Mexicans.[74]

How can this largess be explained, especially in view of New Mexico's minimal impact on national politics? Only 423,317 people lived there in 1930; the state cast only three of Roosevelt's 479 electoral votes in 1932. New Mexico was remote from national life, with an ethnic composition and an economy unlike that of any other state. "It has remained behind the walls of the Rockies," said the *American Mercury* in 1934, "a state *in* but not *of* the United States."[75] New Mexico clearly had some extraordinary means for attracting the attention of New Dealers in faraway Washington. A key factor was political leadership in the state, notably U.S. Senator Bronson Cutting and Governor Clyde Tingley.

"God forbid!" wrote a Fort Sumner Republican to Holm Bursum in 1928, "that the Republican party should make the grievous mistake of sending an 'Independent' from New Mexico to the U.S. Senate to join . . . that bunch of Socialists whose highest ambition seems to be never to miss an opportunity to knife the Republican party and to annoy the Republican administration by their wild visionary schemes."[76] The "grievous mistake" was made that year as voters sent Cutting to the Senate with a large majority. Although Cutting had little loyalty to political parties ("Is he a Democrat or a Republican?" asked the Senate's sergeant-at-arms in one popular story), his attitude about government was consistent throughout his political career. In 1932, when FDR was "describing Hoover's spending as 'most reckless and extravagant,' " Cutting was urging deficit spending. When Democratic Congressman Dennis Chavez favored a 25 percent cut in federal expenditures during the 1932 campaign, Cutting countered that "what we do need is an immediate expansion of employment on a colossal scale by the Federal government." In the *Congressional Record* of the Seventy-third Congress, Cutting favored public ownership of all utilities. Later, he cited the failure to nationalize the banks during the crisis of March 1933 as "President Roosevelt's greatest mistake." In spite of the president's friendship since their days together at Groton, Cutting became "a searching progressive critic of the New Deal." He led a vigorous opposition in 1934 to the president's slash of veteran's benefits; he proposed a sweeping old-age pension plan; he advocated massive federal aid to education; he criticized Democrats for a lack of social reforms. "It is going to require a great deal more dealing of the new deal," he contended during the 1934 campaign. "There will have to be a great amount of additional public work done in order to provide employment and this will have to be done all over the country."[77] Cutting was convinced that the federal government was the only instrument powerful enough to energize the economy and bring political support for progressive causes.

The Roosevelt administration maintained an ambivalent attitude toward the enigmatic Cutting, but both impulses served to increase federal efforts in the senator's state. On the one hand, Cutting's political strength at home and his ability to dramatize major issues in ways unflattering to Democrats inclined the administration toward substantial support for the local party. Clyde Tingley made strikingly effective use of this impulse. On the other hand, Cutting was in many instances the leader of, and at all times beloved by, a small though powerful group of Senate progressives. George W. Norris, Robert LaFollette, Jr., Hiram Johnson, Gerald Nye, Edward Costigan, Robert Wagner, Huey Long (in his calmer moments), and a few others—all formed a forceful left wing in the upper chamber. Although sometimes critical of Roosevelt for not going far enough in restructuring the American economy, the great majority of their votes lined up behind administration programs. As the New Deal gradually lost its initial consensus in Congress and in 1934 there rose a "resurgence on the right,"[78] the president could ill afford to permanently alienate these progressives. This was especially true for the progressive Republicans, several of whom had become national symbols as intrepid defenders of "the little man." As a recognized member of this important Senate faction, Bronson Cutting's opinions were heeded more by White House strategists than many of those in the large, amorphous Democratic majority.[79]

Such a national role, however, undermined Cutting's program for reform at the state level. "By switching his Progressive party into 'fusion' with this or that party, [Cutting] virtually controlled every New Mexico election result from 1916 to his death," complained former governor George Curry.[80] But Cutting's control was negative; his money and influence could defeat opponents but rarely elect one of his own. Although Cutting strengthened his national position by taking his Progressive-Republican faction out of the GOP in 1932 in support of Roosevelt and Seligman, the 1933 legislature showed the weakness of the Progressives at the state level.[81] Conservative Republicans remained implacably hostile. "Under no circumstances should [he] be allowed to return [to the party]," wrote a leader to Richard Dillon. And though his position seemed so close to the liberal Democrats that Clinton Anderson urged Jim Farley in July 1934 to "put the support of the Democratic organization behind [Cutting]," Cutting remained a Republican.[82]

Holm Bursum, J. H. Harvey, Ed Safford, and Lem White—once

leading names in New Mexico politics—held a conference in the summer of 1934 with the exclusive purpose of blocking Cutting's senatorial renomination. The Simms family, upper-class New Mexicans who married into the Mark Hanna dynasty, joined in the bid to stop him. The barons, however, had lost their authority during the depression. Middle-ranking Republicans were quick to nominate the only one among them with a chance for victory. After his renomination by a Republican party dominated by Cutting Progressives, the senator began a monumental campaign against the strongest Democrat in New Mexico, Congressman Dennis Chavez.[83] The contest was a "scrambled egg," declared the *Albuquerque Tribune*: "We have the Republican party running on a Roosevelt platform. The Democratic party, though Rooseveltian, is attracting anti-Cutting Republicans. . . . Democrats here and there are espousing the cause of Senator Cutting."[84] Before the election, the two New Mexico members of the National Republican Committee endorsed Chavez. "Party lines have been wiped out," said *Collier's*, "everybody is either for or against Cutting."[85]

This remarkable campaign tells us much about Cutting and politics. The senator's strength went to the wellsprings of life in New Mexico. He had come to Santa Fe at the age of twenty-two, almost dead with tuberculosis. As he recovered and grew older, Cutting's noblesse oblige background led him to paternalist welfare ideas and concern for the underprivileged. His youthful shyness was countered by a penchant for shocking statements, by the compulsiveness of an eccentric. These assets enabled him to articulate the frustrations of New Mexicans whose anguish lay not in the depression so much as in their disadvantages in the American economy. After statehood, they had lived as a separate part of the nation. The country seemed luxurious and satisfied in ways denied New Mexicans during the twenties. The New Deal, especially Cutting's version of it, indicated government could change that.

To Spanish-speaking farmers in adobe villages, the wealthy Cutting became a symbol for American affluence and comfort—the new world they desired to embrace. On the other hand, his appreciation of New Mexico's heritage reinforced their love for the Spanish-dominated past. "Cutting's signed picture hung in many humble Spanish American homes," wrote Erna Fergusson. "Many young people went from such homes to school or college on scholarships administered from [his] own desk. Small churches were presented with altars or bells."[86] Cutting's wealth seemed to have a Latin conscience. For other New Mexicans

—workers, small storekeepers, poor farmers on the plains—Cutting offered alternatives to the bitterness that grew from years of hardship. Their suffering was caused by selfish manipulation of the economy by private interests, a manipulation ending in disaster in 1929. He told them that "there is a fundamental need of national planning" to assure each a fair income.[87]

With this emphasis, Cutting increasingly turned toward Washington after 1929 when the Labor Commission fight marked the end of Republican harmony in New Mexico. His state organization became choked with "cast-off politicians," more interested in money and power than ideology. Roosevelt pointed to "the crowd that [Cutting] traveled with in New Mexico" as the reason for administration support of Chavez. Cutting preferred cooperation with a lackluster conservative, Democratic Governor Seligman, if he could not dominate the Republicans. The vindication of his ideas during early New Deal days made him believe that he did not need the party organization. His confidence as a leading architect of the new government in America led him to overlook political concerns such as patronage. "He . . . has never asked me for anything," wrote Harold Ickes, surprised that the senator demanded no jobs for his support of Roosevelt.[88] Although Cutting's national stature brought attention to New Mexico, it has been apparent to several observers that it weakened the cause of the Progressives in state government.[89]

Cutting's popularity was tested to its limits in 1934. Chavez was a superb campaigner. Even though many Democrats supported Cutting, their state ticket was united whereas the Republican ticket was not. In effect, it was Cutting against the entire Democratic organization. Nevertheless, when the air cleared, Cutting was elected—the only man in his party to win statewide office between 1930 and 1950. Even though he won by only 2,284 votes, Cutting reversed strong Democratic trends. He carried the Spanish-American counties against one of their brothers. He carried the mining-labor counties. He made inroads into the solidly Democratic east side.[90] Speculation at once intensified that Cutting would be the Republican nominee to oppose Roosevelt in 1936. He was dictator of the state GOP and the only individual there who could compete in popularity with the New Deal.[91]

Bronson Murray Cutting, however, had enjoyed his last victory. In May 1935, he died in a plane disaster enroute to Washington. With him passed a possible coalition of New Mexico's poor under the Republican banner.[92] His bitter, personal criticism of party leaders had created divisions that would last twenty years. Progressives were no match for conservative Republicans after Cutting. The men who had been close to the Senator—Maurice Miera, Severino Trujillo, Brian B. Dunn, Herman and Jesus Baca—never regained influence. The 1936 election crushed the GOP; no state Democrat won by less than 20,000 votes.[93] Many Republicans, though, counted it a victory to be rid of their left wing. "We took care of the Progressive Republicans," Holm Bursum, Jr., boasted, "and God took care of Cutting."[94]

Death had also taken the Democratic leader in 1933. Unlike the Republican experience, the passing of Governor Arthur Seligman did not weaken the party's appeal. In fact, according to Jack Holmes, it allowed full expression "to the forces seeking to achieve a new balance."[95] Among these forces since 1929 had been the Spanish-American and Anglo workers' struggle for a political voice. Since the depression ruined the right wing in New Mexico, the real battles shifted leftward toward assistance for these "forgotten New Mexicans." Because of the federal emergency measures, state political issues became less important during the first thousand days of the New Deal. Forced into this bizarre situation was Seligman's lieutenant governor, Andrew W. Hockenhull, a friendly conservative from the plains along the Texas border. William Keleher, a contemporary in politics, suggests that Hockenhull did not want to be governor, and this sentiment surely increased during the confusion of the first New Deal years. "Andy," as Democrats called him affectionately, was glad to leave the governor's office on 1 January 1935.[96]

The man who moved into that office was a new type of politician, responsive to changes wrought by the depression and representative of "the forces seeking to achieve a new balance." Clyde K. Tingley had been born near London, Ohio. He had worked as a locomotive fireman, a machinist, and in a small motor company before coming to New Mexico. Having married into wealth, Tingley decided upon a political career. He was first elected to the Albuquerque City Commission in 1922 and soon came to be known as "Mr. Mayor." "Albuquerque has a one man form of government—Tingley," laughed the Herald in 1924. Long before the New Deal, Tingley became famous for his pragmatic politics, his grand visions, and his love of large projects. As "Mayor" he constructed the Albuquerque zoo, the Rio Grande baseball park, Tingley Beach, the West Mesa airport, and purchased much land for recreational parks.[97]

Raised in the working class, he had a crude though good nature. Talking politics among city workers or chewing and puffing cigars behind the commission table, Tingley had the brash confidence of an urban boss. "Tingley was a rough diamond," Albuquerque's A. R. Hebenstreit said, "but his very crudities attracted men." The governor became notorious for a simple honesty with friends and brutal abuse for enemies. "Tingley liked to hire and fire employees," Keleher recalls in his memoirs. "Nothing gave him more pleasure than to give a deserving politician a job. Few things gave him more satisfaction than firing a man he considered disloyal to him personally or politically."[98]

Above all, the tenth governor liked action. "He never read a book completely" and dismissed the barons' style of formal speeches and pleasantries. "I want the ain't vote," he declared in 1934, "and I ain't going to quit saying ain't." Tingley relished the back-room talk of politicians hungry for patronage and willing to bend his way for it. Here lay the immediate appeal of his New Deal:

> As he saw it, Washington was at long last appropriating money for projects which he could understand: making money available to put men back to work; and putting to practical use the upper echelon philosophy of bulk vote getting. Plans, specifications, blue prints, as Tingley well knew, could quickly be transformed into PWA and WPA projects.[99]

Believing that New Mexico votes could best be found in Washington, Tingley made twenty-three trips to see Roosevelt. Having accompanied the governor on one of these, A. T. Hannett recalled that "Tingley was at his best during the audience with Hopkins. His diamond in the rough approach was far more effective than mine." According to Senator Clinton Anderson, Tingley amused Roosevelt with his violence to the English language. "The President got a kick out of him," Anderson told Erna Fergusson, "and tolerated some abuses just because he was such a strange and odd person."[100]

Tingley's attitudes caused a great shift in power to the state's executive branch. Legislators, party bosses, and baron financiers had dominated government until the New Deal. In 1935, Tingley had "a firm grip at all times" over the House and Senate. Proposals to increase his authority studded Tingley's address to the Legislature. He asked for (and received) the right to classify all state employees and fix their salary and hours, and for a powerful Bureau of Revenue, appointed by the governor, with authority for all tax collection. "It is probable that few executives in the public service in this country are invested with such extensive powers," concluded the *New Mexico Tax Bulletin*.[101] In spite of opposition from most Democratic leaders, Tingley was powerful enough by 1937 to persuade legislators to pass a constitutional amendment allowing him to run for a third term, though voters later disapproved.[102]

Another reason for Tingley's strength was his role as intermediary between the public and the federal government. Early in 1935, he announced that "no one will go hungry in New Mexico during my Administration." Because of his aggressive use of federal programs, Tingley was able to break through the helplessness of his predecessors. When Mrs. Josie Driver, whose property had been destroyed in a flood near Roswell, appealed to the governor as a last resort, Tingley saw that the Federal Disaster Loan Corporation would help. His pressure on Senator Carl Hatch in June 1937 sent CCC workers to Fort Sumner after another flood. "This rainy season has been the most critical that [the town of] Hatch has faced since 1921," wrote J. H. McLaughlin for the Chamber of Commerce. "However, due to your cooperation, the assistance of the ERA and the CCC, have placed us in some degree of safety."[103]

When federal officials were slow to act, Tingley or some high official would appear on the scene to comfort citizens and recommend action. In short, Tingley used the strategy of cutting through bureaucracies and tight budgets to help citizens directly. To him the depression was psychological, not economic. It could be reversed by immediate results. If a budget deficit or some other problem cropped up, Tingley was certain that an administrator somewhere could juggle it out of existence. He wanted the gratitude of his constituents, not the pleasures of an orderly administration. Tingley, then, concentrated on gaining federal programs for New Mexicans and became a symbol for democratic action in time of need.

The federal programs, however, had their more sordid side. Tingley and the Democrats used them against their enemies at every opportunity. Soon after his inauguration, Tingley received a list of the political activities of every state employee during the 1934 campaign. The Democrats then began employment practices far more partisan than those before the Tingley administration. "During the period 1935–40," Jack Holmes observed, "one could normally find on the roster of state officers and employees [of the federal programs] from a third to a half of the county chairmen and a considerably larger number of precinct chairmen and other party operatives whose activities or connections assured them of state employment."[104] In October 1938, the works program broke into what *Time* called "the hottest WPA scandal of the year." Seventy-three employees were indicted by an Albuquerque grand jury for the creation of a political machine that shook down foremen and assigned partisan duties to workers. Heading the list of accused was Fred G. Healy, former WPA administrator in New Mexico. Also charged were the son-in-law of U.S. Senator Dennis Chavez and his sister, cousin, nephew, and secretary. Although only five were convicted, there was little doubt that the works program was honeycombed with profiteers. "It is too apparent," read the grand jury's report, "that too many persons seeking personal and political gains have violated legal and moral codes."[105]

Although Tingley served only four years in the governor's office, he must be considered the most important New Mexico Democrat in the New Deal years. It was under his leadership that the new patterns of politics were inaugurated. Immediate action, not long-range planning, was Tingley's strength. It was his emphasis on the practical needs of New Mexicans and on tangible government that cemented local support for the Democratic party. His ability to attract federal programs set high standards for future politicians. He was among the first to represent the urban areas of the state. He was the first governor to support labor's right to collective bargaining. After a disturbance at Dawson in 1935, Frank Hefferly, an official of the United Mine Workers, noted that "for the first time in history so far as I recall, during labor troubles in New Mexico, under the administration of Governor Clyde Tingley, the state militia was not utilized against the mine workers and labor."[106]

Because of these developments and the national New Deal, the Democrats received massive majorities from eastern New Mexico workers and Spanish-Americans in the river valleys. Nevertheless, few pieces of positive legislation were passed to assist either group. Organized labor had to rely on federal assistance. The state Labor Commission became so inactive that the Santa Fe County clerk complained to Tingley that it had not met for nine months though the law imposed quarterly sessions. "Political parties in New Mexico have a poor record for fulfillment of labor pledges," concluded two historians during the forties. "The Legislature [has not been] interested in adequate labor legislation," was the assessment of economist Nathaniel Wollman.[107] The prolabor policies of the national administration drew workers into the Democratic column, and state Democrats closely identified themselves with the New Deal.

At the same time, Tingley had a gruff disdain for most Spanish-speaking citizens. "He insulted me by insulting my people when he said that none of mine were competent for white collar work in FERA offices," a Spanish-American legislator told Jack Holmes."[108] Little was done by the legislature for farmers in northern New Mexico or for improved educational facilities for Spanish-speaking citizens. Again, it was the national New Deal and, more important, the death of Bronson Cutting that made Democrats out of most Spanish-Americans.[109] These events and a rush of Anglos into eastern New Mexico convinced Democratic leaders that they could weaken the practice of ethnic politics that had prevailed since statehood. Governor Tingley called the legislature into special session on 22 August 1938. At the top of the agenda was a direct-primary bill that would replace the convention system for state nominations. Spanish-American leaders overwhelmingly opposed the change because their people had been guaranteed influence and, indeed, a number of offices each election in the conventions. It was easy to see the day when their fortunes would be decided by great numbers of Anglos. In spite of their opposition, the direct primary was adopted—certainly a symbolic burial of the old politics in New Mexico. The New Deal had ended the hold of the Republicans on Spanish-Americans, but they received a smaller role in politics in return.[110]

The New Deal did little to strengthen the economic structure of New Mexico. Per capita income remained two-thirds of the national average, and 51.5 percent of the rural population earned less than $100 during 1938. Total cash receipts from farm marketings in 1939 were $50,002,000, down $18 million from 1929. The impact of the Agricultural Adjustment Administration was mixed. Only cotton farmers, the main target of the AAA in New Mexico, benefitted substantially from federal efforts. Sixteen hundred cotton farmers signed contracts in 1933 and received $700,000 for plowing up 30,395 acres, one-fourth of their total acreage. During the 1933–34 season, New Mexicans grew 17,913 bales, a fraction of the 1928–32 average yield of 91,300 bales. Stringent federal controls over other domestic cotton farmers along with a severe drought drove the market price per bale from $37.42 in 1934 to $85.00 by 1935. Other than for cotton, federal programs seemed to have little influence on prices or farm values. The value of wheat, corn, and hogs under contract actually fell between 1933 and 1934. The average farm nationally was worth $31.16 per acre in 1935, almost eight times the value in New Mexico. Nor did federal payments constitute a major portion of income for many farmers. For example, the average gross receipts from the 63 row-crop farms in Curry County was $1,334 during 1934. AAA contracts provided only $133 of this income. "One of the most important accomplishments of the

AAA in New Mexico," a federal administrator concluded in the face of continuing low prices, "has been to show farmers how to organize and work together."[111]

The rest of the economy similarly remained depressed. Mining industries continued their decline. Urban employment fell by 17 percent during the recession of 1937–38. Oil, tourists, and federal employment kept the economy alive in the thirties and would for many years thereafter. New Mexico continued as an economic colony of the United States, providing raw materials and slim markets in return for government support.[112]

Though it did not transform the state economically, the New Deal had several effects on other areas of life in New Mexico. The left and right wings of the Republican party, so strong in 1929, were eliminated as political forces by 1936. The right was discredited by the depression; the left was destroyed by Cutting's disregard for the Republican organization and his untimely death. Although having almost no state program or ideology, the Democrats emerged triumphant through their political use of federal monies. If Bronson Cutting was the philosopher-king of the New Deal in New Mexico, Clyde Tingley was its practical engineer. We have been told by Roosevelt admirers that the success of the New Deal swept away irrelevant theories, economic dictums, and Republican detachment in favor of an emphasis on the daily lives of people, on action without excuses, and on politics as a helping hand to needy friends. Tingley and the Democrats understood well this kind of New Deal.

State government also shifted directions. The New Deal was a response to the problems of an industrial society that had made existing governments archaic. In spite of rhetoric in the twenties from Richard Dillon that state government should be run by "the principles of business," this was never the case if he meant efficient management and intelligent planning. No private corporation could have survived if its affairs were as haphazard as those of the state of New Mexico. The scant resources from ill-conceived taxes drained into dozens of unproductive outlets. Public officials had little concern about the performance of state employees. Formal job training was nonexistent. For even the highest positions, the important qualifications were political activity and mindless obedience to the prevailing faction. Public opinion concluded that government was peripheral to the main interests of society and warranted attention only when collecting taxes. State government was rarely a positive force in affairs.[113] As a result, talented aspirants were undoubtedly discouraged by the artificial quality of public life during the New Era twenties.

The New Deal, of course, changed many of these characteristics. Between 1935 and 1938, we find work projects and large social programs characteristic of the modern, federal government in New Mexico. Increasingly, though, the state was encouraged to assume welfare burdens and to adapt many of the federal efforts to its own needs. Emergency measures of the first New Deal years expanded many state agencies, giving them enormous amounts of money in comparison with state support. For the first time, these agencies played a crucial role in the solution of pervasive social problems. National administrators had tried to keep the relief structure nonpartisan as it grew up overnight. They encouraged professionalism and public relations to improve the public's mood. In early 1935, the New Deal began to focus on structural changes at the state level. The Great Depression had shown the inadequacy of state government in respect to size, organization, and activities. The years between 1935 and 1938 resulted in more contracts between federal officials and state politicians. Local ideas influenced national policies in ways they never did before 1935. In return, legislators were pressured into some reforms at the state level and adopted several on their own. The problem of the national administration was to centralize authority enough on the state level so that officials there could organize the security and welfare programs needed in the depression's wake. State agencies that had existed before the depression were quite successful in maturing into professional services. Entirely new state programs usually failed or were discontinued.

Because the federal government made a long-range commitment to employ many New Mexicans and state government became a vital part of the nation's antidepression efforts, public affairs became the center of attention and discussion. Political activity reached an all-time high as eighty percent of New Mexico's eligibles voted in 1936.[114] Social welfare and economic security suddenly loomed as major concerns for government, although the private sector retained most of its prerogatives. Although it did little to ancitipate new situations or solve fundamental economic problems, the New Deal created a federal and state government to meet the immediate tragedies of the Great Depression.

---

1. *Santa Fe New Mexican*, 8 November 1932.

2. Ernestine Evans, *New Mexico Election Returns, 1911–69* (Santa Fe, 1969), unpaged; Jack Holmes, *Politics in New Mexico* (Albuquerque, 1967), pp. 198–218; Dwight Ramsay, "A Statistical Survey of the Voting Behavior in New Mexico" (M.A. thesis, University of New Mexico, 1952), pp.

13, 46–47; Charles B. Judah, *The Republican Party in New Mexico*, Division of Government Research Bulletin, No. 20 (University of New Mexico, 1949), p. 2.

3. Herbert T. Hoover, "History of the Republican Party in New Mexico" (Ph.D. diss., University of Oklahoma, 1966), pp. 137–59; Holmes, *Politics in New Mexico*, p. 159; Ramsay, "Statistical Survey of Voting," p. 3.

4. John T. Russell, "New Mexico: A Problem of Parochialism in Transition," *American Political Science Review* 30 (1930): 286; Alfred G. Cordova, "Octaviano Ambrosio Larrazolo, the Prophet of Transition in New Mexico: An Analysis of his Political Life" (M.A. thesis, University of New Mexico, 1950), pp. 69–71, 89; Paul Walter, "Octaviano A. Larrazolo," *New Mexico Historical Review* 7 (1932): 97–99; the quotation is from Hoover, "The Republican Party," p. 152. "Governors were to execute that policy which was already formed," Jack Holmes contends in *Politics in New Mexico* (p. 180), "and they were to consult with the Old Guard when it was not."

5. Holmes, *Politics in New Mexico*, pp. 145–74; Ralph E. Twitchell, *The Leading Facts of New Mexican History*, 5 vols. (Cedar Rapids, Iowa, 1912–17), 5:412; H. B. Hening, ed., *George Curry, 1861–1947, An Autobiography* (Albuquerque, 1958), pp. 284–310; Clinton P. Anderson and Milton Viorst, *Outsider in the Senate* (New York, 1970), pp. 11–13; Robert Thompson and Charles B. Judah, *Arthur T. Hannett: Governor of New Mexico*, Division of Government Research Bulletin, No. 26 (University of New Mexico, 1950), p. 8.

6. Arthur T. Hannett, *Sagebrush Lawyer* (New York, 1964), p. 128.

7. Hoover, "History of the Republican Party," pp. 121–22; Twitchell, *Leading Facts of New Mexican History*, 5:413 n. 1107.

8. Holmes, *Politics in New Mexico*, pp. 148–53, 187–97; Thomas C. Donnelly, *Government of New Mexico* (Albuquerque, 1947), p. 115. A good statement about the role of government by a "baron" appears in Reel One, No. 498, Albert Bacon Fall Papers (Zimmerman Library Archives, University of New Mexico).

9. Richard C. Dillon, *Budget Presented to the Eighth Legislature* (Santa Fe, 1927); *New Mexico Tax Bulletin*, June 1927, p. 1, May, 1928, p. 5; *New Mexico Highway Journal* 5 (1927): 1; Ralph Edgel, "New Mexico Population," *New Mexico Business*, October 1958, p. 8; Ross Calvin and Paul Walter, *The Population of New Mexico*, Division of Government Research Bulletin, No. 10 (University of New Mexico, 1947), p. 13; James B. Swayne, "A Survey of the Economic, Political and Legal Aspects of the Labor Problem in New Mexico" (M.A. thesis, University of New Mexico, 1936), p. 98; R. Clyde White, *Administration of Public Welfare* (Dallas, 1940), p. 72; Helen B. Ellis, *Public Welfare Problems in New Mexico*, Division of Government Research Bulletin, No. 18 (University of New Mexico, 1948), p. 9; New Mexico Child Welfare Service, *Bulletin #1* (Santa Fe, 1921); Margaret Reeves, *Child Welfare News*, 7 January 1927, unpaged; Margaret Reeves to Richard Dillon, 19 May 1928; Dillon to Margaret Ruoff, 7 May 1928, Dillon Papers (Zimmerman Library Archives, University of New Mexico); Reginald J. Eyre, "The Origin of Independent Offices and Agencies of the State of New Mexico" (M.A. thesis, University of New Mexico, 1956), pp. 7–8; Robert W. Larson, *New Mexico's Quest for Statehood, 1846–1912* (Albuquerque, 1968), pp. 272–86.

10. *Santa Fe New Mexican*, 20 May 1927; "Address to Various Unions," 21 August 1928, file marked "Political Speeches," Dillon Papers; Ellis A. Davis, ed., *The Historical Encyclopedia of New Mexico* (Albuquerque, 1945), p. 167; Charles B. Judah, *Governor Richard C. Dillon: A Study in New Mexico Politics*, Division of Government Research Bulletin, No. 19 (University of New Mexico, 1948), pp. 27, 37; Vorley M. Rexroad, "The Two Administrations of Governor Richard Dillon" (M.A. thesis, University of New Mexico, 1947); Dillon to James Mussatti, 1 August 1927, Dillon Papers; *New Mexico State Tribune*, 27 October, 1927.

11. A. E. James, "Report on the Fiscal Policies of New Mexico," *New Mexico Tax Bulletin* 8 (1929): 26.

12. *Santa Fe New Mexican*, 19 October 1928; U.S. Treasury, Bureau of Internal Revenue, *Statistics of Income for 1928* (Washington, D.C., 1930), pp. 72, 175, 314; *Statistics of Income for 1926* (Washington, D.C. 1928), p.314; *New Mexico Tax Bulletin 13* (1934): 59–60, 17 (1938): 73; 10 (1931): 66; O. V. Wells, "Agriculture in New Mexico," in Frederick C. Irion, ed., *New Mexico and Its Natural Resources*, Division of Government Research Bulletin, No. 55 (University of New Mexico, 1959), p. 62; "Address Delivered at the Valmora Reception . . . in Chicago," 20 November 1929, Dillon Papers.

13. Gustav L. Seligmann, Jr., "The Political Career of Bronson Cutting" (Ph.D. diss., University of Arizona, 1967), pp. 17–39; His Friends and Comrades in New Mexico, *Bronson Cutting, 1888–1935, U.S. Senator* (Santa Fe, 1939), pp. 18–19; Arthur Schlesinger, Jr., *The Politics of Upheaval* (Boston, Mass., 1960), p. 139; William Keleher, *Memoirs, 1892-1969; A New Mexico Item* (Santa Fe, 1969), pp. 165–66. For the primary accounts of Cutting on which I base my summary of his views: Frederick R. Barkley, "Bronson Cutting: Blue-Blooded Buccanneer," in Ray Tucker and Frederick R. Barkley, *Sons of the Wild Jackass* (Boston, 1932), pp. 196–229; Haniel Long, *Pinon Country* (New York, 1941), pp. 138–45; Owen P. White, "Cutting Free," *Collier's*, 27 October 1934, p. 24; "Correspondence-Bronson Cutting," a file in the Miguel A. Otero Papers (Zimmerman Library Archives, University of New Mexico).

14. Donald C. Rider, *Municipal Development in New Mexico*, Division of Government Research Bulletin, No. 66 (University of New Mexico, 1964), p. 3; Paul Walter, "Rural-Urban Migration in New Mexico," *New Mexico Business Review* 8 (1939): 132; *New Mexico Tax Bulletin* 10 (1931): 95–96; Swayne, "The Labor Problem in New Mexico," p. 8; J. E. Seyfried, "Illiteracy Trends in New Mexico," *University of New Mexico Bulletin*, Vol. 8, No. 1 (15 March 1934), pp. 32–36. Illiteracy, Seyfried said, "in the United States Census Reports . . . was defined as inability to write and to read in any language" (p. 7). New Mexico would have had at least a 40 percent illteracy rate if English alone had been the criterion.

15. Francis McGarity, "Bronston Cutting, Senator from New Mexico" (M.A. thesis, Columbia University, 1934), p. 40.

16. "I have been a Republican and hope that I always shall be one." From Prospero S. Baca, *Book of Personal Verses*, copied by T. M. Pearce, Box 174 (Zimmerman Library Archives, University of New Mexico). John T. Russell, "Racial Groups in the New Mexico Legislature," *Annals of the American Academy of Political and Social Sciences* 195 (1938): 70.

17. Judah, *Governor Richard Dillon*, p. 24; Charles J. Bayard, "The Southern Colorado Coal Strike of 1927–8 and New Mexico's Preventative Measures" (M.A. thesis, University of New Mexico, 1949), p. 82; *New Mexico State Tribune*, 27 October 1927; *Santa Fe New Mexican*, 1 January 1929; *New Mexico Blue Book* (Santa Fe, 1929), pp. 43–44; *New Mexico Tax Bulletin* 8 (1929): 57–58, 61–63, 68; Richard C. Dillon, *Message . . . to the Ninth Legislature* (Santa Fe, 1929), unpaged; Swayne, "The Labor Problem in New Mexico," pp. 93–98; Rexroad, "Two Administrations of Dillon," pp. 136–37. For unfavorable views of Cutting's methods: Hannett, *Sagebrush Lawyer*, pp. 132–57, 165–76; Robert G. Thompson, "The Administration of Governor Arthur T. Hannett" (M.A. thesis, University of New Mexico, 1949), p. 133.

18. Hoover, "Republican Party in New Mexico," p. 158.

19. Judan, *Governor Richard Dillon*, p. 28. For details, see Rexroad, "Two Administrations of Dillon," pp. 110–23, 131–36; Andrea A. Parker, "Arthur Seligman and Bronson Cutting: Coalition Government in New Mexico, 1930–3" (M.A. thesis, University of New Mexico, 1969), pp. 9, 29; Warren Beck, *New Mexico: A History of Four Centuries* (Norman, Okla., 1962), pp. 310–12; *Albuquerque Journal*, 9 March 1929; Holmes, *Politics in New Mexico*, pp. 166–68.

20. E. E. Maes, "The Labor Movement in New Mexico," *New Mexico Business Review* 4 (1939): 139.

21. *New Mexico Tax Bulletin*, December 1928, p. 10; 10 (1931): 95–96; 13 (1934): 60; Thomas C. Donnelly, ed., *Rocky Mountain Politics* (Albuquerque, 1940), p. 225; R. F. Hare, "The Agricultural Industry in New Mexico," *New Mexico Tax Bulletin*, October 1928, p. 20; Frank D. Reeve, *History of New Mexico*, 3 vols. (New York, 1961), 2:227; Paul Beckett, *The Soil Conservation Problem in New Mexico*, Division of Government Research Bulletin, No. 2 (University of New Mexico, 1946), p. 14.

22. *New Mexico.Tax Bulletin* 10 (1931): 3, 121–24; 11 (1932): 75; 12 (1933): 27; 13 (1934): 60; Swayne, "The Labor Problem in New Mexico," p. 18; Y. S. Leong et al., *Technology, Employment, and Output per Man in Copper Mining*, WPA Report No. E-12 (Washington, D.C., 1940), p. 222; F. G. Tryon et al., *Coal: Employment and Related Statistics*, WPA Report No. E-4 (Philadelphia, 1937), p. 1.

23. William J. Parrish, *The Charles Ilfeld Company: A Study of the Rise and Decline of Mercantile Capitalism in New Mexico* (Cambridge, Mass., 1961), p. 253.

24. Herbert J. Hagerman, "How the Depression Is Affecting New Mexico," *New Mexico Tax Bulletin* 10 (1931): 122.

25. Margaret Reeves to Arthur Seligman, 15 June 1932; Minutes of the State Board of Public Welfare, 10 March 1932; Citizens of Lumberton, A Petition Drawn by Father T. Meyer, to Seligman, 26 January 1931, Governor Arthur Seligman Papers (New Mexico State Archives and Records Center, Santa Fe).

26. *Santa Fe New Mexican*, 9 August 1932. An overview of the entire tax situation at this time appears in Rupert F. Asplund, "Tax Crisis in New Mexico," *New Mexico Business Review* 2 (1933): 4–5.

27. John Webb and Malcom Brown, *Migrant Families*, WPA Research Monograph No. 18 (Washington, D.C., 1938), p. 152; Margaret Reeves to Seligman, 26 January 1931; Report . . . filed by Annida Slaves, field representative of the Child Welfare Service, "Dept. of Public Welfare" file; "Confidential Report" of the Executive Conference of Relief and Welfare Representatives in Los Angeles, 20 December 1931, Arthur Seligman Papers.

28. Owen P. White, "Membership in Both Clubs," *American Mercury* 25 (1932): 187–88; Parker, "Arthur Seligman and Bronson Cutting," pp. 18, 55; Edward Lahart, "The Career of Dennis Chavez as a Member of Congress, 1930–4" (M.A. thesis, University of New Mexico, 1958), p. 30; Jonathan R. Cunningham, "Bronson Cutting" (M.A. thesis, University of New Mexico, 1940), pp. 165–66. The 1930 Democratic platform contained little that was controversial: see *Santa Fe New Mexican*, 19 September 1930.

29. Winnifred Berninghaus of Taos to Andrew Hockenhull, 21 November 1933, Governor Hockenhull Papers (New Mexico State Archives and Records Center).

30. Arthur Seligman, *Message . . . to the Tenth Legislature* (Santa Fe, 1931), pp. 11–12; Rupert F. Asplund and Albert K. Nohl, *New Mexico's Tax Structure*, Division of Government Research Bulletin, No. 4 (University of New México, 1946), pp. 6, 12–14; *New Mexico Tax Bulletin* 10 (1931): 26-30; 12 (1933): 32; 13 (1934): 161.

31. Holmes, *Politics in New Mexico*, pp. 169–70; Davis, *Historical Encyclopedia of New Mexico*, p. 167; Parker, "Arthur Seligman and Bronson Cutting," p. 6; Paul Walter, "Necrology: Arthur Seligman," *New Mexico Historical Review* 7 (1933): 311.

32. Seligman, *Message to the Eleventh Legislature* (Santa Fe, 1933), unpaged; Parker, "Arthur Seligman and Bronson Cutting," p. 78. Seligman's attitudes are well expressed in a letter to Harold Hurd, 13 September 1932, Seligman Papers. For the helplessness of the Democratic state administrations: J. L. Burkholder, "Bringing National Relief to New Mexico," *New Mexico Business Review* 2 (1933): 10–11.

33. Swayne, "The Labor Problem in New Mexico," pp. 52–55; Holmes, *Politics in New Mexico*, pp. 168–69; Asplund and Nohl, *New Mexico's Tax Structure*, pp. 6, 19.

34. *Santa Fe New Mexican*, 13 March 1933; J. P. Jones, "Possibilities of Revenue from an Income Tax Levy for New Mexico," *New Mexico Business Review* 1 (1932): 140–43; J. F. Zimmermann, "Taxation and Governmental Reorganization for New Mexico," ibid., 3 (1934): 11–43; *New Mexico Tax Bulletin* 12 (1933): 39–41, 46.

35. Parker, "Arthur Seligman and Bronson Cutting," p. 29.

36. *Raton* (N.M.) *Range*, 23 June 1932; Anderson and Viorst, *Outsider in the Senate*, p. 26.

37. *New Mexico Tax Bulletin* 10 (1931): 84; Burkholder, "Bringing National Relief," pp. 10–11.

38. Donnelly, *Government of New Mexico*, p. 148; Ernest K. Lindley, *The Roosevelt Revolution: The First Phase* (New York, 1933), pp. 15–16; *New Mexico Health Officer*, January 1932, p. 3; B. Tober, "Cost of County Health Work," ibid., July 1932, p. 1; "Passing Thoughts on Budgets as They Pass," ibid., July 1932, p. 1; Margaret Reeves, "Federal Relief in New Mexico," *New Mexico Tax Bulletin* 13 (1933): 105–9.

39. Reeves, "Federal Relief in New Mexico," p. 107; Arthur E. Burns, "The Federal Emergency Relief Administration," *Municipal Yearbook, 1937* (Chicago, 1937), p. 393; FERA, *Monthly Report*, 22 May 1933 to 30 June 1933, p. 17, 1 January to 31 January 1934, p. 30; Erna Fergusson, "Clyde Tingley," an incomplete and unpublished manuscript, p. 127, Erna Fergusson Papers (Zimmerman Library Archives, University of New Mexico).

40. "The Administration of Federal Relief in New Mexico," *New Mexico Tax Bulletin* 13 (1934): 101–2; Corrington Gill, "The Civil Works Administration," *Municipal Yearbook, 1937*, p. 426; Arthur E. Burns and Edward A. Williams, *Federal Work, Security, and Relief Programs*, WPA Research Monograph, No. 24 (Washington, D.C., 1941), p. 136; Harry Hopkins, *An Appraisal of the Results of the Works Progress Administration* (Washington, D.C., 1938), p. 4. One of the problems of studying these early New Deal days comes in the discrepancy in statistics for federal grants. The first three citations in this footnote all list different figures for the CWA expenditure. In the text, I have used the Burns and Williams figure ($2,356,221) for the federal share because a search of local budgets for this fiscal year revealed some contributions that force the CWA's total upward and are probably reflected in the higher figures.

41. Reeves, "Federal Relief in New Mexico," p. 107; "Administration of Federal Relief in New Mexico," pp. 101–2.

42. Works Progress Administration, *Urban Workers on Relief*, WPA Research Monograph, No. 4, 2 vols. (Washington, D.C., 1936), 2: 84. Albuquerque had the lowest median age for men on relief of the 79 cities and more unskilled workers than the national average (pp. 2:28, 34, 43, 88); Enid Baird and Hugh P. Brinton, *Average General Relief Benefits, 1933–8* (Washington, D.C., 1940), p. 77.

43. Arthur E. Burns and Peyton Kerr, "Survey of Work-Relief Wage Policies," *American Economic Review 28* (1937): 713-17. The minutes of the State Board of Public Welfare, 13 February 1934, Hockenhull Papers, has a good discussion of the relationship between relief agencies.

44. FERA, *New Mexico Relief Bulletin*, 14 June 1934, p. 1, 23 August 1934, p. 1; Ed Swope to Hockenhull, 8 December 1933 until 15 January 1934; Rio Arriba Democrats to Hockenhull, undated, in "Relief," 1934" file, Hockenhull Papers.

45. FERA, *New Mexico Relief Bulletin*, 24 January 1935, pp. 1–2; Genevieve T. Chavez to Clyde Tingley, 9 February 1935, Governor Tingley Papers (New Mexico State Archives and Records Center). Mrs. D. Chavez to Burnham Miller, 13 March 1935, Tingley Papers, discusses another removal of evidence from the state relief offices. On "federalizing" the relief structure: Burns and Williams, *Federal Work, Security and Relief Programs*, p. 56. n. 6.

46. John D. Clark, "Discussion of Bott's Article on the Taylor Grazing Act," *New Mexico Business Review 5* (1936): 19; C. M. Botts, "The Taylor Grazing Act," ibid., p. 17; H. S. Kent, "The Agricultural Situation," ibid., 4 (1935): 45–46. For descriptions of the lack of communication between local officials and those in Washington, see: FERA, *New Mexico Relief Bulletin*, 7 June 1934, p. 2; *New Mexico Bulletin for the WPA*, Fall 1935, p. 12.

47. "Report from Riley Mapes," State Board of Public Welfare, 17 March 1934; Mapes to Morris Lewis, 20 March 1934, Hockenhull Papers; WPA, *Bulletin*, 15 December 1935, p. 6.

48. Eshrev Shevky, "Rural Rehabilitation in New Mexico," *New Mexico Business Review* 5 (1936): 6–9. Eighty percent of the 3,384 clients receiving "loans" in New Mexico were expected not to pay the money back. Also see WPA, *Report on the Works Program*, p. 46.

49. George I. Sanchez, *Forgotten People: A Study of New Mexico* (Albuquerque, 1940), pp. 35, 84; *New Mexico Tax Bulletin* 8 (1929): 84.

50. *New Mexico Tax Bulletin* 10 (1931): 135; "The Late Springer," ibid., 12 (1933): 77; Parker, "Arthur Seligman and Bronson Cutting," p. 83; *New Mexico Highway Journal*, January 1927, p. 39; *New Mexico Magazine*, February 1934, p. 36; Charles Brice to Dillon, 21 April 1928, Dillon Papers.

51. *Albuquerque Journal*, 28 March 1932; J. D. Macy, "New Mexico's Recovery Road Program," *New Mexico Magazine*, July 1933, pp. 14–15. *New Mexico Tax Bulletin* 14 (1935): 3, 34; V. O. Key, *Administration of Federal Grants to States* (Chicago, 1937), p. 327. Monthly statistics appear in the *New Mexico Magazine* for all the New Deal years. See list of political activities of state employees, anonymously authored, in file "state employees," Tingley Papers.

52. C. B. Wivel, "The Professionalization of Public Service," *New Mexico Business Review* 8 (1939): 62. Another critique of public service appears in Frederick C. Irion, "New Mexico: The Political State," in Frank Jonas, ed., *Western Politics* (Salt Lake City, 1961), p. 245.

53. *New Mexico Health Officer*, August 1934, p. 7; J. Rosslyn Earp, "Ninth Biennial Report, 1935–6," *New Mexico Health Officer*, December 1936, p. 64; FERA, *New Mexico Relief Bulletin*, 4 April 1934, p. 2, 14 April 1934, p. 1, 14 May 1934, pp. 1–2.

54. According to the list of state employees and their political activities given to Governor Tingley in early 1935 (see note 51 above), the Bureau of Child Welfare was among the least cooperative. "Does not cooperate with Democratic Party," the author asserted about Margaret Reeves. "Judge from Director [i.e., Reeves]" is written below each other name. Although Tingley replaced Reeves in the relief shuffle of 1935, it was remarkable that she had remained for the first two years of the New Deal.

55. Reeves to Clinton P. Anderson, 10 April 1934; Reeves to Hockenhull, 5 July 1934; Hockenhull to each county commission, 18 September 1934; Hockenhull to Byron O. Beall, 29 September 1934, Hockenhull Papers; Key, *Administration of Federal Grants to States*, p. 352. Reluctance of legislators to spend money for relief or social services is pointed out in Henry Watters to Hockenhull, 20 April 1934, Hockenhull Papers.

56. William E. Leuchtenburg, *Franklin D. Roosevelt and the New Deal, 1932-1940* (New York, 1963), pp. 65–69, 77, 84–85, 91–94.

57. P. G. Beck and M. C. Forster, *Six Rural Problem Areas—Relief, Resources, and Rehabilitation*, FERA Research Monograph No. 1 (Washington, D.C., 1935), p. 104.

58. Franklin D. Roosevelt, "Annual Message from the President to the Congress," 74th Cong., 1st sess., January 1935, *House Misc. Doc. 1*, pp. 1–8. The implications of these changes are discussed in Burns and Williams, *Federal Work, Security, and Relief Programs*, p. 51.

59. Harry L. Hopkins, *Inventory: An Appraisal of the Results of the Works Progress Administration* (Washington, D.C., 1938), p. 58; *WPA Bulletin for New Mexico*, March 1936, pp. 1, 25; Emerson Ross, "The Works Progress Administration," *Municipal Yearbook, 1937*, pp. 438, 446; Nathaniel Wollman, *An Appraisal of New Mexico Labor Legislation*, Division of Government Research Bulletin, No. 24 (University of New Mexico, 1950), p. 51; Burns and Williams, *Federal Work, Security, and Relief Programs*, pp. 23, 38–39, 61–63; Burns and Kerr, "Survey of Work-Relief Wage Policies," pp. 713–21. Protests about WPA restrictions appear in Arthur McKinney to Clyde Tingley, 5 December 1935; "MASS MEETING HELD IN COURTHOUSE AT ROSWELL, NEW MEXICO," 24 March 1937, in "NMR&SA" file, Tingley Papers.

60. John A. Salmond, *The Civilian Conservation Corps, 1933–42: A New Deal Case Study* (Durham, N.C., 1967), p. 219; Tom L. Popejoy, "Functions and Purposes of the NYA," *New Mexico Business Review* 5 (1963): 82–86; WPA, *Employment on Work Projects in March, 1936* (Washington, D.C., 1936), p. 129; *National Emergency Council Newsletter*, 20 May 1937, p. 2.

61. Fay Guthrie, "Administration of the New Mexico Relief and Security Authority," *New Mexico Business Review* 6 (1937): 69.

62. Ibid., pp. 73–74. Harry Hopkins to Clyde Tingley, 15 January 1935, Tingley Papers; Irene Conrad, "The Bureau of Child Welfare," *New Mexico Health Officer*, December 1935, p. 3; FERA, *New Mexico Relief Bulletin*, 24 January 1935, p. 1; "New Mexico Relief and Security Authority," *New Mexico Tax Bulletin* 16 (1936): pp. 9–10. Tngley wrote many letters to county officials about the NMR&SA in its file for 1935, Tingley Papers.

63. *New Mexico Tax Bulletin* 14 (1935): 188-89; 15 (1936): 9, 132–33, Guthrie, "NMR&SA," p. 69; Rupert F. Asplund, "The Social Security Act and State Revenue," *New Mexico Business Review* 5 (1936): 107–13.

64. Robert C. Lowe, *State Public Welfare Legislation*, WPA Research Monograph, No. 20 (Washington, D.C., 1939), p. 215; Marietta Stevenson, *Public Welfare Administration* (New York, 1939), p. 313; Guthrie, "NMR&SA," pp. 74–75; Donnelly, *Government in New Mexico*, p. 149; *New Mexico Tax Bulletin* 17 (1938): 114–15, 143; "Dept. Public Welfare—District Conference Report," 30 July 1937, and D.P.W., "Relief Statistics, 1937," pp. 6–7, Tingley Papers.

65. Holmes, *Politics in New Mexico*, p. 204. Although the author is referring to the special session of 1934 and the regular one of 1935, the conclusion applies well to the next two sessions.

66. *New Mexico Tax Bulletin* 13 (1934): 66–67, 159–60; Vernon G. Sorrell, "Two Years of the Sales Tax in New Mexico," *New Mexico Business Review* 5 (1936): 184; Holmes, *Politics in New Mexico*, pp. 203–4.

67. Jack Campbell, "Problems of Oil and Gas Conservation in New Mexico," in Frederick C. Irion, ed., *New Mexico and Its Natural Resources*, Division of Government Research Bulletin, No. 55 (University of New Mexico, 1959), p. 43; *Laws of New Mexico*, 1935 (Santa Fe, 1935), chap. 72,

pp. 137–51. The file of the Oil Commission reveals many hearings and judgments issued during the late thirties. All too often, however, the cases seem to have been brought by jealous oilmen against others, and the commission to have become a regulatory agency designed to ensure stability in the oil industry. See the commission file (Zimmerman Library, University of New Mexico) and *New Mexico Tax Bulletin* 14 (1935): 33–41.

68. Thomas C. Donnelly, "Public Health Administration in New Mexico," *University of New Mexico Bulletin*, vol. 1, no. 2 (Albuquerque, 1938), p. 5. Carl Beck, *Health Survey of the State of New Mexico* (unpublished manuscript, 1934); *New Mexico Health Officer*, Auguat 1934, p. 6; J. Rosslyn Earp, "Ninth Biennial Report, 1935–6," ibid., December 1936, pp. 50, 54; Earp, "The Public Health Program in New Mexico," *New Mexico Business Review* 7 (1937): 120; Earp to Frank Vesely, 8 May 1935, (State Documents Section, Zimmerman Library, University of New Mexico); Myrtle Greenfield, *A History of Public Health in New Mexico* (Albuquerque, 1962), pp. 13–48.

69. Wollman, *An Appraisal of New Mexico Labor Legislation*, pp. 50–51; *New Mexico Tax Bulletin* 17 (1938): 141; Clinton P. Anderson, "First Annual Report of the Unemployment Compensation Commission," [Santa Fe, 1938] (Zimmerman Library, University of New Mexico).

70. Sanchez, *Forgotten People*, p. 63; Donnelly, *Government in New Mexico*, pp. 254–57; FERA, *New Mexico Relief Bulletin*, 7 June 1934, p. 2; 14 June 1934, p. 1; *New Mexico Tax Bulletin* 14 (1935): 100; Beckett, *Soil Conservation Problem in New Mexico*, p. 17; H. C. Stewart, "Soil Conservation Activities in the Southwest," *New Mexico Business Review* 7 (1938): 182.

71. Rexroad, "The Two Administrations of Governor Dillon," pp. 109–10; Richard C. Dillon, *Budget Presented to the Eighth Legislature* (Santa Fe, 1927), p. 36; Donnelly, *Rocky Mountain Politics*, p. 228; Davis, *Historical Encyclopedia of New Mexico*, p. 13; State Tourist Bureau, "Annual Report for 1938" (Santa Fe, 1939), p. 4.

72. C. W. Carson, "Address at the Conference on Business and Government," *New Mexico Business Review* 4 (1935): 96–97; S. R. DeBoer, "Second Progress Report of the New Mexico State Planning Board" (Santa Fe, 1935), p. 10; DeBoer, "State Planning Accomplishments and Suggestions for Future Development" (Denver, 1936), pp. 8–12.

73. Herbert J. Hagerman, "Ducking and Cutting—An Uncensored Review," *New Mexico Tax Bulletin* 11 (1932): 202–3.

74. Anne Geddess, *Trends in Relief Expenditures, 1910–1935*, WPA Research Monograph, No. 10 (Washington, D.C., 1937), p. 88; Leonard J. Arrington, *The Changing Economic Structure of the Mountain West*, Utah State University, Monograph Series 10, No. 3 (Logan, Utah, 1963), pp. 35-36, 46-47.

75. Janet Spiess, "Feudalism and Senator Cutting," *American Mercury* 33 (1934): 372.

76. H. B. Hensley to Holm O. Bursum, 1 August 1928, file on "Political Matters, 1926–9," Bursum Papers (Zimmerman Library Archives, University of New Mexico).

77. *Santa Fe New Mexican*, 6 August 1934; "Tingley," p. 220, Fergusson Papers; David A. Shannon, *Between the Wars: America, 1919–41* (Boston, 1965), p. 144; Seligmann, "The Political Career of Bronson Cutting," pp. 178–79, 205–6; *New Mexico State Tribune*, 7 October 1932; Arthur Schlesinger, Jr., *The Coming of the New Deal* (Boston, 1958), p. 5. The "searching progressive" quotation comes from a letter to the author from Professor David R. McCoy, 24 November 1970. For Cutting's views cited in text, see U.S. Congress, Senate, *Congressional Record*, 73d Cong., 2d Sess., 1934, 78, pt. 8:8051–52, pt. 11: 12047–52; *New York Times*, 9 January 1934; Cunningham, "Bronson Cutting," p. 212; Owen P. White, "Membership in Both Clubs," p. 189; R. W. Hogue, "Senator Cutting's Last Fight," *New Republic* 83 (1935): 77; Leuchtenburg, *Franklin Roosevelt and the New Deal*, p. 122.

78. Schlesinger, *The Coming of the New Deal*, p. 421; James M. Burns, *Roosevelt: The Lion and the Fox* (New York, 1956), pp. 202–8.

79. This argument is elaborated at length in William Pickens, "Cutting vs. Chavez: A Reply to Wolf's Comments," *New Mexico Historical Review* 47 (1972): 337–59.

80. Hening, *George Curry*, p. 272.

81. Parker, "Arthur Seligman and Bronson Cutting," p. 22; Cunningham, "Bronson Cutting," p. 172; "Message from the Roosevelt-Dillon Club, Albuquerque," printed handbill in "Political Affairs,

1932" file, Dillon Papers; Beck, *New Mexico*, p. 311; *New Mexico State Tribune*, 23 September 1932.

82. Henry Wilson to Dillon, 23 November 1932, Dillon Papers; Seligmann, "Political Career of Bronson Cutting," p. 214.

83. Holmes, *Politics in New Mexico*, pp. 172–73; M. A. Otero to Carl Hatch, 11 May 1934, Box 11, Otero Papers; Richard Beaupre, "The 1934 Senatorial Election in New Mexico" (M.A. thesis, University of New Mexico, 1969), p. 31 Cunningham, "Bronson Cutting," pp. 185–86, 190; "Tingley," p. 261, Fergusson Papers; Lahart, "The Career of Dennis Chavez," pp. 105–6; Fleta Springer, "Through the Looking Glass," *New Republic* 80 (1934): 357–58.

84. *Albuquerque Tribune,* 2 October 1934.

85. Owen P. White, "Cutting Free," *Collier's*, 27 October 1934, p. 28.

86. "Tingley," pp. 221–22, Fergusson Papers. On Cutting and Spanish Americans, see: Patricia C. Armstrong, *A Portrait of Bronson Cutting through His Papers*, Division of Government Research Bulletin, No. 57 (University of New Mexico, 1959), p. 39; Spiess, "Feudalism and Senator Cutting," p. 373; Long, *Piñon Country*, pp. 138–42; Donnelly, *Rocky Mountain Politics*, p. 233.

87. *Cong. Record*, (Senate), 73d Cong., 2d sess., 1934, 78, pt. 8:8052; Seligmann, "Political Career of Bronson Cutting," pp. 186–87, 205–6; Cunningham, "Bronson Cutting," pp. 212–13; *Santa Fe New Mexican*, 5 September 1934.

88. Interview with Judge Irwin Moise, 31 December 1970. Judge Moise worked for the National Recovery Administration in Washington from 1934 through 1936. Harold L. Ickes, *The Secret Diary of Harold L. Ickes, 1933–1936* (New York, 1953), pp. 27, 359; Keleher, *Memoirs*, p. 168; Lahart, "Career of Dennis Chavez," p. 97; Seligmann, "Cutting," pp. 236–37; Arthur M. Schlesinger, Jr., *The Politics of Upheaval* (Boston, 1960), p. 140; Beaupre, "Senatorial Election of 1934," pp. 89–92; Raymond Moley, *After Seven Years* (New York, 1939), p. 126.

89. Donnelly, *Rocky Mountain Politics*, p. 247.

90. Cunningham, "Bronson Cutting," pp. 187–90; "Tingley," pp. 265–66, Fergusson Papers; Evans, *New Mexico Election Returns, 1911-69,* unpaged; William Pickens, "Cutting vs. Chavez: Battle of the Patrones in New Mexico, 1934," *New Mexico Historical Review* 4; 6 (1971): 24.

91. Diogenes, "The New Mexico Campaign: A Struggle between Two 'Outlander Baronies,' " *Literary Digest*, 3 November 1934, p. 13; Spiess, "Feudalism and Senator Cutting," p. 374; Pickens, "Reply to Wolf," pp. 345–47.

92. "Cutting and Leadership," *Common Sense,* June 1935, p. 2.

93. Republicans could hardly be found in the 1937 legislature. Only "the senator and two representatives of Taos County—represented the minority, and even they were but the current winners of the endless factional disputes of that county" (Holmes, *Politics in New Mexico*, p. 199).

94. Hannet, *Sagebrush Lawyer*, p. 216.

95. Holmes, *Politics in New Mexico*, p. 204.

96. Keleher, *Memoirs*, p. 133; Davis, *Historical Encyclopedia of New Mexico*, p. 167.

97. Holmes, *Politics in New Mexico*, pp. 198–205; "Tingley," pp. 1–2, 77, 100, 150, 157–63, 173–74, 242–43, Fergusson Papers. Many landmarks around the state bear Tingley's name, indicating his desire for a mark in New Mexico history (a not uncommon impulse among notable politicians).

98. "Tingley," p. 76, Fergusson Papers; Keleher, *Memoirs*, pp. 122, 136.

99. Keleher, *Memoirs*, pp. 120–21, 133, 140; "Tingley," p. 271, Fergusson Papers.

100. C. P. Anderson to Erna Fergusson, 17 May 1955, Fergusson Papers. Tingley's relationship with FDR was, according to Senator Anderson, "the greatest contribution [he] made to our public building program in New Mexico." Hannett, *Sagebrush Lawyer*, p. 219; Kelcher, *Memoirs*, p. 140; Anderson and Viorst, *Outsider in the Senate*, pp. 28–30.

101. Holmes, *Politics in New Mexico*, p. 208; *New Mexico Tax Bulletin* 14 (1935): 2–3, 34.

102. Keleher, *Memoirs*, pp. 141–45; Holmes, *Politics in New Mexico*, p. 208.

103. J. H. McLaughlin to Tingley, 9 September 1935; W. L. Robbins to Tingley, 29 January 1935; Josie Driver to Tingley, 13 June 1937; Tingley to Driver, 16 June 1937; Tingley to Hatch, 4 June 1937;

Hatch to Tingley, 6 June 1937; Charles Allison to Tingley, 12 June 1937; C. F. Knight to Tingley, 3 September 1935, Tingley Papers.

104. Holmes, *Politics in New Mexico*, p. 213.

105. *Time*, 31 October 1938, p. 11; Ernest B. Fincher, "The Spanish Americans as a Political Factor in New Mexico" (Ph.D. diss., New York University, 1950), p. 154; *Santa Fe New Mexican*, 20, 21 October 1938.

106. Frank Hefferly to Robert Montgomery, 31 July 1936; Hefferly to Tingley, 14 October 1935; J. Davis to Tingley, 4 July 1936, Tingley Papers; Richard Stephenson, "The Use of Troops in Labor Disputes in New Mexico" (M.A. thesis, University of New Mexico, 1952), p. 104; F. O. Matthieson, "The New Mexico Workers' Case," *New Republic* 82 (1935): 361–63; "Tingley," p. 209, Fergusson Papers; Keleher, *Memoirs*, pp. 207–24.

107. Frank Ortiz to Tingley, 3 January 1936, Tingley Papers; Thomas C. Donnelly and James Swayne, "The Labor Record of Political Parties in New Mexico," *New Mexico Business Review* 5 (1936): 236; Wollman, *Appraisal of New Mexico Labor Legislation*, p. 64.

108. Holmes, *Politics in New Mexico*, pp. 205–6.

109. Ibid., pp. 199–205; Ramsay, "A Statistical Survey of the Voting Behavior in New Mexico," pp. 61, 63.

110. Beck, *New Mexico*, p. 309; Hannett, *Sagebrush Lawyer*, pp. 165–76; Thompson, "The Administration of Governor Arthur Hannett," pp. 22–24, 86, 90–91; Paul Beckett and Walter L. McNutt, *The Direct Primary in New Mexico*, Division of Government Research Bulletin, No. 7 (University of New Mexico, 1947), pp. 2–8; Fincher, "Spanish Americans as a Political Factor," pp. 177–79; Paul Thiel, "New Mexico's Bilingual Politics and Factional Disputes," *Southern Observer*, February 1954, pp. 22–27; Russell, "Racial Groups in the New Mexico Legislature," p. 67.

111. G. R. Quessenberry, "The AAA in New Mexico," *New Mexico Business Review* 5 (1936): 47.

112. Ellis, *Public Welfare Problems*, p. 5; Wells, "Agriculture in New Mexico," p. 62; Leong, *Technology, Employment, and Output per Man in Copper Mining*, p. 222; Mabel Graham, "The Trend of Employment in New Mexico," *New Mexico Business Review* 7 (1938): 217; L. H. Hauter, "New Mexico's Part in the Agricultural Adjustment Program," ibid., 3 (1934): 49–50; G. L. Guthrie, "Discussion about Quessenberry's Article," ibid., 5 (1936): 53; "New Mexico and the Census of Agriculture," ibid., p. 53; R. S. Kifer and H. L. Stewart, *Farming Hazards in the Drought Area*, WPA Research Monograph, No. 16 (Washington, D.C., 1938), p. 74, 118–19. For other indications of the changing economic picture, see Phillip A. Larson, "A Comparison of Property Values with Assessed Values in the City of Albuquerque," *New Mexico Business Review* 7 (1938): 163; State Tax Commission, *Twelfth Biennial Report* (1936–1938), pp. 99–100; U.S. Dept of the Treasury, *Statistics of Income for 1938* (Washington, D.C., 1939), pt. 1, pp. 80, 236; Hugh Sawyers, "The Story of Oil in New Mexico," *New Mexico Tax Bulletin* 17 (1938): 49–50.

113. A good example of New Mexico's lack of initiative can be seen in development of the federal program for vocational education begun in 1917 with the Smith-Hughes Act. For a discussion of how such education was organized, financed, and accepted by four medium-sized American cities, see Selden C. Menefee, *Vocational Training and Employment of Youth*, WPA Research Monograph, No. 25 (Washington, D.C. 1942). Although this was exactly the kind of education many adolescents in New Mexico needed, the state received very little from the 1917, 1927, 1934, or 1936 vocational education legislation because it would not meet the small matching requirements (see "Announcement from D. W. Rockey, State Supervisor of Trade and Industrial Education, April 30, 1930," in the Dillon Papers). Work in vocational agriculture was carried on by only twenty-six teachers in 1933. See Arthur Seligman, *Budget Presented to the Tenth Legislature* (Santa Fe, 1931), p. 38. In Seligman's *Budget Presented to the Eleventh Legislature* (1933) for the next two fiscal years, the vocational education effort in New Mexico received only $86,494 for each year. The state paid 26 percent of that figure (pp. 152–53). "The ratio of state to Federal funds available is one of the lowest in the entire U.S.," Seligman stated (p. 153). The situation remained virtually the same during the New Deal years. Since there was little federal pressure for such programs, state officials were content to do the minimum. See *New Mexico Tax Bulletin* 15 (1936): 49–51; 17 (1938): 137–38.

114. Hoover, "The Republican Party in New Mexico," p. 163.

Robert E. Burton

The New Deal in Oregon

AMONG THE STATES OF THE PACIFIC NORTHWEST, OREGON PRE-sented an excellent opportunity for experimentation and reform during the New Deal. Virtually untouched by industrialization and with a population of only 953,786 in 1930, the state remained part of what Richard L. Neuberger called "America's last frontier" and Franklin D. Roosevelt described as "a land of opportunity."[1] Both of these descriptions suggested that the New Deal in Oregon would concentrate upon the management and development of natural resources, in addition to short-term measures designed to effect relief and recovery. Oregon's economy, dominated by agriculture and the lumber industry, was well suited for programs in crop control, conservation, and reclamation. Moreover, the state's shipping industry, an important segment of which was devoted to foreign trade, would directly profit from reciprocal trade agreements. But perhaps most important of all was the prospect of harnessing the power of the Columbia River, not only to provide inexpensive hydroelectric power for domestic consumers but also to encourage the growth of industry.

If the federal government had much to offer the states during the 1930s, New Dealers also hoped that the stimulus of national reform would inspire "little new deals" throughout the country. On the surface, at least, Oregon's political heritage of nonpartisan progressivism seemed to offer the promise of innovation in state government. Such had certainly been the case with the celebrated "Oregon System" for which the state won national renown. Though the shadow of nativism and normalcy fell across Oregon in the 1920s, the progressive tradition did not suffer total eclipse.[2] With the unprecedented crisis of the 1930s and the inauguration of the New Deal, there were those in Oregon who confidently predicted a return to the spirit of reform because, as one Democratic party official put it, Oregon and the West believed in "liberal and progressive ideas regardless of party."[3]

Even before the Great Depression of the 1930s descended upon Oregon, the state faced economic problems. During the decade of the 1920s, Oregon had experienced a decline in economic growth and recurring but mild depressions in the lumber industry. Indicative of the general economic malaise of the twenties was the more dramatic fact that between 1927 and 1929 Oregon had the highest rate of business failures in the nation.[4] These economic difficulties may have anticipated, but scarcely matched, the devastation of the depression that followed the stock market crash of 1929.

Oregon did not feel the full intensity of the depression until 1933. In that year, unquestionably the darkest of the thirties in Oregon, unemployment reached its highest figure, with an estimated 59,000 unemployed. Especially hard hit was the lumber industry, which accounted for 53 percent of all those classified as industrial workers. In 1933, employment in the manufacture of lumber and timber products had plunged to 40 percent of the 1929 level.[5] Equally serious was the plight of those engaged in agriculture. The total cash income of Oregon farmers dropped from $136,000,000 in 1929 to $49,000,000 in 1933, and forced farm sales reached a high of 41.3 per thousand in 1933. With unemployment and depressed farm prices, the per capita income of Oregonians declined. The payroll in manufacturing went from $86,000,000 to $34,000,000 between 1929 and 1933, and individual incomes in Oregon in 1933 fell to 55.8 percent of the 1929 level.[6] As incomes fell, delinquencies in taxes climbed from $4,000,000 in 1929 to $40,000,000 in 1933.[7]

During the winter of 1932-33, Oregon was seized with a mood of grim desperation. State authorities officially reported 21,210 families on relief, a figure that did not accurately represent the actual number of Oregonians who were in need of assistance.[8] Reports from county officials in the late fall of 1932 conveyed a picture of suffering and deprivation. After a trip through six southern Oregon counties, a relief worker concluded that there was "serious danger of physical depletion and malnutrition among large numbers of children and adults." From Tillamook County, on the Oregon coast, came word that savings bank deposits were completely depleted and that "children [had] drawn their savings to buy food for the family." Union County, in northeastern Oregon, fared no better. Noting that all the banks had closed in that county, a relief official reported that most of the homeowners and farmers were subject to foreclosure and were unable to pay taxes.[9] In February 1933, Congressman Walter Pierce summarized the feelings of many Oregonians when he confessed to a constituent, "We are on the verge of collapse. I am just wondering what is going to happen."[10]

Faced with the most serious crisis in state history, Oregon had neither the resources nor the creative leadership to meet the challenge. Governor Julius Meier, who was elected as an independent in 1930, offered words of sympathy and reassurance to Oregonians, but little in the way of concrete assistance. Meier, a nominal Republican and respected Portland merchant, asserted that the nation's ills could only be solved by economy in government. In February 1932, he told the Bankers' Club of New York that under President Herbert Hoover the country had been "on a spending debauch [and] orgy of extravagance." What the nation needed, Meier argued, was government "run by business men on business principles."[11]

Acting on his own prescription, Meier had earlier commenced a program of austerity in government spending. Upon entering office in 1931, the governor encountered a budget deficit of $2,500,000. Under Meier's direction, the state legislature in 1931 and again in 1933 slashed spending to the point where the deficit was cut by 50 percent. This was accomplished by a sharp reduction in the appropriations for higher education, funds for soldiers' bonuses, and the salaries of state employees.[12] Oregon legislators, in fact, were so economy-minded that they cut more from the budget of 1933 than the governor had recommended. Henry M. Hanzen, Meier's budget director and a proponent of reduced spending, declared the legislative session of 1933 "the worst" in state history. This was so because the legislators acted like "a lot of wild jackasses who believed they heard the call of the people and were willing to destroy anything and everything so long as they could make a showing of saving a nickel."[13]

Believing that the responsibility for relief and welfare services should be borne by charitable organizations and county government, Governor Meier offered only token relief for the unemployed. In December 1930, Meier created a temporary State Emergency Employment Commission, which, in turn, was succeeded by a State-Wide Relief Council in 1932. Both organizations, which served as advisory bodies to the governor, were charged with the administrative task of coordinating county efforts in financing relief.[14] Before long it became painfully evident that Oregon's counties could not shoulder the burden of relief. Total county revenues declined from approximately $18,000,000 in 1929 to $9,000,000 in 1933 while welfare expenditures increased from roughly $1,000,000 to

$3,000,000 in the same period.[15] In the fall of 1932, the State-Wide Relief Council reported that county government could no longer bear responsibility for unemployment relief. At the same time, it predicted that $6,204,812 would be required for relief in 1933, an amount over and above the reported funds within the various Oregon counties.[16]

Despite this evidence to the contrary, Meier nevertheless continued publicly to assure Oregonians there was no need for alarm. On 20 June 1932, he announced that the state had "practically everything necessary to meet the existing emergency."[17] Eight days later, however, he expressed a more realistic evaluation when he privately wired President Hoover that federal assistance was necessary. "We must have help from the federal government," explained Meier, "if we are to avert suffering . . . and possible uprisings."[18] The governor's fear of "possible uprisings" did not materialize, but Oregonians did express their disenchantment with Republican leadership at the polls in 1932.

In party registration and voting, Oregonians over the years favored the Republican party. Between 1900 and 1932, the Republicans always enjoyed a two-to-one registration ratio over Democrats and several times a majority of three to one.[19] With the exception of the three-way presidential contest of 1912, when Woodrow Wilson carried Oregon with 34 percent of the vote, Republican presidential candidates easily carried the state. But in 1932, Oregon voters reversed this pattern and gave Franklin D. Roosevelt 53 percent of the popular vote at a time when Democratic registration stood at 32 percent. On the state level, Democrats captured the mayoralty of Portland and two of Oregon's three congressional districts. In the Third Congressional District (Portland), Charles H. Martin won reelection after having served one term in Congress; in eastern Oregon, Walter M. Pierce captured the Second Congressional District for the party for the first time in Oregon history. Despite these victories, Republican Senator Frederick Steiwer won reelection; and although Democrats increased their representation in the state legislature, Republicans remained firmly in control of both houses of the legislature.[20]

The state Democratic party, moribund for several years, came alive with Roosevelt's victory in 1932. "The tide has turned," exclaimed the *Oregon Democrat,* an official party publication that made its debut in January 1933. "Democrats learned the formula for success," the magazine noted, "organization, leadership, and a clearly defined progressive program."[21] Most important, the national Democratic victory had given Oregon Democrats a unity of purpose. Without exception, those Democrats elected to office in 1932 identified their candidacies with Franklin Roosevelt and campaigned on the yet unfulfilled promise of a "new deal."

Following the election, Democratic party leaders optimistically predicted that, with the help of the Democratic administration in Washington, they could forge a New Deal coalition on the state level that would give them outright control of Oregon politics. A New Deal coalition in Oregon, as envisioned by party leaders, would consist of two groups: farmers and industrial workers, represented by the Grange and the State Federation of Labor, in league with the state Democratic party.[22] Meanwhile, as Democrats set about to arrange that coalition, Republicans controlled state government during the first two years of the New Deal.

Although Governor Meier had campaigned against Franklin Roosevelt in the presidential contest of 1932, he cooperated with the federal government in administering several early New Deal measures in Oregon. A State Emergency Relief Committee, established by the legislature in 1933, worked with Harry Hopkins and the Federal Emergency Relief Administration in distributing nearly $15,000,000 from mid-1933 to January 1935. The governor and the state legislature, however, continued to stress economy in government and only reluctantly met the FERA's requirement that the state provide matching funds to qualify for federal grants.[23] To supplement relief, the legislature created a State Commission for Self-Help and Rehabilitation and enacted an old-age pension act during its session of 1933, but allocated no funds for either program. Instead, the already overburdened counties were required to administer and finance both programs, neither of which functioned effectively.[24]

Many New Deal measures enacted by Congress in the so-called Hundred Days (9 March–16 June 1933) proved popular in Oregon. The Agricultural Adjustment Act received an enthusiastic welcome from Oregon farmers.[25] Government payments under crop adjustment and production control contracts increased from $71,000 in 1933 to $4,685,000 in 1934 and, in the long run, helped to push Oregon's total cash income in agriculture from $49,777,000 in 1933 to $120,621,000 in 1937. During this period, the AAA negotiated a total of 35,590 production control and soil conservation contracts, the preponderant number of which went to wheat farmers in eastern Oregon.[26] In addition, the Farm Credit Administration assisted farmers by providing loans for the refinancing of farm mortgages and other debts. Distributing funds through the Federal Land Bank of Spokane, the FCA eventually granted over 10,000 loans in the amount of $36,000,000 between 1933 and 1938.[27]

Also immediately helpful to Oregon was the Civil Works Administration, Public Works Administration, and Civilian Conservation Corps. Established as an emergency measure in 1933, the CWA expended $6,527,264 in Oregon between November 1933 and March 1934 on over 1,800 projects, most of which centered upon the renovation of school buildings, parks, and playgrounds.[28] In 1933, the PWA, with an appropriation of over $32,000,000, began construction of Bonneville and Grand Coulee Dams on the Columbia River. The Bonneville project alone provided employment for 4,484 men by March 1935, and became the most ambitious federal program in Oregon during the New Deal.[29] The Civilian Conservation Corps was naturally important to a state that possessed about one-fifth of the nation's stand of timber. By September 1933, the CCC was operating 39 camps in Oregon with employment for 4,596. Over the first three years of its existence there, the CCC provided jobs for 13,000 and expended $2,000,000 in wages. The contributions of the CCC in Oregon were many, but most notable was its work in the prevention of forest fires, reforestation, and the construction of parks, trails, and lookout towers.[30]

Set against the success of these programs was the operation of the National Recovery Act in Oregon. The NRA had only limited application in a state without a large industrial concentration, but Oregon's lumber industry offered an opportunity for experimentation. From the outset, however, NRA code agreements negotiated with lumber producers were ineffective. In part, the codes failed because of the large number of small, independent lumber partnerships that refused to cooperate with NRA officials.[31] On the other hand, there was strong political opposition from the large lumber producers who disliked, among other things, the collective bargaining provisions of section 7(a) of the NRA. C. C. Crow, the conservative owner and editor of the influential *Crow's Pacific Coast Lumber Digest,* declared that the "whole NRA program [was] the worst misfortune that [had] ever befallen the United States."[32] And there were complaints from other quarters. "The only thing they have failed to cover in our Code," an automobile dealer asserted, "was to make the public buy new cars and to make it compulsory that the dealer make a profit."[33] Shortly before the Supreme Court declared the NRA unconstitutional, Congressman Walter Pierce reported: "My mail is full of letters about N.R.A., most of them objecting to its continuance."[34]

In spite of criticism of the NRA and a few other measures,[35] Oregon benefited considerably from the New Deal in 1933 and 1934. The Oregon Democratic party was not so fortunate. Particularly destructive of party morale was the distribution of patronage by the Roosevelt administration. With Republicans in control of state government and the administration of relief, programs like the FERA, CWA, and PWA produced more jobs for Republicans than Democrats. Democratic Congressman Walter Pierce expressed anger and frustration over the appointments made by Harry Hopkins. Because Hopkins was so obsessed with administering the FERA in a nonpartisan fashion, Pierce told one correspondent, he appointed "only reactionary republicans," a condition that prevailed "not only in Oregon, but clear through to the Atlantic Coast."[36] Also distressing to Democrats was Republican domination of the CWA. In 1934, the *Oregon Democrat* found that of 19 CWA positions in Multnomah County, 15 were held by Republicans. The remaining four were divided between three Democrats, two of whom had changed their party registration to Democratic in 1932, and one independent who had campaigned for Hoover against Roosevelt. Describing the apportionment of jobs under the CWA in Oregon, the magazine lamented, "The big warm nest built by Democracy was filled with a weird assortment of Republican cuckoo eggs."[37]

Far more serious than the patronage situation, both for Democratic unity and the creation of a New Deal coalition in Oregon, was a contest between liberals and conservatives for domination of the party. The various factions of the party had closed ranks behind Roosevelt in 1932, but as the New Deal began to take shape, dissension grew. The intraparty struggle first surfaced during the summer of 1933 and, unfortunately for Oregon Democrats, continued over the decade. Although the party dispute ranged over several issues, it grew to its greatest intensity on the question of New Deal reforms and, most specifically, the public power program of the Roosevelt administration as it applied to the development of the Columbia River valley.

Despite growing party division, Democrats improved their political position in 1934. Congressman Charles H. Martin was elected governor, but only after one of the most tumultuous contests in state history. After surviving a bitter primary fight, Martin narrowly won election over Peter Zimmerman, a liberal Republican who ran as an independent on a platform similar to that of Upton Sinclair's EPIC plan for California. Republicans captured the Third Congressional District vacated by Martin, but Walter Pierce was reelected and Democrats won control of the lower house of the state legislature for the first time since 1878.[38]

Democratic victories in 1934 provided the party with an unparalleled opportunity to reshape Oregon politics. Yet the election did nothing to restore harmony, and before long the party was torn apart by an incorrigible factionalism. As the battle raged, conservatives, who controlled the party apparatus during the 1930s, eventually moved to a position of opposition to President Roosevelt and the programs of the New Deal. As a result, voters in Oregon who stood behind the national administration came to view the state Democratic party and its leaders as reactionary. Under the circumstances, Republicans and Democrats alike, in an attempt to secure the benefits of the New Deal, frequently exercised an independence of party and a nonpartisanship reminiscent of the progressive era in Oregon. Republican Senator Charles L. McNary, who was minority leader of the Senate during the New Deal, established a reputation for cooperation with the Roosevelt administration and thereby gained bipartisan support in senatorial campaigns during the New Deal.[39] In some circles, McNary was known as the "Republican New Dealer," and though he was not a strong advocate of public power, the political image he projected on that issue was sufficiently favorable to bring him the backing of public power forces during the 1930s.[40]

Democratic party factionalism in Oregon presented a number of problems to New Dealers in Washington, but none was more rancorous than that of patronage. Caught between the liberal and conservative factions after the election of 1934, the Roosevelt administration tried to placate each group but succeeded only in alienating both. Typical of the disappointment expressed by Oregon Democrats during the New Deal was the complaint of one conservative who described himself as a "loyal party man." Why, he asked, should the party faithful "be required to continually spend time, effort and money in behalf of our party without hope of reward."[41] In 1938, a liberal observed: "Frankly, our whole group here is getting pretty weary of everlastingly battling for the New Deal, and yet seeing virtually every key Federal post in the hands of the opposition."[42] In 1942, the *Oregon Democrat* agreed that the lack of patronage had severely hampered effective party organization. "The absolute failure of the big shots in Washington to play ball with the state organization in passing out jobs . . . caused the organization efforts, and everything that goes with it, to be shot to hell."[43]

But it was not the patronage wrangle that basically prevented party organization or unity. Rather, it was party schism over New Deal reforms. At the center of this controversy was Governor Charles Martin. Although Martin had campaigned as a champion of the New Deal, and continued to insist that he supported the national Democratic administration, his actions belied his words. Those Democrats and others who had voted for him on the supposition that he would cooperate with President Roosevelt and move in the direction of a "little new deal" for Oregon became the governor's strongest critics and most vocal opponents. Before the end of his first year in office, Martin was at sword's point with the Democratic majority in the lower house of the legislature. "My most virile enemies in the legislature are Democrats and most ardent supporters are Republicans," complained the governor.[44]

The problems that Martin faced as governor from 1935 to 1939 would have taxed the most skillful politician. Under pressure, however, he exhibited an unfortunate lack of political acumen and a fondness for blunt language that repeatedly attracted charges of ruthlessness. Known as "Old Ironpants" by friends and foes, the seventy-two-year-old governor had retired from the Army with the rank of major general after forty years of service in 1927. According to critics, Martin was a reactionary whose love of rigid military discipline and unquestioned obedience led him to administer state government like a "Neanderthal man, swinging a club at any who [dared] to disagree with him."[45]

During his tenure, Martin eventually opposed several New Deal programs, but it was his conservative stance on public power, relief and welfare, and labor relations that provoked the most controversy. The issue of public power, long important in Oregon politics, flared anew when the U. S. Army Corps of Engineers began construction of Bonneville and Grand Coulee Dams in 1933. Still unresolved at that time were two important questions: what type of agency would distribute the power produced at these dams, and would private or public interests be the chief beneficiary of the new power?

The Oregon Grange and the State Federation of Labor generally favored the creation of a Columbia Valley Authority, a federal agency patterned after the Tennessee Valley Authority. Among other things, such an agency would ensure the federal distribution of the power from the dams that would be allocated principally for farms and homes in Oregon. In addition, either the state or the federal government would build transmission lines from Bonneville, thus providing electricity at cost to domestic consumers.

An opposite view was held by utility companies, the Portland Chamber of Commerce, and industrial interests. While favoring the federal development of the Columbia River, these groups maintained that the dams should be separately administered by the U. S. Army Corps of Engineers and the Bureau of Reclamation. Even though those who held this position argued that the power produced at the dams should serve both private and public use, it was evident that inexpensive power for industrial purposes distributed by private utility companies was their prime concern.[46]

Construction of Bonneville Dam was not completed until 1937, and in the interim Martin demonstrated his militant opposition to the proposal for a CVA and the position of the Grange and the State Federation of Labor on the primary use of power produced by the dam. In 1935, the governor vetoed a bill passed by the legislature that would have required the state to build power lines from Bonneville to distribute electricty to domestic consumers at cost. The legislation, which had the warm endorsement of Secretary of Interior Harold Ickes, would have also established a State Power Commission.[47] Moreover, Martin tried unsuccessfully to block the appointment of CVA proponent J. D. Ross as Bonneville Dam administrator and testified before the House Rivers and Harbors Committee against the proposed CVA.[48]

More than any other single issue, the governor's stand on public power destroyed the possibility of a Democratic coalition with farmers and industrial workers in Oregon. At the same time, public power remained the most contentious issue dividing Oregon Democrats during the New Deal. Congressman Walter Pierce, an apostle of the CVA and paladin of the public power movement in Oregon, became the leading antagonist of Martin in the power feud. "I think the old fello [sic] should be reprimanded by the people of Oregon," declared Pierce.[49] Joining Pierce in denouncing Martin's attitude on public power was Harold Ickes, who, after a long battle with the governor, exploded, "Martin is at heart no New Dealer."[50]

If Martin was hostile to New Deal power policy, he was no more sympathetic to New Deal legislation that touched on the problem of relief and welfare. In 1935, during his first year as governor, Congress passed the Social Security Act and the Emergency Relief Appropriations Act. Under the latter legislation, the Works Progress Administration was established with an appropriation of nearly $5,000,000,000 for work relief.

Martin disliked both measures. Social Security, he said, was rapidly "driving [the] country into national socialism." Concerning federal relief, the governor asserted that the funds for the WPA should not have been allocated because "democratic nations have lost their moral force through pampering their people."[51] Firm in the conviction that the federal dole was detrimental to the American character, Martin told Harry Hopkins he could "keep his money out of Oregon."[52]

Because of the governor's attitude toward Social Security, Oregon only fitfully, and after much delay, cooperated with the Roosevelt administration in providing matching funds for old-age assistance, aid to the blind and crippled, and care for dependent mothers and children. Initially, Martin refused to allow the allocation of existing state revenues for these programs, insisting that a state sales tax be adopted to provide the needed revenue. Twice the legislature referred a sales tax initiative to Oregonians; twice the initiative was defeated. Only then did the governor turn to other sources for matching funds.[53]

Not unexpectedly, the administration of state relief under Martin was marked by dissension and chaos. When federal relief assistance from the FERA was ended in 1935, the Oregon legislature set aside $5,500,000 from liquor revenues and the general fund for support of indigent relief, old-age pensions, and other relief and welfare activities. Although the state assumed greater responsibility in the administration of relief, the counties were required to contribute an amount equal to that provided by the state for the various relief programs, a totally unrealistic requirement because of the sharp reduction in county revenues during the 1930s.[54]

Describing himself as a "Hoover Democrat," Martin maintained that relief was a problem for counties and cities, not the state or national governments. The governor quarreled with the State Relief Commission, on one occasion refused to approve the distribution of funds already earmarked for relief, and reviled those who were recipients of welfare.[55] Although Martin's salary as governor and army retirement pension gave him an income of over $1,100 per month, he argued that those unable to work because of physical or mental impairments needed no more than $10 per month to care for themselves. For the able-bodied unemployed, there should be no state assistance, said the governor, because the "need for the necessities of life will force these people to get some kind of work and care for themselves."[56] When a suggestion was made that the aged and feeble-minded wards of the state be chloroformed, Martin commended the idea. If 900 of the 969 inmates at the Fairview Home in Salem were "put out of their misery," the governor argued, it would save the state $300,000 on the next biennial budget.[57]

Anxious to see the end of the state relief program, Martin declared in 1936 that the depression was over in Oregon. Consequently, there was no longer any need for relief payments. Speaking of relief recipients, Martin asked rhetorically, "Are we going to feed them for the rest of our lives? Hell! Let them work!"[58] The governor also ordered the chairman of the

State Relief Commission to close down the Roosevelt Transient Camp at Roseburg. Transient camps, said Martin, were in reality "Tramp Camps," and the occupants "should be kept moving out of our state the same as criminals."[59]

Already under attack for his position on public power and relief and welfare, Governor Martin further antagonized New Dealers in Oregon and Washington, D. C., by his actions and words concerning labor disputes in the lumber industry. The collective bargaining provisions of the NRA had earlier led to a few strikes in Oregon, but it was not until the nationwide conflict between the AFL and the CIO erupted that the state was engulfed by labor warfare. Central to the AFL-CIO struggle in Oregon was a two year battle (1935–37) during which the Lumber and Sawmill Worker's Union broke with the AFL, reconstituted itself as the International Woodworkers of America, and affiliated with the CIO. What followed was a series of bitter jurisdictional disputes between the AFL and the CIO, disputes that frequently led to serious strikes. In 1937, for example, the CIO won election as the collective bargaining agent at the Inman-Poulson Lumber Mill in Portland. The NLRB officially designated the CIO as the bargaining unit, but the AFL refused to recognize the election or the action of the NLRB. Consequently, the AFL picketed the mill and boycotted all lumber products produced by CIO workers. For over four months, the mill was paralyzed by violent clashes between AFL and CIO workers.[60]

In responding to the labor turmoil, Martin emphasized law and order, staunchly defended the lumber operators against striking workers, excoriated union organizers (especially the CIO), and condemned New Deal labor legislation. In 1935, the governor ordered the state police to protect strikebreakers and in 1936 clashed with Secretary of Labor Frances Perkins and the National Labor Relations Board over the arbitration of labor disputes in Oregon.[61] Moreover, Martin resisted attempts by union leaders to organize state employees and served notice that "the only privilege accorded state employes [sic] in joining a union organization [would] be that of paying dues and enjoying . . . fraternal satisfactions."[62]

From Governor Martin's point of view, the Wagner Act and the NLRB had encouraged class warfare that threatened to destroy democratic government. "I do not intend," Martin warned, "that the bolshevik-soviet system shall be introduced into this state."[63] The NLRB was a "tool of 'labor royalists' and racketeers" who had led workingmen astray. These forces, Martin said, "want to do away with the capitalist system. They are playing the same game as they played in Italy and Germany–strikes, confusion and turmoil." Nevertheless, asserted the governor, "The Italians wouldn't submit; they organized their blackshirts. The Germans wouldn't submit; so they had their brownshirts and Hitler. I don't believe Americans will submit."[64]

During the disruptive strike at the Inman-Poulsen Lumber Mill in Portland in 1937, Martin directed a withering barrage of criticism against the NLRB and Frances Perkins, whom he called "that miserable Secretary of Labor." Martin blamed the strike on the NLRB and accused it of conducting "Kangaroo courts." After asserting that the Wagner Act should be "wiped off the books," Martin said that he would like to "kick the pants off the National Labor Relations Board."[65] Those who continued to picket the mill were, in the governor's opinion, lawbreakers, and he therefore told law enforcement officers to "Crack their damn heads! Those fellows are there for nothing but trouble–give it to them!"[66]

Governor Martin's antagonism to public power, relief and welfare, and federal labor legislation was obviously inimical to the creation of a cooperative federalism between Oregon and the New Deal. But the governor did not oppose all New Deal measures, though he may have at times given the impression; and between 1935 and 1939, several federal programs functioned effectively in Oregon. The achievements of the New Deal in reclamation and conservation were most important to Oregon. The Bureau of Reclamation, for example, completed 696 miles of canals and drains in reclamation projects, primarily in eastern Oregon. The Owyhee project, at a cost of $4,800,000, was among the more notable efforts. The Land Utilization Division of the Department of Agriculture initiated a number of important land management programs to restore cut-over land to forest cover, establish recreational and wildlife refuges, and encourage controlled range usage. In all, 183,500 acres came under land management projects in Oregon.[67]

In addition to these endeavors, the U.S. Army Corps of Engineers completed 19 major projects in Oregon, including improvement of the harbors at Coos Bay and the mouth of the Columbia River. The Bureau of Public Roads, in cooperation with the Oregon State Highway Department, constructed over 1,200 miles of roads and spent in excess of $20,000,000 in Oregon. In August 1936, there were 6,103 employed in highway construction. And, though Governor Martin disapproved of the WPA, it nevertheless functioned with a minimum of criticism and performed a valuable service by providing employment for hundreds of Oregonians. From its inception in 1935 to June 1939, the WPA expended over

$46,000,000 in Oregon. Aside from construction projects on highways and buildings, the National Youth Administration, which operated under the auspices of the WPA, spent $917,620 to provide work projects for high school and college students.[68] In terms of money spent on these and other federal programs, Oregon received very favorable treatment during the New Deal. Indeed, on a per capita basis, the state ranked eleventh in the amount of funds expended by major New Deal agencies.[69]

The beneficial effects of these expenditures and the physical accomplishments of several federal projects, however, did not accrue to the Oregon Democratic party. Governor Martin's recalcitrant attitude on reform, in fact, thoroughly discredited the Democratic party as a vehicle for change during the 1930s. Political opposition to Martin, which had grown since he entered office, reached its most powerful and organized form in 1937. In that year Republicans, Democrats, and Socialists joined to create the Oregon Commonwealth Federation, a nonpartisan "league of progressives." Although the OCF advocated many liberal programs, and strongly supported the New Deal, its major emphasis was on public power, a cause that it advocated until its end in 1942. On the other hand, the OCF's immediate adversary was Governor Martin. At its first convention, the OCF passed a resolution denouncing the "tyranny of the Martin regime" and pledged itself to cooperation with the New Deal.[70]

Although the OCF was fired with enthusiasm, there was little it could do to establish a friendly atmosphere for New Deal reforms in Oregon. By 1937–38, the domestic legislation of the Roosevelt administration had about run its course. But the OCF did make good on its promise to see Governor Martin retired from office. When Martin announced for a second term as governor in 1938, the OFC endorsed liberal State Senator Henry Hess, Martin's opponent in the Democratic gubernatorial primary. Allied with the OFC against Martin was the Oregon Grange, the State Federation of Labor, and liberal Democrats. Two weeks before the primary, Senator George Norris and Secretary Ickes sent letters of endorsement to Hess. The letters were given wide publicity and interpreted as a repudiation of Martin by President Roosevelt. The combined force of the governor's enemies in Oregon, coupled with the opposition of Norris and Ickes, resulted in Martin's defeat.[71]

Unfortunately for Democrats, it was too late to make political amends to Oregon voters. In the general election of 1938, Oregon followed a national trend and put Republicans back into office. Hess lost the gubernatorial election to Republican Charles Sprague, and Democrats, after maintaining their majority in the lower house of the legislature in 1936, lost twenty-five seats in 1938 to occupy a minority position once again. Democrat Nan Wood Honeyman, who was elected from the Third Congressional District in 1936, failed to win reelection in 1938. Only Walter Pierce survived the Democratic debacle to remain in office until 1943.[72] Oregonians also demonstrated their anger over the protracted labor strife between the AFL and the CIO by adopting an anti-picketing initiative in 1938. The anti-picketing law, according to one reporter, nullified the Wagner Act in Oregon and was "the most severe anti-labor law ever enacted in America."[73]

From the perspective of national history, it is tempting to think of the New Deal as an event that profoundly and uniformly influenced the entire nation. This view has been so pervasive that, among similar interpretations, the New Deal has been described as the "Third American Revolution."[74] But the impact of the New Deal upon Oregon fell far short of revolution. At the same time, Oregon's socioeconomic and political patterns were altered during the 1930s, if not in a radical manner.

Although the Reciprocal Trade Agreement negotiated during the 1930s and short-term measures designed to control production in agriculture contributed to the economic recovery of Oregon, the state's economy was not fundamentally changed by the New Deal. World War II, however, did bring some diversification to the economy. Government contracts for shipbuilding at Portland, the establishment of aluminum reduction plants and electroprocess industries, food processing, and other industries, all aimed at meeting the production demands of the war, collectively broadened the economy. The total number of workers employed in manufacturing industries in Oregon increased 85 percent between 1939 and 1954. The power produced at Bonneville Dam after 1937 assisted new industries in Oregon, but economic growth during and after the war did not remake the state into a replica of industrial areas in other parts of the nation. Actually, Oregon remained heavily dependent upon products from its farms and forests. The lumber industry, which surpassed farm products as the mainstay of the economy in 1940, employed 63 percent of those classified as industrial workers in the mid-1950s.[75] In 1964, that figure had dropped to 48.7 percent, but the lumber industry still employed more people than any other economic activity in Oregon.[76]

During the 1930s, Oregon produced no progressive labor legislation. If anything, labor lost ground in Oregon during the New Deal. In addition to Governor Martin's opposition to federal labor legislation and the anti-picketing law of 1938, labor suffered when the legislature refused to broaden the provisions of the workmen's compensation law, initially enacted in 1913.[77] In later years, the picture changed somewhat. World War II brought workers to new Oregon industries, and union membership increased nearly 300 percent between 1935 and 1953.[78] As labor gained in influence and power in Oregon, it also received more attention. In 1943, Oregon expanded the provisions of its workmen's compensation law, but it was not until 1959 that the legislature established an independent Department of Employment. Finally, in 1961, Oregon created a Labor-Management Relations Board.[79]

The influence of New Deal programs in the field of social security and welfare did have a significant effect on Oregonians, but the state was not immediately won over to matching programs. Although Oregonians undoubtedly recognized the desirability of such measures, they were reluctant to pay for them. In 1938, for instance, Oregon voters seemed of two minds when they simultaneously approved a Townsend Plan but refused to adopt a transaction tax to finance the measure. And, on five occasions since the 1930s, a sales tax provision has been placed before the voters, and each time it was defeated by substantial margins.[80] Nevertheless, the New Deal marked a point of departure in Oregon's attention to welfare problems. Beginning in 1939, when the legislature put relief and welfare on a regular basis by establishing a permanent Public Welfare Commission, Oregon has assumed greater responsibility in this area. In 1945, a retirement system for state employees was inaugurated, and counties no longer bear the lion's share of relief payments.[81]

The larger trends in Oregon politics were not immediately changed as a result of the depression. Republican domination of state politics was only temporarily broken in the 1930s, and after the Republican landslide of 1938, the GOP continued to control state politics during the decade of the 1940s. In part, Oregon Republicans weathered the political storm of the 1930s because they quickly accommodated themselves to the New Deal. Like Senator Charles McNary, those Republicans elected in 1938 cooperated with the New Deal. Governor Charles Sprague, who succeeded Martin, was regarded as a progressive. Sprague endorsed the New Deal's public power program and proved far more friendly to President Roosevelt than had Martin. Homer Angell, who defeated Nan Wood Honeyman in 1938, was an active friend of labor, a consistent supporter of the Townsend Plan, and an advocate of most New Deal reform legislation.[82] Representing the Third Congressional District, a center of union strength and Democratic by registration since 1938, Angell repeatedly won the endorsement of the State Federation of Labor during the 1940s. While a Republican, Senator Wayne Morse generally conformed to the same pattern. In the senatorial campaign of 1944, Morse ran against a conservative Democrat who attacked organized labor and New Deal reforms. At heart, Morse did not oppose the New Deal; in fact, his service on the National War Labor Board (1942–44) and the favorable reputation he had established with labor made him an attractive candidate to New Deal liberals in Oregon. But as a newcomer to active Republican politics, he bowed to the established, conservative wing of the GOP and resorted to campaign rhetoric critical of the New Deal. Morse nonetheless won the endorsement of the Oregon State Federation of Labor, the AFL, and the CIO, a development that caused conservative Republicans to charge he was a "New Dealer masquerading as a republican."[83]

It is true that the Oregon Democratic party did not become ascendant as a result of the New Deal, but the 1930s brought some political change in Oregon. Democratic registration, never higher than 30 percent of the state's voters between 1900 and 1930, climbed to 48 percent in 1938. Even though those who registered as Democrats did not consistently vote the Democratic ticket, their numerical strength was not diminished after the 1930s. More significant for the future of Oregon politics was the fact that the depression spawned a new generation of liberal Democrats who were anxious to lead the party in a new direction. Following World War II, when the Oregon Republican party moved to the right, many former OCF members, in alliance with newcomers to Oregon, successfully revitalized the Democratic party along liberal lines. By 1956, Democrats finally came to dominate state politics.[84]

Even though the depression may have made long-range contributions to Democratic resurgence in the 1950s, the New Deal did not transform Oregon's political culture. Reforms adopted during the progressive movement in Oregon destroyed party responsibility so that Oregonians adopted a habit of voting for the man, not the party label. This was true before and after the New Deal. Thus, in 1972, when registered Democrats outnumbered Republicans by over 200,000, the GOP held most major offices in Oregon.

While the New Deal certainly left its mark on Oregon, it did not prompt a revolution in habits of thought. The New Deal helped to bring about some political change, World War II modified the state's economy, and Oregon assumed greater responsibility for public services and welfare. Despite all this, the force of tradition has remained strong in Oregon.[85]

1. Richard L. Neuberger, *Our Promised Land* (New York, 1938), p.44.

2. Representative of progressivism during the 1920s was the gubernatorial administration of Democrat Walter M. Pierce (1923–27). Although elected with the votes of the Ku Klux Klan in 1922, Pierce otherwise demonstrated a progressive posture by his crusade for prison reform, conservation, development of a state-owned hydroelectric program, and a graduated income tax for Oregon. See Gerald Schwartz, "Walter M. Pierce and the Tradition of Progressive Reform: A Study of Eastern Oregon's Great Democrat" (Ph.D. diss., Washington State University, 1969), pp. 68-86.

3. *Oregon Democrat,* 21 March 1933, p. 11.

4. Dorothy O. Johansen and Charles M. Gates, *Empire of the Columbia: A History of the Pacific Northwest* (New York, 1967), p. 502; Earl Pomeroy, *The Pacific Slope: A History of California, Oregon, Washington, Idaho, Utah, and Nevada* (New York, 1965), pp. 294–95.

5. E. B. Mittleman, *Occupational Characteristics of Workers on Relief* (Salem, Ore., 1936), p. 6; *Report of Executive Committee State-Wide Relief Council to Honorable Julius L. Meier* (Salem, Ore., 1933), p. 7.

6. U.S. Office of Government Reports, Statistical Section, "Oregon: Federal Loans and Expenditures 1933-1939," II, Report No. 10 (n.p., 1939), pp. 5, 7, 10, typed mimeo. copy in Special Collections, University of Oregon (hereafter cited as "Oregon: Federal Loans and Expenditures 1933-1939"); Mittleman, *Occupational Characteristics of Workers on Relief,* p. 5.

7. State Tax Commission, *Twelfth Biennial Report of the State Tax Commission* (Salem, Ore., 1934), pp. 48–50; *Statement of Taxes Collected and Unpaid on County Tax Rolls of 1933–1934* (Salem, Ore., 1934).

8. Mittleman, *Occupational Characteristics of Workers on Relief,* p. 29. A subcommittee appointed by the State Relief Committee in 1933 reported 30,000 families on relief. The committee also concluded that there were "unknown thousands of additional unemployed who are self-sustaining or who have yet not exhausted their personal resources." See *Report of the Committee Appointed by Governor Julius L. Meier to Study Relief Needs of the State of Oregon* (n.p., 1933), p. 4, in Special Collections, University of Oregon.

9. "Confidential Report and Recommendations to Executive Committee, Governor's State-Wide Relief Council, 1932"; "Confidential Report on Unemployment Conditions in Clatsop, Tillamook, Lincoln, and Coos Counties, October, 1932"; Paul V. Maris, "Report of Administration of Relief Work in Union County, October 29, 1932," Oregon State-Wide Relief Council Papers (University of Oregon).

10. Walter M. Pierce to Bayard T. Merrill, 18 February 1933, Pierce Papers (University of Oregon).

11. *Portland Oregonian,* 4, 5 February 1932.

12. *Oregon Voter,* 7 March 1931, pp. 3–6; 18 April 1931, p. 1; 16 December 1933, pp. 3–4; 23 March 1935, pp. 10–11; "News and Notes," *Commonwealth Review,* April 1933, pp. 40–41.

13. Henry M. Hanzen to Charles L. McNary, 4 April 1933, Hanzen Papers (University of Oregon).

14. Herman Kehrli, "Public Welfare and County Finances in Oregon, 1928–1937," *Commonwealth Review,* March 1939, p. 6; [State Emergency Employment Commission], *Unemployment in Oregon* (Salem, Ore., 1931), p. 1.

15. Kehrli, "Public Welfare and County Finances," p. 4.

16. *Report of Executive Committee State-Wide Relief Council*, p. 11.

17. Ibid., p. 15

18. Quoted in James T. Patterson, *The New Deal and the States: Federalism in Transition* (Princeton, N.J., 1969), p. 31

19. Registration statistics are from the *Oregon Blue Books*.

20. Secretary of State, *Abstract of Votes 1932* (Salem, 1933).

21. *Oregon Democrat*, 20 January 1933, p. 4.

22. Ibid., p. 8; 21 March 1933, p. 10; 6 April 1933, p. 3.

23. U.S. Division of Research, Statistics, and Finance, "FERA Grants May 23, 1933 through June 30, 1935," (n.p., 8 July 1935), typed mimeo. copy in Special Collections, University of Oregon. To provide the revenue for matching funds under FERA, the legislature approved a state sales tax to become effective if approved by the voters. In May 1934, the sales tax measure was overwhelmingly defeated, 64,677 to 156,182. *Oregon Voter*, 16 December 1933, pp. 3-4; Secretary of State, *Abstract of Votes May 19, 1934* (Salem, 1934).

24. The Old-Age Pension Act became effective on 1 January 1934. Pension payments under the act differed greatly because they were dependent upon the resources of the various counties. During 1934, payments ranged from $12.64 per month in Multnomah county to $4.86 per month in Curry County. The statewide average for 1934 was $10.64 per month. See Herman Kehrli, "The Operation of the Oregon Old-Age Pension Act," *Commonwealth Review*, January 1935, pp. 205–21. For the operation of the Self-Help and Rehabilitation commission, see *First Biennial Report of the State Commission for Self-Help and Rehabilitation* (Salem, Ore., 1934).

25. In the nationwide wheat referendum of May 1935, Oregon farmers voted 86 percent in favor of the AAA program. In October 1935, corn-hog producers in Oregon voted 85 percent in favor of an adjustment program for 1936. See "Oregon: Federal Loans and Expenditures 1933–1939," p. 11.

26. National Emergency Council, "Oregon: Narrative Review of Agency Operations 1933–1938," Report No. 4 (n.p., 1938), pp. 1–2, typed mimeo. copy in Special Collections, University of Oregon (hereafter cited as NEC, "Oregon: Narrative Review of Agency Operations 1933–1938").

27. "Oregon: Federal Loans and Expenditures 1933–1939," p. 11.

28. Burton E. Palmer, "The CWA in Oregon," *Commonwealth Review*, July 1934, pp. 134–39.

29. "The P.W.A. Program in Oregon," in NEC, "Oregon: Narrative Review of Agency Operations 1933–1938," p. 1.

30. "The Civilian Conservation Corps," ibid., pp. 1–5.

31. For a detailed study of NRA lumber codes in Oregon, see Algernon C. Dixon, "History of Code of Fair Competition for the Lumber and Timber Products Industry" (unpublished manuscript, University of Oregon, 1935).

32. C. C. Crow to Pierce, 10 April 1935, Pierce Papers. For other complaints about NRA lumber codes, see Frank D. Overholser to Pierce, 24 February 1934; M. Peterson to Pierce, 30 May 1934; R. J. Darling to Pierce, 23 February 1935; and M. C. Woodward to Pierce, 6 April 1935, ibid.

33. J. D. Loder to Pierce, 22 April 1935, ibid.

34. Pierce to Kenneth Murhard, 18 April 1935, ibid.

35. Henry M. Hanzen claimed that the operation of the Home Owners' Loan Corporation in Oregon in 1933 and 1934 was a failure; even given the depression, said Hanzen, it was easier to get a loan from private companies than the HOLC (Hanzen to James W. Mott, 23 March 1934, Hanzen Papers).

36. Pierce charged that the FERA director for Oregon, Edgar B. Freed, was a Republican who was appointed by Hopkins because the wives of Freed and Hopkins were close friends. Pierce also asserted: "I have been to Harry Hopkins in person with all sorts of complaints [about the administration of FERA in Oregon] and after presenting them I have been told that he did not believe a word of it and that the work in Oregon is satisfactory to him" (Pierce to F. L. Young 2 January 1934, Pierce Papers).

37. *Oregon Democrat*, 6 January 1934, p. 9; 21 January 1934, p. 9.

38. Secretary of State, *Abstract of Votes 1934* (Salem, 1935); Richard L. Neuberger, "The Northwest Goes Leftish," *New Republic,* 7 November 1934, p. 357.

39. According to one of McNary's biographers, the senator established a better relationship with Franklin D. Roosevelt than any other president he had known (see Roger T. Johnson, "Charles L. McNary and the Republican Party during Prosperity and Depression" [Ph.D. diss., University of Wisconsin, 1967].

40. John D. Phillips, "Charles L. McNary: Progressive Ideology and Minority Politics During the New Deal" (M.A. thesis, University of Oregon, 1963) p. 57.

41. Dellmore Lessard to Pierce, 12 May 1937, Pierce Papers.

42. Monroe Sweetland to E. L. Oliver, 5 December 1938, Oregon Commonwealth Federation Papers (University of Oregon).

43. *Oregon Democrat,* November 1942, p. 7. The inability of Oregon Democrats to benefit measurably from the New Deal is not without parallel. Party factionalism and disputes over patronage, in addition to other problems, also marked other state Democratic parties during the New Deal. For a useful guide to state Democratic troubles during the 1930s, see James T. Patterson, "The New Deal and the States," *American Historical Review* 73 (1967): 70–84.

44. Charles H. Martin to Paul R. Kelty, 21 November 1935, Martin Papers (Oregon Historical Society, Portland).

45. Oregon State Federation of Labor, *Review of the Political Situation in Oregon: An Analysis of the Position of Candidates on Vital Issues* (Portland, Ore., 1938), p. 3.

46. Herman C. Voeltz, "Proposals for a Columbia Valley Authority: A History of Political Controversy" (Ph.D. diss., University of Oregon, 1960), pp. 65–67, 195–212.

47. Charles H. Martin, "Achievements of the 1935 Legislature," *Commonwealth Review,* March–May 1935, pp. 5–8.

48. Daniel M. Ogden, "The Development of Federal Power Policy in the Pacific Northwest" (Ph.D. diss., University of Chicago, 1949, pp. 227–28; Pierce to S. Stephenson Smith, 2 June 1937, Pierce Papers; *Portland Oregonian,* 20 July 1937, p. 8. See also "Resume of Conversation Between President Roosevelt and Governor Charles H. Martin, 28 September '37," typed transcript in Wallace S. Wharton Papers (Oregon State Archives, Salem). Wharton was Martin's budget director and executive secretary.

49. Pierce to Tom Quigley, 26 May 1937, Pierce Papers.

50. Harold Ickes to Henry Hess, 14 May 1938, Oregon Commonwealth Federation Papers.

51. *Roseburg Times,* 15 January 1936; *Salem Capital Journal,* 14 October 1938.

52. Neuberger, *Our Promised Land,* p. 314.

53. The state legislature required Oregon counties to contribute half of the state's matching fund requirements under the different Social Security programs (see Glen Leet, "Social Security In Oregon," *Commonwealth Review,* November 1935, pp. 141–62).

54. Kehrli, "Public Welfare and County Finances," pp. 6–7; "Report of the Budget Director to State Relief Committee, June 25, 1936," Wharton Papers.

55. In 1936, several members of the State Relief Commission resigned in protest because of Martin's unsympathetic attitude toward relief. See Cecila L. Gaven to Martin, 16 June 1936; E. R. Byson to Martin, 17 June 1936; Judd Greenman to Martin, 29 June 1936, Governor's File (Oregon State Archives); *Portland Oregonian,* 13, 14 June 1936.

56. *Salem Capital Journal,* 14 July 1936.

57. Ibid., 12 March 1936; *Portland Oregonian,* 18 March 1936.

58. *Portland Oregonian,* 13 June 1936.

59. Ibid., 15 January 1936; *Roseburg Times,* 15 January 1936.

60. Vernon H. Jensen, *Lumber and Labor* (New York, 1945), pp. 203–24.

61. Pomeroy, *The Pacific Slope,* p. 243; Martin and Joseph K. Carson to Frances Perkins, 2 (telegram), 13 November 1936, Martin Papers.

63. "Statement by Charles H. Martin at Salem—November 28, 1936," Wharton Papers.

64. *Portland Oregonian,* 18 December 1937.

65. Ibid., 7, 8, 9 December 1937; "Radio Speech of Governor Charles H. Martin, December 6, 1937," Martin Papers.

66. *Portland Oregonian,* 18 December 1937.

67. "Oregon: Federal Loans and Expenditures 1933–1937," pp. 43, 47.

68. Ibid., pp. 45–46; "National Youth Administration In Oregon," Bureau of Public Roads in Oregon"; "Physical Accomplishment on WPA Projects," in NEC, "Oregon: Narrative Review of Agency Operations 1933–1937."

69. Leonard Arrington, "The New Deal in the West: A Preliminary Statistical Inquiry," *Pacific Historical Review* 38 (1969): 315.

70. "Program of the Oregon Commonwealth Federation," April, 1937, Oregon Commonwealth Federation Papers; Jill H. Herzig, "The Oregon Commonwealth Federation: The Rise and Decline of a Reform Organization" (M.A. thesis, University of Oregon, 1963).

71. Harold L. Ickes, *The Secret Diaries of Harold L. Ickes,* 3 vols. (New York, 1953–54), 2:493, 500; *Portland Oregonian,* 17, 18 May 1938; Secretary of State, *Abstract of Votes: Democratic and Republican Primary Elections, May 20, 1938* (Salem, Ore., 1938).

72. Secretary of State, *Abstract of Votes 1938* (Salem, Ore., 1939). In a telephone conversation with James A. Farley after his defeat, Martin tried to assure the postmaster general of his loyalty to the Democratic party: "I want you to understand I really am a Democrat," said Martin (typed transcript of telephone conversation between Martin and Farley, 15 July 1938, Wharton Papers). Nevertheless, in the general elections of 1938, Martin campaigned for the Republican candidates against Hess and Honeyman. After the election, the chairman of the Multnomah County Republican Central Committee wrote Martin, thanking him for his help in the campaign: "I want to express to you my very great appreciation for your support given to the Republican cause in the recent campaign in which we were engaged with the Oregon New Deal contingent of the Democratic Party" (Fred W. Brown to Martin, 13 November 1938 Martin Papers).

73. Richard L. Neuberger, "Who Are the Associated Farmers?", *Survey Graphic* 28 (1939): 517.

74. Carl N. Degler, *Out of Our Past: The Forces That Shaped Modern America* (New York, 1959), p. 379.

75. Lester G. Seligman, "Political Change: Legislative Elites and Parties in Oregon," *Western Political Quarterly* 17 (1964): 177–79.

76. John M. Swarthout and Kenneth R. Gervais, "Oregon: Political Experiment Station," in Frank H. Jonas, ed., *Politics in the American West* (Salt Lake City, 1969), p. 303.

77. Victor P. Morris, "Some Proposed Changes in the Oregon Workmen's Compensation Law," *Commonwealth Review,* January 1941, pp. 220–29.

78. Seligman, "Political Change," p. 177.

79. Secretary of State, *Oregon Blue Book 1963–1964* (Salem, Ore., 1964), pp. 56, 70, 73.

80. Swarthout and Gervais, "Oregon: Political Experiment Station," p. 320.

81. *Oregon Blue Book 1963–1964,* pp. 81–82.

82. Angel, who represented the Third Congressional District from 1939 to 1955, prided himself on nonpartisanship: "I realize that Multnomah County is heavily Democratic," he wrote a fellow Republican, "but many of my best supporters belong to the Democratic party which i believe is due to the fact that . . . I represent all the people" (Angell to Ralph J. Anderson, 12 May y 1954, Homer D. Angell Papers [University of Oregon]). For a review of Angell's career, see *Portland Oregonian,* 26 January 1964.

83. "Do the Republicans of Oregon Want to Put a New Dealer in the Senate?", typed manuscript of radio address by C. C. Crow, 29 April 1944, Hanzen Papers. For a critical analysis of Morse's political maneuverings in the 1944 senatorial campaign, see A. Robert Smith, *The Tiger in the Senate: A Biography of Senator Wayne Morse* (New York, 1962), pp. 100–106.

84. Swarthout and Gervais, "Oregon: Political Experiment Station," pp. 301–2, 311–12.

85. This assessment agrees with the suggestion of James T. Patterson, who, in a study of the impact of the New Deal upon the states, concluded there was as much change as continuity on the state level between the progressive era and the 1960s (see Patterson, "The New Deal and the States," p. 85).

Bruce M. Stave

Pittsburgh and the New Deal

PITTSBURGH ENTERED THE 1930s AS A CITY IN ECONOMIC AND EN-vironmental decay and political stagnation; it departed the decade in largely the same condition. Perhaps this is attributable to the fact that the accomplishments "of the New Deal program so far as it dealt with cities . . . were singularly limited" in improving urban life.[1] Yet within this apparent continuity, a good deal of change occurred in the relationship of the city to the federal government, in its political condition, in the status of the workers in its major industry, and in its attitude toward future development. This seeming paradox may be explained by the limits on change placed by the magnitude of the Steel City's urban and economic problems, the nature of those individuals dealing with these problems, and goals of the New Deal program itself.

The advent of the 1930s brought to Pittsburgh a long-term Democratic political tradition. Although the New Deal failed to place the state of Pennsylvania in the iron grip of the Democratic party, no Republican presidential candidate carried the city from 1932 through the 1960s, and all of Pittsburgh's mayors have been Democrats since the early thirties.

Roosevelt's victory in Pittsburgh in 1932, despite his loss of the state, was the first time the city had voted for a Democratic presidential candidate since 1856. Until the New Deal triumph, Pittsburgh had been a staunch Republican bastion in a staunch Republican state and remained under the control of a mighty GOP machine. The Republican machine, founded by Squire Tommy Steele in 1863, passed on to the control of his nephew, Christopher Lyman Magee. In alliance with a young contractor, William

Flinn, Magee consolidated the Republican hegemony over the city that lasted, on the surface at least, until the 1930s. Magee took his job as boss seriously, allegedly studying Tammany Hall after the downfall of Boss Tweed to make certain that he would avoid the New York City politician's mistakes. It was during this period of Magee control that Lincoln Steffens labeled Pittsburgh as "a city ashamed."[2]

By the 1920s, political control of the Republican party—and the city —rested with the family of Andrew Mellon, with William Larimer Mellon as steward of its political fortunes. Adhering to his policy of limiting a mayor to one term, he forced William A. Magee (Boss Christopher Magee's nephew) from office in 1925. However, Mellon spent his political credit on a losing attempt to install both metropolitan government and voting machines in the Pittsburgh area. As a result, Mayor Charles Kline, after serving one term and building his own machine, ran for and won a second term in 1929. He was the last Republican mayor elected in Pittsburgh; scandal in his administration and the coming of the Great Depression made the chances for a Republican mayoralty victory in 1933 less likely than usual. Meanwhile, of course, FDR triumphed a year earlier.[3]

The Roosevelt victory was all the more significant because of the weakness of the Democratic party in Pittsburgh. Only 3 percent of the city's registered voters in 1929 were Democratic, and as late as 1933 the figure stood at 18 percent; not until 1936 did the Democrats have a registration majority. The party organization had been accustomed to living off the patronage crumbs offered to it by the entrenched Republicans. As Democratic leader David L. Lawrence remarked: "Prior to 1932, just a few old faithfuls stuck by the party. It was a long gap between Wilson and FDR. Before 1932 Democrats always played for minority places." The party was so weak, in fact, that Republicans had to be persuaded to sit as Democratic election judges because not enough Democrats were available for work on election day.[4]

Despite these odds, the Democratic victory in 1932 was not as unlikely as the registration figures and organization weakness indicate. The party had done very well in the 1930 congressional elections, and, in 1931, David L. Lawrence, with Republican support, had polled over 120,000 votes in a race for county commissioner. Although he lost the election, this occurred at a time when the average Democratic vote for that office rarely exceeded 10,000. Moreover, as can be seen in both table 1 and figure 1, a Democratic trend had been building up through the 1920s that culminated

TABLE 1

DEMOCRATIC PERCENTAGE OF PITTSBURGH
PRESIDENTIAL AND MAYORALTY VOTE, 1912-69

Election Years	Presidential Vote	Mayoralty Vote
1912-13	26*	. . . †
1916-17	37	. . . †
1920-21	20	31
1924-25	44‡	6§
1928-29	48	32
1932-33	58	57
1936-37	71	57
1940-41	62	51
1944-45	61	53
1948-49	61	61
1952-53	56	62
1956-57	52	65
1959 //	. . . .	63
1960-61	67	67
1964-65	75	62
1968-69#	62	65

SOURCE. The presidential vote for 1912–48 was obtained from the *Pennsylvania Legislative Manuals* and *Handbooks* for the appropriate years; percentages were computed from the totals by the author. The 1952–68 presidential percentages were obtained from Richard Scammon, *America Votes*, vols. 1, 2, 4, 6, 8. The mayoralty vote through 1941 (except 1921) and the 1965 and 1969 figures were obtained from the appropriate Pittsburgh postelection-day newspapers, and percentages were computed by the author; the 1921 vote is from A. H. Kerr, *The Mayors and Recorders of Pittsburgh, 1861–1951* (Pittsburgh, 1952). Mayoralty figures for 1945–61 are from the files of Nicholas Stabile of Pittsburgh.

*In 1912, the Republican candidate, William Howard Taft, won 22 percent of Pittsburgh's vote, and Theodore Roosevelt's combined vote was 38 percent; Eugene V. Debs's share was 13 percent.

†In 1913 and 1917, Pittsburgh mayoralty elections were nonpartisan.

‡The listed 44 percent is the total vote for Democrat John W. Davis, who received 8 percent, and Progressive Robert La Follette, who won 36 percent. See text for the effect of the La Follette vote.

§In 1925, a Prohibition, nonpartisan candidate received 18 percent of the total vote.

//A special mayoralty election was held in 1959 after David L. Lawrence left office to become Pennsylvania's governor.

#In 1969, an anti-organization candidate, Peter Flaherty, won the Democratic primary and subsequently the mayoralty election.

in the FDR win. Correlation voting analysis has shown that, in Pittsburgh, the New Deal coalition had roots in La Follette's 1924 vote as well as in the 1928 drawing power of Al Smith. The urban ethnic working class began shifting to the Democratic party before the depression and FDR's New Deal; the period of critical realignment covered several elections rather than one critical election, that of 1932.[5]

One of the groups that realigned late, but then became solidly Democrat-

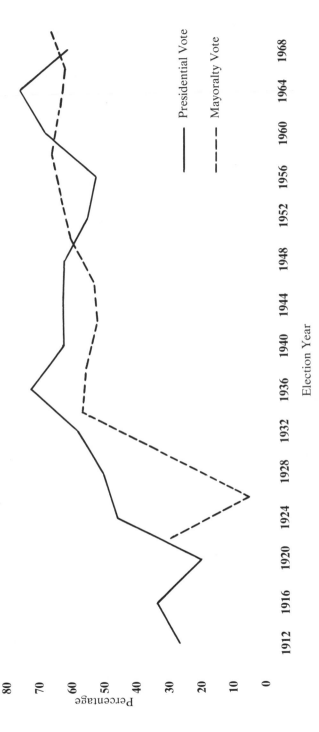

Fig. 1. Democratic percentage of presidential vote, 1912-1968, and mayoralty vote, 1921-1969, city of Pittsburgh. For information about elections, see table 1.

ic, was the city's Negroes; in so doing, black residents of Pittsburgh's ghetto were in the vanguard of a nationwide trend. As indicated in table 2 and figures 2 and 3, Pittsburgh's blacks, crowded into the central city Third and Fifth Wards of its Hill District, voted below the city's 1932 Democratic average, with the Fifth ward maintaining its adherence to the GOP in presidential elections until 1936; blacks did not vote Democratic for mayor until 1937. After 1936 to the end of the 1960s, however, black voting for both president and mayor was far above the city Democratic percentage and the Democratic proportion in the least Negro wards.[6]

In 1932, the Democratic organization made a special effort to win over the staunchly Republican but economically depressed Negro voters. Keeping in mind that in the two Negro wards of the city registration was approximately 80 and 88 percent Republican, respectively, the Democrats jumped at an offer by Robert Vann to bring the black vote into the party fold. Vann, a Negro attorney and editor and publisher of the widely circulated black newspaper, the *Pittsburgh Courier*, appeared bitter toward Republican leadership. Four years earlier, after serving as director of publicity for the Colored Voters Division of the Republican National Committee, he had been refused an assistant attorney generalship for which he had been mentioned. Under FDR, he achieved this position, after campaigning for the New York governor and telling Negro audiences: "My friends, go home and turn Lincoln's picture to the wall. The debt has been paid in full."[7]

Young blacks, less bound by the tradition of previous generations who might have remembered slavery, spread the gospel of the Democracy. One Democratic precinct committeeman visited churches Sunday after Sunday and told Negro congregations that the "Republicans gave you freedom but nothing else." Facing an extreme registration deficit—less than 2,800 Democrats were registered in the two most Negro wards, with the Republicans having a four to one advantage—Vann's organization worked fervently; FDR's New Deal helped. During the 1933 primary election, Democratic leaders Joseph F. Guffey and David L. Lawrence, upon the recommendation of Vann, announced the appointment of five local Negroes to the Pittsburgh office of the Home Owners' Loan Corporation. Vann's *Pittsburgh Courier* campaigned vigorously for the Democratic organization's candidate for mayor, William Nissley McNair, and also made clear its general election choice; as one result, the Republicans refused to grant the *Courier* traditional election advertising.[8]

Moreover, during the primary campaign, Vann and McNair charged that in the economically depressed Negro Fifth Ward, voters who tried to register as Democrats were threatened with being cut from the relief rolls. Erasures in the registration books appeared to bear out the claim that police herded fifty voters of the Fifth Ward, Seventeenth District, who registered as Democrats back to the board and forced them to change their registration or lose their relief aid. McNair attacked such acts by noting, "That's not only commercializing charity. It's prostituting charity!" Charges of this type of activity continued during the general election. To counter widespread rumors of Republican vote-buying—as high as ten dollars a vote—Vann's *Pittsburgh Courier* had told its readers to "take the money, put it in your pocket and then go to the polls and vote the straight Democratic ticket for the protection of yourself, your home, your children."[9]

Despite the Democrats' failure to carry either of the Negro wards, Paul Ford Jones, of the City-County Colored Democratic Committee, was not disheartened. Although the Negro wards voted less Democratic than they had in the 1932 presidential election, they voted significantly more Democratic than they had in the 1929 mayoralty race (see table 2 and figures 2 and 3). Jones told his coworkers, "Despite the intimidation of the Police Department, racketeer's money and whiskey, our Democratic organization not only succeeded in keeping down the Republican majority, but actually carried some of the districts conceded [to] the G.O.P. in the campaign." Two weeks after the election, black Democrats organized a permanent party organization in the city's Third Ward. The shift to the Democratic party among Negroes in Pittsburgh is highlighted by the fact that in that ward more than half of the precinct committeemen elected as Republicans in 1934 served in that position as Democrats by 1938. This indicates that control of the ward remained in the hands of the same individuals, although they had shifted party allegiance. Among the primary recipients of Democratic relief and public housing programs, black voters in Pittsburgh and elsewhere, regardless of the New Deal's lack of civil rights legislation, wedded themselves to the party of Franklin Delano Roosevelt.[10]

The president's coattails were so inviting that the strategy of the 1933 mayoralty campaign had Democrats attacking Mayor John S. Herron and Republican machine politics but more emphatically linking the local party and its candidate, William Nissley McNair, to the New Deal. Full-page

TABLE 2

DEMOCRATIC PERCENTAGE OF PITTSBURGH PRESIDENTIAL AND MAYORALTY VOTE, 1928-69, FOR MOST AND LEAST NEGRO WARDS AND CITY

President

	1928	1932	1936	1940	1944	1948	1952	1956	1960	1964	1958
Most Negro											
3rd Ward	46	58	90	85	84	81	83	83	90	96	90
5th Ward	38	47	76	77	78	76	76	68	78	95	91
Mean	42	53	83	81	81	79	80	76	84	96	91
Least Negro											
29th Ward	35	65	68	51	48	52	46	45	64	71	55
30th Ward	45	55	63	50	49	52	50	51	62	74	60
Mean	40	60	66	51	49	52	48	48	63	73	58
City	48	58	71	62	61	61	56	52	67	75	62

Mayor

	1929	1933	1937	1941	1945	1949	1953	1957	1959*	1961	1965	1969
Most Negro												
3rd Ward	6	37	86	73	71	83	84	85	89	89	85	83
5th Ward	12	48	66	71	64	81	76	75	82	81	79	83
Mean	9	43	76	72	68	82	80	80	86	85	82	83
Least Negro												
29th Ward	49	72	49	38	44	51	53	59	57	62	58	63
30th Ward	48	67	49	40	44	52	57	58	58	60	61	70
Mean	49	69	49	39	44	52	55	59	58	61	60	67
City	32	57	57	51	53	61	62	65	63	67	62	65

SOURCE. Voting returns were compiled from same sources as noted in table 1.

*A special mayoralty election was held in 1959 after David L. Lawrence left office to become Pennsylvania's governor.

N.B. The figures below indicate the percentage of nonwhite, almost totally Negro population living in the 3rd, 5th, 29th, and 30th wards from 1930 to 1960.

	1930	1940	1950	1960
3rd Ward	40.0	51.0	73.0	92.0
5th Ward	54.0	70.0	78.0	85.0
29th Ward	.06	.02	.10	.10
30th Ward	.18	.08	.30	.50

(1930 and 1940 figures from Bureau of Social Research, Federation of Social Agencies of Pittsburgh and Allegheny County, *Social Facts about Pittsburgh and Allegheny County*, Vol. 1, *Pittsburgh Wards* (Pittsburgh, 1945); figures for 1950 and 1960 from Pittsburgh Commission on Human Relations, "Population by Color and Ward with Recent Change, Pittsburgh, 1950 and 1960," mimeograph, 3 March 1961.)

Although it cannot be said that all black voters cast their ballot in the exact percentage of the listing for the 3rd and 5th wards, the black population proportions are large enough to provide a general impression of black voting in Pittsburgh, discounting other variables.

In only three instances—the 1932 presidential election in the Most Negro wards and the 1952 and 1956 presidential elections for the Least Negro wards—did the two wards being measured in each instance vote differently, so that one was Republican and one Democratic; hence, the mean must be viewed with care in those cases.

Voting statistics begin with 1928 because wards 29 and 30 did not join the city of Pittsburgh until one year earlier. Incorporation dates for various Pittsburgh neighborhoods can be found in William G. Willis, *The Pittsburgh Manual* (Pittsburgh, 1950), p. xxvi, and can be compared with ward boundaries listed on p. xxiv of the same volume.

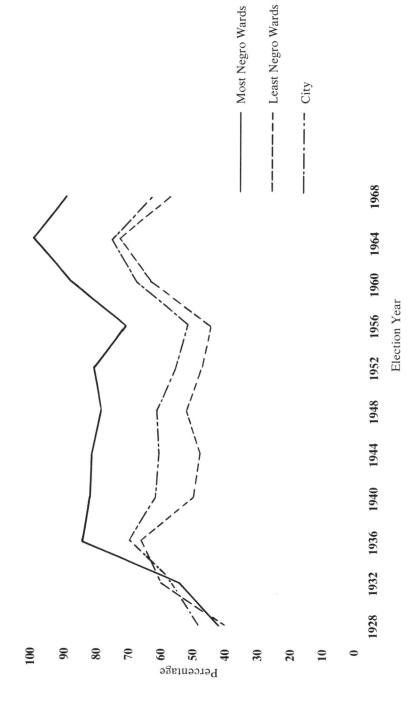

Fig. 2. Democratic percentage of presidential vote in Most and Least Negro wards and city of Pittsburgh, 1928-1968. See table 2 for information about wards.

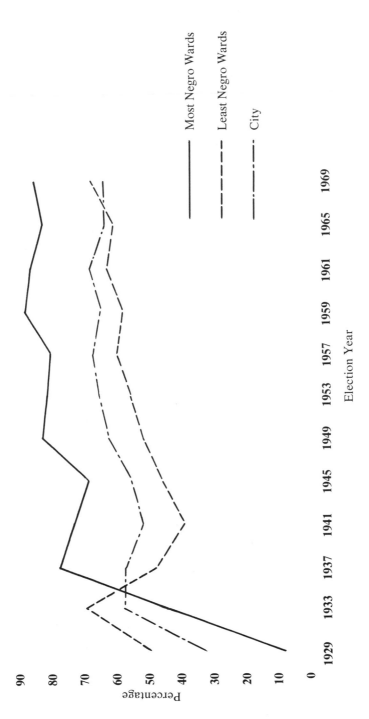

Fig. 3. Democratic percentage of mayoralty vote in Most and Least Negro wards and city of Pittsburgh, 1929-1969. See table 2 for information about wards.

advertisements asked that votes be cast for the Roosevelt Democracy; next to every photograph of McNair was one of Roosevelt. A Democratic candidate for city council informed a meeting that "every vote cast in the Republican primary is a vote cast against Roosevelt, a vote against the New Deal, and a vote for the return to power of such reactionary interests and political industrialists as Andrew Mellon." McNair, himself, kept mentioning FDR. At a major campaign rally, he declared, "I am as confident of becoming the next Mayor of Pittsburgh as I am that FDR will pull this country out of the depression before many months have elapsed." The *Pittsburgh Press* editorialized that McNair, like Roosevelt a year earlier, stood as a focal point for "those who are sick of the old order, who want a New Deal for Pittsburgh as well as the nation." As a *New York Times* correspondent remarked, "The proverbial visitor from Mars might indeed get the notion that it is Mr. Roosevelt himself who is running for Mayor of Pittsburgh."[11]

The popularity of the New Deal program was so great that the Republican mayoralty candidate found himself apologizing for a campaign slur against it. During a speech to the Twenty-seventh Ward Republican workers, William H. Coleman, Republican county leader, lashed out at Roosevelt and the NRA. Coleman attacked the president for "destroying cotton, wheat and hogs while people are starving" and added: "The N.R.A. is wrong and never will succeed. The first ones to destroy it will be the Democrats themselves." John S. Herron, the Republican standard-bearer and the man who replaced scandal-plagued Charles Kline as mayor, quickly rebutted Coleman's comment. He declared, "The N.R.A. deserves the support of every man and woman in Pittsburgh interested in Recovery" and referred to his being honorary chairman of the local NRA parade held in the city. However, David L. Lawrence, who midwifed the birth of the powerful Pittsburgh Democratic party from its inception and served as its leader until his death during the 1960s, seized upon the issue and declared that voters would cast their ballots for "N.R.A. and other important issues." Apparently, Republicans thought the Coleman statement was the greatest blunder of the campaign. He later defended himself by announcing, "I am one of those Republicans who opposed the New Deal philosophy in Washington. I so expressed myself in October, 1933 and my good friend John S. Herron, then a candidate for mayor of Pittsburgh, and many of his supporters believed that my speech contributed much to his defeat. I could not help it. I was afraid of the destruction of my country."[12]

The administration in Washington viewed favorably the attention paid to the New Deal in Pittsburgh and encouraged the local party to make the connection between city and national politics. At the beginning of the mayoralty campaign, James A. Farley, en route from Columbus, Ohio, to New York City, briefly stopped at the Pittsburgh railway station. When he was met by McNair, Lawrence, and other Democrats, Farley emphasized that a Pittsburgh victory and a large Democratic turnout in Philadelphia during the 1933 elections would greatly influence the possibility of party victory for governor and senator in 1934. He remarked, "Washington, naturally, is much interested in Mr. McNair's campaign. We hope Pittsburgh does as well for him as it did for President Roosevelt and we are informed that there is an excellent chance for his election." Mayor Herron did not appreciate Washington's interference and bitterly warned Republicans, "If Farley were to take charge of City Hall we know what would happen to Republican workers."[13]

Although Republicans repeatedly labeled their opponents as Pittsburgh Democrats seeking office, not Roosevelt candidates, many others agreed with Democratic politician James Malone that McNair was the "personification of the New Deal in the Administration of the affairs of the city of Pittsburgh." The Republicans, citing FDR's lack of support for that year's Democratic mayoralty candidate in New York City, where he said he would back no local candidate, claimed that this stand applied to Pittsburgh as well. However, the Pittsburgh Democrats premised their campaign on this linkage between Roosevelt and the local candidate; it worked so well that it became the strategy for the 1934 gubernatorial and senatorial election throughout the state.[14]

In light of such strong attachment of the Democrats to FDR during the campaign, Joseph F. Guffey's postelection comment that the victory was an approval of "the gospel of government laid down by Roosevelt" is not surprising; nor is McNair's retrospective remark "They were voting for Roosevelt—they didn't care anything about me." It was also easy for contemporary observers to agree with the editors of the Pittsburgh *Sun-Telegraph* that the election results "showed that the Democratic tidal wave of 1932 hadn't spent its force," or to concur with the columnist for the Pittsburgh *Post-Gazette* who declared, "Both independent and organization wards were turning in votes that savored strongly of the Roosevelt vote last year." In fact, however, correlation voting analysis has shown that the McNair mayoralty vote in 1933 had a substantially different mass base than did the FDR vote in Pittsburgh a year earlier. The new mayor appealed not to lower- and working-class ethnics, as did FDR, but to an upper-income, native white population. The same individuals who voted for the New Deal in 1932 did not vote in large number for the Democratic mayoralty candidate in 1933 despite the attempt to link McNair to Roosevelt. Thus, the 1933 election was a classic case of campaign rhetoric differing from the reality of election returns.[15]

The Democratic organization by slating and supporting McNair, who had been an unsuccessful perennial candidate for office prior to 1933 and was well known and well liked by the city's independent voters, triumphed as a result of the support of those voters and thereby retarded its own consolidation. The mayor's vote, lying outside the growing Democratic strength generated by La Follette and culminating with Roosevelt, represented the vote of a citizenry disillusioned with a jaded Republican machine; it did not portend a mass base that would support a newly invigorated Democratic machine nor did it encourage the mayor to cooperate with the party organization. Although promising a "New Deal at City Hall" and pledging to show the nation that Pittsburgh stood squarely behind President Roosevelt's program of national recovery, McNair did nothing of the kind. In fact, he opposed New Deal measures and on the local level broke with David L. Lawrence and the Democratic organization over Republican appointments to his cabinet and patronage in general. Under the influence of a select group of "blue stockings" who had supported him in his campaign, and who more often than not were Republicans, the mayor appointed Republicans as well as Democrats, and hired and fired at machine-gun pace. Frustrated in its attempt to grab hold of the city payroll, Lawrence's patronage-starved regular organization, which many thought had slated McNair in the belief he could be controlled easily, attempted to enact legislation to rip him from office by substituting a city commissioner in his place; the action failed.[16]

Thus, until he resigned in 1936, McNair and the Democratic machine battled incessantly. To compensate for the loss of city patronage, the Democratic organization looked to county and especially federal work-relief patronage to strengthen itself internally. In this manner, the urban-federal relationship based on relief played a major role in the restructuring of Pittsburgh politics; it allowed a Democratic machine to replace a Republican machine.

The relief program in Pennsylvania during the New Deal years was riddled with politics. Just as the Democrats accused the Republicans of using relief as a weapon in Negro wards during the 1933 mayoralty campaign, they also attacked Republican use of the Civil Works Administration. Since the GOP controlled the state house until 1935, Democrats complained bitterly about Republican control of relief. Joseph Guffey warned Harry Hopkins, the federal relief administrator, that the Pittsburgh CWA was not taking care of the unemployed but required a prospective jobseeker to see his Republican ward chairman before being assigned a position. Guffey's sister, Emma Guffey Miller, Pennsylvania's national committeewoman, received dozens of letters from irate Democrats such as one expressing the hope that "some way may be found to put this Federal Relief in the hands of some real Americans in Pittsburgh instead of the Republican organization."[17]

Once the Democrats had elected a governor, the Pittsburgh party, as well as the state organization, took political advantage of the WPA, and the Republicans responded quickly. Gifford Pinchot, who had been criticized by Guffey for his handling of the CWA while governor, attacked the Democratic control of the WPA. Noting generally that federal work relief in Pennsylvania "had been sold into political bondage," Pinchot specifically cited Pittsburgh as an example. Basing his charges on an article from the anti–New Deal *Pittsburgh Post-Gazette*, the former governor told how the Pittsburgh district WPA director, John F. Laboon, advised his foremen and supervisors: "I'll tell you right now that any W.P.A. worker who is not in sympathy with the W.P.A. program and the Roosevelt Administration will be eliminated from the WPA payrolls in the district as quickly as I can act. I want you to report all such cases to me without delay." Subsequently claiming that he was misquoted—that the statement applied only to supervisors and not to workers—Laboon was hounded by his remark until he left office to assume a county job. Meanwhile, friends of the Democratic state WPA administrator would remark, "Oh, it's plenty political right here in Pittsburgh . . . Regular ward politics. But the Republicans would do the same thing if they had W.P.A., wouldn't they?"[18]

After 1935, the GOP had no chance to prove whether it would or not. Democratic party workers were rewarded with the best WPA jobs such as foremen, supervisors, and timekeepers; they found ready acceptance if they had a truck to hire out to WPA; they advanced their friends to the better positions on work relief through contacts with supervisory personnel and ward chairman. Most significant, employment with the work relief agency marked the first rung on a ladder of public employment for many

Democratic precinct workers who formed the sinews of the party organization as it began to consolidate its almost four-decade hegemony over Pittsburgh. If the federal government emerged as the chief factor in restructuring Pittsburgh politics, it also played a leading role in attempting to solve the city's problems that had been exacerbated by the onset of the depression.[19]

In 1917, Theodore Roosevelt told a local Chamber of Commerce audience:

> There is no more typical American city than Pittsburgh. And Pittsburgh, by its Americanism, gives a lesson to the entire United States. Pittsburgh has not been built up by talking about it. Your tremendous concerns were built by men who actually did work. You made Pittsburgh ace high when it could have been deuce high. There is not a Pittsburgh man who did not earn his success through his deeds.[20]

Although for the former president, Pittsburgh, by the time of World War I, was "ace high," in actuality it was on its way toward economic stagnation. Industrial overspecialization, already the region's economic characteristic by the early years of the twentieth century, cast an indelible stamp on its later development; a steel mill built in 1911 remained the city's newest plant for decades; no new construction took place in Pittsburgh's downtown for nearly two decades prior to the 1940s; its population growth rate from 1910 through 1940 appeared sluggish in contrast to the earlier boom years covering the final two decades of the nineteenth century and the first of the twentieth; its environment suffered. Breathing in the Steel City's air during the 1920s, a newly arrived immigrant allegedly remarked that she didn't like "the smell of America"; and H. L. Mencken, no newly arrived immigrant himself, saw in Pittsburgh a "scene so dreadfully hideous, so intolerably bleak and forlorn that it reduced the whole aspiration of man to a macabre and depressing joke."[21]

Even if Mencken exaggerated and the story of the immigrant woman was apocryphal, the plight of Pittsburgh and Pittsburghers, especially with the advent of the Great Depression, offered little to envy. Unemployment, which was a problem in 1929 even before the depression, reached epidemic proportions by 1933. Over 25,000 Pittsburghers were reported out of work or laid off in April, 1930, but nine months later, the figure was almost 79,000. By 1933, 15.7 percent of all Pittsburgh whites and 43.4 percent of the city's blacks could be found on the relief rolls. The highly industrialized city quickly felt the brunt of the depression.[22]

Families suffered evictions from their homes, with the largest number coming in the spring of 1932. Several minor riots resulted when tenants organized to move an evicted family's furniture back in as soon as it was moved out; squalid shantytowns sprang up throughout the city. Clergymen like Father James R. Cox and Father Charles Own Rice worked to aid the desperate. In addition to organizing 15,000 for a "March of the Jobless" on Washington in January 1932 and threatening to form a "Jobless Party" if neither the Democrats nor the Republicans brought relief to the poor, Cox's church sponsored a soup kitchen that reputedly served more than two million free meals and provided other services. Likewise, Rice's Catholic Radical Alliance established a "house of hospitality" that served as a refuge for the poor and unemployed; it fed more than 800 daily, slept 300 nightly, and operated its own clinic. Other efforts included private welfare agencies, during the winter of 1931–32, arranging for the unemployed to sell apples on the city's streets without a license.[23]

The business leaders of the city attempted to cope with its problems as they had been used to doing for several decades. Wedded to a belief in voluntarism and private enterprise, seventy-five businessmen gathered at the invitation of Howard Heinz and R. B. Mellon in February 1931, to discuss the plight of Pittsburgh's unemployed. The Allegheny County Emergency Association and its "Pittsburgh Plan" grew out of this meeting. The plan advocated that corporations and individuals make voluntary contributions to be used for the payment of wages to previously unemployed residents; they would work on much needed municipal or semipublic improvements that otherwise could not be undertaken because of lack of financial resources. The municipality or institution that would benefit by the work furnished would pay for materials and skilled labor; the association would supply and pay for all other labor. In May 1932, Pittsburgh's public works director reported city improvements costing more than $2.3 million, almost half of which had been provided by the Allegheny County Emergency Association. However, the association was short-lived, exhausting its resources before that date.[24]

None of these attempts at private initiative to cope with the depression succeeded in alleviating the massive problem of unemployment that faced the city. Across the state in Philadelphia and in other communities nationwide, "the needs of the unemployed overwhelmed traditional community

institutions even when organized at peak efficiency." Although private
relief organizations shouldered the economic burden resulting from the
early impact of the Great Depression, the cost of relief passed on to state
and primarily national agencies; in 1922, private funds had supplied more
than 54 percent of all direct relief aid in Allegheny County, of which
Pittsburgh was the central area, but in 1935 they provided less than 1
percent; in 1931 private agencies had expended one million dollars for
work relief, whereas in 1937 the federal government spent more than 20
times that amount. Pittsburgh's need for economic relief worked to alter
that city's relationship with the federal government, although the full
impact of this change did not occur until a reluctant mayor, elected under
the New Deal banner, left office in 1936.[25]

When private funds and later state allocations began to run dry, many
must have found themselves in agreement with the Roman Catholic bishop
of Pittsburgh, who remarked that "the federal government will have to put
up the money, or—well, God help us all!" The federal government did put
up the money, first with the Civil Works Administration and later with
the Works Progress Administration. During January 1934, its peak month
of employment, the CWA put 319,000 Pennsylvanians to work. However,
two months later, work relief funds allocated to Allegheny County were
exhausted, and the program ended in the Pittsburgh area after an expenditure of $4,300,000 for wages. As the federal cutback lopped off 27,000
men and women from the CWA payroll, the state relief program took up
some of the slack, but it remained for the WPA to make the greatest federal
impact on the relief issue. In Pennsylvania, it employed more persons and
more funds than in any other state with the exception of New York. The
program, however, developed slowly in Pittsburgh because of the opposition to it by Mayor McNair, who, once in office, displayed a great distaste
for economic planning and expansion of federal power even though he had
run as a New Deal candidate.[26]

Although the city council wished to take advantage of the increasing
largess of the federal government, McNair refused to act quickly—and
some times to act at all. He did not limit his opposition to relief measures to
federal attempts alone. In July 1934, he vetoed a $500,000 city bond issue
to provide food, clothing, fuel, and shelter for Pittsburgh's needy. In
September of the same year, he refused to give his consent to a
$24,000,000 Public Works Administration project for Pittsburgh. Six
months later McNair designated President Roosevelt's $4,800,000,000
work relief program (Emergency Relief Appropriation Act) as "wholesale

bribery of the electorate. He [FDR] is paving the way to have himself re-elected in 1936 by spending tremendous sums of money and as long as he spends it, who is going against Santa Claus?"[27]

When the city council met to formulate a request for a sizeable allotment to Pittsburgh of the almost five-billion-dollar WPA appropriation, the mayor, along with his director of public works, appeared before the body and urged a delay in making the request for federal funds, because, in McNair's opinion, the city could do the same without federal aid by issuing private contracts. The pair reasoned that almost any time the government might shut off the funds, and that by using federal money the city was forcing men on to relief because only those on the relief rolls qualified for WPA assignments. The fear of losing federal funds was so great, however, that one councilman demanded a private conference at the time of the hearing to stifle any publicity that indicated Pittsburgh did not desire WPA money.[28]

McNair continued to obstruct the WPA's development in Pittsburgh; when the federal government cut off all direct financial aid to local areas, as the Works Progress Administration moved into full swing, the mayor's actions brough the city close to financial disaster. Pennsylvania's Democratic governor, George Earle, elected in 1934, threatened to stop all state aid to Pittsburgh's direct relief cases unless McNair cooperated with the federal work program. Only after the city council pleaded with the governor and circumvented the mayor's opposition, did Earle agree to continue state contributions. Finally McNair backed down and gave the go-ahead to the WPA in Pittsburgh—but only halfheartedly. Thus, just as the United States Conference of Mayors, organized in 1933 to lobby for federal aid to the cities, vigorously went about its task, the mayor of Pittsburgh opposed such assistance.[29]

As a result of McNair's recalcitrance, in the early days of the WPA, Allegheny County stood at the bottom of all Pennsylvania counties in placing men and women with the federal work-relief program despite FDR's plea that projects be expedited in Massachusetts, New Jersey, New York, and Pennsylvania "where we have the largest number of unemployed." Early Works Progress Administration projects had to center outside of the city, in the county's suburban and rural areas. Nevertheless, by the end of 1937, after McNair, who had unexpectedly resigned in October 1936, was replaced for more than a year by his cooperative successor, organization Democrat Cornelius D. Scully, a total of $69.5 million had been spent on WPA work in Allegheny County, with the federal government providing $62 million and local sponsors $7.5 million. By the time of Scully's own election in 1937, WPA had undertaken more than 530 miles of highway improvements; laid 33 miles of waterlines and 71 miles of sewers; built or improved 81 parks, playgrounds, and athletic fields; produced over a million garments and pieces of bedding; taught 2,200 adults to read and write; and constructed, using salvaged stones, massive bear pits for the city's Highland Park Zoo. In the realm of relief to the unemployed, Pittsburgh and its surrounding area had grown accustomed to a close relationship with the federal government.[30]

Washington also aided the city after the Saint Patrick's Day flood of 1936. Waters at Pittsburgh's Point (the confluence of the Allegeny, Monongahela, and Ohio Rivers) reached 36.4 feet, leaving thousands homeless and causing an estimated $150 to $200 million in damage. Congress, prodded by Pittsburgh's Chamber of Commerce, passed a Flood Control Act; nine dams were to be built at the headwaters of the strategic rivers to contain their flow. The businessmen of the Steel City readily saw the value of federal aid in that instance.[31]

The implementation of the Wagner-Steagall National Housing Act of 1937 also strengthened the national-urban nexus. Although a Housing Division had been established under the Public Works Administration in 1933, its cautious supervision by Harold Ickes and the inadequate amount of funds allocated to projects limited its effectiveness. The National Housing Act created the United States Housing Authority; it took over PWA projects and was authorized to make sixty-year loans at low interest to local housing authorities for slum clearance and housing projects. Pittsburgh, as one of the forty-six cities that already had an official housing authority, was prepared to take advantage of the provisions of the act.[32]

Probably no city in the United States needed modern, low-cost housing more than Pittsburgh. If the national average of one-third substandard housing shocked the country, a 1934 report indicated that of Pittsburgh's 160,000 families, 40 percent comprising 265,000 people lived in substandard homes. No less than 22,366 dwellings needed major repairs (or demolition), and 56,491 were rated substandard for various reasons; only 40 percent of the city's homes were reported in good condition. Earlier in 1928, the housing problem had captured the attention of several civic organizations, such as the Chamber of Commerce, the Federation of Social Agencies, and the Civic Club, which formed the Pittsburgh Housing Association. Its purpose was "to secure facts about housing, to press for better enforcement of safety and sanitation regulations including the elimination of unsafe and unsanitary housing, and to co-operate with other public and private agencies in raising housing standards."[33]

The city, as well as this voluntary organization, displayed an interest in the problem. When McNair was elected mayor in 1933, he appointed George E. Evans, a builder by profession who would later be called "the father of Pittsburgh housing," to the post of superintendent of the Bureau of Building Inspection. His bureau inspector estimated that a rough total of 10,000 Pittsburgh homes were in such bad shape that they had to be immediately razed. Beginning in 1934, both the Bureau of Building Inspection and the Bureau of Sanitation began demolishing homes at the rate of over 500 a year; these, however, were not replaced and the Pittsburgh Housing Association noted three years later that no new supply of low-rent houses had been built to counteract the effects of normal obsolescence and the city's demolition. As a result of municipal policy, Pittsburgh's housing shortage was increased.[34]

Nevertheless, as early as 1935 steps were taken to provide public low-cost housing in Pittsburgh. When the first federal low-rent housing program was launched by the Housing Division of the PWA, the Pittsburgh City Council, to which Evans had been elected, established a local housing authority with power to construct or operate low-cost houses under the Pennsylvania Municipal Authority Act. The act subsequently proved inadequate to meet the housing problem, although the preliminary planning for PWA aid ultimately proved quite useful. Evans and the others considering the housing program had determined that plans for Pittsburgh's low-rent projects should include slum clearance; once the Wagner-Steagall Act passed, the Pittsburghers had at their fingertips the necessary facts and figures to apply for a loan and subsidies. Moreover, less than a week before the signing of the national law, the city council created the Housing Authority of the City of Pittsburgh as prescribed by the act; it was the first in the state. Immediately, Mayor Scully appointed a five-man authority, composed of a black state legislator, a businessman, the president of the Building Trades Council of Pittsburgh, a University of Pittsburgh history professor who also served as the city's director of the Department of Welfare, and Evans. After a loan of $40,000 from the eager city administration to tide it over until federal funds were forthcoming, the housing authority received a tentative allotment of $10,000,000 from the USHA within two months; four months later it received another $3,500,000.[35]

Even before the municipal loan was made available, the authority employed an executive director, agreed to pay a stenographer $2 a session for taking minutes, purchased $443 worth of furniture, and obtained telephone service. Three weeks after these essentials of a going business had been provided, the authority bought a new typewriter. It was thus equipped to deal with Washington, and by June 1938 the authority's initial application for a loan was approved by the New Deal administration.[36]

Community acceptance of the authority and the projects it built was not universal. When acquiring land, it encountered hostility from an Owners and Tenants League, organized by Father Charles Owen Rice. The Catholic clergyman felt that the authority was destroying a stable community of small homeowners and that the imposition of a public apartment house complex in an already overcrowded neighborhood was not in the interests of stable family life. Rice's complaints were many: he attacked the authority for

> its indifferent attitude towards the interests and problems of the poor people. The low prices paid for the homes were unjust. Many of the homes were in no sense slums. The shortage of housing made it impossible for tenants to find satisfactory homes elsewhere. The homeowners who were on relief were removed from the rolls until they spent the money which the Authority paid them for their homes; in consequence, they received no benefit whatever from the sale.[37]

The authority took action to meet these complaints by promising preference in the new projects to site occupants, by permitting a representative of the league to join negotiations between its agents and the owner, and by removing an area from the project that the protesters claimed should not be classified as a slum. Finally, it won the agreement of the State Department of Public Assistance to permit the owners who were on relief to reinvest in other homes. Through Rice's activity, local residents received $1,000 more on the average for their homes than the original figure offered by the government.

Once the projects were built, opposition arose as a result of unfounded fears. Many Pittsburghers, initially at least, preferred to remain in substandard dwellings rather than move to the new projects because rumor had it that lights would be turned off by a master switch at 10 P.M., no visitors would be permitted to remain after that hour, and all gates would be locked except for one main entrance where latecomers would be scrutinized and perhaps cross-examined by housing-authority police. Fact overcame the fear of "Big Brother" once the first tenants moved into the projects.[38]

Another problem faced the authority when it undertook to guarantee Negroes against discrimination in hiring. All authority-approved contracts contained a provision that the contractor would employ blacks as 4.5 percent of his skilled and semiskilled and 29 percent of his unskilled workers. These proportions corresponded to the ratio of Negro to white workers in the area according to the 1930 census. Nevertheless, it took a good deal of prodding by the Pittsburgh authority and the USHA before contractors would comply. They generally met the unskilled requirements, but hired considerably below the skilled quota, complaining that the unions were not supplying enough Negroes for such jobs. The unions countered that skilled blacks were in short supply, but black workers charged the unions with discrimination. The housing authority occasionally tried withholding $5 a day from a contractor for each black worker that he was short of his quota but this punitive measure generally did not increase the black proportion.[39]

The number of black occupants of the projects, however, ranged well over the Negroes' proportion of 9.3 percent of the city's total population of 671,000. By August of 1941, four low-rent housing projects had been built by the authority and 56 percent of the 10,669 residents were black. By 1944, because of the substandard and overcrowded conditions of Negro dwellings, 12.3 percent of the city's black population had been rehoused, compared with 1.6 percent of the white population. Until public housing was built, the Negroes had been unable to move from the city's worst homes: vacancy rates for Negro housing were practically nil; a 1937 report of Pittsburgh housing noted that blacks paid $4.40 per room per month for dwellings that were usually in much worse condition than those rented by white families for $4.23 per month. Thus, as Roy Lubove has noted, public housing was as much a response to the needs of Pittsburgh's growing Negro urban population, which was not accommodated by the traditional housing market, as it was to depression unemployment and the decline in property values that facilitated large-scale slum clearance. Unfortunately, cost considerations forced construction of long box-shaped apartment houses, plain in exterior design, which were to become the New Deal's contribution to Pittsburgh's growing ghetto.[40]

The establishment of the housing authority, and the city's cooperation with it, serves as a prime example of the increasing federal-urban relationship that developed during the New Deal Decade. In the case of public housing, it was not simply the magnitude of the problem created by the depression but also the manner in which the housing policy was framed that forced those wedded to voluntarism to look to government assistance. The PWA housing program was highly centralized in Washington, but the United States Housing Act of 1937 was an attempt, even if a reluctant one, at decentralization. As a result of legal considerations, the New Dealers formulated the program out of necessity, not choice, so that "the federal government was to retreat to the role of lender and spender while the local government would be the initiator and operator." Such an arrangement made the program more acceptable to those previously opposed to government action. Although the Washington-based USHA determined major policy, in practice the Pittsburgh Authority made many, although admittedly often less important, decisions affecting the program. If it was true, as one contemporary observer remarked, that "the Pittsburgh Housing Authority was unable to rise beyond the status of junior partner," it was equally true that local obstacles often blunted federal policy, as exemplified by the inability of blacks to receive their quota of skilled jobs in constructing the projects. Thus, the increased federal-urban relationship harbored a growing local-center tension at its core.[41]

For the management of Pittsburgh's main industry, this tension increased with the federal government's passage of section 7(a) of the National Industrial Recovery Act in 1933 and the National Labor Relations (Wagner-Connery) Act in 1935; both played a major role in the unionization of the city's steelworkers. Whereas section 7(a) gave rise to the establishment of many company unions to meet its collective bargaining requirement, the Wagner Act inspired bona fide unionization; it served as a backdrop for the efforts of John L. Lewis to organize industrial workers. Once Lewis established the Committee for Industrial Organization (CIO) in the fall of 1935, he made unionization of the steel industry a prime goal.[42]

On 4 June 1936, a major step in this direction was taken when the Amalgamated Association of Iron, Steel, and Tin Workers, an AFL-chartered union, agreed to affiliation with the CIO and to the establishment of a Steel Workers Organizing Committee (SWOC). As a result, Lewis and the CIO gained control over the drive to unionize steel. With Philip Murray at SWOC's helm, the committee settled down to the hard battle ahead in rented offices on the thirty-sixth floor of Pittsburgh's Grant Building—the same building that housed several large steel corporations. Then, a month after the agreement with the Amalgamated Association, SWOC sponsored a memorial service in Homestead, across the Monongahela River from Pittsburgh, for the steelworkers slain forty-four years earlier during the famous Homestead strike against the Carnegie Steel Corporation. That strike exemplified the intense antilabor feeling that continued to a large extent to permeate management in the steel industry. It was in opposition to this sentiment that P. T. Fagan, a Pittsburgh labor leader and chairman of the memorial ceremony, proclaimed, "Let the blood of those labor pioneers who were massacred here be the seed of this new organization in 1936."[43]

As a result of the efforts of Fagan and his fellow unionists, the steel drive flourished. By the end of the summer of 1936, SWOC's Pittsburgh office had 166 paid professional organizers and 3,000 volunteers advocating its cause in the area's plants. A friendly national and state Democratic administration supported its efforts, and in turn SWOC and the CIO vigorously aided Roosevelt's 1936 campaign for president. Moreover, although unemployment was still high, the steel industry was in the midst of an upturn in 1936; many felt that the corporations, which were just beginning to see a profit after a long period of drought, might be willing to deal with a union like SWOC rather than face a strike. The industry also had grown concerned about the increased militancy of the company unions, which were demanding greater independence, higher wages, and better working conditions. A breakthrough came with the 2 March 1937 agreement between SWOC and United States Steel. It provided for a minimum $5.00-a-day wage, a 40-hour-work week, the recognition of SWOC as the collective bargaining agent for employees who were its members, and the promise not to interfere with the right of employees to become members of the union and not to discriminate against those who did join.[44]

Although there was violent resistance to a settlement by the so-called Little Steel corporations, the industry moved well on its way toward unionization. By May 1937, SWOC, which was less than a year old, had over 300,000 members, many in the Pittsburgh area. Mayor Cornelius D. Scully proclaimed that the March agreement's impact on the city "accomplished an inestimable public service to Pittsburgh and the nation. [The] contract appears to have opened what will be a new era in relations between management and labor. . . . The general wage increase in the steel industry will add millions of dollars to the Pittsburgh district, and will raise the standard of living of scores of thousands of our citizens." The consequences of the steel settlement also made Pittsburgh an intensely union town in all facets of its economy, cementing the steel union to the Democratic party, which midwifed its birth, and bringing a seemingly militant labor constituency into its place within the New Deal–inspired corporate state.[45]

In postdepression years, unionization was the rule, not the exception, and housing reform was but a minor facet of the attempt to change the environment of Pittsburgh. Ironically, this urban reform effort was a product of the alliance of David L. Lawrence's depression-born Democratic machine with the city's Republican businessmen. While the machine was deeply rooted in the New Deal, the attitudes of the city's business elite toward government involvement in local affairs shifted from one of distrust at the beginning of the depression decade to one of acceptance by the end of the New Deal era. In 1931, the businessman gathered, at the behest of Richard B. Mellon, to fight the depression with the weapon of voluntarism, the Allegheny County Emergency Association. In 1943, Richard K. Mellon summoned a meeting that gave rise to the establishment of the Allegheny Conference on Community Development (ACCD), the organization in the vanguard of Pittsburgh's urban "Renaissance." It employed public resources for the benefit of corporate welfare and used urban renewal to rebuild Pittsburgh's downtown in the image desired by the city's business elite.[46]

By the end of the 1930s and the early 1940s, the magnitude of the city's problems—its automobile-strangled and dilapidated downtown area, polluted skies, swollen rivers, and inability to attract new industry—had grown so great that government assistance was the only answer. The depression had exacerbated, and the New Deal had by no means solved, the problems of Pittsburgh; it did, however, establish firmly the inability of voluntarism to cope with the problems of the nation's cities. Moreover, in the case of Pittsburgh, Wallace K. Richards, one of the individuals most influential in the early postwar redevelopment of the city, was a veteran New Dealer. He had been executive secretary of the Sub-Marginal Land Program, which was responsible for the redevelopment of areas damaged by drought and soil erosion. Subsequently Richards joined the Resettlement Administration in 1935 to supervise the planning and construction of the New Deal's Greenbelt community in Maryland. Even after leaving that project and becoming director of the Pittsburgh Regional Planning Association (PRPA) in 1937, Richards maintained contact with the New Deal program. In the Steel City, he became Richard King Mellon's close associate and civic adviser when Mellon assumed the presidency of the PRPA in 1941. In that capacity, Richards helped to enlarge the scope of Mellon's interest in public problems, and he mediated between the business interests of the city, represented by Mellon, and the politicians, represented by David L. Lawrence. It was during Lawrence's first mayoralty campaign in 1945 that he met Richards. Lawrence, on a campaign fact-finding trip, visited several cities where rebuilding programs were under way. Whether it is an indicator of Lawrence's lack of awareness of planning in Pittsburgh, or merely an example of how the politicians and the city's elite were separated before he became mayor, it was not until Lawrence reached New York that he learned of Richards's activities. When he returned to Pittsburgh, Lawrence met Richards and became all the more determined to work with the ACCD.[47]

This partnership of business elite and New Deal–rooted Democratic machine brought to the city much-needed smoke control, urban renewal and a new downtown area, an improved highway system, and other elements of the famed Pittsburgh "Renaissance." But in terms of social change and improvement, the "Renaissance" was quite limited in its approach, just as the New Deal program had been a decade earlier. Both were geared to reforming a system, but not substantially changing it. Although the New Deal decade did see a change in the business elite's attitudes toward government assistance, it did not change that group's view of what a city should be—that is, of how Pittsburgh should serve the industrial and commercial interests of the community. Likewise, though the New Deal did help to transfer political power from the Republican to the Democratic party, it did not change the substance of urban politics in Pittsburgh: the Republican party, as did the Democratic, would have readily cooperated in the "Renaissance" movement; the Democratic party, on the other hand, had created a political organization not unlike the solidly entrenched GOP machine it replaced after 1933.[48]

The decade of the thirties maintained as much continuity with the past in Pittsburgh as it brought substantive change. The New Deal did not bring economic recovery; in 1940, 17 percent of the city's labor force was still seeking work. Recovery came with World War II. Yet, as the National Resources Committee's report, *Our Cities: Their Role in the National Economy*, proclaimed for Pittsburgh and the rest of urban America, it was

the Federal Government that has had to assume the major burdens of providing emergency relief for the city as well as the farm, of stimulating public works in the Nation's urban centers, and even of reviving insolvent municipal finances.

The New Deal did introduce relief and flood control programs that strengthened the city's ties with the federal government and a public housing program that did the same, while unfortunately simultaneously perpetuating an old problem by relocating Pittsburgh's black ghetto-dwellers into "long boxed shaped apartment houses."[49]

The problem of racial discrimination in Pittsburgh's construction industry that gave rise to massive demonstrations during the late 1960s found a parallel in the public-housing hiring practices of the late 1930s. Post–New Deal decision-making that affected the future development of the city remained in the hands of the same industrial elite that had been shaping Pittsburgh's destiny throughout the twentieth century; they were, however, more disposed to using public rather than private resources for private interests. After the depression decade, the city's voters and politicians more than likely considered themselves Democratic rather than Republican; its steelworkers would consider themselves staunch union supporters. Thus, during the 1930s, Pittsburgh had been shaken by depression, had grown accustomed to an expanding federal government, had witnessed a successful union organizing drive, and had realigned its voting habits while maintaining the same power structure. Although the quality of urban life and environment might change for some, primarily a portion of the city's white population, with the Pittsburgh "Renaissance," this change would not occur until after the New Deal era had long passed; the roots of this change, however, could be located in the depression decade.[50]

I would like to thank the University of Connecticut Research Foundation for a grant that assisted me in the preparation of this essay.

1. Charles N. Glaab and A. Theodore Brown, *A History of Urban America* (New York, 1967), p. 304. A more recent survey of urban America similarly concludes: "Taken as a whole, however, and judged by its accomplishments, the federal response to depression in the cities was conservative. The New Deal urban policy neither envisaged nor produced a radical transformation of metropolitan form and structure" (Zane L. Miller, *The Urbanization of Modern America: A Brief History* [New York, 1973], pp. 168–69).

2. Joseph F. Guffey, *Seventy Years on the Red Fire Wagon* (privately printed, 1952), p. 75; George Swetnam, *The Bicentennial History of Pittsburgh and Allegheny County*, 2 vols. (Pittsburgh, 1955), 1:209–10; Lincoln Steffens, *The Shame of the Cities* (New York, 1957), pp. 104–5, 115–17.

3. For a brief introduction to Pennsylvania's post–Civil War politics, see Edward F. Cooke and G. Edward Janosik, *Guide to Pennsylvania Politics* (New York, 1957), pp. 6–12. For a detailed study of the weakening of Republican power in the state, see Samuel J. Astorino, "The Decline of the Republican Dynasty in Pennsylvania, 1929–1934" (Ph.D. diss., University of Pittsburgh, 1962) especially pp. 68–80, and *New York Times*, 5 April, 25 June, 1931, 8 May 1932.

4. *Pittsburgh Press*, 18 September 1933; David L. Lawrence to Marvin McIntyre, 14 April 1936 (telegram), OF 300, Roosevelt Papers (Franklin D. Roosevelt Library); interview, David L. Lawrence, 14 April 1964.

5. *Pittsburgh Post-Gazette*, 4 November 1931; for a detailed analysis, see Bruce M. Stave, *The New Deal and the Last Hurrah: Pittsburgh Machine Politics* (Pittsburgh, 1970), pp. 35–40. Using the Spearman rank order formula, it was found that the coefficients of correlation between presidential

votes for La Follette, Smith, and Roosevelt (1932), respectively, and foreign stock (1930) for all city wards was .55, .87, .67. The same votes correlated with native stock (1930) indicated coefficients of correlation of −.27, −.70, and −.40 respectively, and with median rental (highest to lowest wards, 1930) −.60, −.64, −.57. These statistics help locate the source of the New Deal coalition in the ethnic, working-class wards and indicate that it was building throughout the 1920s. For several important articles dealing with the question of critical elections, critical periods, and political realignment during the period discussed, see Jerome M. Clubb and Howard W. Allen, eds., *Electoral Change and Stability in American Political History* (New York, 1971). Also pertinent are: Michael P. Rogin and John L. Shover, *Political Change in California* (Westport, Conn., 1970); John L. Shover, "The Emergence of a Two Party System in Republican Philadelphia, 1924–1936," paper delivered before the eighty-sixth meeting of the American Historical Association, New York City, 29 December 1971; and John M. Allswang, *A House for All Peoples* (Lexington, Ky., 1971). A revised version of Shover's paper was published in the *Journal of American History* 60 (1973–74): 985–1002. While Shover's studies adhere to the critical period theory, Allswang's investigation of Chicago finds that in that city the La Follette candidacy had little effect on building the New Deal coalition and that 1928 was the most significant election of the period, i.e., a critical election. He does, however, note that the La Follette movement played a greater role in realigning the voting of Jews and Germans than it did for other ethnic groups.

6. For an over-all view of black politics and realignment during the New Deal, see: Martin Kilson, "Political Change in the Negro Ghetto, 1900–1940's," in Nathan I. Huggins et al., eds., *Key Issues in the Afro-American Experience* (New York, 1971), pp. 167–92. This will be expanded upon in Kilson's forthcoming book *Politics in Black America: Crisis and Change in the Negro Ghetto*; see Table 2 for black population statistics.

7. Guffey, *Red Fire Wagon*, pp. 70–71; Arthur M. Schlesinger, Jr., *The Politics of Upheaval* (Boston, 1960), pp. 430–36; Ruth L. Simmons, "The Negro in Recent Pittsburgh Politics" (M.A. thesis, University of Pittsburgh, 1945), pp. 7, 10–11; interview with Emma Guffey Miller, 27 April 1964.

8. Interview with committeeman who served Pittsburgh's Fifth Ward, First District, in 1932; *Pittsburgh Press*, 18 September 1933; *New Deal Newspaper* (Pittsburgh), 20 August 1933, Allegheny County Democratic Committee Headquarters File, 1933. This newspaper was the official organ of the City-County Colored Democratic Committee. For example of the *Pittsburgh Courier's* support of the Democrats, see issue of 9 September 1933; for Vann's career, see Andrew Buni, *Robert L. Vann of the Pittsburgh Courier: Politics and Black Journalism* (Pittsburgh, 1974).

9. *Pittsburgh Press*, 11–13 September 1933; *Pittsburgh Courier*, 4 November 1933.

10. *Pittsburgh Courier*, 11, 18 November 1933. Lists used in the comparison of the 1934 Republican committeemen with the 1938 Democratic ones were obtained from the spring primary election return books located at the Allegheny County Board of Elections, Pittsburgh, Pennsylvania, and available in Record Group 65:10, Archives of Industiral Society, Hillman Library, University of Pittsburgh. For varying interpretations of the New Deal's treatment of blacks, see Bernard Sternsher, ed., *The Negro in Depression and War* (Chicago, 1969); Schlesinger, *The Politics of Upheaval*, pp. 425–38; Raymond Wolters, *Negroes and the Great Depression: The Problem of Economic Recovery* (Westport, Conn., 1970); and Christopher G. Wye, "The New Deal and the Negro Community: Toward a Broader Conceptualization," *Journal of American History* 59 (1972): 621–39.

11. *Pittsburgh Press*, 25, 31 August, 22 September 1933; *Pittsburgh Sun-Telegraph*, 12 September 1933; *New York Times*, 5 November 1933.

12. *Pittsburgh Press*, 22, 25–26 October 1933; Speeches of William S. Coleman, undated speech mss. and undated clipping from the *Pittsburgh Post-Gazette*, Record Group 64:18, Archives of Industrial Society.

13. *Pittsburgh Press*, 1, 19 October 1933.

14. *Pittsburgh Press*, 24–25, 28 October 1933; Edward J. Flynn, *You're the Boss: The Practice of American Politics* (New York, 1962), pp. 151–53; Edwin B. Bonner, "The New Deal Comes to Pennsylvania: The Gubernatorial Election of 1934," *Pennsylvania History* 27 (1960): 51, 58, 66.

15. *Pittsburgh Sun-Telegraph*, 23 October, 8 November 1933; *Pittsburgh Post-Gazette*, 8 November 1933, 20 February 1935. For a detailed analysis, see Stave, *The New Deal and the Last*

Hurrah, pp. 78–81. The disparity of the McNair and Roosevelt votes indicates that one must consider both national and local elections when investigating political realignment. The trend on the two levels is not always concomitant. For a discussion of off-year elections and their importance in realignment, see Jerome M. Clubb and Howard W. Allen, "The Cities and the Election of 1928: Partisan Realignment," *American Historical Review* 74 (1969): 1205–20.

16. *Pittsburgh Press*, 8 November 1933. A detailed study of the ripper effort can be found in chapter 4 of Stave, *The New Deal and the Last Hurrah*. According to David L. Lawrence, one of the reasons that McNair was slated as the Democratic mayoralty candidate in 1933 was that he was Protestant, whereas the most likely candidate, Lawrence, himself, was Catholic. The Democrats feared being hurt by the religious issue; interview, David L. Lawrence, 14 April 1964.

17. For the politics of relief in the state, see: Priscilla Ferguson Clement, "The Works Progress Administration in Pennsylvania, 1935–1940," *Pennsylvania Magazine of History and Biography* 95 (1971): 244–60, and Richard C. Keller, "Pennsylvania's Little New Deal" (Ph.D. diss., Columbia University, 1960); clipping, Joseph F. Guffey Papers (Washington and Jefferson College, Washington, Pa.); William P. Shaw to Emma Guffey Miller, 20 December 1933, Women's Division Correspondence, Pennsylvania, Emma Guffey Miller, 1933–35, National Democratic Committee Papers (Franklin D. Roosevelt Library).

18. Gifford Pinchot to FDR, 21 December 1935, PPF 289, Roosevelt Papers; *Pittsburgh Post-Gazette*, 18, 20 December 1935; Lorena Hickok to Harry Hopkins, 10 October 1936, Hickok Reports (November 1935–November 1936 File), Hopkins Papers (Franklin D. Roosevelt Library); Searle Charles, *Minister of Relief: Harry Hopkins and the Depression* (Syracuse, 1963), pp. 192–94.

19. See Stave, *The New Deal and the Last Hurrah*, chapter 7, for detailed information about precinct committeemen and the development of the Democratic machine in Pittsburgh. Interviews with 103 Democratic committeemen who served during the 1930s revealed that one-third were on work relief at some point during the depression decade; all but four of these served with the WPA. Patronage continued to play an important role in the building of the Pittsburgh Democratic organization. Only 7 percent of the Democratic precinct committeemen elected in 1934 held public payroll jobs in 1927 before the advent of the New Deal, but by 1940, 48 percent were on the public payroll; almost 78 percent of the Democratic committeemen elected in 1962 were payrollers. On the other hand, the Republican proportion of payroller committeemen elected in 1934 remained at about 18 percent between 1927 and 1940, and less than 6 percent of those elected in 1962 served on the payroll.

20. Stefan Lorant, *Pittsburgh: The Story of an American City* (Garden City, N.Y., 1964), p. 364.

21. Roy Lubove, *Twentieth Century Pittsburgh: Government, Business, and Environmental Change* (New York, 1969), pp. 62–63; Jeanne R. Lowe, *Cities in a Race with Time: Progress and Poverty in America's Renewing Cities* (New York, 1967), pp. 112–13, 123; Lorant, *Pittsburgh*, p. 328.

22. U.S. Bureau of the Census, *Special Census of Unemployment, General Report, 1931* (Washington, 1932); *Pittsburgh Press*, 21 March 1931; Monroe N. Work, ed., *Negro Year Book, 1937–1938* (Tuskegee Institute, Ala., 1937), p. 21.

23. Lubove, *Twentieth Century Pittsburgh*, pp. 69, 82; Neil Betten, "Charles Owen Rice: Pittsburgh Labor Priest, 1936–1940," *Pennsylvania Magazine of History and Biography* 94 (1970): 522–23, 529; *Pittsburgh Sun-Telegraph*, 1 December 1930.

24. See Samuel P. Hays, "The Politics of Reform in Municipal Government in the Progressive Era," *Pacific Northwest Quarterly* 55 (1964): 157–69, and Lubove, *Twentieth Century Pittsburgh*, for the decision-making role that Pittsburgh's business elite has played in the city's affairs. With regard to the Allegheny County Emergency Association, see: clippings from *Pittsburgh Press*, 21 March 1931, 7 February, 17, 19 June 1932, File of Pittsburgh's Unemployed, Pennsylvania Division, Carnegie Library, Pittsburgh, and Ralph Carr Fletcher and Katherine A. Biehl, "Work Relief and Work Programs in Allegheny County, 1920–1937," *Federator* 13 (1938): 121.

25. For the story of Philadelphia, see Bonnie Fox Schwartz, "Unemployment Relief in Philadelphia, 1930–1932: A Study of the Depression's Impact on Voluntarism," *Pennsylvania Magazine of History and Biography* 92 (1969): 86–108, reprinted in Bernard Sternsher, ed., *Hitting Home: The Great Depression in Town and Country* (Chicago, 1970), pp. 60–84. For a detailed study of relief as

well as politics in Pittsburgh during the 1930's, see Stave, *The New Deal and the Last Hurrah*; Ralph Carr Fletcher and Katharine A. Biehl, "Trends in Direct Relief Expenditure in Allegheny County, 1920–1937," *Federator* 13 (1938): 67–72, and Fletcher and Biehl, "Work Relief and Work Programs," pp. 121–26.

26. Report of Lorena Hickok, 7–17 August 1933, August-28 October 1933 File, Hopkins Papers; Fletcher and Biehl, "Work Relief and Work Programs," p. 122; Commonwealth of Pennsylvania, Bureau of Research and Statistics, *Pennsylvania Public Assistance Statistics: Summary, 1932–1940* (Harrisburg, 1940), pp. 1–2; *Pittsburgh Press*, 30 March 1934; *Pittsburgh Post-Gazette*, 15 August 1934, Relief Work Division File, Pennsylvania Division, Carnegie Library, Pittsburgh. The WPA in Pennsylvania is studied with attention to the workings of American federalism in Clement, "The Works Progress Administration in Pennsylvania, 1935–1940."

27. City of Pittsburgh, *Municipal Record, 1934* (Pittsburgh, 1935), 445–46, 549–53; *Pittsburgh Post-Gazette*, 17, 18 September 1934; *Pittsburgh Press*, 16 March 1935. Sixty-nine of McNair's 83 vetoes were overridden, 8 tabled, 6 upheld (*Municipal Record, 1933–1937* [Pittsburgh, 1934–38]).

28. *Municipal Record, 1935* (Pittsburgh, 1936), p. 267.

29. *Pittsburgh Press*, 29 November, 1, 4 December 1935; *Municipal Record, 1936*, pp. 660, 673–79; Blake McKelvey, *The Emergence of Metropolitan America, 1915–1966* (New Brunswick, N.J., 1968), p. 83.

30. *Pittsburgh Press*, 11, 19, 22–23, 31 October 1935; FDR to Comptroller General McCarl, 14 October 1935 (cablegram), OF 444c, WPA File, 16–30 September 1935, Roosevelt Papers; *Pittsburgh Press*, 28 October 1937. It has been noted that "by the mid–1930s federal intervention touched on almost every aspect of municipal policy. One count in 1936 revealed 500 points of contact between the federal bureaucracy and the cities in the fields of planning, zoning, education, health, internal improvements, relief, and housing" (Miller, *The Urbanization of Modern America*, p. 161). For a history of federal-city relations prior to the New Deal that indicates that the New Deal did not bring about a sharp change in this relationship, see Daniel J. Elazar, "Urban Problems and the Federal Government: A Historical Inquiry," *Political Science Quarterly* 82 (1967): 505–25.

31. Lorant, *Pittsburgh*, p. 369.

32. Glaab and Brown, *History of Urban America*, pp. 300–302; McKelvey, *Emergency of Metropolitan America*, p. 96.

33. Housing Authority of the City of Pittsburgh, *The First Seven Years* (Pittsburgh, 1944), pp. 3–4, and M. Nelson McGeary, *The Pittsburgh Housing Authority*, Pennsylvania State College Studies, No. 14 (State College, Pa., 1943), p. 6, in the records of the Housing Authority of the City of Pittsburgh, 1937–1953 (A66:8), Archives of Industrial Society.

34. McGeary, *Pittsburgh Housing Authority*, pp. 6–7; *The First Seven Years*, p. 5; Pittsburgh Housing Association, *Housing in Pittsburgh, 1934–1937* (Pittsburgh, 1937), pp. 9–10, Housing Authority Records (A66:8), Archives of Industrial Society.

35. McGeary, *Pittsburgh Housing Authority*, pp. 7–8; *The First Seven Years*, p. 8. The personnel of the authority quickly changed. When, as a result of a technicality, black state legislator Homer Brown resigned from the position, he was replaced by his law partner, also a Negro, Richard F. Jones. Dr. Brynjolf J. Hovde, University of Pittsburgh professor and Department of Welfare head, became administrator of the authority in August 1938 and was replaced by the president of Carnegie Institute of Technology, Dr. Robert E. Doherty, as an authority member.

36. *The First Seven Years*, p. 10.

37. Betten, "Charles Owen Rice," p. 531; McGeary, *Pittsburgh Housing Authority*, pp. 19–20. Rice later became chairman of Pittsburgh's Fair Rent Committee, which processed thousands of complaints against the Public Housing Authority and other agencies during World War II.

38. McGeary, *Pittsburgh Housing Authority*, pp. 19–20; *The First Seven Years*, p. 23.

39. McGeary, *Pittsburgh Housing Authority*, pp. 30–31.

40. Bureau of Social Research, Federation of Social Agencies of Pittsburgh and Allegheny County, *Social Facts about Pittsburgh and Allegheny County*, 1. *Pittsburgh Wards* (Pittsburgh, 1945); *The First Seven Years*, pp. 59, 24; *Housing in Pittsburgh, 1934–1937*, p. 17; Lubove, *Twentieth Century Pittsburgh*, p. 85; McGeary, *Pittsburgh Housing Authority*, pp. 17–18. Wye, "The New Deal and the

Negro Community," does an especially good job in demonstrating the disruptive effects government housing projects had on Cleveland's black community during the depression decade. Oscar Newman, an architect who is an expert on housing projects, has pointed out to the author that cost considerations are not the lone determinants that lead to the aesthetic drabness of government-sponsored low-cost housing. He contends that those who are not directly subsidized in their rent payments or home ownership would resent aesthetically pleasing housing for the poor. As a result, policy-makers have tended toward the architecturally conservative structure. For Newman's views on housing projects and crime, see Oscar Newman, *Defensible Space: Crime Prevention through Urban Design* (New York, 1972).

41. For examples of how the city cooperated with the authority, see McGeary, *Pittsburgh Housing Authority*, pp. 32–34, and Lubove, *Twentieth Century Pittsburgh*, pp. 69–70; Charles Abrams, *The City Is the Frontier* (New York, 1965), pp. 245–46; McGeary, *Pittsburgh Housing Authority*, pp. 85–86.

42. William E. Leuchtenburg, *Franklin D. Roosevelt and the New Deal, 1932–1940* (New York, 1963), pp. 106–11, 150–51, 239.

43. Irving Bernstein, *Turbulent Years: A History of the American Worker, 1933–1941* (Boston, 1970), pp. 440–41, 452, 434; Leuchtenburg, *Franklin D. Roosevelt and the New Deal*, p. 239; *Pittsburgh Post-Gazette*, 6 July 1936.

44. *Bulletin Index* (Pittsburgh), 27 August 1936; Bernstein, *Turbulent Years*, pp. 448–49, 456; *Pittsburgh Press*, 3 March 1937.

45. *Pittsburgh Press*, 9 May 1937; Leuchtenburg, *Franklin D. Roosevelt and the New Deal*, p. 240; *Pittsburgh Press*, 3 March 1937.

46. For the story of the Pittsburgh "Renaissance," see Lorant, *Pittsburgh*, chapter 10, by David L. Lawrence as told to John P. Robin and Stefan Lorant; Lowe, *Cities in a Race with Time*, chapter 3; Lubove, *Twentieth-Century Pittsburgh*, chapters 6 and 7; Miller, *The Urbanization of Modern America*, chap. 7. The idea of Pittsburgh's business elite using public resources for corporate welfare to establish a "reverse welfare state" is Lubove's.

47. Lorant, *Pittsburgh*, pp. 381, 407–8; Lowe, *Cities in a Race with Time*, pp. 125–26, 132–33; Wallace K. Richards to Eleanor Roosevelt, 28 October 1937 (summary memo), PPF 2; Eleanor Roosevelt to Miss LeHand for FDR, 4 November 1937 (memo), FDR to Eleanor Roosevelt, 6 November 1937, OF 1568 Misc., Roosevelt Papers. The same urban crisis that plagued industrial Pittsburgh as it emerged from the depression also haunted a commercial city like Boston. Professor Charles Trout has noted that in 1940 Boston had an unemployment rate second only to Pittsburgh and Cleveland; its textile and shoe industries were collapsing; its industrial equipment was obsolete; business was fleeing its high tax rate; its wharf facilities were decaying; and its type of industry was not prepared to snatch the coming military contracts. See comments by the author on Charles Trout's paper, "The New Deal in Boston," delivered at the session "Findings, Techniques, and Opportunities in Urban History: The 1930's," April 1972 meeting of the Organization of American Historians. Comments in possession of the author.

48. For the limitations of the Pittsburgh "Renaissance," see Lubove, *Twentieth Century Pittsburgh*, chapters 6 and 7; Lowe, *Cities in a Race with Time*, pp. 130–31; Miller, *The Urbanization of Modern America*, pp. 196–98. In 1945, the Republican-oriented ACCD, in order to aid the party's candidate for mayor, attempted to delay until election time an announcement by the GOP governor that funds were forthcoming for "Renaissance" projects. Lawrence, however, announced that he would support the ACCD program and was glad that the state finally saw fit to assist Pittsburgh.

49. See *Social Facts about Pittsburgh* for the percentage of those still seeking work in 1940; National Resources Committee, *Our Cities*, pamphlet reprint of foreword to report *Our Cities: Their Role in the National Economy* (Washington, D.C., September 1937), p. 2. By 1960, Bedford Dwellings, one of the original public housing units, was 98.4 percent black-occupied (see table, page 242, of Stave, *The New Deal and the Last Hurrah*).

50. For a summary of the "Black Monday" demonstrations against Pittsburgh's construction industry, see John P. Moody, "Monday Report: Anatomy of Black Protest," *Pittsburgh Post-Gazette*, 15 September 1969; David L. Lawrence found the source of much of Pittsburgh's post–World War II development in the programs of the 1930s (Lorant, *Pittsburgh*, p. 450).

Lyle W. Dorsett

Kansas City and the New Deal

UNTIL THE EVE OF THE NEW DEAL, MOST AMERICANS WHO HAD not traveled in the Midwest had one image of Kansas City, Missouri: it was an "overgrown cow town." Citizens on the two coasts were not even aware that Kansas City was in Missouri; Kansas City, of course, must be in Kansas. Although there were many industries in the western Missouri city that served the midland farm states, Kansas City was thought of as a grain and livestock center that turned out a beefsteak that was good charcoal-broiled medium rare. Not until the 1930s did the western Missouri city gain national recognition. Beginning in the early thirties, newspapers and national circulation slick magazines began to publish feature articles and editorials on Thomas Joseph Pendergast, the Democratic chieftain of the city. Attention also focused on the city's night life, where a new brand of jazz—Kansas City jazz—was being nurtured in the bars and nightclubs.

Journalists were interested in the big Irishman who kept Kansas City Democratic during the twenties while other sections of the state made a habit of electing Republicans. Similarly, reporters and feature story writers were intrigued by the nightclubs and speakeasies where Bennie Moten and Count Basie played, and where blues singers such as Julia Lee performed nightly. Kansas City night life became synonymous with the Pendergast machine because Boss Tom's organization (for a cut, of course) allowed the saloons and nightclubs to flourish around the clock during prohibition. Interspersed among the jazz joints in downtown Kansas City were gambling dens where one could feed slot machines and play poker and roulette. On several streets, men could answer the beck and call of the half-clothed prostitutes who yelled from windows on the second floor of hotels and asked them to come upstairs for a few hours of entertainment.[1]

Kansas City's Chamber of Commerce did not frown upon the "wide open" image the community was getting. It was, after all, good for business because it attracted tourists and conventions. Yet the chamber of commerce could not advertise the night life because it was in direct violation of the law. What the business leaders did boast of, however, was the relative homogeneity of the population. The chamber proudly proclaimed that Kansas City was "the most American city" in the United States.[2] In a period of adverse reaction to immigration, and a concern over the black migrations to cities, the fact that Kansas City's population had less that ten percent blacks, and less than seven percent foreign-born citizens, seemed to be a good selling point.

If the "most American city" image was not enough to brag about, Tom Pendergast and the chamber of commerce proudly pointed to the fact that Department of Justice statistics revealed that their city had the lowest crime rate of any city in its class.[3] This distinction was achieved under the Pendergast-controlled police department, and it quieted the critics of the Pendergast machine who maintained corruption was eating out the heart of the city government—although no evidence was uncovered until the late thirties to substantiate such charges.

Perhaps the most noteworthy fact about Kansas City on the eve of the New Deal was that unlike most cities it was weathering the depression unusually well. James T. Patterson has observed that "the depression staggered state and local officials, and it was years before they recovered from the blow."[4] In Kansas City, this simply was not true. The depression, far from staggering local officials, gave them an opportunity to unite the community toward local improvements and the Pendergast machine. Tom Pendergast and his hand-picked city manager, Henry F. McElroy, came up with the idea of a "Ten-Year Plan" for Kansas City and Jackson County. The plan called for a bond issue of nearly fifty million dollars that would provide the community with a monumental public works program. The unemployed would be put to work, and the city and county would be modernized and beautified.

Large bond issues seldom fared well at the polls in Kansas City. But this time Pendergast gained widespread support before taking the proposal to the voters. A Civic Improvement Committee of One Thousand was appointed. The chairman of the committee was Conrad H. Mann, president of the chamber of commerce. Besides the chamber of commerce, every important civic organization was represented. The committee, in conjunction with city officials, studied hundreds of possible projects and their costs. Ultimately, the committee recommended a ten-year works program that would cost nearly fifty million dollars.[5]

The campaign to win voter approval of the Ten-Year Plan was headed by Conrad Mann, City Manager McElroy, and Jackson County Judge Harry S Truman. Emphasizing the fact that the construction programs would relieve unemployment, stimulate industry, and beautify the community, these men won the support of business leaders and the public at large. The plan was submitted to the voters in 1931 and adopted by an overwhelming four-to-one margin.[6]

Immediately, the city and county were buzzing with construction projects. Streets, roads, and airport runways were repaired and improved; Brush Creek (a stream that carried sewage through the city to the Blue River) was paved with concrete; and construction began on a new city hall, county courthouse, police station, and baseball stadium for the Triple A "Blues."[7] Whenever possible, labor-saving equipment was put aside so that the maximum number of men could be taken off the unemployment rolls.[8]

The public works program did not begin without criticism. Cries of anger and disgust arose when it was learned that the Ready-Mixed Concrete Company (owned by Pendergast) was providing most of the cement for the projects. Some citizens were especially disturbed to see Brush Creek being paved—and with Pendergast's cement at that. But though Boss Pendergast was making a fortune on the projects, even his most outspoken critics admitted he provided an excellent product at a competitive price.[9]

Despite the criticisms, the vast majority of people were pleased. Before construction actually began on the building program, the Pendergast organization signed up twenty-two thousand men for work. An engineering journal reported that in 1933 fifteen thousand men were put to work at one time doing hand jobs that previously had been done by machines. By early 1933, nearly two million dollars were spent on wages, and not one bank or business in Kansas City was borrowing from the Reconstruction Finance Corporation. Neither unemployment nor business failure affected Kansas City as adversely as other major cities. The machine was carrying the city through the depression with a minimum of hardship.[10]

Consequently, by the early thirties Thomas Joseph Pendergast was the most powerful Democrat in Missouri. His organization had weathered the Republican-dominated twenties, and his public works program made him even more popular once the depression began. By the 1930s, Pendergast had transformed Kansas City into what was popularly known as "Tom's Town."

He had achieved this feat by gradually expanding the ward organizations of his older brother, James. "Alderman Jim," as the elder Pendergast was popularly known, arrived in Kansas City in the late nineteenth century. He eventually owned saloons in the city's North End and West Bottoms, where the working classes lived. The North End housed the Italian immigrants, and the West Bottoms was populated by the Irish, as well as black and native white American workers.

Alderman Jim quickly became well known, loved, and respected by the area's working-class population. Through his two saloons, he provided the workers with free lunches of cheese, garlic bologna, and hard rolls. He also provided free banking services. In a period when greenbacks were scarce, Alderman Jim always kept enough money in the safe to cash the workers' checks, and he would keep a portion stashed away at no charge if asked. Always sincerely interested in the fate of the destitute poor and those who were temporarily down and out, the saloon keeper put out a sideboard of free turkey and all the trimmings every Christmas. Throughout the year, he gave away food, fuel, and clothing to the needy. He was often at police headquarters putting up bail bond for indigents and workers who had been arrested. During the years 1892 to 1920, while he was on the city council representing the largest working-class ward in the city, he used the patronage at his disposal to help the unemployed and to repay those who knocked on doors at election time for him.[11]

Alderman Jim died in 1911, and his younger brother, Thomas, inherited the machine. Immediately, Tom Pendergast set out to expand the organization so that it would encompass the entire city. He continued to provide welfare services for the underprivileged, but he wanted to extend his power into the middle- and upper-class neighborhoods as well. Pendergast recognized that you do not give handouts to the middle and upper classes. They do not need welfare. "People work for a party because they can get a job or get a favor," said Boss Tom, "special privilege gets the votes."[12] The master broker gave illegal tax breaks to businessmen, large and small. He did thousands of favors for Kansas Citians such as geting a student admitted to a university or fixing a traffic ticket. He established political clubs in all middle-class wards. These clubs were actually social clubs with organized baseball and bowling, as well as bridge tournaments and picnics and dances. Those who took advantage of the Pendergast-sponsored social activities were expected to get out the vote at election time. Those who accepted larger favors contributed to the election campaign treasury.

By astutely dispersing patronage and special favors to a variety of interest groups and individuals, Pendergast built a well-disciplined organization that delivered impressive Democratic victories in Kansas City during the second half of the 1920s and throughout the 1930s. At the same time, the Kansas City boss extended his machine outside of Kansas City into rural Jackson County. His success in making inroads into the county was due largely to the leadership of Harry S Truman. A native of the county, Truman appealed to its WASP constituents because he was a Baptist and an American Legionnaire. Serving as an administrative judge from the early twenties until he went to the United States Senate in 1935, Truman controlled the purse strings and patronage of the county government. With this dual power, Truman was able to build a powerful organization for Pendergast, and thereby add to the already sizable Democratic voting block from Kansas City.[13]

Inasmuch as Democrats in Saint Louis and other parts of the state had no dependable organizations, Pendergast could deliver the largest block of votes in Missouri. His position grew still stronger in the election year of 1932. The census of 1930 indicated that Missouri's congressional districts needed to be reapportioned, but the legislature failed to agree upon the new boundaries before the 1932 elections. As a result, all candidates for Congress had to run at large in the primaries and general election that year.

Because Pendergast maintained a dependable machine that could deliver thousands of votes to favored candidates, Democrats from every corner of the state descended upon him for support. This unusual set of circumstances gave Pendergast the power to control the state party machinery in 1932, and thereby dictate which presidential candidate Missouri's delegates would back at the national convention. It was at this point that Pendergast first ingratiated himself with Franklin D. Roosevelt and set the stage for the New Deal's impact on Kansas City.

As early as fall, 1931, Pendergast publicly announced his endorsement of Roosevelt for the presidential nomination. The Kansas City boss had been in New York, and when he returned home, he told newsmen that the Missouri delegation would back Senator James A. Reed as a favorite son if Reed wanted to enter the race; but otherwise the delegates would be for Roosevelt.[14] After conferences with James Farley and Roosevelt, Pendergast organized the Missouri delegation so that it would support Reed but release votes to New York's governor on each ballot.[15]

After the convention, Farley informed Missouri Senator Bennett Clark that a share of the federal patronage usually reserved for senators was going to Pendergast. This was promised to the Kansas City boss before the convention, Farley recalled, because "he was with us from the start." According to Farley, Roosevelt felt indebted to the Kansas City boss, and hoped to do all that he could to repay him for his loyalty.[16]

Another circumstance that drew Roosevelt and Kansas City's machine closer together was the city's public works program. Months before the New Deal could have any impact on Kansas City, the community had a marked impact on the New Deal. Not only did Kansas City serve as a power base for Pendergast, who in turn helped Roosevelt win the nomination, but the Missouri city's relief programs became the inspiration and model for part of the New Deal. City Manager McElroy boasted that he gave Harry Hopkins the idea for the Civil Works Administration, which was inaugurated late in 1933.[17] It is impossible to prove precisely how much influence McElroy had on Hopkins, but as early as July 1933, the New Deal relief administrator had investigators in Kansas City. They were there to examine the city's work relief programs, which employed thousands of men by disposing of as much labor-saving machinery as possible.[18] Also, in October of that year, just before Hopkins broached the CWA idea to Roosevelt, Hopkins himself traveled to Missouri and conferred with Harry Truman, who was at that time reemployment director on work relief programs.[19]

Kansas City made an imprint on the New Deal, but it was faint in comparison to the New Deal's mark on the city. The most striking New Deal legacy is the community's skyline. Whoever approaches Kansas City by automobile or airplane is struck by a complex of skyscrapers in the heart of the business district. Among them are the city hall, the county courthouse, and the police station. The construction costs of these buildings, as well as the city's beautiful and functional convention hall and municipal auditorium (which covers a square city block), were paid for in part by federal grants through the agencies of the PWA, the CWA, and the WPA. Viewed as a whole, these structures gave Kansas City an unusually attractive, modern face-lifting. The building complex also provided the community with facilities for conventions, sports events, and city and county business, and these facilities were far superior to those in most cities of comparable size in the country.

Not as apparent, but certainly as important, was the federal money that helped build sewer extensions in several sections of the city. Federal grants also made it possible to construct a new waterworks system and to install the most modern flood protection devised to that time. Extensions were added to several hospitals, and parks and playgrounds mushroomed throughout the city. Several trafficways and boulevards, as aesthetically pleasing as they were functional, were completed with federal aid under New Deal programs. Similarly, one of the nation's most expensive county highway systems was brought to completion with the help of New Deal agencies and funds.[20]

The New Deal certainly beautified and modernized Kansas City, and the legacy remains there for anyone to see. Less tangible than buildings and streets, but to the unemployed much more vital, were the thousands of jobs that became available. The CWA, which lasted less than a year, employed over 110,000 men and women in Missouri, with a lion's share going to Kansas City and surrounding areas. The WPA, however, which lasted much longer, employed more people in Kansas City than the CWA did in the entire state.[21]

One reason that so many federal jobs were created in Kansas City was that the director of federal work relief for the state was Matthew S. Murray, a Kansas Citian and close friend of Thomas J. Pendergast. Harry Hopkins controlled the federal relief programs at the national level, and he appointed directors for each state. Theoretically, the senators from each state recommended a candidate for the state directorship to Hopkins, and he rubber-stamped the recommendation. But in Missouri, the reality was that Pendergast told Senators Truman and Clark whom he wanted, and that was Matthew S. Murray. Hopkins, Farley, and even Roosevelt knew that Murray was Pendergast's man. They cooperated willingly though because Pendergast had a favor coming for his loyalty at the national convention.[22]

The state director of work relief programs was a powerful person. A fair director could distribute jobs and programs largely on the basis of need, but, unfortunately, many state directors used the position as a political weapon. They rewarded loyal party workers with soft or high-paying jobs, channeled an inordinate amount of funds into their home counties, and even coerced rank-and-file employees to vote for favored candidates in primaries and general elections.[23]

Missouri's Matthew Murray was no exception. A loyal member of the Pendergast machine, he was described by one of Boss Tom's lieutenants as "extra close to T. J. [Pendergast], and has proven himself LOYALTY itself to the man. Murray came here thru Willie Ross of the Ross Construction Company [of which Pendergast was part owner], off the State Highway Department. . . . He was unknown to T.J.P. Yet, he played ball, made good and soon was a schooled and close mouthed public official."[24] That Kansas City's political machine was given complete control of federal work relief programs was abundantly clear. Citizens in the state who were unemployed and seeking federal assistance often wrote to the governor, hoping he could help them find a position with the WPA. Governor Guy B. Park always replied to such pleas by saying that the person must get in touch with Matthew S. Murray inasmuch as he "will be in complete charge of Federal work relief in Missouri."[25] Even Senator Harry S Truman bowed to the Pendergast machine before helping his constituents find federal jobs. To a man seeking senatorial aid in finding WPA employment, Truman replied: "If you will send us endorsements from the Kansas City Democratic Organization, I shall be glad to do what I can for you."[26]

The federal work relief programs became powerful weapons in Pendergast's political arsenal. In Kansas City, Jackson County, and throughout the entire state, foremen and timekeepers on WPA projects became organizers for the machine. In city, state, and national elections WPA workers were pressured to vote for the Pendergast Democracy. Some foremen bought drinks for their workers and then "asked" them to vote for the machine's candidates. Others told them to vote the party line or forfeit their jobs. In the words of one observer, WPA in Missouri was "literally a stench."[27]

To those who were discriminated against, the WPA was undoubtedly a stench. But to those thousands of men and women who were fortunate enough to work and keep their families from cold and malnutrition, the WPA smelled like spring flowers. One group of Kansas Citians—the blacks—especially benefited from the Pendergast machine's administration of federal work programs. In many states across the nation, blacks were denied equal access to federal relief. In many places, they were the last hired and the first fired; and in some communities, they were paid less than whites for doing identical jobs with equal qualifications. Throughout much of the South, for example, state directors of emergency relief and work relief maintained two relief and wage scales—one for blacks and another for whites.[28] Although Harry Hopkins, Aubrey Williams, and the other national administrators of relief programs deplored such action and tried to prohibit it, the programs were directed at the local level and it was impossible to oversee all of them.

In Kansas City, the black community shared the benefits from the New Deal because the local directors refused to discriminate. In fact, from the formative years of the Pendergast machine in the 1890s, blacks had been an integral part of the organization. And being an integral part meant, to the Pendergasts, having an equal share in patronage and spoils. The *Call*, a black newspaper in Kansas City, continually criticized Roosevelt and the New Deal administrators for discrimination. In Kansas City and Jackson County, however, the editor admitted his people were treated fairly. Indeed, they not only had an equitable number of jobs through the PWA, the CWA, and the WPA, but they had their own people in supervisory posts as well. Similarly, federal grants provided for the construction of parks, swimming pools, and recreation facilities in black neighborhoods. But even more important, the *Call* editor noted, was the fact that during the depression the death rate of the city's blacks declined more than one-third. Despite the economic crisis, the death rate declined so dramatically because two new hospitals were constructed for blacks.[29]

Everything, of course, did not run smoothly all of the time in Kansas City. There were instances where blacks felt that they did not have their fair share of workers on a construction job. There was, too, an outspoken minority of dyed-in-the-wool Republicans continually charging that there were graft and waste. On a few occasions, administrators for General Hugh Johnson grew angry when they discovered that some companies doing federal work were not flying the blue eagle of the NRA. The national administration pressed companies that were on federal projects to cooperate with the NRA. Missouri's Democratic leaders, however, were divided on its merits. Senator Bennett Clark bitterly disliked the NRA. Pendergast, on the other hand, tried to be noncommittal. The result was that Kansas City businessmen were less than enthusiastic in their support of the NRA, and there was little mourning when the Supreme Court declared it unconstitutional.[30]

Section 7(a) of the NIRA and the Wagner Act both caused heated controversy in the western Missouri city. These federal acts guaranteed the right of labor to organize and bargain collectively. Throughout the 1930s, when many employers were cutting wages, unions organized under their new shield of federal protection. In several industries, unions called strikes in an attempt to assert their new power and force higher wages. After 1935, Tom Pendergast grew as antibusiness as Franklin Roosevelt. The Kansas City boss supported the International Ladies' Garment Workers Union in a suit against the Donnelly Garment Company, which had tried to prevent unionization of its workers. And the cause of the American Federation of Labor was frequently championed by Boss Pendergast. The AFL embraced a majority of the city's union members—most of whom were Democrats.[31]

Despite altercations, which were inevitable when so many people were affected by so many federal agencies and laws, the majority of citizens felt that Kansas City and the New Deal were on a honeymoon. The fruits of that love affair were most clearly manifested in the large amount of federal aid that went to Kansas City and, in turn, the enormous majorities for Roosevelt and his New Dealers that were cast in Kansas City.

In the final analysis, it can be said that the New Deal had a far-reaching impact on Kansas City. Thousands of unemployed persons—men and women, black and white, from all walks of life—found employment on federal payrolls. Workers in numerous industries found security in the protection of New Deal labor legislation. The metropolitan area was markedly improved by sewage, water, and transportation facilities that were expanded through federal programs. The Pendergast machine, far from being destroyed by the New Deal, was given the power to direct federal spending in work relief, thus enabling Boss Pendergast to build a powerful statewide organization during the 1930s.[32] At the same time, the city beautiful movement, which had been inspired by progressive newspaper editors in the late nineteenth century, finally came to completion with the new city and county buildings and the park and boulevard projects.[33]

It should be remembered, too, that although the New Deal had a great impact on Kansas City, the second largest city in Missouri had some impact on the New Deal. The city's political machine put the state's delegates to the national convention behind Roosevelt in 1932 and again in 1936. The machine also helped deliver large blocks of votes to Roosevelt and his supporters at election time. And the public works program of the city influenced Harry Hopkins and the design of federal public works programs beginning with CWA.

At nearly the same time that New Deal relief and recovery programs were being phased out, when American industry was expanding to meet the needs of preparedness, Boss Pendergast went to prison and his machine collapsed. It must be understood that although President Roosevelt played a significant role in Pendergast's fall, the New Deal was not responsible. Historians and political scientists often insist that the rise of the welfare state with the New Deal destroyed the city bosses. This just was not true in Kansas City. Corruption in the machine was the cause of Pendergast's downfall.[34]

In 1936, Pendergast threw his support behind Lloyd Stark for governor. Stark had courted the Kansas City boss since 1932 in hopes of winning the machine's backing in 1936. Soon after his inauguration in 1937, Stark began using the state patronage to build his own organization. Inasmuch as he could not under state law succeed himself as governor four years later, Governor Stark set his sights on the Democratic senatorial nomination in 1940. The problem he faced was unseating Senator Truman, who had been elected in 1934 with Pendergast's strong backing. Not only was Pendergast perfectly happy with Truman, the public was too. It occurred to Stark that if he could thoroughly discredit Boss Tom and transfer the stigma of discredit to Truman, he could win the senatorial primary in 1940.

Stark was aware of election irregularities and illegal gambling and prostitution in Kansas City. He also believed Pendergast had accepted graft in settling a major insurance claims case some years earlier. The governor consequently launched a reform crusade against the boss. Stark went to Washington, D.C., talked to Secretary of the Treasury Henry Morgenthau, Jr., and subsequently sparked federal investigations of Pendergast's income. With the cooperation of Federal District Attorney Maurice Milligan, investigations of election returns were held. Ultimately, Stark had Milligan, the Federal Bureau of Investigation, and the Treasury Department all investigating Pendergast's activities.

Then in 1938, Stark pitted his state organization against Pendergast's in the state Supreme Court race. Stark, in boss fashion, coerced state employees to work for his candidate. Pendergast, in his typical style, coerced the men and women with WPA jobs to work for his candidate. It was a close race, but Stark won. He won not only because he had a good organization but also because he had been exposing gambling and corruption in Kansas City and linking it directly to Pendergast.

Stark's victory in 1938 made President Roosevelt take notice. Evidently a new power was emerging in Missouri's Democracy, and Pendergast's days were numbered. Soon after the election, District Attorney Milligan's term was to expire. Senator Truman tried to block the reappointment, but Roosevelt insisted on retaining Milligan.

Roosevelt's decision to desert his old ally Pendergast in favor of the governor, who was gaining in power and prestige, destroyed the Pendergast machine. Milligan and the other federal agents pressed their investigations with vigor. In April 1939, Pendergast was charged with income tax evasion. The tiring boss pleaded guilty, and was sentenced to a term in the penitentiary. The boss who had thrown his machine behind Roosevelt in

1932 saw a grateful president bestow countless favors upon him until 1938. However, as soon as Roosevelt was convinced that Pendergast was losing his grasp on Missouri's voters, he quickly changed his loyalty.

Governor Stark's calculated gamble never paid off, however. He did succeed in sending Pendergast to prison and in destroying the boss's machine. But after Pendergast and several of his henchmen went to jail, Milligan too decided to cash in on the anti-Pendergast sentiment. Both Milligan and Stark ran against Truman in the senatorial primary in 1940. Both men claimed credit for bringing reform to Missouri, and both tried to place the disgrace of Boss Tom on Harry Truman. Many Missouri Democrats, however, felt Pendergast had been "stabbed in the back." They especially felt that Stark had bitten the hand that fed him. Consequently, they sent Truman back to the Senate—not realizing, of course, that as they watched the New Deal curtain fall, they were helping raise the curtain for the Fair Deal.[35]

1. For descriptions of Kansas City night life, see Nat Hentoff and Albert J. McCarthy, *Jazz* (New York, 1959), pp. 189–230; and Carey James Tate, "Julia Lee," *Second Line,* January–February 1960, pp. 9–12, 20; Carey James Tate, "Kansas City Night Life," *Second Line,* November –December 1961, pp. 9–12, 32.

2. Jerome Beatty, "A Political Boss Talks about His Job," *American Magazine,* February 1933, p. 31, tells about the image of the city that the chamber of commerce attempted to create.

3. Lyle W. Dorsett, *The Pendergast Machine* (New York, 1968), p. 123.

4. James T. Patterson, *The New Deal and the States: Federalism in Transition* (Princeton, N.J., 1969), p. 26.

5. A. Theodore Brown, *The Politics of Reform: Kansas City's Municipal Government, 1925–1950* (Kansas City, Mo., 1958), pp. 40–43.

6. Ibid.

7. Timothy K. Evans, "Matthew S. Murray, Director of Public Works" (unpublished seminar paper, University of Missouri, Kansas City, 1970).

8. Dorsett, *Pendergast Machine,* p. 109.

9. Brown, *Politics of Reform,* p. 40.

10. Ibid., pp. 45–47, 168.

11. Lyle W. Dorsett, "Alderman Jim Pendergast," Missouri Historical Society *Bulletin* 21 (1964–65): 3–16; Dorsett, *The Pendergast Machine,* chaps. 1 and 2.

12. Beatty, "A Political Boss," p. 113.

13. For details on the Truman-Pendergast relationship, see Lyle W. Dorsett, "Truman and the Pendergast Machine," *Midcontinent American Studies Journal,* Fall 1966, pp. 16–27.

14. *Missouri Democrat,* 18 September 1931.

15. Dorsett, *Pendergast Machine,* pp. 105–7.

16. Franklin D. Mitchell, *Embattled Democracy: Missouri Democratic Politics, 1919–1932* (Columbia, Mo., 1968) pp. 145–47.

17. William Reddig, *Tom's Town: Kansas City and the Pendergast Legend* (Philadelphia and New York, 1947), pp. 182–83.

18. Corrington Gill to Sherrard Ewing, 17 July 1933, Box 88, Harry Hopkins Papers (Franklin D. Roosevelt Library).

19. Arthur M. Schlesinger, Jr., *The Coming of the New Deal* (Boston, 1959), p. 269.

20. Reddig, *Tom's Town,* p. 182.

21. *Missouri Democrat,* 2 February 1934.

22. For details on the appointment of Murray, see Dorsett, *Pendergast Machine,* chap. 8.

23. The WPA files in the National Archives in Washington, D.C., are filed by states. The files labeled "Political Coercion" reveal the politics and corruption involved in the work relief programs.

24. Jim Hurst to Lloyd C. Stark, 11 July 1935, Box 309, Stark Papers (Western Historical Manuscripts Collection, University of Missouri—Columbia).

25. Guy B. Park to Mrs. Hester B. Miller, 21 June 1935, Box 56, Park Papers (Western Historical Manuscripts Collection, University of Missouri—Columbia).

26. Harry S Truman to L. T. Slayton, 5 February 1935 (photocopy), Box 54, Jesse W. Barrett Papers (Western Historical Manuscripts Collection, University of Missouri—Columbia).

27. Evans, "Murray," pp. 11–13; Dorsett, *Pendergast Machine,* p. 116.

28. See Allen F. Kifer, "The Negro under the New Deal, 1933–1941" (Ph.D. dissertation, University of Wisconsin, 1961.)

29. *Kansas City Call,* 8 July 1938, 27 July, 3 August 1934, 3 July, 19, 30 October, 6 November 1936,21, 28 October 1938.

30. Duane Meyer, *The Heritage of Missouri: A History* (St. Louis, 1963), p. 626.

31. Reddig, *Tom's Town,* pp. 54, 302.

32. For some time, historians and political scientists have assumed that the New Deal destroyed the bosses and political machines. See, for example, the entire issue of *Annals of the American Academy of Political and Social Science,* May 1964, devoted to bosses and machines, and Walter Johnson, *1600 Pennsylvania Avenue* (Boston and Toronto, 1963). The widely read novel by Edwin O'Connor, *The Last Hurrah,* has no doubt contributed to the belief that the New Deal weakened or destroyed the bosses and their machines. Research into this subject suggests that the New Deal did not destroy the bosses. See Bruce M. Stave *The New Deal and the Last Hurrah: Pittsburgh Machine Politics* (Pittsburgh, 1970), and Lyle Dorsett, *Pendergast Machine.*

33. For a detailed study of the "city beautiful" movement in Kansas City, see William H. Wilson, *The City Beautiful Movement in Kansas City* (Columbia, Mo., 1964).

34. See Dorsett, *Pendergast Machine,* chaps. 8 and 9.

35. Ibid.

Notes on the Editors and Contributors

John Braeman, professor of history at the University of Nebraska—Lincoln, is the author of *Albert J. Beveridge: American Nationalist*.

Robert H. Bremner is professor of history at Ohio State University, the author of *From the Depths: The Discovery of Poverty in the United States* and *American Philanthropy*, and the editor of *Children and Youth in America: A Documentary History*.

David Brody teaches history at the University of California—Davis and is the author of *Steelworkers in America: The Nonunion Era, The Butcher Workmen*, and *Labor in Crisis: The Steel Strike of 1919*.

Keith L. Bryant, Jr., of the University of Wisconsin—Milwaukee, is the author of *Alfalfa Bill Murray* and *Arthur E. Stilwell, Promoter with a Hunch*.

Robert E. Burton, who teaches at the California State Polytechnic University at San Luis Obispo, has written *Democrats of Oregon: The Pattern of Minority Politics, 1900–1956*.

F. Alan Coombs, who is working on a biography of Senator Joseph C. O'Mahoney of Wyoming, is a member of the history department at the University of Utah.

Lyle W. Dorsett is professor of history at the University of Denver, author of *The Pendergast Machine*, and editor of *The Challenge of the City, 1860–1910*.

Harold Gorvine, a Harvard Ph.D. who formerly taught at Oakland University, Rochester, Michigan, is presently chairman of the history department at Akiba Hebrew Academy, Merion Station, Pennsylvania.

Robert F. Hunter teaches at Virginia Military Institute and is the author of *The Turnpike Movement in Virginia, 1816–1860*.

Richard C. Keller, chairman of the history department at Millersville State College, Millersville, Pennsylvania, was visiting professor at the University of Sussex, England, 1969–1970.

Michael P. Malone, who teaches at Montana State University, is the author of *C. Ben Ross and the New Deal in Idaho*.

David J. Maurer, of Eastern Illinois University, is working on a study of relief programs and policies in Ohio during the Great Depression.

John Robert Moore is professor in, and chairman of, the history department at the University of Southwestern Louisiana, has served as Senior Fulbright-Hays lecturer in Taiwan, China, and has written *Senator Josiah William Bailey of North Carolina: A Political Biography*.

William Pickens, presently a graduate student in history at the University of California—Davis, has contributed articles to the *New Mexico Historical Review*.

Bruce M. Stave, of the University of Connecticut, is the author of *The New Deal and the Last Hurrah: Pittsburgh Machine Politics*, editor of *Urban Bosses, Machines, and Progressive Reformers*, and co-editor of *The Discontented Society: Interpretations of 20th Century American Protest*. In 1974, he was awarded a National Endowment for the Humanities Fellowship to study urban reform in twentieth-century Hartford, Connecticut.

James F. Wickens, who teaches at Chabot College, Hayward, California, has written *Themes in United States History* and *American Highlights*.

Index